... One of them created our
Dominican H. Upmann, so you
could forget Havana.
That's One-Upmannship

Never Before Was There Such A Cigar...

Fuente Fuente OpusX®

"We will never rush the hands of time."

ARTURO FUENTE®

The Reigning Family Of Premium Cigars

www.cigarfamily.com

CIGAR
Aficionado's

BUYING GUIDE

4TH EDITION

RATINGS & PRICES
FOR MORE THAN
1200 CIGARS

M. SHANKEN COMMUNICATIONS, INC.
NEW YORK

Cigar Aficionado's Buying Guide
4th Edition

Editor & Publisher . . . . Marvin R. Shanken

Executive Editor . . . . Michael Moaba
Managing Editor . . . . Gordon Mott
Editorial Director, Books . . . . Ann Berkhausen
Associate Editor . . . . Amy Lyons
Assistant Editor . . . . Steffanie Diamond Brown

Creative Director . . . . Martin Leeds
Art Director . . . . Ellen Diamant
Cover Photography . . . . Jeff Harris

Director of Business Development . . George Brightman
Marketing Manager . . . . Connie McGilvray
Advertising Director, Luxury Goods . James J. Archambault Jr.
Associate, Business Development . . . Britta Jensen

Director of Advertising Services . . . Elizabeth Ferrero
Advertising Services Manager . . . . . Virginia Juliano

Director of Circulation . . . . Laura Zandi

ISBN: 1-881659-49-6
ISSN: 1096-3359
PUBLISHED BY M. SHANKEN COMMUNICATIONS, INC.
387 Park Avenue South, New York, NY 10016
For subscriptions to *Cigar Aficionado*, please write to the address above or call: (800) 992-2442
Visit our website at: www.cigaraficionado.com
Distributed by Running Press Book Publishers
125 South Twenty-Second Street, Philadelphia, PA 19103-4399

LANDMARK TASTE

Since 1929

ROYAL JAMAICA

If There Were A Better Way To Make A Cigar,
We'd Find It. . .Then We'd Smoke It.

HENNESSY
Martini

Discover this classic. Combine 2 oz. of Hennessy V.S and a squeeze of lemon over ice.
Stir gently, don't shake. Strain into a chilled martini glass. Or ask your bartender.

Foreword

Welcome to the fourth edition of *Cigar Aficionado's* Buying Guide.

This year our guide contains ratings for over 1,200 cigars. The main listings, organized by score within size categories, include complete tasting notes and updated prices. There are also listings by size and country, and by brand. Preceding this is some general information which will help you to purchase, understand and enjoy your cigars.

In addition, we have compiled a list of over 3000 leading tobacconists around the world where *Cigar Aficionado* is sold. That list includes major cigar retailers across the United States and in the major foreign capitals.

The guide to cigar-friendly restaurants focuses specifically on places that have responded to our questionnaires; the list includes over 1,400 cigar-friendly dining establishments, bars, nightclubs, coffee bars, and more. We ask that you please let us know immediately if a restaurant's cigar policy has changed. Also, we have provided a postcard that we invite you to fill out and drop in the mail if your favorite cigar-friendly restaurant was not included in this book.

Finally, *Cigar Aficionado* invites you to visit us on the World Wide Web— at **www.cigaraficionado.com**—where you will find additional information about cigar-friendly restaurants and current information about cigars, business, sports, travel, and much more.

We hope this guide enhances your smoking pleasure. Enjoy.

Marvin R. Shanken
Editor & Publisher

Table of Contents

Shape, Size and Color

Today's cigar smokers are educated consumers. They are aware that there is an enormous selection of cigars available on the market today, and they want to know what they are buying. While most cigar smokers will always have their absolute favorite cigar, they want to experience all the different cigar sizes and tobacco fillers and be able to converse knowledgeably on the subject. It can be very confusing at times, but fortunately, there is an accepted vocabulary and certain basic criteria that apply to all hand-rolled cigars.

The criteria are fairly simple: brand, wrapper, color, and size and shape. Of course, country of manufacture is important too, but today tobacco is a global commodity and cigars made in the Dominican Republic may contain tobacco from Cameroon, Mexico and Nicaragua. Therefore, it may be important to you to understand the origins of tobacco in your cigar because a particular type may create a certain flavor that you like.

Let's start with the brand name. The brand is the designation given by the manufacturer to a particular line of cigars. Punch, Partagas, Macanudo, Montecristo and Davidoff are just a few well-known names. You'll find these names on the cigar band, which is generally wrapped around the "head," or the closed end, of the cigar.

However, depending on which country you're in, even those well-known names can be a source of confusion. Some brands were first produced in Cuba. After Castro's revolution in 1959, many cigar manufacturers fled, believing they could take their brand names with them. The Cubans argued the brands belonged to the country. So today, you have a Punch made in Cuba and one made in Honduras; a Partagas in Cuba and a Partagas in the Dominican Republic. The dual origin problem also affects Romeo y Julieta, La Gloria Cubana, Fonseca, H. Upmann and El Rey del Mundo, Cohiba and Montecristo. You can usually determine which is which by a small Habano or Havana inscribed on the band.

Color refers to the shade of the outer wrapper leaf. In the past, manufacturers used dozens of terms for the wrapper leaves which were grown in Cuba, Sumatra, Brazil and the United States; U.S. cigar makers often described eight to ten different shades. Today, there are six major color grades in use. And wrapper leaf is grown today not only in the countries mentioned above, but in Ecuador, Nicaragua, Honduras and Cameroon as well.

Here are the six basic shades:

- **Double Claro**: Light green, and often called *candela*. The leaves are cured with heat to fix the chlorophyll in the leaf. They often taste slightly sweet. At at one time a majority of American market cigars came with a light-green wrapper, but claro claro is not as popular today.
- **Claro**: A light tan color, usually grown under shade tents. Claro is prized for its neutral flavor qualities.
- **Colorado Claro or Natural**: Light brown to brown. It is most often sun-grown.
- **Colorado - Colorado Maduro**: Brown to reddish brown. It is also usually shade-grown and has rich flavor and a subtle aroma.
- **Maduro**: From the Spanish word for "ripe," it refers to the extra length of time needed to produce a rich, dark-brown wrapper. A maduro should be silky and oily, with a rich strong flavor and mild aroma. There are several processes used to create maduro; one involves "cooking" the leaves in a pressure chamber, the other uses long, hotter-than-normal fermentation in huge bulks.

Colors

Double Claro

Claro

Colorado Claro or Natural

Colorado

Colorado Maduro

Maduro

Oscuro

Parejos
(straight-sided cigars)

CIGARS SHOWN ACTUAL SIZE

Corona

Corona Gorda

Churchill

Double Corona (8 1/2")

12

SHAPE, SIZE AND COLOR

Robusto

Petit Corona

Panetela

Lonsdale

A world beyond other cigars

Figurados

CIGARS SHOWN ACTUAL SIZE

Pyramid

Belicoso

Perfecto

Culebra

A maduro wrapper usually produces a slightly sweet taste.

• **Oscuro**: Meaning dark, it is also called *negro* or black in tobacco-producing countries. It usually is left on the plant the longest, and it is matured or sweated the longest.

You've seen the brand you're looking for, you've spotted the color wrapper you like to smoke, now it's time to get down to choosing a size and shape. In Spanish, the word *vitola* conveniently covers both concepts, but in English we're left describing both size (girth and length) and shape. Most cigars come in boxes with a front mark that tells you the shape of the cigar such as Punch Double Corona or H. Upmann Lonsdale. As you come to know shapes, you also can make some assumptions about size, such as knowing that a double corona is not a short, thin cigar.

It's unfortunate that there is so much confusion about size and shape when there needn't be. But after several generations of every manufacturer independently deciding which size name went with which length and girth, there is no simple logic to the definitions. In fact, haphazard naming conventions have resulted in the same word, such as Churchill, being used by different manufacturers for cigars of different sizes. If any single statement can be made about the standards of different countries, it is that Cuban standards tend to be more uniform. That's because there is one body governing the state-owned tobacco company in Cuba, and it oversees the entire industry there.

The basic measurement standard, however, is the same. The only variations are whether it is expressed in metric or U.S. customary systems. Length, therefore, is listed in inches or centimeters and girth or diameter, or ring gauge as it commonly known, is in 64ths of an inch or millimeters. A classic corona size, for example, is 6 by 42, which means it is six inches long and 42/64ths of an inch thick.

If you're searching for common denominators to use as a starting point for shape, it helps to know that all cigars can be divided into two categories: parejos, or straight sides, and figurados, or irregular shapes.

Simply put, parejos are straight-sided cigars, the kind with which most smokers are familiar. There are three basic groups in this category: coronas, panatelas and lonsdales.

Listed below are some standard size names with their standard sizes in parentheses.

• **Coronas** (6 inches by 42 or 44 ring gauge) have traditionally been the manufacturer's benchmark against which all other cigars are measured. Coronas have an open "foot" (the end you light) and a closed "head" (the end you smoke); the head is most often rounded. A Churchill normally measures 7 by 47. A robusto is 5 by 50. A double corona is 7 1/2 by 49. In other words, these are all variations on the corona theme.

• **Panetelas** (7 x 38) are usually longer than coronas, but they are dramatically thinner. They also have an open foot and closed head.

• **Lonsdales** (6 3/4 by 42) are thicker than panatelas, but longer than coronas.

The irregular shapes, or figurados, encompass every out-of-the ordinary-shaped cigar. The following list comprises the major types:

• **Pyramid**: It has a pointed, closed head and widens to an open foot.

• **Belicoso**: A small pyramid-shaped cigar with a rounded head rather than a point.

• **Torpedo**: A shape with a pointed head, a closed foot and a bulge in the middle.

• **Perfecto**: This looks like the cigar in cartoons with two closed rounded ends and a bulge in the middle.

• **Culebra**: Three panatelas braided together.

• **Diademas**: A giant cigar 8 inches or longer. Most often it has an open foot, but occasionally it will come with a perfecto or closed foot.

Remember, even with these "classic" irregular shapes, there are variations among manufacturers. Some cigars called belicosos look like pyramids, and some called torpedos look like pyramids because they do not have a perfecto tip. Confusing? Yes, it is.

Unfortunately, it really is self-defeating to try to talk about "classic"

Prometheus

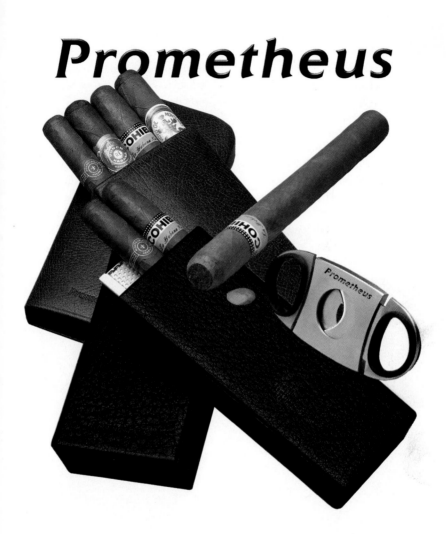

www.prometheuskkp.com

or "normal" ranges for any cigars on the market today. The basic shape designations can vary so greatly from company to company that they make little sense. Once you've become comfortable with the terminology, however, ask your tobacconist what the exact dimensions are of the cigar you like to smoke. Use that as your base to branch out to bigger or smaller, longer or shorter cigars. And, don't assume because you like a Churchill from one company that you're going to get the same-size cigar with that name from another manufacturer.

There are some other designations that are worth knowing because they refer to the style of packing. An 8-9-8 designation, for instance, simply means that the cigars are stacked in three rows inside the box, eight on the bottom, nine in the middle and eight on top. They usually come in a distinctive round-sided box. Amatista refers to a glass jar of 50 cigars, originally packaged by H. Upmann, which was developed for smokers who wanted a "factory fresh" smoke. Finally, there are tubos, cigars that are packed in aluminum, glass or even wooden tubes; a tightly sealed tube will keep cigars fresh for a long period of time. Some cigars are also box-pressed, meaning they are put inside a box so tightly that they acquire a soft, squarish appearance.

GENTYL & HYERS

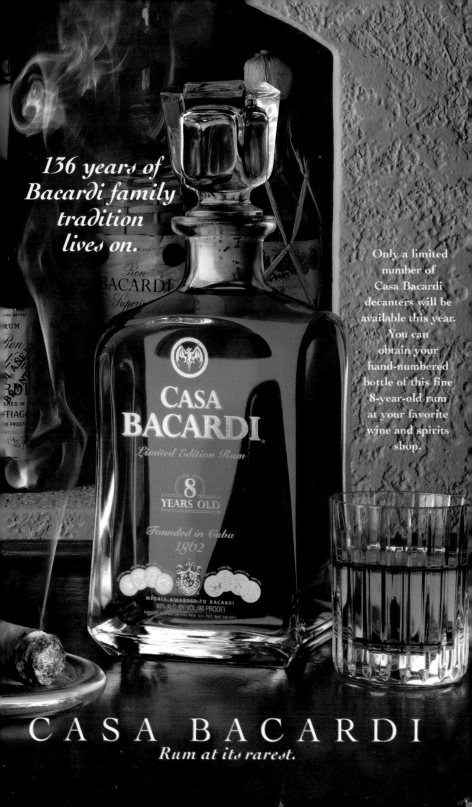

$ About 7 Astral Cigars / dozen

A WEEK OF ROMANTIC BLISS? OR 100% CUBAN-SEEDED,

HAND-ROLLED, ECUADORIAN-WRAPPED, PRECISELY AGED,

MASTER-BLENDED CIGARS? ANYONE HAVE A LIGHTER?

Taste

We all know that individuals are attracted to different taste sensations, and the taste of a cigar is no exception. We all have our personal preferences—but anyone can learn to distinguish a bad cigar from an excellenct one.

While smoking a cigar is the central act in appreciating it, there's more to it than just putting it in your mouth and puffing away. Professional tobacco experts and experienced smokers practice some basic steps in connoisseurship that are worth every cigar lover's effort to master.

Forming an overall impression of a cigar means using all of your senses:

MICHAEL O'NEIL

Michael Douglas

sight, touch, smell, taste, and even your hearing. First, sight and touch go hand in hand. The first thing that you do when you remove a cigar from a box, or from your humidor, is inspect it. Even if this act is only subconscious, the appearance and feel of the cigar wrapper tell a story, and several lessons about taste can be learned from the outside of any cigar. Then, listen to it. Roll the cigar between fingers in order to determine the moisture content of the wrapper and the filler. It should be firm, but should give a little when squeezed, and there shouldn't be any rustling or crackling of the leaves.

A wrapper does not make or break a cigar. But it plays an important role because it provides texture and beauty, and is your first contact with the personality and character of a cigar. Even before you light up, seeing and feeling a wrapper with nice silky oil and without visual blemishes should give you certain expectations. Wrapper appearance will vary depending upon where the leaf was grown.

The best wrappers from Cuba are indeed like silk, with exceedingly close cell structure—they don't feel like vegetable matter because their surface is so smooth. These wrappers have an elasticity and strength often lacking in

Demi Moore

wrapper leaves from other countries.

By contrast, a Cameroon wrapper shows oil in its bumpy surface, called "tooth" in the tobacco industry. These bumps are a good sign that great taste and aroma will follow, even if the texture of the leaf isn't silky. Wrappers from Connecticut and Ecuador are somewhat close in surface texture, though not in color. Better Ecuadoran leaf has less tooth, is smooth to the touch, and has a mattelike appearance. The Connecticut wrapper shows more color depth, a bit more tooth, and a nice shine.

Despite the differences in oils, seeing oil in any wrapper leaf indicates that the cigar has been well-humidified (oil secretes from tobacco at 70 to 72 percent humidity) and that the smoke should be relatively cool. A cool smoke is a tastier one, because it means the tobacco isn't carbonizing or overheating, which can limit the flavors.

If you see cracks or ripples in the surface of the wrapper leaf, you know that the cigar was exposed to cycles of over-humidification and excessive dryness. This, too, is important. If the cigar is forced through rapid cycles of expansion and contraction, the internal construction is destroyed. A cigar

STEPHEN WAYDA

Sylvester Stallone

with internal damage will smoke unevenly, or "plug," drawing unevenly. This may still occur due to faulty construction, but your chances are better with a perfect wrapper than with a broken one.

After lighting your cigar, look at the ash. According to most cigar experts, a white ash is better than a gray one. This is not merely an aesthetic issue; better soil produces whiter ash and more taste. Soil can be manipulated through fertilization, but if too much magnesium (a key ingredient in producing white ash) is added to the mix, the ash will flake, and nobody wants a messy cigar, even if the ash is white. Gray ash may hint at deficiencies in the soil, thus in the flavor.

A final visual cue is the burn rate. You can taste a cigar that is burning improperly because an uneven burn distorts the flavor of the blend. Simply put, a cigar is designed to burn different tobaccos evenly throughout the length of the smoke. A cigar may start off mild and grow stronger or change in some other way; these changes can be attributed to the location of the tobaccos. Thus, if a cigar burns unevenly, the delicate balance designed to produce a particular fla-

vor or taste is disturbed, and the cigar will not taste right.

The sense of taste is located mainly on the tongue and to a lesser degree on the roof of the mouth. There exist only four basic tastes: sweet, sour, salty and bitter. Every-thing else is either a combination of these four or a combination of taste and aroma. Although food flavor descriptors are now being used, most tobacco men stick with words like acidic, salty, bitter, sweet, bite, sour, smooth, heavy, full-bodied, rich, and balanced. Aroma too is important, and most cigar makers not only taste for flavors, but smell for aroma at the same time.

It takes many different types of tobacco to come up with a blend of tastes that works. And to reach a consistent taste, one that stays the same year after year, is the most difficult task for any cigar maker. No two leaves of tobacco are the same, and no two cigars can be the same year to year.

Cigar makers utilize different tobaccos to try to compensate for nature. They continually seek a blend that will achieve consistency and at the same time create some flavor complexity. A good blend uses tobaccos from different geographic zones, varieties, grades and harvests, so that the cigar will be complete and balanced.

Achieving this balance is difficult. There are an infinite number of variables that can alter the taste of any blend: soil, tobacco variety, climate, ground condition, curing, the harvester, fermentation, manufacturing process, and the humidity of the cigar.

Michael Richards

Two especially important factors in taste are aging and construction. Aging provides smoothness, richness and roundness—qualities you won't find in a cigar right from the roller's table.

Even with the finest blend in the world, a poorly constructed cigar will be less enjoyable than a perfectly made cigar of only modest blend. A loose draw (a cigar that burns fast, letting a lot of smoke pass through quickly because it is underfilled) will increase smoking temperature, destroying taste. A tight draw, on the other hand, reduces the sensitivity of the taste buds; drawing less smoke means having less to taste. Moreover, a tight draw may extinguish more frequently, and relighting makes a cigar harsh.

The variability of cigars may be one of the most essential things a consumer should remember. Cigars are handmade products, produced by skilled artisans in quantities of anywhere from 100 to 300 a day, depending on the size of the cigar and the manufacturing process. Like any handmade item, cigars are subject to human error. A bit too much tobacco here, a bit too little there, or a fatigued hand applying the wrong amount of pressure can completely alter the final product. All manufacturers inadvertantly let the occasional faulty cigar slip through their quality control system and reach the marketplace. What should a consumer do? Accept the reality, throw out the cigar and light up a new one. It's extremely unlikely that the next one will be flawed unless you are smoking a second-rate brand.

And, once you're smoking your favorite cigar, you won't even have to think about the complex set of processes that brought the cigar to your hand. It will most likely taste as great as the last one, and you'll already be looking forward to the next one.

STEPHEN WAYDA

Only Rémy

RÉMY MARTIN
FINE CHAMPAGNE COGNAC

Rémy XO Spécial. Only 1st crus of Cognac, Old Cognac blend, aged up to 35 years. Exceptionally smooth and long lasting.

Cutting and Lighting

Cutting and lighting are more than just essential steps in cigar smoking; when done with ease and perfection the ritual is a sign of a true connoisseur. It is important for a cigar smoker to master the procedure because an improper cut can destroy a cigar. The smoke can become hot, the cigar may burn unevenly, or the wrapper leaf may unravel—allowing bits of unsightly tobacco to lodge in the smoker's teeth. When a cigar smoker is comfortable with his technique he can sit back and enjoy a smoke with confidence.

Each smoker has a favorite way to snip off the end of a cigar. A ritual so personal is subject to inflexible opinions about right and wrong methods, and the choice of method is often traceable to the mentor who taught a given smoker to appreciate

JEFF HARRIS

cigars. Regardless of method, though—whether wedge, guillotine, scissors, bull's-eye, piercer, knife or teeth—the quality of the cutting tool often relates directly to the quality of the cut. And there are a few basic rules that can lead to a perfect cut.

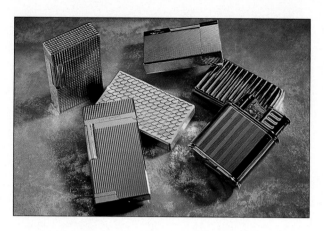

If mistakes are made in the cut, it may be because the smoker doesn't understand how cigars are made. All premium handmade cigars are closed off at one end (called the "head") in the manufacturing process. In some cases, this closure is made with a separate piece of the tobacco leaf called a "cap," usually cut from the same wrapper leaf that's on the cigar. It is secured with a special vegetable-base glue. Others are finished off with a "flag," a piece of leaf that is part of the same wrapper leaf but has been shaped with a knife to be wrapped around the head end of the cigar, which is secured with the same kind of glue. The latter technique is obvious in some cigars because instead of being smoothed out underneath the flag, the leaf is twisted off in a pigtail. In all cases, the cap or flag closes off the wrapper and binder leaves that hold the filler leaves together in the "bunch."

The goal of a guillotine or scissors cut is to clip off enough of the end to expose the filler leaves, but to leave enough of the cap or flag on to keep the wrapper on the cigar. That usually means a cut of about two millimeters, or about one-sixteenth of an inch. If you're not into metrics or rulers, another safe gauge is to look for the "shoulder" of the cigar. In a flat-end cigar, it may be quite noticeable; in a rounded end, it's a little harder to find but basically it's where the curve of the end straightens out. In a well-made cigar, the cap or flag usually extends over the shoulder. A cut made at the shoulder, or just a touch above, may be perfect.

Guillotine cutters must be kept sharp. Once they become dull, the blade begins to "push" the tobacco leaves, often tearing the side of the cigar away from the blade. To achieve a clean cut with a single-blade guillotine, the cigar should be positioned against the far side of the opening, the blade brought to rest against the cigar, and the end snipped with a sharp or quick thrust. Most single-blade guillotines also have a pocket for the blade; these must be regularly cleaned of tobacco pieces, or the blade may jam. Beware of inexpensive guillotine cutters with a single blade; they can damage cigars.

Double-bladed guillotines eliminate the problem of the cigar's far side being torn by an improper stroke of the blade. Be sure the cigar is flush against one blade before attempting to make a cut. The cutting motion should be crisp. These cutters should also be cleaned, but their design usually prevents jamming; an annual cleaning should be enough.

Scissors are more problematic. A good scissors must be properly balanced between the handles and the clipping edges. If not, it is very hard to hold the cigar steady against one of the cutting blades to get a clean cut. Also, if the hinge doesn't allow for a long movement of your fingers, it can be very hard to get a straight cut across the end of the cigar. But again, the same principle applies—you want to cut off enough of the cigar to expose the filler leaves without removing all of the cap.

One of the most popular cutters today leaves a V-shaped wedge in the end of the cigar. A greater surface area of the filler bunch is exposed than in a straight cut across

the end. But smokers who like to chew the end of their cigars should be wary of a wedge cut. If too much pressure is applied to the end of the

cigar, the wedge can collapse. This causes an accumulation of moisture and tars, and can make the draw tighter. If you pull too hard on the cigar, it can make the cigar smoke hotter and harsher.

Two other types of cutters, a bull's-eye and a piercer, accomplish the same basic cut: putting a hole in the end of the cigar without damaging the cap's adhesion to the cigar. The bull's-eye uses a hollow-tip cutter that is turned in a quick circular motion. Experts advise against making the hole too deep; a too-deep cut can draw the air and smoke down toward the middle of the cigar, making it smoke hotter. The same caution

JEFF HARRIS

should be used with the piercer, which often looks like an auger.

Many people swear by a simple knife or one-sided razor blade. Although the free blade requires a steady hand, the depth and angle of the cut, especially in a V-shaped wedge, can be gauged precisely according to the smoker's preference. The key to a successful knife cut is the sharpness of the blade. But unlike some guillotine cutters, a knife blade can be sharpened on a whetstone.

No article on cutting would be complete without the simplest cutting device of all: your teeth. This way is certainly convenient—you always have your teeth with you. But experts, many of whom incidentally make a living selling fancy cutters in addition to cigars, argue that only the very skilled teeth cutter can ensure a good, clean cut every time. They argue you can't see the cigar, you don't know exactly where the cut is being made, and you run the risk of tearing the cap and wrapper. There is also an element of bad manners; spitting out the tobacco can be unsightly. But in a pinch, teeth always work.

Let's dispel a few myths about lighting cigars. Yes, the use of a wooden match or a cedar strip called a "spill" is elegant, and it can be effective. But it's often time-consuming and unwieldy because it takes more than one match to properly light a cigar. Therefore, any good butane lighter is an efficient cigar smoker's companion.

The one caveat concerns fluid lighters. While lighter manufacturers dispute this, it is a fact that oil-based fluids can impart a taste to a cigar, so you must be careful not to draw too heavily when using this type of lighter. Fluid lighters are dependable, though, and tend to have a lot of lights in them.

Now you're ready to light. Cool smoke is the goal of a perfect light. There is a simple rule to follow: Never let the cigar touch the flame. When you light up, hold the cigar at a 45-degree angle above the flame, just far enough away so that the tip of the flame dances up to the cigar but never quite touches it. Then, to assure a proper light, rotate the cigar in your hand so that the foot of the cigar lights all the way around. When a lightly burning

JEFF HARRIS

CIGAR Introductory Offer

Aficionado

CIGAR Aficionado

LIGHTING UP WITH **DANNY DEVITO**

RATING 54 CIGARS
HAVANA, 1959: AN EXCLUSIVE PHOTO ESSAY
GOLF'S GREATEST HUSTLER
PLUS: HOLIDAY GIFT GUIDE.
AND MUCH MORE

☐ 6 issues (1 year) $19.95

☐ 12 issues (2 years) $35.95

Name (please print)

Address

City   State   Zip

☐ Check enclosed   ☐ Bill me

Charge to: ☐ VISA ☐ MasterCard ☐ Amex

Card #   Exp. Date

Signature   48PA0

Call Toll Free
1-800-992-2442

Please allow 4-6 weeks for delivery of first issue. Canada: $25.95 including GST, in U.S. funds.
All other foreign: $48.00 in U.S. funds.

BUSINESS REPLY MAIL

FIRST-CLASS MAIL   PERMIT NO. 1302 BOULDER, CO

POSTAGE WILL BE PAID BY ADDRESSEE

CIGAR AFICIONADO
P.O. BOX 51091
BOULDER, CO 80323-1091

ring surrounds the tip of the cigar and begins to creep toward the center of the foot, blow out lightly through the cigar. Not everyone does this, but it makes sense; rather than breathing a first puff of lighter (or match-born sulfur) gases into the cigar, your first exhalation will rid the tobacco of these unwanted flavors.

Then you are ready to begin smoking. Do so by continuing to rotate the cigar as you take your first few puffs. This will regulate the burn, ensure that it is even and prevent "tunneling," which is when one side of the cigar burns faster than the other. This technique applies to all forms of lighting: matches, cedar strips, or lighters.

Some people wonder if a cigar should be relit if it goes out. Even with a perfect lighting job, a cigar may go out occasionally. While smoking a cigar at a rate of one puff a minute can ensure a smooth, cool smoke, sometimes that isn't feasible. You may be on the telephone, or in a conversation with someone, and just forget to keep puffing. If your cigar goes out, by all means, relight it— just use the same caution in lighting it as you would with a fresh cigar. However, be aware that after a couple of relights, a cigar can begin to get harsh.

If you insist on spills or matches, there are a few rules to follow. You may use a candle to light a spill, but never use a candle to light a cigar; wax vapors can ruin its taste. If you're using matches, long ones are preferable. If you use short ones, strike two at one time, let the sulfur burn off and then commence lighting—by using two, you get a broader flame and make it easier to get an even light.

Lighters are the most portable source of fire, and most can be lit with one hand while the other holds the cigar. A good lighter should have a certain heft; some are cut from solid blocks of brass and feel like it. But as important as the weight is the feel in your hand, like a good knife. It should be balanced and fit the size of your palm.

Opening the lighter should be effortless. The cap should swing open smoothly, and the hinge mechanism should be silent. (A hollow or clunky sound can indicate inferior materials.) Once it is opened, the cap should swing fully away from the body of the lighter; otherwise the flame may not be accessible, especially if you're lighting a bigger cigar. The flame should be adjustable, and should be fat, again something that is more important for a cigar smoker than a cigarette smoker. Some cigar lighters actually have two flames.

In the end, the goal is to have a trouble-free light. Since you'll be using it frequently, look for a lighter that feels comfortable and works in all situations including windy ones. If a lighter is not only functional but attractive, you'll be carrying it around like a pocket watch forever.

Storing and Carrying Cigars

The cigar revolution of the 1990's has spawned a surge in humidor sales. One of the hallmarks of a true cigar aficionado is ownership of a well-made humidor that will provide the special environment needed to care for precious cigars.

A humidor should maintain a cigar at its peak of "smokability." This isn't simple, because a humidor must re-create the tropical or semi-tropical environment in which most cigar tobacco is grown and where most fine, hand-rolled premium cigars are manufactured and aged. Makeshift tropical environments—like a steamy bathroom or a zippered plastic bag with a moist paper towel—don't work well.

A cigar is composed of multiple layers of tobacco. In an inconsistently humid environment like a shower stall, the outside of the cigar will dry once the mist is cut off, but the inside of the cigar will still be damp. The inside "bunch" of tobacco will swell while the wrapper contracts and splits open, destroying your investment.

The most crucial characteristic of a fine humidor is that it provides a consistently tropical environment (about 68-70 degrees Fahrenheit and 70-72 percent humidity) over a long period of time. Remember, this doesn't only mean how often you need to add water to the humidification system; it also means that 20 years from now the box lid hasn't

Savinelli "Rosewood Weave" humidor.

JEFF HARRIS

warped and the hinges still open easily and quietly. Reputable humidor manufacturers include Diamond Crown, Davidoff, Danny Marshall, Dunhill, Elie Bleu, Michel Perrenoud, and Savinelli. Excellent larger humidors, really standing floor cases and even credenza size boxes, are also being made today by manufacturers such as J. Pendergast, Kreitman-Thelan, Vinotemp and others.

The components of a good humidor can be judged easily. Starting from the inside of the box, look for details like perfectly squared and fitted seams. You shouldn't see any glue, and a gap in a joint spells trouble because it provides an exit for moisture, eventually resulting in warping. Cedar is the best wood for the inside of a humidor because of its ability to enhance the aging process. It allows the various tobaccos in a cigar the chance to "marry" so that the cigar is not composed of separate tobacco flavors, but of subtle nuances of taste.

The rim of the box should be constructed uniformly, with tight tolerances, so that the lid closes with the solid feel of a Mercedes Benz car door. An inner lip, especially a lower one, will protect cigars from dry outside air. This is all the more necessary in a box without a lock, because only the weight of the lid will keep it tightly shut. A humidor lid should never close like a safe, however, because if no air were allowed to circulate, musty smells would destroy your cigars. The entire box should be balanced, both when left closed and when opened. (The last thing you want is to have your box tumble off the desk because the lid is too heavy or bounces when lifted.)

Of course, a perfectly constructed box is worthless if it has no means of providing humidity. At one time old apple cores were thought to do this nicely, but modern humidification systems are more reliable. Most humidifiers rely on some variety of sponges, chemical compounds, or plain bottles to provide moisture. However, remember that prime cigar aging demands constant humidity levels. Usually, humidor instruction manuals proclaim low maintenance. But once you've prepared the humidor for use—try wiping the interior with a damp cloth before loading it up with cigars—you should rely as much on the "feel" of the cigars inside as on the humidification system. If the cigars feel dry even though the humidity gauge reads 70 percent, you should check the device.

Other practical features, in order of importance, are: a tray, which provides the owner the option of storing cigars at more than one level so that they are exposed to varying degrees of humidity (always place parched cigars as far as possible from the humidification device so they will regain humidity slowly, then move them closer to the device); slots or wells drilled into box sides, allowing a unit to breath while preventing separation and warping of veneer; and lid magnets for holding

Davidoff "Macassar" humidor.

cutting instruments, which are occasionally added to humidors. A hygrometer, while fancy-looking, is seldom accurate even in the most expensive desk-top models.

The appearance of your humidor is entirely up to you. A deep, rich lacquer finish is beautiful and functional and should be judged as you would the finish of a dining-room table. Also, a felt bottom will serve as protection for both the box and the surface where it sits. Handles are often helpful additions, especially on larger units.

Keep in mind that in a home or office, a humidor shouldn't overwhelm its surroundings. Deciding where to put your new purchase before buying it might help you find a humidor that will both look good and function well. If you made the right choice, twenty years from now— when your son starts to covet your

humidor—you will know for certain that your investment was worthwhile. You didn't buy a mere "box."

Another key question is what to do with cigars when you travel across the country, or across town for a big dinner. The best travel humidors and cigar cases are designed to keep cigars in perfect, smokable condition. Constructed of little more than metal, wood, leather and thread, they are just as simple and refined as what they protect. Do not ignore this parallel truth: your cigars and what you put them in should both be well-conceived products of a basic but nearly flawless design.

Cases, whether telescoping, multifingered, open (without separate cigar dividers), tubular or some combination of the above, should always do at least two things exceptionally well: protect and hold your

JONATHAN L. SMITH

Cigar Aficionado humidor by Elie Bleu, Paris.

cigars. The equation is simple—you want whatever cigars you smoke most often to fit easily into your cigar case.

If you smoke a longer cigar, a telescoping case will be necessary. And if you smoke various ring gauges during the course of the same day, avoid fingered cases which are constructed to hold specific ring gauges and will not stretch to hold larger sizes.

If you smoke the same ring gauge consistently, a fingered case is a good bet because it will keep your cigars from rolling around or rubbing against the interior of the case, especially when you get down to the last cigar. Open cases have no safeguards to prevent your cigars from rattling around once you've removed one or two.

If you'll be stowing a two-, three-, or four-fingered case in your glove compartment for your drive to and from the office or for weekend jaunts in the country, any good quality case will do. Thick leather, of almost any hide, is tough and will resist the minor jostling caused by potholes and traffic jams.

If upon your arrival at work you're going to remove the case from the car and stow it in your coat pocket, be sure that it will fit. Most four-fingered models are very wide, and unless your chest size and tailor are cooperative, you might look like you're packing a weapon.

Aside from a standard check for stitch quality and uniform construction—with no rough edges showing—

The Macanudo Ash

The ash always tells you if a cigar is well-constructed. And the longer, finer and more even the ash is, the finer the leaves are and the longer they have been aged. With that in mind, Macanudo is the only cigar-maker that still spends the time and effort it takes to age its Connecticut Shade wrapper leaves a second time. Just as the Cuban cigar-makers used to do decades ago.

MACANUDO®
True Cigar Taste

picking out a leather case that will protect your cigars is an easy task. A good case should slide open with minimal effort (test this by putting some of your own cigars into the case), and should be lined, to protect your cigars from leathery aromas and prevent the wrapper leaf from catching on any rough inner hide.

Cigar cases come in a variety of shapes and sizes.

you do, never store a partially smoked cigar in a case—the aroma will linger, affecting every cigar placed in the case long after this careless mistake.

Unlike cases, travel humidors are too big for local commuting. The smallest models hold five Churchill-size cigars (one more cigar than the largest standard case), and are much too big to fit in a jacket pocket. The advantage to this bulk is that a travel humidor will keep cigars fresh much longer than all pocket-sized cases because it comes with a humidification unit.

Choosing a cigar case is much like buying new shoes: quality (which includes durability), fit, ease of use, and style are the most important factors, in that order.

If your travel entails bumping (literally) into strangers, take more care in selecting a case—or consider a wooden or silver tube. Tubes are both bulky and heavy, but they can certainly take more abuse than leather, and they will keep a cigar fresh for up to 72 hours. If you mind the extra weight but still need heavy-duty protection, opt for a telescoping case with very thick leather.

Once you've selected a case or tube suitable for your needs, use it wisely. Slide fresh cigars into your case in the morning, and be sure to remove any unsmoked cigars at night, returning them to storage in your humidor. Most cases will not keep cigars fresh for more than a day. And whatever

Even though a travel humidor is designed for a multiday trip and a case is not, your expectations for both products should be similar. Again, remember the size and shape of your cigars, and be certain that the box will accommodate them. Then inspect the details. Look for features like solid rear hinges, preferably of the "piano" variety, which stretch the length of the box. Also, be certain that the humidification unit inside the box will stay put while you sprint to catch a plane or toss your luggage into the back of a taxicab.

If all goes well, both you and your cigars will arrive in fine condition, ready to smoke away the troubles of an all-too-fast modern age.

EXPERIENCE
THE ULTIMATE FINISH.

THE CLASSIC CHOICE FOR A GOOD CIGAR.

Buying Cigars

A favorite story among cigar merchants, as told by the late Zino Davidoff, concerns the destruction of the Dunhill shop in London during the German blitz of World War II. In the aftermath of the bombing the store manager's first priority—at 2 a.m.—was to inform Prime Minister Winston Churchill that his cigars were safe. We should all be so lucky as to receive such devoted attention!

In reality, with the large number of cigar customers today, it is very hard for a tobacconist to get to know his clientele personally. However, a good tobacconist is still the best resource a cigar smoker can have. So

Havana Studios, California

THERE ARE NO MAPS
TO WHERE LIFE WILL TAKE YOU.

BUT WE'RE BUILDING THE
CARS AND TRUCKS
TO GET YOU THERE.

We drive to work. We head out on vacation.

We ferry the kids around town all day long.

And whatever the destination,

we all want to enjoy the journey.

When we're ready to buy, we talk to our friends.

We kick the tires. We look under the hood.

And still we all wonder,

"Will it last? Is it reliable?"

We carry groceries. We carry luggage.

We carry life.

And we all want to be safe doing it.

Building lots of cars and trucks

makes us a car company.

Building the cars and trucks you count on

wherever life takes you—

that's what makes us GM.

GM ® **General Motors.**

CHEVROLET   PONTIAC   OLDSMOBILE   BUICK   CADILLAC   GMC

PEOPLE IN
MOTION

take the time to get to know yours. Make sure that he knows what you like to smoke. Maybe over time you'll get lucky; when he receives a shipment of hard-to-get cigars, he'll put aside a few for you.

Having a hometown tobacconist doesn't solve the question of what you do when you're on the road. Being in a strange city without cigars can be frustrating. What should you look for when judging whether a tobacconist has his act together?

If you ask a tobacconist for cigars and he shows you into a walk-in humidor where moist air caresses your face, and you almost need a sweater because the temperature is right around 70 degrees, you know you're in the right place. Tobacconists who take the time, trouble and expense to construct a properly humidified environment where cigars are kept in perfect smoking condition are definitely worth the detour. If you are at all in doubt about the storage conditions, ask to pick up a cigar. Feel it. If it is supple and its oils are clearly

intact, then you can pretty much rest assured that the cigar you buy will be ready to smoke.

What are some of the trouble signs? First of all, if you are shown a glass counter display case that looks like it's been there forever, be sure to check out the cigars. Some of the humidification units in this type of display case are not very efficient, or they require regular maintenance that they may not always get. The evidence will be in the cigars themselves. Again, there is no substitute for asking to feel a cigar. If you're not allowed to touch, be suspicious.

Arnold's Tobacco Shop, New York City

You may also want to ask about the freshness of the cigars. If the store looks as if it pays more attention to gifts and magazines than to smokables, you may not have any idea how long the cigars in the display case have been there. A store with heavy traffic will turn over its inventory more frequently. In high-volume outlets, even counter-style humidification units may be completely satisfactory because consumer demand forces the owner to pay attention to his cigars.

Some additional factors are important if you are trying to establish a long-term relationship with a tobacconist. Is he willing to entertain your requests for special orders, or does he insist that you try one of his "store brands"? The latter phenomenon may indicate that the tobacconist is most interested in selling what he has in stock. On the other hand, if you're smoking a particular brand, and the tobacconist says he has several brands that are similiar to your favorite, try them out. You're likely to get a cigar that you like, and in the future you'll have an alternative if for some reason the store runs out of your preferred smoke.

Today, it's important to find a tobacconist who is following the cigar market closely. Because of the boom in cigar sales in the last few years, new brands and sizes are coming on the market monthly. A good tobacconist will know what's available and what kind of tobacco is being used in the cigar, and if he or she knows your preferences, he may be able to recommend some new cigars that suit your taste.

There's another new factor to consider in any visit to a retailer. Around the country, one of the most common retailer complaints is how customers treat cigars on the shelf. Although we do recommend that you ask to touch cigars, touching does not require squeezing so hard the wrapper breaks. A gentle pressure on the cigar tells you all you need to know about its condition. You should also be considerate of the shopper behind you. You may have seen tobacco men breathe deeply from the open foot of a cigar, but don't try it yourself. First of all, the average consumer doesn't have a clue what he's smelling for. And if you have the urge to try the smell test in a retail environment, think about the guy coming in after you or the dozens who've been there before you. It's not necessary to determine the quality or condition of the cigar.

Cigar smokers of the world -

Hot Tip

SIGN IN
WHAT'S NEW
FORUMS
CIGAR RATINGS
RETAILERS
RESTAURANTS
PEOPLE
CIGAR STARS
WALL STREET
THE LIBRARY
TRAVEL
DRINKS
THE GOOD LIFE
EVENTS
SPORTS/GAMING
SUBSCRIBE

CIGAR
Aficionado

special selection

contact us | subscribe | site index

Scores & Tasting Notes

Search More Than 1,000 Cigar Ratings

For the first time, our entire database of ratings--every cigar we've rated since our first issue in Autumn 1992--is completely searchable. And if you sign in, you can use our Personal Humidor function, which lets you save and print a customized list of your favorite smokes. You'll also qualify to win free cigars!

Marvin Shanken

Live Chat

Marvin R. Shanken, editor and publisher of Cigar Aficionado, welcomes you online with a live Q&A session. Ask him about the magazine, the JFK humidor, the state of the cigar industry or anything else that piques your interest. If you can't be there, submit questions in advance.

Weekly Poll

The Burning Question

What's the most-improved cigar producing country? Submit your answer to our first Weekly Poll right now. We'll post a new question each Monday, and also report the results of the previous week's poll.

you have a new virtual home!

Cigar Aficionado, your source for the most in-depth information on hand-made cigars and the artisans who make them is on the World Wide Web. Find a wealth of information online including:

- **Cigar Ratings**
- **Retail Tobacconists**
- **Cigar Friendly Restaurants**
- **Live Chats**
- **Bulletin Boards**
- **Lifestyle Information**
- **Publicly Traded Cigar Companies**
- **Betting Lines and Scores**
- **People of *Cigar Aficionado* - industry stars as well as other fascinating personalities**

It's all here plus much more!
Please visit us at:
http://www.cigaraficionado.com

Cognacs and Brandies

Somewhere in the medieval past, a distiller took grapes—the fruit of the vine—and transformed them into a fine distilled spirit. Today, that spirit is known as Cognac when it comes from a small, clearly defined area known by that name in France; Armagnac when it's from the region of that name near Cognac; or simply brandy when it comes from anywhere else.

Cognac is considered the pinnacle of grape brandies. On its label you may find a variety of designations indicating origin, aging and blend. If the town of Cognac is the center of a bull's-eye, then the six areas where

CHARLES SEESSELBERG

MADUROS
ESPECIALES

Maduro No. III

Maduro No. II

Maduro No. I

MADE WITH PRIDE AT LA FLOR DOMINICANA CIGAR FACTORY

FOR ADDITIONAL INFORMATION CALL 1-800-543-7131

is aged less than four and a half years; V.S.O.P., is aged more than four and a half years; and X.O., or Napoleon, which indicates Cognacs aged more than six and a half years. After aging, one of the real arts of Cognac comes into play—the blending. A master blender will often use grapes from a variety of regions or sources to arrive at a consistent final product. A designation of "Fine Champagne" means 50 percent of the grapes come from the Grande Champagne. If all the grapes are from either the Grande or Petite Champagne regions, the Cognac label may state this. Some Cognac makers also produce extra special Cognacs with names like Martell Extra, Rémy Martin Louis XIII, Hennessey Paradis, Courvoisier Initiale Extra, and Hine Triomphe. While all of these contain Cognacs that are aged considerably longer than six and a half years, even up to 70 years in some cases, they are legally bound only to have no Cognac less than six and a half years old. Names of other outstanding producers include Delamain, Frapin, Pierre Ferrand, A.E. Dor, A. de Fussigny, A. Hardy, and Louis Royer.

Armagnac is similar to Cognac but only goes through a single distillation. It is considered a bit rougher than Cognac but purists

grapes for use in Cognac can be grown extend in roughly concentric circles out from the center. At the center is Grande Champagne, a small area from which the best Cognacs are considered to come. Then there is Petit Champagne, which despite its name is larger than Grande Champagne. The other four areas in descending order of quality are Borderies, Fins Bois, Bons Bois and Boi Communs or Ordinaries.

Today, most Cognac comes from a single grape variety, Ugni Blanc, and after fermentation the grapes go through a double distillation. Then Cognac is aged in French oak barrels. There are three designations which indicate length of aging: V.S., which

JONATAHN SMITH

THE CONSISTENTLY PERFECT CIGAR.

Every Leaf.
Every Roll.
Every Draw.
Every Montague.®
Only Montague.

For more information regarding Montague
premium handmade long filler cigars,
please call 1-800-367-3677

Two producers, Carneros Alambic and Germain-Robin, are producing pot still products; as the brandies get more barrel aging, they are being blended into top quality products. Recently, Paul Masson also launched an aged brandy into the U.S. market.

The simple grape-based spirits that do not undergo significant barrel aging include grappa, a clear liquid, and various forms of marc, a spirit made from the leftover grape must after the harvest.

Grappas are primarily Italian, although some American producers, such as Sebastiani, have been creating fine grappas. They have strong grape flavors, and are clean, striking spirits. In recent years, grappas made from single grape varieties, often with even more pronounced flavors, have arrived on the market.

believe it has a truer "grapey" flavor. It is also aged in oak barrels, and unlike Cognac, it can be bottled with a specific vintage date. Some brands to consider are Sempe, Larressingle, Darroze, and Marquis de Caussade.

Spanish brandy is also a fine spirit. These brandies use a different grape variety, and are often richer and darker in appearance with a sweeter flavor on the palate. Top brands include Cardenal Mendoza, Lepanto, Duque de Alba, and Carlos X.

American brandy has made huge strides in the last 10 years.

Cognac, though, is the traditional choice in many countries for the perfect accompaniment to a great cigar. The intensity of the spirit is an especially good match for a robust hand-rolled cigar. Add a cup of coffee, and you have what the French call the "Three C's": Coffee, Cognac, and Cigars.

COURTNEY GRANT WINSTON

Port

I t's almost a standard scene in any Victorian novel or play: the English gentlemen retire to the drawing room for a glass of Port and a cigar. A reflection of the cigar's glowing ember shimmers in the dark, nearly black, liquid in their glasses.

Port is a fortified wine. Port begins like any other wine—on a grapevine. But to be called Port, the vineyards, known as *quintas*, must be located in Portugal's Upper Douro Valley. The grapes are harvested and then crushed in shallow open concrete containers called *lagars* or in stainless steel vats. The wines are fermented to about 5 percent alcohol and then brandy is added to bring the solution to about 20 percent alcohol. The fortifi-

cation process preserves the natural sweetness in the wine.

There are several different types of Port. Vintage Port is designated by the producer or shipper, and is a statement on the overall quality of the vintage. The decision is made in the spring following the

JEFF HARRIS

Dunhill Completes The Hand

AGED CIGARS

second winter of the harvest. For instance, the 1985 vintage was declared in the spring of 1987. The producers taste the wine frequently. If a vintage is declared, the wines must be aged in wood casks for two years before bottling.

Vintage years are usually declared two or three times a decade, although not all the major houses agree on any single year. In the '60s, vintages were declared in 1960, 1963, 1966 and by a few houses in 1967; the '70s brought 1970, 1975 and 1977 and two houses in 1978; in the '80s, a banner decade, vintages were declared in 1980, 1982, 1983 and 1985. A dry spell of six years followed. Now, both 1991 and 1992 have been declared vintage years.

The top producers of vintage Port are Graham, Fonseca, Taylor and Quinta do Noval, although the latter is better known for its rare Nacional. Other producers include Cockburn, Croft, Dow, Ferreira, Sandeman and Warre. Great Ports can last a lifetime. Ports from the 1963 vintage, for instance, have not reached their peak, and 1955 and 1945 are still drinking marvelously.

If a vintage is not declared, then the fortified wine may be used in Ports known as "late bottled vintage" or "vintage character" or saved for nonvintage or tawny Ports. "Late bottled vintage port" carries a vintage date, and receives more barrel-aging before bottling so that it is ready to drink sooner than the classic vintage Port. Most Ports may be blended from the wines of several different vineyards, but single vineyard Ports have also become common on the market. Some of the better ones are Ferreira's Quinta do Seixo 1983, Offley Boa Vista 1983 and the 1987 and 1991 Taylor Quinta de Vargellas.

In addition, Port producers make tawny Ports that have received even more wood-aging. They are designated as 10-year-old, 20-year-old and 40-year-old, although this refers to the average age of the fortified wines used in the blend, not the absolute age of the blend. They tend to be lighter and show a nuttier, more mature character. Finally, there is the nonvintage Port category, which is much less expensive. It's hard to separate the various designations in this category; some producers call it "ruby Port," others "vintage character." In general, it should have about five years of barrel-aging to smooth it out. Nearly every Port producer makes a nonvintage port, and most cost less than $15 a bottle. Look for Churchill's Finest Reserve, Noval LB and Fonseca Bin 27.

When last seen, the photographer's assistant was boarding the Orient Express and wearing an enigmatic smile. **PARTAGAS**® Limited Reserve

Once you find one, never let it go.

CHAPTER 8

Scotch and Irish Whiskey

I f there is a spirit that "marries" its flavors perfectly with cigars, Scotch is certainly the top candidate. This concoction of water and peat-smoked, malted barley is often redolent of smoky, charcoal-like flavors that go well with a fine cigar.

Most Scotch whisky is blended, often using dozens of fine malt spirits from distinct distilleries that are then blended with neutral grain spirits. The proportion of nonbarley grain spirits in a blended Scotch is a closely guarded secret, often passed down from one family generation or master blender to the next. Blends can vary in taste, and descriptors such as dry, sweet, smooth, smoky, peaty,

salty, complex, balanced, clean and soft are used to describe the taste. The exact character of blended Scotch is determined by the barley malt, the ratio of malt to neutral spirits and the length and type of aging. Some blended Scotch brands include Chivas Regal; Crown Royal; Dewars; J&B; Cutty Sark; Johnnie

JEFF HARRIS

Walker Red, Black and Blue; White Horse; Grants; Clan MacGregor; Passport and Teacher's.

A real phenomenon in the United States is the rise in popularity of single malt Scotch whiskies. Several brands are part of any well-stocked bar today: Glenfiddich, Glenlivet, The Macallan, Highland Park, Glenmorangie, Aberlour, the Dalmore, Cardhu, and Laphroaig. A host of others, rarer and harder to find, evoke images of ancient Scotland: Talisker, Lagavulin, Bunnahabhain, Bruichladdich, Oban, and Edradour. Single malts differ from blended Scotches in that they are the product of a single distillery, so the inherent character of that distillery shines through. The distillery's home region is also a contributing factor; the big five are Islay, Speyside, Lowlands, Highlands, and Campbeltown, and each is considered to have its own distinguishing features. Single malts also exhibit the differences between the two different types of barrels used in aging Scotch: old Sherry barrels or Bourbon barrels. Each imparts its own character, but it is generally agreed that Sherry casks

impart a slight sweetness to a Scotch whisky while Bourbon is more neutral. Irish whiskey also occupies a favorite niche in the world of grain-based spirits. In the United States, the two most widely available are Jameson's and Old Bushmills. Most Irish whiskey is triple-distilled, creating a more neutral-tasting spirit than most Scotch whisky. Also, Old Bushmills is primarily a grain spirit with only a small touch of malt. Recently, Old Bushmills created an all single malt product called Bushmills Malt.

Serious Scotch drinkers, especially single malt aficionados, prefer their beverage neat or at most, on the rocks. But Scotch and water or Scotch and soda are certainly accepted drinks. Given Scotch's popularity in the postwar years, bartenders also created a host of exotic Scotch-based cocktails: Rob Roy (Scotch and sweet vermouth) and Rusty Nail (Scotch and Drambuie) are just two.

But if you're intent on exploring the marriage of peat-smoked barley and a fine hand-rolled cigar, stick to the unadulterated versions.

Rum

Like a great cigar, rum is a child of the tropics. But its origins are at least 3,000 years older. The fermented juice of sugar cane was produced first in Asia, made its way through North Africa to Spain and finally arrived in the New World. It was a barter commodity that helped drive the slave trade and much of commerce in the seventeenth and eighteenth centuries.

The majority of rum is of the clear or white variety. It is the fuel for a host of fun cocktails that starts with rum and cola, moves on through Daiquiris, Planter's Punch and Piña Coladas, and ends with mixtures of just about any fruit juice known to man. Rum is the ultimate mixable.

But in recent years, the world has discovered what Latins have known

JEFF HARRIS

When You Find Fonseca, You've Found the Best.

for centuries: a dark, aged rum offers the same enjoyment and smooth character as an aged Cognac, single malt Scotch or Bourbon. After about five years of aging in charred oak barrels, the natural molasses colors turn amber and golden, and the flavors of maturity—vanilla, nuts, spices—come out on the palate.

Rum begins as molasses, using the by-product that remains after the crystallized sugar has been removed from sugar cane stalk. (There are other methods using cane juice and syrup, but they tend not to produce a product of equal quality.) This fact puts rum producers one step ahead of whiskey or vodka makers; in these grain-based products, starches from the grains must first be transformed into sugar.

The range of fermentation and distillation techniques that follows is remarkably diverse, making the word rum almost impossible to define. Some rum makers use a natural, slow fermentation of up to 12 days; others use a controlled fermentation with a secret yeast that produces results in a couple of days. Some use pot stills, much like Cognac stills, to refine their raw spirits; others use modern column stills that tend to produce cleaner, more neutral spirits.

Rum is then aged in used white-oak Bourbon barrels, with some charring of the insides to add color and flavor to the rum; the length of aging is determined by the maker's taste preferences. Almost all of the so-called aged or dark rums are blends of rums of different ages. United States law requires that any age statement on the label must refer to the youngest rum used in the blend, so a five-year-old rum cannot contain rums with less than five years of aging, but could include rums up to eight or ten years old.

Some of the aged rums available in America are Appleton Estate (Jamaica), Bacardi Añejo and Bacardi Gold Reserve (Puerto Rico), Bermúdez Aniversario (Dominican Republic), Ron Botran (Guatemala), Brugal (Dominican Republic), Flor de Caña (Nicaragua), Gosling's Black Seal (Bermuda), Mount Gay (Barbados), Myers's Rum (Jamaica), Pampero Aniversario (Venezuela), and Zacapa Centenario (Guatemala).

Connoisseurs can often identify rums based on their country of origin. Puerto Rican rums tend to be light. Barbados, Martinique, Nicaragua, Trinindad, and the Virgin Islands produce medium-bodied rums. And the rums from Bermuda, Guatemala, and Jamaica are usually the heaviest and darkest. The best rums are slow-fermented, distilled in pot stills and aged a long time.

Some professional cigar tasters in the Caribbean use rum to cleanse their palates between cigars. The reason is simple: the flavors and aromas of the tropics enhance the overall experience of smoking a cigar.

Bourbon

Bourbon is America's own, a homegrown whiskey that was invented in frontier-era Kentucky. Legend has it that a "white lightning" maker, Elijah Craig, suffered a warehouse fire that charred some of his shipping barrels. He filled them with freshly distilled spirit anyway.

When the shipment arrived in New Orleans, the liquid had an amber color and a noticeably softer flavor.

Bourbon is a strictly regulated spirit. To be called Bourbon, it must be made from at least 51 percent corn; most distillers use 65 to 75 percent with a percentage of wheat or

other grains often included in the fermentation mash. Bourbon must age a minimum of two years in new white-oak barrels that have been charred. No additives or colors are permitted. Though Bourbon can be made anywhere in the United States, only that made in Kentucky can have Bourbon on the label. Names like Jim Beam, Heaven Hill, Ancient Age, Early Times, Old Crow, Old Grand-Dad, and Wild Turkey are engraved in Bourbon drinkers' minds.

Some other great American whiskeys aren't called Bourbon, but are made in similar fashion, and often taste very much the same, too. Jack Daniel's and George Dickel are two Tennessee whiskeys. Jack Daniel's differs from Bourbon in that it is charcoal-filtered; its upscale brother, Gentleman Jack, receives two charcoal filterings. Both have a sweeter, smokier taste.

There's been a revolution in Bourbon-making during recent years: small-batch and single-barrel products are the fashion of the day. Most Bourbons are blends of several hundred different barrels that have been aged in huge warehouses and then mixed together to get a uniform taste. But "boutique" Bourbons may be a blend of only 20 barrels, or in several cases, are bottled from only one barrel. They usually carry a premium price, although some, like Maker's Mark, are around $20 in most markets. Other well-known brands are Basil Hayden, Booker's 107, Blanton's, Elijah Craig, Hancock's Reserve, Knob Creek, Rock Hill Farms, and Wild Turkey Rare Breed. You'll also find some "cask-strength" Bourbons in this group; they are bottled straight from the barrel without being cut with water, and the proofs may range up to 126.

Drinking Bourbon, whatever its origin, is a ritual that is as personal as shaving. Some people swear Bourbon should be consumed straight, others say cut with water, others insist that a couple of cubes of ice is all you need. The character of the Bourbon will change depending on the amount of water mixed in; some open up with floral and spice flavors, while others just taste watered down. Try your brand each way, and you'll find the right way for you. As for other drinks, Bourbon and ginger ale and the Whiskey Sour (shaken with sugar and lemon juice) are old favorites. And don't forge the Mint Julep, not really much more than Bourbon poured over cracked ice and mint leaves with a little sugar. Purists, however, reject anything but straight, pure Bourbon in their glass.

BUSINESS REPLY MAIL

FIRST-CLASS MAIL   PERMIT NO 1302   BOULDER, CO

POSTAGE WILL BE PAID BY ADDRESSEE

CIGAR
insider

P.O. Box 57602
Boulder, CO 80323-7602

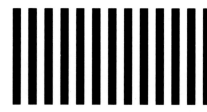

THIS IS A TEST
(SEE ANSWERS BELOW)

How do you spot a counterfeit Fuente Fuente OpusX a mile away?

What are the four top-scoring cigars ever rated?

Tobacco beetles have invaded your humidor. What do you do?

If you missed any of these questions,

call 800-644-4395

and order your subscription to
***Marvin Shanken's Cigar Insider* today.**
Next time, we promise a perfect score.

The cigar book you've been waiting for.

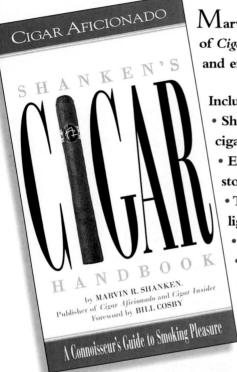

Marvin R. Shanken, editor and publisher of *Cigar Aficionado*, shares his knowledge and enthusiasm in this handy volume.

Includes:
- Shanken's picks of the top 40 cigar brands
- Expert advice on selecting and storing cigars
- The basics of cutting, holding, lighting, & smoking
- Finding a good tobacconist
- Directory of cigar names, sizes and strengths

Plus, the story behind the success of *Cigar Aficionado* magazine!

Published by

CIGAR
Aficionado

RUNNING PRESS
BOOK PUBLISHERS

Shanken's Cigar Handbook is available at bookstores and fine tobacconists everywhere for $24.95
Or call **800-761-4099** to order your copy today!

Visit our Web site at www.cigaraficionado.com
AOL Keyword: Cigar Aficionado

Chapter 11

Cigar Tasting Notes

LISTED BY SIZE AND SCORE

I n this section you will find complete descriptions and tasting notes for more than 1200 of the cigars rated by *Cigar Aficionado* since its founding in 1992—all of which were still available for purchase as this book went to press. They are arranged in these categories:

1) double coronas, Churchills, corona gordas, lonsdales, coronas, robustos, petit coronas, panatelas, and odd-sized, straight-sided cigars
2) unusually shaped cigars such as torpedos and pyramids (grouped together in the figurado category here)
3) a separate listing for the dark-wrapped cigars known as maduros

The cigar's score, arrived at by a panel of senior editors of *Cigar Aficionado* in blind tastings, reflects judgments made in four categories:

Appearance and Construction. The testers look for things like oiliness, firmness and overall consistency of wrapper color. Bulging veins, excessive spotting, marks and a rough finish are defects.

Smoking Characteristics. The way the cigar burns is evaluated; this includes the evenness of the burn and the color of the ash. The cigar's draw is also judged here.

Flavor. The tasters look for mild-, medium- and full-bodied characteristics. A description is then written about the taste of the cigar, which may include everything from cocoa beans and coffee to wet hay and grass. Spiciness is also a key factor. The "finish," or length of time that the flavors stay in the mouth, is noted as well.

Overall Impression. This is the taster's own opinion based on his summary of the cigar's characteristics.

All cigars are rated on a 100 point scale. The scoring system is as follows:
95–100: classic
90–94: outstanding
80–89: very good to excellent
70–79: average to good commercial quality
below 70: don't waste your money
N/A: Not Available

A note on prices: All prices listed here were current at the time of publication. But please be aware that: 1) Cigar prices change frequently. 2) Most prices listed are *manufacturers' suggested retail prices;* tobacconists are free to change any price they wish. Prices for cigars not available in the U.S. are listed in either British pounds sterling (£) or Swiss francs (SF).

The guide is formatted in three different ways. Following the tasting notes, you will find 1) a section with the cigars listed by country of origin and then by score within each size category; 2) an alphabetical listing by brand.

Cigar Tasting Notes

LISTED BY SIZE AND SCORE

Double Corona

Most of the following Double Corona tasting notes appeared in the October 1997 issue of Cigar Aficionado. *Exceptions are indicated by a date in parentheses at the end of the tasting note.*

HOYO DE MONTERREY DOUBLE CORONA **96**
Cuba • *Size:* 7⅝" x 49
Filler/Binder/Wrapper: Cuba
An extraordinary full-bodied smoke. This cigar is filled with cocoa and coffee bean flavors backed up by smooth woody and leathery notes. It has a perfect draw and a toastlike aroma. (03/01/95)
U.K.: £13.70

RAMON ALLONES GIGANTES **94**
Cuba • *Size:* 7⅝" x 49
Filler/Binder/Wrapper: Cuba
This cigar has a smooth, creamy texture with strong pepper and spice notes and a sweet, intense, nutty character on the finish. (03/01/95)
U.K.: £13.35

PARTAGAS LUSITANIA **93**
Cuba • *Size:* 7⅝" x 49
Filler/Binder/Wrapper: Cuba
A powerhouse of flavors. This cigar is filled with an earthy spiciness and strong pepper flavors. There is a hint of cocoa bean. A complex cigar that will age well.
U.K.: £13.70

ARTURO FUENTE CAÑONES **91**
Dominican Republic • *Size:* 8½" x 52 *Filler/Binder:* Dom. Rep. *Wrapper:* Ecuador
A beautiful, medium-bodied cigar. It has a sweet floral character, and sweet spices dominate the flavors. There is a light, leathery note on the finish. U.S.: $5.60

LA GLORIA CUBANA SOBERANOS **91**
U.S.A. • *Size:* 8" x 52 *Filler:* Dom. Rep, Nicaragua *Binder:* Dom. Rep. *Wrapper:* Ecuador
This cigar has strong flavors of spice and leather and delivers a smooth, full-bodied smoke. (03/01/95)
U.S.: $4.60

PUNCH DOUBLE CORONA **91**
Cuba • *Size:* 7⅝" x 49
Filler/Binder/Wrapper: Cuba
This is a strong cigar, with excellent tobacco character and a long finish. It has flavors of spice and leather that give it an earthy, almost herbal, complexity.
(03/01/95) U.K.: £13.50

LEON JIMENES NO. 1 **90**
Dominican Republic • *Size:* 7½" x 50 *Filler/Binder:* Dom. Rep. *Wrapper:* U.S.A./Conn. Shade
This cigar has a great balance. It is filled with a rich coffee bean flavor, and has hints of nuts. It has an overall cedary character, but with a slightly dry woody finish.
U.S.: $5.68

FUENTE FUENTE OPUS X DOUBLE CORONA **89**
Dominican Republic • *Size:* 7⅝" x 49 *Filler/Binder/Wrapper:* Dom. Rep.
A cigar loaded with sweet spice and leather flavors with a solid earthiness. It is well-balanced and smooth, with just a hint of dryness on the finish. U.S.: $14.50

PARTAGAS NO. 10 **89**
Dominican Republic • *Size:* 7½" x 49 *Filler:* Dom. Rep., Mexico *Binder:* Mexico *Wrapper:* Cameroon
A medium-bodied cigar with a solid core of spicy flavors. There are hints of a light, vegetal element on the palate. U.S.: $6.75

Romeo y Julieta Vintage No. 5 **89**

Dominican Republic • *Size:* 7½" x 50 *Filler:* Dom. Rep. *Binder:* Mexico *Wrapper:* U.S.A./Conn. Shade
A medium-bodied cigar that has a light, nutty character with some flavors of mild, sweet spices such as nutmeg. (03/01/95) U.S.: $8.70

Astral Maestro **88**

Honduras • *Size:* 7½" x 52 *Filler/Binder:* Dom. Rep., Nicaragua *Wrapper:* Ecuador
A cigar with a smooth and nutty character. It is a mild to medium smoke with a solid woody finish. U.S.: $7.20

La Gloria Cubana Churchill **88**

U.S.A. • *Size:* 7" x 50 *Filler/Binder:* Dom. Rep., Brazil, Mexico *Wrapper:* Ecuador
Rich and decadent smoke. The wrapper is dark brown, with a great sheen. It is a full-bodied, powerful cigar with fascinating caramel, chocolate flavors and a mouth-filling texture. (12/01/92) U.S.: $4.40

Oscar Supreme **88**

Dominican Republic • *Size:* 8" x 48 *Filler/Binder:* Dom. Rep. *Wrapper:* U.S.A./Conn. Shade
This cigar has solid tobacco flavors and a steely, mineral characteristic that is backed up by a distinct spiciness. (03/01/95) U.S.: $11.55

Por Larrañaga Fabuloso **88**

Dominican Republic • *Size:* 7" x 50 *Filler/Binder:* Dom. Rep. *Wrapper:* U.S.A./Conn. Shade
A mellow, medium-bodied cigar that has some earthy elements, almost flintlike, but with a good solid depth of spicy flavors. (03/01/95) U.S.: $7.50

8-9-8 Collection Churchill **87**

Jamaica • *Size:* 7½" x 49 *Filler:* Dom. Rep., Jamaica *Binder:* Mexico *Wrapper:* U.S.A./Conn. Shade
This is a well-made, medium-bodied cigar. There are hints of nuts on the palate, and there is an overall creamy character with a light, spicy finish. U.S.: $9.75

Ashton Churchill **87**

Dominican Republic • *Size:* 7½" x 52 *Filler/Binder:* Dom. Rep. *Wrapper:* U.S.A./Conn. Shade
A very well-made, medium-bodied cigar. It has peppery flavors, and a pleasant earthiness on the palate with an overall light, sweet herb character. U.S.: $7.75

Aurora Double Corona **87**

Dominican Republic • *Size:* 7½" x 50 *Filler/Binder:* Dom. Rep. *Wrapper:* Cameroon
This is a smooth-tasting cigar with a good balance. There is a sweet spiciness on the palate. It is medium-bodied. U.S.: $5.12

Bauza Fabuloso **87**

Dominican Republic • *Size:* 7½" x 50 *Filler:* Dom. Rep., Nicaragua *Binder:* Mexico *Wrapper:* Ecuador
A cigar with an earthy spiciness. There is a mineral tone with a bite on the finish, but it is a solid cigar. U.S.: $6.00

Cacique Inca #8 **87**

Dominican Republic • *Size:* 7½" x 50 *Filler/Binder:* Dom. Rep. *Wrapper:* U.S.A./Conn. Shade
A mild- to medium-bodied cigar. It has an interesting combination of earthiness and a hazelnut flavor with some coffee grounds and dried orange peel. A little young. U.S.: $5.50

Cuesta-Rey Cabinet No. 1 **87**

Dominican Republic • *Size:* 8½" x 52 *Filler/Binder:* Dom. Rep. *Wrapper:* U.S.A./Conn. Shade
This creamy cigar has a solid core of sweet herbs, with a subtle hint of leather on the palate and finish. U.S.: $6.25

Da Vinci Leonardo **87**

Honduras • *Size:* 8½" x 52 *Filler/Binder:* Dom. Rep., Honduras, Nicaragua *Wrapper:* Ecuador
A creamy nuttiness makes this a well-balanced medium-bodied cigar. There are some light herbal spice flavors on the palate. U.S.: $7.55

DON ASA CHURCHILL 87
Honduras • *Size:* 7½" x 50
Filler/Binder: Honduras
Wrapper: Indonesia
A well-balanced cigar that
should improve with age. It
has a nice, light spiceness on
a mild to medium smoke, and
good tobacco character.
U.S.: $8.00

DON LEO CHURCHILL 87
Dominican Republic • *Size:*
7½" x 50 *Filler/Binder:* Dom.
Rep. *Wrapper:*
U.S.A./Conn. Shade
A pleasant mild- to medium-
bodied cigar. It has some
creamy flavors with an earthy
backbone. It is well balanced
and has a light herbal finish.
U.S.: $5.80

**EL REY DEL MUNDO 87
FLOR DEL MUNDO**
Honduras • *Size:* 7½" x 54
Filler: Dom. Rep, Honduras
Binder/Wrapper: Honduras
Inconsistent. Several tasters
had cigars with too tight a
draw. It does have some
smooth, spicy flavors and a
woody, earthy aftertaste but
may need more aging.
(03/01/95) U.S.: $5.00

**HABANA GOLD STER-
LING VINTAGE PRESI-
DENTE 87**
Honduras • *Size:* 8½" x 52
Filler: Nicaragua
Binder/Wrapper: Ecuador
A well-balanced cigar. It is
smooth-tasting. There are
hints of wood and nuts, and a
light floral character with a
core of sweet spices.
U.S.: $7.75

**LA REGENTA INDIVID- 87
UAL**
Canary Islands • *Size:* 8" x 50
Filler/Binder: Dom. Rep.,
Brazil *Wrapper:*
U.S.A./Conn. Shade
A pleasant, mild- to medium-
bodied cigar. It is creamy and
smooth-tasting, with some
soft herbal and dried orange
peel flavors. U.S.: $8.00

LA REGENTA PREMIER 87
Canary Islands • *Size:* 7½" x
50 *Filler/Binder:* Dom. Rep.,
Brazil *Wrapper:*
U.S.A./Conn. Shade
An earthy quality. It has a
creamy, peppery core of flavors and a sweet, woody finish. U.S.: $7.75

**PLAYBOY BY 87
DON DIEGO CHURCHILL**
Dominican Republic • *Size:*
7¾" x 50 *Filler/Binder:* Dom.
Rep. *Wrapper:*
U.S.A./Conn. Shade
A good, mild- to medium-
bodied smoke. It is well balanced, and there are some
strong toasty flavors with a
hint of herbalness and a
light, earthy finish.
U.S.: $12.50

**SANTA CLARA 1830 87
NO. I**
Mexico • *Size:* 7½" x 52
Filler/Binder/Wrapper: Mexico
A straightforward, medium-
bodied cigar with flavors of
mild spices and a bit of nutti-
ness. (03/01/95) U.S.: $3.00

VUELTABAJO GIGANTE 87
Dominican Republic • *Size:*
8½" x 52 *Filler/Binder:* Dom.
Rep. *Wrapper:*
U.S.A./Conn. Shade
A smooth, creamy tasting
cigar. There are some leath-
ery flavors with a sweet spici-
ness, and a light salty finish.
U.S.: $4.70

C.A.O. CHURCHILL 86
Honduras • *Size:* 8" x 50
Filler: Nicaragua, Mexico
Binder: Honduras *Wrapper:*
U.S.A./Conn. Shade
This is medium-bodied cigar.
It has some solid flavors of
nuts and sweet woods, like
cedar. It has a woody finish.
U.S.: $8.00

**DAVIDOFF SPECIAL 86
SERIES DOUBLE "R"**
Dominican Republic • *Size:*
7½" x 50 *Filler/Binder:* Dom.
Rep. *Wrapper:*
U.S.A./Conn. Shade
A mild, pungent aroma leads
into a toastiness on the
palate. This cigar has a long
finish with cedar, nuts and a
hint of sweetness.
U.S.: $20.00

**DON LINO HAVANA 86
RESERVE CHURCHILL**
Dominican Republic • *Size:*
7½" x 50 *Filler/Binder:* Honduras *Wrapper:*
U.S.A./Conn. Shade
This is a smooth-tasting cigar
with some perfumed aromas,
but a slightly dry, strawlike
finish. (03/01/95) U.S.: $5.06

DON TOMAS SPECIAL EDITION NO. 1 86
Honduras • *Size:* 7½" x 50
Filler: Dom. Rep., Mexico, Nicaragua *Binder:* Mexico *Wrapper:* Indonesia
A cigar with some earthy qualities. There is a light fruity character, with a hint of sweet herbs on the mild- to medium-bodied smoke. U.S.: $6.00

EL REY DEL MUNDO CORONATION 86
Honduras • *Size:* 8½" x 52
Filler: Dom. Rep., Honduras *Binder:* Honduras *Wrapper:* Ecuador
A pleasant, sweet spiciness dominates this mild- to medium-bodied cigar. It has an earthy aroma. U.S.: $5.25

EL RICO HABANO GRAN HABANERO DELUXE 86
Dominican Republic • *Size:* 7¼" x 50 *Filler:* Nicaragua *Binder:* Dom. Rep. *Wrapper:* Ecuador
A spicy, medium- to full-bodied cigar. It has some sweet wood elements on the palate, but lacks good balance. U.S.: $4.10

EXCELSIOR NO. 5 86
Mexico • *Size:* 8" x 50
Filler/Binder: Mexico *Wrapper:* U.S.A./Conn. Shade
This is a solid cigar with nutty, earthy character. It shows some youth, but overall has a smooth creaminess. U.S.: $7.75

HOYO DE MONTERREY PRESIDENTE 86
Honduras • *Size:* 8½" x 52
Filler: Dom. Rep., Honduras, Nicaragua *Binder:* Honduras *Wrapper:* U.S.A./Conn. Shade
A mild- to medium-bodied cigar with an overall sweet tobacco character. There are woody flavors on the palate and the finish. U.S.: $5.50

JOYA DE NICARAGUA VIAJANTE 86
Nicaragua • *Size:* 8½" x 52
Filler/Binder: Nicaragua *Wrapper:* Ecuador
Although this cigar has a medium- to full-bodied style, there is a slightly odd perfumy quality to it. There are some sweet spice flavors. U.S.: $7.00

MATCH PLAY OLYMPIC 86
Dominican Republic • *Size:* 7½" x 50 *Filler/Binder:* Dom. Rep. *Wrapper:* Ecuador
This is a well-made, medium-bodied cigar. It has a pleasant character of wood, and there is a touch of nuttiness on the palate. U.S.: $6.25

PETRUS TABACAGE DC HAVANA 86
Honduras • *Size:* 7¼" x 50
Filler/Binder/Wrapper: Honduras
Young tobacco may have affected this cigar. It has good flavors of spice, nuts and coffee, but it was a little rough. (03/01/95) U.S.: $7.40

ROYAL JAMAICA GIANT CORONA 86
Dominican Republic • *Size:* 7½" x 49 *Filler:* Dom. Rep., Jamaica, Indonesia *Binder:* Cameroon *Wrapper:* Indonesia
A slow start, but this cigar builds to a well-balanced combination of sweet spices, and a light nuttiness on the palate. It has an underlying herbal character, but a rather flat finish. U.S.: $5.25

TABACOS SAN JOSE PRESIDENTE 86
U.S.A. • *Size:* 8" x 52
Filler/Binder: Dom. Rep., Nicaragua, Honduras, Brazil *Wrapper:* Ecuador
A nicely balanced cigar. It has a cedary flavor with some saltiness, and a sweet spice finish. Price N/A

THOMAS HINDS HONDURAN SELECTION PRESIDENTE 86
Honduras • *Size:* 8½" x 52
Filler/Binder: Honduras *Wrapper:* Ecuador
Although this cigar has some construction flaws, it has a creamy, sweet character. It is mild- to medium-bodied. U.S.: $6.65

TROYA CLASICO NO. 72 EXECUTIVE 86
Dominican Republic • *Size:* 7¼" x 50 *Filler/Binder:* Dom. Rep. *Wrapper:* U.S.A./Conn. Shade
This is a mild- to medium-bodied cigar. There are some flavors of nuts with a slightly creamy character. A dry finish. U.S.: $8.60

BERING GRANDE   **85**
Honduras • *Size:* 8½" x 52
Filler: Dom. Rep., Mexico
Binder: Honduras *Wrapper:*
U.S.A./Conn. Shade
This mild- to medium-bodied
cigar has a sweet wood com-
ponent on the palate, with
some hints of herbs and a
smooth creaminess.
U.S.: $3.20

CANONERO "MEDI-   **85**
ANO"
DOUBLE CORONA
Brazil • *Size:* 7½" x 50
Filler/Binder: Brazil *Wrapper:*
Ecuador
A cigar with a mild creami-
ness on the palate. It is well-
balanced, with a woody fin-
ish. U.S.: $5.25

CUESTA-REY CENTEN-   **85**
NIAL COLLECTION
DOMINICAN NO. 1
Dominican Republic • *Size:*
8½" x 52 *Filler/Binder:* Dom.
Rep. *Wrapper:* U.S.A./
Conn. Shade
A well-made cigar. It has a
good balance of creaminess
with an herbal core of fla-
vors. U.S.: $6.50

DANIEL MARSHALL   **85**
DOUBLE CORONA
Dominican Republic • *Size:*
7½" x 50 *Filler/Binder:* Dom.
Rep. *Wrapper:* U.S.A./
Conn. Shade
A mild, herbal and slightly
peppery smoke. It is smooth
on the palate. Well-made
with an herbal character.
U.S.: $6.95

DON LINO CHURCHILL   **85**
Honduras • *Size:* 8" x 50
Filler/Binder: Dom. Rep.
Wrapper: U.S.A./Conn.
Shade
This is a very light-wrapped
cigar with a nice creamy nut-
tiness and some solid tobacco
flavors. (03/01/95)
U.S.: $4.80

DON TOMAS PRESI-   **85**
DENTE
Honduras • *Size:* 7½" x 50
Filler: Dom. Rep., Mexico,
Nicaragua *Binder:* Mexico
Wrapper: Indonesia
A pleasant, mild- to medium-
bodied smoke. It has a good
balance, with a hint of spice
flavors, and a nice woody fin-
ish. U.S.: $5.30

HABANA GOLD BLACK   **85**
LABEL PRESIDENTE
Honduras • *Size:* 8½" x 52
Filler/Binder: Nicaragua
Wrapper: Indonesia
This cigar has a nutty, floral
character, and some spice on
a long, medium-bodied fin-
ish. U.S.: $6.70

JOSÉ BENITO PRESI-   **85**
DENTE
Dominican Republic • *Size:*
7¾" x 50 *Filler:* Dom. Rep.
Binder: Central America
Wrapper: Cameroon
This is a rich-tasting, medium-bodied cigar that has
some creamy coffee flavors
and a core of spiciness.
(03/01/95) U.S.: $5.70

LA FINCA BOLIVARES   **85**
Nicaragua • *Size:* 7½" x 50
Filler/Binder/Wrapper:
Nicaragua
This cigar burned a little hot.
It has some pepper and nut-
meg flavors, but with a rustic
edge to them. (03/01/95)
U.S.: $2.50

LA FLOR DOMINICANA   **85**
PRESIDENTE
Dominican Republic • *Size:*
8" x 50 *Filler/Binder:* Dom.
Rep. *Wrapper:* U.S.A./
Conn. Shade
This is a well-made cigar. It
has a good balance, and some
toastiness on the palate, with
some sweet herb flavors.
U.S.: $8.50

LA HOJA SELECTA   **85**
COSIAC
U.S.A. • *Size:* 7" x 49
Filler/Binder: Dom. Rep.,
Nicaragua *Wrapper:*
U.S.A./Conn. Shade
Another winner from El
Credito Cigars, this is a won-
derfully constructed cigar,
with an attractive medium-
brown wrapper. The La Hoja
Selecta double corona is mild,
with pretty, nutty flavors and
a slightly bitter aftertaste.
(12/01/92) U.S.: $4.20

LA TRADICION CABI-   **85**
NET SERIES DOUBLE
CORONA
U.S.A. • *Size:* 7⅝" x 50
Filler: Dom. Rep., Nicaragua,
Honduras *Binder/Wrapper:*
Ecuador
This cigar is a solid medium-
bodied smoke. But it is a lit-
tle rustic on the palate. Some
wood and spice. U.S.: $5.80

LEMPIRA PRESIDENTE 85
Honduras • *Size:* 7¾" x 50
Filler: Nicaragua, Honduras
Binder: Dom. Rep. *Wrapper:*
U.S.A./Conn. Shade
This is a mild cigar. It has a
light creaminess, and a hint
of wood on the palate. There
is some spice on the finish.
U.S.: $5.80

MAYA VIAJANTES 85
Honduras • *Size:* 8½" x 52
Filler: Nicaragua, Honduras
Binder: Honduras *Wrapper:*
U.S.A./Conn. Shade
This cigar is well-balanced,
with a mix of leather and
light pepper flavors. It has a
creamy texture. U.S.: $6.00

ONYX NO. 852 85
Dominican Republic • *Size:*
8" x 52 *Filler:* Dom. Rep.,
Mexico *Binder:* Indonesia
Wrapper: Mexico
A mild, maduro-style cigar. It
has a core of woody, sweet
tobacco flavors, and good
balance. U.S.: $4.85

PADRÓN EXECUTIVE 85
Nicaragua • *Size:* 7½" x 50
Filler/Binder/Wrapper:
Nicaragua
This is a smooth-smoking
cigar. There is a coffee
ground flavor on the palate,
and an herbal spiciness.
U.S.: $5.00

PLEIADES ALDEBARAN 85
Dominican Republic • *Size:*
8½" x 50 *Filler/Binder:* Dom.
Rep. *Wrapper:*
U.S.A./Conn. Shade
A cigar with a creamy char-
acter. There is a strong flavor

of black pepper, too, with a
light, herbal finish.
U.S.: $14.90

ROYAL JAMAICA 85
CHURCHILL
Dominican Republic • *Size:*
8" x 51 *Filler:* Dom. Rep.,
Jamaica, Indonesia *Binder:*
Cameroon *Wrapper:*
Indonesia
A medium-bodied cigar. It
has a light, salty character,
with a solid earthiness on the
palate. U.S.: $6.50

SOSA MAGNUM 85
Dominican Republic • *Size:*
7¾" x 50 *Filler:* Dom. Rep.
Binder: Nicaragua *Wrapper:*
Ecuador
A well-made cigar. It is quite
mild on the palate, with a
hint of vegetal flavors,
backed up by an earthy component. U.S.: $5.25

AVO NO. 3 84
Dominican Republic • *Size:*
7½" x 50 *Filler/Binder:* Dom.
Rep. *Wrapper:*
U.S.A./Conn. Shade
A young cigar with a slight
gumminess to the wrapper.
But it has an underlying
sweet herbal quality with a
dry, woody finish. U.S.: $7.90

CAMÓRRA 84
DOUBLE CORONA
Honduras • *Size:* 8" x 52
Filler/Binder/Wrapper:
Dom. Rep.
A maduro-style cigar. There
is a sweet tobacco flavor in it,
and a woody quality to the
finish. U.S.: $5.12

CASA BLANCA PRESI- 84
DENTE
Dominican Republic • *Size:*
7½" x 50 *Filler:* Dom. Rep.
Binder: Mexico *Wrapper:*
U.S.A./Conn. Shade
This cigar is a bit dry on the
finish. But there is a hint of
leather flavors, and a light
woodiness. U.S.: $3.25

CERDAN DON JUAN 84
Dominican Republic • *Size:*
7½" x 50 *Filler/Binder:* Dom.
Rep. *Wrapper:*
U.S.A./Conn. Shade
A light creamy character
dominates this cigar. It has a
stemmy quality on the finish.
U.S.: $7.58

CROWN ACHIEVEMENT 84
CHURCHILL
Honduras • *Size:* 8" x 50
Filler: Honduras, Nicaragua,
Costa Rica *Binder:* Dom.
Rep. *Wrapper:* Ecuador
A well-made cigar with an
overall dry character. There
are some vegetal notes, but
with a soft spiciness and a
woody finish. U.S.: $8.50

DAVIDOFF ANIVER- 84
SARIO NO. 1
Dominican Republic • *Size:*
8⅔" x 48 *Filler/Binder:* Dom.
Rep. *Wrapper:*
U.S.A./Conn. Shade
This cigar has some light
spiciness on the palate. But it
is also very dry. U.S.: $23.00

DON LINO COLORADO **84**
PRESIDENTE
Dominican Republic • *Size:*
7½" x 50 *Filler/Binder:* Honduras, Nicaragua *Wrapper:*
U.S.A./Conn. Shade
A very mild, light cigar with some sweet, dry aromas and flavors. (03/01/95)
U.S.: $5.28

H. UPMANN CABINET **84**
SELECTION COLUMBO
Dominican Republic • *Size:*
8" x 50 *Filler/Binder:* Dom.
Rep. *Wrapper:* Indonesia
A cigar with some rustic qualities. It has a sweet, dried fruit character, with a hint of nuts and a slight oiliness on the palate. U.S.: $8.50

LA GLORIA CUBANA **84**
GLORIA INMENSA
Dominican Republic • *Size:*
7½" x 48 *Filler:* Dom. Rep.,
Nicaragua *Binder/Wrapper:*
Ecuador
A very young cigar. The tobacco tastes raw. But it is well made, and there are some toasty elements on the palate. U.S.: $4.45

LICENCIADOS **84**
PRESIDENTE
Dominican Republic • *Size:*
8" x 50 *Filler/Binder:* Dom.
Rep. *Wrapper:*
U.S.A./Conn. Shade
A dry character, but there is a light spiciness and a woody finish. U.S.: $5.05

LICENCIADOS **84**
SOBERANO
Dominican Republic • *Size:*
8½" x 52 *Filler/Binder:* Dom.

Rep. *Wrapper:* U.S.A./
Conn. Shade
A mild- to medium-bodied cigar. There is some spiciness on the finish, and a solid herbal note on the palate.
U.S.: $5.30

MACABI SUPER **84**
CORONA
Dominican Republic • *Size:*
7¾" x 50 *Filler/Binder:* Dom.
Rep. *Wrapper:* U.S.A./
Conn. Shade
This cigar has a flat, dry finish. But there are some nut flavors. Well-made.
U.S.: $5.40

MACANUDO **84**
PRINCE OF WALES
Jamaica • *Size:* 8" x 52
Filler: Dom. Rep., Mexico
Binder: Mexico *Wrapper:*
U.S.A./Conn. Shade
This cigar has elements of sweet dried fruit and herbs on the palate. A mild, dry finish.
U.S.: $7.05

MICUBANO NO. 852 **84**
Nicaragua • *Size:* 8" x 52
Filler/Binder/Wrapper:
Nicaragua
This cigar has a sweet-wood and dried-fruit charater. It is sweet and mild, and finishes on a herbal note. U.S.: $5.75

PAUL GARMIRIAN **84**
DOUBLE CORONA
Dominican Republic • *Size:*
7⅜" x 50 *Filler/Binder:* Dom.
Rep. *Wrapper:*
U.S.A./Conn. Shade
This is a mild- to medium-bodied cigar. It has a dryness

on the palate, with a light, nutty finish. U.S.: $12.65

PETERSON PRESIDENTE **84**
Dominican Republic • *Size:*
7½" x 50 *Filler:* Dom. Rep.
Binder: Ecuador *Wrapper:*
U.S.A./Conn. Shade
A mild- to medium-bodied cigar. It is a little dry on the palate, and there is an herbal note. U.S.: $8.00

PUNCH PRESIDENTE **84**
Honduras • *Size:* 8½" x 52
Filler: Dom. Rep., Honduras,
Nicaragua *Binder:* Honduras
Wrapper: U.S.A./Conn.
Shade
A fairly mild, neutral tasting cigar. There is a hint of nuttiness on a soft, vegetal character. U.S.: $5.50

TE-AMO CEO **84**
Mexico • *Size:* 8½" x 52
Filler/Binder/Wrapper: Mexico
A mild- to medium-bodied cigar with a light, perfumy quality. It ends on a dry note, with a hint of flintiness.
U.S.: $4.25

THE GRIFFIN'S **84**
PRESTIGE
Dominican Republic • *Size:*
7½" x 50 *Filler/Binder:* Dom.
Rep. *Wrapper:*
U.S.A./Conn. Shade
A mild, herbal cigar. It seems a little young. But it is well made. U.S.: $8.50

TRESADO SELECCION **84**
NO. 100
Dominican Republic • *Size:*
8" x 52 *Filler:* Dom. Rep.

Binder: Cameroon *Wrapper:* Indonesia
A little rustic. There is some spice on the palate, and it is pretty well balanced. A dry, woody finish. U.S.: $3.25

V CENTENNIAL PRESIDENTE   84
Honduras • *Size:* 8" x 50
Filler: Dom. Rep., Honduras, Nicaragua *Binder:* Mexico
Wrapper: U.S.A./Conn. Shade
There is a touch of spiciness on an otherwise quite dry cigar. It has a slightly papery finish. U.S.: $7.65

BALLENA SUPREMA DANLI COLLECTION ENCANTO   83
Honduras • *Size:* 8" x 50
Filler: Dom. Rep., Mexico
Binder: Mexico *Wrapper:* U.S.A./Conn. Shade
A nutty character. But the cigar has a light sharpness on the palate, and a papery quality on the finish. U.S.: $4.60

CARRINGTON No. 1   83
Dominican Republic • *Size:* 7½" x 50 *Filler/Binder:* Dom. Rep. *Wrapper:* U.S.A./Conn. Shade
An overall woody character makes this a mild cigar. It is a bit young. U.S.: $5.80

CRUZ REAL No. 14   83
Mexico • *Size:* 7½" x 50
Filler/Binder/Wrapper: Mexico
A well-balanced cigar. There is a hint of a vegetal quality, but with a solid, oily tobacco flavor. It has a dry, wood finish. U.S.: $5.00

DON LEO PRESIDENTE   83
Dominican Republic • *Size:* 8" x 52 *Filler/Binder:* Dom. Rep. *Wrapper:* U.S.A./Conn. Shade
A mild- to medium-bodied cigar. It has a vegetal quality, with a hint of woody flavors. U.S.: $6.20

DON XAVIER CHURCHILL   83
Canary Islands • *Size:* 7½" x 50 *Filler/Binder:* Canary Islands, Dom. Rep., Brazil *Wrapper:* U.S.A./Conn. Shade
While this cigar has some earthy, spicy qualities, it is very dry on the finish. U.S.: $7.25

EL SUBLIMADO CHURCHILL   83
Dominican Republic • *Size:* 8" x 48 *Filler/Binder:* Dom. Rep. *Wrapper:* Ecuador
A solid core of nutty flavors, almost hazelnut in quality. There is an overall herbal character to the cigar, with a firm draw. U.S.: $13.00

FELIPE GREGORIO GLORIOSO   83
Honduras • *Size:* 7¾" x 50 *Filler/Binder/Wrapper:* Honduras
A rustic cigar, with a flinty, papery quality. There is some spice on the finish. U.S.: $9.80

JOSÉ MARTÍ MARTÍ   83
Dominican Republic • *Size:* 7½" x 50 *Filler/Binder:* Dom. Rep. *Wrapper:* U.S.A./Conn. Shade

A medium-bodied cigar. It is very dry on the palate with a sharp woody finish. There are some hints of dried fruit on the palate. U.S.: $4.00

JOSÉ MARTÍ REY DEL REY   83
Nicaragua • *Size:* 8½" x 52
Filler: Dom. Rep., Honduras, Nicaragua *Binder:* Honduras
Wrapper: Ecuador
Although this cigar has some light spice notes on the palate, it has an overall papery quality. A light dry finish. U.S.: $3.25

LA FONTANA MICHELANGELO   83
Honduras • *Size:* 7½" x 52
Filler: Honduras *Binder:* Mexico *Wrapper:* U.S.A./Conn. Shade
This is a very loosely filled cigar with a hot draw. It has dry, strawlike flavors and a very dry, papery finish. (03/01/95) U.S.: $4.35

MACANUDO PRINCE PHILIP   83
Jamaica • *Size:* 7½" x 49
Filler: Dom. Rep., Mexico
Binder: Mexico *Wrapper:* U.S.A./Conn. Shade
A quite mild cigar. It has a papery quality on the palate and the finish. U.S.: $6.00

MACANUDO VINTAGE CABINET SELECTION 1993 I **83**
Jamaica • *Size:* 7½" x 49
Filler: Dom. Rep., Mexico
Binder: Mexico *Wrapper:* U.S.A./Conn. Shade
A pleasant, mild cigar. It has a definite dry wood character on the palate, and a light woody finish. U.S.: $11.50

MANIFIESTO DOUBLE CORONA **83**
Dominican Republic • *Size:* 7½" x 50 *Filler/Binder:* Dom. Rep. *Wrapper:* Indonesia
This cigar is rather flat on the finish. But it has some light notes of spice and wood. Price N/A

NAT SHERMAN LANDMARK SELECTION DAKOTA **83**
Dominican Republic • *Size:* 7½" x 49 *Filler:* Dom. Rep. *Binder:* Mexico *Wrapper:* Cameroon
A slightly rustic cigar. It has a mild to medium body. There is a hint of vegetal quality on the palate, with a dry, woody finish. U.S.: $9.10

DON JUAN PRESIDENTE **82**
Nicaragua • *Size:* 8½" x 50
Filler: Dom. Rep., Nicaragua
Binder: Nicaragua *Wrapper:* U.S.A./Conn. Shade
A dry character. This cigar has some spicy flavors, but finishes quite dry. U.S.: $5.25

F.D. GRAVE CHURCHILL **82**
Honduras • *Size:* 7¼" x 50
Filler: Dom. Rep., U.S.A.,

Honduras *Binder:* U.S.A.
Wrapper: U.S.A./Conn. Broadleaf
This cigar has a hint of orange peel flavors on the palate. But it is quite dry, with a flat, woody finish. U.S.: $3.81

LA UNICA NO. 100 **82**
Dominican Republic • *Size:* 8½" x 52 *Filler/Binder:* Dom. Rep. *Wrapper:* U.S.A./Conn. Shade
A salty character. This cigar has a mild flavor profile with a hint of toastiness, and some creaminess on the palate. U.S.: $5.30

LAS CABRILLAS COLUMBUS **82**
Honduras • *Size:* 8¼" x 52
Filler: Dom. Rep., Mexico
Binder: Mexico *Wrapper:* U.S.A./Conn. Shade
A mild, smooth-tasting cigar with a flinty, mineral quality. There are some light woody flavors on the finish. U.S.: $3.20

SOSA FAMILY SELECTION NO. 9 **82**
Dominican Republic • *Size:* 7¼" x 51 *Filler:* Dom. Rep. *Binder:* Mexico *Wrapper:* U.S.A./Conn. Shade
This cigar is quite mild. It has a dry finish, with some sweet herbal flavors on the palate. U.S.: $5.75

VARGAS CHURCHILL **82**
Canary Islands • *Size:* 7½" x 50 *Filler:* Canary Islands, Dom. Rep. *Binder/Wrapper:* Indonesia

A rustic cigar with some hints of leather and wood on the palate. Overall, it has a vegetal character. U.S.: $6.00

DON MELO PRESIDENTE **81**
Honduras • *Size:* 8½" x 50
Filler/Binder/Wrapper: Honduras
A young, slightly harsh cigar. It has a medium body, and a salty character. U.S.: $7.60

PETRUS TABACAGE DOUBLE CORONA 89 **81**
Honduras • *Size:* 7¾" x 50
Filler: Nicaragua *Binder:* Honduras *Wrapper:* Ecuador
Some inconsistency in construction. This cigar has some good tobacco qualities, with a light nuttiness. U.S.: $7.40

TROYA NO. 72 EXECUTIVE **81**
Dominican Republic • *Size:* 7¼" x 50 *Filler/Binder:* Dom. Rep. *Wrapper:* U.S.A./Conn. Shade
This cigar has a slight metallic taste to it. It seems young. U.S.: $5.80

BELINDA PRIME MINISTER **80**
Honduras • *Size:* 7½" x 50
Filler: Dom. Rep., Honduras
Binder: Honduras *Wrapper:* Ecuador
A very rustic cigar. It has a tough draw, with a very woody character. U.S.: $3.00

NAT SHERMAN **80**
CITY DESK SELECTION
TRIBUNE
Dominican Republic • *Size:*
7½" x 50 *Filler/Binder:* Dom.
Rep., Mexico *Wrapper:*
Mexico
A maduro-style cigar. It has a
very mild character, with a
flat, dry finish. U.S.: $6.50

CANONERO **79**
"CLASSICO"
DOUBLE CORONA
Brazil • *Size:* 7½" x 50
Filler/Binder: Brazil *Wrapper:*
U.S.A./Conn. Shade
This cigar has a very dry,
papery quality. There is a
grassiness on the palate, and
a metallic finish. U.S.: $5.25

TABACOS SAN JOSE **79**
DOUBLE CORONA
U.S.A. • *Size:* 7⅝" x 50
Filler/Binder: Dom. Rep.,
Nicaragua, Honduras, Brazil
Wrapper: Ecuador
This cigar has a heavy, green
vegetable character. It ends
with a rather flinty finish,
with just a hint of wood.
Price N/A

EXCELSIOR INDIVIDUAL **78**
Mexico • *Size:* 8½" x 52
Filler/Binder: Mexico *Wrapper:* U.S.A./Conn. Shade
A mild cigar with some
toasty elements on the
palate. It is also quite dry,
and it has dry, flat finish.
U.S.: $13.50

HABANA GOLD WHITE **78**
LABEL PRESIDENTE
Honduras • *Size:* 8½" x 52
Filler/Binder/Wrapper:
Nicaragua
A flat, rather mild cigar.
There is a hint of woodiness
on the palate and finish.
U.S.: $7.20

TE-AMO CHURCHILL **78**
Mexico • *Size:* 7½" x 50
Filler/Binder/Wrapper: Mexico
A mild, woody cigar. There is
a hint of dark earth on the
finish, but overall it is quite
mild and one-dimensional.
U.S.: $3.95

LA FINCA GRAN FINCA **77**
Nicaragua • *Size:* 8½" x 52
Filler/Binder/Wrapper:
Nicaragua
A cigar with a very dry char-
acter, and almost soapy taste.
It has a very young wrapper,
and it is very mild.
U.S.: $2.75

PUNCH GRAN CRU **77**
PRINCE CONSORT
Honduras • *Size:* 8½" x 52
Filler: Dom. Rep., Honduras,
Nicaragua *Binder:* Honduras
Wrapper: U.S.A./Conn.
Shade
This cigar has a very rough,
dry taste. Although there is a
light herbaceousness, the
cigar finishes with a slight
metallic quality. U.S.: $7.00

MAYA EXECUTIVE **75**
Honduras • *Size:* 7¾" x 50
Filler/Binder: Honduras,
Nicaragua *Wrapper:*
U.S.A./Conn. Shade

A bitter, papery cigar. It is
quite harsh, with some stale
tobacco qualities. U.S.: $5.50

PENAMIL NO. 57 **69**
Canary Islands • *Size:* 7½" x
50 *Filler:* Special Blend
Binder: Dom. Rep. *Wrapper:*
U.S.A./Conn. Shade
It is hard to find something
nice to say about this cigar.
The wrapper was so brittle
that it broke in most of our
smokers' hands. Worse, it
burnt as fast as a quickly
burning fuse. Forget it.
(12/01/92) U.S.: $5.15

Churchill

*Most of the following Churchill
tasting notes appeared in the
February 1998 issue of* Cigar
Aficionado. *Exceptions are
indicated by a date in parentheses at the end of the tasting note.*

PUNCH CHURCHILL **93**
Cuba • *Size:* 7" x 47
Filler/Binder/Wrapper: Cuba
A cigar packed with sweet
spicy flavors of nutmeg and
an earthy complexity on the
palate. It has notes of coffee
beans, leather and cedar.
U.K.: £11.90

BAHIA GOLD **90**
CHURCHILL
Costa Rica • *Size:* 6⅞" x 48
Filler/Binder: Dom. Rep.
Wrapper: Ecuador
A medium- to full-bodied
cigar. It has a strong pepper flavor with some complex earth
and leather notes on the
palate, and it has a sweet wood,
cedary finish. U.S.: $11.00

BAUZA CASA GRANDE 90
Dominican Republic • *Size:*
6¼" x 48 *Filler:* Dom. Rep.,
Nicaragua *Binder:* Mexico
Wrapper: Ecuador
A strong, spicy cigar. There is
a deep complex earthiness
with an overall sweet tobacco
character. It is young enough
that age will improve it.
U.S.: $5.60

**BOLIVAR CORONA 90
GIGANTES**
Cuba • *Size:* 7" x 47
Filler/Binder/Wrapper: Cuba
A cigar filled with spices,
including cinnamon and nut-
meg, and a pleasant sweet-
ness that finishes in a com-
plex earthiness. (09/01/95)
U.K.: £11.90

COHIBA ESPLENDIDOS 90
Cuba • *Size:* 7" x 47
Filler/Binder/Wrapper: Cuba
There is a definite note of
aged cedar taste on this cigar,
with a solid core of spice flavors on the palate. It has a
woody finish. U.K.: £22.25

DON JUAN CHURCHILL 90
Nicaragua • *Size:* 7" x 49
Filler/Wrapper: Nicaragua
Binder: Dom. Rep.
A very smooth-tasting cigar
with flavors of toast and nuts,
and a strong spicy tobacco
finish with a nutmeg quality.
(09/01/95) U.S.: $4.70

**FUENTE FUENTE 90
OPUS X
RESERVA D'CHATEAU**
Dominican Republic • *Size:*
7" x 48 *Filler/Binder/Wrapper:*
Dom. Rep.

A complex spiciness marks
this cigar, and there is a dark,
sweet cocoa element on the
palate. It is full-bodied, and
has a sweet mineral note on
the finish. U.S.: $12.50

PADRÓN CHURCHILL 90
Nicaragua • *Size:* 6⅞" x 46
Filler/Binder/Wrapper:
Nicaragua
A cigar with a core of earthiness. It has some light coffee
bean flavors, and a solid,
sweet, woody finish. A medium-bodied cigar. U.S.: $3.90

**CELESTINO VEGA 89
CHURCHILL**
Indonesia • *Size:* 7¼" x 50
Filler/Binder/Wrapper:
Indonesia
A very well-balanced cigar. It
has a sweet woody character
and a solid nutmeg note on
the palate, with a hint of
leather. U.S.: $2.95

COHIBA CHURCHILL 89
Dominican Republic • *Size:*
7" x 49 *Filler:* Dom. Rep.
Binder: Indonesia *Wrapper:*
Cameroon
This cigar is woody with an
excellent balance. It has a
smooth pepper-and-nut component on the palate, and
there is a sweet, flinty note
on the finish. U.S.: $15.00

CUPIDO CHURCHILL 89
Nicaragua • *Size:* 7" x 47
Filler/Binder: Nicaragua
Wrapper: Indonesia
A medium-bodied cigar. It
has a toasty character and a
sweet herbal note on the

palate. Good balance and a
smooth finish. U.S.: $10.00

**DAVIDOFF ANIVER- 89
SARIO No. 2**
Dominican Republic • *Size:*
7" x 48 *Filler/Binder:* Dom.
Rep. *Wrapper:*
U.S.A./Conn. Shade
A medium-bodied cigar. It is
well made with a core of
light, sweet spice flavors, and
an overall sweet herbal character. There is a touch of
sweet wood on the finish.
U.S.: $18.00

**EL REY DEL MUNDO 89
DOUBLE CORONA**
Honduras • *Size:* 7" x 49
Filler: Dom. Rep *Binder:*
Honduras *Wrapper:* Ecuador
An extremely well-balanced
cigar. It has strong nutty fla-
vors, with a pleasant floral
aroma, and a long, sweet-
wood finish. U.S.: $4.25

**ROMEO Y JULIETA 89
CHURCHILL**
Cuba • *Size:* 7" x 47
Filler/Binder/Wrapper: Cuba
A young cigar. But a solid
core of medium-bodied fla-
vors that include sweet spices
and roasted nuts, and a
strong, sweet, wood finish.
U.K.: £12.60

**ROYAL HONDURAS 89
SOVEREIGN**
Honduras • *Size:* 7" x 48
Filler: Honduras *Binder:*
Dom. Rep. *Wrapper:*
Indonesia
A solid medium-bodied cigar.
It has coffee bean notes, with

a touch of earthiness on the palate. U.S.: $3.90

SAINT LUIS REY 89
CHURCHILL

Cuba • *Size:* 7" x 47
Filler/Binder/Wrapper: Cuba
Although this cigar is quite young, it shows a complex array of toast and roasted nut flavors. There is a hint of light cocoa bean on the palate. N/A

ASHTON CABINET 88
SELECTION No. 8

Dominican Republic • *Size:* 7" x 49 *Filler/Binder:* Dom. Rep. *Wrapper:* U.S.A./Conn. Shade
A mild- to medium-bodied cigar. There are good flavors of spices with an earthy component. The finish is a little dry. U.S.: $10.00

DANIEL MARSHALL 88
CHURCHILL

Dominican Republic • *Size:* 7" x 48 *Filler:* Dom. Rep. *Binder:* Mexico *Wrapper:* U.S.A./Conn. Shade
A good-looking wrapper. The cigar has a smooth, buttery herbal quality, and while it is young, there is some cocoa bean and toast flavor on the palate with a light wood finish. U.S.: $6.95

DIANA SILVIUS 88
CHURCHILL

Dominican Republic • *Size:* 7" x 50 *Filler/Binder:* Dom. Rep. *Wrapper:* U.S.A./Conn. Shade
A cigar with a solid core of peppery tastes. It has excel-

lent balance, with a good cedary finish. U.S.: $10.50

HOYO DE MONTERREY 88
CHURCHILL

Cuba • *Size:* 7" x 47
Filler/Binder/Wrapper: Cuba
This cigar has some exotic spice flavors including nutmeg and cinnamon, but it has a dry finish. (09/01/95) U.K.: £12.05

MAYA CHURCHILL 88
Honduras • *Size:* 6⅞" x 49
Filler/Binder: Honduras
Wrapper: Ecuador
Although this cigar is a bit rustic, there are solid flavors of wood, light coffee bean and cocoa bean. It finishes with a easy woodiness and an hint of earthiness.
U.S.: $5.15

OLIVEROS PREMIUM 88
CORONELES

Dominican Republic • *Size:* 7" x 50 *Filler/Binder:* Dom. Rep. *Wrapper:* Indonesia
There are strong elements of wood and spice on the palate. While still young, this cigar is medium-bodied.
U.S.: $5.05

OLOR COLOSSOS 88
Dominican Republic • *Size:* 7½" x 48 *Filler/Binder:* Dom. Rep. *Wrapper:* U.S.A./Conn. Shade
A spicy cigar with a very nice silky, pepper quality that leads into a fairly neutral finish. (09/01/95) U.S.: $5.15

PETERSON HALLMARK 88
CHURCHILL

Dominican Republic • *Size:* 7" x 48 *Filler:* Dom. Rep. *Binder:* Ecuador *Wrapper:* U.S.A./Conn. Shade
A mild- to medium-bodied cigar. It has good nutty flavors, with some hints of dry herbs and pepper. It's a little dry on the finish. U.S.: $7.65

SAVINELLI E.L.R. 88
No. 1 CHURCHILL

Dominican Republic • *Size:* 7¼" x 48 *Filler/Binder:* Dom. Rep. *Wrapper:* U.S.A./Conn. Shade
A good herbal character. It has a hint of nutty flavors and a firm draw. U.S.: $9.00

TABACOS SAN JOSE 88
CHURCHILL

U.S.A. • *Size:* 7" x 47
Filler/Binder: Dom. Rep., Nicaragua, Honduras, Brazil
Wrapper: Ecuador
Although this cigar is a little dry on the palate, it has excellent sweet tobacco character. There is a ripe apple note, with dried orange peel, and an overall nuttiness.
Price N/A

C.A.O. GOLD 87
CHURCHILL

Nicaragua • *Size:* 7" x 48
Filler/Binder: Nicaragua
Wrapper: Ecuador
A cigar with a sweet perfumy aroma, and a pleasant sweet tobacco character. It has a woody finish and is mild- to medium-bodied. U.S.: $7.50

CASA MARTIN **87**
CHURCHILL
Canary Islands • *Size:* 7" x 46
Filler: Dom. Rep., Nicaragua
Binder: Mexico *Wrapper:*
Ecuador
A very spicy character. This
cigar has good toasty flavors,
but with a dry finish.
U.S.: $4.25

CREDO PYTHAGORAS **87**
Dominican Republic • *Size:*
7" x 50 *Filler/Binder:* Dom.
Rep. *Wrapper:*
U.S.A./Conn. Shade
This is a solid, medium-bodied smoke. It has a peppery
taste softened with a hint of
dried orange peel. It lacks a
bit of depth, and is still
young. U.S.: $8.80

CUESTA-REY ARISTO- **87**
CRAT
Dominican Republic • *Size:*
7¼" x 48 *Filler/Binder:* Dom.
Rep. *Wrapper:*
U.S.A./Conn. Shade
A well-balanced cigar. It has
a creamy element on the
palate, with a sweet woody
flavor. There is a touch of
light earthiness on the palate
and the finish. U.S.: $6.85

DON RENÉ CHURCHILL **87**
Dominican Republic • *Size:*
7¼" x 50 *Filler:* Dom. Rep.
Binder: Honduras *Wrapper:*
Ecuador
A well-balanced cigar. It has
some light, sweet herb fla-
vors, with a woody finish.
U.S.: $4.95

EL REY DEL MUNDO **87**
TAINOS
Cuba • *Size:* 7" x 47
Filler/Binder/Wrapper: Cuba
Uneven construction hurts
this simple mild cigar with a
grassy taste and a light spicy
finish. (09/01/93) Price N/A

GRAND NICA **87**
CHURCHILL
Nicaragua • *Size:* 7" x 52
Filler/Binder: Nicaragua
Wrapper: Brazil
A medium-bodied cigar. It
has some hints of leather, and
a note of sweet grass on the
finish. U.S.: $4.45

JOSÉ BENITO **87**
CHURCHILL
Dominican Republic • *Size:*
7" x 50 *Filler:* Dom. Rep.
Binder: Honduras *Wrapper:*
Cameroon
A well-balanced cigar with a
medium-bodied smoke. It has
a hint of cocoa beans and
leather, and there is a sweet
herbal finish. U.S.: $4.55

LA FONTANA **87**
DA VINCI
Honduras • *Size:* 6⅞" x 48
Filler/Wrapper: Honduras
Binder: Mexico
A mild cigar. It has a pleasing
tangy finish, with some woody
elements on the palate.
U.S.: $3.85

LA REGENTA GRAN **87**
CORONA
Canary Islands • *Size:* 7¼" x
46 *Filler:* Canary Islands,
Dom. Rep. Brazil *Binder:*
Dom. Rep. *Wrapper:*
U.S.A./Conn. Shade

A medium-bodied cigar. It
has a dry, sweet wood character, with a light woody flavor.
U.S.: $7.50

MACANUDO VINTAGE **87**
CABINET SELECTION
1993 XX
Jamaica • *Size:* 7" x 47
Filler/Binder: Mexico, Dom.
Rep. *Wrapper:*
U.S.A./Conn. Shade
A solid medium-bodied cigar.
It has flavors of wood and
spice on a well-balanced
smoke. Quite smooth, it lacks
a bit of depth on the dry fin-
ish. U.S.: $27.50

MONTERO CHURCHILL **87**
Dominican Republic • *Size:*
6⅞" x 46 *Filler/Binder:* Dom.
Rep. *Wrapper:* Ecuador
A cigar with a light herbal
character. It has a creamy texture on the palate, with a hint
of roasted nuts. U.S.: $5.50

PARTICULARES **87**
CHURCHILL
Dominican Republic • *Size:*
6⅞" x 49 *Filler:* Dom. Rep.
Binder: Honduras *Wrapper:*
Ecuador
This cigar is well balanced
with a sweet, mild- to medium-bodied smoke. There is a
light herbal character with a
touch of pepper on the
palate, and a woody finish.
U.S.: $4.00

ROMEO Y JULIETA **87**
CHURCHILL
Dominican Republic • *Size:*
7" x 50 *Filler:* Dom. Rep.
Binder: U.S.A./Conn.
Wrapper: Cameroon

A medium-bodied cigar. It has a strong woody character with a light pepper note on the palate and a floral finish. U.S.: $4.85

SIGNATURE COLLEC- **87**
TION CHURCHILL
Dominican Republic • *Size:* 7¼" x 50 *Filler:* Dom. Rep., Indonesia, Nicaragua *Binder:* Indonesia *Wrapper:* Ecuador This is a well-balanced cigar with a cedary finish. It has a touch of earth and nuts on the palate. U.S.: $6.25

THOMAS HINDS HON- **87**
DURAN SELECTION
CHURCHILL
Honduras • *Size:* 7" x 49 *Filler/Binder:* Honduras *Wrapper:* Ecuador A cigar that has some floral notes on the palate, but with a tang. It is medium-bodied, with a hint of toasted wood, and a slightly sharp finish. U.S.: $5.30

THOMAS HINDS **87**
NICARAGUAN SELEC-
TION CHURCHILL
Nicaragua • *Size:* 7" x 49 *Filler/Binder:* Nicaragua *Wrapper:* Ecuador A smooth-tasting cigar with a core of sweet tobacco flavors. It has a rather flat, dry finish. U.S.: $6.45

TORCEDOR CHURCHILL **87**
Nicaragua • *Size:* 7" x 50 *Filler:* Nicaragua, Honduras *Binder:* Mexico *Wrapper:* Indonesia A cigar that takes a while to get going. But once warm it

has a solid core of spicy flavors, and a medium-length woody finish. U.S.: $3.75

AVO NO. 5 **86**
Dominican Republic • *Size:* 6⅞" x 46 *Filler/Binder:* Dom. Rep. *Wrapper:* U.S.A./Conn. Shade A light herbal character, with a touch of sweet mint on the palate. It finishes a little dry. U.S.: $7.00

BANCES CORONA **86**
INMENSA
Honduras • *Size:* 6¼" x 48 *Filler/Binder:* Honduras, Dom. Rep., Nicaragua *Wrapper:* Ecuador This cigar has a solid spicy core of flavors and a woody finish. It is quite well-made. U.S.: $4.00

CACIQUE CARIBE #7 **86**
Dominican Republic • *Size:* 6⅞" x 46 *Filler/Binder:* Dom. Rep., Nicaragua *Wrapper:* Ecuador A cigar with a pleasant, herbal character and a mild to medium body. There are good spicy elements on the palate with a dry wood finish. U.S.: $4.80

CARA MIA CHURCHILL **86**
Canary Islands • *Size:* 7" x 50 *Filler:* Brazil, Dom. Rep., Canary Islands *Binder:* Canary Islands *Wrapper:* U.S.A./Conn. A well-balanced, medium-bodied smoke, with some light coffee notes and a sweet woodiness, but a short, dry finish. U.S.: $8.00

CARLOS TORAÑO **86**
DOMINICAN SELECTION
CARLOS VI
Dominican Republic • *Size:* 7" x 48 *Filler:* Dom. Rep. *Binder:* Mexico *Wrapper:* U.S.A./Conn. Shade A mild- to medium-bodied cigar. It has a herbal character, but with a very dry taste and finish. U.S.: $5.75

CUESTA-REY **86**
CENTENNIAL
COLLECTION
DOMINICAN NO. 2
Dominican Republic • *Size:* 7¼" x 48 *Filler/Binder:* Dom. Rep. *Wrapper:* U.S.A./Conn. Shade This is a smooth, and creamy cigar. It has a hint of leather on the palate. It is mild- to medium-bodied. U.S.: $5.40

DIANA SILVIUS 2000 **86**
Dominican Republic • *Size:* 6¼" x 47 *Filler/Binder:* Dom. Rep. *Wrapper:* U.S.A./Conn. Shade A mild- to medium-bodied cigar. It has an herbal character, with a dry wood note on the palate. U.S.: $8.40

DOMINO PARK **86**
CHURCHILL
Dominican Republic • *Size:* 7¼" x 50 *Filler:* Dom. Rep., Indonesia *Binder/Wrapper:* Indonesia A well-made cigar. It has a cocoa bean note on the palate and a good balance. It has a woody finish. U.S.: $3.35

DON JUAN PLATINUM 86
CHURCHILL
Nicaragua • *Size:* 7" x 49
Filler/Binder: Dom. Rep.
Wrapper: U.S.A./Conn.
Shade
A mild- to medium-bodied
cigar. It has some light roast-
ed nut flavors on the palate
and the finish. U.S.: $5.00

DUNHILL CABRERAS 86
Dominican Republic • *Size:*
7" x 48 *Filler/Binder:* Dom.
Rep., Brazil *Wrapper:*
U.S.A./Conn. Shade
A well-balanced cigar, with a
mild character. It is creamy
and herbal, with a bit of a
tang on the finish.
U.S.: $9.95

HABANICA SERIE 747 86
Nicaragua • *Size:* 7" x 47
Filler/Binder/Wrapper:
Nicaragua
This cigar is a little rustic.
But it is mild- to medium-
bodied, with a good salty
character, and a bit of earthi-
ness on the finish.
U.S.: $7.50

HOYO DE MONTERREY 86
EXCALIBUR NO. 2
Honduras • *Size:* 6¾" x 47
Filler/Binder: Honduras, Dom.
Rep., Nicaragua *Wrapper:*
U.S.A./Conn. Shade
This cigar has a hint of toast
flavors and a nice creamy
character. There are some
herbal hints on the palate
and the finish. U.S.: $4.95

INDIAN TABAC 86
ANNIVERSARY LTD.
RESERVE "BUFFALO"
Dominican Republic • *Size:*
7" x 47 *Filler:* Nicaragua,
Honduras *Binder:* Mexico
Wrapper: Ecuador
A creamy and smooth-tasting
cigar. There is a hint of nutti-
ness, and a woody finish.
U.S.: $8.00

LA GIANNA HAVANA 86
CHURCHILL
Nicaragua • *Size:* 7" x 49
Filler/Binder: Nicaragua
Wrapper: Ecuador
This a mild- to medium-bodied cigar. It is smooth-tasting
with a dry spice character
and a hint of nuts, and earth
flavors. U.S.: $5.95

LA RESERVA NO. 2 86
Honduras • *Size:* 6½" x 48
Filler: Dom. Rep., Honduras
Binder: Ecuador *Wrapper:*
U.S.A./Conn. Shade
A straightforward, smooth-
smoking cigar with an attrac-
tive dark-brown wrapper. It
has ample mild spice and
pepper flavors. (09/01/93)
Price N/A

MONTESINO GRAN 86
CORONA
Dominican Republic • *Size:*
6¾" x 48 *Filler/Binder:* Dom.
Rep., Brazil *Wrapper:*
U.S.A./Conn. Sun-Grown
This well-made, light-bodied
cigar comes on quickly with a
mild creaminess, but overall
is slightly grassy and has a
tangy finish. (09/01/93)
U.S.: $3.90

NAT SHERMAN HOST 86
SELECTION HAMPTON
Honduras • *Size:* 7" x 50
Filler/Binder: Honduras
Wrapper: Ecuador
A mild cigar with a sweet
tobacco character. There is a
hint of spice. U.S.: $5.90

ROLY VALENTINOS 86
Honduras • *Size:* 7" x 49
Filler: Ecuador *Binder:* Dom.
Rep., Brazil *Wrapper:*
Ecuador, Indonesia
A mild- to medium-bodied
cigar. It has a strong herbal
character with a long, woody
finish. Price N/A

SIGNET BUCKINGHAM 86
Dominican Republic • *Size:*
7" x 48 *Filler/Binder:* Dom.
Rep. *Wrapper:*
U.S.A./Conn. Shade
A mild- to medium-bodied
cigar. It has a creamy character with a light, roasted nut
flavor. U.S.: $10.60

TAMBORIL SUMATRA 86
CHURCHILL
Dominican Republic • *Size:*
7" x 47 *Filler/Binder:* Dom.
Rep. *Wrapper:* Indonesia
There is a hint of nutty flavors in this medium-bodied
cigar. It has a solid woodiness, and a woody finish.
U.S.: $7.00

TEMPLE HALL NO. 700 86
Jamaica • *Size:* 7" x 49
Filler/Binder: Mexico, Dom.
Rep. *Wrapper:*
U.S.A./Conn. Shade
This is a very well-made
cigar. There are notes of
hazelnut and dried orange

peel on the palate, and it has a good balance. It's a bit dry on the finish. U.S.: $7.80

YUMURI CHURCHILL 86
Dominican Republic • *Size:* 7" x 48 *Filler/Binder:* Dom. Rep. *Wrapper:* U.S.A./Conn. Shade
Although this cigar has a vegetal character, there are some underlying flavors of spice. It has a papery finish. U.S.: $6.50

ASHTON PRIME 85
MINISTER
Dominican Republic • *Size:* 6⅛" x 48 *Filler/Binder:* Dom. Rep. *Wrapper:* U.S.A./Conn. Shade
This cigar has some light spiciness on the palate with a light, woody, slightly dry finish. U.S.: $7.15

BACCARAT CHURCHILL 85
Honduras • *Size:* 7" x 50 *Filler:* Honduras *Binder:* Mexican *Wrapper:* Ecuador
This mild cigar has a light spiciness, with a slightly grassy finish. U.S.: $3.35

CABALLEROS 85
CHURCHILL
Dominican Republic • *Size:* 7" x 50 *Filler/Binder:* Dom. Rep. *Wrapper:* U.S.A./Conn. Shade
A nice mild-tasting cigar. It has light herbalness, and hints of spicy flavors. A dry finish. U.S.: $4.20

CAMACHO CHURCHILL 85
Honduras • *Size:* 7" x 48 *Filler/Binder/Wrapper:* Honduras
A cigar with a fine floral aroma, and flavors of toast and nuts, but with a fairly flat, dry finish. (09/01/95) U.S.: $3.35

CREDO MAGNIFICANT 85
Dominican Republic • *Size:* 6⅛" x 46 *Filler/Binder:* Dom. Rep. *Wrapper:* U.S.A./Conn. Shade
Although this cigar is young, it has some dried orange peel flavors. There are some soft vegetal elements on the finish. U.S.: $6.60

DA VINCI MEZZANOTE 85
Nicaragua • *Size:* 7" x 48 *Filler:* Dom. Rep., Nicaragua *Binder:* Nicaragua *Wrapper:* Ecuador
This is a salty cigar. It has additional notes of roasted nuts, and is mild- to medium-bodied. U.S.: $5.95

DON DIEGO 85
MONARCH TUBES
Dominican Republic • *Size:* 7¼" x 46 *Filler/Binder:* Dom. Rep. *Wrapper:* U.S.A./Conn. Shade
A mild- to medium-bodied cigar with a strong dose of spice and leather, but a fairly dry taste on the palate and the finish. U.S.: $6.00

DOUBLE HAPPINESS 85
ECSTASY
Philippines • *Size:* 7" x 47 *Filler/Binder:* Philippines *Wrapper:* Brazil
There is an earthy quality to this cigar. But it lacks complexity and is quite mild, with a flat finish. U.S.: $5.80

EL RICO HABANO 85
DOUBLE CORONA
U.S.A. • *Size:* 7" x 47 *Filler:* Dom. Rep., Ecuador, Nicaragua *Binder/Wrapper:* Ecuador
The oily, dark brown wrapper gives a full-bodied smoke with an earthy aroma. It has some spice, but also has a youthful harshness. (09/01/95) U.S.: $3.85

FELIPE II RESERVA X 85
Honduras • *Size:* 7" x 48 *Filler/Binder:* Nicaragua *Wrapper:* Indonesia
This is a cigar with a medium to full body. There is some inconsistency in taste, but it has an earthy complexity on the palate. U.S.: $8.70

GILBERTO OLIVA 85
CHURCHILL
Nicaragua • *Size:* 7" x 50 *Filler/Binder:* Dom. Rep., Nicaragua *Wrapper:* Ecuador
A young cigar. It has a sharp woody finish, but with some solid floral notes, and a hint of leather. Should improve with age. U.S.: $4.40

MACANUDO VINTAGE No. 1 1988 — **85**

Jamaica • *Size:* 7½" x 49 *Filler:* Jamaica, Dom. Rep. Mexico *Binder:* Mexico *Wrapper:* U.S.A./Conn. Shade

This is a well-made medium-bodied cigar with some flavors of nuts and a light spiciness. (09/01/95) U.S.: $14.00

MATCH PLAY PRESTWICK — **85**

Dominican Republic • *Size:* 6⅞" x 46 *Filler/Binder:* Dom. Rep. *Wrapper:* Ecuador

A mild- to medium-bodied cigar. It is nutty and herbal. It is still young, and there is a bit of bite. U.S.: $5.75

MONTECRISTO CHURCHILL — **85**

Dominican Republic • *Size:* 7" x 48 *Filler/Binder:* Dom. Rep. *Wrapper:* U.S.A./Conn. Shade

A mild- to medium-bodied smoke. It has a nutty and creamy character. A little rough on the finish. U.S.: $9.50

NAT SHERMAN GOTHAM SELECTION No. 500 — **85**

Dominican Republic • *Size:* 7" x 50 *Filler/Binder:* Dom. Rep. *Wrapper:* U.S.A./Conn. Shade

A mild- to medium-bodied cigar with a creamy character. It is smooth tasting with a hint of coffee bean flavor. U.S.: $9.60

NAT SHERMAN EXCHANGE SELECTION OXFORD 5 — **85**

Dominican Republic • *Size:* 7" x 49 *Filler:* Dom. Rep. *Binder:* Mexico *Wrapper:* U.S.A./Conn. Shade

A well-balanced, mild- to medium-bodied cigar. It has a creamy character, with a light coffee ground taste. A smooth tasting cigar. U.S.: $9.60

ONYX No. 646 — **85**

Dominican Republic • *Size:* 6⅝" x 46 *Filler:* Dom. Rep., Mexico *Binder:* Indonesia *Wrapper:* Mexico

A maduro cigar with roasted nut and coffee bean flavors that finishes with sweet spice notes. (09/01/95) U.S.: $3.65

PUNCH DELUXE SERIES CHATEAU L — **85**

Honduras • *Size:* 7¼" x 54 *Filler/Binder:* Honduras, Nicaragua, Dom. Rep. *Wrapper:* Ecuador

This cigar has a good draw with a nice rich, spicy taste, and a slightly woody finish. (09/01/95) U.S.: $4.95

RAMON ALLONES REDONDOS — **85**

Dominican Republic • *Size:* 7" x 49 *Filler:* Dom. Rep., Mexico *Binder:* Mexico *Wrapper:* Cameroon

There is a hint of spiciness on an otherwise quite mild flavor profile. The cigar has a generally light vegetal character. U.S.: $6.00

ROMEO Y JULIETA VINTAGE No. 4 — **85**

Dominican Republic • *Size:* 7" x 48 *Filler:* Dom. Rep. *Binder:* Mexico *Wrapper:* U.S.A./Conn. Shade

This is a nice, mild cigar that has some mild spice and coffee flavors, but with a slightly dry finish. (09/01/95) U.S.: $8.00

SANTA DAMIANA SELECCION No. 100 — **85**

Dominican Republic • *Size:* 6¼" x 48 *Filler/Binder:* Dom. Rep. *Wrapper:* U.S.A./Conn. Shade

A very pleasant well balanced cigar. It is creamy and smooth on the palate. U.S.: $8.50

SANTA ROSA CHURCHILL — **85**

Honduras • *Size:* 7" x 50 *Filler/Binder:* Honduras *Wrapper:* U.S.A./Conn. Shade

A taste of wood on the palate. It is well balanced, although it finishes quite dry. U.S.: $5.75

SAVINELLI ORO 750 CHURCHILL — **85**

Dominican Republic • *Size:* 7" x 47 *Filler/Binder:* Dom. Rep. *Wrapper:* Indonesia

There is a light leathery flavor to this cigar, with some herbal spiciness. A woody finish. U.S.: $6.75

Sosa Churchill 85
Dominican Republic • Size:
7" x 49 Filler: Dom. Rep.
Binder: Brazil Wrapper:
Ecuador
This is a well-made cigar. It
has some vegetal notes on
the palate with an overall
woody character. U.S.: $4.80

V Centennial 85
Churchill
Honduras • Size: 7" x 48
Filler: Dom. Rep., Honduras,
Nicaragua Binder: Mexico
Wrapper: U.S.A./Conn.
Shade
A mild- to medium-bodied
cigar. It is woody and dry, but
has a smooth herbal flavor on
the palate. U.S.: $7.00

V.M. Santana 85
Connecticut
Churchill
Dominican Republic • Size:
7¼" x 50 Filler/Binder: Dom.
Rep. Wrapper:
U.S.A./Conn.
A good oily wrapper. The
cigar seems a little young,
with some green flavors, but
there are hints of roasted
nuts in an otherwise vegetal
character. U.S.: $8.60

Arturo Fuente 84
Churchill
Dominican Republic • Size:
7" x 48 Filler/Binder: Dom.
Rep. Wrapper: Cameroon
A mild- to medium-bodied
cigar. It has a strong cedary
component, with a light
sweet tobacco taste.
U.S.: $4.35

Arturo Fuente 84
Double Chateau
Fuente
Dominican Republic • Size:
6¾" x 48 Filler/Binder: Dom.
Rep. Wrapper: U.S.A./Conn.
Shade
This cigar has a nice, long,
spicy finish. But there is a
strong dryness on the palate,
and a dry wood character.
U.S.: $4.45

Aurora Bristol 84
Especial
Dominican Republic • Size:
6⅜" x 48 Filler/Binder: Dom.
Rep. Wrapper: Cameroon
A slightly tight, mild cigar
with a pleasant earthy quality
and some nutty flavors. Some
inconsistency noted.
(09/01/95) U.S.: $3.12

Camorra Limited 84
Reserve Churchill
San Remo
Honduras • Size: 7" x 48
Filler/Binder: Honduras
Wrapper: Ecuador
This is a mild cigar. It has a
leathery flavor on the palate,
with a light, flat finish.
U.S.: $5.00

Carrington No. 5 84
Dominican Republic • Size:
6⅞" x 46 Filler/Binder: Dom.
Rep. Wrapper:
U.S.A./Conn. Shade
This cigar has some nut flavors. It is well balanced, and
although it is constructed a
little roughly, it performs
well. U.S.: $5.40

Fighting Cock 84
C.O.D.
Philippines • Size: 7" x 47
Filler/Binder: Philippines
Wrapper: Indonesia
This is a mild cigar. It has a
flat texture on the palate,
with hints of wood and a lit-
tle paper. U.S.: $4.60

Flor de Farach 84
Churchill
Nicaragua • Size: 7" x 48
Filler: Dom. Rep., Nicaragua,
Honduras Binder: Honduras
Wrapper: Ecuador
A medium-bodied cigar.
While smooth-tasting over-
all, it still has the bite of
youth. Earthy notes combine
with sweet herbs. U.S.: $2.00

H. Upmann 84
Corona Imperiales
Dominican Republic • Size:
7" x 46 Filler/Binder: Dom.
Rep. Wrapper: Indonesia
A cigar with a strong woody
character. There is an earthy
quality to the smoke that is
mild- to medium-bodied.
U.S.: $5.25

H. Upmann 84
Monarch Tube
Dominican Republic • Size:
7" x 47 Filler/Binder: Dom.
Rep. Wrapper: Indonesia
This cigar has a rough wrapper and a firm draw. It has a
slightly sour taste with a core
of spicy and nutty flavors.
(09/01/95) U.S.: $6.00

HABANA GOLD 84
BLACK LABEL
CHURCHILL
Honduras • *Size:* 7½" x 46
Filler/Binder: Nicaragua,
Honduras *Wrapper:* Ecuador
This easy-draw cigar has
some spice on the palate and
a flinty finish that ends a bit
dry. (09/01/95) U.S.: $5.70

HAVANA CLASSICO 84
CONNECTICUT SHADE
CHURCHILL
Dominican Republic • *Size:*
7¼" x 50 *Filler:* Dom. Rep.,
Indonesia, Colombia
Binder: Ecuador *Wrapper:*
U.S.A./Pennsylvania
A cigar with a mild, herbal
character. It is mild- to medi-
um-bodied, with a smooth
finish. U.S.: $7.75

HOJA CUBANA 84
CHURCHILL
Nicaragua • *Size:* 7" x 50
Filler: Nicaragua *Binder:*
Dom. Rep. *Wrapper:* Ecuador
A light toast-flavored cigar,
like roasted wheat. It has
some dryness on the finish
and the palate. U.S.: $7.40

HOYO DE MONTERREY 84
CUBAN LARGOS
Honduras • *Size:* 7¼" x 47
Filler/Binder: Honduras, Dom.
Rep., Nicaragua *Wrapper:*
Ecuador
A rustic cigar with a strong
herbal character. It is medi-
um-bodied. U.S.: $2.80

HURRICANOS 84
CHURCHILL
Honduras • *Size:* 7" x 49
Filler: Nicaragua, Honduras

Binder: Honduras *Wrapper:*
Ecuador
A maduro-style cigar. It has
some dark, bitter cocoa
tastes, with a hot peppery
character. U.S.: $2.50

IMPERIO CUBANO 84
CHURCHILL
U.S.A. • *Size:* 7" x 48 *Filler:*
Dom. Rep. *Binder:* Mexico
Wrapper: Ecuador
A young wrapper. The cigar
has a sweet wood finish, with
some herbal flavors on the
palate. U.S.: $6.80

LA FINCA VALENTINO 84
Nicaragua • *Size:* 6¾" x 48
Filler/Binder/Wrapper:
Nicaragua
A quite mild cigar, with a
light floral character, and
some light spicy flavors. A
little rustic. U.S.: $2.25

LICENCIADOS 84
CHURCHILL
Dominican Republic • *Size:*
7" x 50 *Filler/Binder:* Dom.
Rep. *Wrapper:*
U.S.A./Conn. Shade
A cigar with a light spiciness.
It is mild- to medium-bodied,
and has a dry wood finish.
U.S.: $4.85

LONE WOLF VINTAGE 84
SERIES CHURCHILL
Dominican Republic • *Size:*
6¾" x 48 *Filler/Binder:* Dom.
Rep. *Wrapper:* Indonesia
There are some strong hints
of spiciness in this cigar. It
has a very woody finish and a
slightly vegetal character.
U.S.: $7.00

MONTECRUZ NATURAL 84
CLARO NO. 200
Dominican Republic • *Size:*
7¼" x 46 *Filler/Binder:* Dom.
Rep., Brazil *Wrapper:*
U.S.A./Conn. Shade
A mild- to medium-bodied
cigar with a good texture. It
has a somewhat vegetal char-
acter, with a dry wood finish.
U.S.: $5.30

MONTECRUZ 84
SUN-GROWN NO. 200
Dominican Republic • *Size:*
7¼" x 46 *Filler/Binder:* Dom.
Rep., Brazil *Wrapper:*
Indonesia
A pleasant, mild cigar. It has
dried citrus flavors, although
there is a salty note on the
palate, too. It has an overall
vegetal character. U.S.: $5.30

OROSI ORO 700 84
Nicaragua • *Size:* 7" x 50
Filler/Binder: Nicaragua
Wrapper: Ecuador
Although this cigar is quite
rustic, there is a strong, sweet
wood component to it. There
is a mineral quality to the
finish. U.S.: $4.60

PETRUS TABACAGE 84
CHURCHILL 90
Honduras • *Size:* 7" x 50
Filler/Binder: Nicaragua
Wrapper: Ecuador
A mild- to medium-bodied
cigar. It has some coffee notes
with a light herbal character.
U.S.: $6.40

PRIMERA DE **84**
NICARAGUA CHURCHILL
Nicaragua • *Size:* 7" x 50
Filler: Nicaragua, Honduras
Binder: Mexico *Wrapper:*
Indonesia
A mild- to medium-bodied
cigar. There is a spicy herbal
taste on the palate, although
it is still a bit green. A light
wood finish. U.S.: $3.75

PUNCH DOUBLE **84**
CORONA
Honduras • *Size:* 6¼" x 48
Filler/Binder: Honduras, Dom.
Rep., Nicaragua *Wrapper:*
U.S.A./Conn. Shade
This cigar is quite young.
There is a hint of nuts, but
otherwise it is flat on the
palate. U.S.: $3.75

PUNCH GRAN CRU **84**
MONARCA
Honduras • *Size:* 6¼" x 48
Filler/Binder: Honduras, Dom.
Rep., Nicaragua *Wrapper:*
U.S.A./Conn. Shade
A mild- to medium-bodied
cigar. It has a strong herbal-
ness, and a creamy texture.
U.S.: $7.50

SANTA DAMIANA **84**
SELECCION NO. 800
Dominican Republic • *Size:*
7" x 50 *Filler/Binder:* Dom.
Rep. *Wrapper:* U.S.A./
Conn. Shade
A pleasant mild- to medium-
bodied cigar with a creamy,
smooth character and flavors
of nuts, a touch of spice and a
dry finish. (09/01/95) U.S.:
$9.50

TAMBORIL CHURCHILL **84**
Dominican Republic • *Size:*
7" x 47 *Filler/Binder:* Dom.
Rep. *Wrapper:*
U.S.A./Conn. Shade
A cigar with some light vegetal notes, with an undertone
of pepper. It is mild and still
quite young. U.S.: $7.00

THOMAS HINDS **84**
CABINET SELECTION
CHURCHILL
Nicaragua • *Size:* 7" x 49
Filler/Binder/Wrapper:
Nicaragua
An interesting, red-wine
note on the palate. The cigar
has a woody character with
hints of burnt toast on the
palate. U.S.: $5.70

TROYA NO. 63 **84**
CHURCHILL
Dominican Republic • *Size:*
6⅞" x 46 *Filler/Binder:* Dom.
Rep. *Wrapper:*
U.S.A./Conn. Shade
Although this cigar is still
young, it has some solid spicy
and woody flavors. It is medi-
um-bodied. U.S.: $5.20

BELINDA RAMON **83**
Honduras • *Size:* 7¼" x 47
Filler: Dom. Rep., Honduras
Binder: Honduras *Wrapper:*
Ecuador
A light perfumed aroma.
This cigar has a mild charac-
ter, with solid woody flavors
on the palate and a woody
finish. U.S.: $2.75

CUESTA-REY CABINET **83**
NO. 898
Dominican Republic • *Size:*
7" x 49 *Filler/Binder:* Dom.
Rep. *Wrapper:*
U.S.A./Conn. Shade

A cigar with a slightly dry
character. There is a hint of
vegetalness on the palate,
with a rich, almost meaty
note. U.S.: $4.85

DON LINO ORO **83**
CHURCHILL
Dominican Republic • *Size:*
6⅞" x 46 *Filler/Binder/Wrap-
per:* Dom. Rep.
This cigar has a very woody
character, with a touch of
earthiness. It is salty on the
palate. A bit rustic.
U.S.: $5.06

DON XAVIER **83**
GRAND CORONA
Canary Islands • *Size:* 7" x 46
Filler/Binder: Canary Islands,
Dom. Rep., Brazil *Wrapper:*
U.S.A./Conn. Shade
A cigar with a creaminess
and a light nuttiness on the
palate. It is quite mild and
flat-tasting. U.S.: $7.00

DUNHILL PERAVIAS **83**
Dominican Republic • *Size:*
7" x 50 *Filler/Binder:* Dom.
Rep., Brazil *Wrapper:*
U.S.A./Conneticut Shade
A well-made cigar with a dry,
woody character. It has some
light, spicy tones on the
palate. U.S.: $8.25

HOYO DE MONTERREY **83**
DOUBLE CORONA
Honduras • *Size:* 6¼" x 48
Filler/Binder: Honduras,
Nicaragua, Dom. Rep.
Wrapper: Ecuador
An oily wrapper with some
strong spicy elements and a
creamy character with a
slightly dry finish. (09/01/95)
U.S.: $3.75

JOYA DE NICARAGUA CHURCHILL — 83

Nicaragua • *Size:* 6⅞" x 49
Filler: Nicaragua *Binder:* Nicaragua *Wrapper:* Ecuador
This cigar is quite rustic. But it has some solid flavors of spice, with a slightly salty character. U.S.: $4.75

JUAN CLEMENTE CHURCHILL — 83

Dominican Republic • *Size:* 6⅞" x 46 *Filler/Binder:* Dom. Rep. *Wrapper:* U.S.A./Conn. Shade
A cigar with an herbal quality on the palate. There is a hint of nuts, but also a light, dry grassiness. Well made. U.S.: $8.25

LA DILIGENCIA CHURCHILL — 83

Honduras • *Size:* 7" x 48
Filler: Nica., Hon., Dom. Rep. *Binder:* Dom. Rep. *Wrapper:* U.S.A./Conn.
A mild- to medium-bodied cigar with some nut and spice flavors on the palate. A little dry. U.S.: $5.65

LA FLOR DOMINICANA CHURCHILL RESERVA ESPECIAL — 83

Dominican Republic • *Size:* 6⅞" x 49 *Filler/Binder:* Dom. Rep. *Wrapper:* U.S.A./Conn. Shade
A light vegetal character marks this cigar. It also has a quite dry finish. U.S.: $7.20

LA GLORIA CUBANA CHURCHILL — 83

Dominican Republic • *Size:* 7" x 50 *Filler:* Dom. Rep., Nicaragua
Binder: Nicaragua
Wrapper: Ecuador
There are some earthy flavors on an otherwise quite salty taste. It is a rustic cigar, with some medium- to full-bodied smoke. U.S.: $4.40

LAS CABRILLAS DE SOTO — 83

Honduras • *Size:* 6⅞" x 50 *Filler/Binder:* Mexico, Dom. Rep. *Wrapper:* U.S.A./Conn. Shade
Although this cigar is a little rustic, it has a toasty, almost burnt coffee ground flavor. U.S.: $2.60

LEON JIMENES NO. 2 — 83

Dominican Republic • *Size:* 7" x 47 *Filler/Binder:* Dom. Rep. *Wrapper:* U.S.A./Conn. Shade
This cigar combines a salty note with an herbal character. There is a touch of harshness on the palate, probably from youthfulness, and a light woody finish. U.S.: $4.56

PARTAGAS CHURCHILL DELUXE — 83

Cuba • *Size:* 7" x 47
Filler/Binder/Wrapper: Cuba
A medium-bodied cigar. There are strong hints of wood on the palate, but it is extremely dry-tasting with a dry finish. SF: 13.60

TRESADO SELECCION NO. 200 — 83

Dominican Republic • *Size:* 7" x 48 *Filler:* Dom. Rep. *Binder:* Cameroon *Wrapper:* Indonesia
A mild, smooth cigar with a floral character and a woody finish. (09/01/95) U.S.: $2.85

V CENTENNIAL 500 SERIES CHURCHILL — 83

Honduras • *Size:* 7" x 48
Filler/Binder: Dom. Rep., Nicaragua, Honduras *Wrapper:* U.S.A./Conn. Shade
A quite mild cigar. It has a light vegetal character with a light wheat tone. There is a woody finish. U.S.: $8.40

ZINO GOLD LINE VERITAS — 83

Honduras • *Size:* 7" x 49 *Filler/Binder:* Honduras *Wrapper:* U.S.A./Conn. Shade
This is a pleasant, mild cigar. It has a woody character, with a touch of creaminess. U.S.: $8.50

BALLENA SUPREMA DANLI COLLECTION ALMA — 82

Honduras • *Size:* 7" x 47
Filler: Dom. Rep. Mexico *Binder:* Mexico *Wrapper:* U.S.A./Conn. Shade
A young cigar. It has a tartness on the palate with a woody character, and finishes with a woody taste. U.S.: $4.40

CUBITA 2000   **82**
Dominican Republic • *Size:*
7" x 50   *Filler/Binder:* Dom.
Rep.   *Wrapper:* U.S.A./
Conn. Shade
While this cigar is well made,
it has a sharp peppery taste
that then turns into a sweet-
ish flavor. (09/01/95)
U.S.: $6.15

DA VINCI   **82**
GINEVRA DE BENCI
Honduras • *Size:* 7" x 48
Filler/Binder: Dom. Rep.,
Honduras, Nicaragua   *Wrap-*
per: Ecuador
While this cigar has a light
flowery note, it is not very
well balanced. There is a
pencil-lead and wood finish.
U.S.: $7.15

DON LEO   **82**
DOUBLE CORONA
Dominican Republic • *Size:*
7" x 48   *Filler/Binder:* Dom.
Rep.   *Wrapper:*
U.S.A./Conn. Shade
This is a well-made cigar.
However, there is slight
metallic tang and a slightly
vegetal character. U.S.: $5.40

ENCANTO CHURCHILL   **82**
NATURAL
Honduras • *Size:* 7" x 50
Filler/Binder/Wrapper: Honduras
This is a nice-looking cigar
with an easy draw. There is a
saltiness on the palate and a
slight earthy character, but it
finishes a little harsh.
U.S.: $5.75

FELIPE GREGORIO SUN-   **82**
TUOSO
Honduras • *Size:* 7" x 48
Filler/Binder/Wrapper: Hon-
duras
There are hints of earthiness,
and a light touch of spice.
But it is quite mild.
U.S.: $8.70

FONSECA 10-10   **82**
Dominican Republic • *Size:*
7" x 50   *Filler:* Dom. Rep.
Binder: Mexico   *Wrapper:*
U.S.A./Conn. Shade
A light spicy cigar, but it
seems quite young. There is
also a dry quality to the
smoke, and a flat finish.
U.S.: $5.25

HOYO DE MONTERREY   **82**
EXCALIBUR BANQUET
Honduras • *Size:* 6¾" x 48
Filler: Nicaragua, Honduras,
Dom. Rep.   *Binder:* Hon-
duras   *Wrapper:*
U.S.A./Conn. Shade
Showed inconsistency. This
cigar has a mild spiciness but
was hampered by apparently
young tobacco and a slightly
hot finish. (09/01/95)
U.S.: $7.50

HOYO DE MONTERREY   **82**
SULTAN
Honduras • *Size:* 7¼" x 54
Filler/Binder: Honduras,
Nicaragua, Dom. Rep.
Wrapper: Ecuador
This medium- to full-bodied
cigar has some spiciness, but
is dominated by dry, balsa-
wood flavors that have a
faint vegetal quality.
(09/01/95) U.S.: $4.65

LA UNICA NO. 200   **82**
Dominican Republic • *Size:*
7" x 49   *Filler/Binder:* Dom.
Rep.   *Wrapper:*
U.S.A./Conn. Shade
A smooth-tasting cigar with
a mild body. It has a slight
vegetal quality, with a hearty
earthiness on the palate.
U.S.: $4.65

PUNCH GRAN CRU   **82**
DIADEMAS
Honduras • *Size:* 7¼" x 54
Filler/Binder: Honduras,
Nicaragua, Dom. Rep   *Wrap-*
per: Ecuador
This cigar has some peppery
and spicy notes, but ends on
the vegetal side with a dry
finish. (09/01/95) U.S.: $6.25

VUELTABAJO   **82**
CHURCHILL
Dominican Republic • *Size:*
7" x 48   *Filler:* Dom. Rep.
Binder: Dom. Rep.,   *Wrap-*
per: U.S.A./Conn. Shade
This is a mild- to medium-
bodied cigar. It has a woody
character, with a bit of tang
on the finish, which suggests
it is still young. U.S.: $4.15

DON MELO CENTE-   **81**
NARIO
Honduras • *Size:* 7" x 48
Filler/Binder/Wrapper: Honduras
There are some hints of
roasted coffee grounds, and
light leather. But this cigar
has a harsh note on the
palate, with a sharp, tangy
finish. U.S.: $16.00

LA FLOR DOMINICANA 81
MAMBISES
Dominican Republic • *Size:*
6⅞" x 48 *Filler/Binder:* Dom.
Rep. *Wrapper:*
U.S.A./Conn. Shade
A mild, creamy cigar. It is
not very complex, but it is
light and pleasant with some
light nut flavors. U.S.: $6.95

LA MAXIMILIANA PER- 81
FECTUS
Honduras • *Size:* 7" x 50
Filler: Nicaragua *Binder:*
Honduras *Wrapper:* Indone-
sia
A salty character. This is a
mild cigar with a slight, sweet
tobacco taste. U.S.: $4.50

PAUL GARMIRIAN 81
CHURCHILL
Dominican Republic • *Size:*
7" x 48 *Filler/Binder:* Dom.
Rep. *Wrapper:* U.S.A./Conn.
Shade
A cigar dominated by dry-
tasting tobacco. It is quite
young, with a touch of spice
on the palate. But it has a
flat, balsa wood finish.
U.S.: $10.80

PLEIADES SIRIUS 81
Dominican Republic • *Size:*
6⅞" x 46 *Filler/Binder:* Dom.
Rep. *Wrapper:* U.S.A./Conn.
Shade
This cigar had draw prob-
lems. It also had very dry flavors including orange peel,
and a touch of spice on the
finish. (09/01/95) U.S.: $8.15

ST. GEORGE 81
CHURCHILL
Dominican Republic • *Size:*
7" x 48 *Filler/Binder:* Dom.
Rep. *Wrapper:* Indonesia
Inconsistent construction
marred this cigar. It has a
woody character with some
woody flavors on the palate.
U.S.: $8.00

SOSA FAMILY 81
SELECTION NO. 8
Dominican Republic • *Size:*
7" x 48 *Filler:* Dom. Rep.,
Nicaragua *Binder:* Mexico
Wrapper: U.S.A./Conn.
A cigar with a light herbal
character and a faint hint of
spice on the palate. But it is
quite tangy and sharp-tasting.
U.S.: $5.30

BALLENA SUPREMA 80
SAN ANDRES
COLLECTION
CONCORDIA
Mexico • *Size:* 7" x 48
Filler/Binder: Mexico *Wrapper:* U.S.A./Conn. Shade
A cigar with vegetal character. It is quite mild and bland.
There is a papery quality to
the smoke, and a light, dry
wood finish. U.S.: $4.30

CERDAN CHURCHILL 80
Dominican Republic • *Size:* 7"
x 46 *Filler/Binder:* Dom. Rep.
Wrapper: U.S.A./Conn. Shade
This is a very salty cigar. It
has some dry wood character
and a woody finish.
U.S.: $7.18

EL RICO HABANO 80
DOUBLE CORONA
Dominican Republic • *Size:*
7" x 47 *Filler:* Nicaragua
Binder: Dom. Rep. *Wrapper:*
Ecuador
This is a very rustic cigar
with a loose draw. It is hot
and peppery, with a slightly
burnt taste, although there is
a solid core of spice.
U.S.: $3.85

HOYO DE MONTERREY 80
EXCALIBUR NO. 1
Honduras • *Size:* 7¼" x 54
Filler/Binder: Honduras,
Nicaragua, Dom. Rep *Wrap-
per:* U.S.A./Conn. Shade
This cigar had an unusual
flower-like aroma, a very
grassy flavor element and a
dry finish. (09/01/95)
U.S.: $5.30

LEMPIRA CHURCHILL 80
Honduras • *Size:* 7" x 48
Filler/Binder: Honduras, Dom.
Rep. *Wrapper:* U.S.A./
Conn. Shade
This cigar lacks balance. It
has some light woodiness, but
overall it is quite dry with a
slight gumminess on the lips.
U.S.: $5.50

SIGLO 21 21-4 80
Dominican Republic • *Size:*
7" x 48 *Filler/Binder:* Dom.
Rep. *Wrapper:* U.S.A./Conn.
An odd, almost rosemary-like
flavor. The cigar has a woody
character, but it finishes a
little bitter. U.S.: $6.00

EL REY DEL MUNDO 79
CORONA INMENSA
Honduras • *Size:* 7¼" x 47
Filler: Dom. Rep., Honduras
Binder: Honduras *Wrapper:*
Ecuador
A very rustic cigar. It is mild-
to medium-bodied, with a
rough exterior. U.S.: $2.00

HOMBRE DE ORO 79
CHURCHILL
Dominican Republic • *Size:*
7" x 50 *Filler:* Dom. Rep.,
Nicaragua *Binder:* Mexico
Wrapper: Indonesia
A very rustic cigar. It has a
salty character, and a dry
finish. U.S.: $4.50

MACABI DOUBLE 79
CORONA
Dominican Republic • *Size:*
6⅞" x 49 *Filler:* Dom. Rep.
Binder: Mexico *Wrapper:*
U.S.A./Conn.
A cigar with a very dry,
papery character. It is quite
mild, with a balsa wood note
on the palate. U.S.: $5.00

MiCUBANO NO. 748 79
Nicaragua • *Size:* 8" x 47
Filler/Binder/Wrapper:
Nicaragua
A cigar with a strong vegetal
character. It is very flat on
the palate, and has a dry,
woody finish. U.S.: $4.75

ORNELAS CHURCHILL 79
Mexico • *Size:* 7" x 49
Filler/Binder/Wrapper: Mexico
A very rustic cigar. It has a
loose fill, and an overall
dusty taste. U.S.: $6.50

PUNCH CASA GRANDE 79
Honduras • *Size:* 7¼" x 46
Filler/Binder: Honduras, Dom.
Rep., Nicaragua *Wrapper:*
Ecuador
A straightforward cigar. It has
a strong vegetal character,
with an earthy aroma. A quite
dry, woody finish. U.S.: $2.80

VARGAS PRESIDENTE 79
Canary Islands • *Size:* 6¾" x
46 *Filler:* Canary Islands,
Dom. Rep. *Binder/Wrapper:*
Indonesia
A mild smoke with a very
rustic, rough wrapper. There
are a few mild flavors of
herbs, but a very dry woody
finish. U.S.: $5.25

AVO XO MAESTOSO 78
Dominican Republic • *Size:*
7" x 48 *Filler/Binder:* Dom.
Rep. *Wrapper:* U.S.A./
Conn. Shade
This cigar is very mild and
very dry. It is flat, with a dry,
herbalness on the palate.
U.S.: $11.20

BALLENA SUPREMA 78
SAN ANDRES COLLECTION
ESPERANZA
Mexico • *Size:* 7" x 50
Filler/Binder: Mexico *Wrap-
per:* U.S.A./Conn.
A very rustic cigar. It has a
dry wood character and it is
slightly bitter. U.S.: $4.50

COTICAS 78
DOUBLE CORONA
Dominican Republic • *Size:*
7" x 48 *Filler/Binder:* Dom.
Rep *Wrapper:* Indonesia
A very rustic cigar. There is a
strong salty component and a
little bitterness on the finish.
U.S.: $5.00

FLOR DE FILIPINAS 78
CHURCHILL
Philippines • *Size:* 7" x 47
Filler/Binder/Wrapper: Philip-
pines
A loose fill created a hot
smoke. It has a strong vegetal
character. U.S.: $2.20

SANTA CLARA 1830 78
NO. II
Mexico • *Size:* 6½" x 48
Filler/Binder/Wrapper: Mexico
This cigar has an extremely
rough, sandpapery wrapper. It
also has a very dry character,
with a balsa-wood flavor and
a papery finish. (09/01/95)
U.S.: $2.75

TE-AMO PRESIDENTE 76
Mexico • *Size:* 7" x 50
Filler/Binder/Wrapper: Mexico
This cigar has a strong, dry,
grassy character with a very
dry finish. U.S.: $3.75

Corona Gorda

*Most of the following Corona
Gorda tasting notes appeared in
the Winter 1996/97 issue of
Cigar Aficionado. Exceptions
are indicated by a date in
parentheses at the end of the
tasting note.*

HOYO DE MONTERREY 92
EPICURE NO. 1
Cuba • *Size:* 5⅝" x 46
Filler/Binder/Wrapper: Cuba
A well-balanced cigar with a
powerful, full-bodied spiciness. There is a complex
earthiness on the palate with
hints of nutmeg. A long finish. U.K.: £9.55

PADRÓN 1964 **92**
ANNIVERSARY SERIES EXCLUSIVO
Nicaragua • *Size:* 5½" x 50
Filler/Binder/Wrapper:
Nicaragua
This is an excellent cigar. It is filled with smooth spice flavors. There's a hint of ripe berries and a strong earthy, leathery finish. Well made with a beautiful wrapper.
U.S.: $8.20

FUENTE FUENTE **91**
OPUS X
FUENTE FUENTE
Dominican Republic • *Size:* 5⅝" x 46 *Filler/Binder/Wrapper:* Dom. Rep.
A powerhouse of flavors, including cocoa and coffee beans and roasted nuts, as well as some sweet spices such as nutmeg. It has a dark, oily wrapper. U.S.: $9.00

ROMEO Y JULIETA **91**
EXHIBICION NO. 3
Cuba • *Size:* 5⅝" x 46
Filler/Binder/Wrapper: Cuba
A hint of youth, but this is a full-bodied, flavorful cigar. Strong hints of cinnamon and coffee beans on a smooth, easy draw. Will improve with age.
U.K.: £8.90

BELINDA CABINET **89**
Honduras • *Size:* 5⅝" x 45
Filler: Dom. Rep., Honduras
Binder: Honduras *Wrapper:* Ecuador
An attractive, medium-bodied cigar with a smooth spiciness and creamy, coffee flavor. (06/01/94) U.S.: $2.25

COHIBA SIGLO IV **89**
Cuba • *Size:* 5⅝" x 46
Filler/Binder/Wrapper: Cuba
This cigar has a solid coffee bean character and is loaded with a core of spiciness. It is medium- to full-bodied with a smooth, leathery finish.
U.K.: £13.10

EL RICO HABANO **89**
GRAN CORONA
Dominican Republic • *Size:* 5¾" x 46 *Filler:* Nicaragua, Ecuador *Binder:* Dom. Rep.
Wrapper: Ecuador
An excellent cigar. It has a solid spiciness and a core of earthy, woody flavors that linger on the finish. Well made with a nice, oily wrapper. U.S.: $3.40

HOYO DE MONTERREY **89**
EXCALIBUR NO. 3
Honduras • *Size:* 6¼" x 50
Filler/Binder: Honduras
Wrapper: U.S.A./Conn. Shade
A good, solid smoke with toasty aromas and nice flavors of coffee and roasted nuts that finish on a cedary note. (06/01/94) U.S.: $4.75

LEMPIRA TORO **89**
Honduras • *Size:* 6" x 50
Filler: Honduras, Nicaragua
Binder: Dom. Rep. *Wrapper:* U.S.A./Conn. Shade
A rich, earthy cigar. It has flavors of roasted nuts, coffee beans and a hint of cocoa. There is a little spice on a medium finish. U.S.: $5.00

AVO NO. 2 **88**
Dominican Republic • *Size:* 6" x 50 *Filler/Binder:* Dom. Rep. *Wrapper:* U.S.A./Conn. Shade
A simple, well-made cigar with nutmeg and cedary flavors and a nice, medium-length finish. (06/01/94)
U.S.: $7.10

DON LINO HAVANA **88**
RESERVE TORO
Dominican Republic • *Size:* 5½" x 46 *Filler/Binder:* Honduras *Wrapper:* U.S.A./Conn. Shade
A very spicy , medium- to full-bodied cigar. It has notes of dried citrus on the palate with rich flavors of coffee beans and spice. U.S.: $4.80

EL REY DEL MUNDO **88**
CHOIX SUPREME
Honduras • *Size:* 6⅛" x 49
Filler: Dom. Rep., Honduras
Binder: Honduras *Wrapper:* Ecuador
A predominantly nutty character marks this medium- to full-bodied cigar. It has flavors of chestnuts on the palate, and a pleasant spicy and coffee bean finish. U.S.: $4.00

FLOR DE FLOREZ CABI- **88**
NET SELECTION FLOREZ FLOREZ
Nicaragua • *Size:* 5¼" x 46
Filler/Binder/Wrapper:
Nicaragua
This is a smooth-tasting cigar with a mild flavor. There are hints of spice and a note of cocoa beans. The finish holds this cigar back. U.S.: $6.00

OLOR PACO **88**
Dominican Republic • *Size:*
6" x 50 *Filler/Binder:* Dom.
Rep. *Wrapper:*
U.S.A./Conn. Shade
An unusual floral character
makes this an attractive
cigar. There are flavors of
coffee, ripe berries and mild,
sweet spices. There is a rich,
woody finish. U.S.: $4.20

PARTAGAS LIMITED **88**
RESERVE REGALE
Dominican Republic • *Size:*
6¼" x 47 *Filler:* Mex., Jam.,
Dom. Rep. *Binder:* Mexico
Wrapper: Cameroon
A well-made cigar that has a
solid tobacco core with mild,
spicy flavors and finish.
(06/01/94) U.S.: $17.50

SOSA GOVERNOR **88**
Dominican Republic • *Size:*
6" x 50 *Filler:* Dom. Rep.
Binder: Honduras *Wrapper:*
Ecuador
A well-made cigar. It has a
mild- to medium-bodied
smoke that has hints of spice
and some coffee beans, and a
woody finish. U.S.: $4.50

V CENTENNIAL **88**
NUMERO 2
Honduras • *Size:* 6" x 50
Filler: Dom. Rep., Honduras,
Nicaragua *Binder:* Mexico
Wrapper: U.S.A./Conn.
Shade
A full-flavored cigar, with
sweet components of dried
fruit and a solid core of nutti-
ness. It should improve with
some aging. U.S.: $6.00

ASHTON **87**
DOUBLE MAGNUM
Dominican Republic • *Size:*
6" x 50 *Filler/Binder:* Dom.
Rep. *Wrapper:*
U.S.A./Conn. Shade
A well-made cigar that has a
nutty character over a solid
spicy core. There is a slight
herbal dryness on the finish.
U.S.: $8.50

BOLIVAR CORONA **87**
EXTRA
Cuba • *Size:* 5⅝" x 46
Filler/Binder/Wrapper: Cuba
Another Cuban cigar with
some inconsistencies. It has a
solid earthy core of flavors
with some spice and wood on
the finish. U.K.: £8.15

CARA MIA TORO **87**
Canary Islands • *Size:* 6" x 50
Filler/Binder: Canary Islands,
Dom. Rep., Brazil *Wrapper:*
U.S.A./Conn. Shade
A cigar with an earthy char-
acter and a solid core of mild
spices, coffee beans and
leather flavors. A medium to
short finish. U.S.: $7.00

CUESTA-REY CENTEN- **87**
NIAL COLLECTION
DOMINICAN NO. 60
Dominican Republic • *Size:*
6" x 50 *Filler/Binder:* Dom.
Rep. *Wrapper:*
U.S.A./Conn. Shade
A solid cigar with a core of
straightforward tobacco fla-
vors. It has a nutty character
with some notes of sweet
herbs and mild spices.
U.S.: $5.40

DA VINCI MONALISA **87**
Honduras • *Size:* 6" x 50
Filler: Honduras, Nicaragua,
Dom. Rep. *Binder:* Dom.
Rep. *Wrapper:* Ecuador
A medium-bodied cigar with
a complex herbal earthiness.
There are strong nutty flavors
on a creamy texture.
U.S.: $6.95

DON LEO ROBUSTO **87**
Dominican Republic • *Size:*
5½" x 50 *Filler/Binder:* Dom.
Rep. *Wrapper:*
U.S.A./Conn. Shade
A medium-bodied smoke
with a pleasant tang. It has
hints of nuts and a dry fruit
character. There is a bit of
spice on the finish.
U.S.: $5.40

DON TOMAS SPECIAL **87**
EDITION NO. 500
Honduras • *Size:* 5½" x 46
Filler: Dom. Rep., Nicaragua
Binder/Wrapper: Honduras
A very well-balanced cigar. It
has leather and spices and
strong hints of nuts on the
palate. It has a smooth tex-
ture on the finish.
U.S.: $4.25

EL REY DEL MUNDO **87**
GRAN CORONAS
Cuba • *Size:* 5⅝" x 46
Filler/Binder/Wrapper: Cuba
An earthy, rich-tasting cigar
with cinnamon notes. It's a
little rustic, but a smooth
woody finish balances out
the cigar. SF: 9

H. UPMANN 87
CHURCHILL
Dominican Republic • *Size:* 5⅝" x 46 *Filler/Binder:* Dom. Rep. *Wrapper:* Indonesia
A solid spicy smoke. It has some saltiness on the palate and an earthy core with some wood flavors on the finish. U.S.: $4.35

HABANICA SERIE 546 87
Nicaragua • *Size:* 5¼" x 46 *Filler/Binder/Wrapper:* Nicaragua
A beautiful, oily sheen on this dark brown wrapper. It has complex flavors of cocoa and anise, with an earthy spiciness. A short finish. U.S.: $6.00

HOYO DE MONTERREY 87
CORONA
Honduras • *Size:* 5⅝" x 46 *Filler/Binder:* Honduras, Nicaragua, Dom. Rep. *Wrapper:* Ecuador
A very spicy cigar with an earthy character. There are flavors of nuts and cedar on the medium- to full-bodied smoke. Finishes a bit dry. U.S.: $3.15

HOYO DE MONTERREY 87
GOVERNOR
Honduras • *Size:* 6⅛" x 50 *Filler/Binder:* Honduras, Nicaragua, Dom. Rep. *Wrapper:* Ecuador
A good cigar with a core of herbal and earthy notes. It's well made with some spice and wood on the finish. U.S.: $3.60

LA GLORIA CUBANA 87
EXTRA
U.S.A. • *Size:* 6¼" x 46 *Filler:* Dom. Rep., Nica. *Binder:* Nicaragua *Wrapper:* Ecuador
A toasty, floral aroma with a solid pepper-spice core of flavors give character to this full-bodied cigar. (06/01/94) U.S.: $3.75

NAT SHERMAN 87
GOTHAM SELECTION NO. 711
Dominican Republic • *Size:* 6" x 50 *Filler/Binder:* Dom. Rep. *Wrapper:* U.S.A./Conn. Shade
A smooth-tasting, well-balanced cigar. It has a creamy character with coffee bean and mild nut flavors, and with a mild, light spice finish. U.S.: $8.60

PARTAGAS ALMIRANTE 87
Dominican Republic • *Size:* 6¼" x 47 *Filler:* Jam., Dom. Rep., Mex. *Binder:* Mexico *Wrapper:* Cameroon
A flavorful cigar with a medium-bodied spiciness. It has a slightly dry finish. (06/01/94) U.S.: $5.70

PETERSON TORO 87
Dominican Republic • *Size:* 6" x 50 *Filler:* Dom. Rep. *Binder:* Ecuador *Wrapper:* U.S.A./Conn. Shade
This is a smooth, medium- to full-bodied cigar. It has flavors of the earth, with leathery notes on the palate. Will benefit from aging. U.S.: $7.55

PUNCH PUNCH 87
Cuba • *Size:* 5⅝" x 46 *Filler/Binder/Wrapper:* Cuba
An earthy character overpowers some spiciness. A good draw on a medium-bodied smoke. U.K.: £8.80

ROMEO Y JULIETA 87
VINTAGE NO. 2
Dominican Republic • *Size:* 6" x 46 *Filler:* Dom. Rep. *Binder:* Mexico *Wrapper:* U.S.A./Conn. Shade
This is a medium-bodied cigar that has solid tobacco flavors and hints of cedar and coffee. (06/01/94) U.S.: $7.30

ROYAL JAMAICA 87
DIRECTOR
Dominican Republic • *Size:* 6" x 45 *Filler:* Jamaica *Binder:* Indonesia *Wrapper:* Cameroon
This cigar has straightforward flavors of cedar and herbs, with a medium-length finish. (06/01/94) U.S.: $4.75

SAVINELLI E.L.R. 87
DOUBLE CORONA
Dominican Republic • *Size:* 6" x 50 *Filler/Binder:* Dom. Rep. *Wrapper:* U.S.A./Conn. Shade
A medium-bodied cigar with some solid leather and coffee bean notes. It has a mild finish. U.S.: $8.25

ARTURO FUENTE 86
FLOR FINA 8-5-8
Dominican Republic • *Size:* 6" x 47 *Filler/Binder:* Dom. Rep. *Wrapper:* Cameroon

A strong peppery flavor dominates this cigar. There is a dusty, earthy quality to the finish that is a little dry. U.S.: $3.50

CUBITA NO. 700 **86**
Dominican Republic • *Size:* 6" x 50 *Filler/Binder:* Dom. Rep. *Wrapper:* U.S.A./Conn. Shade The cigar exhibits some youth. But there is a rich, earthy quality to the flavors with leather and woody tastes on a medium-length finish. U.S.: $5.65

DON MELO CORONA **86**
EXTRA
Honduras • *Size:* 5½" x 46 *Filler/Binder/Wrapper:* Honduras
A spicy smoke. It has a woody character and a medium body, but some vegetal notes on the finish. U.S.: $4.90

DON TOMAS CORONA **86**
Honduras • *Size:* 5½" x 50 *Filler/Binder/Wrapper:* Honduras
A nice, brown wrapper on a cigar that has pleasant cinnamon-spice and cedar flavors with a smooth aftertaste. (06/01/94) U.S.: $3.80

LICENCIADOS TORO **86**
Dominican Republic • *Size:* 6" x 50 *Filler/Binder:* Dom. Rep. *Wrapper:* U.S.A./Conn. Shade A straightforward, medium-bodied cigar. It has a light nuttiness and an herbal character. A woody finish. U.S.: $4.75

MONTECRISTO **86**
CORONA GRANDE
Dominican Republic • *Size:* 5¼" x 46 *Filler/Binder:* Dom. Rep. *Wrapper:* U.S.A./Conn. Shade This is a medium-bodied cigar with a fresh, clean character. There are hints of spice and a dry woody finish. U.S.: $8.00

NAT SHERMAN VIP **86**
SELECTION CARNEGIE
Dominican Republic • *Size:* 6" x 48 *Filler/Binder:* Dom. Rep. *Wrapper:* U.S.A./Conn. Shade An earthy cigar with solid spice and roasted coffee-bean flavors. It burns well and has a good draw. (06/01/94) U.S.: $8.10

PAUL GARMIRIAN **86**
CONNOISSEUR
Dominican Republic • *Size:* 6" x 50 *Filler/Binder:* Dom. Rep. *Wrapper:* U.S.A./Conn. Shade A pleasant smooth-smoking cigar. There is a solid spiciness in this cigar, and it has a woody finish. Should improve with age. U.S.: $10.20

PUROS INDIOS **86**
CORONA GORDA
Honduras • *Size:* 6" x 50 *Filler:* Brazil, Dom. Rep., Nicaragua *Binder/Wrapper:* Ecuador
A core of earthiness, with a spicy character. This cigar is great looking with an oily dark wrapper. It has a clean,

sweet woody finish. U.S.: $4.75

SANTA ROSA TORO **86**
Honduras • *Size:* 6" x 50 *Filler/Binder:* Honduras *Wrapper:* Ecuador
This cigar shows its youth. The slight bite and young wood tastes should mellow with age. Medium- to full-bodied, and it is well made. U.S.: $5.50

TE-AMO TORO **86**
Mexico • *Size:* 6" x 50 *Filler/Binder/Wrapper:* Mexico
Although this cigar has some coarse qualities, it is filled with a peppery core of flavors that mellow as it smokes. U.S.: $3.20

BERING HISPANOS **85**
Honduras • *Size:* 6" x 50 *Filler/Binder:* Honduras, Mexico, Dom. Rep. Nicaragua *Wrapper:* U.S.A./Conn. Shade
This cigar has a creamy core that has a straightforward saltiness. There are hints of earth and a woodiness on the finish. U.S.: $2.50

C.A.O. CORONA **85**
GORDA
Honduras • *Size:* 6" x 50 *Filler:* Nicaragua, Mexico *Binder:* Honduras *Wrapper:* U.S.A./Conn. Shade Another young cigar. It is well made, but there is a strong, sharp vegetal character. There are hints of dried orange peel and pepper notes. U.S.: $6.98

CASA BLANCA DELUXE 85
Dominican Republic • *Size:*
6" x 50 *Filler:* Dom. Rep.
Binder: Mexico *Wrapper:*
U.S.A./Conn. Shade
A mild, mellow smoke.
There are some hints of
sweet herbs, wood and
leather on a mild finish.
U.S.: $3.00

DAVIDOFF NO. 5000 85
Dominican Republic • *Size:*
5⅝" x 46 *Filler/Binder:* Dom.
Rep. *Wrapper:*
U.S.A./Conn. Shade
A smooth-tasting cigar with
some wood and herbal notes
on the palate. It has a light
body on the finish.
U.S.: $11.00

DON ASA CORONA 85
Honduras • *Size:* 5½" x 50
Filler/Binder/Wrapper: Honduras
An attractive medium-brown
wrapper. It is a mellow smoke
with a nutty character, some
exotic eastern spices, but
with a hint of vegetal notes
on the finish. U.S.: $3.80

DON LINO TORO 85
Honduras • *Size:* 5½" x 46
Filler/Binder: Honduras
Wrapper: U.S.A./Conn.
Shade
This is an easy-smoking, mild
cigar. It has some herbal and
nut flavors on the palate and
a slightly drying finish.
U.S.: $3.60

DUNHILL CONDADOS 85
Dominican Republic • *Size:*
6" x 48 *Filler/Binder:* Dom.

Rep., Brazil *Wrapper:*
U.S.A./Conn. Shade
This is a very nice, mellow
smoke. It has a strong herbal
character and a mild, spicy
finish. U.S.: $6.90

FLOR DE FLOREZ 85
CORONA
Nicaragua • *Size:* 6" x 50
Filler/Binder: Honduras
Wrapper: U.S.A./Conn.
Shade
A medium-bodied smoke
with a creamy texture and a
light spicy flavor. U.S.: $5.00

HABANICA SERIE 646 85
Nicaragua • *Size:* 6" x 46
Filler/Binder/Wrapper:
Nicaragua
A pretty dark brown colorado
wrapper. It has sweet spice
flavors, and as it warms up a
sweet woody character comes
out. A short finish holds it
back. U.S.: $6.90

MONTECRUZ 85
SUN-GROWN NO. 201
Dominican Republic • *Size:*
6¼" x 46 *Filler/Binder:* Dom.
Rep., Brazil *Wrapper:*
Cameroon
This cigar is a bit rough, but
it delivers a spicy, medium-
bodied flavor and a slightly
hot finish. (06/01/94)
U.S.: $4.60

PUNCH DELUXE SERIES 85
CHATEAU M
Honduras • *Size:* 5¾" x 46
Filler/Binder: Honduras,
Nicaragua, Dom. Rep.
Wrapper: Ecuador
A nice-looking cigar with a
medium-brown wrapper.

There are hints of cocoa
bean and leather on a medium-bodied smoke. Finishes a
bit dry. U.S.: $3.65

ROMANTICOS 85
LEONARDO
Dominican Republic • *Size:*
6" x 50 *Filler/Binder:* Dom.
Rep. *Wrapper:*
U.S.A./Conn. Shade
A mild cigar with a smooth,
creamy taste. There are hints
of herbs, but it has a very
short finish. U.S.: $5.75

SAINT LUIS REY 85
SERIE A
Honduras • *Size:* 6" x 50
Filler/Binder/Wrapper: Hon-
duras
This is a rich-tasting cigar.
Flavors of toast and coffee
beans with some hints of
leather on the rather short
finish. U.S.: $4.45

THOMAS HINDS 85
NICARAGUAN
SELECTION
SHORT CHURCHILL
Nicaragua • *Size:* 6" x 50
Filler/Binder/Wrapper:
Nicaragua
A well-made cigar with a
solid medium-bodied smoke.
It has a creamy texture and
finishes a bit woody and flat.
U.S.: $6.40

BLAIR ROBUSTO 84
Honduras • *Size:* 6" x 50
Filler/Binder: Honduras
Wrapper: Ecuador
This cigar showed some
inconsistency. It had a salty
character. There are flavors
of sweet herbs on the palate.
U.S.: $5.20

DON DIEGO GRANDE **84**
Dominican Republic • *Size:*
6" x 50 *Filler/Binder:* Dom.
Rep. *Wrapper:*
U.S.A./Conn. Shade
A pleasant, mild cigar. It has
some hints of nutty flavors
and a clean, fresh finish.
U.S.: $5.25

DON TOMAS TORO **84**
Honduras • *Size:* 5½" x 46
Filler: Honduras, Nicaragua
Binder/Wrapper: Honduras
A creamy cigar with nut and
herbal spiciness. It's a little
young with a dry finish.
U.S.: $3.60

JOYA DE NICARAGUA **84**
TORO
Nicaragua • *Size:* 6" x 50
Filler/Binder: Nicaragua
Wrapper: Ecuador
A mild- to medium-bodied
cigar. It has nutty and sweet
spice notes and feels a bit oily
on the palate. A mild, dry
woody finish. U.S.: $4.60

MACABI **84**
CORONA EXTRA
Dominican Republic • *Size:*
6" x 50 *Filler:* Dom. Rep.,
Nicaragua *Binder:* Mexico
Wrapper: U.S.A./Conn.
Shade
This cigar seems fairly dry on
the palate. There are some
sweet pepper flavors, and it
also finishes dry. U.S.: $4.70

TRESADO SELECCION **84**
NO. 300
Dominican Republic • *Size:*
6" x 46 *Filler:* Dom. Rep.
Binder: Cameroon *Wrapper:*
Indonesia

This cigar has a salty character. There are hints of cedar
and pepper. U.S.: $2.75

VARGAS RESERVA **84**
SENADORES
Canary Islands • *Size:* 5½" x
46 *Filler:* Canary Islands,
Dom. Rep. *Binder/Wrapper:*
Indonesia
Inconsistent performance. At
its best, some hints of sweet
spices and a woody finish.
U.S.: $5.00

CABAÑAS ROYALE **83**
Dominican Republic • *Size:*
5⅝" x 46 *Filler/Binder:* Dom.
Rep. *Wrapper:* Mexico
A rough, dark wrapper produces a spicy smoke with
solid tobacco flavors, but a
slightly vegetal finish.
(06/01/94) U.S.: $4.15

DON XAVIER CORONA **83**
Canary Islands • *Size:* 5⅝" x
46 *Filler/Binder:* Canary
Islands, Dom. Rep., Brazil
Wrapper: U.S.A./Conn.
Shade
A mild cigar. It has a light
body with a clean, woody fin-
ish. U.S.: $6.50

EL REY DEL MUNDO **83**
ROBUSTO LARGA
Honduras • *Size:* 6" x 50
Filler: Dom. Rep., Honduras
Binder/Wrapper: Honduras
Inconsistent. A medium-bod-
ied cigar with a dried herbal,
tobacco character. (06/01/94)
U.S.: $4.25

H. UPMANN MAGNUM **83**
Cuba • *Size:* 5⅝" x 46
Filler/Binder/Wrapper: Cuba
Very inconsistent. Three
tasters had a loose fill with a
quick burn. Some pepper and
spiciness at its best. But not
up to par. U.K.: £9.45

JUAN CLEMENTE **83**
CLUB SELECTION
NO. 1
Dominican Republic • *Size:*
6" x 50 *Filler/Binder:* Dom.
Rep. *Wrapper:*
U.S.A./Conn. Shade
A pleasant mild cigar with a
light cedary aroma and some
hints of nuts and sweet herbs
on the palate. A light finish.
U.S.: $10.05

MAYA MAYA **83**
Honduras • *Size:* 6" x 50
Filler/Binder: Honduras,
Nicaragua *Wrapper:*
U.S.A./Conn. Shade
There are strong elements of
dry spices and woodiness on
this slow-starting cigar. It has
a salty character and is rather
roughly constructed.
U.S.: $4.40

OSCAR NO. 500 **83**
Dominican Republic • *Size:*
5½" x 50 *Filler/Binder:* Dom.
Rep. *Wrapper:*
U.S.A./Conn. Shade
Showed some inconsistency.
But tasters noted a light- to
medium-bodied smoke with a
creamy texture and some
spiciness. U.S.: $9.05

Santa Damiana Seleccion No. 300 — 83

Dominican Republic • *Size:* 5½" x 46 *Filler/Binder:* Dom. Rep. *Wrapper:* U.S.A./Conn. Shade
This cigar shows evidence of young tobacco. It has some sharp vegetal edges, but there are flavors of coffee beans on its medium-bodied smoke. U.S.: $6.90

MiCubano No. 650 — 82

Nicaragua • *Size:* 6" x 50 *Filler/Binder/Wrapper:* Nicaragua
A slightly vegetal character masks some spicy notes on the palate. A short finish. U.S.: $3.85

Nat Sherman Exchange Selection Trafalgar 4 — 82

Dominican Republic • *Size:* 6" x 47 *Filler:* Dom. Rep., Mexico *Binder:* Mexico *Wrapper:* U.S.A./Conn. Shade
This cigar shows some youth. It has a smooth round character with some herbal flavors and a hint of pepper. A papery finish. U.S.: $8.00

Petrus Tabacage Corona Sublime 89 — 82

Honduras • *Size:* 5½" x 46 *Filler/Binder:* Honduras *Wrapper:* Ecuador
A quite mild cigar with a mild herbal character and a very dry finish. U.S.: $4.70

Te-Amo Satisfaction — 82

Mexico • *Size:* 6" x 46 *Filler/Binder/Wrapper:* Mexico

A cigar with some pepper flavors. But it is dominated by a dry, vegetal character. U.S.: $2.85

Thomas Hinds Honduran Selection Short Churchill — 82

Honduras • *Size:* 6" x 50 *Filler/Binder:* Honduras *Wrapper:* Ecuador
A cigar with a cedary character. There are hints of pepper and a bit of sweetness on the mild- to medium-bodied smoke. U.S.: $4.70

Vueltabajo Toro — 82

Dominican Republic • *Size:* 6" x 50 *Filler/Binder:* Dom. Rep. *Wrapper:* U.S.A./Conn. Shade
This cigar has a very drying effect on the palate. It is mild, with small hints of nuts and a floral note, with a dry woody finish. U.S.: $4.00

Cacique Apache — 81

Dominican Republic • *Size:* 6" x 50 *Filler/Binder:* Dom. Rep. *Wrapper:* U.S.A./Conn. Shade
A very herbal cigar with some grassy notes on the palate. It is light and has some nuttiness on the finish. U.S.: $4.20

Hoyo de Monterrey Excalibur No. 4 — 81

Honduras • *Size:* 5⅝" x 46 *Filler/Binder:* Honduras, Nicaragua, Dom. Rep. *Wrapper:* U.S.A./Conn. Shade
A very mild-tasting cigar. It has a hint of vanilla and pepper, but a paper-thin charac-

ter. There are hints of grassiness and herbal flavors. U.S.: $4.10

Cruz Real No. 19 — 80

Mexico • *Size:* 6" x 50 *Filler/Binder/Wrapper:* Mexico
This is a rustic cigar. Mild flavors of spice and dried fruit are present, but it has a very dry, woody finish. U.S.: $4.15

Match Play Turnberry — 80

Dominican Republic • *Size:* 6" x 50 *Filler/Binder:* Dom. Rep. *Wrapper:* Ecuador
The cigar has some bite to it. There are hints of pepper and dry nuts, but some raw flavors of mint on the finish. U.S.: $5.50

Carrington No. 7 — 79

Dominican Republic • *Size:* 6" x 50 *Filler/Binder:* Dom. Rep. *Wrapper:* U.S.A./Conn. Shade
A coarse cigar with a vegetal character. It is very mouth-drying, with a flat, dry woody finish. U.S.: $5.20

La Finca Joya — 79

Nicaragua • *Size:* 6" x 50 *Filler/Binder/Wrapper:* Nicaragua
While there are some hints of nutty flavors, this is a very rough, rustic cigar with some sharp tastes on the finish. U.S.: $2.25

Santa Clara 1830 No. VI — 79

Mexico • *Size:* 6" x 50 *Filler:* Mexico, Nicaragua *Binder/Wrapper:* Mexico

There are some earthy and spicy flavors in this cigar. But it showed inconsistent construction and ended up very dry and woody on the finish. U.S.: $2.50

HENRY CLAY   **78**
BREVAS A LA CONSERVA
Dominican Republic • *Size:* 5⅝" x 46 *Filler/Binder:* Dom. Rep. *Wrapper:* U.S.A./Conn. Shade
A very rustic cigar. It is a bit hot on the palate, and there are funky, earthy flavors, with a flat, dry woody finish. U.S.: $3.50

TORCEDOR TORO   **78**
Nicaragua • *Size:* 6" x 50 *Filler/Binder:* Nicaragua *Wrapper:* Honduras
A poorly constructed cigar. It is rough and coarse, with a strong salty component and a dry, vegetal character. U.S.: $3.50

TESOROS DE COPAN   **77**
CORONA
Honduras • *Size:* 5¼" x 46 *Filler/Binder:* Honduras *Wrapper:* Ecuador
A cigar with a vegetal character. It seems young and green, and has a very drying element on the palate. U.S.: $5.00

Lonsdale

Most of the following Lonsdale tasting notes appeared in the Autumn 1996 issue of Cigar Aficionado. *Exceptions are indicated by a date in parentheses at the end of the tasting note.*

COHIBA SIGLO III   **95**
Cuba • *Size:* 6" x 42 *Filler/Binder/Wrapper:* Cuba
A great addition to a great line of cigars. It is gorgeous to look at with its rich brown, smooth wrapper and gives loads of pleasure with every puff. An opulent smoke with great finesse and class. (03/01/93) U.K.: £11.75

QUINTERO CHURCHILL **92**
Cuba • *Size:* 6½" x 42 *Filler/Binder/Wrapper:* Cuba
A powerful, full-bodied cigar with a deep nutty aroma and strong flavors of clove and nutmeg, with a cocoa-like finish. (03/01/94) Price N/A

PARTAGAS LIMITED   **91**
RESERVE ROYALE
Dominican Republic • *Size:* 6¾" x 43 *Filler:* Mex., Dom. Rep., Jamaica *Binder:* Mexico *Wrapper:* Cameroon
This cigar is packed with spice and pepper flavors. It is well-made and has a lingering finish. (03/01/94) U.S.: $17.00

RAFAEL GONZALES   **91**
LONSDALE
Cuba • *Size:* 6½" x 42 *Filler/Binder/Wrapper:* Cuba

A dark-brown wrapper burns evenly on this full-bodied cigar, which has flavors of coffee and cocoa and a solid spicy core. (03/01/94) U.K.: £8.45

SANCHO PANZA   **91**
MOLINAS
Cuba • *Size:* 6½" x 42 *Filler/Binder/Wrapper:* Cuba
A well-balanced cigar with smooth spiciness. There are hints of dark coffee flavors and dried citrus notes, with a long spicy finish. U.K.: £8.45

COHIBA SIGLO V   **90**
Cuba • *Size:* 6⅝" x 43 *Filler/Binder/Wrapper:* Cuba
This cigar has a white peppery taste and is loaded with coffee and cream flavors. It is well balanced with a medium to full body and a cedary finish. U.K.: £16.50

H. UPMANN LONSDALE **90**
Cuba • *Size:* 6½" x 42 *Filler/Binder/Wrapper:* Cuba
A well-made, full-bodied cigar that has an earthy aroma and complex flavors of spice and dried fruits. (03/01/94) Price N/A

LA GLORIA CUBANA   **90**
MEDAILLE D'OR NO. 2
Cuba • *Size:* 6⅔" x 43 *Filler/Binder/Wrapper:* Cuba
A well-made cigar that burns beautifully. It is well balanced and has a core of leathery flavors with a perfumed character, and a long, earthy finish. SF: 13.4

ROMEO Y JULIETA **90**
CORONA GRANDE
Cuba • *Size:* 6½" x 42
Filler/Binder/Wrapper: Cuba
This is a full-bodied, rich
smoke. It has cedar and spice
flavors, including nutmeg,
and an overall pepper spice
character with a long, coffee
bean finish. SF: 9.2

TROYA NO. 45 CETRO **90**
Dominican Republic • *Size:*
6¼" x 44 *Filler/Binder:* Dom.
Rep. *Wrapper:*
U.S.A./Conn. Shade
This cigar has a medium
body with a solid spicy flavor
and a rich, almost leathery
mouth feel on the finish.
(03/01/94) U.S.: $4.40

DAVIDOFF NO. 4000 **89**
Dominican Republic • *Size:*
6" x 42 *Filler/Binder:* Dom.
Rep. *Wrapper:*
U.S.A./Conn.
A firm cigar with attractive
aromas and elegant coffee
and nut flavors. (03/01/94)
U.S.: $10.25

DAVIDOFF GRAND CRU **89**
NO. 1
Dominican Republic • *Size:*
6" x 42 *Filler/Binder:* Dom.
Rep. *Wrapper:*
U.S.A./Conn. Shade
A beautiful brown wrapper
on a finely constructed cigar
that delivers a spicy pepper
flavor and a cedary finish.
(03/01/94) U.S.: $10.75

HOYO DE MONTERREY **89**
LE HOYO DES DIEUX
Cuba • *Size:* 6" x 42
Filler/Binder/Wrapper: Cuba

A spicy, well-rolled cabinet
cigar with rich flavors and an
earthy aftertaste. (03/01/94)
U.K.: £9.20

V CENTENNIAL CETRO **89**
Honduras • *Size:* 6½" x 44
Filler/Binder: Dom. Rep.,
Mex., Nica., Hon. *Wrapper:*
U.S.A./Conn. Shade
A medium-bodied cigar with
a core of earthy flavors that
have a hint of spiciness. It
finishes smoothly. (03/01/94)
U.S.: $5.00

ARTURO FUENTE **88**
SPANISH LONSDALE
Dominican Republic • *Size:*
6½" x 42 *Filler/Binder:* Dom.
Rep. *Wrapper:* Cameroon
A cigar filled with earthy,
spicy flavors. It's well-made
and has a long, smooth finish. (03/01/94) U.S.: $3.20

LA GLORIA CUBANA **88**
MEDAILLE D'OR NO. 1
U.S.A. • *Size:* 6¼" x 43
Filler/Binder: Dom. Rep.,
Nicaragua *Wrapper:*
Ecuador
A rich, full-bodied smoke
with leathery, earthy notes
and a solid spicy and coffee
core of flavors. (03/01/94)
U.S.: $3.75

MONTECRISTO NO. 1 **88**
Cuba • *Size:* 6½" x 42
Filler/Binder/Wrapper: Cuba
A medium- to full-bodied
cigar with some mellow spiciness. It is smooth and well
balanced with a floral character and some hints of cedar.
U.K.: £9.60

PARTAGAS NO. 1 **88**
Cuba • *Size:* 6⅝" x 43
Filler/Binder/Wrapper: Cuba
This cigar showed the incon-
sistency of young tobacco.
Some tasters noted solid
spices with a strong earthy
core of flavors. Needs aging.
SF: 11

PARTAGAS 8-9-8 **88**
Cuba • *Size:* 6⅝" x 43
Filler/Binder/Wrapper: Cuba
Another cigar with some
youthful characteristics. But
it also is rich and full-bodied
with a good, solid hazelnut
quality on the palate and a
woody finish. Will improve
with age. U.K.: £10.35

PARTAGAS 8-9-8 **88**
Dominican Republic • *Size:*
6⅞" x 44 *Filler:* Dom. Rep.,
Mexico *Binder:* Mexico
Wrapper: Cameroon
A well-made cigar with a
smooth taste. It has notes of
nuts and spices, with a strong
hint of herbs. It has a medium body and a pleasant finish. U.S.: $6.25

PARTAGAS NO. 1 **88**
Dominican Republic • *Size:*
6¼" x 43 *Filler:* Dom. Rep.,
Mexico *Binder:* Mexico
Wrapper: Cameroon
This is a well-balanced,
smooth smoke with a solid
spicy core and a touch of
earthiness on the palate.
There is a light, woody finish. U.S.: $5.55

SAINT LUIS REY 88
LONSDALE
Cuba • *Size:* 6½" x 42
Filler/Binder/Wrapper: Cuba
This is a solid, spicy cigar with a sweet cocoa-bean backbone. A touch rustic, but very rich and tasty. SF: 9.6

SAVINELLI E.L.R. 88
No. 3 LONSDALE
Dominican Republic • *Size:* 6¼" x 43 *Filler/Binder:* Dom. Rep. *Wrapper:* U.S.A./Conn. Shade
A medium- to full-bodied cigar. It has a solid, earthy and leathery character with a hint of sweet herbs and a hazelnut finish. U.S.: $7.25

BERING PLAZA 87
Honduras • *Size:* 6" x 43
Filler: Mex., Dom. Rep., Hon. *Binder:* Honduras
Wrapper: Mexico
A solid-smoking cigar with pepper flavors that come through a good, easy draw. (03/01/94) U.S.: $1.75

BOLIVAR INMENSA 87
Cuba • *Size:* 6⅝" x 43
Filler/Binder/Wrapper: Cuba
A well-made cigar with good balance and a core of red spices. But it finishes a little dry. U.K.: £9.00

EL REY DEL MUNDO 87
LONSDALE
Cuba • *Size:* 6⅜" x 42
Filler/Binder/Wrapper: Cuba
A full-flavored cigar with some sweet spice and cedar wood flavors. It also has some undertones of earth and leather. But it showed inconsistency. U.K.: £8.45

JOYA DE NICARAGUA 87
No. 1
Nicaragua • *Size:* 6⅝" x 44
Filler/Binder: Nicaragua
Wrapper: Ecuador
A sweet nut flavor dominates this medium-bodied cigar. It has solid notes of herbs that build into spicy flavors, and it has a spicy finish. U.S.: $4.25

LA FINCA ROMEO 87
Nicaragua • *Size:* 6½" x 42
Filler/Binder/Wrapper: Nicaragua
A cigar with a creamy texture. It has plenty of nutty flavors on the palate and a sweet, cedary finish. U.S.: $2.00

LICENCIADOS 87
EXCELENTE
Dominican Republic • *Size:* 6¾" x 43 *Filler/Binder:* Dom. Rep. *Wrapper:* U.S.A./Conn. Shade
A well-made cigar with spice and nuts on the mid-palate with a woody, slightly short finish. U.S.: $4.05

MONTECRISTO No. 1 87
Dominican Republic • *Size:* 6½" x 44 *Filler/Binder:* Dom. Rep. *Wrapper:* U.S.A./Conn. Shade
A solid medium-bodied cigar. It has a core of cocoa bean flavors, with hints of sweet spices and a pleasant, sweet wood finish. U.S.: $7.50

MONTESINO No. 1 87
Dominican Republic • *Size:* 6¾" x 43 *Filler/Binder:* Dom. Rep. *Wrapper:* U.S.A./Conn. Shade

A cigar with a spicy attack on the palate, but with a short finish. Well-made. (03/01/94) U.S.: $3.40

PADRÓN PALMA 87
Honduras • *Size:* 6⁷⁄₁₆" x 42
Filler/Binder/Wrapper: Nicaragua
A cool, smooth smoke with strong hints of roasted coffee flavors. It also has some sweet spices on the palate with a perfumed, but rather short, finish. U.S.: $2.90

PARTAGAS HUMITUBE 87
Dominican Republic • *Size:* 6¾" x 43 *Filler:* Dom. Rep.
Binder: Mexico *Wrapper:* Cameroon
This cigar comes across as quite rustic with some good spiciness. It has a smoothness on the palate, with a sweet woody character. U.S.: $6.50

POR LARRAÑAGA 87
CETROS
Dominican Republic • *Size:* 6⅞" x 42 *Filler/Binder:* Dom. Rep. *Wrapper:* U.S.A./Conn. Shade
A nice, smooth-tasting cigar. It has some hints of toastiness on the palate and there is a good creamy texture. U.S.: $5.50

RAMON ALLONES "B" 87
Dominican Republic • *Size:* 6½" x 42 *Filler:* Dom. Rep., Mexico *Binder:* Mexico
Wrapper: Cameroon
A smooth brown wrapper leads to a mild, medium-bodied spiciness with cedar and coffee flavors. (03/01/94) U.S.: $5.50

THOMAS HINDS NICARAGUAN SELECTION LONSDALE **87**

Nicaragua • *Size:* 6⅓" x 43
Filler/Binder/Wrapper:
Nicaragua
A nice oily wrapper. This cigar has solid notes of coffee grounds and a good spiciness, with a slight mineral finish.
U.S.: $5.80

8-9-8 COLLECTION LONSDALE **86**

Jamaica • *Size:* 6½" x 42
Filler: Jamaica, Dom. Rep.
Binder: Mexico *Wrapper:*
U.S.A./Conn. Shade
A very well-made cigar. It has some solid notes of spice and nuts on the palate that finish a bit short and on the dry, woody side. U.S.: $8.25

ASHTON 8-9-8 **86**

Dominican Republic • *Size:*
6½" x 44 *Filler/Binder:* Dom.
Rep. *Wrapper:* U.S.A./
Conn. Shade
A very pleasant, creamy cigar. It has strong flavors of nuts, with hints of leather and nutmeg. U.S.: $6.60

AVO NO. 1 **86**

Dominican Republic • *Size:*
6⅔" x 42 *Filler:* Dom.Rep.
Binder: Dom. Rep. *Wrapper:*
U.S.A./Conn. Shade
This is a medium-bodied cigar that needs some aging. But it is smooth and woody with a slight floral aroma. There are nuts and dried citrus flavors on the palate.
U.S.: $6.90

BAUZA MEDAILLE D'ORO NO. 1 **86**

Dominican Republic • *Size:*
6⅞" x 44 *Filler:* Dom. Rep. ,
Nicaragua *Binder:* Mexico
Wrapper: Ecuador
A very peppery cigar with a solid woody core of flavors. It has a smooth taste.
U.S.: $4.95

DON DIEGO LONSDALE **86**

Dominican Republic • *Size:*
6⅝" x 42 *Filler/Binder:* Dom.
Rep. *Wrapper:* U.S.A./
Conn. Shade
A good, medium-bodied cigar. It has a touch of pepper at first, which rounds out to a creamy, toasty character with a hint of spiciness.
U.S.: $4.10

DON MELO CORONA GORDA **86**

Honduras • *Size:* 6¼" x 44
Filler/Binder/Wrapper: Honduras
An oily, dark wrapper makes this an attractive cigar. It is a bit dry on the palate, with some hints of leathery and earthy flavors. U.S.: $5.40

ENCANTO ELEGANTE **86**

Honduras • *Size:* 7" x 44
Filler/Binder/Wrapper: Honduras
Some inconsistency in construction for this cigar. But it is very spicy, with a nice earthy texture. There are hints of citrus fruit and a tanginess on the finish.
U.S.: $4.75

MACANUDO VINTAGE CABINET SELECTION 1993 II **86**

Jamaica • *Size:* 6⁹⁄₁₆" x 43
Filler: Dom. Rep., Jamaica,
Mexico *Binder:* Mexico
Wrapper: U.S.A./Conn. Shade
This is a good mild- to medium-bodied cigar with a strong element of nuttiness on the palate. It finishes a little dry, but has a woody character. U.S.: $10.50

MONTE CANARIO IMPERIALES **86**

Canary Islands • *Size:* 6½" x 42 *Filler:* Canary Islands, Dom. Rep. *Binder:* Dom. Rep. *Wrapper:* U.S.A./
Conn. Shade
A medium-bodied cigar with a sweet herbal character. It has hints of leather and earthiness with a smooth finish. U.S.: $5.50

MONTE CANARIO NUNCIO **86**

Canary Islands • *Size:* 6¼" x 44 *Filler:* Canary Islands, Dom. Rep. *Binder:* Dom. Rep. *Wrapper:* U.S.A./
Conn. Shade
A well-made cigar with a good balance of flavors that include dried citrus and leather notes. It has a woody finish. U.S.: $5.75

PETRUS TABACAGE NO. II 89 **86**

Honduras • *Size:* 6¼" x 44
Filler: Nicaragua *Binder:*
Honduras *Wrapper:* Ecuador
A very nice smooth-tasting cigar. It has some strong hints of leather with a spicy, floral finish. U.S.: $5.20

PRIMO DEL REY   86
SELECCION No. 1
Dominican Republic • *Size:*
6¹³⁄₁₆ x 42   *Filler:* Dom. Rep.,
Brazil   *Binder:* U.S.A.
Wrapper: Indonesia
A pleasant medium-bodied
smoke. It has some sweet
pepper and earth notes on
the palate, and a woody finish. U.S.: $2.60

RAMON ALLONES   86
CRYSTALS
Dominican Republic • *Size:*
6¼" x 42   *Filler:* Dom. Rep.,
Mexico   *Binder:* Mexico
Wrapper: Cameroon
This cigar is a bit rough, but
it has a good woody character
and flavor elements of nuts
and mild spices with a slightly mineral finish. U.S.: $5.90

SAINT LUIS REY   86
LONSDALE
Honduras • *Size:* 6½" x 44
Filler/Binder/Wrapper: Honduras
A medium-bodied cigar that
is a bit coarse, but it's packed
with complex sweet herb and
toast-like flavors. It ends a bit
dry. U.S.: $3.90

SANTA ROSA CETROS   86
Honduras • *Size:* 6" x 42
Filler/Binder/Wrapper: Honduras
Mild nut and spice flavors
dominate this cigar that
starts a bit slow, but builds to
a smooth, pleasant smoke.
(03/01/94) U.S.: $4.00

TRESADO SELECCION   86
No. 400
Dominican Republic • *Size:*
6⅝" x 44   *Filler:* Dom. Rep.
Binder: Cameroon   *Wrapper:*
Indonesia
Some inconsistency. But a
cigar with good balance and
sweetish character. It has
hints of coffee bean flavors
and a sweet wood character.
U.S.: $2.50

TROYA No. 54   86
ELEGANTE
Dominican Republic • *Size:*
7" x 43   *Filler/Binder:* Dom.
Rep.   *Wrapper:*
U.S.A./Conn. Shade
This is a well-balanced and
smooth-tasting cigar. It has
some flavors of toast and
cream. U.S.: $4.80

VERACRUZ RESERVE   86
ESPECIAL
Mexico • *Size:* 6½" x 42
Filler/Binder/Wrapper: Mexico
A light-tasting cigar that
smokes easily with some spicy
flavors. (03/01/94) Price N/A

ARTURO FUENTE   85
SELECCION PRIVADA
No. 1
Dominican Republic • *Size:*
6¾" x 44   *Filler/Binder:* Dom.
Rep.   *Wrapper:* Cameroon
This is a smooth, well-bal-
anced cigar. It has a light
peppery flavor with hints of
sweet nuts. U.S.: $3.65

BELINDA CORONA   85
GRANDE
Honduras • *Size:* 6¼" x 44
Filler/Binder: Honduras
Wrapper: Ecuador

This cigar has a short finish.
But it has a creamy texture
with smooth flavors of nuts
and an earthy herbalness.
U.S.: $2.25

C.A.O. LONSDALE   85
Honduras • *Size:* 7" x 44
Filler: Nicaragua, Mexico
Binder: Honduras   *Wrapper:*
U.S.A./Conn. Shade
A nice, well-balanced cigar.
It has a strong cedarwood fin-
ish and some hints of leather
and sweet spices on the
palate. U.S.: $5.78

CUESTA-REY   85
CABINET No. 95
Dominican Republic • *Size:*
6¼" x 42   *Filler:* Dom. Rep.
Binder: Dom.Rep.   *Wrapper:*
Cameroon
A pleasant, spicy cigar. It has
some hints of chocolate and
earthiness on the palate, but
ends with a rather dry, woody
finish. U.S.: $3.85

CUESTA-REY   85
CABINET No. 1884
Dominican Republic • *Size:*
6¼" x 44   *Filler/Binder:* Dom.
Rep.   *Wrapper:* U.S.A./
Conn. Shade
A mild- to medium-bodied
cigar with a smooth taste of
nuts and herbs. It has a mild
spicy finish. U.S.: $4.35

DON ASA   85
CETROS No. 2
Honduras • *Size:* 6½" x 44
Filler/Binder/Wrapper: Honduras
A very well-balanced and
harmonious cigar with hints
of sweet spices, woodiness
and a slightly herbal flavor. A
dry finish. U.S.: $6.00

DON LINO HAVANA RESERVE NO. 1 — 85

Dominican Republic • *Size:* 6½" x 44 *Filler/Binder:* Honduras *Wrapper:* U.S.A./Conn. Shade

A mild, smooth-tasting cigar. It has a creamy texture with some herb and wood flavors, and a bit of saltiness. A woody finish. U.S.: $4.18

DON TOMAS SPECIAL EDITION NO. 200 — 85

Honduras • *Size:* 6½" x 44 *Filler:* Dom. Rep., Nicaragua *Binder/Wrapper:* Honduras

This is a mellow smoke with a strong nutty component. Showed some inconsistency in performance. It has some solid coffee-like flavors. U.S.: $4.60

DON VITO CAPO — 85

Canary Islands • *Size:* 6¾" x 44 *Filler/Binder:* Dom. Rep. *Wrapper:* U.S.A./Conn. Shade

A well-made cigar with an oily wrapper. It has a creamy texture, with a solid pepper spice core, and a sweet cedar finish. U.S.: $6.25

HOYO DE MONTERREY NO. 1 — 85

Honduras • *Size:* 6½" x 43 *Filler/Binder:* Honduras, Nicaragua, Dom. Rep. *Wrapper:* Ecuador

A very well-made cigar with a pleasant floral character. There is a bit of young tobacco evident on the palate, and it should improve with age. U.S.: $3.55

MACABI NO. 1 — 85

Dominican Republic • *Size:* 6¾" x 44 *Filler:* Dom. Rep., Nicaragua *Binder:* Mexico *Wrapper:* U.S.A./Conn. Shade

A young cigar that starts out slow, but it warms up to pleasant flavors of sweet herbs with an overall creamy texture. U.S.: $4.40

MACANUDO BARON DE ROTHSCHILD — 85

Jamaica • *Size:* 6½" x 42 *Filler:* Dom. Rep., Jamaica, Mexico *Binder:* Mexico *Wrapper:* U.S.A./Conn. Shade

A very well-made cigar. It has a creamy texture on a mild body, with a slight tang. It has a slightly dry finish. U.S.: $4.95

NAT SHERMAN GOTHAM SELECTION NO. 1400 — 85

Dominican Republic • *Size:* 6¼" x 44 *Filler/Binder:* Dom. Rep. *Wrapper:* U.S.A./Conn. Shade

A spicy smoke with a white peppery note. It has a slightly earthy quality, with a woody finish, and some hints of coffee bean on the palate. It burns well. U.S.: $7.50

PRIMO DEL REY CHAVON — 85

Dominican Republic • *Size:* 6½" x 41 *Filler:* Dom. Rep., Brazil *Binder:* U.S.A. *Wrapper:* Indonesia

This cigar starts out quite salty, but it builds into a solid core of spiciness with hints of nutmeg. A woody finish. U.S.: $2.10

PUNCH LONSDALE — 85

Honduras • *Size:* 6½" x 43 *Filler/Binder:* Honduras, Nicaragua, Dom. Rep. *Wrapper:* Ecuador

A pleasant, mild- to medium-bodied cigar. It has a mild, woody character with a slightly dry wood finish. U.S.: $3.55

RAMON ALLONES PRIVADA A — 85

Dominican Republic • *Size:* 7" x 45 *Filler:* Dom. Rep., Mexico *Binder:* Mexico *Wrapper:* Cameroon

A pleasant, mild- to medium-bodied smoke with a light creaminess, a hint of nuts and spices, and a fresh finish. U.S.: $5.95

SANTA CLARA 1830 NO. III — 85

Mexico • *Size:* 6⅝" x 43 *Filler/Binder/Wrapper:* Mexico

This cigar starts slowly, but it builds to some nutty flavors with a smooth-tasting orange peel quality. It is a medium-bodied smoke. U.S.: $2.50

SOSA FAMILY SELECTION NO. 1 — 85

Dominican Republic • *Size:* 6¾" x 43 *Filler/Binder:* Dom. Rep. *Wrapper:* U.S.A./Conn. Shade

A solid peppery cigar, but it lacks depth. There are some vegetal notes on a rather short finish. U.S.: $4.75

THOMAS HINDS HONDURAN SELECTION SUPREMOS 85

Honduras • *Size:* 6⅗" x 43
Filler/Binder: Honduras
Wrapper: Ecuador
This is an herbal cigar dominated by a woody character. It has some hints of spice on the palate, and is a mild- to medium-bodied smoke.
U.S.: $4.10

ZINO MOUTON CADET NO. 1 85

Honduras • *Size:* 6½" x 44
Filler/Binder/Wrapper: Honduras
A medium-bodied cigar with a hint of sweet spice on the palate. It is dominated by an herbal character with a dry woody finish. U.S.: $7.25

ASTRAL LUJOS 84

Honduras • *Size:* 6½" x 44
Filler: Dom. Rep., Nicaragua
Binder/Wrapper: Honduras
A mild-tasting cigar with a strong dry, herbal character. Some inconsistency in performance. It has a hint of earthiness on a dry finish.
U.S.: $5.75

CARA MIA LONSDALE 84

Canary Islands • *Size:* 6½" x 42 *Filler/Binder:* Canary Island, Brazil, Dom. Rep.
Wrapper: U.S.A./Conn. Shade
A smooth-tasting cigar with some mild hints of cream, and a meaty note. It has an overall floral character.
U.S.: $6.50

CASA BLANCA LONSDALE 84

Dominican Republic • *Size:* 6½" x 42 *Filler:* Dom. Rep., Brazil *Binder:* Mexico *Wrapper:* U.S.A./Conn. Shade
A very young cigar. It has some cinnamon and dried citrus elements on the palate, and there are some strong woody notes. Needs to be aged. U.S.: $2.75

CUESTA-REY CAPTIVA 84

Dominican Republic • *Size:* 6¾6" x 42 *Filler/Binder:* Dom. Rep. *Wrapper:* U.S.A./Conn. Shade
A mild- to medium-bodied cigar dominated by woody flavors. It has a hint of nuttiness on the palate.
U.S.: $5.40

DIANA SILVIUS CORONA 84

Dominican Republic • *Size:* 6½" x 42 *Filler/Binder:* Dom. Rep. *Wrapper:* U.S.A./Conn. Shade
This is a well-made cigar. It has some solid notes of cedar and tobacco character with a slightly tangy finish.
U.S.: $7.95

DON JUAN NUMERO UNO 84

Nicaragua • *Size:* 6⅝" x 44 *Filler:* Nicaragua, Dom. Rep. *Binder:* Mexico *Wrapper:* U.S.A./Conn. Shade
A decent medium-bodied cigar. It has some vegetal notes and a salty character, but there are some hints of nuts on the palate.
U.S.: $3.75

DON LINO NO. 1 84

Honduras • *Size:* 6½" x 44
Filler/Binder: Honduras
Wrapper: U.S.A./Conn. Shade
A well-made, medium-bodied cigar dominated by sweet herbal notes. While there are some leathery tones on the finish, it is dry. U.S.: $3.60

DON TOMAS CORONA GRANDE 84

Honduras • *Size:* 6½" x 44
Filler/Binder/Wrapper: Honduras, Nicaragua*Filler:* Honduras, Nicaragua *Binder/Wrapper:* Honduras
This is a soft, spicy cigar with a creamy character. It is medium-bodied and has a woody finish. U.S.: $6.45

DON XAVIER LONSDALE 84

Canary Islands • *Size:* 6⅝" x 42 *Filler/Binder:* Canary Islands, Dom. Rep., Brazil *Wrapper:* U.S.A./Conn. Shade
A mild cigar with a good creamy texture. It has mild flavors of herbs. U.S.: $6.00

F.D. GRAVE LONSDALE 84

Honduras • *Size:* 6¼" x 44
Filler: Dom. Rep., Honduras, U.S.A. *Binder/Wrapper:* U.S.A.
A cigar with a good woody character and a soft touch of sweet herbs. A pleasant aroma with hints of mint.
U.S.: $3.30

HOYO DE MONTERREY AMBASSADOR · 84

Honduras • *Size:* 6¼" x 44
Filler/Binder: Honduras, Nicaragua, Dom. Rep.
Wrapper: Ecuador
This mild- to medium-bodied cigar has some sweet, mild spice flavors. It is a bit dry on the finish. U.S.: $2.40

JOSÉ MARTÍ PALMA · 84

Dominican Republic • *Size:* 7" x 42 *Filler:* Dom. Rep.
Binder: Mexico *Wrapper:* U.S.A./Conn. Shade
A pleasant, nutty cigar with a very creamy character. It is a light-tasting, mild cigar with an attractive wrapper. U.S.: $3.50

JUAN CLEMENTE CLUB SELECTION NO. 3 · 84

Dominican Republic • *Size:* 7" x 44 *Filler/Binder:* Dom. Rep. *Wrapper:* U.S.A./Conn. Shade
Good core of sweet herb and nut flavors. It has a slightly dry finish. U.S.: $9.55

JUAN CLEMENTE GRAN CORONA · 84

Dominican Republic • *Size:* 6" x 42 *Filler/Binder:* Dom. Rep. *Wrapper:* U.S.A./Conn. Shade
This cigar has a woody aroma and flavor and, as it gets going, takes on a rustic, earthy character. (03/01/94) U.S.: $5.98

LA UNICA NO. 300 · 84

Dominican Republic • *Size:* 6¾" x 44 *Filler/Binder:* Dom. Rep. *Wrapper:* U.S.A./ Conn. Shade
An oily wrapper. This mild- to medium-bodied cigar has a sweet spicy character with some light coffee-like flavors. U.S.: $4.40

MONTECRUZ SUN-GROWN NO. 210 · 84

Dominican Republic • *Size:* 6½" x 42 *Filler/Binder:* Dom. Rep., Brazil *Wrapper:* Indonesia
A pleasant mild- to medium-bodied smoke. It has a light brown wrapper and a strong mineral character with a hint of spice. U.S.: $4.25

NAT SHERMAN LANDMARK SELECTION ALGONQUIN · 84

Dominican Republic • *Size:* 6¾" x 43 *Filler:* Dom. Rep. *Binder:* Mexico *Wrapper:* Cameroon
This is a pleasant, full-bodied cigar that is a bit hot, but has a core of spiciness. (03/01/94) U.S.: $7.90

OLOR LONSDALE · 84

Dominican Republic • *Size:* 6½" x 42 *Filler/Binder:* Dom. Rep. *Wrapper:* U.S.A./Conn. Shade
A cigar with a pleasant floral note on the finish. It has some nut and herb flavors. U.S.: $4.25

PRIMO DEL REY SELECCION NO. 2 · 84

Dominican Republic • *Size:* 6¼" x 42 *Filler:* Dom. Rep., Brazil *Binder:* U.S.A. *Wrapper:* Indonesia

This is a solid, medium-bodied cigar with a good earthy character and some sweet wood and herbal flavors. A nice, easy smoke. U.S.: $2.35

PUNCH AMATISTA · 84

Honduras • *Size:* 6¼" x 44 *Filler/Binder:* Honduras, Nicaragua, Dom. Rep.
Wrapper: Ecuador
There are some flavors of dried citrus fruit, with an overall woody character. It has a slightly herbal finish. U.S.: $2.40

ROMEO Y JULIETA PALMA · 84

Dominican Republic • *Size:* 6" x 43 *Filler:* Dom. Rep., Brazil *Binder:* U.S.A./Conn. Broadleaf *Wrapper:* Cameroon
Mild pepper flavors show through in this medium-bodied cigar. (03/01/94) U.S.: $3.95

ROYAL JAMAICA CORONA GRANDE · 84

Dominican Republic • *Size:* 6½" x 42 *Filler:* Jamaica *Binder:* Cameroon *Wrapper:* Indonesia
This cigar has a very salty character. There are hints of black pepper and some cedarwood, but it finishes quite dry. U.S.: $4.25

TESOROS DE COPAN CETROS · 84

Honduras • *Size:* 6¼" x 44 *Filler:* Nicaragua *Binder/Wrapper:* Honduras
A decent yellow-brown wrapper. This cigar still has

some grassy notes on the palate, with touches of wood and earth flavors. A dry woody finish. U.S.: $5.10

THE GRIFFIN'S NO. 300 84
Dominican Republic • *Size:* 6¼" x 44 *Filler/Binder:* Dom. Rep. *Wrapper:* U.S.A./Conn. Shade
This cigar has leathery flavors and a mild spiciness on the palate. It is well balanced and has a sweet, woody finish. U.S.: $5.75

ZINO GOLD LINE TRADITION 84
Honduras • *Size:* 6¼" x 44 *Filler/Binder:* Honduras *Wrapper:* Ecuador
A well-balanced cigar that should improve with age. It has some herb and nut flavors on a creamy core. A dry finish. U.S.: $6.80

AL CAPONE CORONA GRANDE 83
Nicaragua • *Size:* 6¼" x 43 *Filler/Binder:* Nicaragua *Wrapper:* Brazil
This cigar has a smooth, cedary flavor with some notes of sweet coffee. It is medium-bodied and finishes with a slightly woody note. U.S.: $3.50

BACCARAT LUCHADORES 83
Honduras • *Size:* 6" x 43 *Filler/Binder/Wrapper:* Honduras
A cigar that uses sweet gum to secure the wrapper. Not for everybody, but it's well-

made, with solid tobacco flavors. (03/01/94) U.S.: $2.75

BAUZA JAGUAR 83
Dominican Republic • *Size:* 6½" x 42 *Filler:* Dom. Rep., Nicaragua *Binder:* Mexico *Wrapper:* Ecuador
There is a hint of spiciness on the palate of this fairly straightforward cigar. It rounds out on the finish with a sweet woody note. U.S.: $4.70

CANARIA D'ORO LONSDALE 83
Dominican Republic • *Size:* 6½" x 43 *Filler:* Dom. Rep., Mexico *Binder/Wrapper:* Mexico
A medium-bodied cigar with hints of spice and wood on the palate, and a woody finish. U.S.: $3.15

CUBITA 8-9-8 83
Dominican Republic • *Size:* 6¼" x 43 *Filler/Binder:* Dom. Rep. *Wrapper:* U.S.A./Conn. Shade
A light, easy-smoking cigar with medium-bodied smoke. It has hints of anise and pepper, but with an overall paper-like, or dry woody character. U.S.: $5.40

CUESTA-REY CENTENNIAL COLLECTION DOMINICAN NO. 4 83
Dominican Republic • *Size:* 6½" x 42 *Filler/Binder:* Dom. Rep. *Wrapper:* U.S.A./Conn. Shade
A cigar with a noted salty character. It has some strong

vegetal notes and a mouth-drying finish. U.S.: $4.95

DON TOMAS CETROS 83
Honduras • *Size:* 6½" x 44 *Filler:* Honduras, Nicaragua *Binder/Wrapper:* Honduras
A light and simple cigar. It has some vegetal character and a bit of tang on the palate. A dry finish. U.S.: $3.00

DUNHILL DIAMANTES 83
Dominican Republic • *Size:* 6⅝" x 42 *Filler/Binder:* Dom. Rep., Brazil *Wrapper:* U.S.A./Conn. Shade
A nice-looking Conn. shade wrapper. This cigar has some earthy qualities, but overall it has a slightly vegetal character with a dry woody finish. U.S.: $6.25

GILBERTO OLIVA NUMERO 1 83
Honduras • *Size:* 6½" x 44 *Filler/Binder:* Dom. Rep., Nicaragua *Wrapper:* Ecuador
A young cigar. But it has some good spicy flavors and a smooth, creamy texture. Give it time. U.S.: $3.95

H. UPMANN LONSDALE 83
Dominican Republic • *Size:* 6⅝" x 42 *Filler/Binder:* Dom. Rep. *Wrapper:* Indonesia
A slightly rustic cigar with some spiciness on the palate. It has a vegetal character and a woody finish. U.S.: $4.10

LEON JIMENES NO. 3   **83**
Dominican Republic • *Size:*
6½" x 42   *Filler/Binder:* Dom.
Rep.   *Wrapper:*
U.S.A./Conn. Shade
A very yellow wrapper on a
cigar that has a dry and
herbal character. There is a
hint of curry spice on its
mild- to medium-bodied
smoke. U.S.: $4.16

MONTESINO   **83**
CESAR NO. 2
Dominican Republic • *Size:*
6¼" x 44   *Filler/Binder:* Dom.
Rep.   *Wrapper:*
U.S.A./Conn. Shade
This cigar burns well with a
firm draw. It has a strong
woody character with a
woody finish. There are hints
of spiciness. U.S.: $3.15

NAT SHERMAN   **83**
EXCHANGE SELECTION
BUTTERFIELD 8
Dominican Republic • *Size:*
6½" x 42   *Filler:* Dom. Rep.
Binder: Mexico   *Wrapper:*
U.S.A./Conn. Shade
A straightforward cigar with
hints of nuttiness and
creaminess and a touch of
spice, but with a very dry,
neutral finish. U.S.: $7.40

PADRÓN AMBASSADOR   **83**
Honduras • *Size:* 6⅞" x 42
Filler/Binder/Wrapper:
Nicaragua
A mild- to medium-bodied
smoke with solid flavors of
nuts and herbs. U.S.: $3.10

PADRÓN 1964   **83**
ANNIVERSARY SERIES
SUPERIOR
Honduras • *Size:* 6" x 42
Filler/Binder/Wrapper:
Nicaragua
This cigar has a strong herbal
character. There are some
hints of cocoa and leather on
the palate with a perfume-
like aroma. Mild. U.S.: $7.30

RAMON ALLONES   **83**
TRUMPS
Dominican Republic • *Size:*
6¾" x 43   *Filler:* Dom. Rep.,
Mexico   *Binder:* Mexico
Wrapper: Cameroon
A rustic cigar. It has a smooth
taste with some sweet notes,
and a woody finish. U.S.: $4.50

SANTA ROSA CORONA   **83**
Honduras • *Size:* 6½" x 44
Filler/Binder/Wrapper: Honduras
A dry woodiness dominates
this medium-bodied cigar. It
has some strong vegetal flavors. U.S.: $4.25

LA FLOR DOMINICANA   **82**
ALCALDE
Dominican Republic • *Size:*
6½" x 44   *Filler/Binder:* Dom.
Rep.   *Wrapper:* U.S.A./
Conn. Shade
A nicely made cigar with a
slightly peppery taste. It has a
sharp finish. U.S.: $5.50

SANTA DAMIANA   **82**
SELECCION NO. 700
Dominican Republic • *Size:*
6½" x 42   *Filler/Binder:* Dom.
Rep.   *Wrapper:* U.S.A./
Conn. Shade

This cigar shows some youth.
But it has a creamy texture
with a backbone of pepper
flavors. A woody finish.
U.S.: $6.35

TE-AMO RELAXATION   **82**
Mexico • *Size:* 6⅝" x 44
Filler/Binder/Wrapper: Mexico
A rather rustic cigar with
straightforward, dry vegetal
flavors. It has a dry, balsa-
wood finish. U.S.: $2.95

TEMPLE HALL NO. 625   **82**
Jamaica • *Size:* 6½" x 42
Filler: Dom. Rep., Mexico,
Jamaica   *Binder:* Mexico
Wrapper: U.S.A./Conn.
Shade
This has some sweet spice
notes on a very woody char-
acter. It is mild- to medium-
bodied and has a rather neu-
tral finish. U.S.: $6.85

BACCARAT NO. 1   **81**
Honduras • *Size:* 7" x 44
Filler/Wrapper: Honduras
Binder: Mexico
This cigar has sweet gum on
the wrapper. While some-
what neutral, it has a mild
nuttiness and creaminess that
is pleasant. U.S.: $3.05

HOYO DE MONTERREY   **81**
CHURCHILL
Honduras • *Size:* 6¼" x 45
Filler/Binder: Honduras,
Nicaragua, Dom. Rep.
Wrapper: Ecuador
A cigar that shows its youth.
It has some hot spiciness and
a dry finish. It's well made
and should improve with age.
U.S.: $3.35

OSCAR NO. 300 — 81

Dominican Republic • *Size:* 6¼" x 44 *Filler/Binder:* Dom. Rep. *Wrapper:* U.S.A./ Conn. Shade
A fairly roughly made cigar. It has strong hot spices on the palate and tends to be a bit harsh, with a vegetal, woody finish. U.S.: $8.25

PUNCH PUNCH — 81

Honduras • *Size:* 6¼" x 45 *Filler/Binder:* Honduras, Nicaragua, Dom. Rep. *Wrapper:* Ecuador
A relatively mild cigar with a sharp spiciness and vegetal flavors, and a balsa-wood finish. U.S.: $3.35

TE-AMO CELEBRATION — 81

Mexico • *Size:* 6¹¹⁄₁₆ x 44 *Filler/Binder/Wrapper:* Mexico
A mild, herbal cigar. There's a bit of a perfume quality to it. The finish is dry. U.S.: $3.80

NAT SHERMAN MAN- — 80
HATTAN
SELECTION GRAMERCY

Dominican Republic • *Size:* 6¼" x 43 *Filler:* Dom. Rep. *Binder/Wrapper:* Mexico
This cigar has a salty character. It has some herbal and wood flavors, and a woody, earthy finish. U.S.: $5.10

TE-AMO NEW YORK — 80
PARK AVENUE

Mexico • *Size:* 6⅝" x 42 *Filler/Binder/Wrapper:* Mexico
A young cigar with a strong vegetal character. There is some hot spiciness on the palate, but it burns quickly. U.S.: $2.90

VUELTABAJO LONSDALE — 80

Dominican Republic • *Size:* 7" x 43 *Filler/Binder:* Dom. Rep. *Wrapper:* U.S.A./ Conn. Shade
A rather flat neutral cigar. It has a vegetal and dry woody character. There is a hint of spice on the palate. U.S.: $4.00

LAS CABRILLAS — 79
PONCE DE LEON

Honduras • *Size:* 6⅝" x 44 *Filler:* Nicaragua, Mexico *Binder:* Mexico *Wrapper:* U.S.A./Conn. Shade
This is a very rough, rustic cigar. It is mild, but with a dry papery character and an overall grassy flavor. U.S.: $2.40

BANCES CAZADORES — 78

Honduras • *Size:* 6¼" x 43 *Filler:* Nicaragua *Binder:* Mexico *Wrapper:* Ecuador
Hints of coffee and cocoa, but this cigar turns hot and has some slight vegetal flavors. (03/01/94) U.S.: $1.75

ORNELAS LTD. — 78
COGNAC

Mexico • *Size:* 6¼" x 42 *Filler/Binder/Wrapper:* Mexico
A strange-tasting cigar. It warms up to a pungent sweetness, but has a slightly harsh finish. U.S.: $11.00

ORNELAS NO. 1 — 78

Mexico • *Size:* 6¼" x 44 *Filler/Binder/Wrapper:* Mexico
A very rustic cigar with a rough-looking wrapper. It has a very salty character and a hint of wood on the finish. U.S.: $4.75

PAUL GARMIRIAN — 78
LONSDALE

Dominican Republic • *Size:* 6½" x 42 *Filler/Binder:* Dom. Rep. *Wrapper:* U.S.A./ Conn. Shade
This cigar is dominated by balsa wood and grassy elements. It has a very harsh attack and finishes very dry in the mouth. U.S.: $8.70

SOSA LONSDALE — 78

Dominican Republic • *Size:* 6½" x 43 *Filler:* Dom. Rep. *Binder:* Honduras *Wrapper:* Ecuador
A dull greenish-brown wrapper. It has funky flavors of wet hay and earthy dried herbs, and finishes quite dry on the palate. U.S.: $4.30

CAMACHO NO. 1 — 76

Honduras • *Size:* 7" x 44 *Filler/Binder:* Honduras *Wrapper:* Ecuador
This is a very rustic cigar with a rough wrapper. It has some hints of spice, but has an earthy, funky character with a bark-like finish. Inconsistent. U.S.: $3.10

CRUZ REAL NO. 1 — 76

Mexico • *Size:* 6⅝" x 42 *Filler/Binder/Wrapper:* Mexico
A rough cigar. It is hot, and while it has some pepper notes on the palate, it also has an earthy funkiness. U.S.: $3.90

ORNELAS NO. 1   **69**
VANILLA
Mexico • *Size:* 6¾" x 44
Filler/Binder/Wrapper: Mexico
Beware. Not for connoisseurs. The vanilla flavoring is perfume-like and sickly sweet, and tastes more like pipe tobacco. In a humidor, it contaminates other cigars. If you must, keep it separately.
U.S.: $6.75

Corona

Most of the following Corona tasting notes appeared in the Spring 1996 issue of Cigar Aficionado. *Exceptions are indicated by a date in parentheses at the end of the tasting note.*

BOLIVAR CORONA   **91**
Cuba • *Size:* 5½" x 42
Filler/Binder/Wrapper: Cuba
A rich, earthy cigar with a solid core of nuts and spices and a very smooth balance. A long spicy finish.
U.K.: £7.55

EL REY DEL MUNDO   **91**
CORONA DE LUXE
Cuba • *Size:* 5½" x 42
Filler/Binder/Wrapper: Cuba
Although a little young, this cigar exhibits great spice, including cinnamon, and a strong earthy finish that lasts. Very well-made. SF: 8

H. UPMANN CORONA   **91**
Cuba • *Size:* 5½" x 42
Filler/Binder/Wrapper: Cuba
Always a great smoke for a corona. The H. Upmann is bursting with complex coffee,

roasted nut and tobacco flavors. Buy a box and enjoy. (03/01/93) U.K.: £7.55

LA FINCA CORONA   **91**
Nicaragua • *Size:* 5½" x 42
Filler/Binder/Wrapper: Nicaragua
A rich-tasting cigar with a lot of depth. It has flavors of spice, raisins and cedar. It is well-balanced and has a smooth finish. U.S.: $1.75

MONTESINO   **91**
DIPLOMATICO
Dominican Republic • *Size:* 5½" x 43 *Filler/Binder:* Dom. Rep. *Wrapper:* U.S.A./Conn. Shade
A very well-made cigar. It has an earthy depth, with delicious sweet spice flavors of cinnamon and strong nut elements, including walnuts. A smooth, long-lasting finish. U.S.: $2.85

ARTURO FUENTE DON   **90**
CARLOS RESERVA NO. 3
Dominican Republic • *Size:* 5½" x 44 *Filler/Binder:* Dom. Rep. *Wrapper:* Cameroon
This cigar has a full-bodied character. There are hints of sweet spices with a solid core of cedar wood and a sweet nutmeg component. A spicy finish. U.S.: $7.25

HOYO DE MONTERREY   **90**
LE HOYO DU ROI
Cuba • *Size:* 5½" x 42
Filler/Binder/Wrapper: Cuba
A full-bodied, rich cigar with nutmeg and earthy flavors. It is very well-balanced with a long, cedery finish. U.K.: £8.15

PUROS INDIOS NO. 4   **90**
ESPECIAL
Honduras • *Size:* 5½" x 44
Filler: Brazil, Nicaragua, Dom. Rep. *Binder/Wrapper:* Ecuador
A rich, full-bodied cigar filled with nutmeg and cinnamon spices, with a great nutty character on the palate. It has an long, earthy finish with a hint of cocoa. U.S.: $3.25

CASA BLANCA   **89**
CORONA
Dominican Republic • *Size:* 5½" x 42 *Filler:* Dom. Rep., Brazil *Binder:* Mexico *Wrapper:* U.S.A./Conn. Shade
A good-tasting cigar with notes of spice and cedar. It has excellent oils in the wrapper and a smooth, herb-like character on the finish. U.S.: $2.50

PUNCH CORONA   **89**
Cuba • *Size:* 5½" x 42
Filler/Binder/Wrapper: Cuba
This is a spicy cigar with some leather notes. It finishes with a dry, woody flavor. U.K.: £7.20

RAMON ALLONES   **89**
CORONA
Cuba • *Size:* 5½" x 42
Filler/Binder/Wrapper: Cuba
A cigar with a firm draw. It has fancy chocolate and almond flavors, but shows its youth despite a solid tobacco core. U.K.: £7.40

ROMEO Y JULIETA **89**
CORONA
Cuba • *Size:* 5½" x 42
Filler/Binder/Wrapper: Cuba
A slightly rough boxed cigar.
It has good spice and a dose
of nut flavors with a smooth,
leathery finish. U.K.: £7.55

SAVINELLI **89**
EXTRAORDINAIRE
Dominican Republic • *Size:*
5½" x 44 *Filler/Binder:* Dom.
Rep. *Wrapper:*
U.S.A./Conn. Shade
This medium-bodied cigar
has a smooth, creamy nut
element, and solid tobacco
flavors in an earthy core. It
has a long, spicy finish with
wood notes. U.S.: $7.00

CREDO ANTHANOR **88**
Dominican Republic • *Size:*
5¾" x 42 *Filler/Binder:* Dom.
Rep. *Wrapper:*
U.S.A./Conn. Shade
A good medium-bodied cigar.
It has flavors of dried orange
peel with a nutty, spicy com-
ponent and a well-balanced
finish. U.S.: $5.85

DAVIDOFF GRAND CRU **88**
No. 2
Dominican Republic • *Size:*
5⅝" x 43 *Filler/Binder:* Dom.
Rep. *Wrapper:*
U.S.A./Conn. Shade
A well-made, medium-bod-
ied cigar with excellent spice
flavors, including nutmeg.
There's a solid, nutty core
and a pleasant finish.
U.S.: $9.25

LA GLORIA CUBANA **88**
GLORIAS
U.S.A. • *Size:* 5½" x 43
Filler: Dom. Rep., Nicaragua
Binder: Nicaragua *Wrapper:*
Ecuador
A solid, medium-bodied cigar
with strong spice and cedar
notes, and flavors of choco-
late. It has a strong spicy fin-
ish. U.S.: $3.25

LEMPIRA CORONA **88**
Honduras • *Size:* 5½" x 42
Filler: Honduras, Nicaragua
Binder: Dom. Rep. *Wrapper:*
U.S.A./Conn. Shade
A rustic cigar with a pleasant
cedary finish. It has flavors of
nutmeg and cinnamon.
U.S.: $3.30

MONTECRISTO NO. 3 **88**
Cuba • *Size:* 5½" x 42
Filler/Binder/Wrapper: Cuba
A smooth but full-bodied
cigar with a solid core of exotic spices, including cinnamon
and nutmeg, and a pleasing
cedary finish. U.K.: £8.45

OLOR MOMENTO **88**
Dominican Republic • *Size:*
5½" x 43 *Filler/Binder:* Dom.
Rep. *Wrapper:*
U.S.A./Conn. Shade
A sweet finish on a medium-
bodied cigar. This cigar has a
roasted chestnut flavor and
creamy, herbal character with
mild spices. U.S.: $3.30

PADRÓN 1964 **88**
ANNIVERSARY SERIES
CORONA
Honduras • *Size:* 6" x 42
Filler/Binder/Wrapper:
Nicaragua
Although it is slightly tight,
this cigar is packed with good
spices and a hint of choco-
late. It's well-balanced with a
medium-bodied smoke.
U.S.: $6.80

PUNCH CAFE ROYAL **88**
Honduras • *Size:* 5⅝" x 44
Filler/Binder: Honduras,
Nicaragua, Dom.Rep. *Wrapper:* Ecuador
This cigar has good nut flavors, including hints of
chestnuts. It has a mild, spicy
finish and is well-balanced
overall. U.S.: $3.65

AVO NO. 7 **87**
Dominican Republic • *Size:*
6" x 44 *Filler/Binder:* Dom.
Rep. *Wrapper:*
U.S.A./Conn. Shade
This cigar, a medium-bodied
smoke, offers some herbal
notes followed by strong
chestnut flavors and an overall toast-like character.
U.S.: $6.75

BELINDA **87**
BREVA CONSERVA
Honduras • *Size:* 5½" x 43
Filler: Dom. Rep., Honduras
Binder: Honduras *Wrapper:*
Ecuador
A cigar with medium-bodied
character. It has solid flavors
of nuts and a core of spici-
ness. There is a good toasty
finish. U.S.: $1.75

BERING CORONA ROYALE   87

Honduras • *Size:* 6" x 41
Filler/Binder: Honduras, Mexico, Dom. Rep, Nicaragua
Wrapper: Mexico
This is a medium-bodied cigar with a solid spicy core of flavors. It has a leathery aroma and a pleasing tobacco character. U.S.: $1.95

C.A.O. CORONA   87

Honduras • *Size:* 6" x 42
Filler: Nicaragua, Mexico
Binder: Honduras *Wrapper:* U.S.A./Conn. Shade
This cigar has a firm draw, but a pleasant toasty, creamy character. There's a bit of dry straw in the flavor, but it has a well-balanced finish.
U.S.: $4.98

CARRINGTON NO. 2   87

Dominican Republic • *Size:* 6" x 42 *Filler/Binder:* Dom. Rep. *Wrapper:* U.S.A./Conn. Shade
This smooth-tasting cigar has a light, spicy character, with some earthy tones.
U.S.: $5.00

CUESTA-REY CENTENNIAL COLLECTION DOMINICAN NO. 5   87

Dominican Republic • *Size:* 5½" x 43 *Filler/Binder:* Dom. Rep. *Wrapper:* U.S.A./Conn. Shade
A well-balanced cigar that shows a pleasing smooth, creamy texture with hints of spice and leather and solid tobacco flavors. U.S.: $4.65

DON DIEGO CORONA MAJOR TUBES   87

Dominican Republic • *Size:* 5½" x 42 *Filler/Binder:* Dom. Rep. *Wrapper:* U.S.A./Conn. Shade
A firm draw on a medium-bodied cigar. It has a creamy tobacco character and some hints of a toast-like flavor.
U.S.: $3.85

HOYO DE MONTERREY CAFE ROYAL   87

Honduras • *Size:* 5⅝" x 43
Filler/Binder: Honduras, Nicaragua, Dom. Rep.
Wrapper: Ecuador
This is a well-made cigar with an oily wrapper. It has a smooth herbal core of flavors with a good woody finish.
U.S.: $3.65

MACANUDO VINTAGE NO. 3 1988   87

Jamaica • *Size:* 5⁹⁄₁₆" x 43
Filler: Dom. Rep., Jam.
Binder: Mexico *Wrapper:* U.S.A./Conn. Shade
Although some tightness was noted in the draw, this cigar has a good creamy texture with a strong flavor of chestnuts and a pleasant toasty finish. U.S.: $11.00

MONTECRISTO NO. 3   87

Dominican Republic • *Size:* 5½" x 44 *Filler/Binder:* Dom. Rep. *Wrapper:* U.S.A./Conn. Shade
A well-made, medium-bodied cigar with a solid, nutty character. It has some smooth herb and sweet spice flavors, including nutmeg.
U.S.: $6.00

MONTECRUZ SUN-GROWN NO. 220   87

Dominican Republic • *Size:* 5½" x 42 *Filler/Binder:* Dom. Rep., Brazil *Wrapper:* Cameroon
This cigar delivers a creaminess with a backbone of spicy flavors. It has a medium-bodied character. U.S.: $4.15

NAT SHERMAN LANDMARK SELECTION HAMPSHIRE   87

Dominican Republic • *Size:* 5½" x 42 *Filler:* Jam., Mex., Dom. Rep. *Binder:* Mexico *Wrapper:* Cameroon
This is a good-looking cigar with solid tobacco flavors, some notes of chestnuts and chocolate with a mild, peppery finish. U.S.: $7.10

NAT SHERMAN METROPOLITAN SELECTION ANGLERS   87

Dominican Republic • *Size:* 5½" x 43 *Filler/Binder:* Dom. Rep. *Wrapper:* U.S.A./Conn. Shade
An earthiness dominates this cigar. The medium-bodied smoke has rich flavors of leather and toast and a pleasant woody finish. U.S.: $5.80

ROMEO Y JULIETA VINTAGE NO. 1   87

Dominican Republic • *Size:* 6" x 43 *Filler:* Dom. Rep. *Binder:* Mexico *Wrapper:* U.S.A./Conn. Shade
A cigar with a smooth, creamy texture. It has a touch of sweet spices and nutmeg, and a floral character. U.S.: $7.00

SANTA CLARA 1830 NO. V 87

Mexico • *Size:* 6" x 43
Filler/Binder/Wrapper: Mexico
A well-made cigar packed with spices, it has a toasty herbal character, with hints of nuts and coffee. A smooth, easy smoke. U.S.: $2.25

TROYA NO. 27 CORONA 87

Dominican Republic • *Size:* 5½" x 42 *Filler/Binder:* Dom. Rep. *Wrapper:* U.S.A./Conn. Shade
A good, solid medium-bodied cigar. It has hints of nuts and flowers. It is smooth and mellow. U.S.: $3.80

ASHTON AGED MADURO NO. 20 86

Dominican Republic • *Size:* 5½" x 44 *Filler/Binder:* Dom. Rep. *Wrapper:* U.S.A
This cigar has sweet herbal notes and a pleasant toasty flavor. U.S.: $6.75

BANCES BREVAS 86

Honduras • *Size:* 5½" x 43
Filler/Binder: Honduras, Nicaragua, Dom. Rep.
Wrapper: Ecuador
A cigar with a flinty character on the palate. There are some spicy pepper flavors and a nice cedary finish.
U.S.: $1.50

CRUZ REAL NO. 2 86

Mexico • *Size:* 6" x 42
Filler/Binder/Wrapper: Mexico
A tart smoke with some slightly vegetal tones, but a spicy backbone that includes

hints of black pepper.
U.S.: $3.60

FELIPE GREGORIO SERENO 86

Honduras • *Size:* 5¾" x 42
Filler/Binder/Wrapper: Honduras
This is a medium-bodied cigar with an earthy character. It has some nut and herb flavors with a smooth, well-balanced finish. U.S.: $6.80

FONSECA 8-9-8 86

Dominican Republic • *Size:* 6" x 43 *Filler/Binder:* Dom. Rep. *Wrapper:* U.S.A./Conn. Shade
This cigar has a nice nutty flavor with hints of spice and dried orange peel, and a strong woody finish.
U.S.: $4.15

H. UPMANN CORONA 86

Dominican Republic • *Size:* 5½" x 42 *Filler/Binder:* Dom. Rep. *Wrapper:* Indonesia
A medium-bodied cigar with a tangy character and a mild spice note on the palate. A slighty earthy finish.
U.S.: $3.60

HABANA GOLD BLACK LABEL CORONA 86

Honduras • *Size:* 6" x 44
Filler/Binder: Nicaragua
Wrapper: Indonesia
A mild cigar with a creamy character. It has some leather and toast notes with a smooth herbal finish.
U.S.: $4.75

HOYO DE MONTERREY SUPER HOYO 86

Honduras • *Size:* 5½" x 44
Filler: Nica., Hon., Dom. Rep. *Binder:* Honduras
Wrapper: Ecuador
A young-tasting cigar. It has a pungent earthy aroma, with some vegetal flavors and a slightly toasty taste.
U.S.: $2.60

JOSÉ BENITO PALMA 86

Dominican Republic • *Size:* 6" x 43 *Filler:* Dom. Rep. *Binder:* Honduras *Wrapper:* Cameroon
Even-keeled corona with medium-bodied, fresh, creamy, tobacco aromas and flavors and a light aftertaste. A good everyday corona. (03/01/93) U.S.: $3.80

JUAN CLEMENTE CLUB SELECTION NO. 4 86

Dominican Republic • *Size:* 5¾" x 42 *Filler/Binder:* Dom. Rep. *Wrapper:* U.S.A./Conn. Shade
A good-looking, medium-bodied cigar. It has good spice and herb flavors and shows a solid construction.
U.S.: $8.85

LICENCIADOS NO. 4 86

Dominican Republic • *Size:* 5¾" x 43 *Filler/Binder:* Dom. Rep. *Wrapper:* U.S.A./Conn. Shade
A mild- to medium-bodied cigar. It has some rich creamy flavors and a solid core of nuttiness, with a woody finish. U.S.: $3.40

MACABI 86
MEDIA CORONA
Dominican Republic • *Size:*
5½" x 43 *Filler:* Dom. Rep.,
Nicaragua *Binder:* Mexico
Wrapper: U.S.A./Conn.
Shade
A well-balanced cigar with a
good floral character. It has
nut and spice flavors and a
light, woody finish.
U.S.: $3.50

MACANUDO 86
DUKE OF DEVON
Jamaica • *Size:* 5½" x 42
Filler: Dom. Rep., Jamaica
Binder: Mexico *Wrapper:*
U.S.A./Conn. Shade
A straightforward, mild- to
medium-bodied cigar with
solid notes of nuts and light
coffee flavors, and a good
cedary finish. U.S.: $4.80

PADRÓN LONDRES 86
Nicaragua • *Size:* 5½" x 42
Filler/Binder: Nicaragua
Wrapper: Ecuador
A rich-tasting cigar some
dark, sweet flavors like
chocolate. But a very firm
draw was noted. U.S.: $2.15

PARTAGAS CORONA 86
Cuba • *Size:* 5½" x 42
Filler/Binder/Wrapper: Cuba
Another cigar that exhibits
signs of youthfulness. But it
has a spicy core of flavors and
an interesting herbal and
woody finish. U.K.: £7.55

PARTAGAS NO. 2 86
Dominican Republic • *Size:*
5¾" x 43 *Filler:* Dom. Rep.,
Mexico *Binder:* Mexico
Wrapper: Cameroon

This cigar has a rough-looking wrapper. But it has some
nut and spice flavors on the
palate, and a dry woody finish. U.S.: $5.15

PARTAGAS SABROSOS 86
Dominican Republic • *Size:*
5⅞" x 43 *Filler/Binder:* Mexico, Dom. Rep. *Wrapper:*
Cameroon
A rustic cigar that had a
loose draw, some strong
grassy flavors and a wood
component. U.S.: $5.45

PAUL GARMIRIAN 86
CORONA
Dominican Republic • *Size:*
5½" x 42 *Filler/Binder:* Dom.
Rep. *Wrapper:*
U.S.A./Conn. Shade
A good-tasting, medium-bodied cigar with baked bread
flavors of cinnamon and nutmeg. There is a sweet tobacco character with a slightly
leathery finish. U.S.: $9.55

RAMON ALLONES 86
PRIVADA D
Dominican Republic • *Size:*
5" x 42 *Filler/Binder:* Mexico, Dom. Rep. *Wrapper:*
Cameroon
This is more of a petite corona in size, but if you're into
spicy, peppery food, try this
one. With a dark-brown
wrapper and a slow draw, it's
medium-bodied with a
strong, spicy, savory style.
(03/01/93) U.S.: $5.15

SANTA ROSA NO. 4 86
Honduras • *Size:* 5½" x 42
Filler/Binder: Honduras
Wrapper: Ecuador

A good medium-bodied
smoke. It has a flinty character, but a core of nuttiness,
and a smooth herbal texture.
U.S.: $3.50

THOMAS HINDS 86
HONDURAN SELECTION
CORONA
Honduras • *Size:* 5½" x 42
Filler/Binder: Honduras
Wrapper: Ecuador
Although it has a mild finish,
this cigar has some leather
and floral notes, with a hint
of chocolate. U.S.: $3.15

VUELTABAJO CORONA 86
Dominican Republic • *Size:*
5¼" x 42 *Filler/Binder:* Dom.
Rep. *Wrapper:*
U.S.A./Conn. Shade
A good draw leads into a
medium-bodied smoke with
solid tobacco flavors. It has a
peppery finish with a cedary
character. U.S.: $3.60

AURORA NO. 4 85
Dominican Republic • *Size:*
5¼" x 42 *Filler/Binder:* Dom.
Rep. *Wrapper:* Cameroon
A mild cigar with a pleasing
woody spiciness and a hint of
nuts. U.S.: $2.84

BAUZA GRECOS 85
Dominican Republic • *Size:*
5½" x 42 *Filler:* Dom. Rep.,
Nicaragua *Binder:* Mexico
Wrapper: Cameroon
A spicy cigar with a light
backbone of nut flavors and
mild chocolate. It is still
young. U.S.: $4.30

CAMACHO 85
NACIONALES
Honduras • *Size:* 5½" x 44
Filler/Binder/Wrapper: Honduras
Tasters noted a sweet tobacco taste with a floral character. There's a bit of spice with a mild, earthy finish.
U.S.: $2.45

DON DIEGO CORONA 85
Dominican Republic • *Size:* 5⅝" x 42 *Filler/Binder:* Dom. Rep. *Wrapper:* U.S.A./Conn. Shade
A smooth-tasting, mild cigar that has some floral notes and a slight nutty flavor, but an overall papery character.
U.S.: $3.60

DON MELO 85
PETIT CORONA
Honduras • *Size:* 5½" x 42 *Filler:* Honduras, Nicaragua *Binder/Wrapper:* Honduras
This cigar has a medium-bodied character. There are flavors of nuts and a hint of leather and coffee. A short finish. U.S.: $4.30

DUNHILL TABARAS 85
Dominican Republic • *Size:* 5½" x 42 *Filler/Binder:* Dom. Rep., Brazil *Wrapper:* U.S.A./Conn. Shade
This is a mellow cigar with a smooth, mild texture filled with creamy notes and some light, nutty flavors.
U.S.: $6.60

DUNHILL VALVERDES 85
Dominican Republic • *Size:* 5½" x 42 *Filler/Binder:* Dom. Rep., Brazil *Wrapper:* U.S.A./Conn. Shade
A creamy-tasting cigar. It is medium-bodied with solid spice and herbal flavors and a light, woody finish.
U.S.: $5.50

EL RICO HABANO 85
CORONA
U.S.A. • *Size:* 5½" x 42 *Filler:* Dom. Rep., Nicaragua *Binder:* Nicaragua *Wrapper:* Ecuador
Loads of flavor in this middle-of-the-road cigar. Oily with a rich-brown wrapper, it shows enticing aromas and flavors of coffee and cinnamon and a rich long finish. (03/01/93) U.S.: $3.25

H. UPMANN 85
CORONA MAJOR TUBE
Dominican Republic • *Size:* 5⅛" x 42 *Filler/Binder:* Dom. Rep. *Wrapper:* Indonesia
A solid, medium-bodied smoke. Strong earthy notes dominate hints of nuts and sweet spices. U.S.: $4.10

HOYO DE MONTERREY 85
CORONA
Cuba • *Size:* 5½" x 42 *Filler/Binder/Wrapper:* Cuba
A pleasant cigar that shows signs of youth. It has spicy flavors, but overall a woody, herbal character with some bite. U.K.: £7.55

HOYO DE MONTERREY 85
EXCALIBUR NO. 5
Honduras • *Size:* 6¼" x 43 *Filler:* Nica., Hon., Dom. Rep. *Binder:* Honduras *Wrapper:* Ecuador
This is always a very good cigar. Medium brown colored, it's firmly made with a sure and even draw. Plenty of chocolate, spice aromas and flavors. (03/01/93)
U.S.: $4.35

LA FLOR DOMINICANA 85
INSURRECTO
Dominican Republic • *Size:* 5½" x 42 *Filler/Binder:* Dom. Rep. *Wrapper:* U.S.A./Conn. Shade
A mild cigar with solid tobacco flavors and character. A bit of spice on the finish. This cigar was rated under the brand name Los Libertadores. U.S.: $4.00

LEON JIMENES NO. 4 85
Dominican Republic • *Size:* 5⁹⁄₁₆" x 42 *Filler/Binder:* Dom. Rep. *Wrapper:* U.S.A./Conn. Shade
A cigar with a medium-bodied smoke. It has a light spiciness with a cedary aroma. U.S.: $3.76

MAYA PETIT CORONA 85
Honduras • *Size:* 5½" x 42 *Filler/Binder:* Honduras, Nicaragua *Wrapper:* U.S.A./Conn. Shade
A medium-bodied cigar that offers hints of earthiness and herbs. It has toasty notes in the aroma and on the palate.
U.S.: $3.30

Montecruz Sun-Grown Tubos — 85

Dominican Republic • *Size:* 6" x 42 *Filler/Binder:* Dom. Rep., Brazil *Wrapper:* Indonesia

Although tasters noted a pleasant, nutty complexity, this cigar finished with a metallic taste. But it has a good earthy spiciness and a touch of sweet tobacco flavor. U.S.: $4.55

Tresado Seleccion No. 500 — 85

Dominican Republic • *Size:* 5½" x 42 *Filler:* Dom. Rep. *Binder:* Cameroon *Wrapper:* Indonesia

A woody character dominates this cigar. It has some hints of pepper and a fairly neutral finish. U.S.: $2.25

Ashton Corona — 84

Dominican Republic • *Size:* 5½" x 44 *Filler/Binder:* Dom. Rep. *Wrapper:* U.S.A./Conn. Shade

A nice, mild cigar with some light spicy flavors and a pleasant herbal character. U.S.: $6.00

Canaria d'Oro Corona — 84

Dominican Republic • *Size:* 5½" x 43 *Filler:* Dom. Rep., Mexico *Binder/Wrapper:* Mexico

A mild cigar with a decent draw. It is rustic-looking but provides some light nuttiness and dry, woody finish. U.S.: $3.00

El Rey del Mundo Habana Club — 84

Honduras • *Size:* 5½" x 42 *Filler:* Dom. Rep., Honduras *Binder:* Honduras *Wrapper:* Ecuador

A smooth-tasting cigar with a hint of nuts and a floral character. It ends with a dry finish. U.S.: $3.50

El Sublimado Corona — 84

Dominican Republic • *Size:* 6" x 44 *Filler/Binder:* Dom. Rep. *Wrapper:* U.S.A./Conn. Shade

A very yellow wrapper. This mild- to medium-bodied cigar has straw-like herbal notes with a creamy coffee flavor and a light woody finish. U.S.: $3.00

Henry Clay Brevas — 84

Dominican Republic • *Size:* 5½" x 42 *Filler/Binder:* Dom. Rep. *Wrapper:* U.S.A./Conn. Shade

There is a some spice in this cigar, with some coffee flavors. It has a slightly earthy quality on the dry finish. U.S.: $3.20

José Martí Corona — 84

Dominican Republic • *Size:* 5½" x 42 *Filler:* Dom. Rep. *Binder:* Mexico *Wrapper:* U.S.A./Conn. Shade

A smooth, mellow cigar with a creamy texture and mild herbal character. U.S.: $2.50

Knockando No. 3 — 84

Dominican Republic • *Size:* 5¾" x 41 *Filler/Binder:* Dom. Rep. *Wrapper:* U.S.A./Conn. Shade

Aptly named after the single malt Scotch, this cigar has an appealing nutty character. It's well made with a surefire draw and gives plenty of pleasure until the last puff. (03/01/93) U.S.: $6.75

La Unica No. 500 — 84

Dominican Republic • *Size:* 5½" x 42 *Filler/Binder:* Dom. Rep. *Wrapper:* U.S.A./Conn. Shade

A greenish-brown cigar with a slightly rough construction. It has a weedy character with some mild wood on the finish. U.S.: $4.15

Las Cabrillas Magellan — 84

Honduras • *Size:* 6" x 42 *Filler:* Nicaragua, Mexico *Binder:* Mexico *Wrapper:* U.S.A./Conn. Shade

A medium-bodied cigar with a balsa-wood tone, and a dry, papery finish. There's a touch of white-pepper flavor. U.S.: $2.10

Licenciados Supreme Maduro No. 200 — 84

Dominican Republic • *Size:* 5" x 42 *Filler/Binder:* Dom. Rep. *Wrapper:* U.S.A./Conn. Shade

A good maduro cigar. It has flavors of coffee and cola, with a solid spicy finish and an overall mild character. U.S.: $4.40

MiCubano No. 542 **84**
Nicaragua • *Size:* 5" x 42
Filler/Binder/Wrapper:
Nicaragua
All tasters noted a tight draw
on this otherwise medium-
bodied cigar. It has some
smooth, creamy flavors with
a hint of earthiness.
U.S.: $3.75

Por Larrañaga **84**
Nacionales
Dominican Republic • *Size:*
5½" x 42 *Filler/Binder:* Dom.
Rep. *Wrapper:*
U.S.A./Conn. Shade
This is a well-balanced,
medium-bodied cigar. It has
some good hints of nuts with
a creamy texture. U.S.: $5.00

Primo del Rey **84**
Seleccion No. 4
Dominican Republic • *Size:*
5½" x 42 *Filler/Binder:* Dom.
Rep. *Wrapper:* Indonesia
This cigar has a light, salty
character with some mild,
light tobacco flavors and an
earthy finish. U.S.: $2.00

Punch No. 75 **84**
Honduras • *Size:* 5½" x 43
Filler: Nica., Hon., Dom.
Rep. *Binder/Wrapper:*
Ecuador
Although there is a hint of a
vegetal quality, this cigar has
a solid peppery core. It needs
time to age. U.S.: $2.60

Sosa Brevas **84**
Dominican Republic • *Size:*
5½" x 43 *Filler:* Dom. Rep.
Binder: Honduras *Wrapper:*
Ecuador

A cigar with some vegetal
notes on the palate, but it
finishes with a light spiciness
and earthiness. U.S.: $3.50

Thomas Hinds **84**
Nicaraguan Selec-
tion Corona
Nicaragua • *Size:* 5½" x 42
Filler/Binder/Wrapper:
Nicaragua
A cigar dominated by some
woody flavors with a creamy
texture. There is a smoothness here with a light, spicy
finish. U.S.: $5.00

8-9-8 Collection **83**
Corona
Jamaica • *Size:* 5½" x 42
Filler: Jamaica, Dom. Rep.
Binder: Mexico *Wrapper:*
U.S.A./Conn. Shade
A medium-bodied smoke
with a smooth texture and
some spice, but an overall
dry, papery character.
U.S.: $7.75

Caballeros Corona **83**
Dominican Republic • *Size:*
5¼" x 43 *Filler/Binder:* Dom.
Rep. *Wrapper:*
U.S.A./Conn. Shade
A cigar with a creamy texture and mild character. It
has an easy-smoking buttery
flavor with a slightly cedary
finish. U.S.: $3.60

Joya de Nicaragua **83**
No. 6
Nicaragua • *Size:* 6" x 42
Filler/Binder/Wrapper:
Nicaragua
This cigar is rustic, with
slightly sour herbal flavors,
although it has a touch of

spice on the finish.
U.S.: $3.75

La Hoja Selecta **83**
Cetros de Oro
U.S.A. • *Size:* 5¼" x 43
Filler/Binder: Dom. Rep.,
Mexico, Brazil *Wrapper:*
U.S.A./Conn. Shade
Straightforward corona with
pleasing herbal, tobacco
character. Very handsome
and well-constructed but per-
haps a little one-dimensional
in flavor. (03/01/93)
U.S.: $3.90

Nat Sherman **83**
City Desk Selection
Gazette
Dominican Republic • *Size:*
6" x 42 *Filler/Binder/Wrap-*
per: Dom. Rep.
A maduro cigar. It has an
earthy character with flavors
of nuts and herbs and a solid
tobacco core. U.S.: $5.30

Punch Deluxe Series **83**
Royal Coronation
Honduras • *Size:* 5¼" x 44
Filler/Binder: Honduras,
Nicaragua, Dom. Rep.
Wrapper: Ecuador
This medium-bodied cigar
has some vegetal notes with a
leathery flavor, and some
spice on a long finish. Shows
its youth. U.S.: $3.10

ROMEO Y JULIETA CORONA 83
Dominican Republic • *Size:* 5½" x 44 *Filler:* Dom. Rep., U.S.A. *Binder:* U.S.A./Conn. Broadleaf *Wrapper:* Cameroon
A good everyday smoke you won't get bored with. The wrapper is a little rough and uneven in color, but there's plenty of spicy, nutmeg and tobacco aromas and flavors. (03/01/93) U.S.: $3.80

V CENTENNIAL CORONA 83
Honduras • *Size:* 5½" x 42 *Filler:* Honduras, Dom.Rep., Nicaragua *Binder:* Mexico *Wrapper:* U.S.A./Conn. Shade
Some inconsistency noted. This cigar shows some nutty flavors and a bit of spice, but a flat finish. U.S.: $4.00

ZINO GOLD LINE DIAMONDS 83
Honduras • *Size:* 5½" x 40 *Filler/Binder:* Honduras *Wrapper:* U.S.A./Conn. Shade
A small cigar. It has a light, mild character with some nutty flavors and a smooth woody finish. U.S.: $5.00

PETERSON CORONA 82
Dominican Republic • *Size:* 5¾" x 43 *Filler:* Dom. Rep. *Binder:* Ecuador *Wrapper:* U.S.A./Conn. Shade
A rather rustic, rough cigar. It has a straw-like character and a dry spice finish. U.S.: $7.30

PLEIADES ORION 81
Dominican Republic • *Size:* 5¾" x 42 *Filler/Binder:* Dom. Rep. *Wrapper:* U.S.A./Conn. Shade
This cigar has a dry, papery character with some hints of grass on an otherwise creamy texture. U.S.: $6.95

DON JUAN CETRO 80
Nicaragua • *Size:* 6" x 43 *Filler:* Nicaragua *Binder:* Dom. Rep. *Wrapper:* U.S.A./Conn. Shade
A mild cigar. It has some decent tobacco components, but overall is a little rough, and a vegetal character dominates. U.S.: $3.30

TE-AMO MEDITATION 80
Mexico • *Size:* 6" x 42 *Filler/Binder/Wrapper:* Mexico
A cigar with a tight draw and salty character with flavors of straw and paper. A hint of pepper spice on the finish. U.S.: $2.60

LA REGENTA NO. 3 78
Canary Islands • *Size:* 5⅝" x 42 *Filler/Binder:* Dom. Rep., Brazil *Wrapper:* U.S.A./Conn. Shade
Slightly difficult to draw and even harder to get any serious flavor. Extremely mild in character with a light coffee and cream character and a short aftertaste. (03/01/93) U.S.: $6.50

Robusto

Most of the following Robusto tasting notes appeared in the August 1997 issue of Cigar Aficionado. *Exceptions are indicated by a date in parentheses at the end of the tasting note.*

BOLIVAR ROYAL CORONA 95
Cuba • *Size:* 5" x 50 *Filler/Binder/Wrapper:* Cuba
A powerful, spicy smoke with rich, earthy flavors of leather, sweet spices like cinnamon and nutmeg and a dash of chocolate. It delivers a smooth, nutty, long-lasting finish. (12/01/94) U.K.: £8.35

HOYO DE MONTERREY EPICURE NO. 2 92
Cuba • *Size:* 4⅞" x 50 *Filler/Binder/Wrapper:* Cuba
A deep spiciness dominates this cigar. There is an overtone of sweet cocoa bean and hints of nutmeg and cinnamon. A sweet cedar, coffee bean finish. U.K.: £8.95

PARTAGAS SERIE D NO. 4 92
Cuba • *Size:* 4⅞" x 50 *Filler/Binder/Wrapper:* Cuba
This is a wonderully balanced cigar with a medium to full body. There are deep elements of earthiness and leather on the palate, and it has a long, smooth, but very spicy, finish. U.K.: £8.90

ROMEO Y JULIETA EXHIBICION No. 4 **92**
Cuba • *Size:* 5" x 48
Filler/Binder/Wrapper: Cuba
A wonderful combination of sweet spices such as cinnamon, roasted nuts and a strong earthy quality. It has a spicy and woody finish.
U.K.: £7.90

COHIBA ROBUSTO **91**
Cuba • *Size:* 4⅞" x 50
Filler/Binder/Wrapper: Cuba
A beautiful oily wrapper. This cigar has some youth, but it is powerfully spicy with a solid leathery, earthy backbone of flavors. A long spicy finish. U.K.: £13.60

FUENTE FUENTE OPUS X ROBUSTO **91**
Dominican Republic • *Size:* 5¼" x 50 *Filler/Binder/Wrapper:* Dom. Rep.
A beautiful colorado wrapper. This cigar is packed with earthy flavors of leather and coffee beans, and has a solid core of sweet spices. It is complex, with a sweet wood, and cedar finish.
U.S.: $10.50

RAMON ALLONES SPECIALLY SELECTED **91**
Cuba • *Size:* 4⅞" x 50
Filler/Binder/Wrapper: Cuba
A full-bodied cigar. It smokes beautifully, and it has a smooth palate of flavors, including a spicy earthiness and a hint of toasted nuts, and a sweet, cedar finish.
U.K.: £8.15

EL RICO HABANO HABANO CLUB **90**
Dominican Republic • *Size:* 5" x 48 *Filler:* Nicaragua *Binder:* Dom. Rep. *Wrapper:* Ecuador
An excellent cigar. There is good balance of earthiness and spiciness on a full-bodied smoke. There is a hint of leather on the finish. Should improve with age.
U.S.: $3.25

JOYA DE NICARAGUA CONSUL **90**
Nicaragua • *Size:* 4½" x 52
Filler/Binder: Nicaragua *Wrapper:* Ecuador
This cigar has rich flavors of cocoa bean and cedar wood. There is a deep, earthy spiciness on the palate. Some inconsistency held this cigar back. U.S.: $4.00

JUAN LOPEZ SELECCION No. 2 **90**
Cuba • *Size:* 4⅞" x 50
Filler/Binder/Wrapper: Cuba
This cigar has excellent balance. There is a strong peppery core of flavor, with a pleasant sweet coffee-ground character and an earthy finish. Price N/A

MACANUDO VINTAGE CABINET SELECTION 1993 VIII (CRYSTAL) **90**
Jamaica • *Size:* 5½" x 50
Filler/Binder: Mexico, Dom. Rep. *Wrapper:* U.S.A./Conn. Shade
A medium-bodied cigar with a solid herbal character and some creaminess on the palate. There is solid spicy

core of flavors on an otherwise woody finish.
U.S.: $12.50

ASTRAL BESO **89**
Honduras • *Size:* 5" x 52
Filler: Nicaragua, Dom. Rep. *Binder:* Dom. Rep. *Wrapper:* Ecuador
A well-made cigar with a smooth, leathery quality. It has flavors of coffee beans and a pleasant cedary finish.
U.S.: $5.25

C.A.O. GOLD ROBUSTO **89**
Nicaragua • *Size:* 5" x 50
Filler/Binder: Nicaragua *Wrapper:* Ecuador
A cigar with a strong herbal spiciness and a long earthy finish. It has a medium- to full-bodied character and is well made. U.S.: $5.70

MONTECRISTO ROBUSTO **89**
Dominican Republic • *Size:* 4¾" x 50 *Filler/Binder:* Dom. Rep. *Wrapper:* U.S.A./Conn. Shade
Strong elements of sweet spices, including raw cinnamon. This cigar also has a dry, woody finish. U.S.: $8.25

ENCANTO ROTHSCHILD 88
Honduras • *Size:* 4½" x 50
Filler/Binder/Wrapper: Honduras
This cigar comes with an attractive brown wrapper. It has rich, spicy flavors with notes of coffee beans and a long aftertaste. (12/01/94) U.S.: $4.50

HABANICA SERIE 550 88
Nicaragua •Serie *Size:* 5" x 50 *Filler/Binder/Wrapper:* Nicaragua
A mild- to medium-bodied cigar. It has flavors of hazelnuts and coffee beans, and a good, sweet wood finish. U.S.: $6.40

JOSÉ MARTÍ ROBUSTO 88
Nicaragua • *Size:* 4⅝" x 50 *Filler/Binder:* Nicaragua, Honduras, Dom. Rep. *Wrapper:* Ecuador
A spicy cigar. It has a medium to full body, and a complex earthy core of flavors including roasted nuts and coffee beans. A quite woody finish. U.S.: $2.00

LA UNICA NO. 400 88
Dominican Republic • *Size:* 4½" x 50 *Filler/Binder:* Dom. Rep. *Wrapper:* U.S.A./Conn. Shade
A well-made cigar. It has a sweet tobacco component with a hint of cocoa bean, and an overall creamy herbal quality. U.S.: $4.10

LEON JIMENES 88
ROBUSTO
Dominican Republic • *Size:* 5" x 50 *Filler/Binder:* Dom.

Rep. *Wrapper:* U.S.A./Conn. Sahde
A cigar with a spicy character. There is a good balance of earth and cedar flavors with some sweet spiciness on the finish. U.S.: $4.64

MACANUDO VINTAGE 88
CABINET SELECTION
1993 V
Jamaica • *Size:* 5½" x 49 *Filler/Binder:* Mexico, Dom. Rep. *Wrapper:* U.S.A./Conn. Shade
This cigar has a solid spicy core, and a very smooth taste. It lacks a little bit of complexity on an otherwise dry, woody finish. U.S.: $11.00

MONTECRUZ 88
SUN-GROWN ROBUSTO
Dominican Republic • *Size:* 4½" x 49 *Filler/Binder:* Dom. Rep. *Wrapper:* Indonesia
A well-made cigar with a solid, medium-bodied smoke. It has an herbal character, and a hint of sweet pepper on the palate. Good balance. U.S.: $3.50

PUNCH 88
SUPER ROTHSCHILD
Honduras • *Size:* 5¼" x 50 *Filler:* Hon., Nica., Dom. Rep. *Binder:* Honduras *Wrapper:* U.S.A./Conn. Shade
A solid mild- to medium-bodied cigar. There is a flinty quality on the palate, with a backbone of good tobacco flavors, and a good, woody finish. U.S.: $3.95

SAVINELLI E.L.R. 88
ROBUSTO
Dominican Republic • *Size:* 5" x 49 *Filler/Binder:* Dom. Rep. *Wrapper:* U.S.A./Conn. Shade
This cigar has loads of pepper, with a solid herbal character to round it out. Good balance, and shows some aging potential. U.S.: $7.50

SOSA WAVELL 88
Dominican Republic • *Size:* 4¾" x 50 *Filler/Binder:* Dom. Rep. *Wrapper:* Ecuador
A medium-bodied cigar. It has sweet flavors, with a hint of cocoa bean and nice earthy and spicy components. U.S.: $4.30

THE GRIFFIN'S 88
ROBUSTO
Dominican Republic • *Size:* 5" x 50 *Filler/Binder:* Dom. Rep. *Wrapper:* U.S.A./Conn. Shade
This cigar has an excellent balance. There are flavors of hazelnuts and hints of dried orange peel, and solid earthy backbone. U.S.: $6.50

5 VEGAS ROBUSTO 87
Nicaragua • *Size:* 5" x 50 *Filler:* Dom. Rep., Nicaragua *Binder/Wrapper:* Indonesia
This is a smooth and well-balanced cigar. There are flavors of herbal spices, and some earth and leather components on the finish. U.S.: $3.60

8-9-8 COLLECTION ROBUSTO 87

Jamaica • *Size:* 5½" x 49
Filler: Jamaica, Dom. Rep.
Binder: Mexico *Wrapper:*
U.S.A./Conn. Shade
This is a mild cigar. It has a
palate with flavors of wood
and spices, and a hint of
dried orange peel. There is a
woody finish. U.S.: $9.25

ARTURO FUENTE DON CARLOS ROBUSTO 87

Dominican Republic • *Size:*
5" x 50 *Filler/Binder:* Dom.
Rep. *Wrapper:* Cameroon
A beautifully made cigar. It
has strong flavors of coffee
beans and rich spices, but it
has a little dryness on the finish. U.S.: $8.00

ASHTON CABINET SELECTION NO. 6 87

Dominican Republic • *Size:*
5½" x 52 *Filler/Binder:* Dom.
Rep. *Wrapper:* U.S.A./
Conn. Shade
A well-made cigar. It is very
smooth-tasting with a creamy
core of flavors. There are
notes of herbs and coffee
beans. U.S.: $9.00

ASHTON MAGNUM 87

Dominican Republic • *Size:*
5" x 50 *Filler/Binder:* Dom.
Rep. *Wrapper:* U.S.A./
Conn. Shade
A very well-balanced cigar
with a smooth, creamy character. There are solid hints of
toastiness and leather and a
cedary finish. U.S.: $6.50

AURORA ROBUSTO 87

Dominican Republic • *Size:*
5" x 50 *Filler/Binder:* Dom.
Rep. *Wrapper:* Cameroon
A nicely made cigar. It has a
solid spiciness on the palate,
and a good woody finish.
U.S.: $4.08

BAUZA ROBUSTO 87

Dominican Republic • *Size:*
5½" x 50 *Filler:* Dom. Rep.,
Nicaragua *Binder:* Mexico
Wrapper: Ecuador
A solid cigar with a good
tobacco character. There are
hints of nuttiness on the
palate and a woody finish.
U.S.: $5.60

DA VINCI MADONNA 87

Honduras • *Size:* 5" x 50
Filler: Nicaragua, Honduras,
Dom. Rep. *Binder:* Dom.
Rep. *Wrapper:* Ecuador
A well-balanced cigar. It is
spicy with a hint of cedar on
the palate, and it has a good
woody finish. U.S.: $6.55

DAVIDOFF SPECIAL SERIES "R" 87

Dominican Republic • *Size:*
4⅞" x 50 *Filler/Binder:* Dom.
Rep. *Wrapper:* U.S.A./
Conn. Shade
A cigar with some solid spice
notes, but it has a bit of sourness on the finish and a dry
wood character. (12/01/94)
U.S.: $11.00

DON JUAN ROBUSTO 87

Nicaragua • *Size:* 5" x 50
Filler: Nicaragua *Binder:*
Dom. Rep. *Wrapper:*
U.S.A./Conn. Shade

A well-balanced cigar. It has
nut and herbal flavors, with a
touch of saltiness. It is medium-bodied. U.S.: $3.30

EL SUBLIMADO ROBUSTO 87

Dominican Republic • *Size:*
4½" x 50 *Filler/Binder:* Dom.
Rep. *Wrapper:* Honduras
A light perfume-like quality
makes this cigar attractive. It
has a nutty character, with a
light woodiness on the finish.
U.S.: $9.00

HABANA GOLD WHITE LABEL ROBUSTO 87

Honduras • *Size:* 5" x 50
Filler/Binder/Wrapper:
Nicaragua
A very dark, almost maduro
style wrapper. It has flavors of
sweet tobacco, and a hint of
nuts on the palate. A bit rustic. U.S.: $5.20

IMPERIO CUBANO ROBUSTO 87

U.S.A. • *Size:* 5" x 50 *Filler:*
Dom. Rep. *Binder:* Nicaragua
Wrapper: Ecuador
There are some hints of spice
in an otherwise light vegetal
character. A smooth, good-
looking wrapper. U.S.: $5.20

LA FLOR DOMINICANA 87 ROBUSTO RESERVA ESPECIAL

Dominican Republic • *Size:*
5" x 48 *Filler/Binder:* Dom.
Rep. *Wrapper:* U.S.A./
Conn. Shade
This is a well-balanced mild
cigar. On the palate, there is
a spiciness combined with a
light nutty quality, and a dry
woodiness. U.S.: $6.75

**MACANUDO VINTAGE 87
CABINET SELECTION
1993 IV**
Jamaica • *Size:* 4½" x 47
Filler/Binder: Mexico, Dom.
Rep. *Wrapper:* U.S.A./
Conn. Shade
A mild- to medium-bodied
cigar with a solid core of
leather and wood. There are
some hints of spice on the
palate and the finish.
U.S.: $10.00

PADRÓN 3000 87
Nicaragua • *Size:* 5½" x 52
Filler/Binder/Wrapper:
Nicaragua
This is a good solid cigar.
There are strong elements of
earthiness, and a lightly per-
fumed quality. It has an
earthy finish. U.S.: $3.85

PARTAGAS ROBUSTO 87
Dominican Republic • *Size:*
4½" x 49 *Filler/Binder:* Mexico, Dom. Rep. *Wrapper:*
Cameroon
There are some subtle hints
of spiciness in this medium-
bodied cigar. It is straightforward and well-made, with a
slight touch of wood on the
finish. U.S.: $5.15

**POR LARRAÑAGA 87
ROBUSTO**
Dominican Republic • *Size:*
5" x 50 *Filler/Binder:* Dom.
Rep. *Wrapper:* U.S.A./
Conn.
A solid, medium-bodied
cigar. It has a very pro-
nounced nutty character and
a dry woody finish, with a
smooth taste. U.S.: $6.00

**PUROS INDIOS 87
COLORADO ROTHSCHILD**
Honduras • *Size:* 5" x 50
Filler: Nicaragua, Dom. Rep.,
Brazil *Binder/Wrapper:*
Ecuador
Although this cigar shows
some youth, it has an oily
wrapper with a solid core of
coffee bean, spice and toast
flavors. U.S.: $3.80

**ROLY COLORADO 87
ROTHSCHILD**
Honduras • *Size:* 5" x 50
Filler: Dom. Rep., Brazil
Binder/Wrapper: Ecuador
This is a full-bodied cigar
with a strong earthy charac-
ter. There is some roasted nut
and leather on the palate. It's
a little dry. Price N/A

**SIGNATURE 87
COLLECTION ROBUSTO**
Dominican Republic • *Size:*
5" x 50 *Filler:* Dom. Rep.,
Nicaragua, Indonesia
Binder/Wrapper: Ecuador
A sweet woodiness that sug-
gests cedar. This is an earthy
cigar with some nuttiness and
a coffee bean character on
the palate. A woody finish.
U.S.: $5.25

**THOMAS HINDS 87
CABINET SELECTION
ROBUSTO**
Nicaragua • *Size:* 5" x 50
Filler/Binder/Wrapper:
Nicaragua
A well-balanced cigar with a
mix of leather and sweet
spice flavors on the palate.
U.S.: $4.95

TORCEDOR ROBUSTO 87
Nicaragua • *Size:* 5" x 50
Filler: Nicaragua, Honduras
Binder: Mexico *Wrapper:*
Indonesia
This cigar has good earthy
quality, and some sweetness
on the finish. U.S.: $3.25

**V CENTENNIAL 87
ROBUSTO**
Honduras • *Size:* 5" x 50
Filler: Dom. Rep., Honduras,
Nicaragua *Binder:* Mexico
Wrapper: U.S.A./Conn.
Shade
A creamy, smooth, mild- to
medium-bodied cigar. It has
light, but spicy flavors, and is
very well made. U.S.: $5.00

**ARTURO FUENTE 86
ROTHSCHILD**
Dominican Republic • *Size:*
4½" x 50 *Filler/Binder:* Dom.
Rep. *Wrapper:* Cameroon
This cigar has an earthy,
sweet spice character with
hints of cocoa bean and coffee. There is hint of youth on
the finish, and its wrapper is
a bit rough. U.S.: $3.15

C.A.O. ROBUSTO 86
Honduras • *Size:* 4½" x 50
Filler: Nicaragua, Mexico
Binder: Honduras *Wrapper:*
U.S.A./Conn. Shade
Although this cigar has some
vegetal notes on the palate, it
is creamy, with a pleasant
light pepper finish. U.S.:
$5.60

CREDO ARCANE 86
Dominican Republic • *Size:* 5" x 50 *Filler/Binder:* Dom. Rep. *Wrapper:* U.S.A. /Conn. Shade
A pleasant, mild cigar. There is hint of sweet gum on the wrapper. It is quite herbal on the palate, and finishes with a dry wood taste. U.S.: $7.10

DIANA SILVIUS 86
ROBUSTO
Dominican Republic • *Size:* 4⅞" x 52 *Filler/Binder:* Dom. Rep. *Wrapper:* U.S.A./ Conn. Shade
This is a smooth, creamy cigar. It has a mild- to medium-body smoke, with a solid spicy-wood finish. U.S.: $8.10

DOMINO PARK 86
ROBUSTO
Dominican Republic • *Size:* 5" x 50 *Filler:* Dom. Rep., Nicaragua *Binder:* Ecuador *Wrapper:* Indonesia
Although this cigar has a touch of youth, there are also hints of earthiness on the palate and the finish. U.S.: $2.95

DON LINO 86
COLORADO ROTHSCHILD
Dominican Republic • *Size:* 4½" x 50 *Filler/Binder/ Wrapper:* Dom. Rep.
A light spiciness on a mild- to medium-bodied cigar. There are some spice and wood flavors on the palate and a dry wood finish. U.S.: $4.30

EL REY DEL MUNDO 86
ROTHSCHILD
Honduras • *Size:* 5" x 50 *Filler:* Dom. Rep., Honduras *Binder:* Honduras *Wrapper:* Ecuador
A cigar with a nutty character. It has a litte bit of a metallic tone on the finish, but there are also dry wood notes. U.S.: $3.75

FREE CUBA ROBUSTO 86
Nicaragua • *Size:* 5" x 50 *Filler:* Dom. Rep. *Binder:* Nicaragua *Wrapper:* Indonesia
Although this cigar is a little rustic, it has a dark, rich wrapper that delivers some coffee bean flavors, with a very mild finish. U.S.: $4.50

H. UPMANN CABINET 86
SELECTION CORSARIO
Dominican Republic • *Size:* 5½" x 50 *Filler/Binder:* Dom. Rep. *Wrapper:* Indonesia
This is a straightforward, medium-bodied cigar. There is a good balance of leathery and earthy flavors, with a hint of mild spice on the finish. U.S.: $6.90

H. UPMANN CABINET 86
SELECTION ROBUSTO
Dominican Republic • *Size:* 4¾" x 50 *Filler/Binder:* Dom. Rep. *Wrapper:* Indonesia
A very smooth-tasting cigar with good balance. It lacks some depth but has an interesting note of ripe cheese, and a woody finish. U.S.: $6.35

H. UPMANN PEQUEÑOS 86
NO. 100
Dominican Republic • *Size:* 4½" x 50 *Filler/Binder:* Dom. Rep. *Wrapper:* Indonesia
This cigar is a little rustic with a salty character. But it has some good earthy tones, with a slight mineral cast and a smooth tobacco finish. U.S.: $3.00

HOYO DE MONTERREY 86
ROTHSCHILD
Honduras • *Size:* 4½" x 50 *Filler/Binder:* Honduras, Nicaragua, Dom. Rep. *Wrapper:* Ecuador
A good medium-bodied cigar. It has some earthy notes on the palate, and a light toastiness with a sweet spice finish. U.S.: $2.80

LICENCIADOS WAVELL 86
Dominican Republic • *Size:* 5" x 50 *Filler/Binder:* Dom. Rep. *Wrapper:* U.S.A./ Conn. Shade
A well-made, mild- to medium-bodied cigar. It has an herbal character and a light, toasty finish. U.S.: $4.50

NAT SHERMAN 86
VIP SELECTION ASTOR
Dominican Republic • *Size:* 4½" x 50 *Filler/Binder:* Dom. Rep. *Wrapper:* U.S.A./ Conn. Shade
A light cigar with a smooth draw and a mild, spicy flavor that turns to a dried-wood character on the finish. (12/01/94) U.S.: $5.90

NAT SHERMAN HOST SELECTION HOBART 86
Honduras • *Size:* 5" x 50 *Filler:* Honduras *Binder:* Mexico *Wrapper:* U.S.A./ Conn. Shade
A cigar with light, grassy flavors and a smooth, mild finish that contains some medium spiciness. (12/01/94) U.S.: $4.80

PADRÓN 2000 86
Nicaragua • *Size:* 5" x 50 *Filler/Binder/Wrapper:* Nicaragua
This cigar is medium-bodied. It has some spicy flavors on the palate, but it finishes a little dry. U.S.: $3.15

PLAYBOY BY DON DIEGO ROBUSTO 86
Dominican Republic • *Size:* 5" x 50 *Filler/Binder:* Dom. Rep. *Wrapper:* U.S.A./ Conn. Shade
A cigar with a light, mild character. It has some notes of light spices, dry woodiness on the palate, and a light woody finish. U.S.: $6.50

ROLY COLORADO CLARO ROTHSCHILD 86
Honduras • *Size:* 5" x 50 *Filler:* Dom. Rep., Brazil *Binder/Wrapper:* Ecuador
This is a well-made cigar with a slightly firm draw. There are flavors of toast, nuts and coffee beans, with a peppery finish. Price N/A

ROMANTICOS EROS 86
Dominican Republic • *Size:* 5" x 52 *Filler/Binder:* Dom.

Rep. *Wrapper:* U.S.A./ Conn. Shade
A well-made cigar with a smooth, creamy character. It has some peppery flavors with a mild- to medium-bodied smoke. U.S.: $5.60

ROMEO Y JULIETA VINTAGE NO. 3 86
Dominican Republic • *Size:* 4½" x 50 *Filler:* Dom. Rep. *Binder:* Mexico *Wrapper:* U.S.A./Conn. Shade
Good balance. This creamy cigar has an overall herbal quality, with a smooth, even smoke. U.S.: $7.70

SOSA FAMILY SELECTION NO. 5 86
Dominican Republic • *Size:* 5" x 50 *Filler/Binder:* Dom. Rep. *Wrapper:* U.S.A./Conn. Shade
A creamy, smooth-tasting cigar. There is a good dash of pepper in the flavors. U.S.: $4.90

TEMPLE HALL NO. 550 86
Jamaica • *Size:* 5½" x 49 *Filler:* Dom. Rep., Jamaica *Binder:* Mexico *Wrapper:* U.S.A./Conn. Shade
This is a well-made cigar with a light wrapper. There are some earthy tones here, with a slight vegetal hint on the finish. U.S.: $7.35

VUELTABAJO ROBUSTO 86
Dominican Republic • *Size:* 4¾" x 52 *Filler/Binder:* Dom. Rep. *Wrapper:* U.S.A./ Conn. Shade

A cigar with a nutty character. It is mild- to medium-bodied, with some spice on the palate, and hints of wood on the finish. U.S.: $3.80

ARTURO FUENTE CHATEAU FUENTE 85
Dominican Republic • *Size:* 4½" x 50 *Filler/Binder:* Dom. Rep. *Wrapper:* U.S.A./ Conn. Shade
A mild- to medium-bodied cigar. It has a mix of herbal and dry wood flavors on the palate, and a slighty dry, woody finish. U.S.: $3.35

CALLE OCHO GORDITO 85
Dominican Republic • *Size:* 5" x 50 *Filler:* Dom. Rep., Nicaragua, Mexico, Indonesia *Binder/Wrapper:* Ecuador
A decent, middle-of-the-road cigar. There is a perfumy character, with a light woody finish. Some inconsistency was noted in the construction. U.S.: $5.50

DON LINO COLORADO ROBUSTO 85
Dominican Republic • *Size:* 5½" x 50 *Filler:* Nicaragua, Honduras *Binder:* U.S.A./ Conn. Broadleaf *Wrapper:* U.S.A./Conn. Shade
A firm, well-made cigar with solid, nutty flavors and a woody character, yet a hot, almost metallic finish. (12/01/94) U.S.: $4.34

DON MELO NOM PLUS 85
Honduras • *Size:* 4¼" x 50
Filler/Binder/Wrapper: Honduras
There is a touch of spiciness on this mild- to medium-bodied cigar. It has a bit of dryness on the palate, but there is an overall woody character. U.S.: $5.10

EL SUBLIMADO 85
REGARDETE
Dominican Republic • *Size:* 4½" x 50 *Filler/Binder:* Dom. Rep. *Wrapper:* U.S.A./Conn. Shade
Some inconsistencies in this cigar. Overall, it has a mild character with some spicy flavors and a decent, smooth finish. (12/01/94) U.S.: $8.00

FONSECA 5-50 85
Dominican Republic • *Size:* 5" x 50 *Filler:* Dom. Rep. *Binder:* Mexico *Wrapper:* U.S.A./Conn. Shade
This is a mild cigar. It has a straightforward vegetal character. It is smooth tasting with a light mineral tone on the finish. U.S.: $4.75

GILBERTO OLIVA 85
ROBUSTO
Honduras • *Size:* 5½" x 50 *Filler/Binder:* Dom. Rep., Nicaragua *Wrapper:* Ecuador
A cigar with rustic qualities. But there is a spicy core of flavors, with an overall earthy character. U.S.: $4.60

HAVANA CLASSICO 85
CONNECTICUT SHADE
ROBUSTO
Dominican Republic • *Size:* 5" x 50 *Filler:* Dom. Rep., Mexico, Indonesia *Binder:* Ecuador *Wrapper:* U.S.A./Conn. Shade
A creamy cigar with a touch of coffee and toastiness on the palate. It has a fresh, clean finish, with a touch of herbaceousness. U.S.: $6.30

JUAN CLEMENTE 85
ROTHSCHILD
Dominican Republic • *Size:* 4⅞" x 50 *Filler/Binder:* Dom. Rep. *Wrapper:* U.S.A./Conn. Shade
This cigar showed some inconsistency. It has a mild- to medium-body, with a dry, woody character, and some light pepper flavors. U.S.: $7.65

LA FLOR DOMINICANA 85
MACEO
Dominican Republic • *Size:* 5" x 48 *Filler/Binder:* Dom. Rep. *Wrapper:* U.S.A./Conn. Shade
A nice, mellow cigar with a salty character. There is a sweet woodiness, and a light finish. U.S.: $6.50

LA GIANNA ROBUSTO 85
Nicaragua • *Size:* 5" x 50 *Filler/Binder:* Nicaragua *Wrapper:* Ecuador
Although this cigar has a stemmy character, there are solid elements of herbs and nuts on the palate. A medium-bodied cigar. U.S.: $4.60

LA GLORIA CUBANA 85
WAVELL
U.S.A. • *Size:* 5" x 50 *Filler:* Dom. Rep., Nicaragua *Binder:* Nicaragua *Wrapper:* Ecuador
A cigar with a clean finish, mild spiciness and some exotic floral flavors on the palate. (12/01/94) U.S.: $3.70

MACANUDO 85
CRYSTAL CAFE
Jamaica • *Size:* 5½" x 50 *Filler/Binder:* Mexico, Dom. Rep. *Wrapper:* U.S.A./Conn. Shade
A mild- to medium-bodied cigar with some herbal character. But it also has hints of an earthy finish, with a touch of leather. Well-made. U.S.: $5.95

MACANUDO 85
HYDE PARK CAFE
Jamaica • *Size:* 5½" x 49 *Filler:* Dom. Rep., Jamaica *Binder:* Mexico *Wrapper:* U.S.A./Conn. Shade
This cigar has a very smooth taste. It has a herbal character, with some smooth creaminess. U.S.: $5.20

MACANUDO VINTAGE 85
NO. 5 1988
Jamaica • *Size:* 5½" x 49 *Filler:* Dom. Rep., Jamaica *Binder:* Mexico *Wrapper:* U.S.A./Conn. Shade
A light, easy-smoking cigar that tends toward some grassy and straw flavors. (12/01/94) U.S.: $13.50

ROYAL JAMAICA **85**
ROBUSTO
Dominican Republic • *Size:*
4½" x 49 *Filler:* Jamaica,
Dom. Rep., Indonesia
Binder: Cameroon *Wrapper:*
Indonesia
This is a solid, earthy cigar. It
is medium-bodied, and the
flavors include coffee beans
with a hint of pepper.
U.S.: $3.50

TAMBORIL **85**
SUMATRA ROBUSTO
Dominican Republic • *Size:*
5" x 52 *Filler/Binder:* Dom.
Rep. *Wrapper:* Indonesia
A good, mild cigar. It has a
creaminess on the palate
with some solid sweet-spice
elements. U.S.: $6.00

THOMAS HINDS **85**
NICARAGUAN SELEC-
TION ROBUSTO
Nicaragua • *Size:* 5" x 50
Filler/Binder/Wrapper:
Nicaragua
A medium-bodied cigar with
strong elements of earthiness.
It is complex, but with a
slight metallic edge on the
finish. U.S.: $6.00

V.M. SANTANA **85**
CONNECTICUT COL-
LECTION ROBUSTO
Dominican Republic • *Size:*
5" x 50 *Filler/Binder:* Dom.
Rep. *Wrapper:* U.S.A./
Conn. Shade
Although this cigar is a bit
green, it has some strong
spicy elements and a hint of
wood on the finish.
U.S.: $6.95

V.M. SANTANA SUMA- **85**
TRA COLLECTION
ROBUSTO
Dominican Republic • *Size:*
5" x 50 *Filler/Binder:* Dom.
Rep. *Wrapper:* Indonesia
A quite salty cigar with some
good cedary elements on the
finish. It is pretty well-bal-
anced. U.S.: $6.65

BELINDA **84**
MEDAGLIA D'ORO
Honduras • *Size:* 4⅝" x 50
Filler: Dom. Rep., Honduras
Binder: Honduras *Wrapper:*
Ecuador
This cigar looks a little rustic.
But there are some woody
elements on the palate, with
a slightly dry, woody finish.
U.S.: $2.50

CUESTA-REY CENTEN- **84**
NIAL COLLECTION
DOMINICAN NO. 7
Dominican Republic • *Size:*
4½" x 50 *Filler/Binder:* Dom.
Rep. *Wrapper:* U.S.A./
Conn. Shade
A mild- to medium-bodied
cigar. It has a slight dry
herbal character, and woody
finish. It has a very smooth
taste. U.S.: $4.75

DON LINO ROBUSTO **84**
Honduras • *Size:* 5½" x 50
Filler/Binder: Sumatra *Wrapper:* U.S.A./Conn. Shade
There is a tart, almost sour
quality to this cigar. It has
some dry, grassy flavors that
turn to soft, creamy notes on
the finish. (12/01/94)
U.S.: $4.16

DON MANOLO **84**
SERIES III ROBUSTO
Dominican Republic • *Size:*
5" x 50 *Filler/Binder:* Dom.
Rep. *Wrapper:* Indonesia
This is a young cigar. It has
hints of nuttiness, but it is
largely grassy and papery.
U.S.: $6.50

DON XAVIER ROBUSTO **84**
Canary Islands • *Size:* 4⅝" x
50 *Filler:* Brazil, Dom. Rep.,
Canary Islands *Binder:*
Canary Islands *Wrapper:*
U.S.A./Conn. Shade
This is a rustic cigar. It has a
strong vegetal tone, with a
hint of leather on the finish
that rounds out the cigar.
U.S.: $6.50

DUNHILL ROMANAS **84**
Dominican Republic • *Size:*
4½" x 50 *Filler/Binder:* Dom.
Rep. *Wrapper:* U.S.A./
Conn. Shade
A cigar with flavors of spice
and a toasted, almost burnt,
aroma. (12/01/94)
U.S.: $6.60

FELIPE GREGORIO **84**
ROBUSTO
Honduras • *Size:* 5" x 50
Filler/Binder/Wrapper: Honduras
A cigar with a dry finish and
an overall salty character. It
has hints of nuts and some
herbal elements on the
palate. U.S.: $7.60

JOSÉ BENITO ROTH- **84**
SCHILD
Dominican Republic • *Size:*
4¾" x 50 *Filler:* Dom. Rep.

Binder: Honduras *Wrapper:* Cameroon
This cigar starts slowly, but offers pleasant spice flavors on a smooth texture. (12/01/94) U.S.: $4.15

JUAN CLEMENTE CLUB SELECTION No. 2 84
Dominican Republic • *Size:* 4½" x 46 *Filler/Binder:* Dom. Rep. *Wrapper:* U.S.A./ Conn. Shade
Inconsistent. Some tasters noted strong spicy and cedar flavors. Others found it harsh and sour. (12/01/94) U.S.: $8.70

MACABI 84
ROYAL CORONA
Dominican Republic • *Size:* 5" x 50 *Filler/Binder:* Dom. Rep. *Wrapper:* U.S.A./ Conn. Shade
A mild- to medium-cigar with straightforward ele-ments. It's a little simple with a dry wood, almost papery note but it is light and fresh. U.S.: $4.40

MATCH PLAY CYPRESS 84
Dominican Republic • *Size:* 4¾" x 50 *Filler/Binder:* Dom. Rep. *Wrapper:* Ecuador
A woody character. This cigar has some hints of light spices on a medium-bodied smoke. U.S.: $4.50

NAT SHERMAN MAN- 84
HATTAN SELECTION
SUTTON
Dominican Republic • *Size:* 5½" x 49 *Filler:* Dom. Rep. *Binder/Wrapper:* Mexico

This cigar has a nutty taste, with a strong woody quality on the finish. U.S.: $5.50

PUNCH GRAN CRU 84
ROBUSTO
Honduras • *Size:* 5¼" x 50 *Filler/Binder:* Honduras, Nicaragua, Dom. Rep. *Wrapper:* U.S.A./Conn. Shade
A smooth-tasting cigar with an earthy character, dry on the palate, but a bit of a min-eral finish. U.S.: $5.50

PUNCH ROTHSCHILD 84
Honduras • *Size:* 4½" x 50 *Filler/Binder:* Honduras, Nicaragua, Dom. Rep. *Wrapper:* Ecuador
This is a solid cigar with good tobacco qualities. There is a hint of burnt coffee, and a very woody finish. U.S.: $2.80

ROMEO Y JULIETA 84
ROTHSCHILD
Dominican Republic • *Size:* 5" x 50 *Filler:* Dom. Rep., Brazil *Binder:* U.S.A./Conn. Broadleaf *Wrapper:* Cameroon
This is a very mild cigar with a dry, papery flavor, although it offers a hint of spice. (12/01/94) U.S.: $4.05

SANTA DAMIANA 84
SELECCION No. 500
Dominican Republic • *Size:* 5" x 50 *Filler/Binder:* Dom. Rep. *Wrapper:* U.S.A./Conn. Shade
A very creamy and smooth-tasting cigar. It has a mild to

medium body, and some creamy flavors. U.S.: $7.50

TABACOS SAN JOSE 84
ROBUSTO
U.S.A. • *Size:* 5" x 50 *Filler/Binder:* Dom. Rep., Nicaragua, Honduras, Brazil *Wrapper:* U.S.A./Conn. Shade
A mild- to medium-bodied cigar with a creamy texture. A touch of pepper rounds out the core of smooth flavors. It's a little dry on the finish. Price N/A

THOMAS HINDS HON- 84
DURAN SELECTION
ROBUSTO
Honduras • *Size:* 5" x 50 *Filler/Binder:* Honduras *Wrapper:* Ecuador
A light finish on an other-wise creamy and spicy cigar. It has some vegetal hints on the palate, and may be a bit young. U.S.: $3.70

AROMAS DE SAN 83
ANDREAS ROBUSTO
Mexico • *Size:* 5" x 50 *Filler/Binder/Wrapper:* Mexico
This rustic cigar is young. But it has some spice and herbs on the palate. U.S.: $4.35

AVO No. 9 83
Dominican Republic • *Size:* 4¾" x 48 *Filler/Binder:* Dom. Rep. *Wrapper:* U.S.A./Conn. Shade
A cigar with earthy aromas, but with slightly sour, acidic flavors. (12/01/94) U.S.: $6.25

AVO XO INTERMEZZO 83

Dominican Republic • *Size:* 5½" x 50 *Filler/Binder:* Dom. Rep. *Wrapper:* U.S.A./ Conn. Shade

A cigar with a salty taste. There is also a bit of dryness on the palate, and a dry, woody finish. U.S.: $9.50

CANARIA D'ORO INMENSO 83

Dominican Republic • *Size:* 5½" x 49 *Filler:* Dom. Rep., Mexico *Binder/Wrapper:* Mexico

A definite woody character dominates this cigar. It is quite smooth on the palate, and there is a good balance of flavors. U.S.: $3.25

DON ALBERTO RESERVA GRAND CRUZ 83

Dominican Republic • *Size:* 5" x 50 *Filler/Binder:* Dom. Rep. *Wrapper:* Indonesia

A rustic cigar with some earthy flavors. It 's a medium-bodied smoke with a slightly dried-out finish. Price N/A

DON LINO HAVANA RESERVE ROBUSTO 83

Dominican Republic • *Size:* 5½" x 50 *Filler:* Conn. broadleaf *Binder:* Sumatra *Wrapper:* U.S.A./Conn. Shade

Grassy flavors tend to dominate this mild cigar with a firm draw. (12/01/94) U.S.: $4.88

DON TOMAS INTERNATIONAL NO. 2 83

Honduras • *Size:* 5½" x 50 *Filler:* Mexico, Nicaragua,

Dom. Rep. *Binder:* Dom. Rep. *Wrapper:* Indonesia

A mild cigar that has some herbal qualities, but lacks complexity. A pleasant, easy smoke. U.S.: $4.80

DUNHILL CORONA EXTRA 83

Canary Islands • *Size:* 5½" x 50 *Filler/Binder:* Canary Islands *Wrapper:* Cameroon

A pleasant, mild cigar. It has an herbal creaminess, with a hint of wood on the finish. U.S.: $7.60

EL REY DEL MUNDO ROBUSTO 83

Honduras • *Size:* 5" x 54 *Filler/Binder/Wrapper:* Honduras

A quite unattractive wrapper. Inconsistencies in the draw were noted, but otherwise it has some woody, spicy flavors. (12/01/94) U.S.: $3.75

HURRICANOS ROBUSTO 83

Honduras • *Size:* 5" x 50 *Filler:* Nicaragua, Honduras *Binder:* Honduras *Wrapper:* Ecuador

An easy draw on an interesting combination of pepper flavors with a papery character. It has a light wood finish. U.S.: $1.95

LA REGENTA NO. 2 ROBUSTO 83

Canary Islands • *Size:* 4¾" x 50 *Filler/Binder:* Dom. Rep., Brazil, Canary Islands *Wrapper:* U.S.A./Conn. Shade

A mild- to medium-bodied cigar. It has a hint of toasty

flavors, but a very dry wood finish. U.S.: $6.75

LAS CABRILLAS CORTEZ 83

Honduras • *Size:* 4¾" x 50 *Filler/Binder:* Mexico, Dom. Rep. *Wrapper:* U.S.A./ Conn. Shade

A mild cigar. There are some hints of nuttiness, but the tobacco tastes young. U.S.: $2.00

PARTAGAS NATURALES 83

Dominican Republic • *Size:* 5½" x 50 *Filler/Binder:* Mexico, Dom. Rep. *Wrapper:* Cameroon

This medium-bodied cigar has a slightly vegetal character, that ends with a somewhat smoother herbal finish. It has some hints of woodiness throughout. U.S.: $5.15

PLEIADES PLUTON 83

Dominican Republic • *Size:* 5" x 50 *Filler/Binder:* Dom. Rep. *Wrapper:* U.S.A./ Conn. Shade

Quite creamy. There is a smooth spiciness on the palate, but it has a fairly neutral, flat finish. U.S.: $8.70

PUNCH GRAN CRU SUPERIOR 83

Honduras • *Size:* 5½" x 48 *Filler/Binder:* Honduras, Nicaragua, Dom. Rep. *Wrapper:* U.S.A./Conn. Shade

A cigar with herbal character, that warms up quickly with sweet herb and wood flavors on a mild body. U.S.: $5.00

TROYA NO. 18 83 ROTHCHILD
Dominican Republic • *Size:* 4½" x 50 *Filler/Binder:* Dom. Rep. *Wrapper:* U.S.A./ Conn. Shade
A cigar with a strong salty character, and a vegetal quality. There is some pepper on the medium-bodied smoke. U.S.: $4.30

VARGAS ROBUSTO 83
Canary Islands • *Size:* 4¾" x 50 *Filler:* Canary Islands, Dom. Rep. *Binder/Wrapper:* Indonesia
Although the wrapper may be a little young, the cigar has some solid notes of spiciness with a touch of nuttiness on the finish. U.S.: $5.25

BACCARAT ROTH- 82 SCHILD
Honduras • *Size:* 5" x 50 *Filler/Wrapper:* Honduras *Binder:* Mexico
A sweet gum flavors this cigar. It has some solid tobacco tastes, and it is quite spicy and young. Not for everyone, but quite good. U.S.: $2.85

CABALLEROS ROTH- 82 SCHILD
Dominican Republic • *Size:* 5" x 50 *Filler/Binder:* Dom. Rep. *Wrapper:* U.S.A./ Conn. Shade
This cigar has strong notes of spice on the palate and some good woodiness on the finish, but everything is slightly out of balance. The cigar is too young. U.S.: $3.60

CAMACHO MONARCA 82
Honduras • *Size:* 5" x 50 *Filler/Binder/Wrapper:* Honduras
A rustic cigar that has a fairly strong grassy element. There is a mineral tone to the flavors. Quite mild. U.S.: $3.10

DUNHILL ALTAMIRAS 82
Dominican Republic • *Size:* 5" x 48 *Filler/Binder:* Dom. Rep., Brazil *Wrapper:* U.S.A./Conn. Shade
This is a mild cigar, with a simple herbalness. It has a slight woody aftertaste. U.S.: $8.60

NAT SHERMAN LAND- 82 MARK SELECTION VAN-DERBILT
Dominican Republic • *Size:* 5" x 47 *Filler:* Dom. Rep. *Binder:* Mexico *Wrapper:* Cameroon
A somewhat rustic cigar. It has a sweet-pepper quality, but is quite mild overall with a flat finish. U.S.: $8.30

OROSI ORO 550 82
Nicaragua • *Size:* 5" x 50 *Filler/Binder:* Nicaragua *Wrapper:* Ecuador
A slightly rough cigar. It's young, with a mild simple character, that has some elements of herbalness. U.S.: $3.40

PAUL GARMIRIAN EPI- 82 CURE
Dominican Republic • *Size:* 5½" x 50 *Filler/Binder:* Dom. Rep. *Wrapper:* U.S.A./Conn. Shade

A cigar with a largely vegetal character. There is a hint of toastiness on the palate, and some wood on the finish. U.S.: $9.55

TE-AMO TORITO 82
Mexico • *Size:* 4¾" x 50 *Filler/Binder/Wrapper:* Mexico
This cigar is a little young. There is a strong woodiness on the palate and finish. U.S.: $2.50

ZINO MOUTON CADET 82 NO. 6
Honduras • *Size:* 5" x 50 *Filler/Binder:* Honduras *Wrapper:* U.S.A./Conn. Shade
A cigar that is light and mild on the palate. There are some perfumy qualites to it, and it ends up dry, with a cedar wood overtone. U.S.: $7.50

BALLENA SUPREMA 81 SAN ANDRES COLLEC-TION CORDURA
Mexico • *Size:* 5" x 52 *Filler/Binder:* Mexico *Wrapper:* U.S.A./Conn. Shade
A cigar with an strong herbal character. There is some creaminess, but there is also a slighty harsh youthfulness, and a sharp woody finish. U.S.: $4.00

CAMÓRRA ROMA 81
Honduras • *Size:* 5" x 50 *Filler/Binder:* Honduras *Wrapper:* Ecuador
A very mild, young cigar with some papery qualities. It warms up a bit to have some hints of nuts. U.S.: $4.48

EXCELSIOR NO. 3   **81**
Mexico • *Size:* 5½" x 52
Filler/Binder: Mexico *Wrapper:* U.S.A./Conn. Shade
A cigar with inconsistent construction. It seems quite young, with a vegetal harshness, but there are some spicy hints. U.S.: $5.75

LA TRADICION CABINET SERIES ROSADO ROBUSTO   **81**
U.S.A. • *Size:* 5" x 50 *Filler:* Dom. Rep., Nicaragua, Honduras *Binder/Wrapper:* Ecuador
A well-made cigar. It is very woody, but the cigar has some definite youthful notes of light ammonia with a vegetal character. U.S.: $5.40

PAUL GARMIRIAN ROBUSTO   **81**
Dominican Republic • *Size:* 5" x 50 *Filler/Binder:* Dom. Rep. *Wrapper:* U.S.A./Conn. Shade
This cigar is dominated by a grassy tone. There is a vegetal flavor note, and a neutral, light, woody finish.
U.S.: $9.10

PETERSON ROBUSTO   **81**
Dominican Republic • *Size:* 4¾" x 50 *Filler:* Dom. Rep. *Binder:* Ecuador *Wrapper:* U.S.A./Conn. Shade
This is a young cigar that has a trace of ammonia. But it warms up to a woody character on a mild smoke.
U.S.: $7.40

BERING ROBUSTO   **80**
Honduras • *Size:* 4¾" x 50
Filler: Dom. Rep., Nicaragua, Mexico, Honduras *Binder:* Honduras *Wrapper:* U.S.A./Conn. Shade
This is a young cigar. It has pleasant woody flavors on the palate, but lacks some depth. U.S.: $2.65

CRUZ REAL NO. 24   **80**
Mexico • *Size:* 4½" x 50
Filler/Binder/Wrapper: Mexico
Another cigar with young tobacco. It has an easy draw on a mild-bodied smoke, but it's basically flat on the finish. U.S.: $3.60

DON TOMAS ROTHSCHILD   **80**
Honduras • *Size:* 4½" x 50
Filler/Binder: Mexico, Nicaragua, Dom. Rep. *Wrapper:* Honduras
This mild-bodied cigar has a salty, woody character. There is a slight hint of nuts on the palate, and a woody finish.
U.S.: $3.40

DON TOMAS SPECIAL EDITION NO. 300   **80**
Honduras • *Size:* 5" x 50
Filler: Nicaragua, Dom. Rep. *Binder:* Mexico *Wrapper:* Honduras
A very dry tasting cigar. It seems young, and it has a woody finish. U.S.: $4.50

HABANA GOLD BLACK LABEL ROBUSTO   **80**
Honduras • *Size:* 5" x 50
Filler/Binder: Nicaragua *Wrapper:* Indonesia

This cigar is quite young, with a slightly gummy wrapper. There is a strong mineral bite on the finish.
U.S.: $4.80

LEMPIRA ROBUSTO   **80**
Honduras • *Size:* 5" x 50
Filler: Honduras, Nicaragua *Binder:* Dom. Rep. *Wrapper:* U.S.A./Conn. Shade
A very mild cigar. It has a dry wood, papery taste, with a light, vegetal element on the palate. U.S.: $3.70

PAUL GARMIRIAN NO. 2   **80**
Dominican Republic • *Size:* 4¾" x 48 *Filler/Binder:* Dom. Rep. *Wrapper:* U.S.A./Conn. Shade
A cigar that shows some harshness of youth. It is very well made, and it smokes well, but there is a dryness on the palate and some grassiness. U.S.: $8.45

TAMBORIL ROBUSTO   **80**
Dominican Republic • *Size:* 5" x 52 *Filler/Binder:* Dom. Rep. *Wrapper:* U.S.A./Conn. Shade
This cigar has a loose draw. It is straightforward and mild, but with a slightly grassy flavor and a neutral finish.
U.S.: $6.00

CARRINGTON NO. 6   **78**
Dominican Republic • *Size:* 4½" x 50 *Filler/Binder:* Dom. Rep. *Wrapper:* U.S.A./Conn. Shade
Mediocre construction mars this young cigar. There is a chalky dryness on the palate

that has some grassy flavors. A balsa wood finish. U.S.: $5.00

DON MANOLO SERIES II ROBUSTO   78
Dominican Republic • *Size:* 5" x 50   *Filler/Binder:* Dom. Rep.   *Wrapper:* U.S.A./ Conn. Shade
A cigar with a very dry character. There is a hint of balsa wood on the palate, and a touch of ammonia. A rough wrapper. U.S.: $6.50

LA TRADICION CABINET SERIES NATURAL ROBUSTO   78
U.S.A. • *Size:* 5" x 50   *Filler:* Dom. Rep., Nicaragua, Honduras   *Binder:* Ecuador   *Wrapper:* U.S.A./Conn. Shade
A very mild, herbal cigar with a touch of staleness on the finish. U.S.: $5.40

CRUZ REAL NO. 25   77
Mexico • *Size:* 5½" x 52   *Filler/Binder/Wrapper:* Mexico
A rather rustic cigar with a veiny, bumpy wrapper. It is very papery, and there's some gumminess from poorly aged wrapper. U.S.: $4.25

DON ALBERTO SUPERIOR HABANA ROBUSTO   77
Dominican Republic • *Size:* 5" x 50   *Filler/Binder:* Dom. Rep.   *Wrapper:* Ecuador
This is a very mild cigar. It has a strong vegetal character, and a light balsa-wood, papery finish. Price N/A

HABANA GOLD STERLING VINTAGE ROBUSTO   77
Honduras • *Size:* 5" x 50   *Filler:* Nicaragua   *Binder/Wrapper:* Ecuador
This cigar is quite salty, and it has a flinty aspect of youth. It is rough and rustic. U.S.: $5.50

LA FINCA ROBUSTO   77
Nicaragua • *Size:* 4½" x 50   *Filler/Binder/Wrapper:* Nicaragua
A very rustic cigar. It does have some toasty flavors, with a hint of herbal spices. But there's a touch of bitterness on the finish. U.S.: $2.00

DON ALBERTO ORO DE HABANA ROBUSTO   76
Dominican Republic • *Size:* 5" x 50   *Filler/Binder:* Dom. Rep.   *Wrapper:* Ecuador
This is a very mild and somewhat young cigar. It has a papery quality on the palate, and shows some signs of inadequate construction. Price N/A

ORNELAS ROBUSTO   75
Mexico • *Size:* 4¾" x 49   *Filler/Binder/Wrapper:* Mexico
A cigar with a pipe-like tobacco quality. It is poorly made with a loose draw. It has a waxy quality, and a strong, sweet aroma. Not for everyone. U.S.: $4.75

PETRUS TABACAGE ROTHSCHILD   74
Honduras • *Size:* 4¾" x 50   *Filler/Binder/Wrapper:* Honduras
A consistently underfilled cigar. It burns hot with harsh, chemical flavors and has a dry, balsa-wood, papery character. (12/01/94) U.S.: $4.60

LA HOJA SELECTA PALAIS ROYAL   72
U.S.A. • *Size:* 4¼" x 50   *Filler/Binder:* Dom. Rep., Bra., Mex.   *Wrapper:* U.S.A./ Conn. Shade
Inconsistency hurts this cigar. The wrapper is uneven and the entire cigar is loosely rolled. It smokes too fast and gives very grassy, strawlike flavors. Not a complete write off, but it could be better. (09/01/92) U.S.: $3.95

SANTA CLARA 1830 ROBUSTO   72
Mexico • *Size:* 4½" x 50   *Filler:* Mexico, Honduras   *Binder/Wrapper:* Mexico
This cigar is quite young and raw. There is a cardboard quality to the taste. A very rustic cigar. U.S.: $2.25

MONTE CANARIO ROBUSTO   70
Canary Islands • *Size:* 4¾" x 50   *Filler/Binder:* Dom. Rep., Brazil, Canary Islands   *Wrapper:* U.S.A./Conn. Shade
A poorly made cigar. It is loose and underfilled. There's very little taste in this cigar. U.S.: $5.50

Petit Corona

Most of the following Petit Corona tasting notes appeared in the December 1997 issue of Cigar Aficionado. Exceptions are indicated by a date in parentheses at the end of the tasting note.

COHIBA SIGLO I　93
Cuba • *Size:* 4" x 40
Filler/Binder/Wrapper: Cuba
A lot of flavor in a small cigar. Beautifully crafted with a rich chocolate wrapper, it is soft-textured and sumptuous to smoke, with dark chocolate and spice aromas and flavors. (03/01/93) U.K.: £6.65

FUENTE FUENTE　92
OPUS X PERFECXION
NO. 5
Dominican Republic • *Size:* 4⅞" x 40　*Filler/Binder/Wrapper:* Dom. Rep.
An excellent full-bodied smoke, with flavors of nutmet, sweet cocoa and some sweet cedar wood notes on the finish. U.S.: $7.50

ROMEO Y JULIETA　92
CEDROS NO. 3
Cuba • *Size:* 5" x 42
Filler/Binder: Cuba　*Wrapper:* Cuba/Shade Grown
A full-bodied, flavor-filled cigar. It has dark sweet flavors of cocoa beans, with a hint of coffee, a sweet woody character and a solid core of earthiness. U.K.: £6.20

BOLIVAR　90
PETIT CORONA
Cuba • *Size:* 5" x 42
Filler/Binder: Cuba　*Wrapper:* Cuba/Shade Grown
Although this cigar is a little young, it has excellent spice notes, including a hint of nutmeg, with a sweet undertone of cocoa beans. Good balance. U.K.: £6.10

MONTECRISTO NO. 4　90
Cuba • *Size:* 5" x 42
Filler/Binder: Cuba　*Wrapper:* Cuba/Shade Grown
A well-made cigar. It has a strong spiciness, a complex earthiness with hints of dark roasted coffee on the palate, and a long, spicy finish. U.K.: £6.25

PARTAGAS LIMITED　90
RESERVE EPICURE
Dominican Republic • *Size:* 5" x 38　*Filler/Binder:* Mexico, Dom. Rep.　*Wrapper:* Cameroon
This cigar has a solid woodiness on the palate. There is a hint of anise. It has a flat finish. U.S.: $11.50

GRAND NICA TORAÑO　89
Nicaragua • *Size:* 5" x 42
Filler/Binder: Nicaragua
Wrapper: Brazil
A solid earthiness dominates this cigar. It has sweet spicy flavors, and solid cedar wood finish. U.S.: $3.65

PARTAGAS NO. 4　89
Dominican Republic • *Size:* 5" x 38　*Filler/Binder:* Mexico, Dom. Rep.　*Wrapper:* Cameroon

A well-balanced cigar with a medium body. It has a hint of coffee grounds and toastiness with a light, sweet tobacco finish. U.S.: $4.10

PARTAGAS　89
PETIT CORONA
Cuba • *Size:* 5" x 42
Filler/Binder/Wrapper: Cuba
A beautiful, oily wrapper leads into a smoke with excellent leather and sweet spice flavors. It has a light, smooth finish. (06/01/95)
U.K.: £6.10

BAUZA PETIT CORONA　88
Dominican Republic • *Size:* 5" x 38　*Filler:* Dom. Rep., Nicaragua　*Binder:* Mexico
Wrapper: Ecuador
A mild- to medium-bodied cigar with a sweet spice component, almost cinnamon-like, on the palate. It ends a bit dry and flat. U.S.: $4.00

C.A.O. PETIT CORONA　88
Honduras • *Size:* 5" x 40
Filler: Nicaragua, Mexico
Binder: Honduras　*Wrapper:* U.S.A./Conn. Shade
This cigar has flavors of nuts and pepper. A smooth creaminess on the palate with a light herbal character. It is well-made with a good wrapper. U.S.: $4.38

HOYO DE MONTERREY　88
DEMITASSE
Honduras • *Size:* 4" x 39
Filler: Honduras, Dom. Rep., Nicargua　*Binder:* Hoduras
Wrapper: U.S.A./Conn.
Excellent small cigar. The medium- to full-bodied

smoke has some solid spiciness, and a light woodiness on the finish. U.S.: $1.30

HOYO DE MONTERREY 88 EXCALIBUR NO. 7
Honduras • *Size:* 5" x 43
Filler/Binder: Honduras, Nicaragua, Dom. Rep.
Wrapper: U.S.A./Conn. Shade
A pleasant cigar with an earthy complexity. At its core, there are smooth, creamy pepper flavors. It ends on a rich leathery note. (06/01/95) U.S.: $3.80

HOYO DE MONTERREY 88 LE HOYO DU PRINCE
Cuba • *Size:* 5" x 40
Filler/Binder: Cuba *Wrapper:* Cuba/Shade Grown
This full-bodied cigar has an earthy complexity with a roasted cocoa bean flavor. It's a little rustic looking, but performs well. U.K.: £6.20

ROMEO Y JULIETA 88 PETIT CORONA
Cuba • *Size:* 5" x 42
Filler/Binder: Cuba *Wrapper:* Cuba/Shade Grown
A solid cigar with flavors of nuts. It has a smooth quality on the palate with a light, earthy, herbal character. Well-made. U.K.: £6.10

AVO NO. 8 87
Dominican Republic • *Size:* 5½" x 40 *Filler/Binder:* Dom. Rep. *Wrapper:* U.S.A./ Conn. Shade
This cigar has pleasant floral aromas. There are sweet nutmeg flavors, and a hint of

coffee beans and creaminess on the palate. (06/01/95) U.S.: $6.25

BACCARAT PETIT 87 CORONA
Honduras • *Size:* 5½" x 42
Filler/Wrapper: Honduras
Binder: Mexico
Although it showed some inconsistency, this cigar had a well-balanced, smooth taste, and contained solid notes of spice and coffee. (06/01/95) U.S.: $2.45

FLOR DE FLOREZ CABI- 87 NET SELECTION CORO- NITA
Nicaragua • *Size:* 5" x 42
Filler/Binder/Wrapper: Nicaragua
Although this cigar lacks a bit of balance, it has excellent flavors of dark coffee, and a solid earthy character. U.S.: $5.00

HABANA GOLD 87 BLACK LABEL PETIT CORONA
Honduras • *Size:* 5" x 42
Filler/Binder: Nicaragua
Wrapper: Indonesia
A well-made cigar with dark brown wrapper. There is a strong peppery quality to it, with a sweet, earthy core of flavors. U.S.: $3.25

MACANUDO 87 HAMPTON COURT
Jamaica • *Size:* 5¾" x 43
Filler: Dom. Rep., Jamaica, Mexico *Binder:* Mexico
Wrapper: U.S.A./Conn. Shade

A very well-made mild cigar. It has a good draw and an even burn, and solid flavors of tobacco and sweet wood. A coffee bean character comes out on the finish. (06/01/95) U.S.: $4.95

MONTECRUZ SUN- 87 GROWN CEDAR AGED
Dominican Republic • *Size:* 5" x 42 *Filler/Binder:* Dom. Rep., Brazil *Wrapper:* Indonesia
A cigar with sweet wood and a light, sweet spicy character. There are some hints of cocoa on the finish. Generally mild. U.S.: $4.00

PALMAREJO 87 PETIT CORONA
Dominican Republic • *Size:* 5⅛" x 42 *Filler/Binder:* Dom. Rep. *Wrapper:* Indonesia
A smooth, very well-balanced cigar. It has solid core of woodiness, and there is some good spice flavors. Price N/A

PLEIADES ANTARES 87
Dominican Republic • *Size:* 5½" x 40 *Filler/Binder:* Dom. Rep. *Wrapper:* U.S.A./ Conn. Shade
A mellow cigar that has an interesting aroma of roasting meat. There are fruity flavors reminiscent of mango and a smooth nutty finish. (06/01/95) U.S.: $6.35

ZINO **87**
MOUTON CADET NO. 5
Honduras • *Size:* 5" x 42
Filler/Binder: Honduras
Wrapper: U.S.A./Conn.
Shade
A bit salty, but with a perfumed herbal character. It has an earthy finish.
U.S.: $5.25

CANONERO "MEDIANO" POTRA **86**
Brazil • *Size:* 4¼" x 38
Filler/Binder: Brazil *Wrapper:* Ecuador
A smallish cigar. It has a smooth creaminess on the palate with strong hints of herbs. There are also some toast and nut notes on the palate. U.S.: $2.50

DAVIDOFF **86**
GRAND CRU NO. 4
Dominican Republic • *Size:* 4⅞" x 41 *Filler/Binder:* Dom. Rep. *Wrapper:* U.S.A./Conn. Shade
A cigar with strong hints of spice and pepper. It has an earthy undertone and a hint of nuttiness. U.S.: $6.00

DAVIDOFF NO. 2000 **86**
Dominican Republic • *Size:* 5" x 43 *Filler/Binder:* Dom. Rep. *Wrapper:* U.S.A./Conn. Shade
A smooth-tasting cigar with a creamy quality. It has some flavors of nuts, with a woody finish. U.S.: $7.30

EL RICO HABANO **86**
PETIT-HABANO
Dominican Republic • *Size:* 5" x 40 *Filler:* Nicaragua

Binder: Dom. Rep. *Wrapper:* Ecuador
A cigar with a strong vegetal character, and a quite dry finish. U.S.: $3.15

H. UPMANN **86**
PEQUEÑOS NO. 300
Dominican Republic • *Size:* 4½" x 42 *Filler/Binder:* Dom. Rep. *Wrapper:* Indonesia
A relatively mild cigar. It has some sweet tobacco notes, and good balance.
U.S.: $2.75

JOSÉ MARTÍ **86**
PETIT LANCERO
Nicaragua • *Size:* 4½" x 38 *Filler:* Dom. Rep., Honduras, Nicaragua *Binder:* Honduras *Wrapper:* Ecuador
A spicy cigar with a strong woody component on the palate and the finish. It has a good balance, with a hint of earthiness. U.S.: $1.25

LA REGENTA NO. 5 **86**
Canary Islands • *Size:* 4½" x 42 *Filler/Binder:* Dom. Rep., Brazil *Wrapper:* U.S.A./Conn. Shade
A well-balanced cigar with a creamy texture, and some wood and spice flavors.
U.S.: $6.00

PAUL GARMIRIAN **86**
PETIT CORONA
Dominican Republic • *Size:* 5" x 43 *Filler/Binder:* Dom. Rep. *Wrapper:* U.S.A./Conn. Shade
A medium body smoke has creamy and mild spice qualities, and a mild woody finish. (06/01/95) U.S.: $7.25

PUNCH PETIT CORONA **86**
DEL PUNCH
Cuba • *Size:* 5" x 42 *Filler/Binder/Wrapper:* Cuba
A cigar with a very sweet flavor profile that includes butterscotch and burnt caramel. It has a very woody component on the finish.
(06/01/95) U.K.: £5.80

THE GRIFFIN'S **86**
NO. 500
Dominican Republic • *Size:* 5¹⁄₁₆" x 43 *Filler/Binder:* Dom. Rep. *Wrapper:* U.S.A./Conn. Shade
A mild- to medium-bodied cigar. It has some flavors of herbs, with a slight hint of spiciness. U.S.: $5.10

AURORA CORONA **85**
Dominican Republic • *Size:* 5" x 38 *Filler/Binder:* Dom. Rep. *Wrapper:* Cameroon
A mild- to medium-bodied cigar with some herbs and sweet wood flavors. It ends up a little dry on the finish. U.S.: $2.40

AURORA SUBLIMES **85**
Dominican Republic • *Size:* 5" x 38 *Filler/Binder:* Dom. Rep. *Wrapper:* Cameroon
A cigar with a very woody character. There is a hint of earth and spice on the palate, but with a dry finish. U.S.: $3.60

DAVIDOFF **85**
GRAND CRU NO. 3
Dominican Republic • *Size:* 5" x 43 *Filler/Binder:* Dom. Rep. *Wrapper:* U.S.A./Conn. Shade

A cigar with a mild, nutty finish. It has a pleasant floral character, but there are some dry, herbal notes on the palate. U.S.: $8.25

H. UPMANN 85
PETIT CORONA
Dominican Republic • *Size:* 5¹⁄₁₆" x 42 *Filler/Binder:* Dom. Rep. *Wrapper:* Indonesia
A bit rustic. The cigar has a salty character, with a solid tobacco flavor. U.S.: $3.20

H. UPMANN TUBOS 85
GOLD TUBE
Dominican Republic • *Size:* 5¹⁄₁₆" x 42 *Filler/Binder:* Dom. Rep. *Wrapper:* Indonesia
A medium-bodied cigar with a light salty character and a light earthy finish. U.S.: $4.10

HABANA GOLD 85
WHITE LABEL
PETIT CORONA
Honduras • *Size:* 5" x 42 *Filler/Binder:* Nicaragua *Wrapper:* NIcaragua
A cigar with a woody character, and a hint of dark roasted coffee beans on the palate. Good balance, and a woody finish. U.S.: $3.85

HOYO DE MONTERREY 85
EXCALIBUR NO. 6
Honduras • *Size:* 5½" x 38 *Filler/Binder:* Honduras, Nicaragua, Dom. Rep. *Wrapper:* U.S.A./Conn. Shade
Some inconsistency in this cigar. A loose, hot draw was

noted by several tasters. But there are some earthy tobacco flavors, and the cigar settles down after a brief harshness. (06/01/95) U.S.: $3.95

JUAN CLEMENTE 85
CORONA
Dominican Republic • *Size:* 5" x 42 *Filler/Binder:* Dom. Rep. *Wrapper:* U.S.A./Conn. Shade
A cigar with a solid herbal character. It has some eastern spices on the palate, and has a bit of youthfulness, suggesting it will improve.
U.S.: $5.45

MACANUDO 85
PETIT CORONA
Jamaica • *Size:* 5" x 38 *Filler:* Dom. Rep.,Jamaica *Binder:* Mexico *Wrapper:* U.S.A./Conn. Shade
A solid, middle-of-the-road cigar. It has some earthiness on the palate, with a slight dry wood character. Nice wrapper. U.S.: $3.65

PUNCH ELITE 85
Honduras • *Size:* 5¼" x 44 *Filler/Binder:* Honduras, Nicaragua, Dom. Rep. *Wrapper:* Ecuador
This cigar is a medium-bodied smoke. There are nutmeg and burnt spice flavors, and an overall woody character. (06/01/95) U.S.: $1.65

SANCHO PANZA 85
NON PLUS
Cuba • *Size:* 5" x 42 *Filler/Binder/Wrapper:* Cuba
Although this cigar shows some nice flavors of coffee

and cream, it lacks complexity and depth in its medium-bodied smoke. (06/01/95) U.K.: £5.95

SOSA FAMILY SELEC- 85
TION NO. 4
Dominican Republic • *Size:* 5" x 40 *Filler/Binder:* Dom. Rep. *Wrapper:* U.S.A./ Conn. Shade
A well-balanced cigar. There is a sweet tobacco taste on the palate, with a hint of earthiness. Inconsistent construction. U.S.: $3.00

VARGAS CREMAS 85
Canary Islands • *Size:* 4⅞" x 39 *Filler:* Dom. Rep. *Binder/Wrapper:* Indonesia
This is a decent medium-bodied cigar. It has some toasty and sweet spice notes, but a light woody finish. U.S.: $4.50

ARTURO FUENTE 84
PETIT CORONA
Dominican Republic • *Size:* 5" x 38 *Filler/Binder:* Dom. Rep. *Wrapper:* Cameroon
A well-balanced cigar. It is quite mild, and has a slightly papery finish. U.S.: $2.85

BERING IMPERIAL 84
Honduras • *Size:* 5¼" x 42 *Filler/Wrapper:* Mexico, Dom. Rep., Honduras *Binder:* Honduras
This is a mild cigar. It has some light earthy flavors backed up by a hint of spice, and ends with a somewhat dry finish. (06/01/95) U.S.: $2.95

CARLOS TORAÑO NICARAGUAN SELECTION **84**
Nicaragua • *Size:* 5" x 42
Filler/Binder: Nicaragua
Wrapper: Indonesia
There are some nutty flavors, with an underlying earthiness. But the finish is quite dry and papery. U.S.: $3.65

DON MELO CREMAS **84**
Honduras • *Size:* 4½" x 42
Filler/Binder/Wrapper: Honduras
A cigar with dark earthy flavors. But it has an underlying vegetal note. Dry on the palate. U.S.: $4.20

LA FLOR DOMINICANA MACHETEROS **84**
Dominican Republic • *Size:* 4" x 40   *Filler/Binder:* Dom. Rep.   *Wrapper:* U.S.A./Conn. Shade
A cigar that is dry on the palate. It is a mild- to medium-bodied. There is some herbal spice and woodiness on the finish. U.S.: $3.50

LA GLORIA CUBANA MINUTOS **84**
Dominican Republic • *Size:* 4½" x 40   *Filler:* Dom. Rep., Nicaragua   *Binder/Wrapper:* Ecuador
A well-made, mild- to medium-bodied cigar with some vegetal notes on the palate. U.S.: $2.70

LEON JIMENES NO. 5 **84**
Dominican Republic • *Size:* 5" x 38   *Filler/Binder:* Dom. Rep.   *Wrapper:* U.S.A./Conn. Shade

This is a cigar with some herbal character, with a hint of leather on the finish. U.S.: $3.04

MONTECRUZ SUN-GROWN NO. 230 **84**
Dominican Republic • *Size:* 5" x 42   *Filler/Binder:* Dom. Rep., Brazil   *Wrapper:* Cameroon
A nice cigar with medium body. Although it has some light spice and citrus flavors, it finishes a bit flat and dry. (06/01/95) U.S.: $3.70

PIO VI PETIT CORONA **84**
U.S.A. • *Size:* 5⅛" x 40
Filler: Honduras, Dom. Rep.
Binder: Indonesia *Wrapper:* Brazil
A mild- to medium-bodied smoke with a light herbal character, and pleasant sweetness on the palate. U.S.: $5.75

QUINTERO MEDIAS CORONAS **84**
Cuba • *Size:* 5" x 40
Filler/Binder/Wrapper: Cuba
This cigar showed some rough construction, but it has nice flavors of sweet spice and dry cedar wood. (06/01/95) Price N/A

TROYA CLASICO NO. 27 CORONA **84**
Dominican Republic • *Size:* 5½" x 42   *Filler/Binder:* Dom. Rep.   *Wrapper:* U.S.A./Conn. Shade
A cigar with a flinty character, and a toasty aroma with some nutty flavors. A dry finish. (06/01/95) U.S.: $7.20

DON TOMAS BLUNT **83**
Honduras • *Size:* 5" x 42
Filler: Dom. Rep., Mexico, Nicaragua   *Binder:* Mexico
Wrapper: Indonesia
This is a well-made cigar with a dry woody character. There is hint of mustiness on the palate. U.S.: $3.25

HABANA GOLD STERLING VINTAGE PETIT CORONA **83**
Honduras • *Size:* 5" x 42
Filler: Nicaragua
Binder/Wrapper: Ecuador
This is a mild cigar, with a sweetish wood quality and some vegetal notes. U.S.: $4.00

HOYO DE MONTERREY NO. 55 **83**
Honduras • *Size:* 5¼" x 43
Filler/Binder: Honduras, Nicaragua, Dom. Rep.
Wrapper: Ecuador
A slightly rustic, middle-of-the-road smoke that has some spicy flavors, and a bit of dryness on the palate. (06/01/95) U.S.: $1.65

POR LARRAÑAGA PETIT CETROS EN CEDRO **83**
Dominican Republic • *Size:* 5" x 38   *Filler/Binder:* Dom. Rep.   *Wrapper:* U.S.A./Conn. Shade
This cigar has some sweet-wood notes on the palate. But it is quite light with a hint of vegetalness. U.S.: $4.25

ROYAL JAMAICA 83
PETIT CORONA
Dominican Republic • *Size:*
5" x 40 *Filler:* Jamaica,
Dom. Rep., Sumatra *Binder:*
Java *Wrapper:* Cameroon
A mild cigar with a tight
draw. It has some soft,
creamy flavors with nutty
components. (06/01/95)
U.S.: $3.55

DON DIEGO 82
PETIT CORONA
Dominican Republic • *Size:*
5⅛" x 42 *Filler/Binder:* Dom.
Rep. *Wrapper:* U.S.A./
Conn.
There is a hint of hot, spicy
pepper in this cigar, but it is
dominated by a dry woodi-
ness, and a woody finish.
U.S.: $3.20

FONSECA 2-2 82
Dominican Republic • *Size:*
4¼" x 40 *Filler:* Dom. Rep.
Binder: Mexico *Wrapper:*
U.S.A./Conn. Shade
A well-made cigar. It is quite
mild, with a touch of salti-
ness, and a light papery taste.
U.S.: $2.95

HOYO DE MONTERREY 82
SABROSO
Honduras • *Size:* 5" x 40
Filler/Binder: Honduras, Dom.
Rep., Nicaragua *Wrapper:*
U.S.A./Conn. Shade
This cigar had a slightly
gummy wrapper, and suffered
from poor construction. It
was sharp on the palate, and
had a vegetal character.
U.S.: $1.30

MONTECRUZ NATURAL 82
CLARO CEDAR AGED
Dominican Republic • *Size:*
5" x 42 *Filler/Binder:* Dom.
Rep., Brazil *Wrapper:*
U.S.A./Conn. Shade
Although this cigar has some
creamy qualities, there is still
a little bit of youth. It has a
slightly vegetal finish.
U.S.: $4.00

NAT SHERMAN 82
VIP SELECTION BAR-
NUM GLASS TUBE
Dominican Republic • *Size:*
5½" x 42 *Filler/Binder:* Dom.
Rep. *Wrapper:* U.S.A./
Conn. Shade
A light-bodied cigar with
some slightly sour, acidic
tones, and a vegetal character that is balanced on the
finish with a touch of spice.
(06/01/95) U.S.: $8.50

TAMBORIL CORTADITO 82
Dominican Republic • *Size:*
5" x 38 *Filler/Binder:* Dom.
Rep. *Wrapper:* U.S.A./
Conn. Shade
This is a mild cigar with
some woody flavors. It ends
up with some vegetal notes,
and a bit of sharpness.
U.S.: $4. 00

FONSECA COSACOS 81
Cuba • *Size:* 5⅓" x 42
Filler/Binder/Wrapper: Cuba
A very rough, unattractive
wrapper. The cigar is loosely
filled, and has a grassy, sour
flavor. (06/01/95) Price N/A

H. UPMANN 81
PETIT CORONA
Cuba • *Size:* 5" x 42
Filler/Binder/Wrapper: Cuba
A cigar with a very tight
draw. Although it has some
nice citrus-style flavors, it
ended up lacking complexity.
(06/01/95) U.K.: £6.15

PAUL GARMIRIAN 81
No. 5
Dominican Republic • *Size:*
4" x 40 *Filler/Binder:* Dom.
Rep. *Wrapper:* U.S.A./
Conn. Shade
Although this cigar has a
hint of spiciness on the finish, it has a very flat character, with some bite on the
palate. U.S.: $5.85

CARRINGTON No. 4 80
Dominican Republic • *Size:*
5½" x 40 *Filler/Binder:* Dom.
Rep. *Wrapper:* U.S.A./
Conn. Shade
A rough wrapper on this mild
cigar gives a dried out character to the flavors. It tastes
of paper, and some spice on a
hot finish. (06/01/95)
U.S.: $4.80

FLOR DE FILIPINAS 80
HALF CORONA
Philippines • *Size:* 4" x 39
Filler/Binder: Philippines
Wrapper: Indonesia, Philip-
pines
A cigar with a very salty
character, and a lot of dryness
on the palate. U.S.: $1.45

NAT SHERMAN HOST 80 SELECTION HAMILTON
Honduras • *Size:* 5½" x 42
Filler: Honduras *Binder:*
Mexico *Wrapper:* U.S.A./
Conn. Shade
A cigar with a very mild
tobacco character. There are
flavors of orange peel and
some spice but with a dry fin-
ish. (06/01/95) U.S.: $4.20

TE-AMO NO. 4 80
Mexico • *Size:* 5" x 42
Filler/Binder/Wrapper: Mexico
A strong vegetal quality, with
a hint of overripe leaves.
There are some hints of wood
and light spice on the finish.
U.S.: $2.35

CORTESIA NO. 1 79
Honduras • *Size:* 5½" x 40
Filler/Binder: Honduras,
Nicaragua, Dom. Rep.
Wrapper: Ecuador
A loose fill creates a hot
draw, and fills the mouth
with a dry, woody, balsa-like
flavor. It also has a metallic
finish. (06/01/95) Price N/A

PETRUS TABACAGE 78 GREGORIUS
Honduras • *Size:* 5" x 42
Filler/Binder: Honduras
Wrapper: Ecuador
This cigar smoked well, but it
has a gummy wrapper, with a
bit of harshness on the finish.
U.S.: $4.00

JUAN CLEMENTE 76 DEMI-CORONA
Dominican Republic • *Size:*
4" x 40 *Filler/Binder:* Dom.
Rep. *Wrapper:* U.S.A./
Conn. Shade

This cigar had inconsistent
construction with a loose fill.
It is very mild with a balsa-
wood character, and some
harshness. U.S.: $4.90

TORCEDOR NO. 4 76
Nicaragua • *Size:* 5" x 42
Filler: Nicaragua, Honduras
Binder: Mexico *Wrapper:*
Indonesia
A medium- to full-bodied
cigar. There is a sweet earthy
quality to this cigar. It has a
one-dimensional, flat finish.
U.S.: $2.75

Panetela

*Most of the following Panetela
tasting notes appeared in the
May/June 1997 issue of* Cigar
Aficionado. *Exceptions are
indicated by a date in parentheses at the end of the tasting
note.*

ARTURO FUENTE 91 PETIT LANCERO
Dominican Republic • *Size:*
6" x 38 *Filler/Binder/Wrap-
per:* Dom. Rep.
A beautiful, reddish-brown
wrapper and an easy, elegant
draw. Complex flavors of
robust spices with undertones
of cedar and leather produce
a rich, full character.
(09/01/94) U.S.: $9.50

COHIBA 89 CORONA ESPECIAL
Cuba • *Size:* 6" x 38
Filler/Binder/Wrapper: Cuba
A firm, well-made cigar produces well-rounded flavors of
spices and nuts and has a
solid tobacco character with

an earthy, chocolaty finish.
(09/01/94) U.K.: £12.25

AVO NO. 6 88
Dominican Republic • *Size:*
6½" x 36 *Filler/Binder:* Dom.
Rep. *Wrapper:* U.S.A./
Conn. Shade
This is a very well-balanced
cigar. It is smooth, with an
earthy core of flavors and
nice spicy notes throughout.
U.S.: $6.25

HOYO DE MONTERREY 88 LE HOYO DU DAUPHIN
Cuba • *Size:* 6" x 38
Filler/Binder/Wrapper: Cuba
A beautiful light brown, oily
wrapper. It is a smooth, well-
balanced smoke with solid
flavors of herbs and pepper,
and a nice spicy finish.
U.K.: £8.05

ROYAL JAMAICA BUC- 88 CANEER
Dominican Republic • *Size:*
5½" x 30 *Filler:* Dom. Rep,
Jamaica, Indonesia *Binder:*
Cameroon *Wrapper:*
Indonesia
A deep earthiness marks this
cigar. It has hints of dried
orange peel and toasty flavors, with a good cedary finish. U.S.: $2.90

V CENTENNIAL 88 NUMERO 1
Honduras • *Size:* 7½" x 38
Filler: Dom. Rep., Honduras,
Nicaragua *Binder:*
Nicaragua *Wrapper:*
U.S.A./Conn. Shade
A beautiful, oily, brown
wrapper delivers a rich spici-
ness and a medium body with

a bit of a tang. (09/01/94)
U.S.: $6.00

AVO XO PRELUDIO 87
Dominican Republic • *Size:*
6" x 40 *Filler/Binder:* Dom.
Rep. *Wrapper:* U.S.A./
Conn. Shade
A smooth, brown wrapper. It
has some cedar-wood flavors
and a spicy backbone.
(09/01/94) U.S.: $9.00

BELINDA BELINDA 87
Honduras • *Size:* 6½" x 36
Filler/Binder: Honduras,
Nicaragua, Dom. Rep.
Wrapper: Ecuador
This cigar has a sweet spice
character with some leathery
notes. It is medium-bodied
with a nutty finish. U.S.: $2.00

CUESTA-REY 87
CABINET NO. 2
Dominican Republic • *Size:*
7" x 36 *Filler/Binder:* Dom.
Rep. *Wrapper:* Cameroon
A dark-brown wrapper pro-
duces a nice, mild spiciness
with a slightly sweet, cocoa
finish. (09/01/94) U.S.: $4.50

DUNHILL SAMANAS 87
Dominican Republic • *Size:*
6½" x 38 *Filler/Binder:* Dom.
Rep., Brazil *Wrapper:*
U.S.A./Conn. Shade
A solid, mild- to medium-
bodied cigar. It has good
spice flavors, and a somewhat
dry wood finish. U.S.: $5.65

EL REY DEL MUNDO 87
TINOS
Honduras • *Size:* 5½" x 38
Filler/Binder: Honduras,
Nicaragua, Dom. Rep.
Wrapper: Ecuador
A solid, medium-bodied cigar
with a core of nut and wood
flavors. It has a hint of spice
on the otherwise woody fin-
ish. U.S.: $2.50

JOSÉ BENITO PETITE 87
Dominican Republic • *Size:*
5½" x 38 *Filler:* Dom. Rep.
Binder: Honduras *Wrapper:*
Indonesia
This cigar has a solid coffee
bean flavor, and an overall
smooth herbal character. It
has an earthy finish.
U.S.: $3.80

LA FLOR DOMINICANA 87
DEMI TASSE
Dominican Republic • *Size:*
5" x 30 *Filler/Binder:* Dom.
Rep. *Wrapper:* U.S.A./
Conn. Shade
This cigar has a mild, salty
character. There some inter-
esting floral notes with some
roasted nut flavors.
U.S.: $2.50

LA GLORIA CUBANA 87
PANETELA DELUXE
U.S.A. • *Size:* 7" x 37 *Filler:*
Dom. Rep., Nicaragua
Binder/Wrapper: Ecuador
This cigar has strong, deli-
cious, spicy notes, but it fin-
ishes a bit short and flat.
(09/01/94) U.S.: $3.10

MONTECRISTO ESPE- 87
CIAL NO. 2
Cuba • *Size:* 6" x 38
Filler/Binder/Wrapper: Cuba
A beautifully made cigar. It
has youthful characteristics.
But there are strong hints of
earth, with solid leather and
wood flavors. U.K.: £8.35

PAUL GARMIRIAN 87
PANETELA
Dominican Republic • *Size:*
7½" x 38 *Filler/Binder:* Dom.
Rep. *Wrapper:* U.S.A./
Conn. Shade
A full-flavored smoke with
some spice and toasted-nut
notes. It is elegant and well-
balanced, but has a tight
draw. (09/01/94) Price N/A

PUROS INDIOS NO. 5 87
ESPECIAL COLORADO
Honduras • *Size:* 5" x 36
Filler: Nicaragua, Dom. Rep.,
Brazil *Binder/Wrapper:*
Ecuador
This cigar has a beautiful oily
sheen. It has a perfumed
quality with a core of nutmeg
and earthy flavors, and a long
finish. U.S.: $3.10

5 VEGAS PANETELA 86
Nicaragua • *Size:* 6" x 38
Filler: Dom. Rep., Nicaragua
Binder/Wrapper: Indonesia
A smooth-tasting cigar
despite its youth. There are
flavors of nuts and cinnamon
spices. It has a woody finish.
U.S.: $3.28

CUESTA-REY **86**
CENTENNIAL COLLECTION DOMINICAN NO. 3

Dominican Republic • *Size:* 7" x 36 *Filler/Binder:* Dom. Rep. *Wrapper:* U.S.A./ Conn. Shade
A well-made cigar with a light-brown wrapper. It has mild, spicy flavors and a smooth, flinty aftertaste. (09/01/94) U.S.: $4.95

DAVIDOFF NO. 2 **86**

Dominican Republic • *Size:* 6" x 38 *Filler/Binder:* Dom. Rep. *Wrapper:* U.S.A./ Conn. Shade
A well-balanced cigar. It has a light woody character, with some smooth nuttiness on the palate. U.S.: $10.25

DON TOMAS **86**
SPECIAL EDITION NO. 400

Honduras • *Size:* 7" x 36 *Filler/Binder/Wrapper:* Honduras
A smooth-drawing cigar with a mellow tobacco character that is backed up by a mild spiciness. (09/01/94) U.S.: $4.50

JUAN CLEMENTE 530 **86**

Dominican Republic • *Size:* 5" x 30 *Filler/Binder:* Dom. Rep. *Wrapper:* U.S.A./ Conn. Shade
A pleasant small cigar. It has hints of pepper and sweet wood, and an overall woody character. U.S.: $4.90

LA FINCA FLORA **86**

Nicaragua • *Size:* 7" x 36 *Filler/Binder/Wrapper:* Nicaragua
A medium-bodied cigar with some spicy flavors and a well-balanced presence in the mouth. (09/01/94) U.S.: $2.00

MAYA PALMA FINA **86**

Honduras • *Size:* 6⅞" x 36 *Filler/Binder:* Honduras, Dom. Rep. *Wrapper:* U.S.A./ Conn. Shade
This cigar has a good, solid draw and mild flavors of spices and nuts. (09/01/94) U.S.: $3.70

MONTECRISTO ESPECIAL **86**

Cuba • *Size:* 7½" x 38 *Filler/Binder/Wrapper:* Cuba
This is a smooth-tasting cigar with solid notes of pepper spice and a pleasant cedarwood finish. (09/01/94) U.K.: £10.35

ROLY PETIT CETRO **86**

Honduras • *Size:* 5" x 36 *Filler:* Dom. Rep. , Brazil *Binder/Wrapper:* Ecuador
This is a medium- to full-bodied cigar. It has a good draw, and a solid spicy core of flavors. It will improve with age. Price N/A

THE GRIFFIN'S **86**
NO. 400

Dominican Republic • *Size:* 6" x 38 *Filler/Binder:* Dom. Rep. *Wrapper:* U.S.A./ Conn. Shade
This cigar starts out slow, perhaps because of youth.

But it has some nutty flavors, with a slightly leathery finish. U.S.: $5.25

THE GRIFFIN'S PRIVILEGE **86**

Dominican Republic • *Size:* 5" x 32 *Filler/Binder:* Dom. Rep. *Wrapper:* U.S.A./ Conn. Shade
A medium-bodied cigar with a long finish. It has some rich spice notes on the palate. U.S.: $4.30

TORCEDOR PANETELA **86**

Nicaragua • *Size:* 5" x 36 *Filler:* Nicaragua, Honduras *Binder:* Mexico *Wrapper:* Indonesia
A medium-bodied cigar with a dried-orange-peel note on the palate, and a touch of burnt or very dark coffee on the finish. U.S.: $2.50

ZINO **86**
MOUTON CADET NO. 4

Honduras • *Size:* 5⅛" x 30 *Filler/Binder:* Honduras *Wrapper:* U.S.A./Conn. Shade
This is a solid cigar with an herbal character. It has a strong woodiness on the palate and a woody finish. U.S.: $4.30

ARTURO FUENTE **85**
PANETELA FINA

Dominican Republic • *Size:* 7" x 38 *Filler/Binder:* Dom. Rep. *Wrapper:* Cameroon
A cigar with fine aromas and a spicy flavor that has notes of nuts and sweet wood. (09/01/94) U.S.: $3.45

ASHTON CORDIAL **85**

Dominican Republic • *Size:*
5" x 30 *Filler/Binder:* Dom.
Rep. *Wrapper:* U.S.A./
Conn. Shade
A mild cigar. It has some
pleasing flavors of nuts and
sweet wood. Well made.
U.S.: $4.80

CAMÓRRA CAPRI **85**

Honduras • *Size:* 5½" x 32
Filler/Binder: Honduras
Wrapper: Ecuador
This is a well-made cigar. It is
a bit one-dimensional on the
palate, but there are hints of
sweet wood and nuts.
U.S.: $3.12

CARRINGTON NO. 3 **85**

Dominican Republic • *Size:*
7" x 36 *Filler/Binder:* Dom.
Rep. *Wrapper:* U.S.A./
Conn. Shade
An elegant smoke with a
smooth mellowness. A good,
firm draw produces some
mild spice and toast flavors.
(09/01/94) U.S.: $4.80

CUBITA NO. 2 **85**

Dominican Republic • *Size:*
6¼" x 38 *Filler/Binder:* Dom.
Rep. *Wrapper:* U.S.A./
Conn. Shade
A cigar with a solid core of
sweet herb flavors, and a
smooth spiciness on the finish. U.S.: $4.75

DON LINO HAVANA **85**
RESERVE PANETELA

Dominican Republic • *Size:*
7" x 36 *Filler/Binder:* Sumatra *Wrapper:* U.S.A./Conn.
Shade

The draw is a bit tight. There
is some nutty spiciness, but
the flavors tend toward a
vegetal, dry-paper finish.
(09/01/94) U.S.: $4.08

DON TOMAS **85**
PANETELA LARGAS

Honduras • *Size:* 7" x 38
Filler/Binder/Wrapper: Honduras
This cigar has a tight draw,
but it has nut and spice flavors and a solid tobacco core.
(09/01/94) U.S.: $3.80

HABANICA SERIE 638 **85**

Nicaragua • *Size:* 6" x 38
Filler/Binder/Wrapper:
Nicaragua
Although this cigar finishes
with a dry, paper quality,
there is a nice core of spicy
flavors on the palate with a
bit of a bite. U.S.: $5.50

JOYA DE NICARAGUA **85**
NO. 5

Nicaragua • *Size:* 6⅞" x 35
Filler/Binder: Nicaragua
Wrapper: Ecuador
An elegant cigar with a
slightly tight draw. It has fla-
vors of hazelnut and spice,
and a mild woody finish.
U.S.: $3.60

LAS CABRILLAS **85**
PIZARRO

Honduras • *Size:* 5½" x 32
Filler/Binder: Mexico, Dom.
Rep. *Wrapper:* U.S.A./
Conn. Shade
This mild- to medium-bodied
cigar has a good balance of
flavors that tend toward coffee grounds. It has a smooth
taste. U.S.: $1.20

MACANUDO PORTOFI- **85**
NO

Jamaica • *Size:* 7" x 34
Filler: Dom. Rep., Mex., Jam.
Binder: Mexico *Wrapper:*
U.S.A./Conn. Shade
A delicate, light-brown wrap-
per leads to spicy and pep-
pery flavors and a mild,
cedary aftertaste. (09/01/94)
U.S.: $4.95

MONTECRUZ **85**
SUN-GROWN NO. 276

Dominican Republic • *Size:*
6" x 32 *Filler/Binder:* Dom.
Rep., Brazil *Wrapper:*
Indonesia
A cigar with light, peppery
flavors and a nice earthy
character. It is mild.
U.S.: $3.50

NAT SHERMAN **85**
EXCHANGE SELECTION
MURRAY HILL 7

Dominican Republic • *Size:*
6" x 38 *Filler:* Dom. Rep.
Binder: Mexico *Wrapper:*
U.S.A./Conn. Shade
A mild- to medium-bodied
cigar. It has a smooth, creamy
spice character with some flavors of nuts and herbs and a
woody finish. U.S.: $7.30

ORNELAS MATINEE **85**

Mexico • *Size:* 6" x 30
Filler/Binder/Wrapper: Mexico
A rough, rustic cigar with a
tight draw. It has an odd,
mothball-like taste on the
palate, with a mineral finish.
U.S.: $2.50

ROMEO Y JULIETA **85**
SHAKESPEARE
Cuba • *Size:* 6½" x 28
Filler/Binder/Wrapper: Cuba
This cigar has some solid,
spicy notes, but draws a bit
hot from a slightly loose fill.
(09/01/94) Price N/A

ROYAL JAMAICA GAU- **85**
CHO
Dominican Republic • *Size:*
5¼" x 33 *Filler:* Dom. Rep.,
Jamaica, Indonesia *Binder:*
Cameroon *Wrapper:*
Indonesia
A cigar with hints of the
earth, with a slightly leathery
character. It is a nicely bal-
anced, medium-bodied cigar.
U.S.: $1.30

ROYAL JAMAICA **85**
NO. 2 TUBE
Dominican Republic • *Size:*
6½" x 34 *Filler:* Dom. Rep.,
Jamaica, Indonesia *Binder:*
Cameroon *Wrapper:*
Indonesia
This cigar has a hint of salti-
ness and a mineral quality.
There are some spicy, earthy
flavors on the palate and a
dry, woody finish. U.S.: $4.65

SOSA SANTA FE **85**
Dominican Republic • *Size:*
6" x 35 *Filler/Binder:* Dom.
Rep. *Wrapper:* Ecuador
Although this cigar is bit flat
on the palate, it has a core of
herbs and pepper flavors that
end with a hint of spice.
U.S.: $3.50

TESOROS DE COPAN **85**
LINDA
Honduras • *Size:* 5⅝" x 38
Filler: Nicaragua, Honduras
Binder: Honduras *Wrapper:*
Ecuador
A well-made cigar with a
firm but good draw. It has an
herbal quality, with some
spice on the palate and a
woody finish. U.S.: $4.30

ZINO MOUTON **85**
CADET NO. 3
Honduras • *Size:* 5¾" x 36
Filler/Binder: Honduras
Wrapper: U.S.A./Conn.
Shade
This cigar has an herbal tone,
with a hint of nuttiness on
the palate. U.S.: $5.40

ASHTON PANETELA **84**
Dominican Republic • *Size:*
6" x 36 *Filler/Binder:* Dom.
Rep. *Wrapper:* U.S.A./
Conn. Shade
A hint of dryness on the
palate. It has an overall floral
character with some nutty
flavors. U.S.: $5.70

CANARIA D'ORO FINO **84**
Dominican Republic • *Size:*
6" x 31 *Filler:* Mexico, Dom.
Rep. *Binder/Wrapper:* Mexico
A cigar with an earthy and
leathery quality on the
palate. It is a bit salty overall,
with a woody finish.
U.S.: $2.65

CASA BLANCA **84**
PANETELA
Dominican Republic • *Size:*
6" x 36 *Filler:* Dom. Rep.
Binder: Mexico *Wrapper:*
U.S.A./Conn. Shade
A tight draw produces some
hot, vegetal flavors although
some spice comes through on
the finish. (09/01/94)
U.S.: $2.00

LA GLORIA CUBANA **84**
MEDAILLE D'OR NO. 4
Dominican Republic • *Size:*
6" x 32 *Filler:* Dom. Rep.,
Nicaragua *Binder/Wrapper:*
Ecuador
There is a core of spice and
wood flavors in this medium-
bodied cigar. U.S.: $2.60

MONTECRUZ **84**
SUN-GROWN
TUBULARES
Dominican Republic • *Size:*
6⅛" x 36 *Filler/Binder:* Dom.
Rep., Brazil *Wrapper:*
Indonesia
There are strong spice ele-
ments on an otherwise salty
character. It has a touch of
earthiness and a long woody
finish. U.S.: $4.25

NAT SHERMAN **84**
GOTHAM SELECTION
NO. 65
Dominican Republic • *Size:*
6" x 32 *Filler/Binder:* Dom.
Rep. *Wrapper:* U.S.A./
Conn. Shade
A nice-looking medium-bod-
ied cigar. It has an unusual
and pleasant hint of anise
and pepper flavors, with a
dry, woody finish. U.S.: $5.40

NAT SHERMAN MAN- **84**
HATTAN SELECTION
CHELSEA
Dominican Republic • *Size:*
6½" x 38 *Filler:* Dom. Rep.
Binder/Wrapper: Mexico
This is a nice, medium-bodied smoke. There are some
nut and dried fruit elements
on the palate, but it has a
very dry finish. U.S.: $4.80

ROMEO Y JULIETA **84**
BELVEDERE
Cuba • *Size:* 5½" x 39
Filler/Binder/Wrapper: Cuba
A pleasant cigar with some
woody flavors and spicy
notes. A tight draw.
(09/01/94) SF: 3.4

BERING GOLD NO. 1 **83**
Honduras • *Size:* 6¼" x 33
Filler: Dom. Rep., Honduras,
Nicaragua, Mexico *Binder:*
Honduras *Wrapper:* Mexico
A cigar with a light spiciness.
It is generally mild- to medi-
um-bodied, and has a good
balance. U.S.: $2.05

COHIBA LANCERO **83**
Cuba • *Size:* 7½" x 38
Filler/Binder/Wrapper: Cuba
This cigar was too tight.
Great tobacco flavors, but
the draw is simply too hard to
smoke. (09/01/94)
U.K.: £15.20

CREDO JUBILATE **83**
Dominican Republic • *Size:*
5" x 34 *Filler/Binder:* Dom.
Rep. *Wrapper:* U.S.A./
Conn. Shade
There are hints of dry nuts
on an otherwise herbal char-
acter. U.S.: $4.90

DAVIDOFF NO. 1 **83**
Dominican Republic • *Size:*
7½" x 38 *Filler/Binder:* Dom.
Rep. *Wrapper:* U.S.A./
Conn. Shade
The mild, light wrapper
delivers some mild herbal flavors; but there is an unpleas-
ant, short, balsa-wood finish.
(09/01/94) U.S.: $12.25

EL REY DEL MUNDO **83**
ELEGANTE
Cuba • *Size:* 6¾" x 28
Filler/Binder/Wrapper: Cuba
A nice, oily, brown wrapper
shows a solid, spicy-nut core
of flavors, but otherwise this
cigar is a bit bland and one-
dimensional. (09/01/94)
U.K.: £4.60

H. UPMANN NATU- **83**
RALES TUBE
Dominican Republic • *Size:*
6⅛" x 36 *Filler/Binder:* Dom.
Rep. *Wrapper:* Indonesia
A cigar with a vegetal char-
acter. But there are hints of
sweet wood, and a core of
decent tobacco flavors.
U.S.: $4.10

JOSÉ BENITO PANETELA **83**
Dominican Republic • *Size:*
6¾" x 38 *Filler:* Dom. Rep.
Binder: Honduras *Wrapper:*
Indonesia
A very tight draw on this
medium-bodied cigar. It has
solid flavor notes of nuts and
earth. U.S.: $3.80

JUAN CLEMENTE **83**
PANETELA
Dominican Republic • *Size:*
6½" x 34 *Filler/Binder:* Dom.

Rep. *Wrapper:*
U.S.A./Conn. Shade
This cigar has an overall veg-
etal character, but it is light,
simple and straightforward.
U.S.: $5.15

MACANUDO CLAY- **83**
BURNE
Jamaica • *Size:* 6" x 31
Filler: Dom. Rep., Mexico,
Jamaica *Binder:* Mexico
Wrapper: U.S.A./Conn.
Shade
This cigar has a dry wood
character that dominates a
slightly vegetal flavor profile.
U.S.: $3.60

PADRÓN CHICOS **83**
Nicaragua • *Size:* 5½" x 36
Filler/Binder/Wrapper:
Nicaragua
Although this mild- to medium-bodied cigar has some
hearty notes on the palate, it
is dominated by a strong
woodiness that ends with a
dry finish. U.S.: $1.90

PUROS INDIOS NO. 5 **83**
ESPECIAL COLORADO
CLARO
Honduras • *Size:* 5" x 36
Filler: Nicaragua, Dom. Rep.,
Brazil *Binder/Wrapper:*
Ecuador
A young cigar. It shows fla-
vors of spice and dried fruits,
and a very dry finish.
U.S.: $3.10

ZINO 83
MOUTON CADET NO. 2
Honduras • *Size:* 6" x 35
Filler/Binder: Honduras
Wrapper: U.S.A./Conn.
Shade
A well-made cigar. It has a
firm draw, and an overall
herbal character that has a
minty quality to it.
U.S.: $6.10

ASHTON ELEGANTE 82
Dominican Republic • *Size:*
6½" x 35 *Filler/Binder:* Dom.
Rep. *Wrapper:* U.S.A./
Conn. Shade
A mild cigar with some vegetal notes on the palate. It
also has a solid, woody character. U.S.: $6.25

CACIQUE JARAGUA #3 82
Dominican Republic • *Size:*
6¾" x 36 *Filler/Binder:* Dom.
Rep. *Wrapper:* U.S.A./
Conn. Shade
This is a mild cigar with a
light floral character and an
herbal note on the palate.
U.S.: $3.50

DON DIEGO 82
ROYAL PALMAS TUBES
Dominican Republic • *Size:*
6⅛" x 36 *Filler/Binder:* Dom.
Rep. *Wrapper:* U.S.A./
Conn. Shade
This is a mild cigar with a
firm, almost tight draw.
There are hints of dry wood
on the palate and the finish.
U.S.: $4.10

JOYA DE NICARAGUA 82
PETITE
Nicaragua • *Size:* 5½" x 38
Filler/Binder: Nicaragua
Wrapper: Ecuador
A vegetal character domi-
nates this cigar. It is mild,
almost thin on the palate,
with a balsa wood finish.
U.S.: $3.25

LICENCIADOS 82
PANETELA LINDA
Dominican Republic • *Size:*
7" x 38 *Filler:* Dom. Rep.
Binder: Honduras *Wrapper:*
U.S.A./Conn. Shade
A very tight draw limits this
cigar. But the mild, slightly
dry finish has hints of herbs
and nuts. (09/01/94)
U.S.: $3.25

MAYA PETIT 82
Honduras • *Size:* 5¼" x 34
Filler: Honduras, Nicaragua,
Dom. Rep. *Binder:* Dom.
Rep. *Wrapper:* U.S.A./
Conn. Shade
A pleasant, mild- to medium-
bodied cigar. It is very dry on
the palate, and there is a
leafy quality to the taste. It
has a hint of spiciness.
U.S.: $2.65

NAT SHERMAN LAND- 82
MARK SELECTION
METROPOLE
Dominican Republic • *Size:*
6" x 34 *Filler:* Dom. Rep.
Binder: Mexico *Wrapper:*
Cameroon
A straightforward, mild- to
medium-bodied cigar. It has
some herbal notes.
U.S.: $5.70

PETRUS TABACAGE 82
PALMA FINA
Honduras • *Size:* 6" x 38
Filler: Honduras, Nicaragua
Binder: Nicaragua *Wrapper:*
Ecuador
This is a mild cigar with a
firm draw. It has an herbal
character and a light, woody
finish. U.S.: $4.00

PLEIADES MARS 82
Dominican Republic • *Size:*
5" x 28 *Filler/Binder:* Dom.
Rep. *Wrapper:* U.S.A./
Conn. Shade
An unattractive wrapper on
this small, easy drawing cigar.
It has some earthy flavors.
U.S.: $6.35

POR LARRAÑAGA DELI- 82
CADOS
Dominican Republic • *Size:*
6½" x 36 *Filler/Binder:* Dom.
Rep. *Wrapper:* U.S.A./
Conn. Shade
An inconsistent cigar. It has
some smooth tobacco flavors
and a light, dry finish.
(09/01/94) U.S.: $4.00

PUROS INDIOS 82
PETIT PERLA
Honduras • *Size:* 5" x 38
Filler: Nicaragua, Dom. Rep.,
Brazil *Binder/Wrapper:*
Ecuador
A cigar with a loose fill. It
has a spicy character, with a
dry, papery finish. U.S.: $3.35

SOSA FAMILY SELEC- 82
TION NO. 6
Dominican Republic • *Size:*
6¼" x 38 *Filler/Binder:* Dom.
Rep. *Wrapper:* U.S.A./
Conn. Shade

This cigar is dominated by dry herbal flavors that verge on grassy. It is light and easy. U.S.: $4.15

AVO NO. 4 81
Dominican Republic • *Size:* 7" x 38 *Filler/Binder:* Dom. Rep. *Wrapper:* U.S.A./ Conn. Shade
This cigar appears well-made, but a tough draw leads into a dry, one-dimensional flavor. Some pepper notes, but with a bite. (09/01/94) U.S.: $6.50

BACCARAT PANETELA 81
Honduras • *Size:* 6" x 38 *Filler/Wrapper:* Honduras *Binder:* Mexico
This cigar showed some inconsistency with a loose draw. It also was quite mild with a somewhat papery finish. U.S.: $2.45

BANCES UNIQUE 81
Honduras • *Size:* 5½" x 38 *Filler:* Nicaragua *Binder:* Mexico *Wrapper:* Ecuador
This cigar has a firm, solid draw with a decent spiciness. An unattractive wrapper. (09/01/94) U.S.: $1.50

DAVIDOFF NO. 3 81
Dominican Republic • *Size:* 5⅛" x 30 *Filler/Binder:* Dom. Rep. *Wrapper:* U.S.A./ Conn. Shade
This cigar has a sharp metallic note, although it finishes with a touch of wood on the palate. U.S.: $6.50

DUNHILL PANETELA 81
Canary Islands • *Size:* 6" x 30 *Filler/Binder:* Canary Islands *Wrapper:* Cameroon
This cigar is a little rough. But it has a good draw, and has good light spice flavors that finish on a light, nutty note. U.S.: $4.90

NAT SHERMAN MAN- 81
HATTAN SELECTION
TRIBECA
Dominican Republic • *Size:* 6" x 31 *Filler:* Dom. Rep. *Binder/Wrapper:* Mexico
This cigar has a salty character. There are floral notes on an otherwise woody finish. U.S.: $4.40

ORNELAS NO. 6 81
Mexico • *Size:* 5" x 38 *Filler/Binder/Wrapper:* Mexico
There's some rough construction in this cigar. It has some nice spicy flavors on a mild character, with a very dry wood finish. U.S.: $5.25

PARTAGAS NO. 6 81
Dominican Republic • *Size:* 6" x 34 *Filler:* Dom. Rep., Mexico *Binder:* Mexico *Wrapper:* Cameroon
This cigar exhibited some roughness, and uneven construction. It had some spicy flavors, with a very dry finish. U.S.: $4.10

TE-AMO 81
IMPULSE LIGHTS
Mexico • *Size:* 5" x 32 *Filler/Binder/Wrapper:* Mexico
A mild cigar with a solid earthy element on the palate. U.S.: $.90

TE-AMO TORERO 81
Mexico • *Size:* 6³⁄₁₆" x 35 *Filler/Binder/Wrapper:* Mexico
A nice-looking cigar, but with a very tight draw. Some dryness on the palate creates a mild smoothness, yet it lacks flavor. (09/01/94) U.S.: $2.45

AURORA PALMAS 80
EXTRA
Dominican Republic • *Size:* 6¾" x 35 *Filler:* U.S.A./ Conn. Broadleaf *Binder:* Sumatra *Wrapper:* U.S.A./Conn. Broadleaf
This rustic cigar has a burnt taste with some vegetal notes and very little spice. (09/01/94) U.S.: $2.48

DON TITO PANETELA 80
U.S.A. • *Size:* 6⅛" x 37 *Filler:* Honduras, Nicaragua, Dom. Rep. *Binder:* Nicaragua *Wrapper:* Ecuador
A very yellow, rough wrapper. This cigar has a vegetal quality with a dry wood, almost papery finish. U.S.: $4.75

EL RICO HABANO 80
NO. 1
U.S.A. • *Size:* 7½" x 38 *Filler:* Dom. Rep. *Binder:* Nicaragua *Wrapper:* Ecuador
A tight draw with a spicy character and a dry, coffee-bean flavor. (09/01/94) U.S.: $4.10

HOYO DE MONTERREY DELIGHTS — 80

Honduras • *Size:* 6¼" x 37
Filler/Binder: Honduras
Wrapper: U.S.A./Conn.
Shade
This cigar smokes solidly with some straightforward, spice flavors, but with a hot aftertaste and finish. (09/01/94) U.S.: $1.55

MONTE CANARIO PANETELA — 80

Canary Islands • *Size:* 6" x 38
Filler/Binder: Dom. Rep., Brazil, Canary Islands *Wrapper:* U.S.A./Conn. Shade
This is a mild cigar. It has dry balsa-wood finish. A rustic wrapper. U.S.: $5.00

MONTECRUZ SUN-GROWN NO. 281 — 80

Dominican Republic • *Size:* 6" x 28 *Filler/Binder:* Dom. Rep., Brazil *Wrapper:* Indonesia
A cigar with a strong vegetal tone. It is also quite salty on the palate, and has a light, dry wood finish. U.S.: $3.40

ORNELAS NO. 5 — 80

Mexico • *Size:* 6" x 38
Filler/Binder/Wrapper: Mexico
This is a mild cigar with a powder-like taste on the palate. A woody finish. U.S.: $6.00

PARTICULARES PETIT — 80

Honduras • *Size:* 5⅝" x 34
Filler: Honduras, Nicaragua, Dom. Rep. *Binder:* Dom. Rep. *Wrapper:* Ecuador
A rough and rustic cigar. It has a strong vegetal charac-
ter, with a mineral overlay on the palate. It is sharp-tasting. U.S.: $2.50

DON LINO PANATELAS — 79

Honduras • *Size:* 7" x 36
Filler/Binder: Sumatra *Wrapper:* U.S.A./Conn. Shade
A pretty wrapper doesn't deliver. The cigar has a tough draw with bitter flavors and a short, flat finish. (09/01/94) U.S.: $3.76

NAT SHERMAN MANHATTAN SELECTION BEEKMAN — 79

Dominican Republic • *Size:* 5½" x 28 *Filler:* Dom. Rep. *Binder/Wrapper:* Mexico
A very rustic cigar. This cigar has a salty, almost fishy note, with some hints of cigarette taste. Very small and mild. U.S.: $4.10

PLEIADES PERSEUS — 79

Dominican Republic • *Size:* 5" x 34 *Filler:* Dom. Rep. *Binder:* Dom Rep. *Wrapper:* U.S.A./Conn. Shade
A cigar with a strong grassy taste on the palate. It burned hot and had a gritty quality. U.S.: $6.00

DON TOMAS INTERNATIONAL NO. 4 — 78

Honduras • *Size:* 7" x 36
Filler/Binder/Wrapper: Honduras
A very tight draw with hot, harsh spices and a camphor element on the palate. (09/01/94) U.S.: $4.60

NAT SHERMAN EXCHANGE SELECTION ACADEMY 2 — 78

Dominican Republic • *Size:* 5" x 31 *Filler:* Dom. Rep. *Binder:* Mexico *Wrapper:* U.S.A./Conn. Shade
A very mild cigar. There is a light grassy component to the flavor, and a dry, woody finish. U.S.: $5.40

DON JUAN LINDAS — 77

Nicaragua • *Size:* 5½" x 38
Filler: Nicaragua, Mexico
Binder/Wrapper: Nicaragua
An underfilled cigar that burns hot with a bitter, sour presence in the mouth and some dry, grassy flavors. (09/01/94) U.S.: $2.65

VARGAS DIPLOMATICO — 77

Canary Islands • *Size:* 5½" x 36 *Filler:* Canary Islands, Dom. Rep. *Binder/Wrapper:* Indonesia
A rustic, rather flat-tasting cigar. There are some hints of toasty flavors, and some earth on the finish. U.S.: $4.75

DON DIEGO BABIES — 75

Dominican Republic • *Size:* 5¹⁄₁₆" x 33 *Filler/Binder:* Dom. Rep. *Wrapper:* U.S.A./Conn. Shade
A very rustic cigar with a saltiness on the palate. It also has a somewhat flinty aftertaste. U.S.: $1.10

Odd-Sized

Most of the following tasting notes appeared in the March/April 1997 issue of Cigar Aficionado. *Exceptions are indicated by a date in parentheses at the end of the tasting note.*

MONTECRISTO "A" 91
Cuba • *Size:* 9¼" x 47
Filler/Binder/Wrapper: Cuba
A great-looking cigar, with an oily sheen on the wrapper. An excellent draw leads to a sweet spice, nutmeg flavor with an earthy undertone. It has a mild finish that intensifies. Great balance.
U.K.: £25.85

PADRÓN MAGNUM 91
Nicaragua • *Size:* 9" x 50
Filler/Binder/Wrapper: Nicaragua
A smooth, well-balanced medium-bodied smoke. It has strong, solid flavors of nuts and coffee beans. It is a very well-made cigar. U.S.: $6.30

DIAMOND CROWN 90
ROBUSTO NO. 4
Dominican Republic • *Size:* 5½" x 54 *Filler/Binder:* Dom. Rep. *Wrapper:* U.S.A./Conn. Shade
A medium-bodied cigar with an excellent balance of flavors. There is a good tobacco core, with a perfumed, floral character and a nutty finish.
U.S.: $10.50

EL REY DEL MUNDO 89
ORIGINALE
Honduras • *Size:* 5⅝" x 45
Filler/Binder: Honduras
Wrapper: Ecuador
A rich-tasting cigar with flavors of toasted nuts and baked cocoa beans. It has a strong earthy spiciness on the finish. U.S.: $4.00

EVELIO ROBUSTO 89
Honduras • *Size:* 4¾" x 54
Filler: Dom. Rep., Nicaragua
Binder: Nicaragua *Wrapper:* Ecuador
A medium-bodied cigar with a lot of spicy flavors. It has a long finish with hints of leather and the earth.
U.S.: $5.25

ASHTON CABINET 88
SELECTION NO. 7
Dominican Republic • *Size:* 6¼" x 52 *Filler/Binder:* Dom. Rep. *Wrapper:* U.S.A./Conn. Shade
A well-made cigar with solid flavors of pepper and nuts, and a nice creamy character. There are some floral notes, with a bit of tangy youthfulness. U.S.: $9.75

LA GLORIA CUBANA 88
GLORIAS EXTRA
Dominican Republic • *Size:* 6¼" x 46 *Filler/Binder:* Dom. Rep., Nicaragua *Wrapper:* Ecuador
A spicy, medium-bodied cigar. It has good coffee bean flavors on a solid herbal core and a nice spicy finish.
U.S.: $3.75

PUNCH DELUXE SERIES 88
CORONA
Honduras • *Size:* 6¼" x 45
Filler/Binder: Honduras, Nicaragua, Dom. Rep.
Wrapper: Ecuador
This is medium- to full-bodied cigar with a strong sweet spice character. There are notes of sweet herbs, leather and dry cedar with a touch of nuttiness. U.S.: $3.95

PUNCH GRAN CRU 88
BRITANNIA
Honduras • *Size:* 6¼" x 50
Filler/Binder: Honduras, Nicaragua, Dom. Rep. *Wrapper:* U.S.A./Conn. Shade
This medium-bodied cigar is filled with solid tobacco flavors, and is backed with a cedary tone and a straightforward herbalness. U.S.: $5.95

ROMEO Y JULIETA 88
PRESIDENTE
Dominican Republic • *Size:* 7" x 43 *Filler:* Dom. Rep., Brazil *Binder:* U.S.A.
Wrapper: Indonesia
An earthy aroma leads into a well-balanced, medium-bodied cigar. It has flavors of spices and a leathery, woody finish. U.S.: $4.45

DIAMOND CROWN 87
ROBUSTO NO. 5
Dominican Republic • *Size:* 4½" x 54 *Filler/Binder:* Dom. Rep. *Wrapper:* U.S.A./Conn. Shade
A well-made cigar with some characteristics of youth. But there is a solid core of cedar flavors with hints of nuts and a floral undertone. U.S.: $9.50

ORNELAS 250 **87**
Mexico • *Size:* 9½" x 64
Filler/Binder/Wrapper: Mexico
One of the biggest cigars in
the tasting. It's almost too big
to enjoy, but it has a solid
core of sweet spice and nutty
flavors with a creamy aftertaste. U.S.: $31.00

PAUL GARMIRIAN BOM- **87**
BONE
Dominican Republic • *Size:*
3½" x 43 *Filler/Binder:* Dom.
Rep. *Wrapper:* U.S.A./
Conn. Shade
A well-balanced, small
smoke. It has elements of
cream and cedar on the
palate and a solid tobacco
aftertaste. U.S.: $5.85

ROYAL JAMAICA DOU- **87**
BLE CORONA
Dominican Republic • *Size:*
7" x 45 *Filler:* Jamaica
Binder: Cameroon *Wrapper:*
Indonesia
This is a medium- to full-
bodied cigar. It has a very
sweet tobacco character with
a core of sweet spice flavors.
U.S.: $4.85

TE-AMO NEW YORK **87**
LAGUARDIA
Mexico • *Size:* 5" x 54
Filler/Binder/Wrapper: Mexico
A well-made cigar with a
core of spiciness on an otherwise herbal character. It has
some smoked woodiness on
the finish. U.S.: $3.10

8-9-8 COLLECTION **86**
MONARCH
Jamaica • *Size:* 6¼" x 45
Filler: Jamaica, Dom. Rep.

Binder: Mexico *Wrapper:*
U.S.A./Conn. Shade
An elegant cigar. It is a mild,
mellow smoke with a creamy,
light spicy character and a
solid woody finish.
U.S.: $9.00

ARTURO FUENTE **86**
CHATEAU FUENTE
ROYAL SALUTE
Dominican Republic • *Size:*
7⅝" x 54 *Filler/Binder:* Dom.
Rep. *Wrapper:* U.S.A./
Conn. Shade
A well-balanced, medium-
bodied cigar with a creamy,
herbal character and a hint
of woodiness on the finish.
U.S.: $5.75

BERING BARON **86**
Honduras • *Size:* 7¼" x 42
Filler: Dom. Rep., Mexico,
Nicaragua, Honduras
Binder: Honduras *Wrapper:*
Mexico
A cigar with an earthy char-
acter. There are flavors of
sweet spice with a woody fin-
ish. U.S.: $2.35

C.A.O. GOLD **86**
CORONA GORDA
Nicaragua • *Size:* 6½" x 50
Filler/Binder: Nicaragua
Wrapper: Ecuador
A cigar with a suppleness and
a smooth draw. It has an
herbal character with a few
hints of spice, and a slight
earthy, rough finish.
U.S.: $7.10

CASA BLANCA JER- **86**
OBOAM
Dominican Republic • *Size:*
10" x 66 *Filler:* Dom. Rep.,

Brazil *Binder:* Mexico
Wrapper: U.S.A./Conn.
Shade
A huge cigar. But there is
plenty of flavor packed into
it. The cigar has a creamy
character with some hints of
herbs. U.S.: $6.50

DIAMOND CROWN **86**
ROBUSTO NO. 1
Dominican Republic • *Size:*
8½" x 54 *Filler/Binder:* Dom.
Rep. *Wrapper:* U.S.A./
Conn. Shade
This is a very well-balanced,
medium-bodied cigar. It has
nutty flavors, with a slight
floral character and a light
peppery finish. U.S.: $18.00

GILBERTO OLIVA VIA- **86**
JANTE
Nicaragua • *Size:* 6" x 52
Filler/Binder: Dom. Rep.,
Nicaragua *Wrapper:*
Ecuador
A solid, medium-bodied
smoke. It has a creamy char-
acter with some herbal fla-
vors and a peppery note on
the finish. U.S.: $4.60

MONTECRISTO **86**
DOUBLE CORONA
Dominican Republic • *Size:*
6¼" x 50 *Filler/Binder:* Dom.
Rep. *Wrapper:*
U.S.A./Conn. Shade
This is a solid mild- to medium-bodied cigar. It has a
woody character with some
hints of nuts, and a slightly
vegetal finish. U.S.: $8.75

**SANCHO PANZA SAN- 86
CHO**
Cuba • *Size:* 9¼" x 47
Filler/Binder/Wrapper: Cuba
A cigar with very light, mild
characteristics. It has a
cedary note on the palate
with some papery flavors.
U.K.: £18.20

BERING CORONADOS 85
Honduras • *Size:* 5³⁄₁₆" x 45
Filler/Wrapper: Mexico, Dom.
Rep., Nicaragua, Honduras
Binder: Honduras
A mild- to medium-bodied
cigar. It has a perfumed quali-
ty with light, earthy aromas
and a light spiciness.
U.S.: $1.60

**CANARIA D'ORO 85
SUPREMOS**
Dominican Republic • *Size:*
7" x 45 *Filler:* Mexico, Dom.
Rep. *Binder/Wrapper:* Mexico
This is a solid spicy cigar
with an earthy character. It
finishes a little dry. A well-
made smoke. U.S.: $3.60

**EVELIO ROBUSTO 85
LARGA**
Honduras • *Size:* 6" x 54
Filler: Dom. Rep., Nicaragua
Binder: Nicaragua *Wrapper:*
Ecuador
This cigar has evidence of
young tobacco. There are
strong flavors of herbs with
some hints of sweet spice.
Should improve with age.
U.S.: $6.15

JOSÉ MARTÍ REMEDIO 85
Nicaragua • *Size:* 5½" x 45
Filler: Nicaragua, Honduras,

Dom. Rep. *Binder:* Hon-
duras *Wrapper:* Ecuador
This cigar shows medium-
bodied complexity with an
earthy aroma, but it has a
short finish with a bit of dryness. U.S.: $1.75

**NESTOR 747 VINTAGE 85
CABINET SERIES NO. 2**
Honduras • *Size:* 4¾" x 54
Filler: Honduras *Binder:*
Nicaragua *Wrapper:*
Ecuador
Although this cigar has a dry
finish, there some nut and
spice flavors on the palate. It
is a bit young. U.S.: $4.80

**EL REY DEL MUNDO 84
RECTANGULARE**
Honduras • *Size:* 5⅝" x 45
Filler/Binder: Honduras
Wrapper: Ecuador
A medium-bodied cigar with
hints of dried orange peel,
and a mintiness on top of a
solid tobacco character. It is
young. U.S.: $3.50

**MONTECRUZ SUN- 84
GROWN INDIVIDUALES**
Dominican Republic • *Size:*
8" x 46 *Filler/Binder:* Dom.
Rep., Brazil *Wrapper:*
Indonesia
Good balance with a woody,
earthy character and some
sweet white pepper flavors. It
finishes a little flat.
U.S.: $15.00

**TE-AMO NEW YORK 84
WALL STREET**
Mexico • *Size:* 6" x 52
Filler/Binder/Wrapper: Mexico
A medium-bodied cigar with
a decent balance. It has an

herbal character with some
hints of woodiness.
U.S.: $3.60

**BERING 83
CORONA GRANDE**
Honduras • *Size:* 6¼" x 46
Filler/Wrapper: Mexico,
Nicaragua, Dom. Rep., Hon-
duras *Binder:* Honduras
A medium-bodied cigar that
has some woody flavors and
an overall vegetal character.
U.S.: $1.95

**PETRUS TABACAGE 83
NO. IV 89**
Honduras • *Size:* 5⅝" x 38
Filler: Nicaragua *Binder:*
Honduras *Wrapper:* Ecuador
A slightly salty cigar with
some hints of spice on the
palate and a dry finish.
U.S.: $3.50

CRUZ REAL NO. 28 82
Mexico • *Size:* 8½" x 54
Filler/Binder/Wrapper: Mexico
A rustic, rough cigar with a
loose fill. It has a vegetal
pungency, with some hints of
wood and spice. U.S.: $6.35

**EL REY DEL MUNDO 82
CORONA**
Honduras • *Size:* 5⅝" x 45
Filler/Binder: Honduras
Wrapper: Ecuador
This cigar shows some youth.
It has decent flavors, but
overall it is a little rough.
U.S.: $3.25

LAS CABRILLAS BALBOA 82

Honduras • *Size:* 7½" x 54
Filler/Binder: Mexico, Dom.
Rep. *Wrapper:* U.S.A./
Conn. Shade
This is a rustic cigar made
with young tobacco. It has
some spiciness and an overall
herbal character. U.S.: $2.90

ROYAL JAMAICA NO. 1 TUBE 82

Dominican Republic • *Size:*
6" x 45 *Filler:* Jamaica
Binder: Cameroon *Wrapper:*
Indonesia
A cigar with a slightly tight
draw. It is a little rough on
the palate, but it has some
solid tobacco flavors with a
slight earthiness. U.S.: $5.30

EL REY DEL MUNDO ROBUSTO ZAVALLA 81

Honduras • *Size:* 5" x 54
Filler/Binder: Honduras
Wrapper: Ecuador
A cigar with a tight draw. It
has some decent medium-
bodied herbal flavors, but a
flat finish. U.S.: $3.75

JOSÉ MARTÍ MACEO 81

Dominican Republic • *Size:*
6⅞" x 45 *Filler:* Dom. Rep.,
Brazil *Binder:* Mexico
Wrapper: U.S.A./Conn.
Shade
A rustic cigar. There is an
overall creaminess on the
palate, but it has a slightly
grassy undertone. U.S.: $3.75

PLEIADES SATURNE 81

Dominican Republic • *Size:*
8" x 46 *Filler/Binder:* Dom.

Rep. *Wrapper:*
U.S.A./Conn. Shade
A cigar with a strong, dry
herbal character. It is light-
bodied and has a dry wood
finish. U.S.: $10.90

THE GRIFFIN'S NO. 200 81

Dominican Republic • *Size:*
7" x 44 *Filler/Binder:* Dom.
Rep. *Wrapper:*
U.S.A./Conn. Shade
A somewhat harsh cigar with
very dry, papery flavors. It
has some spice on the finish.
U.S.: $6.75

NAT SHERMAN VIP SELECTION MORGAN 80

Dominican Republic • *Size:*
7" x 42 *Filler/Binder:* Dom.
Rep. *Wrapper:* U.S.A./
Conn. Shade
A simple cigar with a light
vegetal character. There is a
hint of nuttiness on an otherwise dry finish. U.S.: $6.60

ROYAL JAMAICA GOLIATH 80

Dominican Republic • *Size:*
9" x 64 *Filler:* Jamaica
Binder: Cameroon *Wrapper:*
Indonesia
Lives up to its name. It's got
an undertone of damp earthiness, and it showed some
inconsistency with a tight
draw. U.S.: $10.00

BERING CASINOS 79

Honduras • *Size:* 7⅛" x 42
Filler: Dom. Rep, Mexico,
Nicaragua, Honduras
Binder: Honduras *Wrapper:*
U.S.A./Conn. Shade

This cigar is dominated by
dry grassy flavors, with a hint
of sweet tobacco on the finish. The construction is a little rough. U.S.: $2.90

PLEIADES NEPTUNE 79

Dominican Republic • *Size:*
7½" x 42 *Filler/Binder:* Dom.
Rep. *Wrapper:*
U.S.A./Conn. Shade
A flat finish and a dry papery
character dominate this cigar.
It is light-bodied, and there is
a hint of a spice on the
palate. U.S.: $9.85

PUNCH AFTER DINNER 74

Honduras • *Size:* 7¼" x 45
Filler/Binder: Honduras,
Nicaragua, Dom. Rep.
Wrapper: Ecuador
A very rustic cigar. It also
had a poor draw. There are
some hints of coffee bean and
spice on the palate, but it was
hard to get past the poor construction. U.S.: $3.00

Figurado

*Most of the following Figurado
tasting notes appeared in the
Winter 1995 issue of* Cigar
Aficionado. *Exceptions are
indicated by a date in parentheses at the end of the tasting
note.*

MONTECRISTO NO. 2 94

Cuba • *Size:* 6⅛" x 52
Filler/Binder/Wrapper: Cuba
The benchmark torpedo. It is
loaded with rich, complex
flavors such as cinnamon,
with strong full-bodied notes
of chocolate and leather, and

a long spicy finish.
U.K.: £11.45

DIPLOMATICOS NO. 2   92
Cuba • *Size:* 6⅛" x 52
Filler/Binder/Wrapper: Cuba
A well-balanced cigar with a
strong earthy characteristic
and a complex core of spicy
flavors that ends in a long
finish. Price N/A

FUENTE FUENTE   92
OPUS X NO. 2
Dominican Republic • *Size:*
6¼" x 52 *Filler/Binder/Wrapper:* Dom. Rep.
A beautiful, oily wrapper.
This cigar has an excellent
draw and is loaded with spice
and nut flavors, with solid
notes of cedar. A long earthy
finish. U.S.: $13.50

PUROS INDIOS   92
PIRAMIDES NO. 1
Honduras • *Size:* 7½" x 60
Filler: Brazil, Dom. Rep.,
Nicaragua *Binder/Wrapper:*
Ecuador
A full-flavored cigar loaded
with sweet earthy flavors
including cocoa and leather,
with a coffee bean character
on the palate. U.S.: $6.50

BOLIVAR   90
BELICOSO FINO
Cuba • *Size:* 5½" x 52
Filler/Binder/Wrapper: Cuba
A beautiful small torpedo.
This full-bodied smoke has a
strong spiciness and sweet
earthy quality with a pleasant
tangy finish. U.K.: £10.00

PUROS INDIOS   90
PIRAMIDES NO. 2
Honduras • *Size:* 6½" x 46
Filler: Brazil, Dom. Rep.,
Nicaragua *Binder/Wrapper:*
Ecuador
This is a rich-tasting pyramid
with lots of spice and nuts on
the palate and a long earthy
finish. Well made with a
smooth draw. U.S.: $5.50

ROMEO Y JULIETA BELI- 90
COSO
Cuba • *Size:* 5½" x 52
Filler/Binder/Wrapper: Cuba
A handsome pyramid with a
gray hue. It draws well and is
full-bodied with a rich, pep-
pery, spicy character and a
long finish. (06/01/93)
U.K.: £10.00

SIGNATURE COLLEC-   90
TION TORPEDO
Dominican Republic • *Size:*
6¼" x 54 *Filler:* Dom. Rep.,
Honduras, Nicaragua
Binder/Wrapper: Ecuador
A very nice medium-bodied
cigar. Nutty flavors, including chestnuts, dominate and
there is a pleasant sweet spice
character with hints of nutmeg. Medium-length finish.
U.S.: $7.95

ARTURO FUENTE   89
HEMINGWAY
SHORT STORY
Dominican Republic • *Size:*
4¼" x 49 *Filler/Binder:* Dom.
Rep. *Wrapper:* Cameroon
This cigar's unique size makes
blind tasting impossible. It is
packed with flavors of pep-
per, spice and espresso coffee.
U.S.: $4.15

ARTURO FUENTE   89
HEMINGWAY SIGNATURE
Dominican Republic • *Size:*
6" x 46 *Filler/Binder:* Dom.
Rep. *Wrapper:* Cameroon
A beautiful dark wrapper. A
smooth, rich cigar with an
earthy combination of spice,
pepper and leather flavors
and a cedary finish.
U.S.: $5.85

ASHTON CABINET   89
SELECTION NO. 10
Dominican Republic • *Size:*
7½" x 52 *Filler/Binder:* Dom.
Rep. *Wrapper:*
U.S.A./Conn. Shade
A mild- to medium-bodied
cigar. It has a delicious combination of creaminess and a
cocoa bean flavor with sweetish tobacco flavors. A slightly
dry woody finish.
U.S.: $15.50

H. UPMANN NO. 2   89
Cuba • *Size:* 6⅛" x 52
Filler/Binder/Wrapper: Cuba
A full-bodied smoke with fla-
vors of cocoa bean and nut-
meg, and a strong nutty core.
A smooth, peppery finish. It
is a little young. U.K.: £10.60

ASHTON CABINET   88
SELECTION NO. 3
Dominican Republic • *Size:*
6" x 46 *Filler/Binder:* Dom.
Rep. *Wrapper:*
U.S.A./Conn. Shade
A medium-bodied cigar with
a creamy texture and a solid
core of nutty flavors that lead
into a light spiciness.
U.S.: $10.50

EL REY DEL MUNDO 88
GRANDES DE ESPAÑA
Cuba • *Size:* 7½" x 38
Filler/Binder/Wrapper: Cuba
Extremely well crafted and
easy to draw. Medium-bodied
with rich, nutty, coffee aromas and flavors and a lingering aftertaste. (06/01/93)
SF: 11

MACABI 88
BELICOSO FINO
Dominican Republic • *Size:*
6¼" x 52 *Filler:* Dom. Rep.,
Nicaragua *Binder:* Mexico
Wrapper: U.S.A./Conn.
Shade
A smooth-tasting cigar with
nice flavors of nuts and cinnamon and a creamy texture.
U.S.: $6.80

OSCAR NO. 700 88
Dominican Republic • *Size:*
7" x 54 *Filler/Binder:* Dom.
Rep. *Wrapper:* U.S.A.
This cigar has a pleasant
herbal aroma, and offers up
flavors of nuts and spice on
the palate. It finishes with
hints of dry spices.
U.S.: $14.20

PAUL GARMIRIAN BELI- 88
COSO
Dominican Republic • *Size:*
6¼" x 52 *Filler/Binder:* Dom.
Rep. *Wrapper:*
U.S.A./Conn. Shade
A medium-bodied cigar with
rich, spicy flavors. It has a
solid, earthy tobacco backbone but lacks a bit of intensity. U.S.: $11.20

PAUL GARMIRIAN CEL- 88
EBRATION
Dominican Republic • *Size:*
9" x 50 *Filler/Binder:* Dom.
Rep. *Wrapper:*
U.S.A./Conn. Shade
A flavor-packed smoke that
burns extremely well. It has
peppery aromas and flavors
and a rich finish. (06/01/93)
U.S.: $23.00

SOSA FAMILY SELEC- 88
TION NO. 2
Dominican Republic • *Size:*
6¼" x 54 *Filler/Binder:* Dom.
Rep. *Wrapper:* U.S.A./
Conn. Shade
A cigar with strong nut and
toast flavors. It has a medium-bodied smoke. A well-made, attractive cigar.
U.S.: $7.00

TEMPLE HALL BELI- 88
COSO
Jamaica • *Size:* 6" x 50
Filler: Jamaica, Dom. Rep.,
Mexico *Binder:* Mexico
Wrapper: U.S.A./Conn.
Shade
A well-balanced, medium-bodied cigar with a light
spiciness that smooths out
through a creamy and nutty
core. A woody finish.
U.S.: $8.10

ASHTON CABINET 87
SELECTION NO. 1
Dominican Republic • *Size:*
9" x 52 *Filler/Binder:* Dom.
Rep. *Wrapper:* U.S.A./
Conn. Shade
Another big cigar, yet it
shows reserve. It's mild and
fresh with light coffee, slight-ly herbal aromas and flavors.
(06/01/93) U.S.: $18.50

ASHTON CABINET 87
SELECTION NO. 2
Dominican Republic • *Size:*
7" x 47 *Filler/Binder:* Dom.
Rep. *Wrapper:*
U.S.A./Conn. Shade
A medium-bodied cigar with
a smooth, creamy texture
that rounds out to straight-forward, nutty flavors with a
touch of spice. U.S.: $12.75

AVO BELICOSO 87
Dominican Republic • *Size:*
6" x 50 *Filler/Binder:* Dom.
Rep. *Wrapper:* U.S.A./
Conn. Shade
This is a mellow cigar with a
medium-bodied smoke. It has
a floral aroma with solid flavors of toasted nuts and a
creamy, sweetish character.
U.S.: $9.00

CARRINGTON NO. 8 87
Dominican Republic • *Size:*
6⅞" x 60 *Filler/Binder:* Dom.
Rep. *Wrapper:* U.S.A./
Conn. Shade
A pleasant, mild smoke with
a creamy texture and a walnut-like flavor with an earthy
finish. U.S.: $6.40

DAVIDOFF 87
SPECIAL SERIES "T"
Dominican Republic • *Size:*
6" x 52 *Filler/Binder:* Dom.
Rep. *Wrapper:* U.S.A./
Conn. Shade
This is a pleasant medium-bodied cigar that has a soft
spicy character and a creamy
texture, but with a flat finish.
U.S.: $13.00

EL REY DEL MUNDO 87
FLOR DE LLANEZA
Honduras • *Size:* 6½" x 54
Filler/Binder: Honduras, Dom.
Rep *Wrapper:* Ecuador
This is a full-flavored cigar
showing good balance and
notes of leather with an
earthy quality. It has a slight-
ly dry, flat finish. U.S.: $7.00

FONSECA TRIANGU- 87
LARE
Dominican Republic • *Size:*
5½" x 56 *Filler:* Dom. Rep.
Binder: Mexico *Wrapper:*
U.S.A./Conn. Shade
A cigar with a mellow quality
and a medium body. It has a
dry spiciness and a pleasant,
creamy texture with a long
finish. U.S.: $7.00

LA FLOR DOMINICANA 87
FIGURADO
Dominican Republic • *Size:*
6½" x 52 *Filler/Binder:* Dom.
Rep. *Wrapper:* U.S.A./
Conn. Shade
A well-balanced, medium-
bodied cigar. It has flavors of
sweet nuts and toast with a
light finish. This cigar was
rated under the brand name
Los Libertadores. U.S.: $7.20

LA GLORIA CUBANA 87
MEDAILLE D'OR NO. 1
Cuba • *Size:* 7⅛" x 36
Filler/Binder/Wrapper: Cuba
Hard to draw, but it burns
evenly and delivers light cof-
fee and clove aromas and fla-
vors. (06/01/93) SF: 10.8

LA GLORIA CUBANA 87
PIRAMIDES
U.S.A. • *Size:* 7¼" x 56
Filler: Dom. Rep., Nicaragua
Binder/Wrapper: Ecuador
This is a medium-bodied
style for this brand. It has
solid spicy flavors and a
woody finish. U.S.: $7.50

MACANUDO 87
DUKE OF WINDSOR
Jamaica • *Size:* 6" x 50
Filler: Jamaica, Dom. Rep.,
Mexico *Binder:* Mexico
Wrapper: U.S.A./Conn.
Shade
This is a mellow cigar with a
mild to medium body. It has
some delicate spice notes on
otherwise woody flavors, and
it has a bit of a tangy finish.
U.S.: $7.25

MONTECRISTO NO. 2 87
Dominican Republic • *Size:*
6" x 50 *Filler/Binder:* Dom.
Rep. *Wrapper:* U.S.A.
A mild- to medium-bodied
cigar with a nice earthy quality and flavors of spice and
nuts with a light, well-balanced finish. U.S.: $12.00

NAT SHERMAN METRO- 87
POLITAN SELECTION
METROPOLITAN
Dominican Republic • *Size:*
7" x 52 *Filler/Binder:* Dom.
Rep. *Wrapper:* U.S.A./
Conn. Shade
A mellow cigar with plenty
of nuttiness on the palate. It
has a slightly balsa-like fin-
ish, but a spiciness compen-
sates for the dryness.
U.S.: $8.70

PARTAGAS CULEBRA 87
Cuba • *Size:* 5¾" x 39
Filler/Binder/Wrapper: Cuba
An unusual cigar in the marketplace, the three-cigar
braid. It has a sweet woody
character and decent con-
struction. It's just odd-look-
ing. U.K.: £11.00

ROMEO Y JULIETA 87
CELESTIAL FINO
Cuba • *Size:* 5¾" x 46
Filler/Binder/Wrapper: Cuba
It looks a little coarse with a
rough wrapper, but this pyramid smokes well, with an
enticing rosemary, spicy character and a smooth texture.
(06/01/93) Price N/A

TROYA NO. 81 TORPEDO 87
Dominican Republic • *Size:*
7" x 54 *Filler/Binder:* Dom.
Rep. *Wrapper:* U.S.A./
Conn. Shade
A well-made medium-bodied
cigar with strong nut and
solid tobacco flavors. It also
has a spicy character with a
ripe finish. U.S.: $6.00

V CENTENNIAL 87
TORPEDO
Honduras • *Size:* 7" x 54
Filler: Dom. Rep., Nicaragua,
Honduras *Binder:* Mexico
Wrapper: U.S.A./Conn. Shade
A well-balanced cigar. It has
some spice and coffee flavors.
A solid, medium-bodied
smoke. U.S.: $8.00

ARTURO FUENTE HEMINGWAY CLASSIC 86
Dominican Republic • *Size:* 7" x 48 *Filler/Binder:* Dom. Rep. *Wrapper:* Cameroon
This cigar has a medium body with a dry spice character. It has a slightly dry finish with a solid core of tobacco flavors. U.S.: $5.75

ARTURO FUENTE HEMINGWAY MASTERPIECE 86
Dominican Republic • *Size:* 9¼" x 52 *Filler/Binder:* Dom. Rep. *Wrapper:* Cameroon
A powerful and rich smoke. Good draw and full-bodied with rich coffee taste and spicy flavors. (06/01/93) U.S.: $12.50

AVO PETIT BELICOSO 86
Dominican Republic • *Size:* 4¼" x 50 *Filler/Binder:* Dom. Rep. *Wrapper:* U.S.A./ Conn. Shade
A medium-bodied cigar with some inconsistency; nuts and nutmeg flavors with notes of cocoa beans. A slightly woody finish. U.S.: $7.10

AVO PYRAMID 86
Dominican Republic • *Size:* 7" x 54 *Filler/Binder:* Dom. Rep. *Wrapper:* U.S.A./ Conn. Shade
This cigar has a sweet spice quality with hints of leather and wood. There is a tanginess on the finish. U.S.: $9.00

C.A.O. TRIANGULARE 86
Honduras • *Size:* 7" x 54 *Filler:* Nicaragua, Mexico

Binder: Honduras *Wrapper:* U.S.A./Conn. Shade
A nice, mild cigar. It has a nutty quality with a good toast-like flavor. U.S.: $7.78

EL SUBLIMADO TORPEDO 86
Dominican Republic • *Size:* 7" x 54 *Filler/Binder:* Dom. Rep. *Wrapper:* U.S.A.
This well-made cigar has some floral aromas and a core of nutty flavors. U.S.: $14.00

FELIPE GREGORIO BELICOSO 86
Honduras • *Size:* 6⅛" x 54 *Filler/Binder/Wrapper:* Honduras
A medium-bodied cigar with medium-length finish. There are earthy flavors with a mild spiciness. U.S.: $10.00

LA GLORIA CUBANA TORPEDO NO. 1 86
U.S.A. • *Size:* 6½" x 54 *Filler:* Dom. Rep., Nicaragua *Binder:* Nicaragua *Wrapper:* Ecuador
This cigar has strong toasty flavors with an earthy leatheryness. But a bit of sourness was noted by several tasters. U.S.: $6.50

PAUL GARMIRIAN BELICOSO FINO 86
Dominican Republic • *Size:* 5½" x 52 *Filler/Binder:* Dom. Rep. *Wrapper:* U.S.A./ Conn. Shade
A cigar with rich spice flavors notes, but with a slightly dry cedary finish. U.S.: $10.55

PETRUS TABACAGE ANTONIUS 86
Honduras • *Size:* 5" x 54 *Filler/Binder:* Honduras, Nicaragua *Wrapper:* Ecuador
A mild- to medium-bodied cigar that has a creamy, salty-nut flavor on the palate and a well-balanced finish. U.S.: $6.60

POR LARRAÑAGA PYRAMID 86
Dominican Republic • *Size:* 6" x 50 *Filler/Binder:* Dom. Rep. *Wrapper:* U.S.A.
This is a mild- to medium-bodied cigar with a light creaminess and a slightly dry woody finish. U.S.: $9.00

SANCHO PANZA BELICOSO 86
Cuba • *Size:* 5½" x 52 *Filler/Binder/Wrapper:* Cuba
A well-made cigar that has an herbal aroma and leather and spice flavors, but it finishes a little dry. U.K.: £9.80

THOMAS HINDS HONDURAN SELECTION TORPEDO 86
Honduras • *Size:* 6" x 52 *Filler/Binder:* Honduras *Wrapper:* Ecuador
A very pleasant, medium-bodied cigar with a core of earthy tobacco flavors and a light finish. U.S.: $6.05

ASTRAL PERFECCION 85
Honduras • *Size:* 7" x 48 *Filler:* Honduras, Nicaragua *Binder/Wrapper:* Honduras
A mild-tasting cigar with some dry wood/paper notes

that round out into a mild spiciness and a woody finish. U.S.: $7.20

EL REY DEL MUNDO 85
FLOR DE LAVONDA
Honduras • Size: 6½" x 52
Filler/Binder: Honduras, Dom. Rep. Wrapper: Ecuador
This is a pleasant, mild smoke. It has light herb-like flavors. U.S.: $4.25

HABANA GOLD 85
BLACK LABEL TORPEDO
Honduras • Size: 6" x 52
Filler/Binder: Nicaragua, Honduras Wrapper: Indonesia
A medium-bodied cigar with nut and spice flavors that end on a slightly vegetal finish. U.S.: $5.70

ROMEO Y JULIETA 85
ROMEO
Dominican Republic • Size: 6" x 46 Filler: Dom. Rep., Brazil Binder: U.S.A. Wrapper: Cameroon
Some hints of exotic spices and coffee bean flavors. It is a little rustic and rough. U.S.: $5.55

ROYAL JAMAICA 85
PARK LANE
Dominican Republic • Size: 6" x 47 Filler: Jamaica, Dom. Rep., Indonesia Binder: Cameroon Wrapper: Indonesia
A good medium-bodied cigar. It has a pleasant spicy flavor with a tangy finish. U.S.: $4.95

TE-AMO FIGURADO 85
Mexico • Size: 6⅝" x 50
Filler/Binder/Wrapper: Mexico
This cigar has a deep earthiness and a strong pepper influence in the flavor, but with a bit of steeliness on the palate and a dry wood finish. U.S.: $3.95

LAS CABRILLAS MAXI- 84
MILIAN
Honduras • Size: 7" x 55
Filler: Nicaragua, Mexico
Binder: Mexico Wrapper: U.S.A./Conn. Shade
A cigar with cedary and slightly baked flavors, including roasted cocoa. A firm draw and a somewhat vegetal finish. U.S.: $3.50

PARTAGAS PRESIDENTE 84
Cuba • Size: 6⅛" x 47
Filler/Binder/Wrapper: Cuba
This cigar shows extreme youth and some inconsistency in the draw. But it has a rich, spicy core of flavors. SF: 10

TE-AMO 84
GRAN PIRAMIDE
Mexico • Size: 7¼" x 54
Filler/Binder/Wrapper: Mexico
A rough-looking cigar. Although it has a slightly vegetal, grassy tone, it also delivers some spicy pepper flavors. U.S.: $4.75

THE GRIFFIN'S 84
NO. 100
Dominican Republic • Size: 7" x 38 Filler/Binder: Dom. Rep. Wrapper: U.S.A./Conn. Shade

Slightly rough and coarse looking, and it doesn't burn evenly. But it has pleasant, creamy, spicy flavors and a delicate texture. (06/01/93) U.S.: $6.25

VUELTABAJO PYRAMIDE 84
Dominican Republic • Size: 7" x 50 Filler/Binder: Dom. Rep. Wrapper: U.S.A./Conn. Shade
A straightforward cigar. It has a mild, creamy character with a touch of pepper. A slightly metallic aftertaste. U.S.: $5.70

ASTRAL FAVORITO 83
Honduras • Size: 7" x 48
Filler: Honduras, Nicaragua
Binder/Wrapper: Honduras
This cigar has a firm draw, a sweet woody quality and a nice nutty flavor, but a slight bitterness on the finish. U.S.: $7.20

DON LINO 83
COLORADO TORPEDO
Dominican Republic • Size: 7" x 48 Filler/Binder: Honduras, Nicaragua Wrapper: U.S.A.
An attractive reddish-brown wrapper. It has some spicy flavors, but an overall grassy, herbal quality and a woody finish. U.S.: $6.56

NAT SHERMAN 83
VIP SELECTION
ZIGFELD FANCY TAIL
Dominican Republic • *Size:*
6¾" x 38 *Filler/Binder:* Dom.
Rep. *Wrapper:* U.S.A./
Conn. Shade
An inconsistent draw. It has
some pleasant toast and spice
notes on the palate, but a dry,
woody finish. U.S.: $5.90

TE-AMO PIRAMIDE 83
Mexico • *Size:* 6¼" x 50
Filler/Binder/Wrapper: Mexico
A cigar with plenty of pepper
taste. It also has a flinty fla-
vor, and some inconsistency
was noted in the draw.
U.S.: $3.60

DUNHILL CENTENAS 82
Dominican Republic • *Size:*
6" x 50 *Filler/Binder:* Dom.
Rep., Brazil *Wrapper:*
U.S.A./Conn. Shade
This cigar is smooth-tasting
with some vegetal flavors and
a touch of spice on the finish.
U.S.: $11.75

ORIENT EXPRESS 82
EXPRESSO
Honduras • *Size:* 6" x 48
Filler: Nicaragua, Mexico
Binder: Dom. Rep. *Wrapper:*
Ecuador
A somewhat rustic and rough
cigar with a tartness on the
palate. A straightforward
smoke. U.S.: $12.50

PADRÓN 1964 82
ANNIVERSARY SERIES
PIRAMIDE
Honduras • *Size:* 6⅞" x 52
Filler/Binder/Wrapper:
Nicaragua

A spicy cigar with plenty of
pepper notes, but it finishes a
little short and harsh.
U.S.: $11.50

SOSA PIRAMIDES 80
Dominican Republic • *Size:*
6½" x 54 *Filler:* Dom. Rep.
Binder: Honduras *Wrapper:*
Ecuador
This is a mild, light cigar
with a loose draw that turns
hot. It finishes with a fairly
dry, burnt wood flavor.
U.S.: $6.75

Maduro

*Most of the following Maduro
tasting notes appeared in the
Summer 1996 issue of* Cigar
Aficionado. *Exceptions are
indicated by a date in parentheses at the end of the tasting
note.*

EL REY DEL MUNDO 91
ROBUSTO SUPREMA
Honduras • *Size:* 7" x 54
Filler: Dom. Rep., Honduras
Binder/Wrapper: Honduras
This cigar has an oily, dark-
brown wrapper and a pleasant combination of
pungent/sweet flavors including chocolate, roasted nuts
and spice. A long finish
enhances this pleasant cigar.
(12/01/93) U.S.: $4.75

DON LINO 90
CHURCHILL MADURO
Honduras • *Size:* 7" x 50
Filler/Binder: Honduras
Wrapper: U.S.A./Conn.
Broadleaf
This cigar has a dark, smooth
wrapper and woody flavors

that turn spicy on the finish.
(12/01/93) U.S.: $4.80

LA GLORIA CUBANA 90
WAVELL MADURO
U.S.A. • *Size:* 5" x 50 *Filler:*
Dom. Rep., Nica., Ecu.
Binder: Ecuador *Wrapper:*
U.S.A./Conn. Shade
A very dark, oily wrapper.
This cigar has a rich, creamy
taste that is filled with sweet,
spicy flavors. (12/01/93)
U.S.: $3.70

BANCES PRESIDENT 89
Honduras • *Size:* 8½" x 52
Filler: Nicaragua, Honduras
Binder: Mexico *Wrapper:*
Ecuador
A cool, big cigar with medi-
um-bodied smoke and flavors
of chocolate, coffee and
sweet spices. (12/01/93)
U.S.: $5.20

LA GLORIA CUBANA 89
CHURCHILL MADURO
U.S.A. • *Size:* 7" x 50 *Filler:*
Dom. Rep., Nicaragua
Binder: Ecuador *Wrapper:*
U.S.A./Conn. Broadleaf
A cigar with an oily, black-
brown wrapper that delivers
rich spicy flavors and
smooth, round tobacco tastes
on a short finish. (12/01/93)
U.S.: $4.40

TRESADO SELECCION 89
NO. 200 MADURO
Dominican Republic • *Size:*
7" x 48 *Filler/Binder:* Dom.
Rep. *Wrapper:* Indonesia
A very well-made cigar with
a good draw. It has flavors of
cloves and other sweet spices
and a solid tobacco taste on

the finish. (12/01/93)
U.S.: $2.85

ARTURO FUENTE   **88**
CHATEAU FUENTE
MADURO
Dominican Republic • *Size:*
4½" x 50 *Filler/Binder:* Dom.
Rep. *Wrapper:* U.S.A./
Conn. Sun-Grown
This rich-tasting cigar has a
smoky, coffee character with
a medium body. (12/01/93)
U.S.: $3.35

CUESTA-REY CABINET   **88**
NO. 1884 MADURO
Dominican Republic • *Size:*
6¾" x 44 *Filler/Binder:* Dom.
Rep. *Wrapper:* U.S.A./
Conn. Broadleaf
This rustic-looking cigar has
strong chocolate flavors and
a smooth earthiness on the
finish. (12/01/93) U.S.: $4.35

JOYA DE NICARAGUA   **88**
MADURO DELUXE
ROBUSTO
Nicaragua • *Size:* 4¼" x 52
Filler/Binder: Nicaragua
Wrapper: Costa Rica
This is a rich-tasting maduro.
It has strong cocoa bean fla-
vors and a long sweet finish.
It is well made with a good
oily wrapper and a good draw.
U.S.: $4.50

ONYX NO. 650   **88**
Dominican Republic • *Size:*
6" x 50 *Filler:* Dom. Rep.,
Mexico *Binder:* Indonesia
Wrapper: Mexico
A very well-made maduro. It
starts out slowly, but builds
into a solid core of sweet
spicy flavors. It has strong

woody elements on the finish. U.S.: $4.00

PADRÓN 3000   **88**
MADURO
Nicaragua • *Size:* 5½" x 52
Filler/Binder/Wrapper:
Nicaragua
A cigar with a strong spicy
character and a range of cof-
fee-style flavors. It is rich-
tasting with an earthy finish.
U.S.: $3.85

SOSA   **88**
CHURCHILL MADURO
Dominican Republic • *Size:*
6¹⁵⁄₁₆ x 49 *Filler:* Dom. Rep.
Binder: Honduras *Wrapper:*
U.S.A./Conn. Broadleaf
This is a light-colored
maduro with an oily wrapper.
It has a combination of
woodiness and sweet herbs,
with a good, earthy finish.
U.S.: $4.80

ASHTON   **87**
AGED MADURO NO. 30
Dominican Republic • *Size:*
6¾" x 44 *Filler/Binder:* Dom.
Rep. *Wrapper:* U.S.A./
Conn. Broadleaf
A lush, dark-brown wrapper
helps deliver a dark chocolate aroma with a light, spicy
flavor on the palate and a
hint of sweetness. An enjoyable, pleasant finish.
(12/01/93) U.S.: $7.50

BANCES CORONA   **87**
INMENSA MADURO
Honduras • *Size:* 6¾" x 48
Filler: Nicaragua, Honduras
Binder: Mexico *Wrapper:*
Ecuador

A well-made maduro with a
smooth, oily wrapper. It has
rich coffee flavors and a light,
almost-sweet taste on the
palate. (12/01/93)
U.S.: $4.00

CASA BLANCA   **87**
DELUXE MADURO
Dominican Republic • *Size:*
6" x 50 *Filler:* Dom. Rep.
Binder: Mexico *Wrapper:*
U.S.A./Conn. Shade
A very dark, well-made
maduro. It has flavors of
dried citrus and cocoa and a
long, peppery finish.
U.S.: $3.00

CRUZ REAL   **87**
NO. 14 MADURO
Mexico • *Size:* 7½" x 50
Filler/Binder/Wrapper: Mexico
This cigar has a sweet, earthy
character. There are flavors
of sweet wood and pepper
with a long finish.
U.S.: $5.00

CUESTA-REY   **87**
CENTENNIAL
COLLECTION
DOMINICAN NO. 2
MADURO
Dominican Republic • *Size:*
7½" x 48 *Filler/Binder:* Dom.
Rep. *Wrapper:* U.S.A./
Conn. Broadleaf
There are well-balanced fla-
vors of leather, nuts and hints
of cocoa and coffee beans. It
has an overall sweet tobacco
character and a mild finish.
U.S.: $5.40

HENRY CLAY   **87**
BREVAS A LA CONSERVA
MADURO
Dominican Republic • *Size:*
5⅝" x 46   *Filler/Binder:* Dom.
Rep., Brazil   *Wrapper:*
U.S.A./Conn. Broadleaf
This is a solid maduro with a
shiny wrapper. It has hints of
cocoa bean and a slight burnt
toast character with some
sweet spice on the finish.
U.S.: $3.50

HOYO DE MONTERREY   **87**
EXCALIBUR NO. 3
MADURO
Honduras • *Size:* 6⅛" x 48
Filler/Binder: Honduras,
Nicaragua, Dom. Rep.
Wrapper: U.S.A./Conn.
Broadleaf
A well-made maduro with a
good, smooth taste. It has a
mild cocoa bean character
with herbal notes, and a long
spicy finish. U.S.: $4.75

LA FINCA   **87**
ROBUSTO MADURO
Nicaragua • *Size:* 4½" x 50
Filler/Binder/Wrapper:
Nicaragua
This cigar has an herbal
character. The medium-bod-
ied smoke has flavors of pep-
per and sweet chocolate, and
a long spicy finish.
U.S.: $2.00

LICENCIADOS   **87**
WAVELL MADURO
Dominican Republic • *Size:*
5" x 50   *Filler/Binder:* Dom.
Rep.   *Wrapper:*
U.S.A./Conn. Broadleaf
A well-made maduro. It has a
sweet character with a cola

flavor and some dark spices.
A medium-length finish.
U.S.: $4.50

PADRÓN   **87**
EXECUTIVE MADURO
Nicaragua • *Size:* 7½" x 50
Filler/Binder/Wrapper:
Nicaragua
A big, well-made maduro. It
has excellent balance, good
mild spice flavors and a
woody, leathery finish.
U.S.: $5.00

PETRUS TABACAGE   **87**
DOUBLE CORONA
Honduras • *Size:* 7¾" x 50
Filler/Binder/Wrapper: Honduras
A well-balanced cigar with a
smooth, cream taste and flavors of citrus and nuts with a
solid tobacco finish.
(12/01/93) U.S.: $7.40

PUNCH PITA MADURO   **87**
Honduras • *Size:* 6⅛" x 50
Filler/Binder: Honduras,
Nicaragua, Dom. Rep.
Wrapper: U.S.A./Conn.
Broadleaf
A smooth-tasting cigar with
solid sweet spice notes and
some deep coffee bean fla-
vors. There are hints of nuts
and wood on the palate. It
has a dry finish. U.S.: $3.60

ROMEO Y JULIETA   **87**
ROTHSCHILD MADURO
Dominican Republic • *Size:*
5" x 50   *Filler/Binder:* Dom.
Rep.   *Wrapper:* U.S.A./
Conn. Broadleaf
A rich, black-brown cigar
with hints of coffee and spice
on the palate. A sightly

woody finish comes through
the medium-bodied smoke.
(12/01/93) U.S.: $4.05

ROYAL JAMAICA   **87**
MADURO CORONA
Dominican Republic • *Size:*
5½" x 40   *Filler:* Jamaica
Binder: Indonesia   *Wrapper:*
Mexico
A smooth-tasting cigar with
a rich, black wrapper. It has
rich coffee and roasted nut
flavors, but a mild finish.
(12/01/93) U.S.: $4.00

SOSA WAVELL MADURO **87**
Dominican Republic • *Size:*
4¾" x 50   *Filler:* Dom. Rep.
Binder: Honduras   *Wrapper:*
U.S.A./Conn. Broadleaf
A cigar filled with spicy flavors and a complex earthy
quality. It smokes well and
has a smooth medium-bodied
finish. U.S.: $4.30

TROYA NO. 18 ROTH-   **87**
SCHILD MADURO
Dominican Republic • *Size:*
4½" x 50   *Filler/Binder:* Dom.
Rep.   *Wrapper:* Ecuador
A light maduro with flavors
of coffee beans and a smooth,
long finish. It is a medium-
bodied smoke. U.S.: $4.30

ARTURO FUENTE   **86**
CORONA IMPERIAL
Dominican Republic • *Size:*
6½" x 46   *Filler/Binder:* Dom.
Rep.   *Wrapper:* U.S.A./
Conn. Sun-Grown
A black-wrapped cigar with
mild spiciness and nutty, cof-
fee flavors. It finishes a bit
hot. (12/01/93) U.S.: $3.70

ASHTON AGED MADURO NO. 50 — 86

Dominican Republic • Size: 7" x 48 Filler/Binder: Dom. Rep. Wrapper: U.S.A./ Conn. Broadleaf
A well-balanced cigar. It has some toast and wood flavors with a hint of cocoa bean, and a short, herbal finish. U.S.: $8.25

CANARIA D'ORO ROTHSCHILD MADURO — 86

Dominican Republic • Size: 4½" x 50 Filler/Wrapper: Mexico, Dominican Republic Binder: U.S.A.
A strong spicy core carries this cigar. The construction is a bit rough and it has dry, woody finish. U.S.: $2.75

EL REY DEL MUNDO FLOR DEL MUNDO MADURO — 86

Honduras • Size: 7¼" x 52 Filler/Binder: Honduras, Dom. Rep. Wrapper: Ecuador
A cigar with a shiny maduro wrapper. It has a core of spicy flavors and hints of cocoa bean, toast and leather on the medium-bodied smoke. A short finish. U.S.: $5.00

ENCANTO TORO MADURO — 86

Honduras • Size: 6" x 50 Filler/Binder/Wrapper: Honduras
A cigar with well-balanced flavors. It has some sweet spice and nut qualities, and a long finish with some spice. U.S.: $5.50

F.D. GRAVE CHURCHILL MADURO — 86

Honduras • Size: 7¾" x 50 Filler: Dom. Rep., Honduras, U.S.A. Binder: U.S.A. Wrapper: U.S.A./Conn. Broadleaf
A smooth-tasting cigar. It has a creaminess and flavors of pepper, licorice and herbs. A good medium-bodied smoke. U.S.: $3.81

FONSECA 5-50 MADURO — 86

Dominican Republic • Size: 5" x 50 Filler: Dom. Rep. Binder: Mexico Wrapper: U.S.A./Conn. Broadleaf
A smooth, almost-black wrapper gives this cigar a range of medium-bodied, spicy flavors that finish with a chocolaty, nutty taste. (12/01/93) U.S.: $4.75

HAVANA CLASSICO ROBUSTO — 86

Dominican Republic • Size: 5" x 50 Filler: Dom. Rep., Mexico, Nicaragua Binder/Wrapper: Ecuador
A medium-bodied cigar with a light woodiness and hints of mild herbs. It has a slightly earthy finish. U.S.: $5.25

HOYO DE MONTERREY GOVERNOR MADURO — 86

Honduras • Size: 6⅛" x 50 Filler/Binder: Honduras, Nicaragua, Dom. Rep. Wrapper: U.S.A./Conn. Broadleaf
A smooth-tasting cigar with flavors of dried citrus and a spicy cedar box character. It

has a light woody finish. U.S.: $3.60

LA UNICA NO. 200 — 86

Dominican Republic • Size: 7" x 49 Filler/Binder: Dom. Rep. Wrapper: U.S.A./ Conn. Broadleaf
A cigar with a sweet flavor profile. There are hints of coffee and pepper. It has a dry, woody finish. U.S.: $4.65

MONTESINO DIPLO-MATICO MADURO — 86

Dominican Republic • Size: 5½" x 42 Filler/Binder: Dom. Rep. Wrapper: U.S.A./ Conn. Sun-Grown
A cigar with sweet flavors that range from exotic floral notes to licorice. An interesting smoke. (12/01/93) U.S.: $2.85

MONTESINO GRAN CORONA MADURO — 86

Dominican Republic • Size: 6¾" x 48 Filler/Binder: Dom. Rep. Wrapper: U.S.A./ Conn. Sun-Grown
This well-made corona draws well and has burnt sugar and spicy flavors on the palate and a short but tangy finish. (12/01/93) U.S.: $3.90

NAT SHERMAN CITY DESK SELECTION TRIBUNE MADURO — 86

Dominican Republic • Size: 7½" x 50 Filler/Binder: Dom. Rep. Wrapper: Mexico
A well-balanced cigar with a spicy sweetness. There are hints of earthiness on the palate and the finish. U.S.: $6.50

ORNELAS **86**
ROBUSTO MADURO
Mexico • *Size:* 4¾" x 49
Filler/Binder/Wrapper: Mexico
A mild- to medium-bodied
cigar with a light spicy char-
acter. There are hints of nut
and cedar box flavors and it
has a woody finish.
U.S.: $6.00

PADRÓN **86**
CHURCHILL MADURO
Nicaragua • *Size:* 6⅞" x 46
Filler/Binder/Wrapper:
Nicaragua
A mild- to medium-bodied
cigar with a combination of
vegetal and herbal elements
that turn into a sweet spici-
ness on the palate and finish.
U.S.: $3.90

PADRÓN **86**
2000 MADURO
Nicaragua • *Size:* 5" x 50
Filler/Binder/Wrapper:
Nicaragua
A rich-tasting maduro with
plenty of spice and hints of
coffee. It has an earthy finish.
U.S.: $3.15

PUNCH DELUXE SERIES **86**
CHATEAU M MADURO
Honduras • *Size:* 6¾" x 46
Filler: Nica., Hon., Dom.
Rep. *Binder/Wrapper:*
Ecuador
This rich-looking maduro
delivers spicy flavors with a
sweetish, burnt chocolate fin-
ish. A nice, well-rounded
cigar. (12/01/93) U.S.: $3.65

PUNCH **86**
DOUBLE CORONA
MADURO
Honduras • *Size:* 6¾" x 48
Filler: Nica., Hon., Dom.
Rep. *Binder:* U.S.A./Conn
Broadleaf *Wrapper:* U.S.A./
Conn. Shade
A well-made cigar with a
smooth draw. It has clean
tobacco flavors and hints of
sweet chocolate and spice on
a mild finish. (12/01/93)
U.S.: $3.75

PUNCH **86**
ROTHSCHILD MADURO
Honduras • *Size:* 4½" x 50
Filler/Binder: Honduras,
Nicaragua, Dom. Rep.
Wrapper: U.S.A./Conn.
Broadleaf
A cigar with an earthy char-
acter. There are hints of
wood and coffee beans on the
palate. It has mild pepper fla-
vors. U.S.: $2.80

PUROS INDIOS **86**
CHURCHILL MADURO
Honduras • *Size:* 7¼" x 52
Filler: Nicaragua, Dom. Rep.,
Brazil, Jamaica *Binder/Wrap-
per:* Ecuador
This cigar has flavors of nuts
and coffee, with a leathery
aroma. The finish is rather
short, but has a touch of
spice. U.S.: $7.40

PUROS INDIOS **86**
CORONA GORDA
MADURO
Honduras • *Size:* 6" x 52
Filler: Nicaragua, Dom. Rep.,
Brazil, Jamaica *Binder/Wrap-
per:* Ecuador

A medium-bodied maduro
cigar with a solid core of pepper spice. There are also
fruity and creamy elements
with a good, woody finish.
U.S.: $4.25

ROYAL JAMAICA **86**
MADURO CHURCHILL
Dominican Republic • *Size:*
8" x 51 *Filler:* Jamaica
Binder: Cameroon *Wrapper:*
Mexico
A good, medium-bodied
cigar. It has a strong sweet
spiciness, with elements of
coffee and cocoa bean flavors.
A spicy finish. U.S.: $6.50

TE-AMO MAXIMO **86**
CHURCHILL MADURO
Mexico • *Size:* 7" x 54
Filler/Binder/Wrapper: Mexico
A cigar that starts out slowly
but has some solid notes of
spice, including dry pepper
flavors, and a hint of roasted
nuts. U.S.: $4.10

TEMPLE HALL **86**
NO. 450 MADURO
Jamaica • *Size:* 4½" x 49
Filler: Mex., Jam., Dom. Rep.
Binder: U.S.A./Conn. Shade
Wrapper: Mexico
A dark-black wrapper with a
slightly tough draw. Rich fla-
vors of coffee and nuts.
(12/01/93) U.S.: $6.75

ARTURO FUENTE **85**
CHURCHILL MADURO
Dominican Republic • *Size:*
7" x 48 *Filler/Binder:* Dom.
Rep. *Wrapper:* U.S.A./
Conn. Sun Grown
This medium-bodied cigar
has a slight sweetness on the

palate and strong flavors of sweet nuts and spice. (12/01/93) U.S.: $4.35

ASHTON 85
AGED MADURO NO. 40
Dominican Republic • *Size:* 6" x 50 *Filler/Binder:* Dom. Rep. *Wrapper:* U.S.A./ Conn. Broadleaf
A cigar with a sweet tobacco character. There are hints of cinnamon and a smooth nuttiness. The finish is light. U.S.: $7.75

C.A.O. 85
CHURCHILL MADURO
Honduras • *Size:* 8" x 50 *Filler:* Nicaragua, Mexico *Binder:* Honduras *Wrapper:* U.S.A./Conn. Broadleaf
A fairly mild cigar. It has some notes of raw nuts and a woody, mild finish. U.S.: $8.00

DON TOMAS PRESI- 85
DENTE MADURO
Honduras • *Size:* 7½" x 50 *Filler/Binder:* Honduras *Wrapper:* U.S.A./Conn. Broadleaf
A good, smooth smoke with peppery spices and a light finish. (12/01/93) U.S.: $6.30

ENCANTO 85
ROTHSCHILD MADURO
Honduras • *Size:* 4½" x 50 *Filler/Binder/Wrapper:* Honduras
A cigar with a perfume-like character. There are some sweet, nutty flavors and a touch of pepper on the finish. U.S.: $4.50

FONSECA 85
10-10 MADURO
Dominican Republic • *Size:* 6¾" x 49 *Filler:* Dom. Rep. *Binder:* Mexico *Wrapper:* U.S.A./Conn. Broadleaf
This cigar has an oily, black wrapper and a light body with slightly sweet flavors. A smooth smoke. (12/01/93) U.S.: $5.25

HABANA GOLD 85
WHITE LABEL
CHURCHILL
Honduras • *Size:* 7" x 52 *Filler/Binder/Wrapper:* Nicaragua
A cigar with a pleasant sweet herbal character and a cedary flavor. It has a smooth finish. U.S.: $6.25

HOYO DE MONTERREY 85
EXCALIBUR NO. 1
MADURO
Honduras • *Size:* 7¼" x 54 *Filler/Binder:* Honduras, Nicaragua, Dom. Rep. *Wrapper:* U.S.A./Conn. Broadleaf
A well-made maduro. This cigar has a hint of nutmeg and sweet spices, with an overall toasty character. It has a mild nutty finish. U.S.: $5.30

HOYO DE MONTERREY 85
EXCALIBUR NO. 2
MADURO
Honduras • *Size:* 7" x 46 *Filler:* Hon., Nica., Dom. Rep. *Binder:* Ecuador *Wrapper:* U.S.A./Conn. Broadleaf
A good, dark wrapper. The cigar has spicy, roasted coffee flavors, but some dry wood and vegetal notes on the finish. (12/01/93) U.S.: $4.95

HOYO DE MONTERREY 85
ROTHSCHILD MADURO
Honduras • *Size:* 4½" x 50 *Filler/Binder:* Honduras, Nicaragua, Dom. Rep. *Wrapper:* U.S.A./Conn. Broadleaf
This cigar has a sweet spice, almost ginger-like, flavor. There are strong notes of nuts on the finish. U.S.: $2.80

HOYO DE MONTERREY 85
SULTAN MADURO
Honduras • *Size:* 7¼" x 54 *Filler/Binder:* Honduras, Nicaragua, Dom. Rep. *Wrapper:* U.S.A./Conn. Broadleaf
A cigar with a well-balanced flavor of bittersweet chocolate around a nutty core. It has a light, spicy finish. U.S.: $4.65

MACANUDO 85
PRINCE PHILIP MADURO
Jamaica • *Size:* 7½" x 49 *Filler:* Mex., Jam., Dom. Rep. *Binder:* U.S.A./Conn. Shade *Wrapper:* Mexico
Rough construction hurt this cigar, but it has peppery flavors and a slightly spicy finish. (12/01/93) U.S.: $6.00

NAT SHERMAN 85
CITY DESK SELECTION
DISPATCH
Dominican Republic • *Size:* 6½" x 46 *Filler/Binder:* Dom. Rep. *Wrapper:* Mexico
This is a solid maduro cigar with dark coffee bean and mild spice flavors. It has a woody finish. U.S.: $5.80

NAT SHERMAN 85
CITY DESK SELECTION
TELEGRAPH
Dominican Republic • *Size:* 6" x 50 *Filler/Binder:* Dom. Rep. *Wrapper:* Mexico
A mild nuttiness dominates this cigar. It has some light spice and pepper notes on the palate and a mild, woody finish. U.S.: $6.00

ONYX NO. 642 85
Dominican Republic • *Size:* 6" x 42 *Filler:* Dom. Rep., Mexico *Binder:* Indonesia *Wrapper:* Mexico
A tight draw limits this cigar, but it has mild, earthy flavors with a sweetish taste. (12/01/93) U.S.: $3.25

ONYX NO. 750 85
Dominican Republic • *Size:* 7½" x 50 *Filler:* Dom. Rep., Mexico *Binder:* Indonesia *Wrapper:* Mexico
A well-constructed cigar, although a tight draw was noted. There are complex flavors of chocolate with an herbal character and a mild coffee finish. U.S.: $4.50

ORNELAS 85
CAFETERO GRANDE
Mexico • *Size:* 6½" x 46 *Filler/Binder/Wrapper:* Mexico
A mild cigar with well-balanced flavors of nuts and toast. It has touch of flintiness on the finish. U.S.: $6.00

PARTAGAS MADURO 85
Dominican Republic • *Size:* 6¼" x 48 *Filler:* Dominican Republic, Mexico *Binder:* U.S.A. *Wrapper:* Mexico
A mild- to medium-bodied smoke. It has attractive spiciness and an herbal, woody finish. U.S.: $5.45

PRIMO DEL REY SELEC- 85
CION NO. 4 MADURO
Dominican Republic • *Size:* 5½" x 42 *Filler:* Dom. Rep. *Binder:* U.S.A./Conn. *Wrapper:* U.S.A./Conn. Broadleaf
A mild-flavored cigar with touches of spice and an earthy finish that make it a straightforward smoke. (12/01/93) U.S.: $2.00

PUNCH DELUXE SERIES 85
CHATEAU L MADURO
Honduras • *Size:* 7¼" x 54 *Filler/Binder:* Honduras, Nicaragua, Dom. Rep. *Wrapper:* U.S.A./Conn. Broadleaf
A cigar with an herbal character. There are hints of buttered toast with a slightly burnt flavor. U.S.: $4.95

ROYAL JAMAICA 85
MADURO CORONA
GRANDE
Dominican Republic • *Size:* 6½" x 42 *Filler:* Jamaica *Binder:* Indonesia *Wrapper:* Mexico
An easy-smoking cigar filled with a solid, rich taste and some sweet flavors. It has a smooth finish. (12/01/93) U.S.: $4.25

SANTA CLARA 1830 85
NO. VI MADURO
Mexico • *Size:* 6" x 51 *Filler/Binder/Wrapper:* Mexico
A pleasant, but basic, maduro with a spicy, chocolate flavor and one of the tasting's longest aftertastes. (12/01/93) U.S.: $2.50

TE-AMO 85
TORITO MADURO
Mexico • *Size:* 4¾" x 50 *Filler/Binder/Wrapper:* Mexico
A cigar with lots of earthy elements and a sweet spiciness. There is a strong woody character on the finish. U.S.: $2.50

V CENTENNIAL 85
ROBUSTO MADURO
Honduras • *Size:* 5" x 50 *Filler:* Dom. Rep., Nicaragua, Honduras *Binder/Wrapper:* Mexico
A medium-bodied cigar with a slightly sweet character. It has mild spice, citrus and wood flavors with a slight saltiness on the finish. U.S.: $5.00

ASHTON AGED **84**
MADURO NO. 60
Dominican Republic • *Size:*
7½" x 52 *Filler/Binder:* Dom.
Rep. *Wrapper:* U.S.A./
Conn. Broadleaf
A big cigar with a medium
body and loads of spice on
the palate, but it finishes dry
and sharp. (12/01/93)
U.S.: $8.75

BELINDA EXCELLENTE **84**
Honduras • *Size:* 6" x 50
Filler: Dom. Rep., Honduras
Binder: Honduras *Wrapper:*
Ecuador
A cigar with a strong woody
character. There are some
light, spicy flavors and a
leather note on the finish.
U.S.: $2.75

C.A.O. **84**
ROBUSTO MADURO
Honduras • *Size:* 4½" x 50
Filler: Nicaragua, Mexico
Binder: Honduras *Wrapper:*
U.S.A./Conn. Broadleaf
There are some hints of pep-
per in this cigar. It has a dry
woodiness on the palate and
some vegetal flavors. It has a
woody finish. U.S.: $5.60

CABAÑAS CORONA **84**
Dominican Republic • *Size:*
5½" x 42 *Filler/Binder:* Dom.
Rep. *Wrapper:* Mexico
A tight draw limits this otherwise well-balanced cigar. It
has spice and nut flavors and
a medium finish. (12/01/93)
U.S.: $3.70

CABAÑAS **84**
EXQUISITO MADURO
Dominican Republic • *Size:*
6½" x 48 *Filler/Binder:* Dom.
Rep. *Wrapper:* Mexico
This brownish-black-wrap-
pered cigar has slightly sweet,
milk-chocolate flavors and a
long finish. (12/01/93)
U.S.: $4.25

CRUZ REAL **84**
NO. 19 MADURO
Mexico • *Size:* 6" x 50
Filler/Binder/Wrapper: Mexico
A mild-tasting maduro with
an earthy, herbal character. It
has some perfume-like flavors
and a woody finish.
U.S.: $4.15

CUESTA-REY **84**
CABINET NO. 95
MADURO
Dominican Republic • *Size:*
6¼" x 42 *Filler/Binder:* Dom.
Rep. *Wrapper:* U.S.A./
Conn. Broadleaf
A firmly packed cigar that
delivers nut and roasted-cof-
fee flavors and has a slightly
sweet finish. (12/01/93)
U.S.: $3.85

DON LINO **84**
ROTHSCHILD MADURO
Honduras • *Size:* 4½" x 50
Filler/Binder/Wrapper: Hon-
duras
A cigar with light touches of
nuts, herbs and a slight hint
of pepper on the finish.
U.S.: $3.84

FLAMENCO **84**
BREVAS A LA CONSERVA
Dominican Republic • *Size:*
5³⁄₁₆" x 42 *Filler/Binder:*
Dom. Rep. *Wrapper:*
U.S.A./Conn. Broadleaf
A medium-bodied cigar that
seems too tightly packed, but
has rich flavors of spice and
pepper. (12/01/93) Price N/A

HABANA GOLD **84**
WHITE LABEL ROBUS-
TO MADURO
Honduras • *Size:* 5" x 50
Filler/Binder/Wrapper:
Nicaragua
A cigar with an overall
woody character. There are
some notes of dried citrus fla-
vors, and sweet herbal notes
with a sweet finish.
U.S.: $5.20

HENRY CLAY **84**
BREVAS FINA MADURO
Dominican Republic • *Size:*
6½" x 48 *Filler/Binder:* Dom.
Rep., Brazil *Wrapper:*
U.S.A./Conn. Broadleaf
A cigar with some hints of
coffee beans, but an overall
herbal character. It has an
earthy finish. U.S.: $3.85

LA UNICA NO. 400 **84**
Dominican Republic • *Size:*
4½" x 50 *Filler/Binder:* Dom.
Rep. *Wrapper:*
U.S.A./Conn. Broadleaf
A slightly rough finish. This
cigar has some woodiness on
the palate with a solid citrus
note. It is well-balanced.
U.S.: $4.10

LAS CABRILLAS **84**
CORTEZ MADURO
Honduras • *Size*: 4¾" x 50
Filler: Nicaragua, Mexico
Binder/Wrapper: Mexico
A mild cigar with some
charred flavors. But it also
has some dry spice and
cedary components on the
palate with a woody finish.
U.S.: $2.00

LICENCIADOS SUPREME **84**
MADURO NO. 400
Dominican Republic • *Size*:
6" x 50 *Filler/Binder*: Dom.
Rep. *Wrapper*:
U.S.A./Conn. Shade
A mild cigar with flavors of
roasted nuts and a complex
espresso and coffee bean
character. It has an excellent
draw, and burns evenly and
smoothly. U.S.: $5.35

ORNELAS **84**
CHURCHILL MADURO
Mexico • *Size*: 7" x 49
Filler/Binder/Wrapper: Mexico
A cigar with a medium-
length finish. It has flavors of
toast and leather with a hint
of cedar wood. U.S.: $6.50

PETRUS TABACAGE **84**
CHURCHILL MADURO 89
Honduras • *Size*: 7" x 50
Filler: Nicaragua *Binder*:
Honduras *Wrapper*: Ecuador
A cigar with flavors of nuts
and a hint of dry citrus. It has
a very dry finish. U.S.: $6.40

PETRUS TABACAGE **84**
NO. II MADURO
Honduras • *Size*: 6¼" x 44
Filler/Binder/Wrapper: Honduras
A rich-tasting cigar filled
with spice and an attractive,
light, fruity aftertaste. However, showed inconsistency.
(12/01/93) U.S.: $5.20

TE-AMO **84**
CHURCHILL MADURO
Mexico • *Size*: 7½" x 50
Filler/Binder/Wrapper: Mexico
A mild cigar with a mellow,
slightly spicy character. It has
a solid pepper note and a
woody finish. U.S.: $3.95

TE-AMO **84**
SATISFACTION MADURO
Mexico • *Size*: 6" x 46
Filler/Binder/Wrapper: Mexico
A cigar with a light, easy
taste. It has some spice on
the palate and a solid woody
finish. U.S.: $2.85

TE-AMO **84**
TORO MADURO
Mexico • *Size*: 6" x 50
Filler/Binder/Wrapper: Mexico
A quite mild cigar with some
hints of cocoa bean and some
vegetal flavors with a dry,
woody finish. U.S.: $3.20

THOMAS HINDS **84**
NICARAGUAN SELECTION
ROBUSTO MADURO
Nicaragua • *Size*: 5" x 50
Filler/Binder/Wrapper:
Nicaragua
This medium-bodied maduro
has very peppery flavors with
a ripe, dried-citrus core, but
with a dry finish. U.S.: $6.50

THOMAS HINDS **84**
NICARAGUAN SELECTION
SHORT CHURCHILL
MADURO
Nicaragua • *Size*: 6" x 50
Filler/Binder/Wrapper:
Nicaragua
A cigar with a mild spiciness.
It has some pepper flavors
and a woody finish.
U.S.: $6.95

TROYA NO. 63 **84**
CHURCHILL MADURO
Dominican Republic • *Size*:
6⅛" x 46 *Filler/Binder*: Dom.
Rep. *Wrapper*: Ecuador
This is a well-balanced cigar
with nutty and leathery fla-
vors. It has a woody finish
with a hint of earthiness.
U.S.: $5.20

V CENTENNIAL **84**
CHURCHILL MADURO
Honduras • *Size*: 7" x 48
Filler: Dom. Rep., Nicaragua,
Honduras *Binder/Wrapper*:
Mexico
A cigar with a light, sweet
perfume-like character and
herbal tones. It has some
spicy flavors and a soft, dry
woody finish. U.S.: $7.00

V CENTENNIAL **84**
NUMERO 2 MADURO
Honduras • *Size*: 6" x 50
Filler: Dom. Rep., Nicaragua,
Honduras *Binder/Wrapper*:
Mexico
An earthy cigar with hints of
dark chocolate and anise. It
has a short but sweet finish.
U.S.: $6.00

ASHTON **83**
AGED MADURO NO. 10
Dominican Republic • *Size:*
5" x 50 *Filler/Binder:* Dom.
Rep. *Wrapper:* U.S.A./
Conn. Broadleaf
This cigar has a spicy core of
flavors and a quite dry, woody
finish. U.S.: $7.25

CASA BLANCA PRESI- **83**
DENTE MADURO
Dominican Republic • *Size:*
7½" x 50 *Filler:* Dom. Rep.
Binder: Mexico *Wrapper:*
U.S.A./Conn. Broadleaf
A well-made maduro. It has a
strong woody element on the
palate with a hint of herbs
and nuts. U.S.: $3.25

LICENCIADOS **83**
TORO MADURO
Dominican Republic • *Size:*
6" x 50 *Filler:* Dom. Rep.
Binder: Honduras *Wrapper:*
U.S.A./Conn. Broadleaf
A rough black wrapper deliv-
ers very spicy flavors. Overall
it is a good cigar with a light
finish. (12/01/93) U.S.: $4.75

MACANUDO **83**
DUKE OF DEVON
MADURO
Jamaica • *Size:* 5½" x 42
Filler: Mex., Jam., Dom. Rep.
Binder: U.S.A./Conn. Shade
Wrapper: Mexico
A big, well-made cigar that
offers mild pepper and toast-
ed nut flavors. (12/01/93)
U.S.: $4.80

SANTA CLARA 1830 **83**
NO. I MADURO
Mexico • *Size:* 7" x 51
Filler/Binder/Wrapper: Mexico

A rustic, medium-brown
wrapper that offers rich, spicy
smoke with a cedary, cinnamon note. A slightly hot finish. (12/01/93) U.S.: $3.00

TE-AMO **83**
PRESIDENTE MADURO
Mexico • *Size:* 7" x 50
Filler/Binder/Wrapper: Mexico
A smooth-tasting cigar with
a solid woody component,
and a mild nuttiness and
light spiciness on the finish.
U.S.: $3.75

THOMAS HINDS **83**
NICARAGUAN SELECTION
CHURCHILL MADURO
Nicaragua • *Size:* 7" x 49
Filler/Binder/Wrapper:
Nicaragua
An unusual cigar. It has a
fresh, herbal aroma that leads
into a sweet spice and dried
orange peel character. It is
mild, with some slightly veg-
etal flavors. U.S.: $7.00

TRESADO SELECCION **83**
NO. 500 MADURO
Dominican Republic • *Size:*
5½" x 42 *Filler/Binder:* Dom.
Rep. *Wrapper:* Indonesia
This brownish maduro-style
cigar has a light, delicate character with a hint of spice on the
palate. (12/01/93) U.S.: $2.25

TROYA NO. 45 **83**
CETRO MADURO
Dominican Republic • *Size:*
6" x 44 *Filler/Binder:* Dom.
Rep. *Wrapper:*
U.S.A./Conn. Broadleaf
Inconsistent construction
hurt this cigar, but some
tasters noted floral flavors

and a peppery finish.
(12/01/93) U.S.: $4.40

CRUZ REAL **82**
NO. 24 MADURO
Mexico • *Size:* 4½" x 50
Filler/Binder/Wrapper: Mexico
A cigar with a slightly rough
wrapper. It has hints of toast
and leather on the palate and
it has a tangy finish.
U.S.: $3.60

ENCANTO **82**
CHURCHILL MADURO
Honduras • *Size:* 6⅞" x 49
Filler/Binder/Wrapper: Hon-
duras
A mild cigar with an herbal
flavor profile. There is a light
spiciness on the palate.
U.S.: $5.75

LAS CABRILLAS BAL- **82**
BOA MADURO
Honduras • *Size:* 7½" x 54
Filler: Nicaragua, Mexico
Binder/Wrapper: Mexico
This cigar has a rough con-
struction. It has some burnt
caramel flavors and a soft
peppery finish. U.S.: $2.90

PETRUS TABACAGE **81**
ROTHSCHILD
MADURO 89
Honduras • *Size:* 4¼" x 50
Filler: Nicaragua *Binder:*
Honduras *Wrapper:* Ecuador
A cigar with a tangy quality
that may denote youth. It has
some herbal, woody charac-
teristics and a touch of sweet-
ness on the palate.
U.S.: $4.60

SANTA ROSA **81**
SANCHO PANZA
MADURO
Honduras • *Size:* 4½" x 50
Filler/Binder: Honduras
Wrapper: U.S.A./Conn.
Broadleaf
A cigar with unusually ripe
fruit flavors. There is an
earthy and woody quality to
the finish. U.S.: $4.75

TE-AMO **81**
ROBUSTO MADURO
Mexico • *Size:* 5½" x 54
Filler/Binder/Wrapper: Mexico
This cigar exhibits some
spicy characteristics, but with
a rather stale, grassy finish.
U.S.: $3.00

LICENCIADOS **80**
NO. 4 MADURO
Dominican Republic • *Size:*
5¾" x 43   *Filler:* Dom. Rep.
Binder: Honduras   *Wrapper:*
U.S.A./Conn. Broadleaf
Inconsistent construction.
But it delivers chocolate and
tobacco flavors even though
it has a short, hot aftertaste.
(12/01/93) U.S.: $3.40

LICENCIADOS PRESI- **80**
DENTE MADURO
Dominican Republic • *Size:*
8" x 50   *Filler:* Dom. Rep.
Binder: Honduras   *Wrapper:*
U.S.A./Conn. Broadleaf
A tough cigar that either
burns quickly and hot or is
too tight to draw. The short
finish has a bite. (12/01/93)
U.S.: $5.05

ORNELAS CAFETERO **79**
CHICO MADURO
Mexico • *Size:* 5½" x 46
Filler/Binder/Wrapper: Mexico
This cigar has a tight draw.
Some tasters noted stale and
burnt-leaf flavors. Overall, it
had a dry, balsa-wood charac-
ter. U.S.: $5.75

PETRUS TABACAGE **78**
CORONA SUBLIME
MADURO 89
Honduras • *Size:* 5½" x 46
Filler: Nicaragua   *Binder:*
Honduras   *Wrapper:* Ecuador
This cigar was very young
with a gummy quality to the
wrapper. But it had some
solid spice notes, with an
overall tangy character.
U.S.: $4.70

CHAPTER 12

Cigars

LISTED BY SIZE AND COUNTRY

RATING	BRAND	SIZE

Double Corona

BRAZIL

85   Canonero "Mediano" Double Corona 7½" x 50

79   Canonero "Classico" Double Corona 7½" x 50

CANARY ISLANDS

87   La Regenta Individual 8" x 50

87   La Regenta Premier 7½" x 50

83   Don Xavier Churchill 7½" x 50

82   Vargas Churchill 7½" x 50

69   Penamil No. 57 7½" x 50

CUBA

96   Hoyo de Monterrey Double Corona 7⅝" x 49

94   Ramon Allones Gigantes 7⅝" x 49

93   Partagas Lusitania 7⅝" x 49

91   Punch Double Corona 7⅝" x 49

DOMINICAN REPUBLIC

91   Arturo Fuente Cañones 8½" x 52

90   Leon Jimenes No. 1 7½" x 50

89   Fuente Fuente Opus X Double Corona 7⅝" x 49

89   Partagas No. 10 7½" x 49

89   Romeo y Julieta Vintage No. 5 7½" x 50

88   Oscar Supreme 8" x 48

88   Por Larrañaga Fabuloso 7" x 50

87   Ashton Churchill 7½" x 52

87   Aurora Double Corona 7½" x 50

87   Bauza Fabuloso 7½" x 50

87   Cacique Inca #8 7½" x 50

87   Cuesta-Rey Cabinet No. 1 8½" x 52

87   Don Leo Churchill 7½" x 50

87   Playboy by Don Diego Churchill 7¼" x 50

87   Vueltabajo Gigante 8½" x 52

86   Davidoff Special Series Double "R" 7½" x 50

86   Don Lino Havana Reserve Churchill 7½" x 50

86   El Rico Habano Gran Habanero Deluxe 7¼" x 50

86   Match Play Olympic 7½" x 50

86   Royal Jamaica Giant Corona 7½" x 49

86   Troya Clasico No. 72 Executive 7¼" x 50

85   Cuesta-Rey Centennial Collection Dominican No. 1 8½" x 52

85   Daniel Marshall Double Corona 7½" x 50

85   José Benito Presidente 7¼" x 50

85   La Flor Dominicana Presidente 8" x 50

85   Onyx No. 852 8" x 52

85   Pleiades Aldebaran 8½" x 50

85   Royal Jamaica Churchill 8" x 51

85   Sosa Magnum 7¾" x 50

84   Avo No. 3 7½" x 50

84   Casa Blanca Presidente 7½" x 50

84   Cerdan Don Juan 7½" x 50

84   Davidoff Aniversario No. 1
     8⅔" x 48

84   Don Lino Colorado Presidente
     7½" x 50

84   H. Upmann Cabinet Selection
     Columbo 8" x 50

84   La Gloria Cubana Gloria Inmensa
     7½" x 48

84   Licenciados Presidente 8" x 50

84   Licenciados Soberano 8½" x 52

84   Macabi Super Corona 7¾" x 50

84   Paul Garmirian Double Corona
     7⅞" x 50

84   Peterson Presidente 7½" x 50

84   The Griffin's Prestige 7½" x 50

84   Tresado Seleccion No. 100 8" x 52

83   Carrington No. 1 7½" x 50

83   Don Leo Presidente 8" x 52

83   El Sublimado Churchill 8" x 48

83   José Martí Martí 7½" x 50

83   Manifiesto Double Corona 7½" x 50

83   Nat Sherman Landmark Selection
     Dakota 7½" x 49

82   La Unica No. 100 8½" x 52

82   Sosa Family Selection No. 9
     7¾" x 51

81   Troya No. 72 Executive 7¾" x 50

80   Nat Sherman City Desk Selection
     Tribune 7½" x 50

HONDURAS

88   Astral Maestro 7½" x 52

87   Da Vinci Leonardo 8½" x 52

87   Don Asa Churchill 7½" x 50

87   El Rey del Mundo Flor del Mundo
     7½" x 54

87   Habana Gold Sterling Vintage Presidente 8½" x 52

86   C.A.O. Churchill 8" x 50

86   Don Tomas Special Edition No. 1
     7½" x 50

86   El Rey del Mundo Coronation
     8½" x 52

86   Hoyo de Monterrey Presidente
     8½" x 52

86   Petrus Tabacage DC Havana
     7¾" x 50

86   Thomas Hinds Honduran Selection
     Presidente 8½" x 52

85   Bering Grande 8½" x 52

85   Don Lino Churchill 8" x 50

85   Don Tomas Presidente 7½" x 50

85   Habana Gold Black Label Presidente
     8½" x 52

85   Lempira Presidente 7¼" x 50

85   Maya Viajantes 8½" x 52

84   Camórra Double Corona 8" x 52

84   Crown Achievement Churchill
     8" x 50

84   Punch Presidente 8½" x 52

84   V Centennial Presidente 8" x 50

83   Ballena Suprema Danli Collection
     Encanto 8" x 50

83   Felipe Gregorio Glorioso 7¾" x 50

83   La Fontana Michelangelo 7½" x 52

82   F.D. Grave Churchill 7¾" x 50

82   Las Cabrillas Columbus 8¼" x 52

81   Don Melo Presidente 8½" x 50

81   Petrus Tabacage Double Corona 89
     7¾" x 50

80   Belinda Prime Minister 7½" x 50

78 Habana Gold White Label Presidente 8½" x 52

77 Punch Gran Cru Prince Consort 8½" x 52

75 Maya Executive 7¼" x 50

JAMAICA

87 8-9-8 Collection Churchill 7½" x 49

84 Macanudo Prince of Wales 8" x 52

83 Macanudo Prince Philip 7½" x 49

83 Macanudo Vintage Cabinet Selection 1993 I 7½" x 49

MEXICO

87 Santa Clara 1830 No. I 7½" x 52

86 Excelsior No. 5 8" x 50

84 Te-Amo CEO 8½" x 52

83 Cruz Real No. 14 7½" x 50

78 Excelsior Individual 8½" x 52

78 Te-Amo Churchill 7½" x 50

NICARAGUA

86 Joya de Nicaragua Viajante 8½" x 52

85 La Finca Bolivares 7½" x 50

85 Padrón Executive 7½" x 50

84 MiCubano No. 852 8" x 52

83 José Martí Rey del Rey 8½" x 52

82 Don Juan President 8½" x 50

77 La Finca Gran Finca 8½" x 52

U.S.A.

91 La Gloria Cubana Soberanos 8" x 52

88 La Gloria Cubana Churchill 7" x 50

86 Tabacos San Jose Presidente 8" x 52

85 La Hoja Selecta Cosiac 7" x 49

85 La Tradicion Cabinet Series Double Corona 7⅜" x 50

79 Tabacos San Jose Double Corona 7⅜" x 50

Churchill

CANARY ISLANDS

87 Casa Martin Churchill 7" x 46

87 La Regenta Gran Corona 7¼" x 46

86 Cara Mia Churchill 7" x 50

83 Don Xavier Grand Corona 7" x 46

79 Vargas Presidente 6¼" x 46

COSTA RICA

90 Bahia Gold Churchill 6⅞" x 48

CUBA

93 Punch Churchill 7" x 47

90 Bolivar Corona Gigantes 7" x 47

90 Cohiba Esplendidos 7" x 47

89 Romeo y Julieta Churchill 7" x 47

89 Saint Luis Rey Churchill 7" x 47

88 Hoyo de Monterrey Churchill 7" x 47

87 El Rey del Mundo Tainos 7" x 47

83 Partagas Churchill Deluxe 7" x 47

DOMINICAN REPUBLIC

90 Bauza Casa Grande 6¼" x 48

90 Fuente Fuente Opus X Reserva d'Chateau 7" x 48

89 Cohiba Churchill 7" x 49

89 Davidoff Aniversario No. 2 7" x 48

88 Ashton Cabinet Selection No. 8 7" x 49

88 Daniel Marshall Churchill 7" x 48

88 Diana Silvius Churchill 7" x 50

88 Oliveros Premium Coroneles 7" x 50

88 Olor Colossos 7½" x 48

88	Peterson Hallmark Churchill 7" x 48	85	Onyx No. 646 6⅝" x 46
88	Savinelli E.L.R. No. 1 Churchill 7¼" x 48	85	Ramon Allones Redondos 7" x 49
87	Credo Pythagoras 7" x 50	85	Romeo y Julieta Vintage No. 4 7" x 48
87	Cuesta-Rey Aristocrat 7¼" x 48	85	Santa Damiana Seleccion No. 100 6¾" x 48
87	Don René Churchill 7¼" x 50	85	Savinelli Oro 750 Churchill 7" x 47
87	José Benito Churchill 7" x 50	85	Sosa Churchill 7" x 49
87	Montero Churchill 6⅞" x 46	85	V.M. Santana Connecticut Churchill 7¼" x 50
87	Particulares Churchill 6⅞" x 49	84	Arturo Fuente Churchill 7" x 48
87	Romeo y Julieta Churchill 7" x 50	84	Arturo Fuente Double Chateau Fuente 6¼" x 48
87	Signature Collection Churchill 7¼" x 50	84	Aurora Bristol Especial 6⅛" x 48
86	Avo No. 5 6⅞" x 46	84	Carrington No. 5 6⅞" x 46
86	Cacique Caribe #7 6⅛" x 46	84	H. Upmann Corona Imperiales 7" x 46
86	Carlos Toraño Dominican Selection Carlos VI 7" x 48	84	H. Upmann Monarch Tube 7" x 47
86	Cuesta-Rey Centennial Collection Dominican No. 2 7¼" x 48	84	Havana Classico Connecticut Shade Churchill 7¼" x 50
86	Diana Silvius 2000 6¾" x 47	84	Licenciados Churchill 7" x 50
86	Domino Park Churchill 7¼" x 50	84	Lone Wolf Vintage Series Churchill 6¾" x 48
86	Dunhill Cabreras 7" x 48	84	Montecruz Sun-Grown No. 200 7¼" x 46
86	Indian Tabac Anniversary Ltd. Reserve "Buffalo" 7" x 47	84	Montecruz Natural Claro No. 200 7¼" x 46
86	Montesino Gran Corona 6¼" x 48	84	Santa Damiana Seleccion No. 800 7" x 50
86	Signet Buckingham 7" x 48	84	Tamboril Churchill 7" x 47
86	Tamboril Sumatra Churchill 7" x 47	84	Troya No. 63 Churchill 6⅞" x 46
86	Yumuri Churchill 7" x 48	83	Cuesta-Rey Cabinet No. 898 7" x 49
85	Ashton Prime Minister 6⅞" x 48	83	Don Lino Oro Churchill 6⅞" x 46
85	Caballeros Churchill 7" x 50	83	Dunhill Peravias 7" x 50
85	Credo Magnificant 6⅞" x 46	83	Juan Clemente Churchill 6⅞" x 46
85	Don Diego Monarch Tubes 7¼" x 46	83	La Flor Dominicana Churchill Reserva Especial 6⅞" x 49
85	Match Play Prestwick 6⅞" x 46		
85	Montecristo Churchill 7" x 48	83	La Gloria Cubana Churchill 7" x 50
85	Nat Sherman Gotham Selection No. 500 7" x 50		
85	Nat Sherman Exchange Selection Oxford 5 7" x 49		

83 **Leon Jimenes No. 2** 7" x 47

83 **Tresado Seleccion No. 200** 7" x 48

82 **Cubita 2000** 7" x 50

82 **Don Leo Double Corona** 7" x 48

82 **Fonseca 10-10** 7" x 50

82 **La Unica No. 200** 7" x 49

82 **Vueltabajo Churchill** 7" x 48

81 **La Flor Dominicana Mambises** 6⅞" x 48

81 **Paul Garmirian Churchill** 7" x 48

81 **Pleiades Sirius** 6⅞" x 46

81 **St. George Churchill** 7" x 48

81 **Sosa Family Selection No. 8** 7" x 48

80 **Cerdan Churchill** 7" x 46

80 **El Rico Habano Double Corona** 7" x 47

80 **Siglo 21 21-4** 7" x 48

79 **Hombre de Oro Churchill** 7" x 50

79 **Macabi Double Corona** 6⅞" x 49

78 **Avo XO Maestoso** 7" x 48

78 **Coticas Double Corona** 7" x 48

HONDURAS

89 **El Rey del Mundo Double Corona** 7" x 49

89 **Royal Honduras Sovereign** 7" x 48

88 **Maya Churchill** 6⅞" x 49

87 **La Fontana Da Vinci** 6⅞" x 48

87 **Thomas Hinds Honduran Selection Churchill** 7" x 49

86 **Bances Corona Inmensa** 6¾" x 48

86 **Hoyo de Monterrey Excalibur No. 2** 6¾" x 47

86 **La Reserva No. 2** 6½" x 48

86 **Nat Sherman Host Selection Hampton** 7" x 50

86 **Roly Valentinos** 7" x 49

85 **Baccarat Churchill** 7" x 50

85 **Camacho Churchill** 7" x 48

85 **Felipe II Reserva X** 7" x 48

85 **Punch Deluxe Series Chateau L** 7¼" x 54

85 **Santa Rosa Churchill** 7" x 50

85 **V Centennial Churchill** 7" x 48

84 **Camórra Limited Reserve Churchill San Remo** 7" x 48

84 **Habana Gold Black Label Churchill** 7½" x 46

84 **Hoyo de Monterrey Cuban Largos** 7¼" x 47

84 **Hurricanos Churchill** 7" x 49

84 **Petrus Tabacage Churchill 90** 7" x 50

84 **Punch Double Corona** 6¾" x 48

84 **Punch Gran Cru Monarca** 6¾" x 48

83 **Belinda Ramon** 7¼" x 47

83 **Hoyo de Monterrey Double Corona** 6¾" x 48

83 **La Diligencia Churchill** 7" x 48

83 **Las Cabrillas De Soto** 6⅞" x 50

83 **V Centennial 500 Series Churchill** 7" x 48

83 **Zino Gold Line Veritas** 7" x 49

82 **Ballena Suprema Danli Collection Alma** 7" x 47

82 **Da Vinci Ginevra de Benci** 7" x 48

82 **Encanto Churchill Natural** 7" x 50

82 **Felipe Gregorio Suntuoso** 7" x 48

82 **Hoyo de Monterrey Excalibur Banquet** 6¾" x 48

82 **Hoyo de Monterrey Sultan** 7¼" x 54

82 **Punch Gran Cru Diademas** 7¼" x 54

81 **Don Melo Centenario** 7" x 48

81 **La Maximiliana Perfectus** 7" x 50

80 Hoyo de Monterrey Excalibur No. 1
7¼" x 54

80 Lempira Churchill 7" x 48

79 El Rey del Mundo Corona Inmensa
7¼" x 47

79 Punch Casa Grande 7¼" x 46

INDONESIA

89 Celestino Vega Churchill 7¼" x 50

JAMAICA

87 Macanudo Vintage Cabinet Selection
1993 XX 7" x 47

86 Temple Hall No. 700 7" x 49

85 Macanudo Vintage No. 1 1988
7½" x 49

MEXICO

80 Ballena Suprema San Andres Collection Concordia 7" x 48

79 Ornelas Churchill 7" x 49

78 Ballena Suprema San Andres Collection Esperanza 7" x 50

78 Santa Clara 1830 No. II 6½" x 48

76 Te-Amo Presidente 7" x 50

NICARAGUA

90 Don Juan Churchill 7" x 49

90 Padrón Churchill 6⅛" x 46

89 Cupido Churchill 7" x 47

87 C.A.O. Gold Churchill 7" x 48

87 Grand Nica Churchill 7" x 52

87 Thomas Hinds Nicaraguan Selection
Churchill 7" x 49

87 Torcedor Churchill 7" x 50

86 Don Juan Platinum Churchill
7" x 49

86 Habanica Serie 747 7" x 47

86 La Gianna Havana Churchill 7" x 49

85 Da Vinci Mezzanote 7" x 48

85 Gilberto Oliva Churchill 7" x 50

84 Flor de Farach Churchill 7" x 48

84 Hoja Cubana Churchill 7" x 50

84 La Finca Valentino 6¼" x 48

84 Orosi Oro 700 7" x 50

84 Primera de Nicaragua Churchill
7" x 50

84 Thomas Hinds Cabinet Selection
Churchill 7" x 49

83 Joya de Nicaragua Churchill
6⅞" x 49

79 MiCubano No. 748 8" x 47

PHILIPPINES

85 Double Happiness Ecstasy 7" x 47

84 Fighting Cock C.O.D. 7" x 47

78 Flor de Filipinas Churchill 7" x 47

U.S.A.

88 Tabacos San Jose Churchill 7" x 47

85 El Rico Habano Double Corona
7" x 47

84 Imperio Cubano Churchill 7" x 48

Corona Gorda

CANARY ISLANDS

87 Cara Mia Toro 6" x 50

84 Vargas Reserva Senadores 5½" x 46

83 Don Xavier Corona 5⅝" x 46

CUBA

92 Hoyo de Monterrey Epicure No. 1
5⅝" x 46

91 Romeo y Julieta Exhibicion No. 3
5⅝" x 46

89 Cohiba Siglo IV 5⅝" x 46

87 Bolivar Corona Extra 5⅝" x 46

87 El Rey del Mundo Gran Coronas
5⅝" x 46

87 Punch Punch 5⅝" x 46

83 H. Upmann Magnum 5⅝" x 46

DOMINICAN REPUBLIC

91 Fuente Fuente Opus X Fuente
Fuente 5⅝" x 46

89 El Rico Habano Gran Corona
5¼" x 46

88 Avo No. 2 6" x 50

88 Don Lino Havana Reserve Toro
5½" x 46

88 Olor Paco 6" x 50

88 Partagas Limited Reserve Regale
6¼" x 47

88 Sosa Governor 6" x 50

87 Ashton Double Magnum 6" x 50

87 Cuesta-Rey Centennial Collection
Dominican No. 60 6" x 50

87 Don Leo Robusto 5½" x 50

87 H. Upmann Churchill 5⅝" x 46

87 Nat Sherman Gotham Selection No.
711 6" x 50

87 Partagas Almirante 6¼" x 47

87 Peterson Toro 6" x 50

87 Romeo y Julieta Vintage No. 2
6" x 46

87 Royal Jamaica Director 6" x 45

87 Savinelli E.L.R. Double Corona
6" x 50

86 Arturo Fuente Flor Fina 8-5-8
6" x 47

86 Cubita No. 700 6" x 50

86 Licenciados Toro 6" x 50

86 Montecristo Corona Grande
5¼" x 46

86 Nat Sherman VIP Selection
Carnegie 6" x 48

86 Paul Garmirian Connoisseur 6" x 50

85 Casa Blanca Deluxe 6" x 50

85 Davidoff No. 5000 5⅝" x 46

85 Dunhill Condados 6" x 48

85 Montecruz Sun-Grown No. 201
6¼" x 46

85 Romanticos Leonardo 6" x 50

84 Don Diego Grande 6" x 50

84 Macabi Corona Extra 6" x 50

84 Tresado Seleccion No. 300 6" x 46

83 Cabañas Royale 5⅝" x 46

83 Juan Clemente Club Selection No. 1
6" x 50

83 Oscar No. 500 5½" x 50

83 Santa Damiana Seleccion No. 300
5½" x 46

82 Nat Sherman Exchange Selection
Trafalgar 4 6" x 47

82 Vueltabajo Toro 6" x 50

81 Cacique Apache 6" x 50

80 Match Play Turnberry 6" x 50

79 Carrington No. 7 6" x 50

78 Henry Clay Brevas a la Conserva
5⅝" x 46

HONDURAS

89 Belinda Cabinet 5⅝" x 45

89 Hoyo de Monterrey Excalibur No. 3
6¼" x 50

89 Lempira Toro 6" x 50

88 El Rey del Mundo Choix Supreme
6⅛" x 49

88 V Centennial Numero 2 6" x 50

87 Da Vinci Monalisa 6" x 50

87   **Don Tomas Special Edition No. 500**
5½" x 46

87   **Hoyo de Monterrey Corona**
5⅜" x 46

87   **Hoyo de Monterrey Governor**
6⅛" x 50

86   **Don Melo Corona Extra** 5½" x 46

86   **Don Tomas Corona** 5½" x 50

86   **Puros Indios Corona Gorda** 6" x 50

86   **Santa Rosa Toro** 6" x 50

85   **Bering Hispanos** 6" x 50

85   **C.A.O. Corona Gorda** 6" x 50

85   **Don Asa Corona** 5½" x 50

85   **Don Lino Toro** 5½" x 46

85   **Punch Deluxe Series Chateau M**
5¼" x 46

85   **Saint Luis Rey Serie A** 6" x 50

84   **Blair Robusto** 6" x 50

84   **Don Tomas Toro** 5½" x 46

83   **El Rey del Mundo Robusto Larga**
6" x 50

83   **Maya Maya** 6" x 50

82   **Petrus Tabacage Corona Sublime 89**
5½" x 46

82   **Thomas Hinds Honduran Selection
Short Churchill** 6" x 50

81   **Hoyo de Monterrey Excalibur No. 4**
5⅝" x 46

77   **Tesoros de Copan Corona** 5¼" x 46

MEXICO

86   **Te-Amo Toro** 6" x 50

82   **Te-Amo Satisfaction** 6" x 46

80   **Cruz Real No. 19** 6" x 50

79   **Santa Clara 1830 No. VI** 6" x 50

NICARAGUA

92   **Padrón 1964 Anniversary Series
Exclusivo** 5½" x 50

88   **Flor de Florez Cabinet Selection Florez Florez** 5¼" x 46

87   **Habanica Serie 546** 5¼" x 46

85   **Flor de Florez Corona** 6" x 50

85   **Habanica Serie 646** 6" x 46

85   **Thomas Hinds Nicaraguan Selection
Short Churchill** 6" x 50

84   **Joya de Nicaragua Toro** 6" x 50

82   **MiCubano No. 650** 6" x 50

79   **La Finca Joya** 6" x 50

78   **Torcedor Toro** 6" x 50

U.S.A.

87   **La Gloria Cubana Extra** 6¼" x 46

Lonsdale

CANARY ISLANDS

86   **Monte Canario Imperiales** 6½" x 42

86   **Monte Canario Nuncio** 6¼" x 44

85   **Don Vito Capo** 6¾" x 44

84   **Cara Mia Lonsdale** 6½" x 42

84   **Don Xavier Lonsdale** 6⅝" x 42

CUBA

95   **Cohiba Siglo III** 6" x 42

92   **Quintero Churchill** 6½" x 42

91   **Rafael Gonzales Lonsdale** 6½" x 42

91   **Sancho Panza Molinas** 6½" x 42

90   **Cohiba Siglo V** 6⅞" x 43

90   **H. Upmann Lonsdale** 6½" x 42

90   **La Gloria Cubana Medaille d'Or
No. 2** 6⅔" x 43

90 **Romeo y Julieta Corona Grande** 6½" x 42

89 **Hoyo de Monterrey Le Hoyo des Dieux** 6" x 42

88 **Montecristo No. 1** 6½" x 42

88 **Partagas 8-9-8** 6⅝" x 43

88 **Partagas No. 1** 6⅝" x 43

88 **Saint Luis Rey Lonsdale** 6½" x 42

87 **Bolivar Inmensa** 6⅝" x 43

87 **El Rey del Mundo Lonsdale** 6⅜" x 42

DOMINICAN REPUBLIC

91 **Partagas Limited Reserve Royale** 6¾" x 43

90 **Troya No. 45 Cetro** 6¼" x 44

89 **Davidoff No. 4000** 6" x 42

89 **Davidoff Grand Cru No. 1** 6" x 42

88 **Arturo Fuente Spanish Lonsdale** 6½" x 42

88 **Partagas 8-9-8** 6⅞" x 44

88 **Partagas No. 1** 6¾" x 43

88 **Savinelli E.L.R. No. 3 Lonsdale** 6¼" x 43

87 **Licenciados Excelente** 6¾" x 43

87 **Montecristo No. 1** 6½" x 44

87 **Montesino No. 1** 6¾" x 43

87 **Partagas Humitube** 6¾" x 43

87 **Por Larrañaga Cetros** 6⅞" x 42

87 **Ramon Allones "B"** 6½" x 42

86 **Ashton 8-9-8** 6½" x 44

86 **Avo No. 1** 6⅔" x 42

86 **Bauza Medaille d'Oro No. 1** 6⅞" x 44

86 **Don Diego Lonsdale** 6⅝" x 42

86 **Primo del Rey Seleccion No. 1** 6¹³⁄₁₆ x 42

86 **Ramon Allones Crystals** 6¾" x 42

86 **Tresado Seleccion No. 400** 6⅝" x 44

86 **Troya No. 54 Elegante** 7" x 43

85 **Arturo Fuente Seleccion Privada No. 1** 6¾" x 44

85 **Cuesta-Rey Cabinet No. 95** 6¼" x 42

85 **Cuesta-Rey Cabinet No. 1884** 6¾" x 44

85 **Don Lino Havana Reserve No. 1** 6½" x 44

85 **Macabi No. 1** 6¾" x 44

85 **Nat Sherman Gotham Selection No. 1400** 6¼" x 44

85 **Primo del Rey Chavon** 6½" x 41

85 **Ramon Allones Privada A** 7" x 45

85 **Sosa Family Selection No. 1** 6¾" x 43

84 **Casa Blanca Lonsdale** 6½" x 42

84 **Cuesta-Rey Captiva** 6³⁄₁₆" x 42

84 **Diana Silvius Corona** 6½" x 42

84 **José Martí Palma** 7" x 42

84 **Juan Clemente Club Selection No. 3** 7" x 44

84 **Juan Clemente Gran Corona** 6" x 42

84 **La Unica No. 300** 6¾" x 44

84 **Montecruz Sun-Grown No. 210** 6½" x 42

84 **Nat Sherman Landmark Selection Algonquin** 6¾" x 43

84 **Olor Lonsdale** 6½" x 42

84 **Primo del Rey Seleccion No. 2** 6¼" x 42

84 **Romeo y Julieta Palma** 6" x 43

84 **Royal Jamaica Corona Grande** 6½" x 42

84 **The Griffin's No. 300** 6¼" x 44

83 **Bauza Jaguar** 6½" x 42

83 **Canaria d'Oro Lonsdale** 6½" x 43

83 **Cubita 8-9-8** 6¾" x 43

83 Cuesta-Rey Centennial Collection Dominican No. 4 6½" x 42

83 Dunhill Diamantes 6⅝" x 42

83 H. Upmann Lonsdale 6⅝" x 42

83 Leon Jimenes No. 3 6½" x 42

83 Montesino Cesar No. 2 6¼" x 44

83 Nat Sherman Exchange Selection Butterfield 8 6½" x 42

83 Ramon Allones Trumps 6¼" x 43

82 La Flor Dominicana Alcalde 6½" x 44

82 Santa Damiana Seleccion No. 700 6½" x 42

81 Oscar No. 300 6¼" x 44

80 Nat Sherman Manhattan Selection Gramercy 6¼" x 43

80 Vueltabajo Lonsdale 7" x 43

78 Paul Garmirian Lonsdale 6½" x 42

78 Sosa Lonsdale 6½" x 43

HONDURAS

89 V Centennial Cetro 6½" x 44

87 Bering Plaza 6" x 43

87 Padrón Palma 6⁹⁄₁₆" x 42

86 Don Melo Corona Gorda 6¼" x 44

86 Encanto Elegante 7" x 44

86 Petrus Tabacage No. II 89 6¼" x 44

86 Saint Luis Rey Lonsdale 6½" x 44

86 Santa Rosa Cetros 6" x 42

85 Belinda Corona Grande 6¼" x 44

85 C.A.O. Lonsdale 7" x 44

85 Don Asa Cetros No. 2 6½" x 44

85 Don Tomas Special Edition No. 200 6½" x 44

85 Hoyo de Monterrey No. 1 6½" x 43

85 Punch Lonsdale 6½" x 43

85 Thomas Hinds Honduran Selection Supremos 6⅔" x 43

85 Zino Mouton Cadet No. 1 6½" x 44

84 Astral Lujos 6½" x 44

84 Don Lino No. 1 6½" x 44

84 Don Tomas Corona Grande 6½" x 44

84 F.D. Grave Lonsdale 6¼" x 44

84 Hoyo de Monterrey Ambassador 6¼" x 44

84 Punch Amatista 6¼" x 44

84 Tesoros de Copan Cetros 6¼" x 44

84 Zino Gold Line Tradition 6¼" x 44

83 Baccarat Luchadores 6" x 43

83 Don Tomas Cetros 6½" x 44

83 Gilberto Oliva Numero 1 6½" x 44

83 Padrón Ambassador 6⅞" x 42

83 Padrón 1964 Anniversary Series Superior 6" x 42

83 Santa Rosa Corona 6½" x 44

81 Baccarat No. 1 7" x 44

81 Hoyo de Monterrey Churchill 6¼" x 45

81 Punch Punch 6¼" x 45

79 Las Cabrillas Ponce de Leon 6⅝" x 44

78 Bances Cazadores 6¼" x 43

76 Camacho No. 1 7" x 44

JAMAICA

86 8-9-8 Collection Lonsdale 6½" x 42

86 Macanudo Vintage Cabinet Selection 1993 II 6⁹⁄₁₆" x 43

85 Macanudo Baron de Rothschild 6½" x 42

82 Temple Hall No. 625 6½" x 42

MEXICO

86 Veracruz Reserve Especial 6½" x 42

85 Santa Clara 1830 No. III 6⅝" x 43

82 **Te-Amo Relaxation** 6⅝" x 44

81 **Te-Amo Celebration** 6¹¹⁄₁₆ x 44

80 **Te-Amo New York Park Avenue** 6⅝" x 42

78 **Ornelas Ltd. Cognac** 6¼" x 42

78 **Ornelas No. 1** 6¾" x 44

76 **Cruz Real No. 1** 6⅝" x 42

69 **Ornelas No. 1 Vanilla** 6¼" x 44

NICARAGUA

87 **Joya de Nicaragua No. 1** 6⅝" x 44

87 **La Finca Romeo** 6½" x 42

87 **Thomas Hinds Nicaraguan Selection Lonsdale** 6⅔" x 43

84 **Don Juan Numero Uno** 6⅝" x 44

83 **Al Capone Corona Grande** 6¼" x 43

U.S.A.

88 **La Gloria Cubana Medaille d'Or No. 1** 6¼" x 43

Corona

CANARY ISLANDS

78 **La Regenta No. 3** 5⅝" x 42

CUBA

91 **Bolivar Corona** 5½" x 42

91 **El Rey del Mundo Corona De Luxe** 5½" x 42

91 **H. Upmann Corona** 5½" x 42

90 **Hoyo de Monterrey Le Hoyo du Roi** 5½" x 42

89 **Punch Corona** 5½" x 42

89 **Ramon Allones Corona** 5½" x 42

89 **Romeo y Julieta Corona** 5½" x 42

88 **Montecristo No. 3** 5½" x 42

86 **Partagas Corona** 5½" x 42

85 **Hoyo de Monterrey Corona** 5½" x 42

DOMINICAN REPUBLIC

91 **Montesino Diplomatico** 5½" x 43

90 **Arturo Fuente Don Carlos Reserva No. 3** 5½" x 44

89 **Casa Blanca Corona** 5½" x 42

89 **Savinelli Extraordinaire** 5½" x 44

88 **Credo Anthanor** 5¾" x 42

88 **Davidoff Grand Cru No. 2** 5⅝" x 43

88 **Olor Momento** 5½" x 43

87 **Avo No. 7** 6" x 44

87 **Carrington No. 2** 6" x 42

87 **Cuesta-Rey Centennial Collection Dominican No. 5** 5½" x 43

87 **Don Diego Corona Major Tubes** 5½" x 42

87 **Montecristo No. 3** 5½" x 44

87 **Montecruz Sun-Grown No. 220** 5½" x 42

87 **Nat Sherman Landmark Selection Hampshire** 5½" x 42

87 **Nat Sherman Metropolitan Selection Anglers** 5½" x 43

87 **Romeo y Julieta Vintage No. 1** 6" x 43

87 **Troya No. 27 Corona** 5½" x 42

86 **Ashton Aged Maduro No. 20** 5½" x 44

86 **Fonseca 8-9-8** 6" x 43

86 **H. Upmann Corona** 5½" x 42

86 **José Benito Palma** 6" x 43

86 **Juan Clemente Club Selection No. 4** 5¼" x 42

86 **Licenciados No. 4** 5¼" x 43

86 **Macabi Media Corona** 5½" x 43

86 **Partagas No. 2** 5¾" x 43

86 **Partagas Sabrosos** 5⅞" x 43

86 **Paul Garmirian Corona** 5½" x 42

86 **Ramon Allones Privada D** 5" x 42

86 **Vueltabajo Corona** 5¾" x 42

85 **Aurora No. 4** 5¼" x 42

85 **Bauza Grecos** 5½" x 42

85 **Don Diego Corona** 5⅝" x 42

85 **Dunhill Tabaras** 5½" x 42

85 **Dunhill Valverdes** 5½" x 42

85 **H. Upmann Corona Major Tube** 5⅛" x 42

85 **La Flor Dominicana Insurrecto** 5½" x 42

85 **Leon Jimenes No. 4** 5⁹⁄₁₆" x 42

85 **Montecruz Sun-Grown Tubos** 6" x 42

85 **Tresado Seleccion No. 500** 5½" x 42

84 **Ashton Corona** 5½" x 44

84 **Canaria d'Oro Corona** 5½" x 43

84 **El Sublimado Corona** 6" x 44

84 **Henry Clay Brevas** 5½" x 42

84 **José Martí Corona** 5½" x 42

84 **Knockando No. 3** 5¾" x 41

84 **La Unica No. 500** 5½" x 42

84 **Licenciados Supreme Maduro No. 200** 5" x 42

84 **Por Larrañaga Nacionales** 5½" x 42

84 **Primo del Rey Seleccion No. 4** 5½" x 42

84 **Sosa Brevas** 5½" x 43

83 **Caballeros Corona** 5¾" x 43

83 **Nat Sherman City Desk Selection Gazette** 6" x 42

83 **Romeo y Julieta Corona** 5½" x 44

82 **Peterson Corona** 5¾" x 43

81 **Pleiades Orion** 5¾" x 42

HONDURAS

90 **Puros Indios No. 4 Especial** 5½" x 44

88 **Lempira Corona** 5½" x 42

88 **Padrón 1964 Anniversary Series Corona** 6" x 42

88 **Punch Cafe Royal** 5⅝" x 44

87 **Belinda Breva Conserva** 5½" x 43

87 **Bering Corona Royale** 6" x 41

87 **C.A.O. Corona** 6" x 42

87 **Hoyo de Monterrey Cafe Royal** 5⅝" x 43

86 **Bances Brevas** 5½" x 43

86 **Felipe Gregorio Sereno** 5¾" x 42

86 **Habana Gold Black Label Corona** 6" x 44

86 **Hoyo de Monterrey Super Hoyo** 5½" x 44

86 **Santa Rosa No. 4** 5½" x 42

86 **Thomas Hinds Honduran Selection Corona** 5½" x 42

85 **Camacho Nacionales** 5½" x 44

85 **Don Melo Petit Corona** 5½" x 42

85 **Hoyo de Monterrey Excalibur No. 5** 6¼" x 43

85 **Maya Petit Corona** 5½" x 42

84 **El Rey del Mundo Habana Club** 5½" x 42

84 **Las Cabrillas Magellan** 6" x 42

84 **Punch No. 75** 5½" x 43

83 **Punch Deluxe Series Royal Coronation** 5¼" x 44

83 **V Centennial Corona** 5½" x 42

83 **Zino Gold Line Diamonds** 5½" x 40

JAMAICA

87   Macanudo Vintage No. 3 1988
5⁵⁄₁₆" x 43

86   Macanudo Duke of Devon   5½" x 42

83   8-9-8 Collection Corona   5½" x 42

MEXICO

87   Santa Clara 1830 No. V   6" x 43

86   Cruz Real No. 2   6" x 42

80   Te-Amo Meditation   6" x 42

NICARAGUA

91   La Finca Corona   5½" x 42

86   Padrón Londres   5½" x 42

84   MiCubano No. 542   5" x 42

84   Thomas Hinds Nicaraguan Selection
Corona   5½" x 42

83   Joya de Nicaragua No. 6   6" x 42

80   Don Juan Cetro   6" x 43

U.S.A.

88   La Gloria Cubana Glorias   5½" x 43

85   El Rico Habano Corona   5½" x 42

83   La Hoja Selecta Cetros de Oro
5¾" x 43

Robusto

CANARY ISLANDS

84   Don Xavier Robusto   4⅝" x 50

83   Dunhill Corona Extra   5½" x 50

83   La Regenta No. 2 Robusto   4¾" x 50

83   Vargas Robusto   4¾" x 50

70   Monte Canario Robusto   4¾" x 50

CUBA

95   Bolivar Royal Corona   5" x 50

92   Hoyo de Monterrey Epicure No. 2
4⅞" x 50

92   Partagas Serie D No. 4   4⅞" x 50

92   Romeo y Julieta Exhibicion No. 4
5" x 48

91   Cohiba Robusto   4⅞" x 50

91   Ramon Allones Specially Selected
4⅞" x 50

90   Juan Lopez Seleccion No. 2   4⅞" x 50

DOMINICAN REPUBLIC

91   Fuente Fuente Opus X Robusto
5¼" x 50

90   El Rico Habano Habano Club
5" x 48

89   Montecristo Robusto   4¾" x 50

88   La Unica No. 400   4½" x 50

88   Leon Jimenes Robusto   5" x 50

88   Montecruz Sun-Grown Robusto
4½" x 49

88   Savinelli E.L.R. Robusto   5" x 49

88   Sosa Wavell   4¾" x 50

88   The Griffin's Robusto   5" x 50

87   Arturo Fuente Don Carlos Robusto
5" x 50

87   Ashton Cabinet Selection No. 6
5½" x 52

87   Ashton Magnum   5" x 50

87   Aurora Robusto   5" x 50

87   Bauza Robusto   5½" x 50

87   Davidoff Special Series "R"
4⅞" x 50

87   El Sublimado Robusto   4½" x 50

87   La Flor Dominicana Robusto Reserva Especial   5" x 48

87   Partagas Robusto 4½" x 49

87   Por Larrañaga Robusto 5" x 50

87   Signature Collection Robusto 5" x 50

86   Arturo Fuente Rothschild 4½" x 50

86   Credo Arcane 5" x 50

86   Diana Silvius Robusto 4⅞" x 52

86   Domino Park Robusto 5" x 50

86   Don Lino Colorado Rothschild 4½" x 50

86   H. Upmann Cabinet Selection Corsario 5½" x 50

86   H. Upmann Cabinet Selection Robusto 4¾" x 50

86   H. Upmann Pequeños No. 100 4½" x 50

86   Licenciados Wavell 5" x 50

86   Nat Sherman VIP Selection Astor 4½" x 50

86   Playboy by Don Diego Robusto 5" x 50

86   Romanticos Eros 5" x 52

86   Romeo y Julieta Vintage No. 3 4½" x 50

86   Sosa Family Selection No. 5 5" x 50

86   Vueltabajo Robusto 4¾" x 52

85   Arturo Fuente Chateau Fuente 4½" x 50

85   Calle Ocho Gordito 5" x 50

85   Don Lino Colorado Robusto 5½" x 50

85   El Sublimado Regardete 4½" x 50

85   Fonseca 5-50 5" x 50

85   Havana Classico Connecticut Shade Robusto 5" x 50

85   Juan Clemente Rothschild 4⅞" x 50

85   La Flor Dominicana Maceo 5" x 48

85   Royal Jamaica Robusto 4½" x 49

85   Tamboril Sumatra Robusto 5" x 52

85   V.M. Santana Connecticut Collection Robusto 5" x 50

85   V.M. Santana Sumatra Collection Robusto 5" x 50

84   Cuesta-Rey Centennial Collection Dominican No. 7 4½" x 50

84   Don Manolo Series III Robusto 5" x 50

84   Dunhill Romanas 4½" x 50

84   José Benito Rothschild 4¾" x 50

84   Juan Clemente Club Selection No. 2 4½" x 46

84   Macabi Royal Corona 5" x 50

84   Match Play Cypress 4¾" x 50

84   Nat Sherman Manhattan Selection Sutton 5½" x 49

84   Romeo y Julieta Rothschild 5" x 50

84   Santa Damiana Seleccion No. 500 5" x 50

83   Avo No. 9 4¾" x 48

83   Avo XO Intermezzo 5½" x 50

83   Canaria d'Oro Inmenso 5½" x 49

83   Don Alberto Reserva Grand Cruz 5" x 50

83   Don Lino Havana Reserve Robusto 5½" x 50

83   Partagas Naturales 5½" x 50

83   Pleiades Pluton 5" x 50

83   Troya No. 18 Rothchild 4½" x 50

82   Caballeros Rothschild 5" x 50

82   Dunhill Altamiras 5" x 48

82   Nat Sherman Landmark Selection Vanderbilt 5" x 47

82   Paul Garmirian Epicure 5½" x 50

81   Paul Garmirian Robusto 5" x 50

81   Peterson Robusto 4¾" x 50

80   Paul Garmirian No. 2 4¾" x 48

80   Tamboril Robusto 5" x 52

78 Carrington No. 6 4½" x 50

78 Don Manolo Series II Robusto
5" x 50

77 Don Alberto Superior Habana
Robusto 5" x 50

76 Don Alberto Oro de Habana Robusto 5" x 50

HONDURAS

89 Astral Beso 5" x 52

88 Encanto Rothschild 4½" x 50

88 Punch Super Rothschild 5¼" x 50

87 Da Vinci Madonna 5" x 50

87 Habana Gold White Label Robusto
5" x 50

87 Puros Indios Colorado Rothschild
5" x 50

87 Roly Colorado Rothschild 5" x 50

87 V Centennial Robusto 5" x 50

86 C.A.O. Robusto 4½" x 50

86 El Rey del Mundo Rothschild
5" x 50

86 Hoyo de Monterrey Rothschild
4½" x 50

86 Nat Sherman Host Selection Hobart
5" x 50

86 Roly Colorado Claro Rothschild
5" x 50

85 Don Melo Nom Plus 4¼" x 50

85 Gilberto Oliva Robusto 5½" x 50

84 Belinda Medaglia d'Oro 4⅝" x 50

84 Don Lino Robusto 5½" x 50

84 Felipe Gregorio Robusto 5" x 50

84 Punch Gran Cru Robusto 5¼" x 50

84 Punch Rothschild 4½" x 50

84 Thomas Hinds Honduran Selection
Robusto 5" x 50

83 Don Tomas International No. 2
5½" x 50

83 El Rey del Mundo Robusto 5" x 54

83 Hurricanos Robusto 5" x 50

83 Las Cabrillas Cortez 4¾" x 50

83 Punch Gran Cru Superior 5½" x 48

82 Baccarat Rothschild 5" x 50

82 Camacho Monarca 5" x 50

82 Zino Mouton Cadet No. 6 5" x 50

81 Camórra Roma 5" x 50

80 Bering Robusto 4¾" x 50

80 Don Tomas Rothschild 4½" x 50

80 Don Tomas Special Edition No. 300
5" x 50

80 Habana Gold Black Label Robusto
5" x 50

80 Lempira Robusto 5" x 50

77 Habana Gold Sterling Vintage
Robusto 5" x 50

74 Petrus Tabacage Rothschild 4¾" x 50

JAMAICA

90 Macanudo Vintage Cabinet Selection
1993 VIII (Crystal) 5½" x 50

88 Macanudo Vintage Cabinet Selection
1993 V 5½" x 49

87 8-9-8 Collection Robusto 5½" x 49

87 Macanudo Vintage Cabinet Selection
1993 IV 4½" x 47

86 Temple Hall No. 550 5½" x 49

85 Macanudo Crystal Cafe 5½" x 50

85 Macanudo Hyde Park Cafe 5½" x 49

85 Macanudo Vintage No. 5 1988
5½" x 49

MEXICO

83 Aromas de San Andreas Robusto
5" x 50

82 Te-Amo Torito 4¼" x 50

81   Ballena Suprema San Andres Collection Cordura 5" x 52

81   Excelsior No. 3 5½" x 52

80   Cruz Real No. 24 4½" x 50

77   Cruz Real No. 25 5½" x 52

75   Ornelas Robusto 4¾" x 49

72   Santa Clara 1830 Robusto 4½" x 50

NICARAGUA

90   Joya de Nicaragua Consul 4½" x 52

89   C.A.O. Gold Robusto 5" x 50

88   Habanica Serie 550 5" x 50

88   José Martí Robusto 4⅝" x 50

87   5 Vegas Robusto 5" x 50

87   Don Juan Robusto 5" x 50

87   Padrón 3000 5½" x 52

87   Thomas Hinds Cabinet Selection Robusto 5" x 50

87   Torcedor Robusto 5" x 50

86   Free Cuba Robusto 5" x 50

86   Padrón 2000 5" x 50

85   La Gianna Robusto 5" x 50

85   Thomas Hinds Nicaraguan Selection Robusto 5" x 50

82   Orosi Oro 550 5" x 50

77   La Finca Robusto 4½" x 50

U.S.A.

87   Imperio Cubano Robusto 5" x 50

85   La Gloria Cubana Wavell 5" x 50

84   Tabacos San Jose Robusto 5" x 50

81   La Tradicion Cabinet Series Rosado Robusto 5" x 50

78   La Tradicion Cabinet Series Natural Robusto 5" x 50

72   La Hoja Selecta Palais Royal 4¼" x 50

Petit Corona

BRAZIL

86   Canonero "Mediano" Potra 4¼" x 38

CANARY ISLANDS

86   La Regenta No. 5 4½" x 42

85   Vargas Cremas 4⅝" x 39

CUBA

93   Cohiba Siglo I 4" x 40

92   Romeo y Julieta Cedros No. 3 5" x 42

90   Bolivar Petit Corona 5" x 42

90   Montecristo No. 4 5" x 42

89   Partagas Petit Corona 5" x 42

88   Hoyo de Monterrey Le Hoyo du Prince 5" x 40

88   Romeo y Julieta Petit Corona 5" x 42

86   Punch Petit Corona del Punch 5" x 42

85   Sancho Panza Non Plus 5" x 42

84   Quintero Medias Coronas 5" x 40

81   Fonseca Cosacos 5⅛" x 42

81   H. Upmann Petit Corona 5" x 42

DOMINICAN REPUBLIC

92   Fuente Fuente Opus X Perfecxion No. 5 4⅞" x 40

90   Partagas Limited Reserve Epicure 5" x 38

89   Partagas No. 4 5" x 38

88   Bauza Petit Corona 5" x 38

87   Avo No. 8 5½" x 40

87	Montecruz Sun-Grown Cedar Aged 5" x 42
87	Palmarejo Petit Corona 5⅛" x 42
87	Pleiades Antares 5½" x 40
86	Davidoff Grand Cru No. 4 4⅝" x 41
86	Davidoff No. 2000 5" x 43
86	El Rico Habano Petit-Habano 5" x 40
86	H. Upmann Pequeños No. 300 4½" x 42
86	Paul Garmirian Petit Corona 5" x 43
86	The Griffin's No. 500 5¹⁄₁₆" x 43
85	Aurora Corona 5" x 38
85	Aurora Sublimes 5" x 38
85	Davidoff Grand Cru No. 3 5" x 43
85	H. Upmann Petit Corona 5¹⁄₁₆" x 42
85	H. Upmann Tubos Gold Tube 5¹⁄₁₆" x 42
85	Juan Clemente Corona 5" x 42
85	Sosa Family Selection No. 4 5" x 40
84	Arturo Fuente Petit Corona 5" x 38
84	La Flor Dominicana Macheteros 4" x 40
84	La Gloria Cubana Minutos 4½" x 40
84	Leon Jimenes No. 5 5" x 38
84	Montecruz Sun-Grown No. 230 5" x 42
84	Troya Clasico No. 27 Corona 5½" x 42
83	Por Larrañaga Petit Cetros en Cedro 5" x 38
83	Royal Jamaica Petit Corona 5" x 40
82	Don Diego Petit Corona 5⅛" x 42
82	Fonseca 2-2 4¼" x 40
82	Montecruz Natural Claro Cedar Aged 5" x 42
82	Nat Sherman VIP Selection Barnum Glass Tube 5½" x 42

82	Tamboril Cortadito 5" x 38
81	Paul Garmirian No. 5 4" x 40
80	Carrington No. 4 5½" x 40
76	Juan Clemente Demi-Corona 4" x 40

HONDURAS

88	C.A.O. Petit Corona 5" x 40
88	Hoyo de Monterrey Demitasse 4" x 39
88	Hoyo de Monterrey Excalibur No. 7 5" x 43
87	Baccarat Petit Corona 5½" x 42
87	Habana Gold Black Label Petit Corona 5" x 42
87	Zino Mouton Cadet No. 5 5" x 42
85	Habana Gold White Label Petit Corona 5" x 42
85	Hoyo de Monterrey Excalibur No. 6 5½" x 38
85	Punch Elite 5¼" x 44
84	Bering Imperial 5¼" x 42
84	Don Melo Cremas 4½" x 42
83	Don Tomas Blunt 5" x 42
83	Habana Gold Sterling Vintage Petit Corona 5" x 42
83	Hoyo de Monterrey No. 55 5¼" x 43
82	Hoyo de Monterrey Sabroso 5" x 40
80	Nat Sherman Host Selection Hamilton 5½" x 42
79	Cortesia No. 1 5½" x 40
78	Petrus Tabacage Gregorius 5" x 42

JAMAICA

87	Macanudo Hampton Court 5¾" x 43
85	Macanudo Petit Corona 5" x 38

MEXICO

80	Te-Amo No. 4 5" x 42

NICARAGUA

89   Grand Nica Toraño 5" x 42

87   Flor de Florez Cabinet Selection Coronita 5" x 42

86   José Martí Petit Lancero 4½" x 38

84   Carlos Toraño Nicaraguan Selection 5" x 42

76   Torcedor No. 4 5" x 42

PHILIPPINES

80   Flor de Filipinas Half Corona 4" x 39

U.S.A.

84   PIO VI Petit Corona 5⅛" x 40

Panetela

CANARY ISLANDS

81   Dunhill Panetela 6" x 30

80   Monte Canario Panetela 6" x 38

77   Vargas Diplomatico 5½" x 36

CUBA

89   Cohiba Corona Especial 6" x 38

88   Hoyo de Monterrey Le Hoyo du Dauphin 6" x 38

87   Montecristo Especial No. 2 6" x 38

86   Montecristo Especial 7½" x 38

85   Romeo y Julieta Shakespeare 6½" x 28

84   Romeo y Julieta Belvedere 5½" x 39

83   Cohiba Lancero 7½" x 38

83   El Rey del Mundo Elegante 6¾" x 28

DOMINICAN REPUBLIC

91   Arturo Fuente Petit Lancero 6" x 38

88   Avo No. 6 6½" x 36

88   Royal Jamaica Buccaneer 5½" x 30

87   Avo XO Preludio 6" x 40

87   Cuesta-Rey Cabinet No. 2 7" x 36

87   Dunhill Samanas 6½" x 38

87   José Benito Petite 5½" x 38

87   La Flor Dominicana Demi Tasse 5" x 30

87   Paul Garmirian Panetela 7½" x 38

86   Cuesta-Rey Centennial Collection Dominican No. 3 7" x 36

86   Davidoff No. 2 6" x 38

86   Juan Clemente 530 5" x 30

86   The Griffin's No. 400 6" x 38

86   The Griffin's Privilege 5" x 32

85   Arturo Fuente Panetela Fina 7" x 38

85   Ashton Cordial 5" x 30

85   Carrington No. 3 7" x 36

85   Cubita No. 2 6¼" x 38

85   Don Lino Havana Reserve Panetela 7" x 36

85   Montecruz Sun-Grown No. 276 6" x 32

85   Nat Sherman Exchange Selection Murray Hill 7 6" x 38

85   Royal Jamaica Gaucho 5¼" x 33

85   Royal Jamaica No. 2 Tube 6½" x 34

85   Sosa Santa Fe 6" x 35

84   Ashton Panetela 6" x 36

84   Canaria d'Oro Fino 6" x 31

84   Casa Blanca Panetela 6" x 36

84   La Gloria Cubana Medaille d'Or No. 4 6" x 32

84 **Montecruz Sun-Grown Tubulares** 6⅛" x 36

84 **Nat Sherman Gotham Selection No. 65** 6" x 32

84 **Nat Sherman Manhattan Selection Chelsea** 6½" x 38

83 **Credo Jubilate** 5" x 34

83 **Davidoff No. 1** 7½" x 38

83 **H. Upmann Naturales Tube** 6⅛" x 36

83 **José Benito Panetela** 6¾" x 38

83 **Juan Clemente Panetela** 6½" x 34

82 **Ashton Elegante** 6½" x 35

82 **Cacique Jaragua #3** 6¾" x 36

82 **Don Diego Royal Palmas Tubes** 6⅛" x 36

82 **Licenciados Panetela Linda** 7" x 38

82 **Nat Sherman Landmark Selection Metropole** 6" x 34

82 **Pleiades Mars** 5" x 28

82 **Por Larrañaga Delicados** 6½" x 36

82 **Sosa Family Selection No. 6** 6¼" x 38

81 **Avo No. 4** 7" x 38

81 **Davidoff No. 3** 5⅛" x 30

81 **Nat Sherman Manhattan Selection Tribeca** 6" x 31

81 **Partagas No. 6** 6" x 34

80 **Aurora Palmas Extra** 6¾" x 35

80 **Montecruz Sun-Grown No. 281** 6" x 28

79 **Nat Sherman Manhattan Selection Beekman** 5½" x 28

79 **Pleiades Perseus** 5" x 34

78 **Nat Sherman Exchange Selection Academy 2** 5" x 31

75 **Don Diego Babies** 5 1/16" x 33

HONDURAS

88 **V Centennial Numero 1** 7½" x 38

87 **Belinda Belinda** 6½" x 36

87 **El Rey del Mundo Tinos** 5½" x 38

87 **Puros Indios No. 5 Especial Colorado** 5" x 36

86 **Don Tomas Special Edition No. 400** 7" x 36

86 **Maya Palma Fina** 6⅞" x 36

86 **Roly Petit Cetro** 5" x 36

86 **Zino Mouton Cadet No. 4** 5⅛" x 30

85 **Camórra Capri** 5½" x 32

85 **Don Tomas Panetela Largas** 7" x 38

85 **Las Cabrillas Pizarro** 5½" x 32

85 **Tesoros de Copan Linda** 5⅝" x 38

85 **Zino Mouton Cadet No. 3** 5¾" x 36

83 **Bering Gold No. 1** 6¼" x 33

83 **Puros Indios No. 5 Especial Colorado Claro** 5" x 36

83 **Zino Mouton Cadet No. 2** 6" x 35

82 **Maya Petit** 5¼" x 34

82 **Petrus Tabacage Palma Fina** 6" x 38

82 **Puros Indios Petit Perla** 5" x 38

81 **Baccarat Panetela** 6" x 38

81 **Bances Unique** 5½" x 38

80 **Hoyo de Monterrey Delights** 6¼" x 37

80 **Particulares Petit** 5⅝" x 34

79 **Don Lino Panatelas** 7" x 36

78 **Don Tomas International No. 4** 7" x 36

JAMAICA

85 **Macanudo Portofino** 7" x 34

83 **Macanudo Clayburne** 6" x 31

MEXICO

85 Ornelas Matinee 6" x 30

81 Ornelas No. 6 5" x 38

81 Te-Amo Impulse Lights 5" x 32

81 Te-Amo Torero 6⁹⁄₁₆" x 35

80 Ornelas No. 5 6" x 38

NICARAGUA

86 5 Vegas Panetela 6" x 38

86 La Finca Flora 7" x 36

86 Torcedor Panetela 5" x 36

85 Habanica Serie 638 6" x 38

85 Joya de Nicaragua No. 5 6⅞" x 35

83 Padrón Chicos 5½" x 36

82 Joya de Nicaragua Petite 5½" x 38

77 Don Juan Lindas 5½" x 38

U.S.A.

87 La Gloria Cubana Panetela Deluxe 7" x 37

80 Don Tito Panetela 6⅞" x 37

80 El Rico Habano No. 1 7½" x 38

Odd-Sized

CUBA

91 Montecristo "A" 9¼" x 47

86 Sancho Panza Sancho 9¼" x 47

DOMINICAN REPUBLIC

90 Diamond Crown Robusto No. 4 5½" x 54

88 Ashton Cabinet Selection No. 7 6¼" x 52

88 La Gloria Cubana Glorias Extra 6¼" x 46

88 Romeo y Julieta Presidente 7" x 43

87 Diamond Crown Robusto No. 5 4½" x 54

87 Paul Garmirian Bombone 3½" x 43

87 Royal Jamaica Double Corona 7" x 45

86 Arturo Fuente Chateau Fuente Royal Salute 7⅝" x 54

86 Casa Blanca Jeroboam 10" x 66

86 Diamond Crown Robusto No. 1 8½" x 54

86 Montecristo Double Corona 6¼" x 50

85 Canaria d'Oro Supremos 7" x 45

84 Montecruz Sun-Grown Individuales 8" x 46

82 Royal Jamaica No. 1 Tube 6" x 45

81 José Martí Maceo 6⅞" x 45

81 Pleiades Saturne 8" x 46

81 The Griffin's No. 200 7" x 44

80 Nat Sherman VIP Selection Morgan 7" x 42

80 Royal Jamaica Goliath 9" x 64

79 Pleiades Neptune 7½" x 42

HONDURAS

89 El Rey del Mundo Originale 5⅝" x 45

89 Evelio Robusto 4¾" x 54

88 Punch Deluxe Series Corona 6¼" x 45

88 Punch Gran Cru Britannia 6¼" x 50

86 Bering Baron 7¼" x 42

85 Bering Coronados 5¹⁄₁₆" x 45

85 Evelio Robusto Larga 6" x 54

85 Nestor 747 Vintage Cabinet Series No. 2 4¾" x 54

84 El Rey del Mundo Rectangulare 5⅝" x 45

83 Bering Corona Grande 6¼" x 46

83 Petrus Tabacage No. IV 89 5⅝" x 38

82 El Rey del Mundo Corona 5⅝" x 45

82 Las Cabrillas Balboa 7½" x 54

81 El Rey del Mundo Robusto Zavalla
5" x 54

79 Bering Casinos 7⅛" x 42

74 Punch After Dinner 7¼" x 45

JAMAICA

86 8-9-8 Collection Monarch 6¼" x 45

MEXICO

87 Ornelas 250 9½" x 64

87 Te-Amo New York LaGuardia
5" x 54

84 Te-Amo New York Wall Street
6" x 52

82 Cruz Real No. 28 8½" x 54

NICARAGUA

91 Padrón Magnum 9" x 50

86 C.A.O. Gold Corona Gorda
6½" x 50

86 Gilberto Oliva Viajante 6" x 52

85 José Martí Remedio 5½" x 45

Figurado

CUBA

94 Montecristo No. 2 6⅛" x 52

92 Diplomaticos No. 2 6⅛" x 52

90 Bolivar Belicoso Fino 5½" x 52

90 Romeo y Julieta Belicoso 5½" x 52

89 H. Upmann No. 2 6⅛" x 52

88 El Rey del Mundo Grandes de
España 7½" x 38

87 La Gloria Cubana Medaille d'Or
No. 1 7⅛" x 36

87 Partagas Culebra 5¾" x 39

87 Romeo y Julieta Celestial Fino
5¾" x 46

86 Sancho Panza Belicoso 5½" x 52

84 Partagas Presidente 6⅛" x 47

DOMINICAN REPUBLIC

92 Fuente Fuente Opus X No. 2
6¼" x 52

90 Signature Collection Torpedo
6¼" x 54

89 Arturo Fuente Hemingway Short
Story 4¼" x 49

89 Arturo Fuente Hemingway Signature
6" x 46

89 Ashton Cabinet Selection No. 10
7½" x 52

88 Ashton Cabinet Selection No. 3
6" x 46

88 Macabi Belicoso Fino 6¼" x 52

88 Oscar No. 700 7" x 54

88 Paul Garmirian Belicoso 6¼" x 52

88 Paul Garmirian Celebration 9" x 50

88 Sosa Family Selection No. 2
6¼" x 54

87 Ashton Cabinet Selection No. 1
9" x 52

87 Ashton Cabinet Selection No. 2
7" x 47

87 Avo Belicoso 6" x 50

87 Carrington No. 8 6⅛" x 60

87 Davidoff Special Series "T" 6" x 52

87 Fonseca Triangulare 5½" x 56

87 La Flor Dominicana Figurado
6½" x 52

87 Montecristo No. 2 6" x 50

87 **Nat Sherman Metropolitan Selection Metropolitan** 7" x 52

87 **Troya No. 81 Torpedo** 7" x 54

86 **Arturo Fuente Hemingway Classic** 7" x 48

86 **Arturo Fuente Hemingway Masterpiece** 9¼" x 52

86 **Avo Petit Belicoso** 4¾" x 50

86 **Avo Pyramid** 7" x 54

86 **El Sublimado Torpedo** 7" x 54

86 **Paul Garmirian Belicoso Fino** 5½" x 52

86 **Por Larrañaga Pyramid** 6" x 50

85 **Romeo y Julieta Romeo** 6" x 46

85 **Royal Jamaica Park Lane** 6" x 47

84 **The Griffin's No. 100** 7" x 38

84 **Vueltabajo Pyramide** 7" x 50

83 **Don Lino Colorado Torpedo** 7" x 48

83 **Nat Sherman VIP Selection Zigfeld Fancy Tail** 6¾" x 38

82 **Dunhill Centenas** 6" x 50

80 **Sosa Piramides** 6½" x 54

HONDURAS

92 **Puros Indios Piramides No. 1** 7½" x 60

90 **Puros Indios Piramides No. 2** 6½" x 46

87 **El Rey del Mundo Flor de Llaneza** 6½" x 54

87 **V Centennial Torpedo** 7" x 54

86 **C.A.O. Triangulare** 7" x 54

86 **Felipe Gregorio Belicoso** 6⅛" x 54

86 **Petrus Tabacage Antonius** 5" x 54

86 **Thomas Hinds Honduran Selection Torpedo** 6" x 52

85 **Astral Perfeccion** 7" x 48

85 **El Rey del Mundo Flor de LaVonda** 6½" x 52

85 **Habana Gold Black Label Torpedo** 6" x 52

84 **Las Cabrillas Maximilian** 7" x 55

83 **Astral Favorito** 7" x 48

82 **Orient Express Expresso** 6" x 48

82 **Padrón 1964 Anniversary Series Piramide** 6⅞" x 52

JAMAICA

88 **Temple Hall Belicoso** 6" x 50

87 **Macanudo Duke of Windsor** 6" x 50

MEXICO

85 **Te-Amo Figurado** 6⅝" x 50

84 **Te-Amo Gran Piramide** 7¼" x 54

83 **Te-Amo Piramide** 6¼" x 50

U.S.A.

87 **La Gloria Cubana Piramides** 7¼" x 56

86 **La Gloria Cubana Torpedo No. 1** 6½" x 54

Maduro

DOMINICAN REPUBLIC

89 **Tresado Seleccion No. 200 Maduro** 7" x 48

88 **Arturo Fuente Chateau Fuente Maduro** 4½" x 50

88 **Cuesta-Rey Cabinet No. 1884 Maduro** 6¾" x 44

88 **Onyx No. 650** 6" x 50

88 **Sosa Churchill Maduro** 6¹⁵⁄₁₆ x 49

87 **Ashton Aged Maduro No. 30** 6¾" x 44

87 **Casa Blanca Deluxe Maduro** 6" x 50

87 **Cuesta-Rey Centennial Collection Dominican No. 2 Maduro** 7½" x 48

87 **Henry Clay Brevas a la Conserva Maduro** 5⅝" x 46

87 **Licenciados Wavell Maduro** 5" x 50

87 **Romeo y Julieta Rothschild Maduro** 5" x 50

87 **Royal Jamaica Maduro Corona** 5½" x 40

87 **Sosa Wavell Maduro** 4¾" x 50

87 **Troya No. 18 Rothschild Maduro** 4½" x 50

86 **Arturo Fuente Corona Imperial** 6½" x 46

86 **Ashton Aged Maduro No. 50** 7" x 48

86 **Canaria d'Oro Rothschild Maduro** 4½" x 50

86 **Fonseca 5-50 Maduro** 5" x 50

86 **Havana Classico Robusto** 5" x 50

86 **La Unica No. 200** 7" x 49

86 **Montesino Diplomatico Maduro** 5½" x 42

86 **Montesino Gran Corona Maduro** 6¾" x 48

86 **Nat Sherman City Desk Selection Tribune Maduro** 7½" x 50

86 **Royal Jamaica Maduro Churchill** 8" x 51

85 **Arturo Fuente Churchill Maduro** 7" x 48

85 **Ashton Aged Maduro No. 40** 6" x 50

85 **Fonseca 10-10 Maduro** 6¾" x 49

85 **Nat Sherman City Desk Selection Dispatch** 6½" x 46

85 **Nat Sherman City Desk Selection Telegraph** 6" x 50

85 **Onyx No. 642** 6" x 42

85 **Onyx No. 750** 7½" x 50

85 **Partagas Maduro** 6¼" x 48

85 **Primo del Rey Seleccion No. 4 Maduro** 5½" x 42

85 **Royal Jamaica Maduro Corona Grande** 6½" x 42

84 **Ashton Aged Maduro No. 60** 7½" x 52

84 **Cabañas Corona** 5½" x 42

84 **Cabañas Exquisito Maduro** 6½" x 48

84 **Cuesta-Rey Cabinet No. 95 Maduro** 6¼" x 42

84 **Flamenco Brevas a la Conserva** 5 9/16" x 42

84 **Henry Clay Brevas Fina Maduro** 6½" x 48

84 **La Unica No. 400** 4½" x 50

84 **Licenciados Supreme Maduro No. 400** 6" x 50

84 **Troya No. 63 Churchill Maduro** 6⅞" x 46

83 **Ashton Aged Maduro No. 10** 5" x 50

83 **Casa Blanca Presidente Maduro** 7½" x 50

83 **Licenciados Toro Maduro** 6" x 50

83 **Tresado Seleccion No. 500 Maduro** 5½" x 42

83 **Troya No. 45 Cetro Maduro** 6" x 44

80 **Licenciados No. 4 Maduro** 5¾" x 43

80 **Licenciados Presidente Maduro** 8" x 50

HONDURAS

91 **El Rey del Mundo Robusto Suprema** 7" x 54

90 **Don Lino Churchill Maduro** 7" x 50

89 **Bances President** 8½" x 52

87 **Bances Corona Inmensa Maduro** 6¼" x 48

87 **Hoyo de Monterrey Excalibur No. 3 Maduro** 6⅛" x 48

87 **Petrus Tabacage Double Corona** 7¾" x 50

87 **Punch Pita Maduro** 6⅛" x 50

86 **El Rey del Mundo Flor del Mundo Maduro** 7¼" x 52

86 **Encanto Toro Maduro** 6" x 50

86 **F.D. Grave Churchill Maduro** 7¾" x 50

86 **Hoyo de Monterrey Governor Maduro** 6⅛" x 50

86 **Punch Deluxe Series Chateau M Maduro** 6¾" x 46

86 **Punch Double Corona Maduro** 6¾" x 48

86 **Punch Rothschild Maduro** 4½" x 50

86 **Puros Indios Churchill Maduro** 7¼" x 52

86 **Puros Indios Corona Gorda Maduro** 6" x 52

85 **C.A.O. Churchill Maduro** 8" x 50

85 **Don Tomas Presidente Maduro** 7½" x 50

85 **Encanto Rothschild Maduro** 4½" x 50

85 **Habana Gold White Label Churchill** 7" x 52

85 **Hoyo de Monterrey Excalibur No. 1 Maduro** 7¼" x 54

85 **Hoyo de Monterrey Excalibur No. 2 Maduro** 7" x 46

85 **Hoyo de Monterrey Rothschild Maduro** 4½" x 50

85 **Hoyo de Monterrey Sultan Maduro** 7¼" x 54

85 **Punch Deluxe Series Chateau L Maduro** 7¼" x 54

85 **V Centennial Robusto Maduro** 5" x 50

84 **Belinda Excellente** 6" x 50

84 **C.A.O. Robusto Maduro** 4½" x 50

84 **Don Lino Rothschild Maduro** 4½" x 50

84 **Habana Gold White Label Robusto Maduro** 5" x 50

84 **Las Cabrillas Cortez Maduro** 4¾" x 50

84 **Petrus Tabacage Churchill Maduro 89** 7" x 50

84 **Petrus Tabacage No. II Maduro** 6¼" x 44

84 **V Centennial Churchill Maduro** 7" x 48

84 **V Centennial Numero 2 Maduro** 6" x 50

82 **Encanto Churchill Maduro** 6⅛" x 49

82 **Las Cabrillas Balboa Maduro** 7½" x 54

81 **Petrus Tabacage Rothschild Maduro 89** 4¾" x 50

81 **Santa Rosa Sancho Panza Maduro** 4½" x 50

78 **Petrus Tabacage Corona Sublime Maduro 89** 5½" x 46

JAMAICA

86 **Temple Hall No. 450 Maduro** 4½" x 49

85 **Macanudo Prince Philip Maduro** 7½" x 49

83 **Macanudo Duke of Devon Maduro** 5½" x 42

MEXICO

87 Cruz Real No. 14 Maduro 7½" x 50

86 Ornelas Robusto Maduro 4¼" x 49

86 Te-Amo Maximo Churchill Maduro 7" x 54

85 Ornelas Cafetero Grande 6½" x 46

85 Santa Clara 1830 No. VI Maduro 6" x 51

85 Te-Amo Torito Maduro 4¼" x 50

84 Cruz Real No. 19 Maduro 6" x 50

84 Ornelas Churchill Maduro 7" x 49

84 Te-Amo Churchill Maduro 7½" x 50

84 Te-Amo Satisfaction Maduro 6" x 46

84 Te-Amo Toro Maduro 6" x 50

83 Santa Clara 1830 No. I Maduro 7" x 51

83 Te-Amo Presidente Maduro 7 " x 50

82 Cruz Real No. 24 Maduro 4½" x 50

81 Te-Amo Robusto Maduro 5½" x 54

79 Ornelas Cafetero Chico Maduro 5½" x 46

NICARAGUA

88 Joya de Nicaragua Maduro Deluxe Robusto 4¼" x 52

88 Padrón 3000 Maduro 5½" x 52

87 La Finca Robusto Maduro 4½" x 50

87 Padrón Executive Maduro 7½" x 50

86 Padrón Churchill Maduro 6⅞" x 46

86 Padrón 2000 Maduro 5" x 50

84 Thomas Hinds Nicaraguan Selection Robusto Maduro 5 " x 50

84 Thomas Hinds Nicaraguan Selection Short Churchill Maduro 6" x 50

83 Thomas Hinds Nicaraguan Selection Churchill Maduro 7" x 49

U.S.A.

90 La Gloria Cubana Wavell Maduro 5" x 50

89 La Gloria Cubana Churchill Maduro 7" x 50

Vintage

CUBA

98 Cabañas No. 751 Alfred Dunhill 6½" x 42

98 Montecristo Seleccion Suprema No. 1 6½" x 42

97 Romeo y Julieta No. 758 Alfred Dunhill Ltd. Seleccion Sun-Grown Breva 6½" x 42

95 H. Upmann No. 4 Alfred Dunhill 6½" x 46

94 H. Upmann No. 22 Alfred Dunhill Seleccion Suprema 4½" x 55

93 La Corona Churchill 6½" x 46

93 Partagas No. 6 Seleccion Superba 4½" x 40

92 Belinda Belinda 5½" x 42

92 Flor de Farach Palmeras 5" x 38

92 Montecristo Seleccion Suprema No. 4 5" x 42

89 Ramon Allones Ideales 6½" x 40

89 Romeo y Julieta Alfred Dunhill Selection Sun-Grown Breva 5½" x 44

87 Ramon Allones No. 66 (Perfecto) 6" x na

86 Henry Clay Corona 5½" x 42

CHAPTER 13

Cigars

LISTED BY BRAND

Brand	Category	Size	Rating

5 Vegas

NICARAGUA

Panetela *Panetela* 6" x 38 • **86**

Robusto *Robusto* 5" x 50 • **87**

8-9-8 Collection

JAMAICA

Churchill *Double Corona* 7½" x 49 • **87**

Corona *Corona* 5½" x 42 • **83**

Lonsdale *Lonsdale* 6½" x 42 • **86**

Monarch *Odd* 6¾" x 45 • **86**

Robusto *Robusto* 5½" x 49 • **87**

Al Capone

NICARAGUA

Corona Grande *Lonsdale* 6¼" x 43 • **83**

Aromas de San Andreas

MEXICO

Robusto *Robusto* 5" x 50 • **83**

Arturo Fuente

DOMINICAN REPUBLIC

Cañones *Double Corona* 8½" x 52 • **91**

Chateau Fuente *Robusto* 4½" x 50 • **85**

Chateau Fuente Maduro *Maduro*
4½" x 50 • **88**

Chateau Fuente Royal Salute *Odd*
7⅝" x 54 • **86**

Churchill *Churchill* 7" x 48 • **84**

Churchill Maduro *Maduro* 7" x 48 • **85**

Corona Imperial *Maduro* 6½" x 46 • **86**

Don Carlos Reserva No. 3 *Corona*
5½" x 44 • **90**

Don Carlos Robusto *Robusto* 5" x 50 • **87**

Double Chateau Fuente *Churchill*
6¾" x 48 • **84**

Flor Fina 8-5-8 *Corona Gorda* 6" x 47 • **86**

Hemingway Classic *Figurado* 7" x 48 • **86**

Hemingway Masterpiece *Figurado*
9¼" x 52 • **86**

Hemingway Short Story *Figurado*
4¼" x 49 • **89**

Hemingway Signature *Figurado*
6" x 46 • **89**

Panetela Fina *Panetela* 7" x 38 • **85**

Petit Corona *Petit Corona* 5" x 38 • **84**

Petit Lancero *Panetela* 6" x 38 • **91**

Rothschild *Robusto* 4½" x 50 • **86**

Seleccion Privada No. 1 *Lonsdale*
6¾" x 44 • **85**

Spanish Lonsdale *Lonsdale* 6½" x 42 • **88**

Ashton

DOMINICAN REPUBLIC

8-9-8 *Lonsdale* 6½" x 44 • **86**

Aged Maduro No. 10 *Maduro* 5" x 50 • 83

Aged Maduro No. 20 *Corona*
5½" x 44 • 86

Aged Maduro No. 30 *Maduro*
6¼" x 44 • 87

Aged Maduro No. 40 *Maduro* 6" x 50 • 85

Aged Maduro No. 50 *Maduro* 7" x 48 • 86

Aged Maduro No. 60 *Maduro*
7½" x 52 • 84

Cabinet Selection No. 1 *Figurado*
9" x 52 • 87

Cabinet Selection No. 2 *Figurado*
7" x 47 • 87

Cabinet Selection No. 3 *Figurado*
6" x 46 • 88

Cabinet Selection No. 6 *Robusto*
5½" x 52 • 87

Cabinet Selection No. 7 *Odd* 6¼" x 52 • 88

Cabinet Selection No. 8 *Churchill*
7" x 49 • 88

Cabinet Selection No. 10 *Figurado*
7½" x 52 • 89

Churchill *Double Corona* 7½" x 52 • 87

Cordial *Panetela* 5" x 30 • 85

Corona *Corona* 5½" x 44 • 84

Double Magnum *Corona Gorda*
6" x 50 • 87

Elegante *Panetela* 6½" x 35 • 82

Magnum *Robusto* 5" x 50 • 87

Panetela *Panetela* 6" x 36 • 84

Prime Minister *Churchill* 6⅛" x 48 • 85

Astral

HONDURAS

Beso *Robusto* 5" x 52 • 89

Favorito *Figurado* 7" x 48 • 83

Lujos *Lonsdale* 6½" x 44 • 84

Maestro *Double Corona* 7½" x 52 • 88

Perfeccion *Figurado* 7" x 48 • 85

Aurora

DOMINICAN REPUBLIC

Bristol Especial *Churchill* 6⅛" x 48 • 84

Corona *Petit Corona* 5" x 38 • 85

Double Corona *Double Corona*
7½" x 50 • 87

No. 4 *Corona* 5¼" x 42 • 85

Palmas Extra *Panetela* 6¼" x 35 • 80

Robusto *Robusto* 5" x 50 • 87

Sublimes *Petit Corona* 5" x 38 • 85

Avo

DOMINICAN REPUBLIC

No. 1 *Lonsdale* 6⅔" x 42 • 86

No. 2 *Corona Gorda* 6" x 50 • 88

No. 3 *Double Corona* 7½" x 50 • 84

No. 4 *Panetela* 7" x 38 • 81

No. 5 *Churchill* 6⅛" x 46 • 86

No. 6 *Panetela* 6½" x 36 • 88

No. 7 *Corona* 6" x 44 • 87

No. 8 *Petit Corona* 5½" x 40 • 87

No. 9 *Robusto* 4¾" x 48 • 83

Belicoso *Figurado* 6" x 50 • 87

Petit Belicoso *Figurado* 4¼" x 50 • 86

Pyramid *Figurado* 7" x 54 • 86

XO Intermezzo *Robusto* 5½" x 50 • 83

XO Maestoso *Churchill* 7" x 48 • 78

XO Preludio *Panetela* 6" x 40 • 87

Baccarat

HONDURAS

Churchill *Churchill* 7" x 50 • 85

Luchadores *Lonsdale* 6" x 43 • 83

No. 1 *Lonsdale* 7" x 44 • 81

Panetela *Panetela* 6" x 38 • 81

Petit Corona *Petit Corona* 5½" x 42 • 87

Rothschild *Robusto* 5" x 50 • 82

Bahia Gold

COSTA RICA

Churchill *Churchill* 6⅞" x 48 • 90

Ballena Suprema

HONDURAS

Danli Collection Alma *Churchill*
7" x 47 • 82

Danli Collection Encanto *Double Corona*
8" x 50 • 83

Ballena Suprema

MEXICO

San Andres Collection Concordia *Churchill*
7" x 48 • 80

San Andres Collection Cordura *Robusto*
5" x 52 • 81

San Andres Collection Esperanza *Churchill*
7" x 50 • 78

Bances

HONDURAS

Brevas *Corona* 5½" x 43 • 86

Cazadores *Lonsdale* 6¼" x 43 • 78

Corona Inmensa *Churchill* 6¼" x 48 • 86

Corona Inmensa Maduro *Maduro*
6¾" x 48 • 87

President *Maduro* 8½" x 52 • 89

Unique *Panetela* 5½" x 38 • 81

Bauza

DOMINICAN REPUBLIC

Casa Grande *Churchill* 6¼" x 48 • 90

Fabuloso *Double Corona* 7½" x 50 • 87

Grecos *Corona* 5½" x 42 • 85

Jaguar *Lonsdale* 6½" x 42 • 83

Medaille d'Oro No. 1 *Lonsdale*
6⅛" x 44 • 86

Petit Corona *Petit Corona* 5" x 38 • 88

Robusto *Robusto* 5½" x 50 • 87

Belinda

HONDURAS

Belinda *Panetela* 6½" x 36 • 87

Breva Conserva *Corona* 5½" x 43 • 87

Cabinet *Corona Gorda* 5⅝" x 45 • 89

Corona Grande *Lonsdale* 6¼" x 44 • 85

Excellente *Maduro* 6" x 50 • 84

Medaglia d'Oro *Robusto* 4⅝" x 50 • 84

Prime Minister *Double Corona*
7½" x 50 • 80

Ramon *Churchill* 7¼" x 47 • 83

Bering

HONDURAS

Baron *Odd* 7¼" x 42 • 86

Casinos *Odd* 7⅛" x 42 • 79

Corona Grande *Odd* 6¼" x 46 • 83

Corona Royale *Corona* 6" x 41 • 87

Coronados *Odd* 5⅜₁₆" x 45 • 85

Gold No. 1 *Panetela* 6¼" x 33 • 83

Grande *Double Corona* 8½" x 52 • 85

Hispanos *Corona Gorda* 6" x 50 • 85

Imperial *Petit Corona* 5¼" x 42 • 84

Plaza *Lonsdale* 6" x 43 • **87**
Robusto *Robusto* 4¼" x 50 • **80**

Blair

HONDURAS
Robusto *Corona Gorda* 6" x 50 • **84**

Bolivar

CUBA
Belicoso Fino *Figurado* 5½" x 52 • **90**
Corona *Corona* 5½" x 42 • **91**
Corona Extra *Corona Gorda* 5⅝" x 46 • **87**
Corona Gigantes *Churchill* 7" x 47 • **90**
Inmensa *Lonsdale* 6⅛" x 43 • **87**
Petit Corona *Petit Corona* 5" x 42 • **90**
Royal Corona *Robusto* 5" x 50 • **95**

C.A.O.

HONDURAS
Churchill *Double Corona* 8" x 50 • **86**
Churchill Maduro *Maduro* 8" x 50 • **85**
Corona *Corona* 6" x 42 • **87**
Corona Gorda *Corona Gorda* 6" x 50 • **85**
Lonsdale *Lonsdale* 7" x 44 • **85**
Petit Corona *Petit Corona* 5" x 40 • **88**
Robusto *Robusto* 4½" x 50 • **86**
Robusto Maduro *Maduro* 4½" x 50 • **84**
Triangulare *Figurado* 7" x 54 • **86**

C.A.O.

NICARAGUA
Gold Churchill *Churchill* 7" x 48 • **87**
Gold Corona Gorda *Odd* 6½" x 50 • **86**
Gold Robusto *Robusto* 5" x 50 • **89**

Caballeros

DOMINICAN REPUBLIC
Churchill *Churchill* 7" x 50 • **85**
Corona *Corona* 5¼" x 43 • **83**
Rothschild *Robusto* 5" x 50 • **82**

Cabañas

DOMINICAN REPUBLIC
Corona *Maduro* 5½" x 42 • **84**
Exquisito Maduro *Maduro* 6½" x 48 • **84**
Royale *Corona Gorda* 5⅝" x 46 • **83**

Cacique

DOMINICAN REPUBLIC
Apache *Corona Gorda* 6" x 50 • **81**
Caribe #7 *Churchill* 6⅛" x 46 • **86**
Inca #8 *Double Corona* 7½" x 50 • **87**
Jaragua #3 *Panetela* 6¼" x 36 • **82**

Calle Ocho

DOMINICAN REPUBLIC
Gordito *Robusto* 5" x 50 • **85**

Camacho

HONDURAS
Churchill *Churchill* 7" x 48 • **85**
Monarca *Robusto* 5" x 50 • **82**
Nacionales *Corona* 5½" x 44 • **85**
No. 1 *Lonsdale* 7" x 44 • **76**

Camórra

HONDURAS

Capri *Panetela* 5½" x 32 • **85**

Double Corona *Double Corona* 8" x 52 • **84**

Limited Reserve Churchill San Remo
Churchill 7" x 48 • **84**

Roma *Robusto* 5" x 50 • **81**

Canaria d'Oro

DOMINICAN REPUBLIC

Corona *Corona* 5½" x 43 • **84**

Fino *Panetela* 6" x 31 • **84**

Inmenso *Robusto* 5½" x 49 • **83**

Lonsdale *Lonsdale* 6½" x 43 • **83**

Rothschild Maduro *Maduro* 4½" x 50 • **86**

Supremos *Odd* 7" x 45 • **85**

Canonero

BRAZIL

"Classico" Double Corona *Double Corona*
7½" x 50 • **79**

"Mediano" Double Corona *Double Corona*
7½" x 50 • **85**

"Mediano" Potra *Petit Corona*
4¼" x 38 • **86**

Cara Mia

CANARY ISLANDS

Churchill *Churchill* 7" x 50 • **86**

Lonsdale *Lonsdale* 6½" x 42 • **84**

Toro *Corona Gorda* 6" x 50 • **87**

Carlos Toraño

DOMINICAN REPUBLIC

Dominican Selection Carlos VI *Churchill*
7" x 48 • **86**

Carlos Toraño

NICARAGUA

Nicaraguan Selection *Petit Corona*
5" x 42 • **84**

Carrington

DOMINICAN REPUBLIC

No. 1 *Double Corona* 7½" x 50 • **83**

No. 2 *Corona* 6" x 42 • **87**

No. 3 *Panetela* 7" x 36 • **85**

No. 4 *Petit Corona* 5½" x 40 • **80**

No. 5 *Churchill* 6⅞" x 46 • **84**

No. 6 *Robusto* 4½" x 50 • **78**

No. 7 *Corona Gorda* 6" x 50 • **79**

No. 8 *Figurado* 6⅞" x 60 • **87**

Casa Blanca

DOMINICAN REPUBLIC

Corona *Corona* 5½" x 42 • **89**

Deluxe *Corona Gorda* 6" x 50 • **85**

Deluxe Maduro *Maduro* 6" x 50 • **87**

Jeroboam *Odd* 10" x 66 • **86**

Lonsdale *Lonsdale* 6½" x 42 • **84**

Panetela *Panetela* 6" x 36 • **84**

Presidente *Double Corona* 7½" x 50 • **84**

Presidente Maduro *Maduro* 7½" x 50 • **83**

Casa Martin

CANARY ISLANDS

Churchill *Churchill* 7" x 46 • **87**

Celestino Vega

INDONESIA

Churchill *Churchill* 7¼" x 50 • **89**

Cerdan

DOMINICAN REPUBLIC

Churchill *Churchill* 7" x 46 • **80**
Don Juan *Double Corona* 7½" x 50 • **84**

Cohiba

CUBA

Corona Especial *Panetela* 6" x 38 • **89**
Esplendidos *Churchill* 7" x 47 • **90**
Lancero *Panetela* 7½" x 38 • **83**
Robusto *Robusto* 4⅞" x 50 • **91**
Siglo I *Petit Corona* 4" x 40 • **93**
Siglo III *Lonsdale* 6" x 42 • **95**
Siglo IV *Corona Gorda* 5⅝" x 46 • **89**
Siglo V *Lonsdale* 6⅝" x 43 • **90**

Cohiba

DOMINICAN REPUBLIC

Churchill *Churchill* 7" x 49 • **89**

Cortesia

HONDURAS

No. 1 *Petit Corona* 5½" x 40 • **79**

Coticas

DOMINICAN REPUBLIC

Double Corona *Churchill* 7" x 48 • **78**

Credo

DOMINICAN REPUBLIC

Anthanor *Corona* 5¼" x 42 • **88**
Arcane *Robusto* 5" x 50 • **86**
Jubilate *Panetela* 5" x 34 • **83**
Magnificant *Churchill* 6⅛" x 46 • **85**
Pythagoras *Churchill* 7" x 50 • **87**

Crown Achievement

HONDURAS

Churchill *Double Corona* 8" x 50 • **84**

Cruz Real

MEXICO

No. 1 *Lonsdale* 6⅝" x 42 • **76**
No. 2 *Corona* 6" x 42 • **86**
No. 14 *Double Corona* 7½" x 50 • **83**
No. 14 Maduro *Maduro* 7½" x 50 • **87**
No. 19 *Corona Gorda* 6" x 50 • **80**
No. 19 Maduro *Maduro* 6" x 50 • **84**
No. 24 *Robusto* 4½" x 50 • **80**
No. 24 Maduro *Maduro* 4½" x 50 • **82**
No. 25 *Robusto* 5½" x 52 • **77**
No. 28 *Odd* 8½" x 54 • **82**

Cubita

DOMINICAN REPUBLIC

2000 *Churchill* 7" x 50 • **82**

8-9-8 *Lonsdale 6¾" x 43 • 83*

No. 2 *Panetela 6¼" x 38 • 85*

No. 700 *Corona Gorda 6" x 50 • 86*

Cuesta-Rey

DOMINICAN REPUBLIC

Aristocrat *Churchill 7¼" x 48 • 87*

Cabinet No. 1 *Double Corona*
8½" x 52 • 87

Cabinet No. 2 *Panetela 7" x 36 • 87*

Cabinet No. 95 *Lonsdale 6¼" x 42 • 85*

Cabinet No. 95 Maduro *Maduro*
6¼" x 42 • 84

Cabinet No. 898 *Churchill 7" x 49 • 83*

Cabinet No. 1884 *Lonsdale 6¾" x 44 • 85*

Cabinet No. 1884 Maduro *Maduro*
6¾" x 44 • 88

Captiva *Lonsdale 6⁷⁄₁₆" x 42 • 84*

Centennial Collection Dominican No. 1
Double Corona 8½" x 52 • 85

Centennial Collection Dominican No. 2
Churchill 7¼" x 48 • 86

Centennial Collection Dominican No. 2
Maduro *Maduro 7½" x 48 • 87*

Centennial Collection Dominican No. 3
Panetela 7" x 36 • 86

Centennial Collection Dominican No. 4
Lonsdale 6½" x 42 • 83

Centennial Collection Dominican No. 5
Corona 5½" x 43 • 87

Centennial Collection Dominican No. 7
Robusto 4½" x 50 • 84

Centennial Collection Dominican No. 60
Corona Gorda 6" x 50 • 87

Cupido

NICARAGUA

Churchill *Churchill 7" x 47 • 89*

Da Vinci

HONDURAS

Ginevra de Benci *Churchill 7" x 48 • 82*

Leonardo *Double Corona 8½" x 52 • 87*

Madonna *Robusto 5" x 50 • 87*

Monalisa *Corona Gorda 6" x 50 • 87*

Da Vinci

NICARAGUA

Mezzanote *Churchill 7" x 48 • 85*

Daniel Marshall

DOMINICAN REPUBLIC

Churchill *Churchill 7" x 48 • 88*

Double Corona *Double Corona*
7½" x 50 • 85

Davidoff

DOMINICAN REPUBLIC

Aniversario No. 1 *Double Corona*
8⅔" x 48 • 84

Aniversario No. 2 *Churchill 7" x 48 • 89*

Grand Cru No. 1 *Lonsdale 6" x 42 • 89*

Grand Cru No. 2 *Corona 5⅝" x 43 • 88*

Grand Cru No. 3 *Petit Corona 5" x 43 • 85*

Grand Cru No. 4 *Petit Corona*
4⅝" x 41 • 86

No. 1 *Panetela 7½" x 38 • 83*

No. 2 *Panetela 6" x 38 • 86*

No. 3 *Panetela* 5⅛" x 30 • **81**

No. 2000 *Petit Corona* 5" x 43 • **86**

No. 4000 *Lonsdale* 6" x 42 • **89**

No. 5000 *Corona Gorda* 5⅝" x 46 • **85**

Special Series Double "R" *Double Corona*
 7½" x 50 • **86**

Special Series "R" *Robusto* 4⅞" x 50 • **87**

Special Series "T" *Figurado* 6" x 52 • **87**

Diamond Crown

DOMINICAN REPUBLIC

Robusto No. 1 *Odd* 8½" x 54 • **86**

Robusto No. 4 *Odd* 5½" x 54 • **90**

Robusto No. 5 *Odd* 4½" x 54 • **87**

Diana Silvius

DOMINICAN REPUBLIC

2000 *Churchill* 6¼" x 47 • **86**

Churchill *Churchill* 7" x 50 • **88**

Corona *Lonsdale* 6½" x 42 • **84**

Robusto *Robusto* 4⅞" x 52 • **86**

Diplomaticos

CUBA

No. 2 *Figurado* 6⅛" x 52 • **92**

Domino Park

DOMINICAN REPUBLIC

Churchill *Churchill* 7¼" x 50 • **86**

Robusto *Robusto* 5" x 50 • **86**

Don Alberto

DOMINICAN REPUBLIC

Oro de Habana Robusto *Robusto*
 5" x 50 • **76**

Reserva Grand Cruz *Robusto* 5" x 50 • **83**

Superior Habana Robusto *Robusto*
 5" x 50 • **77**

Don Asa

HONDURAS

Cetros No. 2 *Lonsdale* 6½" x 44 • **85**

Churchill *Double Corona* 7½" x 50 • **87**

Corona *Corona Gorda* 5½" x 50 • **85**

Don Diego

DOMINICAN REPUBLIC

Babies *Panetela* 5¹⁄₁₆" x 33 • **75**

Corona *Corona* 5⅝" x 42 • **85**

Corona Major Tubes *Corona* 5½" x 42 • **87**

Grande *Corona Gorda* 6" x 50 • **84**

Lonsdale *Lonsdale* 6⅝" x 42 • **86**

Monarch Tubes *Churchill* 7¼" x 46 • **85**

Petit Corona *Petit Corona* 5⅛" x 42 • **82**

Royal Palmas Tubes *Panetela* 6¼" x 36 • **82**

Don Juan

NICARAGUA

Cetro *Corona* 6" x 43 • **80**

Churchill *Churchill* 7" x 49 • **90**

Lindas *Panetela* 5½" x 38 • **77**

Numero Uno *Lonsdale* 6⅝" x 44 • **84**

Platinum Churchill *Churchill* 7" x 49 • **86**

President *Double Corona* 8½" x 50 • **82**

Robusto *Robusto* 5" x 50 • **87**

Don Leo

DOMINICAN REPUBLIC

Churchill *Double Corona* 7½" x 50 • **87**

Double Corona *Churchill* 7" x 48 • **82**

Presidente *Double Corona* 8" x 52 • **83**

Robusto *Corona Gorda* 5½" x 50 • **87**

Don Lino

DOMINICAN REPUBLIC

Colorado Presidente *Double Corona*
7½" x 50 • **84**

Colorado Robusto *Robusto* 5½" x 50 • **85**

Colorado Rothschild *Robusto* 4½" x 50 • **86**

Colorado Torpedo *Figurado* 7" x 48 • **83**

Havana Reserve Churchill *Double Corona*
7½" x 50 • **86**

Havana Reserve No. 1 *Lonsdale*
6½" x 44 • **85**

Havana Reserve Panetela *Panetela*
7" x 36 • **85**

Havana Reserve Robusto *Robusto*
5½" x 50 • **83**

Havana Reserve Toro *Corona Gorda*
5½" x 46 • **88**

Oro Churchill *Churchill* 6⅛" x 46 • **83**

Don Lino

HONDURAS

Churchill *Double Corona* 8" x 50 • **85**

Churchill Maduro *Maduro* 7" x 50 • **90**

No. 1 *Lonsdale* 6½" x 44 • **84**

Panatelas *Panetela* 7" x 36 • **79**

Robusto *Robusto* 5½" x 50 • **84**

Rothschild Maduro *Maduro* 4½" x 50 • **84**

Toro *Corona Gorda* 5½" x 46 • **85**

Don Manolo

DOMINICAN REPUBLIC

Series II Robusto *Robusto* 5" x 50 • **78**

Series III Robusto *Robusto* 5" x 50 • **84**

Don Melo

HONDURAS

Centenario *Churchill* 7" x 48 • **81**

Corona Extra *Corona Gorda* 5½" x 46 • **86**

Corona Gorda *Lonsdale* 6¼" x 44 • **86**

Cremas *Petit Corona* 4½" x 42 • **84**

Nom Plus *Robusto* 4¾" x 50 • **85**

Petit Corona *Corona* 5½" x 42 • **85**

Presidente *Double Corona* 8½" x 50 • **81**

Don René

DOMINICAN REPUBLIC

Churchill *Churchill* 7¼" x 50 • **87**

Don Tito

U.S.A.

Panetela *Panetela* 6⅛" x 37 • **80**

Don Tomas

HONDURAS

Blunt *Petit Corona* 5" x 42 • **83**

Cetros *Lonsdale* 6½" x 44 • **83**

Corona *Corona Gorda* 5½" x 50 • **86**

Corona Grande *Lonsdale* 6½" x 44 • **84**

International No. 2 *Robusto* 5½" x 50 • **83**

International No. 4 *Panetela* 7" x 36 • **78**

Panetela Largas *Panetela* 7" x 38 • **85**

Presidente *Double Corona* 7½" x 50 • **85**

Presidente Maduro *Maduro* 7½" x 50 • **85**

Rothschild *Robusto* 4½" x 50 • **80**

Special Edition No. 1 *Double Corona*
7½" x 50 • **86**

Special Edition No. 200 *Lonsdale*
6½" x 44 • **85**

Special Edition No. 300 *Robusto*
5" x 50 • **80**

Special Edition No. 400 *Panetela*
7" x 36 • **86**

Special Edition No. 500 *Corona Gorda*
5½" x 46 • **87**

Toro *Corona Gorda* 5½" x 46 • **84**

Don Vito

CANARY ISLANDS

Capo *Lonsdale* 6¼" x 44 • **85**

Don Xavier

CANARY ISLANDS

Churchill *Double Corona* 7½" x 50 • **83**

Corona *Corona Gorda* 5⅝" x 46 • **83**

Grand Corona *Churchill* 7" x 46 • **83**

Lonsdale *Lonsdale* 6⅝" x 42 • **84**

Robusto *Robusto* 4⅝" x 50 • **84**

Double Happiness

PHILIPPINES

Ecstasy *Churchill* 7" x 47 • **85**

Dunhill

CANARY ISLANDS

Corona Extra *Robusto* 5½" x 50 • **83**

Panetela *Panetela* 6" x 30 • **81**

Dunhill

DOMINICAN REPUBLIC

Altamiras *Robusto* 5" x 48 • **82**

Cabreras *Churchill* 7" x 48 • **86**

Centenas *Figurado* 6" x 50 • **82**

Condados *Corona Gorda* 6" x 48 • **85**

Diamantes *Lonsdale* 6⅝" x 42 • **83**

Peravias *Churchill* 7" x 50 • **83**

Romanas *Robusto* 4½" x 50 • **84**

Samanas *Panetela* 6½" x 38 • **87**

Tabaras *Corona* 5½" x 42 • **85**

Valverdes *Corona* 5½" x 42 • **85**

El Rey del Mundo

CUBA

Corona De Luxe *Corona* 5½" x 42 • **91**

Elegante *Panetela* 6¼" x 28 • **83**

Gran Coronas *Corona Gorda* 5⅝" x 46 • **87**

Grandes de España *Figurado* 7½" x 38 • **88**

Lonsdale *Lonsdale* 6⅝" x 42 • **87**

Tainos *Churchill* 7" x 47 • **87**

El Rey del Mundo

HONDURAS

Choix Supreme *Corona Gorda*
6⅛" x 49 • **88**

Corona *Odd* 5⅜" x 45 • **82**

Corona Inmensa *Churchill* 7¼" x 47 • **79**

Coronation *Double Corona* 8½" x 52 • **86**

Double Corona *Churchill* 7" x 49 • **89**

Flor de LaVonda *Figurado* 6½" x 52 • **85**

Flor de Llaneza *Figurado* 6½" x 54 • **87**

Flor del Mundo *Double Corona*
7½" x 54 • **87**

Flor del Mundo Maduro *Maduro*
7¼" x 52 • **86**

Habana Club *Corona* 5½" x 42 • **84**

Originale *Odd* 5⅝" x 45 • **89**

Rectangulare *Odd* 5⅝" x 45 • **84**

Robusto *Robusto* 5" x 54 • **83**

Robusto Larga *Corona Gorda* 6" x 50 • **83**

Robusto Suprema *Maduro* 7" x 54 • **91**

Robusto Zavalla *Odd* 5" x 54 • **81**

Rothschild *Robusto* 5" x 50 • **86**

Tinos *Panetela* 5½" x 38 • **87**

El Rico Habano

DOMINICAN REPUBLIC

Double Corona *Churchill* 7" x 47 • **80**

Gran Corona *Corona Gorda* 5¼" x 46 • **89**

Gran Habanero Deluxe *Double Corona*
7¼" x 50 • **86**

Habano Club *Robusto* 5" x 48 • **90**

Petit-Habano *Petit Corona* 5" x 40 • **86**

El Rico Habano

U.S.A.

Corona *Corona* 5½" x 42 • **85**

Double Corona *Churchill* 7" x 47 • **85**

No. 1 *Panetela* 7½" x 38 • **80**

El Sublimado

DOMINICAN REPUBLIC

Churchill *Double Corona* 8" x 48 • **83**

Corona *Corona* 6" x 44 • **84**

Regardete *Robusto* 4½" x 50 • **85**

Robusto *Robusto* 4½" x 50 • **87**

Torpedo *Figurado* 7" x 54 • **86**

Encanto

HONDURAS

Churchill Maduro *Maduro* 6⅞" x 49 • **82**

Churchill Natural *Churchill* 7" x 50 • **82**

Elegante *Lonsdale* 7" x 44 • **86**

Rothschild *Robusto* 4½" x 50 • **88**

Rothschild Maduro *Maduro* 4½" x 50 • **85**

Toro Maduro *Maduro* 6" x 50 • **86**

Evelio

HONDURAS

Robusto *Odd* 4¾" x 54 • **89**

Robusto Larga *Odd* 6" x 54 • **85**

Excelsior

MEXICO

Individual *Double Corona* 8½" x 52 • **78**

No. 3 *Robusto* 5½" x 52 • **81**

No. 5 *Double Corona* 8" x 50 • **86**

Felipe Gregorio

HONDURAS

Belicoso *Figurado* 6⅛" x 54 • **86**

Glorioso *Double Corona* 7¼" x 50 • **83**

Robusto *Robusto* 5" x 50 • **84**

Sereno *Corona* 5¼" x 42 • **86**

Suntuoso *Churchill* 7" x 48 • **82**

Felipe II

HONDURAS

Reserva X *Churchill* 7" x 48 • **85**

F.D. Grave

HONDURAS

Churchill *Double Corona* 7¼" x 50 • 82
Churchill Maduro *Maduro* 7¼" x 50 • 86
Lonsdale *Lonsdale* 6¼" x 44 • 84

Fighting Cock

PHILIPPINES

C.O.D. *Churchill* 7" x 47 • 84

Flamenco

DOMINICAN REPUBLIC

Brevas a la Conserva *Maduro*
5⁵⁄₁₆" x 42 • 84

Flor de Farach

NICARAGUA

Churchill *Churchill* 7" x 48 • 84

Flor de Filipinas

PHILIPPINES

Churchill *Churchill* 7" x 47 • 78
Half Corona *Petit Corona* 4" x 39 • 80

Flor de Florez

NICARAGUA

Cabinet Selection Coronita *Petit Corona*
5" x 42 • 87
Cabinet Selection Florez Florez *Corona
Gorda* 5¾" x 46 • 88
Corona *Corona Gorda* 6" x 50 • 85

Fonseca

CUBA

Cosacos *Petit Corona* 5⅓" x 42 • 81

Fonseca

DOMINICAN REPUBLIC

2-2 *Petit Corona* 4¼" x 40 • 82
10-10 *Churchill* 7" x 50 • 82
10-10 Maduro *Maduro* 6¾" x 49 • 85
5-50 *Robusto* 5" x 50 • 85
5-50 Maduro *Maduro* 5" x 50 • 86
8-9-8 *Corona* 6" x 43 • 86
Triangulare *Figurado* 5½" x 56 • 87

Free Cuba

NICARAGUA

Robusto *Robusto* 5" x 50 • 86

Fuente Fuente Opus X

DOMINICAN REPUBLIC

Double Corona *Double Corona*
7⅝" x 49 • 89
Fuente Fuente *Corona Gorda* 5⅝" x 46 • 91
No. 2 *Figurado* 6¼" x 52 • 92
Perfecxion No. 5 *Petit Corona*
4⅞" x 40 • 92
Reserva d'Chateau *Churchill* 7" x 48 • 90
Robusto *Robusto* 5¼" x 50 • 91

Gilberto Oliva

HONDURAS

Numero 1 *Lonsdale* 6½" x 44 • 83
Robusto *Robusto* 5½" x 50 • 85

Gilberto Oliva

NICARAGUA

Churchill *Churchill* 7" x 50 • **85**
Viajante *Odd* 6" x 52 • **86**

Grand Nica

NICARAGUA

Churchill *Churchill* 7" x 52 • **87**
Toraño *Petit Corona* 5" x 42 • **89**

H. Upmann

CUBA

Corona *Corona* 5½" x 42 • **91**
Lonsdale *Lonsdale* 6½" x 42 • **90**
Magnum *Corona Gorda* 5⅝" x 46 • **83**
No. 2 *Figurado* 6⅛" x 52 • **89**
Petit Corona *Petit Corona* 5" x 42 • **81**

H. Upmann

DOMINICAN REPUBLIC

Cabinet Selection Columbo *Double Corona*
8" x 50 • **84**
Cabinet Selection Corsario *Robusto*
5½" x 50 • **86**
Cabinet Selection Robusto *Robusto*
4¼" x 50 • **86**
Churchill *Corona Gorda* 5⅝" x 46 • **87**
Corona *Corona* 5½" x 42 • **86**
Corona Imperiales *Churchill* 7" x 46 • **84**
Corona Major Tube *Corona* 5⅛" x 42 • **85**
Lonsdale *Lonsdale* 6⅝" x 42 • **83**
Monarch Tube *Churchill* 7" x 47 • **84**
Naturales Tube *Panetela* 6⅛" x 36 • **83**

Pequeños No. 100 *Robusto* 4½" x 50 • **86**
Pequeños No. 300 *Petit Corona*
4½" x 42 • **86**
Petit Corona *Petit Corona* 5⅛₆" x 42 • **85**
Tubos Gold Tube *Petit Corona*
5⅛₆" x 42 • **85**

Habana Gold

HONDURAS

Black Label Churchill *Churchill*
7½" x 46 • **84**
Black Label Corona *Corona* 6" x 44 • **86**
Black Label Petit Corona *Petit Corona*
5" x 42 • **87**
Black Label Presidente *Double Corona*
8½" x 52 • **85**
Black Label Robusto *Robusto* 5" x 50 • **80**
Black Label Torpedo *Figurado* 6" x 52 • **85**
Sterling Vintage Petit Corona *Petit Corona*
5" x 42 • **83**
Sterling Vintage Presidente *Double Corona*
8½" x 52 • **87**
Sterling Vintage Robusto *Robusto*
5" x 50 • **77**
White Label Churchill *Maduro*
7" x 52 • **85**
White Label Petit Corona *Petit Corona*
5" x 42 • **85**
White Label Presidente *Double Corona*
8½" x 52 • **78**
White Label Robusto *Robusto* 5" x 50 • **87**
White Label Robusto Maduro *Maduro*
5" x 50 • **84**

Habanica

NICARAGUA

Serie 546 *Corona Gorda* 5¼" x 46 • **87**

Serie 550 *Robusto* 5" x 50 • **88**
Serie 638 *Panetela* 6" x 38 • **85**
Serie 646 *Corona Gorda* 6" x 46 • **85**
Serie 747 *Churchill* 7" x 47 • **86**

Havana Classico

DOMINICAN REPUBLIC

Connecticut Shade Churchill *Churchill*
7¼" x 50 • **84**

Connecticut Shade Robusto *Robusto*
5" x 50 • **85**

Robusto *Maduro* 5" x 50 • **86**

Henry Clay

DOMINICAN REPUBLIC

Brevas *Corona* 5½" x 42 • **84**

Brevas Fina Maduro *Maduro* 6½" x 48 • **84**

Brevas a la Conserva *Corona Gorda*
5⅝" x 46 • **78**

Brevas a la Conserva Maduro *Maduro*
5⅝" x 46 • **87**

Hoja Cubana

NICARAGUA

Churchill *Churchill* 7" x 50 • **84**

Hombre de Oro

DOMINICAN REPUBLIC

Churchill *Churchill* 7" x 50 • **79**

Hoyo de Monterrey

CUBA

Churchill *Churchill* 7" x 47 • **88**

Corona *Corona* 5½" x 42 • **85**

Double Corona *Double Corona*
7⅞" x 49 • **96**

Epicure No. 1 *Corona Gorda* 5⅝" x 46 • **92**

Epicure No. 2 *Robusto* 4⅞" x 50 • **92**

Le Hoyo des Dieux *Lonsdale* 6" x 42 • **89**

Le Hoyo du Dauphin *Panetela* 6" x 38 • **88**

Le Hoyo du Prince *Petit Corona*
5" x 40 • **88**

Le Hoyo du Roi *Corona* 5½" x 42 • **90**

Hoyo de Monterrey

HONDURAS

Ambassador *Lonsdale* 6¼" x 44 • **84**

Cafe Royal *Corona* 5⅝" x 43 • **87**

Churchill *Lonsdale* 6¼" x 45 • **81**

Corona *Corona Gorda* 5⅝" x 46 • **87**

Cuban Largos *Churchill* 7¼" x 47 • **84**

Delights *Panetela* 6¼" x 37 • **80**

Demitasse *Petit Corona* 4" x 39 • **88**

Double Corona *Churchill* 6¼" x 48 • **83**

Excalibur Banquet *Churchill* 6¼" x 48 • **82**

Excalibur No. 1 *Churchill* 7¼" x 54 • **80**

Excalibur No. 1 Maduro *Maduro*
7¼" x 54 • **85**

Excalibur No. 2 *Churchill* 6¼" x 47 • **86**

Excalibur No. 2 Maduro *Maduro*
7" x 46 • **85**

Excalibur No. 3 *Corona Gorda*
6¼" x 50 • **89**

Excalibur No. 3 Maduro *Maduro*
6⅛" x 48 • **87**

Excalibur No. 4 *Corona Gorda*
5⅝" x 46 • **81**

Excalibur No. 5 *Corona* 6¼" x 43 • **85**

Excalibur No. 6 *Petit Corona* 5½" x 38 • **85**

Excalibur No. 7 *Petit Corona* 5" x 43 • **88**

Governor *Corona Gorda* 6⅛" x 50 • **87**
Governor Maduro *Maduro* 6⅛" x 50 • **86**
No. 1 *Lonsdale* 6½" x 43 • **85**
No. 55 *Petit Corona* 5¼" x 43 • **83**
Presidente *Double Corona* 8½" x 52 • **86**
Rothschild *Robusto* 4½" x 50 • **86**
Rothschild Maduro *Maduro* 4½" x 50 • **85**
Sabroso *Petit Corona* 5" x 40 • **82**
Sultan *Churchill* 7¼" x 54 • **82**
Sultan Maduro *Maduro* 7¼" x 54 • **85**
Super Hoyo *Corona* 5½" x 44 • **86**

Hurricanos

HONDURAS

Churchill *Churchill* 7" x 49 • **84**
Robusto *Robusto* 5" x 50 • **83**

Imperio Cubano

U.S.A.

Churchill *Churchill* 7" x 48 • **84**
Robusto *Robusto* 5" x 50 • **87**

Indian Tabac

DOMINICAN REPUBLIC

Anniversary Ltd. Reserve "Buffalo"
Churchill 7" x 47 • **86**

José Benito

DOMINICAN REPUBLIC

Churchill *Churchill* 7" x 50 • **87**
Palma *Corona* 6" x 43 • **86**
Panetela *Panetela* 6¼" x 38 • **83**
Petite *Panetela* 5½" x 38 • **87**

Presidente *Double Corona* 7¼" x 50 • **85**
Rothschild *Robusto* 4¾" x 50 • **84**

José Martí

DOMINICAN REPUBLIC

Corona *Corona* 5½" x 42 • **84**
Maceo *Odd* 6⅞" x 45 • **81**
Martí *Double Corona* 7½" x 50 • **83**
Palma *Lonsdale* 7" x 42 • **84**

José Martí

NICARAGUA

Petit Lancero *Petit Corona* 4½" x 38 • **86**
Remedio *Odd* 5½" x 45 • **85**
Rey del Rey *Double Corona* 8½" x 52 • **83**
Robusto *Robusto* 4⅝" x 50 • **88**

Joya de Nicaragua

NICARAGUA

Churchill *Churchill* 6⅞" x 49 • **83**
Consul *Robusto* 4½" x 52 • **90**
Maduro Deluxe Robusto *Maduro*
    4¾" x 52 • **88**
No. 1 *Lonsdale* 6⅝" x 44 • **87**
No. 5 *Panetela* 6¼" x 35 • **85**
No. 6 *Corona* 6" x 42 • **83**
Petite *Panetela* 5½" x 38 • **82**
Toro *Corona Gorda* 6" x 50 • **84**
Viajante *Double Corona* 8½" x 52 • **86**

Juan Clemente

DOMINICAN REPUBLIC

530 *Panetela* 5" x 30 • **86**

Churchill *Churchill* 6⅞" x 46 • **83**

Club Selection No. 1 *Corona Gorda*
6" x 50 • **83**

Club Selection No. 2 *Robusto*
4½" x 46 • **84**

Club Selection No. 3 *Lonsdale* 7" x 44 • **84**

Club Selection No. 4 *Corona* 5¼" x 42 • **86**

Corona *Petit Corona* 5" x 42 • **85**

Demi-Corona *Petit Corona* 4" x 40 • **76**

Gran Corona *Lonsdale* 6" x 42 • **84**

Panetela *Panetela* 6½" x 34 • **83**

Rothschild *Robusto* 4⅞" x 50 • **85**

Juan Lopez

CUBA

Seleccion No. 2 *Robusto* 4⅞" x 50 • **90**

Knockando

DOMINICAN REPUBLIC

No. 3 *Corona* 5¼" x 41 • **84**

La Diligencia

HONDURAS

Churchill *Churchill* 7" x 48 • **83**

La Finca

NICARAGUA

Bolivares *Double Corona* 7½" x 50 • **85**

Corona *Corona* 5½" x 42 • **91**

Flora *Panetela* 7" x 36 • **86**

Gran Finca *Double Corona* 8½" x 52 • **77**

Joya *Corona Gorda* 6" x 50 • **79**

Robusto *Robusto* 4½" x 50 • **77**

Robusto Maduro *Maduro* 4½" x 50 • **87**

Romeo *Lonsdale* 6½" x 42 • **87**

Valentino *Churchill* 6¼" x 48 • **84**

La Flor Dominicana

DOMINICAN REPUBLIC

Alcalde *Lonsdale* 6½" x 44 • **82**

Churchill Reserva Especial *Churchill*
6⅞" x 49 • **83**

Demi Tasse *Panetela* 5" x 30 • **87**

Figurado *Figurado* 6½" x 52 • **87**

Insurrecto *Corona* 5½" x 42 • **85**

Maceo *Robusto* 5" x 48 • **85**

Macheteros *Petit Corona* 4" x 40 • **84**

Mambises *Churchill* 6⅞" x 48 • **81**

Presidente *Double Corona* 8" x 50 • **85**

Robusto Reserva Especial *Robusto*
5" x 48 • **87**

La Fontana

HONDURAS

Da Vinci *Churchill* 6⅞" x 48 • **87**

Michelangelo *Double Corona* 7½" x 52 • **83**

La Gianna

NICARAGUA

Havana Churchill *Churchill* 7" x 49 • **86**

Robusto *Robusto* 5" x 50 • **85**

La Gloria Cubana

CUBA

Medaille d'Or No. 1 *Figurado*
7⅛" x 36 • **87**

Medaille d'Or No. 2 *Lonsdale*
6⅔" x 43 • **90**

La Gloria Cubana

DOMINICAN REPUBLIC

Churchill *Churchill* 7" x 50 • **83**

Gloria Inmensa *Double Corona*
7½" x 48 • **84**

Glorias Extra *Odd* 6¼" x 46 • **88**

Medaille d'Or No. 4 *Panetela* 6" x 32 • **84**

Minutos *Petit Corona* 4½" x 40 • **84**

La Gloria Cubana

U.S.A.

Churchill *Double Corona* 7" x 50 • **88**

Churchill Maduro *Maduro* 7" x 50 • **89**

Extra *Corona Gorda* 6¼" x 46 • **87**

Glorias *Corona* 5½" x 43 • **88**

Medaille d'Or No. 1 *Lonsdale*
6¼" x 43 • **88**

Panetela Deluxe *Panetela* 7" x 37 • **87**

Piramides *Figurado* 7¼" x 56 • **87**

Soberanos *Double Corona* 8" x 52 • **91**

Torpedo No. 1 *Figurado* 6½" x 54 • **86**

Wavell *Robusto* 5" x 50 • **85**

Wavell Maduro *Maduro* 5" x 50 • **90**

La Hoja Selecta

U.S.A.

Cetros de Oro *Corona* 5¼" x 43 • **83**

Cosiac *Double Corona* 7" x 49 • **85**

Palais Royal *Robusto* 4¼" x 50 • **72**

La Maximiliana

HONDURAS

Perfectus *Churchill* 7" x 50 • **81**

La Regenta

CANARY ISLANDS

Gran Corona *Churchill* 7¼" x 46 • **87**

Individual *Double Corona* 8" x 50 • **87**

No. 2 Robusto *Robusto* 4¼" x 50 • **83**

No. 3 *Corona* 5⅜" x 42 • **78**

No. 5 *Petit Corona* 4½" x 42 • **86**

Premier *Double Corona* 7½" x 50 • **87**

La Reserva

HONDURAS

No. 2 *Churchill* 6½" x 48 • **86**

La Tradicion

U.S.A.

Cabinet Series Double Corona *Double
Corona* 7⅜" x 50 • **85**

Cabinet Series Natural Robusto *Robusto*
5" x 50 • **78**

Cabinet Series Rosado Robusto *Robusto*
5" x 50 • **81**

La Unica

DOMINICAN REPUBLIC

No. 100 *Double Corona* 8½" x 52 • **82**

No. 200 *Churchill* 7" x 49 • **82**

No. 200 *Maduro* 7" x 49 • **86**

No. 300 *Lonsdale* 6¼" x 44 • **84**

No. 400 *Maduro* 4½" x 50 • **84**

No. 400 *Robusto* 4½" x 50 • **88**

No. 500 *Corona* 5½" x 42 • **84**

Las Cabrillas

HONDURAS

Balboa *Odd* 7½" x 54 • **82**

Balboa Maduro *Maduro* 7½" x 54 • **82**

Columbus *Double Corona* 8¼" x 52 • **82**

Cortez *Robusto* 4¼" x 50 • **83**

Cortez Maduro *Maduro* 4¼" x 50 • **84**

De Soto *Churchill* 6⅞" x 50 • **83**

Magellan *Corona* 6" x 42 • **84**

Maximilian *Figurado* 7" x 55 • **84**

Pizarro *Panetela* 5½" x 32 • **85**

Ponce de Leon *Lonsdale* 6⅝" x 44 • **79**

Lempira

HONDURAS

Churchill *Churchill* 7" x 48 • **80**

Corona *Corona* 5½" x 42 • **88**

Presidente *Double Corona* 7¼" x 50 • **85**

Robusto *Robusto* 5" x 50 • **80**

Toro *Corona Gorda* 6" x 50 • **89**

Leon Jimenes

DOMINICAN REPUBLIC

No. 1 *Double Corona* 7½" x 50 • **90**

No. 2 *Churchill* 7" x 47 • **83**

No. 3 *Lonsdale* 6½" x 42 • **83**

No. 4 *Corona* 5⁹⁄₁₆" x 42 • **85**

No. 5 *Petit Corona* 5" x 38 • **84**

Robusto *Robusto* 5" x 50 • **88**

Licenciados

DOMINICAN REPUBLIC

Churchill *Churchill* 7" x 50 • **84**

Excelente *Lonsdale* 6¾" x 43 • **87**

No. 4 *Corona* 5¾" x 43 • **86**

No. 4 Maduro *Maduro* 5¾" x 43 • **80**

Panetela Linda *Panetela* 7" x 38 • **82**

Presidente *Double Corona* 8" x 50 • **84**

Presidente Maduro *Maduro* 8" x 50 • **80**

Soberano *Double Corona* 8½" x 52 • **84**

Supreme Maduro No. 200 *Corona* 5" x 42 • **84**

Supreme Maduro No. 400 *Maduro* 6" x 50 • **84**

Toro *Corona Gorda* 6" x 50 • **86**

Toro Maduro *Maduro* 6" x 50 • **83**

Wavell *Robusto* 5" x 50 • **86**

Wavell Maduro *Maduro* 5" x 50 • **87**

Lone Wolf

DOMINICAN REPUBLIC

Vintage Series Churchill *Churchill* 6¼" x 48 • **84**

Macabi

DOMINICAN REPUBLIC

Belicoso Fino *Figurado* 6¼" x 52 • **88**

Corona Extra *Corona Gorda* 6" x 50 • **84**

Double Corona *Churchill* 6⅛" x 49 • **79**

Media Corona *Corona* 5½" x 43 • **86**

No. 1 *Lonsdale* 6¼" x 44 • **85**

Royal Corona *Robusto* 5" x 50 • **84**

Super Corona *Double Corona* 7¼" x 50 • **84**

Macanudo

JAMAICA

Baron de Rothschild *Lonsdale* 6½" x 42 • **85**

Clayburne *Panetela* 6" x 31 • **83**

Crystal Cafe *Robusto* 5½" x 50 • **85**

Duke of Devon *Corona* 5½" x 42 • **86**

Duke of Devon Maduro *Maduro*
5½" x 42 • **83**

Duke of Windsor *Figurado* 6" x 50 • **87**

Hampton Court *Petit Corona* 5¼" x 43 • **87**

Hyde Park Cafe *Robusto* 5½" x 49 • **85**

Petit Corona *Petit Corona* 5" x 38 • **85**

Portofino *Panetela* 7" x 34 • **85**

Prince Philip *Double Corona* 7½" x 49 • **83**

Prince Philip Maduro *Maduro*
7½" x 49 • **85**

Prince of Wales *Double Corona*
8" x 52 • **84**

Vintage Cabinet Selection 1993 I *Double Corona* 7½" x 49 • **83**

Vintage Cabinet Selection 1993 II
Lonsdale 6⁹⁄₁₆" x 43 • **86**

Vintage Cabinet Selection 1993 IV
Robusto 4½" x 47 • **87**

Vintage Cabinet Selection 1993 V *Robusto*
5½" x 49 • **88**

Vintage Cabinet Selection 1993 VIII
(Crystal) *Robusto* 5½" x 50 • **90**

Vintage Cabinet Selection 1993 XX
Churchill 7" x 47 • **87**

Vintage No. 1 1988 *Churchill*
7½" x 49 • **85**

Vintage No. 3 1988 *Corona* 5⁹⁄₁₆" x 43 • **87**

Vintage No. 5 1988 *Robusto* 5½" x 49 • **85**

Manifiesto

DOMINICAN REPUBLIC

Double Corona *Double Corona*
7½" x 50 • **83**

Match Play

DOMINICAN REPUBLIC

Cypress *Robusto* 4¾" x 50 • **84**

Olympic *Double Corona* 7½" x 50 • **86**

Prestwick *Churchill* 6⅛" x 46 • **85**

Turnberry *Corona Gorda* 6" x 50 • **80**

Maya

HONDURAS

Churchill *Churchill* 6⅞" x 49 • **88**

Executive *Double Corona* 7¼" x 50 • **75**

Maya *Corona Gorda* 6" x 50 • **83**

Palma Fina *Panetela* 6⅞" x 36 • **86**

Petit *Panetela* 5¼" x 34 • **82**

Petit Corona *Corona* 5½" x 42 • **85**

Viajantes *Double Corona* 8½" x 52 • **85**

MiCubano

NICARAGUA

No. 542 *Corona* 5" x 42 • **84**

No. 650 *Corona Gorda* 6" x 50 • **82**

No. 748 *Churchill* 8" x 47 • **79**

No. 852 *Double Corona* 8" x 52 • **84**

Monte Canario

CANARY ISLANDS

Imperiales *Lonsdale* 6½" x 42 • **86**

Nuncio *Lonsdale* 6¼" x 44 • **86**

Panetela *Panetela* 6" x 38 • **80**

Robusto *Robusto* 4¾" x 50 • **70**

Montecristo

CUBA

"A" *Odd* 9¼" x 47 • **91**

Especial *Panetela* 7½" x 38 • **86**

Especial No. 2 *Panetela* 6" x 38 • **87**

No. 1 *Lonsdale* 6½" x 42 • **88**

No. 2 *Figurado* 6⅛" x 52 • **94**

No. 3 *Corona* 5½" x 42 • **88**

No. 4 *Petit Corona* 5" x 42 • **90**

Montecristo

DOMINICAN REPUBLIC

Churchill *Churchill* 7" x 48 • **85**

Corona Grande *Corona Gorda*
5¼" x 46 • **86**

Double Corona *Odd* 6¼" x 50 • **86**

No. 1 *Lonsdale* 6½" x 44 • **87**

No. 2 *Figurado* 6" x 50 • **87**

No. 3 *Corona* 5½" x 44 • **87**

Robusto *Robusto* 4¼" x 50 • **89**

Montecruz

DOMINICAN REPUBLIC

Natural Claro Cedar Aged *Petit Corona*
5" x 42 • **82**

Natural Claro No. 200 *Churchill*
7¼" x 46 • **84**

Sun-Grown Cedar Aged *Petit Corona*
5" x 42 • **87**

Sun-Grown Individuales *Odd* 8" x 46 • **84**

Sun-Grown No. 200 *Churchill*
7¼" x 46 • **84**

Sun-Grown No. 201 *Corona Gorda*
6¼" x 46 • **85**

Sun-Grown No. 210 *Lonsdale*
6½" x 42 • **84**

Sun-Grown No. 220 *Corona* 5½" x 42 • **87**

Sun-Grown No. 230 *Petit Corona*
5" x 42 • **84**

Sun-Grown No. 276 *Panetela* 6" x 32 • **85**

Sun-Grown No. 281 *Panetela* 6" x 28 • **80**

Sun-Grown Robusto *Robusto* 4½" x 49 • **88**

Sun-Grown Tubos *Corona* 6" x 42 • **85**

Sun-Grown Tubulares *Panetela*
6⅛" x 36 • **84**

Montero

DOMINICAN REPUBLIC

Churchill *Churchill* 6⅞" x 46 • **87**

Montesino

DOMINICAN REPUBLIC

Cesar No. 2 *Lonsdale* 6¼" x 44 • **83**

Diplomatico *Corona* 5½" x 43 • **91**

Diplomatico Maduro *Maduro* 5½" x 42 • **86**

Gran Corona *Churchill* 6¼" x 48 • **86**

Gran Corona Maduro *Maduro*
6¼" x 48 • **86**

No. 1 *Lonsdale* 6¼" x 43 • **87**

Nat Sherman

DOMINICAN REPUBLIC

City Desk Selection Dispatch *Maduro*
6½" x 46 • **85**

City Desk Selection Gazette *Corona*
6" x 42 • **83**

City Desk Selection Telegraph *Maduro*
6" x 50 • **85**

City Desk Selection Tribune *Double
Corona* 7½" x 50 • **80**

City Desk Selection Tribune Maduro
Maduro 7½" x 50 • **86**

Exchange Selection Academy 2 *Panetela*
5" x 31 • **78**

Exchange Selection Butterfield 8 *Lonsdale*
6½" x 42 • **83**

Exchange Selection Murray Hill 7 *Panetela*
6" x 38 • **85**

Exchange Selection Oxford 5 *Churchill*
7" x 49 • **85**

Exchange Selection Trafalgar 4 *Corona
Gorda* 6" x 47 • **82**

Gotham Selection No. 65 *Panetela*
6" x 32 • **84**

Gotham Selection No. 500 *Churchill*
7" x 50 • **85**

Gotham Selection No. 711 *Corona Gorda*
6" x 50 • **87**

Gotham Selection No. 1400 *Lonsdale*
6¼" x 44 • **85**

Landmark Selection Algonquin *Lonsdale*
6¼" x 43 • **84**

Landmark Selection Dakota *Double Corona*
7½" x 49 • **83**

Landmark Selection Hampshire *Corona*
5½" x 42 • **87**

Landmark Selection Metropole *Panetela*
6" x 34 • **82**

Landmark Selection Vanderbilt *Robusto*
5" x 47 • **82**

Manhattan Selection Beekman *Panetela*
5½" x 28 • **79**

Manhattan Selection Chelsea *Panetela*
6½" x 38 • **84**

Manhattan Selection Gramercy *Lonsdale*
6¼" x 43 • **80**

Manhattan Selection Sutton *Robusto*
5½" x 49 • **84**

Manhattan Selection Tribeca *Panetela*
6" x 31 • **81**

Metropolitan Selection Anglers *Corona*
5½" x 43 • **87**

Metropolitan Selection Metropolitan
Figurado 7" x 52 • **87**

VIP Selection Astor *Robusto* 4½" x 50 • **86**

VIP Selection Barnum Glass Tube *Petit
Corona* 5½" x 42 • **82**

VIP Selection Carnegie *Corona Gorda*
6" x 48 • **86**

VIP Selection Morgan *Odd* 7" x 42 • **80**

VIP Selection Zigfeld Fancy Tail *Figurado*
6¼" x 38 • **83**

Nat Sherman

HONDURAS

Host Selection Hamilton *Petit Corona*
5½" x 42 • **80**

Host Selection Hampton *Churchill*
7" x 50 • **86**

Host Selection Hobart *Robusto*
5" x 50 • **86**

Nestor 747 Vintage

HONDURAS

Cabinet Series No. 2 *Odd* 4¾" x 54 • **85**

Oliveros

DOMINICAN REPUBLIC

Premium Coroneles *Churchill* 7" x 50 • **88**

Olor

DOMINICAN REPUBLIC

Colossos *Churchill* 7½" x 48 • **88**

Lonsdale *Lonsdale* 6½" x 42 • **84**

Momento *Corona* 5½" x 43 • **88**

Paco *Corona Gorda* 6" x 50 • **88**

Onyx

DOMINICAN REPUBLIC

No. 642 *Maduro* 6" x 42 • **85**

No. 646 *Churchill* 6⅝" x 46 • **85**

No. 650 *Maduro* 6" x 50 • **88**

No. 750 *Maduro* 7½" x 50 • **85**

No. 852 *Double Corona* 8" x 52 • **85**

Orient Express

HONDURAS

Expresso *Figurado* 6" x 48 • **82**

Ornelas

MEXICO

250 *Odd* 9½" x 64 • **87**

Cafetero Chico Maduro *Maduro* 5½" x 46 • **79**

Cafetero Grande *Maduro* 6½" x 46 • **85**

Churchill *Churchill* 7" x 49 • **79**

Churchill Maduro *Maduro* 7" x 49 • **84**

Ltd. Cognac *Lonsdale* 6¼" x 42 • **78**

Matinee *Panetela* 6" x 30 • **85**

No. 1 *Lonsdale* 6¼" x 44 • **78**

No. 1 Vanilla *Lonsdale* 6¼" x 44 • **69**

No. 5 *Panetela* 6" x 38 • **80**

No. 6 *Panetela* 5" x 38 • **81**

Robusto *Robusto* 4¼" x 49 • **75**

Robusto Maduro *Maduro* 4¼" x 49 • **86**

Orosi

NICARAGUA

Oro 550 *Robusto* 5" x 50 • **82**

Oro 700 *Churchill* 7" x 50 • **84**

Oscar

DOMINICAN REPUBLIC

No. 300 *Lonsdale* 6¼" x 44 • **81**

No. 500 *Corona Gorda* 5½" x 50 • **83**

No. 700 *Figurado* 7" x 54 • **88**

Supreme *Double Corona* 8" x 48 • **88**

PIO VI

U.S.A.

Petit Corona *Petit Corona* 5⅛" x 40 • **84**

Padrón

HONDURAS

1964 Anniversary Series Corona *Corona* 6" x 42 • **88**

1964 Anniversary Series Piramide *Figurado* 6⅛" x 52 • **82**

1964 Anniversary Series Superior *Lonsdale* 6" x 42 • **83**

Ambassador *Lonsdale* 6⅛" x 42 • **83**

Palma *Lonsdale* 6¾₆" x 42 • **87**

Padrón

NICARAGUA

1964 Anniversary Series Exclusivo *Corona Gorda* 5½" x 50 • **92**

2000 *Robusto* 5" x 50 • **86**

2000 Maduro *Maduro* 5" x 50 • **86**

3000 *Robusto* 5½" x 52 • **87**

3000 Maduro *Maduro* 5½" x 52 • **88**

Chicos *Panetela* 5½" x 36 • **83**

Churchill *Churchill* 6⅞" x 46 • **90**

Churchill Maduro *Maduro* 6⅞" x 46 • **86**

Executive *Double Corona* 7½" x 50 • **85**

Executive Maduro *Maduro* 7½" x 50 • **87**
Londres *Corona* 5½" x 42 • **86**
Magnum *Odd* 9" x 50 • **91**

Palmarejo

DOMINICAN REPUBLIC

Petit Corona *Petit Corona* 5⅛" x 42 • **87**

Partagas

CUBA

8-9-8 *Lonsdale* 6⅜" x 43 • **88**
Churchill Deluxe *Churchill* 7" x 47 • **83**
Corona *Corona* 5½" x 42 • **86**
Culebra *Figurado* 5¾" x 39 • **87**
Lusitania *Double Corona* 7⅜" x 49 • **93**
No. 1 *Lonsdale* 6⅜" x 43 • **88**
Petit Corona *Petit Corona* 5" x 42 • **89**
Presidente *Figurado* 6⅛" x 47 • **84**
Serie D No. 4 *Robusto* 4⅞" x 50 • **92**

Partagas

DOMINICAN REPUBLIC

8-9-8 *Lonsdale* 6⅛" x 44 • **88**
Almirante *Corona Gorda* 6¼" x 47 • **87**
Humitube *Lonsdale* 6¼" x 43 • **87**
Limited Reserve Epicure *Petit Corona*
   5" x 38 • **90**
Limited Reserve Regale *Corona Gorda*
   6¼" x 47 • **88**
Limited Reserve Royale *Lonsdale*
   6¾" x 43 • **91**
Maduro *Maduro* 6¼" x 48 • **85**
Naturales *Robusto* 5½" x 50 • **83**
No. 1 *Lonsdale* 6¼" x 43 • **88**

No. 2 *Corona* 5¼" x 43 • **86**
No. 4 *Petit Corona* 5" x 38 • **89**
No. 6 *Panetela* 6" x 34 • **81**
No. 10 *Double Corona* 7½" x 49 • **89**
Robusto *Robusto* 4½" x 49 • **87**
Sabrosos *Corona* 5⅞" x 43 • **86**

Particulares

DOMINICAN REPUBLIC

Churchill *Churchill* 6⅞" x 49 • **87**

Particulares

HONDURAS

Petit *Panetela* 5⅜" x 34 • **80**

Paul Garmirian

DOMINICAN REPUBLIC

Belicoso *Figurado* 6¼" x 52 • **88**
Belicoso Fino *Figurado* 5½" x 52 • **86**
Bombone *Odd* 3½" x 43 • **87**
Celebration *Figurado* 9" x 50 • **88**
Churchill *Churchill* 7" x 48 • **81**
Connoisseur *Corona Gorda* 6" x 50 • **86**
Corona *Corona* 5½" x 42 • **86**
Double Corona *Double Corona*
   7⅜" x 50 • **84**
Epicure *Robusto* 5½" x 50 • **82**
Lonsdale *Lonsdale* 6½" x 42 • **78**
No. 2 *Robusto* 4¼" x 48 • **80**
No. 5 *Petit Corona* 4" x 40 • **81**
Panetela *Panetela* 7½" x 38 • **87**
Petit Corona *Petit Corona* 5" x 43 • **86**
Robusto *Robusto* 5" x 50 • **81**

Penamil

CANARY ISLANDS

No. 57 *Double Corona* 7½" x 50 • 69

Peterson

DOMINICAN REPUBLIC

Corona *Corona* 5¼" x 43 • 82

Hallmark Churchill *Churchill* 7" x 48 • 88

Presidente *Double Corona* 7½" x 50 • 84

Robusto *Robusto* 4¼" x 50 • 81

Toro *Corona Gorda* 6" x 50 • 87

Petrus Tabacage

HONDURAS

Antonius *Figurado* 5" x 54 • 86

Churchill 90 *Churchill* 7" x 50 • 84

Churchill Maduro 89 *Maduro* 7" x 50 • 84

Corona Sublime 89 *Corona Gorda*
 5½" x 46 • 82

Corona Sublime Maduro 89 *Maduro*
 5½" x 46 • 78

DC Havana *Double Corona* 7¼" x 50 • 86

Double Corona *Maduro* 7¼" x 50 • 87

Double Corona 89 *Double Corona*
 7¼" x 50 • 81

Gregorius *Petit Corona* 5" x 42 • 78

No. II 89 *Lonsdale* 6¼" x 44 • 86

No. II Maduro *Maduro* 6¼" x 44 • 84

No. IV 89 *Odd* 5⅜" x 38 • 83

Palma Fina *Panetela* 6" x 38 • 82

Rothschild *Robusto* 4¼" x 50 • 74

Rothschild Maduro 89 *Maduro*
 4¼" x 50 • 81

Playboy by Don Diego

DOMINICAN REPUBLIC

Churchill *Double Corona* 7¼" x 50 • 87

Robusto *Robusto* 5" x 50 • 86

Pleiades

DOMINICAN REPUBLIC

Aldebaran *Double Corona* 8½" x 50 • 85

Antares *Petit Corona* 5½" x 40 • 87

Mars *Panetela* 5" x 28 • 82

Neptune *Odd* 7½" x 42 • 79

Orion *Corona* 5¼" x 42 • 81

Perseus *Panetela* 5" x 34 • 79

Pluton *Robusto* 5" x 50 • 83

Saturne *Odd* 8" x 46 • 81

Sirius *Churchill* 6⅞" x 46 • 81

Por Larrañaga

DOMINICAN REPUBLIC

Cetros *Lonsdale* 6⅞" x 42 • 87

Delicados *Panetela* 6½" x 36 • 82

Fabuloso *Double Corona* 7" x 50 • 88

Nacionales *Corona* 5½" x 42 • 84

Petit Cetros en Cedro *Petit Corona*
 5" x 38 • 83

Pyramid *Figurado* 6" x 50 • 86

Robusto *Robusto* 5" x 50 • 87

Primera de Nicaragua

NICARAGUA

Churchill *Churchill* 7" x 50 • 84

Primo del Rey

DOMINICAN REPUBLIC

Chavon *Lonsdale* 6½" x 41 • **85**

Seleccion No. 1 *Lonsdale* 6¹³⁄₁₆ x 42 • **86**

Seleccion No. 2 *Lonsdale* 6¼" x 42 • **84**

Seleccion No. 4 *Corona* 5½" x 42 • **84**

Seleccion No. 4 Maduro *Maduro*
5½" x 42 • **85**

Punch

CUBA

Churchill *Churchill* 7" x 47 • **93**

Corona *Corona* 5½" x 42 • **89**

Double Corona *Double Corona*
7⅞" x 49 • **91**

Petit Corona del Punch *Petit Corona*
5" x 42 • **86**

Punch *Corona Gorda* 5⅝" x 46 • **87**

Punch

HONDURAS

After Dinner *Odd* 7¼" x 45 • **74**

Amatista *Lonsdale* 6¼" x 44 • **84**

Cafe Royal *Corona* 5⅝" x 44 • **88**

Casa Grande *Churchill* 7¼" x 46 • **79**

Deluxe Series Chateau L *Churchill*
7¼" x 54 • **85**

Deluxe Series Chateau L Maduro *Maduro*
7¼" x 54 • **85**

Deluxe Series Chateau M *Corona Gorda*
5¼" x 46 • **85**

Deluxe Series Chateau M Maduro *Maduro*
6¼" x 46 • **86**

Deluxe Series Corona *Odd* 6¼" x 45 • **88**

Deluxe Series Royal Coronation *Corona*
5¼" x 44 • **83**

Double Corona *Churchill* 6¼" x 48 • **84**

Double Corona Maduro *Maduro*
6¼" x 48 • **86**

Elite *Petit Corona* 5¼" x 44 • **85**

Gran Cru Britannia *Odd* 6¼" x 50 • **88**

Gran Cru Diademas *Churchill*
7¼" x 54 • **82**

Gran Cru Monarca *Churchill* 6¾" x 48 • **84**

Gran Cru Prince Consort *Double Corona*
8½" x 52 • **77**

Gran Cru Robusto *Robusto* 5¼" x 50 • **84**

Gran Cru Superior *Robusto* 5½" x 48 • **83**

Lonsdale *Lonsdale* 6½" x 43 • **85**

No. 75 *Corona* 5½" x 43 • **84**

Pita Maduro *Maduro* 6⅛" x 50 • **87**

Presidente *Double Corona* 8½" x 52 • **84**

Punch *Lonsdale* 6¼" x 45 • **81**

Rothschild *Robusto* 4½" x 50 • **84**

Rothschild Maduro *Maduro* 4½" x 50 • **86**

Super Rothschild *Robusto* 5¼" x 50 • **88**

Puros Indios

HONDURAS

Churchill Maduro *Maduro* 7¼" x 52 • **86**

Colorado Rothschild *Robusto* 5" x 50 • **87**

Corona Gorda *Corona Gorda* 6" x 50 • **86**

Corona Gorda Maduro *Maduro*
6" x 52 • **86**

No. 4 Especial *Corona* 5½" x 44 • **90**

No. 5 Especial Colorado *Panetela*
5" x 36 • **87**

No. 5 Especial Colorado Claro *Panetela*
5" x 36 • **83**

Petit Perla *Panetela* 5" x 38 • **82**

Piramides No. 1 *Figurado* 7½" x 60 • **92**

Piramides No. 2 *Figurado* 6½" x 46 • **90**

Quintero

CUBA

Churchill *Lonsdale* 6½" x 42 • **92**
Medias Coronas *Petit Corona* 5" x 40 • **84**

Rafael Gonzales

CUBA

Lonsdale *Lonsdale* 6½" x 42 • **91**

Ramon Allones

CUBA

Corona *Corona* 5½" x 42 • **89**
Gigantes *Double Corona* 7⅝" x 49 • **94**
Specially Selected *Robusto* 4⅞" x 50 • **91**

Ramon Allones

DOMINICAN REPUBLIC

"B" *Lonsdale* 6½" x 42 • **87**
Crystals *Lonsdale* 6¼" x 42 • **86**
Privada A *Lonsdale* 7" x 45 • **85**
Privada D *Corona* 5" x 42 • **86**
Redondos *Churchill* 7" x 49 • **85**
Trumps *Lonsdale* 6¼" x 43 • **83**

Roly

HONDURAS

Colorado Claro Rothschild *Robusto*
    5" x 50 • **86**
Colorado Rothschild *Robusto* 5" x 50 • **87**
Petit Cetro *Panetela* 5" x 36 • **86**
Valentinos *Churchill* 7" x 49 • **86**

Romanticos

DOMINICAN REPUBLIC

Eros *Robusto* 5" x 52 • **86**
Leonardo *Corona Gorda* 6" x 50 • **85**

Romeo y Julieta

DOMINICAN REPUBLIC

Churchill *Churchill* 7" x 50 • **87**
Corona *Corona* 5½" x 44 • **83**
Palma *Lonsdale* 6" x 43 • **84**
Presidente *Odd* 7" x 43 • **88**
Romeo *Figurado* 6" x 46 • **85**
Rothschild *Robusto* 5" x 50 • **84**
Rothschild Maduro *Maduro* 5" x 50 • **87**
Vintage No. 1 *Corona* 6" x 43 • **87**
Vintage No. 2 *Corona Gorda* 6" x 46 • **87**
Vintage No. 3 *Robusto* 4½" x 50 • **86**
Vintage No. 4 *Churchill* 7" x 48 • **85**
Vintage No. 5 *Double Corona* 7½" x 50 • **89**

Romeo y Julieta

CUBA

Belicoso *Figurado* 5½" x 52 • **90**
Belvedere *Panetela* 5½" x 39 • **84**
Cedros No. 3 *Petit Corona* 5" x 42 • **92**
Celestial Fino *Figurado* 5¾" x 46 • **87**
Churchill *Churchill* 7" x 47 • **89**
Corona *Corona* 5½" x 42 • **89**
Corona Grande *Lonsdale* 6½" x 42 • **90**
Exhibicion No. 3 *Corona Gorda*
    5⅝" x 46 • **91**
Exhibicion No. 4 *Robusto* 5" x 48 • **92**
Petit Corona *Petit Corona* 5" x 42 • **88**
Shakespeare *Panetela* 6½" x 28 • **85**

Royal Honduras

HONDURAS

Sovereign *Churchill* 7" x 48 • **89**

Royal Jamaica

DOMINICAN REPUBLIC

Buccaneer *Panetela* 5½" x 30 • **88**

Churchill *Double Corona* 8" x 51 • **85**

Corona Grande *Lonsdale* 6½" x 42 • **84**

Director *Corona Gorda* 6" x 45 • **87**

Double Corona *Odd* 7" x 45 • **87**

Gaucho *Panetela* 5¼" x 33 • **85**

Giant Corona *Double Corona* 7½" x 49 • **86**

Goliath *Odd* 9" x 64 • **80**

Maduro Churchill *Maduro* 8" x 51 • **86**

Maduro Corona *Maduro* 5½" x 40 • **87**

Maduro Corona Grande *Maduro*
   6½" x 42 • **85**

No. 1 Tube *Odd* 6" x 45 • **82**

No. 2 Tube *Panetela* 6½" x 34 • **85**

Park Lane *Figurado* 6" x 47 • **85**

Petit Corona *Petit Corona* 5" x 40 • **83**

Robusto *Robusto* 4½" x 49 • **85**

St. George

DOMINICAN REPUBLIC

Churchill *Churchill* 7" x 48 • **81**

Saint Luis Rey

CUBA

Churchill *Churchill* 7" x 47 • **89**

Lonsdale *Lonsdale* 6½" x 42 • **88**

Saint Luis Rey

HONDURAS

Lonsdale *Lonsdale* 6½" x 44 • **86**

Serie A *Corona Gorda* 6" x 50 • **85**

Sancho Panza

CUBA

Belicoso *Figurado* 5½" x 52 • **86**

Molinas *Lonsdale* 6½" x 42 • **91**

Non Plus *Petit Corona* 5" x 42 • **85**

Sancho *Odd* 9¼" x 47 • **86**

Santa Clara 1830

MEXICO

No. I *Double Corona* 7½" x 52 • **87**

No. I Maduro *Maduro* 7" x 51 • **83**

No. II *Churchill* 6½" x 48 • **78**

No. III *Lonsdale* 6⅞" x 43 • **85**

No. V *Corona* 6" x 43 • **87**

No. VI *Corona Gorda* 6" x 50 • **79**

No. VI Maduro *Maduro* 6" x 51 • **85**

Robusto *Robusto* 4½" x 50 • **72**

Santa Damiana

DOMINICAN REPUBLIC

Seleccion No. 100 *Churchill* 6¾" x 48 • **85**

Seleccion No. 300 *Corona Gorda*
   5½" x 46 • **83**

Seleccion No. 500 *Robusto* 5" x 50 • **84**

Seleccion No. 700 *Lonsdale* 6½" x 42 • **82**

Seleccion No. 800 *Churchill* 7" x 50 • **84**

Santa Rosa

HONDURAS

Cetros *Lonsdale* 6" x 42 • 86

Churchill *Churchill* 7" x 50 • 85

Corona *Lonsdale* 6½" x 44 • 83

No. 4 *Corona* 5½" x 42 • 86

Sancho Panza Maduro *Maduro*
4½" x 50 • 81

Toro *Corona Gorda* 6" x 50 • 86

Savinelli

DOMINICAN REPUBLIC

E.L.R. Double Corona *Corona Gorda*
6" x 50 • 87

E.L.R. No. 1 Churchill *Churchill*
7¼" x 48 • 88

E.L.R. No. 3 Lonsdale *Lonsdale*
6¼" x 43 • 88

E.L.R. Robusto *Robusto* 5" x 49 • 88

Extraordinaire *Corona* 5½" x 44 • 89

Oro 750 Churchill *Churchill* 7" x 47 • 85

Siglo 21

DOMINICAN REPUBLIC

21-4 *Churchill* 7" x 48 • 80

Signature Collection

DOMINICAN REPUBLIC

Churchill *Churchill* 7¼" x 50 • 87

Robusto *Robusto* 5" x 50 • 87

Torpedo *Figurado* 6¼" x 54 • 90

Signet

DOMINICAN REPUBLIC

Buckingham *Churchill* 7" x 48 • 86

Sosa

DOMINICAN REPUBLIC

Brevas *Corona* 5½" x 43 • 84

Churchill *Churchill* 7" x 49 • 85

Churchill Maduro *Maduro* 6¹⁵/₁₆ x 49 • 88

Family Selection No. 1 *Lonsdale*
6¼" x 43 • 85

Family Selection No. 2 *Figurado*
6¼" x 54 • 88

Family Selection No. 4 *Petit Corona*
5" x 40 • 85

Family Selection No. 5 *Robusto*
5" x 50 • 86

Family Selection No. 6 *Panetela*
6¼" x 38 • 82

Family Selection No. 8 *Churchill*
7" x 48 • 81

Family Selection No. 9 *Double Corona*
7¾" x 51 • 82

Governor *Corona Gorda* 6" x 50 • 88

Lonsdale *Lonsdale* 6½" x 43 • 78

Magnum *Double Corona* 7¾" x 50 • 85

Piramides *Figurado* 6½" x 54 • 80

Santa Fe *Panetela* 6" x 35 • 85

Wavell *Robusto* 4¾" x 50 • 88

Wavell Maduro *Maduro* 4¾" x 50 • 87

Tabacos San Jose

U.S.A.

Churchill *Churchill* 7" x 47 • 88

Double Corona *Double Corona*
7⅞" x 50 • 79

Presidente *Double Corona* 8" x 52 • **86**
Robusto *Robusto* 5" x 50 • **84**

Tamboril

DOMINICAN REPUBLIC

Churchill *Churchill* 7" x 47 • **84**
Cortadito *Petit Corona* 5" x 38 • **82**
Robusto *Robusto* 5" x 52 • **80**
Sumatra Churchill *Churchill* 7" x 47 • **86**
Sumatra Robusto *Robusto* 5" x 52 • **85**

Te-Amo

MEXICO

Celebration *Lonsdale* 6¹¹⁄₁₆ x 44 • **81**
CEO *Double Corona* 8½" x 52 • **84**
Churchill *Double Corona* 7½" x 50 • **78**
Churchill Maduro *Maduro* 7½" x 50 • **84**
Figurado *Figurado* 6⅝" x 50 • **85**
Gran Piramide *Figurado* 7¼" x 54 • **84**
Impulse Lights *Panetela* 5" x 32 • **81**
Maximo Churchill Maduro *Maduro* 7" x 54 • **86**
Meditation *Corona* 6" x 42 • **80**
New York LaGuardia *Odd* 5" x 54 • **87**
New York Park Avenue *Lonsdale* 6⅝" x 42 • **80**
New York Wall Street *Odd* 6" x 52 • **84**
No. 4 *Petit Corona* 5" x 42 • **80**
Piramide *Figurado* 6¼" x 50 • **83**
Presidente *Churchill* 7" x 50 • **76**
Presidente Maduro *Maduro* 7 " x 50 • **83**
Relaxation *Lonsdale* 6⅝" x 44 • **82**
Robusto Maduro *Maduro* 5½" x 54 • **81**
Satisfaction *Corona Gorda* 6" x 46 • **82**
Satisfaction Maduro *Maduro* 6" x 46 • **84**
Torero *Panetela* 6⁹⁄₁₆" x 35 • **81**

Torito *Robusto* 4¾" x 50 • **82**
Torito Maduro *Maduro* 4¾" x 50 • **85**
Toro *Corona Gorda* 6" x 50 • **86**
Toro Maduro *Maduro* 6" x 50 • **84**

Temple Hall

JAMAICA

Belicoso *Figurado* 6" x 50 • **88**
No. 450 Maduro *Maduro* 4½" x 49 • **86**
No. 550 *Robusto* 5½" x 49 • **86**
No. 625 *Lonsdale* 6½" x 42 • **82**
No. 700 *Churchill* 7" x 49 • **86**

Tesoros de Copan

HONDURAS

Cetros *Lonsdale* 6¼" x 44 • **84**
Corona *Corona Gorda* 5¼" x 46 • **77**
Linda *Panetela* 5⅝" x 38 • **85**

The Griffin's

DOMINICAN REPUBLIC

No. 100 *Figurado* 7" x 38 • **84**
No. 200 *Odd* 7" x 44 • **81**
No. 300 *Lonsdale* 6¼" x 44 • **84**
No. 400 *Panetela* 6" x 38 • **86**
No. 500 *Petit Corona* 5¹⁄₁₆" x 43 • **86**
Prestige *Double Corona* 7½" x 50 • **84**
Privilege *Panetela* 5" x 32 • **86**
Robusto *Robusto* 5" x 50 • **88**

Thomas Hinds

HONDURAS

Honduran Selection Churchill *Churchill* 7" x 49 • **87**

Honduran Selection Corona *Corona*
5½" x 42 • **86**

Honduran Selection Presidente *Double Corona* 8½" x 52 • **86**

Honduran Selection Robusto *Robusto*
5" x 50 • **84**

Honduran Selection Short Churchill
Corona Gorda 6" x 50 • **82**

Honduran Selection Supremos *Lonsdale*
6⅔" x 43 • **85**

Honduran Selection Torpedo *Figurado*
6" x 52 • **86**

Thomas Hinds

NICARAGUA

Cabinet Selection Churchill *Churchill*
7" x 49 • **84**

Cabinet Selection Robusto *Robusto*
5" x 50 • **87**

Nicaraguan Selection Churchill *Churchill*
7" x 49 • **87**

Nicaraguan Selection Churchill Maduro
Maduro 7" x 49 • **83**

Nicaraguan Selection Corona *Corona*
5½" x 42 • **84**

Nicaraguan Selection Lonsdale *Lonsdale*
6⅔" x 43 • **87**

Nicaraguan Selection Robusto *Robusto*
5" x 50 • **85**

Nicaraguan Selection Robusto Maduro
Maduro 5" x 50 • **84**

Nicaraguan Selection Short Churchill
Corona Gorda 6" x 50 • **85**

Nicaraguan Selection Short Churchill
Maduro *Maduro* 6" x 50 • **84**

Torcedor

NICARAGUA

Churchill *Churchill* 7" x 50 • **87**

No. 4 *Petit Corona* 5" x 42 • **76**

Panetela *Panetela* 5" x 36 • **86**

Robusto *Robusto* 5" x 50 • **87**

Toro *Corona Gorda* 6" x 50 • **78**

Tresado

DOMINICAN REPUBLIC

Seleccion No. 100 *Double Corona*
8" x 52 • **84**

Seleccion No. 200 *Churchill* 7" x 48 • **83**

Seleccion No. 200 Maduro *Maduro*
7" x 48 • **89**

Seleccion No. 300 *Corona Gorda*
6" x 46 • **84**

Seleccion No. 400 *Lonsdale* 6⅛" x 44 • **86**

Seleccion No. 500 *Corona* 5½" x 42 • **85**

Seleccion No. 500 Maduro *Maduro*
5½" x 42 • **83**

Troya

DOMINICAN REPUBLIC

Clasico No. 27 Corona *Petit Corona*
5½" x 42 • **84**

Clasico No. 72 Executive *Double Corona*
7¼" x 50 • **86**

No. 18 Rothchild *Robusto* 4½" x 50 • **83**

No. 18 Rothschild Maduro *Maduro*
4½" x 50 • **87**

No. 27 Corona *Corona* 5½" x 42 • **87**

No. 45 Cetro *Lonsdale* 6¼" x 44 • **90**

No. 45 Cetro Maduro *Maduro* 6" x 44 • **83**

No. 54 Elegante *Lonsdale* 7" x 43 • **86**

No. 63 Churchill *Churchill* 6⅛" x 46 • **84**

No. 63 Churchill Maduro *Maduro*
6⅛" x 46 • **84**

No. 72 Executive *Double Corona*
7¼" x 50 • **81**

No. 81 Torpedo *Figurado* 7" x 54 • **87**

V Centennial

HONDURAS

500 Series Churchill *Churchill* 7" x 48 • **83**

Cetro *Lonsdale* 6½" x 44 • **89**

Churchill *Churchill* 7" x 48 • **85**

Churchill Maduro *Maduro* 7" x 48 • **84**

Corona *Corona* 5½" x 42 • **83**

Numero 1 *Panetela* 7½" x 38 • **88**

Numero 2 *Corona Gorda* 6" x 50 • **88**

Numero 2 Maduro *Maduro* 6" x 50 • **84**

Presidente *Double Corona* 8" x 50 • **84**

Robusto *Robusto* 5" x 50 • **87**

Robusto Maduro *Maduro* 5" x 50 • **85**

Torpedo *Figurado* 7" x 54 • **87**

V.M. Santana

DOMINICAN REPUBLIC

Connecticut Churchill *Churchill*
7¼" x 50 • **85**

Connecticut Collection Robusto *Robusto*
5" x 50 • **85**

Sumatra Collection Robusto *Robusto*
5" x 50 • **85**

Vargas

CANARY ISLANDS

Churchill *Double Corona* 7½" x 50 • **82**

Cremas *Petit Corona* 4⅜" x 39 • **85**

Diplomatico *Panetela* 5½" x 36 • **77**

Presidente *Churchill* 6¾" x 46 • **79**

Reserva Senadores *Corona Gorda*
5½" x 46 • **84**

Robusto *Robusto* 4¼" x 50 • **83**

Veracruz

MEXICO

Reserve Especial *Lonsdale* 6½" x 42 • **86**

Vueltabajo

DOMINICAN REPUBLIC

Churchill *Churchill* 7" x 48 • **82**

Corona *Corona* 5¾" x 42 • **86**

Gigante *Double Corona* 8½" x 52 • **87**

Lonsdale *Lonsdale* 7" x 43 • **80**

Pyramide *Figurado* 7" x 50 • **84**

Robusto *Robusto* 4¼" x 52 • **86**

Toro *Corona Gorda* 6" x 50 • **82**

Yumuri

DOMINICAN REPUBLIC

Churchill *Churchill* 7" x 48 • **86**

Zino

HONDURAS

Gold Line Diamonds *Corona* 5½" x 40 • **83**

Gold Line Tradition *Lonsdale* 6¼" x 44 • **84**

Gold Line Veritas *Churchill* 7" x 49 • **83**

Mouton Cadet No. 1 *Lonsdale*
6½" x 44 • **85**

Mouton Cadet No. 2 *Panetela* 6" x 35 • **83**

Mouton Cadet No. 3 *Panetela*
5¾" x 36 • **85**

Mouton Cadet No. 4 *Panetela*
5⅛" x 30 • **86**

Mouton Cadet No. 5 *Petit Corona*
5" x 42 • **87**

Mouton Cadet No. 6 *Robusto* 5" x 50 • **82**

CHAPTER 14

Cigar Retailers

The cigar stores that follow are divided into two sections: United States and International. Stores in the United States are listed alphabetically by state, then by metropolitan area, then by city. International stores are listed alphabetically by country, and then by city (or, in the case of Canada, by province and then by city; or, in the case of the Caribbean, by island and then by city).

UNITED STATES

Alabama

Smokin' Joes Discount Tobacco
2914 Pelham Rd. S.
Anniston
(205) 835-9090

Cigar Limited
1027A Opelika Rd.
Auburn
(334) 821-3886

BIRMINGHAM & VICINITY

The Briary
Brookwood Village
Birmingham
(205) 871-2839

Dee's Fine Cigars
2398 Green Springs
Hwy.
Birmingham
(888) 299-0222

J. Blackburn & Co.
3232 Galleria Circle
Birmingham
(205) 985-0409

Puff & Browse
1901 6th Ave.
Birmingham
(205) 251-9251

Tobacco Express
1813 Center Point
Pkwy.
Birmingham
(205) 856-1155

Zachary Scott Cigar Co., Inc.
2402 Canterbury Rd.
Birmingham
(205) 879-0059

Tobacco Express
1405 2nd Ave. SW
Cullman
(205) 775-1212

Tobacco Road
219-A 2nd Ave. SE
Decatur
(205) 355-8065

The Tobacco Express
3290 Florence Blvd.
Florence
(205) 764-7641

Antonelli's
525 Broad St.
Gadsden
(205) 543-7473

HUNTSVILLE & VICINITY

Great Spirits
3022 S. Memorial
Pkwy.
Huntsville
(205) 881-4496

Humidor Pipe Shop, Inc.
2502 Memorial
Pkwy. SW
Huntsville
(205) 539-6431

Tobacco Junction
8890 Hwy. 72 W.
Madison
(205) 890 0557

MOBILE & VICINITY

Tinder Box
212B Fairhope Ave.
Fairhope
(334) 473-1221

Cottage Hill Package Store
6376 Cottage Hill
Rd., Mobile
(334) 660-0166

Tinder Box
3484 Bel Air Mall
Mobile
(334) 473-1221

Tobacco Leaf
6150 Atlanta Hwy.
Montgomery
(334) 277-3880

Tobacco Road
25405 Perdido
Beach Blvd.
Orange Beach
(334) 981-6105

The White House
901D Hwy 231 N.
Ozark
(334) 445-1135

Alaska

ANCHORAGE

Brown Jug
4140 Old Seward
Hwy.
Anchorage
(907) 563-3286

The Great Alaska Tobacco Company
3960 W. Diamond Blvd.
Anchorage
(907) 245-2243

Pete's Tobacco Shop
531 E. 5th Ave.
Anchorage
(907) 274-7473

Tobacco Cache
601 E. Northern Lights Blvd.
Anchorage
(907) 279-9411

....

Super Value Shoppers Forum
1255 Airport Way
Fairbanks
(907) 456-4102

Percy's
214 Front St.
Juneau
(907) 463-3100

Salooney Cigar
80038 Warren
Ketchikan
(907) 225-1493

Ferdinand's Gallery
7th & Broadway
Skagway
(907) 983-2831

Arizona

The Kind Connection
1174 Hwy. 95
Bullhead City
(520) 754-1114

Smoke-n-Guns
322 S. Main
Cottonwood
(520) 634-3216

The Cigar Shop
109 E. Phoenix
Flagstaff
(520) 214-8784

Stag Tobacconist
7700 W. Arrowhead Towne Center
Glendale
(602) 979-7500

J's Smoke Shop
27 S. Acoma Blvd.
Lake Havasu City
(520) 680-2655

MESA

Arizona Premium Cigar
6555-2402 E. Southern Ave.
Mesa
(602) 830-4134

Cigarette & Cigar Outlet
2753 E. Broadway
Mesa
(602) 610-9077

DJ's Smoke Shop
1815 W. 1st Ave.
Mesa
(602) 461-9174

DJ's Smoke Shop
1206 E. Broadway Rd., Mesa
(602) 649-8893
(602) 461-9174

DJ's Smoke Shop
7310 E. Main St.
Mesa
(602) 854-2566

Tinder Box
1312 W. Southern Ave., Mesa
(602) 644-9300

PHOENIX & VICINITY

Arizona Premium Cigar
6920 E. Cave Creek Rd., Cave Creek
(602) 595-6600

Smoker Friendly
9210 W. Peoria
Peoria
(602) 878-3834

Ambassador
10625 N. Tatum Blvd.
Phoenix
(602) 905-1000

Christopher's
2398 E. Camelback
Phoenix
(602) 957-3214

Churchill's Fine Cigars
5021 N. 44th St.
Phoenix
(602) 840-9080

Holy Smokes
9627-A Metro Pkwy. W., Phoenix
(602) 674-8400

Knight Gallery
Paradise Valley Mall, 4550 E. Cactus Rd.
Phoenix
(602) 996-6610

Robusto's Cigar Emporium
214 N. Central Ave.
Phoenix
(602) 716-9446

Smoker Friendly
717 W. Union Hills
Phoenix
(602) 548-3370

Smoker Friendly
12038 N. 35th Ave.
Phoenix
(602) 938-9288

Sportsman's Fine Wine & Spirit
3205 E. Camelback Rd., Phoenix
(602) 955-7730

Stag Tobacconist
9627-A Metro Pkwy. W., Phoenix
(602) 943-7517

Stag Tobacconist
9201 N. 29th Ave.
Phoenix
(602) 943-8519

Stag Tobacconist
3121 N. 3rd Ave.
Phoenix
(602) 265-2748

Tinder Box International
4940 E. Ray Rd.
Phoenix
(602) 961-2203

Ye Old Pipe Shoppe
2017 E. Camelback
Rd., Phoenix
(602) 955-9542

SCOTTSDALE

AZ Wine Co.
2515 N. Scottsdale.
Rd., Scottsdale
(602) 423-9305

DJ's Smoke Shop
1412 N. Scottsdale
Rd., Scottsdale
(602) 946-4509

Ford & Haig
Tobacconist
7076 5th Ave.
Scottsdale
(602) 946-0608

Lonsdales Cigars
23535 N. Scottsdale
Rd., Scottsdale
(602) 585-8330

Smoke 'n' News at
The Borgata
6166 N. Scottsdale
Rd., Scottsdale
(602) 835 6846

Stag Tobacconist
7014 E. Camelback
Scottsdale
(602) 994-4282

The Village Smoke
Shop
8989 E. Via Linda
Scottsdale
(602) 314-9898

Rural Road Liquors
7420 S. Rural Rd.
Tempe
(602) 345-9110

Tempe Tobacco
7 W. Baseline
Tempe
(602) 777-7710

Smoke Signals
427 E. Allen St.
Tombstone
(520) 457-9020

TUCSON

Anthony's Cigar
Emporium
7866 N. Oracle Rd.
Tucson
(520) 531-9155

Crescent Tobacco
Shop & Newsstand
216 E. Congress St.
Tucson
(520) 622-1559

Crescent Tobacco
Shop & Newsstand
7037 E. Tanque-
Berde Rd.
Tucson
(520) 296-3102

The Moon Smoke
Shop
120 W. Grant Rd.
Tucson
(520) 622-7261

Smoker's Haven
Park Mall, 5870 E.
Broadway
Tucson
(520) 747-8989

Tinder Box
3601 E. Broadway
Tucson
(520) 326-7198

Arkansas

The Tobacco Store
521 W. Main St.
Cabot
(501) 974-3179

The Tobacco Shop
121 W. Township
Fayetteville
(501) 444-8311

FORT SMITH

Discount Tobacco
2000 Rogers Ave.
Fort Smith
(501) 494 7740

Midland Smoke
Shop
2908 Midland Rd.
Fort Smith
(501) 783-2696

Taylor Pipe &
Tobacco
5304 Rogers Ave.
Fort Smith
(800) 36-SMOKE

Tobacco Box
Limited
Indian Mall
Jonesboro
(501) 972-6420

LITTLE ROCK &
VICINITY

Tobacco Mart
309 Watson St.
Benton
(501) 315-1888

Gatsby's Fine Cigars
200 N. Bowman
Little Rock
(501) 221-0088

The Pipe &
Tobacco
2908 S. University
Little Rock
(501) 562-7473

Smoke Shoppe
7420 N. Hills Blvd.
North Little Rock
(501) 835-6067

The Tobacco Rack
4512 Camp
Robinson Rd.
North Little Rock
(501) 753-1312

Davis Smoke Shop
East Gate Plaza,
#2 Davis Bldg.
Russellville
(501) 968-6760

Tobacco Express
1606 Hwy. 71 S.
Mena
(501) 394-5060

Stogies Fine Cigars,
Tobacco and Much
More
224 2nd St.
Rogers
(501) 621-6610

California

ANAHEIM VICINITY

Maxwell's Tobacco Shop
2500 E. Imperial
Hwy., Brea
(714) 256-2344

Canyon Smoke Shop Inc.
7941 Beach Blvd.
Buena Park
(714) 739-0894

M K's Cigar Box
19116 Pioneer Blvd.
Cerritos
(310) 865-5111

Albertson's
10051 Valley View
Ave., Cypress
(704) 854-8282

Tobacco Club
5491 Ball Rd.
Cypress
(714) 527-1363

Albertson's
1040 E. Bastanchury
Rd., Fullerton
(714) 257-0460

Red Cloud Fine Cigar
118 W. Wilshire
Ave., Fullerton
(714) 680-6200

Adray's
1809 W. Chapman
Ave., Orange
(714) 978-8500

Albertson's
8440 E. Chapman
Ave., Orange
(714) 771-6996

Aroma Italiano Coffee House
1948 N. Tustin
Orange
(714) 282-2382

Tinder Box
2183 Mall Of
Orange
Orange
(714) 998-0792

Wine Exchange
2368 North Orange
Mall, Orange
(714) 974-1454

Prissy's Smoke Shop
12136 Beach Blvd.
Stanton
(714) 893-0066

Havana House Cigar & Lounge
7020 Greenleaf Ave.
Uptown Whittier
(310) 698-2245

H & H Tobaccos
16170 Leffingwell
Rd., Whittier
(310) 902-9417

Whittier Cigarette & Cigar
11803 Whittier
Blvd.
Whittier City
(310) 695-7870

Smoke Shop
20513 Yorba Linda
Blvd.
Yorba Linda
(714) 695-0532

Akimbo International
8400 Misty Oak
Way, Antelope
(916) 456-7315

BAKERSFIELD

17th St. Cigar Company
1418 17th St.
Bakersfield
(805) 631-9885

Gerry's Fine Cigars
2324 Brundage Lane
Bakersfield
(805) 633-1440

Havana House
8200 Stockdale Hwy.
Bakersfield
(805) 832-2211

Hiland's Gift & Tobacco
East Hill Mall, 3000
Mall View Rd.
Bakersfield
(805) 872-7890

John T's Pipe & Tobacco
84 Valley Plaza
Bakersfield
(805) 832-7002

Bidwell Cigar
243 W. 2nd St.
Chico
(916) 842-8600

Rabbogliatti's
802 W. 5th St.
Chico
(916) 342-9591

COSTA MESA & VICINITY

Alfred Dunhill Limited
South Coast Plaza,
3333 Bristol St.
Costa Mesa
(714) 641-0521

Cheer's Tobacco
1525 Mesa Verde Dr.
Costa Mesa
(714) 662-2880

Long's Drug Store
175 E. 17th St.
Costa Mesa
(714) 631-8860

Meerschaum King
88 Fair Dr.
Costa Mesa
(714) 636-1897

Royal Cigar Society
1909 Harbor Blvd.
Costa Mesa
(714) 646-0550

7 Day Liquors
891 Baker St.
Costa Mesa
(714) 540-2519

Smoke Shack
250 Ogle St.
Costa Mesa
(800) 969-3005

Tinder Box
Crystal Court-South
  Coast Plaza, 3333
  Bear St.
Costa Mesa
(714) 540-8262

H & H Tobacco
18225 S. Brookhurst
Fountain Valley
(714) 962-2927

Beachside Cigars
17852 Quintana
  Lane
Huntington Beach
(714) 848-2447

**Hiland's Gift &
Tobacco**
15931 Goldenwest
  St.
Huntington Beach
(714) 897-1172

**Huntington Beach
Smoke Shop**
7194 Edinger Ave.
Huntington Beach
(714) 841-9929

K & B Cigars
15562 Graham St.
Huntington Beach
(714) 899-9007

Liquor Warehouse
9092 Adams
Huntington Beach
(714) 965-6000

Albertson's
4541 Campus Dr.
Irvine
(714) 854-8282

**Hiland's Gift &
Tobacco**
2272 Michelson
Irvine
(714) 475-9986

Irvine Smoke Shop
165251 Carmen
  Ave., Irvine
(714) 263-8939

Cheer's Tobacco
177 Riverside Ave.
Newport Beach
(714) 650-6510

Lido Cigar Room
3441 Via Lido
Newport Beach
(714) 923-0595

Newport Tobacco
Fashion Island,
  533 Newport
  Centre Dr.
Newport Beach
(714) 644-5153

Portofino Cigars
1000 W. Coast Hwy.
Newport Beach
(714) 650-0166

Romeo Et Juliette
1000 Bristol N.
Newport Beach
(714) 261-7722

Smoke Shop
2781 W. Macarthur
  Blvd., Santa Ana
(714) 557-8730

The Wine Club
2110 E. MacFadden
Santa Ana
(714) 835-6485

**King Cigar &
Cigarettes**
14300 Beach Blvd.
Westminster
(714) 899-7111

D & B's Cigars
1461 S. 4th St.
El Centro
(760) 352-2459

El Centro Liquor
401 State St.
El Centro
(760) 353-4460

Cigar Den
17933 Ventura Blvd.
Encino
(818) 343-5768

John's Cigars
2211 Myrtle Ave.
Eureka
(707) 444-8869

**John T's Unique
Gifts**
1419-B Solano Mall
Fairfield
(707) 426-5566

Harvest Market
171 Boatyard Dr.
Fort Bragg
(707) 964-7000

FRESNO

Cigar Ltd.
4287 W. Swift Ave.
Fresno
(209) 221-0161

Cigar World
4988 N. Fresno St.
Fresno
(209) 227-6210

**Hardwick's Briar
Shoppe**
3402 N. Blackstone
  Ave., Fresno
(209) 228-1389

Havana's
2051 W. Bullard
Fresno
(209) 439-4642

**John T's Pipe &
Tobacco**
581 E. Shaw Ave.
Fresno
(209) 229-4253

**Perfect Blend Fine
Cigars**
1294 N. Wishon
Fresno
(209) 486-0400

Wine Barrel
1105 E. Champlain
  Dr., Fresno
(209) 434-1057

Fetzer Vineyards
3601 Eastside Rd.
Hopland
(707) 744-7600

LAKE TAHOE &
VICINITY

King's Liquor
2227 Lake Tahoe
  Blvd.
South Lake Tahoe
(716) 541-4614

Tourist Liquor
10092 Donner Pass
  Rd., Truckee
(916) 582-3521

LANCASTER & VICINITY

London Pipe & Gift Shop
1120 W. Ave. K
Lancaster
(805) 948-5352

Hiland's Gifts & Tobacco
Antelope Valley
Mall, 1233 W.
Ave. P
Palmdale
(805) 538-9620

LIVERMORE

Jack Kavanagh Liquor/Beverage
4068 East Ave.
Livermore
(510) 443-2434

Jack Kavanagh Liquor/Beverage
1024 E. Stanley
Blvd.
Livermore
(510) 443-9463

Jack Kavanagh Liquor/Beverage
4518 Las Positas Rd.
Livermore
(510) 443-443

LOS ANGELES & VICINITY

Cigar Palace
139 E. Foothill Blvd.
Arcadia
(818) 359-8582

Al's Newsstand
216 S. Beverly Dr.
Beverly Hills
(310) 278-6397

Alfred Dunhill Limited
201 N. Rodeo Dr.
Beverly Hills
(310) 274-5351

Beverly Hills Hotel Signature Shop
9641 Sunset Blvd.
Beverly Hills
(310) 276-2251

Davidoff of Geneva
Via Rodeo, 232 N.
Rodeo Dr.
Beverly Hills
(310) 278-8884

Grand Havana Room
301 N. Canon Dr.
Beverly Hills
(310) 274-8100

Nazareths
350 N. Canon Dr.
Beverly Hills
(310) 271-5863

Thomas Hinds Tobacconist
9632 Santa Monica
Blvd.
Beverly Hills
(310) 275-9702

The Wine Merchant
9701 Santa Monica
Blvd.
Beverly Hills
(310) 278-7322

Cigar Arama
11729 Barrington
Court
Brentwood
(310) 440-0402

Cigar Corner
151 N. Fernando
Blvd., Burbank
(626) 558-1701

The Cigar Shop
1700 N. San
Fernando Blvd.
Burbank
(626) 842-5359

Havana Studios
245 E. Olive Ave.
Burbank
(818) 557-7600

House of Cigar & Gift
144 S. Glenoaks
Blvd., Burbank
(626) 845-3631

Briar Rose
20700 S. Avalon
Blvd., Carson
(310) 538-1018

The Pipe Rack
2020 Ave. of The
Stars, Level 2
Century City
(310) 552-9842

Tinder Box
333 Puente Hills
Mall
City of Industry
(818) 965-7215

Royal Tobacco
7946 E. Florence
Ave., Downey
(310) 928-1113

Ceegar Gallery & Lounge
109 S. Broadway
Glendale
(818) 559-2170

Cigar Box
1325-A Glendale
Galleria
Glendale
(818) 244-3344

Cigar Plus
309½ W. Broadway
Glendale
(818) 547-3771

Garard Fine Cigars
154 S. Brand Blvd.
Glendale
(818) 247-9701

Red Carpet Wines & Spirits/Havana Studios
400 E. Glen Oaks
Blvd., Glendale
(818) 247-5544

Smoke A Cigar Club
318 N. Brand Blvd.
Glendale
(818) CIGAR-97

Cigarette City
5460 Woodruff Ave.
Lakewood
(310) 867-7467

John's Cigar & Spirits
5932 E. Delamo
Blvd.
Lakewood
(310) 421-6815

Chief Tobacco
5535 Woodruff Ave.
Lakewood City
(562) 920-6065

Discount Cigarette
Outlets
16129 Hawthorne
Blvd.
Lawndale
(310) 542-5884

Board Room
5305 E. 2nd St.
Long Beach
(562) 438-5069

C & K Cigars
202 Nieto Ave.
Long Beach
(562) 439-3246

Casillas Cigars
5660 E. Pacific
Coast Hwy.
Long Beach
(562) 498-0210

Churchill's
5844 Naples Plaza
Long Beach
(562) 433-3994

Havana Cigar Club
3939 E. Broadway
Long Beach
(562) 433-8053

Hiland's Gift &
Tobacco
Von's Pavillion
Center, 5937
Spring St.
Long Beach
(310) 425-3258

Joe R. Churchill's
of Long Beach
107 W. Broadway
Long Beach
(562) 491-7300

Marina Tobacco
6244 E. Pacific
Coast Hwy.
Long Beach
(562) 597-0095

Naples Pipe Shop
5662 E. 2nd St.
Long Beach
(562) 439-8515

Salpat/Tobaccoland
2730 El Presidio
Long Beach
(310) 604-4787

Beverage
Warehouse
4935 McConnell
Ave., Los Angeles
(310) 306-2822

Beverly Hills Cigars
5327 E. Beverly Hills
Blvd., Los Angeles
(213) 724-6102

Cigar Source
6230 Wilshire Blvd.
Los Angeles
(310) 456-9628

Country Home
Tobacco
2240 S. Atlantic
Blvd.
Los Angeles
(213) 721-1192

Gift Connections
418 W. 6th St.
Los Angeles
(213) 689-4438

Gourmet Chalet
7880 Sunset Blvd.
Los Angeles
(213) 874-6303

Havana Banana
Cigar
23504 Calabasas Rd.
Los Angeles
(818) 224-4286

Havana Studios
8851 Sunset Blvd.
Los Angeles
(310) 652-4955

Hill Street Cafe &
Cigar
818 N. Hill St.
Los Angeles
(213) 617-1108

Hogie Stogies
201 N. Los Angeles
St., Los Angeles
(213) 622-8745

Jack's Liquor &
Cigars
3720 W. Olympic
Blvd.
Los Angeles
(213) 737-0922

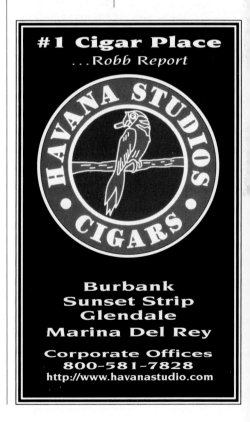

La Plata Cigars Mfg.
1026 S. Grand Ave.
Los Angeles
(213) 747-8561

Mel & Rose Liquor & Deli
8344 Melrose Ave.
Los Angeles
(213) 655-5557

The Tobacco Merchant
7115 Melrose Ave.
Los Angeles
(213) 931-3225

The V-Cut Smoke Shop
8172 Melrose Ave.
Los Angeles
(213) 655-5959

Wally's Liquor
2107 Westwood Blvd.
Los Angeles
(310) 475-0606

'bu Heaven
3900 Cross Creek Rd., Malibu
(310) 456-2924

Bristol Farms
1570 Rosecrans Ave.
Manhattan Beach
(310) 643-5229

Cigar Corner
Manhattan Village,
3200 Sepulveda Blvd.
Manhattan Beach
(310) 545-9775

Manhattan Liquors
1157A Artesia Blvd.
Manhattan Beach
(310) 374-3454

Royal Cigar Society
1145 N. Sepulveda Blvd.
Manhattan Beach
(310) 796-5577

Havana Studios
4325 Glencoe Ave.
Marina Del Rey
(310) 305-0303

Tobacco Trader
4722 ¼ Admiralty Way
Marina Del Rey
(310) 823-5831

Captain Tobacco
2371 E. Colorado Blvd., Pasadena
(818) 795-4714

The Cigar Company
380 S. Lake Ave.
Pasadena
(818) 792-2112

Tinder Box
165 Plaza Pasadena
Pasadena
(818) 449-6479

Big Town Liquors
28733 S. Western Ave.
Rancho Palos Verdes
(310) 833-4401

Bombay Cigar Society
209 Ave. I
Redondo Beach
(310) 798-6568

The Dukes
1630 Pacific Coast Hwy.
Redondo Beach
(310) 792-3853

House of Cigar & Liquor
400 S. Pacific Coast Hwy.
Redondo Beach
(310) 540-7075

The Cigar Place
1427 San Marino Ave.
San Marino
(818) 285-3900

Jerry's Liquor & Wine
2923 Wilshire Blvd.
Santa Monica
(310) 828-5923

M & A Tobacco
1803 Lincoln Blvd.
Santa Monica
(310) 314-9839

Main Smoke
3310 Main St.
Santa Monica
(310) 581-0775

Royal Cigar Society
2814 Main St.
Santa Monica
(310) 581-8555

Tinder Box
2729 Wilshire Blvd.
Santa Monica
(310) 828-2313

Romeo Et Juliette
1198 Pacific Coast Hwy., Seal Beach
(310) 430-2331

Burning Desires
14006 Riverside Dr.
Sherman Oaks
(818) 990-6584

Cigar Gallery
4421 Alamo St.
Simi Valley
(805) 527-7332

JM Enterprises
2235 1st St.
Simi Valley
(805) 582-2454

Fair Oaks Cigar Company
806 Fair Oaks Ave.
South Pasadena
(818) 441-1457

Kappy's
1503 Mission St.
South Pasadena
(213) 682-1163

Jumping Java
12265 Ventura Blvd.
Studio City
(818) 980-4249

Universal City Cigar
3701 Cahuenga Blvd. W.
Studio City
(818) 766-5328

Vendome
11976 Ventura Blvd.
Studio City
(818) 766-5272

Party House
18839 Ventura Blvd.
Tarzana
(818) 342-0355

Mursuli Cigars
10667 Lower Azusa
Rd., Temple City
(818) 444-3443

Cigar House
1378-A Noah Moore
Park Rd.
Thousand Oaks
(805) 374-0082

Cigar Spot
222 W. Hillcrest Dr.
Thousand Oaks
(805) 371-0793

Village Smoke Shoppe
3006 Thousand
Oaks Blvd.
Thousand Oaks
(805) 495-9736

Liberson's International Tobac
10143 Riverside Dr.
Toluca Lake
(818) 985-4310

V-Cut Smoke Shop
10600 Riverside Dr.
Toluca Lake
(818) 766-9593

Beverages, & More!
2775 Pacific Hwy.
Torrance
(310) 257-9022

Cigar Emporium
1305 Sartori Ave.
Torrance
(310) 320-3400

The Cigar Room Tobacconist
22543 Hawthorne
Blvd., Torrance
(310) 375-4420

Tinder Box
71 Del Amo Fashion
Sq.
Torrance
(310) 542-7975

Tinder Box
8621 Santa Monica
Blvd.
West Hollywood
(310) 659-6464

The Big Easy
1922 Westwood
Blvd.
West Los Angeles
(310) 234-3279

The Wine House
2311 Cotner Ave.
West Los Angeles
(310) 479-3731

The Cigar Company
3845-A E. Thousand
Oaks Blvd.
Westlake Village
(805) 494-1886

The Cigar Company
21744 Ventura Blvd.
Woodland Hills
(818) 346-1505

Green Jug Liquor
6307 Platt Ave.
Woodland Hills
(818) 887-9463

Sierra Cigar Company
4863 Topanga
Canyon Blvd.
Woodland Hills
(818) 883-1217

Cigar Box
311 D St.
Marysville
(916) 742-4354

Cigar Man
2012 Yosemite Pkwy.
Merced
(209) 724-9035

MODESTO

Liquor Locker
2020 Standiford
Ave., Modesto
(209) 522-9112

Long Drug Store
2601 Oakdale Rd.
Modesto
(209) 523-4901

Tresetti Wine World
927 11th St.
Modesto
(209) 548-9463

MONTEREY & VICINITY

Carmel Pipe Shop
3574 Oliver Rd.
Carmel
(408) 624-9737

The Humidor
120 Crossroads Blvd.
Carmel
(408) 622-7969

Mediterrean Market
Ocean Ave. &
Mission
Carmel
(408) 624-2022

Big Shot Cigar
380 Foam St.
Monterey
(408) 658-0892

Hellam's Tobacco Shop
423 Alvarado St.
Monterey
(408) 373-2816

Beverages, & More!
423 San Antonio
Rd.
Mountain View
(415) 949-1826

NAPA COUNTY

Baker Street Tobacco
3053 Jefferson
Napa

Brix Restaurant & Market
7377 St. Helena
Hwy., Napa
(707) 944-2749

Baker Street Tobacconist
1150 Main St.
St. Helena
(707) 963-8673

St. Helena Wine Merchant
699 St. Helena Hwy.
St. Helena
(707) 963-7888

Mustards Grill
7399 St. Helena
Hwy.
Yountville
(707) 944-2424

The Humidor Fine Cigars
21 Hampshire Way
Novato
(415) 892-3358

Mingo's Mercantile
40571 Hwy. 41
Oakhurst
(209) 683-4878

OAKLAND & VICINITY

Beverages, & More!
836 San Pablo Ave.
Albany
(510) 525-9582

Juicy News II
3167 College Ave.
Berkeley
(510) 601-8602

Cigarette Store
6942 Village Pkwy.
Dublin
(510) 829-9615

Beverages, & More!
525 Embarcadero
Oakland
(510) 208-5126

Grand Lake Smoke Shop
3206 Grand Ave.
Oakland
(510) 268-4070

JT Enterprise
449 Hegenberger Rd.
Oakland
(510) 687-1818

La Salle Cigars
6218 La Salle Ave.
Oakland
(510) 339-8788

The Piedmont Tobbaconist
17 Glen Ave.
Oakland
(510) 652-PIPE

Quesada's Cigar
699 Lewelling Blvd.
San Leandro
(510) 357-5800

OCEANSIDE & VICINITY

Cardiff Seaside Market
2087 San Elijo Ave.
Cardiff by the Sea
(619) 753-5445

Hiland's Gift & Tobacco
Plaza Camino Real,
2525 El Camino
Real, Carlsbad
(619) 434-2788

Village Cigar & Fine Gift
2959 State St.
Carlsbad
(619) 730-0717

Wine Street
6986 El Camino
Real, La Costa
(619) 431-8455

Puff & Stuff
518 Oceanside Blvd.
Oceanside
(760) 757-3457

Albertson's
151 Woodland
Pkwy.
San Marcos
(760) 736-8880

Pipes & Tobacco
512 E. Vista Way
Vista
(619) 758-9881

Sam's Cigars & Smokeshop
889 S. Santa Fe Ave.
Vista
(760) 726-5749

ORANGE COUNTY SOUTH

The Ritz-Carlton - Gift Shop
One Ritz Carlton
Dana Point
(714) 240-2000

Albertson's
700 S. Coast Hwy.
Laguna Beach
(714) 497-6410

Mr. Bones Fine Cigars
325 Glenneyre
Laguna Beach
(714) 494-8665

Post & Package
412 N. Coast Hwy.
Laguna Beach
(714) 494-5705

Albertson's
26892 La Paz Rd.
Laguna Hills
(714) 643-0511

Laguna Hill Smoke Shop
25614 Alicia Pkwy.
Laguna Hills
(714) 699-2651

Southwest Gift & Tobacco
24155 Laguna Hills
Mall
Laguna Hills
(714) 829-8474

Albertson's
22351 El Torro Rd.
Lake Forest
(714) 581-3440

Tobacco Barn Pipe Shop
23532 El Toro Rd.
Lake Forest
(714) 830-7110

Wine Emporium
22500 Muirlands
Blvd.
Lake Forest
(714) 951-9463

Hiland's Gift & Tobacco
27000 Crown Valley
Pkwy.
Mission Viejo
(714) 347-8665

Southwest Gift & Tobacco
Mission Viejo Mall,
27000 Crown
Valley Pkwy.
Mission Viejo
(714) 347-1442

Innerlimits
508 N. El Camino
Real
San Clemente
(714) 498-0167

Smokin'
647 Camino de los
    Mars
San Clemente
(714) 654-0791

Prestige Cigar
32281 Camino
    Capistrano
San Juan
(714) 496-1199

PALM SPRINGS & VICINITY

Smokes
48400 Seminole Dr.
Cabazon
(909) 849-4343

Tobacco Road
Village Lane, 54200
    N. Circle Dr.
Idyllwild
(909) 659-3930

**Hyatt Grand
Champions Resort**
44-600 Indian Wells
    Lane
Indianwells
(760) 341-1000

Albertson's
78-630 Hwy. 111
La Quinta
(760) 564-5388

The Humidor
73405 El Paseo
Palm Desert
(760) 568-1892

**Palm Desert
Tobacco**
73580 El Paseo
Palm Desert
(760) 340-1954

**Palm Desert
Tobacco**
Palm Desert Town
    Center, 72-840
    Hwy. 111
Palm Desert
(760) 340-3364

Cigar Imports
530 S. Indian
    Canyon Dr.
Palm Springs
(760) 325-0554

Tinder Box
245 S. Palm Canyon
    Dr., Palm Springs
(760) 325-4041

POMONA & VICINITY

**S & S Exclusive
Cigars**
6430 Sunridge Court
Alta Loma
(909) 466-9690

Smoke Shop
8722 Baseline Rd.
Alta Loma
(909) 483-1917

**Claremont Tobacco
House**
272 W. 2nd St.
Claremont
(909) 625-6321

Smoke Shop
590 E. Baseline Rd.
Claremont
(909) 625-1998

Glendora Cigars
614 W. Alosta Ave.
Glendora
(818) 852-2255

**Marty's Cigar &
Divan**
109 W. Foothill
    Blvd.
Glendora
(818) 852-9337

**David's Gift &
Tobacco**
1 Mills Circle
Ontario
(909) 481-2200

Express West
266 N. Euclid Ave.
Pomona
(909) 988-1366

San Dimas Liquor
1427 W. Arrow Hwy.
San Dimas
(909) 599-4744

**Sharon Cigar &
Tobacco**
1371 W. Arrow Hwy.
San Dimas
(909) 305-2199

**Cigar Exchange
International**
134 N. 2nd Ave.
Upland
(909) 946-6782

Liquor Land
965 N. Central Ave.
Upland
(909) 981-2303

S & H Tobacco
101 W. Central Ave.
Walnut
(909) 671-0224

John T's
597 Plaza Dr.
West Covina
(818) 338-8124

**Good Fellas Fine
Cigars**
8034 Haven Ave.
Rancho Cucamonga
(909) 987-3005

RIVERSIDE & VICINITY

**Arnett's Smoke
Shop**
1185 Magnolia Ave.
Corona
(909) 340-2739

**Holy Smoke
Tobacco**
3637 W. Florida
    Ave., Hemet
(909) 925-1945

**Smitty's Smoke
House**
25073 Sunny Mead
    Blvd.
Moreno Valley
(909) 243-6664

**Mission Tobacco
Lounge**
3630 University
    Ave., Riverside
(909) 682-4427

Tinder Box
1283 Galleria at
    Tyler, Riverside
(909) 689-4401

SACRAMENTO & VICINITY

Beverages, & More!
7929 Greenback
  Lane
Citrus Heights
(916) 728-4204

Tinder Box
6144 Sunrise Mall
Citrus Heights
(800) 725-3231

D R Cigars
657 E. Bidwell St.
Folsom
(916) 983-4278

Golden Cigar
35-89 Taylor
Loomis
(916) 652-2010

Duffy's Liquor & Cigar
329 Vernon St.
Roseville
(916) 783-3258

Berkley Fine Wines
515 Pavilions Lane
Sacramento
(916) 929-4422

Beverages, & More!
3106 Arden Way
Sacramento
(916) 481-8657

Briar Patch Smoke Shop
Arden Fair, 1689
  Arden Way
Sacramento
(916) 929-8965

Gerry's Fine Cigars
1100 O St.
Sacramento
(916) 443-7497

Hardwick's Briar Shoppe
1115 Front St., Old
  Sacramento
Sacramento
(916) 498-0450

Rodney's Cigars & Liquor
1000 J St.
Sacramento
(916) 442-5998

Select Wine & Spirits
7485 Rush River Dr.
Sacramento
(916) 393-3132

Tower Pipe & Cigars
2518 Land Park Dr.
Sacramento
(916) 443-8466

Lil' Havana
1011 Mason St.
Vacaville
(707) 447-8678

Grapes & Grains
385 Salinas
Salinas
(408) 424-3482

SAN BERNARDINO & VICINITY

Alpine Liquor Junction
41532 Big Bear Blvd.
Big Bear Lake
(909) 866-2824

Cheefa's Fine Cigars
23360 W. Valencia
  Blvd.
Big Bear Lake
(888) 838-2442

Sam's Smoke Shop
1091 S. Mount
  Vernon
Coulton
(800) 903-7509

Highland Smoke Shop
7291 Boulder Ave.
Highland
(909) 863-1998

Hiland's Gift & Tobacco
212 Inland Center
San Bernardino
(909) 885-8282

Poor Richards Pipe Shop
364 W. Highland
  Ave.
San Bernardino
(909) 883-7031

Hiland's Gift & Tobacco
Mall of Victor
  Valley, 14400 Bear
  Valley Rd.
Victorville
(619) 241-5821

SAN DIEGO & VICINITY

La Villa Del Tobacco
1049 Cordova Dr.
Chula Vista
(619) 482-7658

Royalty Cigar Company
345 3rd Ave.
Chula Vista
(619) 425-8905

San Diego Cigar Company
931 Otay Lakes Rd.
Chula Vista
(619) 482-9295

Tinder Box
Chula Vista Center,
  555 Broadway
Chula Vista
(619) 262-4822

Coronado Tobacco Company
1341 Orange Ave.
Coronado
(619) 437-1565

Albertson's
2707 Via De La
  Valle, Del Mar
(619) 481-8178

Del Mar Hills Liquors
2654 Del Mar
  Heights Rd.
Del Mar
(619) 481-8148

Primo Cigar
2670 Via De La
  Valle, Del Mar
(619) 259-0855

Tinder Box
329 Parkway Plaza
El Cajon
(619) 440-1121

Albertson's
1048 N. El Camino
Real, Encinitas
(760) 943-7738

Beverages, & More!
212 North El
Camino Real
Encinitas
(760) 943-6631

Puff & Stuff
335 1st St.
Encinitas
(619) 753-3839

**Holiday Wine
Cellars**
302 W. Mission
Escondido
(619) 745-1200

**Tinder Box North
County Fair**
200 E. Via Rancho
Pkwy., Escondido
(619) 745-9230

**Bob's Casa Del
Habano**
523 Nautilus St.
La Jolla
(619) 456-6161

Cigar Cellar
1261 Prospect St.
La Jolla
(619) 459-3255

Havana Club
2149 Avenida de la
Playa, La Jolla
(619) 459-7787

**Spirits of St.
Germain**
3251 Holiday Court
La Jolla
(619) 455-1414

Beverages, & More!
8410 Center Drive
La Mesa
(619) 461-6230

Long's Drug Store
4445 Mission Blvd.
Pacific Beach
(619) 273-0440

Albertson's
8510 Genesee Ave.
San Diego
(619) 458-1662

Bad Habits
3850 5th Ave.
San Diego
(619) 298-6340

Beverages, & More!
11475 Carmel
Mountain Road
San Diego
(619) 673-3892

The Black
5017 Newport Ave.
San Diego
(619) 222-5498

**Captain Hunt
Tobacconist**
851-D W. Harbor Dr.
San Diego
(619) 232-2938

**Cuban Cigar
Factory**
360 8th Ave.
San Diego
(619) 238-2496

El Caribe Cigars
322 W. Washington
St., San Diego
(619) 296-5898

Fumar Cigar
1165-A Garnet
San Diego
(619) 270-9227

Jug Liquor
4979 Cass St.
San Diego
(619) 483-1374

Liberty Tobacco
7341 Clairemont
Mesa Blvd.
San Diego
(619) 292-1772

Tinder Box
4465 La Jolla Village
Dr., San Diego
(619) 452-9444

The Wine Bank
363 5th Ave.
San Diego
(619) 234-7487

The Cigar Box
437 S. Hwy. 101
Solana Beach
(619) 350-4500

SAN
FRANCISCO &
VICINITY

Elegant Tobacco
1538-A El Camino
Real, Belmont
(650) 631-0600

**Burlingame
Tobacconist**
1404 Burlingame
Ave.
Burlingame
(415) 343-3300

Beverages, & More!
4915 Junipero Serra
Blvd., Colma
(650) 757-0196

Tinder Box
107-A Serramante
Center
Daly City
(415) 756-1771

**The Foster City
Cigar Company**
999-B Edgewater
Blvd.
Foster City
(888) 606-7300

Telfords Pipe Shop
121 Strawberry
Village
Mill Valley
(415) 388-0440

**Ludwig's Smoke
Shop**
431 San Anselmo
Ave.
San Anselmo
(415) 456-1820

**Alfred Dunhill
Limited (North
America)**
250 Post St.
San Francisco
(415) 781-3368

Another Hennessy's
199 Brannan St.
San Francisco
(415) 777-9403

Ashbury Tobacco
1524 Haight St.
San Francisco
(415) 552-5556

Beverages, & More!
201 Bayshore Blvd.
San Francisco
(415) 648-1233

California Tobacco Center
1501 Polk St.
San Francisco
(415) 885-5479

Cigar Amour
218 Church St.
San Francisco
(415) 252-9871

D & M Liquors
2200 Fillmore
San Francisco
(415) 346-1325

Grant's Pipe Shop
562 Market St.
San Francisco
(415) 981-1000

Griffis & Chester
36 Loraine Court
San Francisco
(415) 576-9902

The Humidor
2201 Union St.
San Francisco
(415) 563-5181

Jim Mate Pipe Shop
575 Geary St.
San Francisco
(415) 775-6634

Lombardi Sports
1600 Jackson St.
San Francisco
(415) 771-0600

Michael's Liquors
2198 Union St.
San Francisco
(415) 921-5700

N A Tobacco
1343 Polk St.
San Francisco
(415) 776-5650

Nob Hill Cigar
699 Sutter St.
San Francisco
(415) 928-5799

Sherlock's Haven
Embarcadero Center
W., 275 Battery St.
San Francisco
(415) 362-1405

Smokin' Cigars
Pier 39
San Francisco
(415) 981-6116

Vendetta
12 Tillman Place
San Francisco
(415) 397-7755

The Wine Club
953 Harrison St.
San Francisco
(415) 512-9088

Tinder Box
139 Hillsdale Mall
San Mateo
(415) 341-4945

Beverages, & More!
750 Francisco Blvd.
W., San Rafael
(415) 456-8367

The Humidor Fine Cigars
3330 North Gate Mall
San Rafael
(415) 898-9990

SAN JOSE & VICINITY

The Cigar Emporium
40835 Fremont
Blvd., Fremont
(510) 226-9900

Rock Stop
39494 Fremont
Blvd., Fremont
(510) 745-8118

Edward's Pipe & Tobacco
4546 El Camino
Real, Los Altos
(415) 941-1228

Beltramo's
1540 El Camino
Real, Menlo Park
(415) 325-2806

Old Knickerbockers
555 Santa Cruz Ave.
Menlo Park
(415) 327-8769

Lil' Havana Cigars
530 Barberlane
Milipitas
(408) 435-0698

John T's
1043 New Park Mall
Newark
(510) 796-7033

Dominion Premium Cigars
2465 E. Bayshore
Rd., Palo Alto
(650) 354-0244

Mac's Smoke Shop
534 Emerson St.
Palo Alto
(650) 323-3724

Old Knickerbocker
480 University Ave.
Palo Alto
(650) 328-7473

Beverages, & More!
5765 Johnson Drive
Pleasanton
(510) 416-2086

Tobacco Loft
Rose Pavilion, 4001-
4 Santa Rita Rd.
Pleasanton
(510) 463-0100

Broadway Tobacconist
2013 Broadway
Redwood City
(415) 261-9657

Ed's Smoke Shop
1221 San Carlos
Ave., San Carlos
(415) 591-6266

Tobacco Club
1683 Laurel St.
San Carlos
(415) 596-8856

Beverages, & More!
14800 Camden Ave.
San Jose
(408) 369-0990

Club Havana Premium Cigars
860 El Paseo De
Saratoga
San Jose
(408) 370-9098

Metro Convenience Center
73 Metro Dr.
San Jose
(408) 437-0393

Mission Pipe Shop
812 Town Country
  Village Dr.
San Jose
(408) 241-8868

Willow Glen Cigars
& Tobacco
1068 Lincoln Ave.
San Jose
(408) 283-9323

Beverages, & More!
4175 Stevens Creek
  Blvd.
Santa Clara
(408) 248-2776

Dante's Premium
Cigars
5259 Stevens Creek
  Blvd., Santa Clara
(408) 261-2277

The Mission City
Cigar Company
791 Franklin St.
Santa Clara
(408) 296-2510

The Wine Club
1200 Coleman Ave.
Santa Clara
(408) 567-0900

Murphy Street
Smoke Shop
114 S. Murphy St.
Sunnyvale
(408) 735-9127

T J Smokes
520 S. Murphy Ave.
Sunnyvale
(408) 450-1102

Jack Kavanagh
Liquor/Beverage
1306 Bockman Rd.
San Lorenzo
(510) 278-4336

SAN LUIS
OBISPO &
VICINITY

Boyd's Tobacco
625 Spring St.
Paso Robles
(805) 239-8701

Sanctuary Tobacco
Shop
1111 Chorro St.
San Luis Obispo
(805) 543-1958

SANTA
BARBARA &
VICINITY

M & R Liquor
1024 Casitas Pass
  Rd., Carpinteria
(805) 684-3110

The Bottle Shop
Liquor
1200 Coast Village
  Rd., Santa Barbara
(805) 969-4466

The Cigar Company
1005 Santa Barbara
  St., Santa Barbara
(805) 962-4427

The Cigar Company
137 E. De Laguerra
Santa Barbara
(805) 962-4427

The Cigar Company
9 W. Carrillo St.
Santa Barbara
(805) 899-4724

Mission Cigar
Company
3204 State St.
Santa Barbara
(805) 569-0064

Santa Barbara Cigar
& Tobacco
10 W. Figueroa St.
Santa Barbara
(805) 963-1979

El Rancho Market
2886 Mission Dr.
Solvang
(805) 688-4300

SANTA CRUZ &
VICINITY

Deer Park Wine &
Spirits
783 Rio Del Mar
  Blvd., Aptos
(408) 688-1228

Avenue Cigars
713 Pacific Ave.
Santa Cruz
(408) 427-9747

Bay Briar Shoppe
2910 Daubenbiss
  Ave., Soquel
(408) 462-1965

J. Whites Tobacco
Company
323-B Town Center
  W., Santa Maria
(805) 928-3693

SIERRA
FOOTHILLS

Old Havana Cigar
Company
329 Riverview Dr.
Auburn
(916) 823-7522

Old Town Cigar
Shop
111 Sacramento St.
Auburn
(916) 887-9533

The Humidor
207 Broad St.
Nevada City
(916) 265-8054

Hang Town
Humidor & Cigar
Co.
135 Placerville Dr.
Placerville
(916) 626-3475

Sonora Cigars
68 N. Washington
  St., Sonora
(209) 533-3569

SONOMA
COUNTY

Sotoyome Tobacco
Company
119 Plaza St.
Healdsburg
(707) 433-3338

Beverages, & More!
2090 Santa Rosa
  Ave., Santa Rosa
(707) 573-1544

The Squire
346 Coddington
  Mall, Santa Rosa
(707) 573-8544

Tinder Box
2048 Santa Rosa
  Plaza, Santa Rosa
(707) 579-4442

STOCKTON &
VICINITY

Fred's Puff N Stuff
228 W. Pine St.
Lodi
(209) 334-1088

Tobacco Leaf
209 Lincoln Center
Stockton
(209) 474-8216

JC Fine Cigars
923 Central Ave.
Tracy
(209) 833-0426

Time For A Gift
3200 S. Naglee Rd.
Tracy
(209) 832-4030

STUDIO CITY &
VICINITY

**Cigar House &
Cigarette**
9905 Topanga
  Canyon Blvd.
Chatsworth
(818) 993-5856

TEMECULA

Albertson's
29530 Rancho
  California Rd.
Temecula
(909) 699-7100

The Cigar Source
27520 Ynez Rd.
Temecula
(909) 676-6708

**Old Towne Smoke
Shoppe**
43139 Business Park
  Dr., Temecula
(909) 699-1918

VENTURA &
VICINITY

Cigar Lovers Too
2173 Ventura Blvd.
Camarillo
(805) 388-8344

Cigar Lovers
2540 Vineyard Ave.
Oxnard
(805) 485-6974

The Cigar Company
3431 Telegraph Rd.
Ventura
(805) 642-7108

John T's
363 S. Mills Rd.
Ventura
(805) 627-9252

**Mandells Liquor &
Wine**
3915 Telegraph Rd.
Ventura
(805) 642-1148

Salzers
5777 Valentine Rd.
Ventura
(805) 639-2160

WALNUT CREEK
& VICINITY

**Danville Cigar and
Fine Gifts**
411 Hartz Ave.
Danville
(510) 831-8899

**Jackson Wine &
Spirits**
3524 Mount Diablo
  Blvd.
Lafayette
(510) 376-6000

Tobacco Loft
1920 Contra Costa
  Blvd.
Pleasant Hill
(510) 686-3440

**Jack Kavanagh
Liquor/Beverage**
21001 San Ramon
  Valley Blvd.
San Ramon
(510) 828-6891

Beverages, & More!
2900 N. Main St.
Walnut Creek
(510) 472-0130

O'Sullivan's Cigars
1628 Locust St.
Walnut Creek
(510) 274-1533

John T's
2183 Mooney Blvd.
Visalia
(209) 627-9252

**Sequoia Cigar
Company**
111 N. Locust Ave.
Visalia
(209) 738-8115

Colorado

**Aspen's Pen
Perfecto**
645 E. Durant St.
Aspen
(800) 250-5089

BOULDER &
VICINITY

The Cigarette Store
1750 15th St.
Boulder
(303) 449-7089

**Harvest Wine &
Spirits**
3075 Arapahoe Ave.
Boulder
(303) 447-9832

**Petty John's Liquor
& Wine**
613 S. Broadway
Boulder
(303) 499-2337

The Cigarette Store
179 W. South
  Boulder Rd.
Lafayette
(303) 665-7870

Smoker Friendly
1705 Freemont Dr.
Canon City
(719) 269-3945

COLORADO SPRINGS & VICINITY

Cheer's Liquor Mart
1105 N. Circle Dr.
Colorado Springs
(719) 574-2244

Cugino's Cigars
12 Lake Circle
Colorado Springs
(719) 338-1341

Hathaway's Mag & Smoke
216 N. Tejon
Colorado Springs
(719) 632-1441

Old West Cigar Company
303 E. Pike Peak Ave.
Colorado Springs
(719) 635-2443

Sherlock's Pipes & Tobacco
3650 Austin Bluffs Pkwy.
Colorado Springs
(719) 598-4444

Smoker Friendly
815 S. Sierra Madre St.
Colorado Springs
(719) 471-0854

Smoker Friendly
4337 N. Academy Blvd.
Colorado Springs
(719) 532-1747

Smoker Friendly
1730 W. Colorado Ave.
Colorado Springs
(719) 444-8805

Smoker Friendly
1150 E. Fillmore
Colorado Springs
(719) 471-1074

Smoker Friendly
2353 E. Platte Place
Colorado Springs
(719) 471-7448

Smoker Friendly
3111 S. Academy
Colorado Springs
(719) 390-5343

Smoker Friendly
5845 Galley Rd.
Colorado Springs
(719) 591-6883

Smoker Friendly
1326 S. Tejon
Colorado Springs
(719) 578-1750

Smokers Friendly
815 S. Sierra Madre St.
Colorado Springs
(719) 471-0854

Southwest Wine & Spirits
1785 S. 8th St.
Colorado Springs
(719) 389-0906

Stag Tobacconist
750 Citadel Dr. E.
Colorado Springs
(719) 596-5363

Smoker Friendly
Security Shopping Center, 362 Main St., Security
(719) 390-5996

DENVER & VICINITY

Cigar Heaven
2295 S. Chambers Rd., Aurora
(303) 743-0204

Argonaut Wine & Liquor
700 E. Colfax
Denver
(303) 831-7788

Cigar & Tobacco World
5227 Leetsdale Dr.
Denver
(303) 321-7308

Cigarette Store
2120 S. Broadway
Denver
(303) 715-1506

Havana's Fine Cigars
2727 E. 2nd Ave.
Denver
(303) 355-2003

Jerri's Tobacco Shops
1616 Glenarm
Denver
(888) 825-3522

Prince Philips
3333 S. Tamarac Dr.
Denver
(303) 695-1959

Smokers Inn
1685 S. Colorado Blvd., Denver
(303) 758-5030

The Stogie Club
4515 E. Colfax
Denver
(303) 388-7864

T Devon Premium Cigars
4992 E. Hampden Ave., Denver
(303) 756-5507

Tewksbury & Company
Writer Square, 1512 Larimer St.
Denver
(303) 825-1880

The Tobacco Leaf
7111 W. Alameda
Denver
(303) 274-8721

Edward Pipe & Tobacco Shop
3439 S. Broadway
Englewood
(303) 781-7662

Evergreen Discount Liquor
3847 Evergreen Pkwy.
Evergreen
(303) 674-6668

Tinder Box
6782 Snowshoe Trail
Evergreen
(303) 674-7930

Arrow Liquor Mart
4301 E. Virginia
Ave., Glendale
(303) 399-2123

**Highlands Ranch
Wine & Spirits**
9455 S. University
Blvd., Highlands
(303) 470-7000

**Baccus Wine &
Spirits**
9265 S. Broadway
Highlands Ranch
(303) 683-5000

Cigarette Express
6630 W. Colfax
Lakewood
(303) 235-2755

**Private Reserve
Cigar Company**
8527 W. Colfax Ave.
Lakewood
(303) 232-6065

Alexander Liquors
11757 W. Kencaryl
Littleton
(303) 979-7837

**Lucas Liquor Super
Store**
8457 S. Yosemite
Littleton
(303) 792-2576

The Nickle Cigar
6679 W. Ken Caryl
Ave., Littleton
(303) 904-8760

**Tony's Wine &
Specialty Beer**
4991 E. Dry Creek
Rd., Littleton
(303) 770-4297

Total Liquors Inc.
6901 S. Broadway
Littleton
(303) 730-3102

Tobacco Haven
10572-B Melody Dr.
Northglenn
(303) 450-0953

Burning Desires
5674 W. 88th Ave.
Westminster
(303) 430-7446

DURANGO &
VICINITY

**Durango Smoke
Shop**
113 W. College Dr.
Durango
(970) 247-9115

Mountain Mama
100 W. Grand Ave.
Mancos
(970) 533-7258

FORT COLLINS

**Edwards Tobacco &
Darts**
3307 S. College
Fort Collins
(970) 226-5311

Fish's Liquor Mart
1007 E. Harmony
Rd., Fort Collins
(970) 223-3348

**Vincent's Old Town
Cigar Club**
238 Linden St.
Fort Collins
(970) 416-5350

Cigarette Store
2692 Hwy. 50 B
Grand Junction
(970) 241-7378

Rem's Place
241 Grand Ave.
Grand Junction
(970) 242-3136

**West Lake Wine &
Spirits**
2024 35th Ave.
Greeley
(303) 330-8466

Smoker Friendly
401 Colorado Ave.
La Junta
(719) 384-8533

PUEBLO

Smoker Friendly
951 US Hwy. 50 W.
Pueblo
(719) 545-3646

Smoker Friendly
401 Greenwood
Pueblo
(719) 543-6846

Smoker Friendly
2211 W. Northern
Pueblo
(719) 566-1760

Smoker Friendly
1326 US Hwy. 50
Bypass
Pueblo
(719) 583-0271

Telluride Liquor
123 E. Colorado
Ave., Telluride
(970) 728-3380

Smoker Friendly
401 N. Commercial
St., Trinidad
(719) 846-7512

VAIL &
VICINITY

Avon Liquor
100 W. Beaver
Creek Blvd.
Avon
(970) 949-4384

**The Baggage
Cheque**
244 Wall St.
Vail
(970) 476-1747

Smoker Friendly
110 W. Midland
Woodland Park
(719) 687-9890

Connecticut

BRIDGEPORT &
VICINITY

Arcade Cigars
1636 Post Rd.
Fairfield
(203) 259-1994

**Golden Leaf Cigar
Shop**
2248 Black Rock
Tpke., Fairfield
(203) 735-3174

Brewers
487 Rte. 111
Monroe
(203) 459-2909

Executive Cigars
446 Main St.
Monroe
(203) 452-9154

Cigar Box
871 Barnum Ave.
Stratford
(203) 378-5989

**For Your
Entertainment**
Trumbull Shopping
  Park, 5065 Main
  St., Trumbull
(203) 373-1014

DANBURY &
VICINITY

CP Royal Tobacco
235 Federal Rd.
Brookfield
(203) 775-6325

Cigar Box
279 Main St.
Danbury
(203) 748-5718

Street Corner News
7 Backus Ave.
Danbury
(203) 622-9831

Archway News
64 Bank St.
New Milford
(203) 355-1557

**Red Rooster
Tobacconist**
6 Queen St.
Newtown
(203) 270-8018

**Carolina Tobacco
Emporium**
606 Enfield St.
Enfield
(860) 253-0441

**The Connecticut
Valley Tobacconist**
337 Hazard Ave.
Enfield
(860) 763-4655

**Greenwich Cigar
Store**
91 Railroad Ave.
Greenwich
(203) 622-9831

U.S. Tobacco
1 Sound Shore Dr.
Greenwich
(203) 622-3626

HARTFORD &
VICINITY

**Connecticut Yankee
Cigar Co.**
78 Maple St.
Bristol
(860) 589-1793

The Aperitif
50 Albany Tpke.
Canton
(203) 693-9373

Up In Smoke
136 Berlin Rd.
Cromwell
(860) 632-1962

Cigar Cellar
771-A Farmington
  Ave., Farmington
(860) 677-1901

**De La Concha of
Hartford**
1 Civic Center Plaza
Hartford
(860) 527-4291

Short Stop Citco
84 Airport Rd.
Hartford
(860) 296-2639

The Tobacco Shop
55 Asylum St.
Hartford
(860) 524-8577

**Select Cigars &
Coffees**
446 Birge Park Rd.
Harwinton
(860) 485-1490

J & J Tobacco
3273 Berlin Tpke.
Newington
(860) 666-0439

**Century Service
Center**
940 Cromwell Ave.
Rocky Hill
(860) 721-1145

**Rocky Hill Cigar
Company**
 781 Cromwell Ave.
Rocky Hill
(860) 571-0110

**Torpedoes Smoke
Shop**
922 Hopmeadow St.
Simsbury
(860) 658-7502

Have A Cigar!
980 Sullivan Ave.
South Windsor
(860) 644-5800

Have A Cigar!
435 Hartford Tpke.
Vernon
(860) 875-6556

**Best Cigar
Company**
769 Farmington
  Ave.
West Hartford
(860) 570-1228

The Cigar Shop
52 La Salle Rd.
West Hartford
(860) 236-5041

JJ's News
255 Main St.
Windsor Locks
(860) 627-9200

**Litchfield Tobacco
Company**
3 West St.
Litchfield
(860) 567-3775

**Carolina Tobacco
Emporium**
374B Middle Tpke.
Manchester
(860) 643-0090

NEW HAVEN &
VICINITY

The Hunter's Shop
635 W. Main St.
Branford
(203) 488-8550

Winslow Cigar Company
470 W. Main St.
Cheshire
(203) 271-3401

The Good Life
9 Foxon Blvd.
East Haven
(203) 468-6773

Guilford News & Tobacco
1016 Boston Post
Rd., Guilford
(203) 453-1349

The Calabash Shoppe
2450 Whitney Ave.
Hamden
(203) 248-6185

Hamden News & Cigars
2367 Whitney Ave.
Hamden
(203) 284-0770

Makayla's Cigar Store
679 Boston Post Rd.
Madison
(203) 245-0469

Tobacco Road Ltd.
1201 Connecticut
Post Mall
Milford
(203) 877-1957

The Hunter's Shop
76 Terrace St.
New Haven
(203) 467-4618

Owl Shop
268 College St.
New Haven
(203) 624-3250

Par Cigars
114 Washington
Ave.
North Haven
(203) 234-6313

The Classic Cigar
517-B Boston Post
Rd., Orange
(203) 799-7833

Wine & Liquor Outlet
528 Boston Post Rd.
Orange
(203) 795-8302

Baybrook Meat & Tobacco
6 Jones Hill Rd.
West Haven
(203) 933-8989

NEW LONDON
& VICINITY

Olive Oyls
77 Main St.
Essex
(203) 767-4909

El Dorado City
744 Long Hill Rd.
Groton
(860) 449-1222

City Cigar & Tobacconist
112 Main St.
Norwich
(860) 892-4927

Tobacco Plaza
1393 Boston Post
Rd., Old Saybrook
(860) 388-4811

Simply Cigars
Crystal Mall, Rtes.
85 & 195
Waterford
(860) 701-0436

NORWALK &
VICINITY

M & M Smoke Shop
85 Washington St..
South Norwalk
(203) 853-9748

Cigar Port
7 Riverside Ave.
Westport
(203) 454-PUFF

Westport Cigar Company
44 Rail Road Place
Westport
(203) 227-8996

Sam's Smoke Junction
71 Oxford Rd.
Oxford
(203) 888-4995

STAMFORD

Bull's Head News & Variety
51 High Ridge Rd.
Stamford
(203) 359-0740

Connecticut Shade Cigar Lounge & Boutique
211 Summer St.
Stamford
(203) 353-1245

Smokin Sounds
1026 High Ridge Rd.
Stamford
(203) 329-2808

WATERBURY &
VICINITY

Stogie's
80 Church St.
Naugatuck
(203) 729-3031

The Smoke Shop
Heritage Inn
Arcade, Heritage
Village
Southbury
(203) 264-5075

The Brass Mills Tobacconist
Brass Mills Mall
Waterbury
(203) 574-7788

The Cigar Pro
5 Broad St.
Wethersfield
(860) 721-1888

Delaware

REHOBOTH &
VICINITY

Tobacco Outlet
Town Square
Shopping Center,
Rte. 113
Millsboro
(302) 934-8045

Rehoboth Cigarette Outlet & Newsstand
2 The Marketplace
Rehoboth
(302) 226-3151

Greybeard's Tobacco And Coffee
203 Rehoboth Ave.
Rehoboth Beach
(302) 227-4972

WILMINGTON & VICINITY

Wine & Spirit Company
4025 Kennett Pike
Greenville
(302) 658-5939

Books & Tobacco
214 Lantana Dr.
Hockessin
(302) 239-4224

Three Sons Smoke Shop
Farmers Market, 110
N. Dupont Hwy.
New Castle
(302) 322-2116

CB Perkins
328 Christiana Mall
Newark
(302) 266-7200

Books & Tobacco
4555 Kirkwood Hwy.
Wilmington
(302) 994-3156

Brandywine Cigarette and Tobacco Outlet
3101 Concord Pike
Wilmington
(302) 478-3362

F & N Liquors
2094 Naamas Rd.
Wilmington
(302) 475-4496

Kreston Liquor Mart, Inc.
904 Concord Ave.
Wilmington
(302) 652-3792

Peco's Liquors
522 Philadelphia
Pike
Wilmington
(302) 762-5230

Tobacco Village
4011-B Concord
Pike
Wilmington
(302) 478-5075

District of Columbia

Calvert Woodley Wines
4339 Connecticut
Ave. NW
Washington, DC
(202) 966-4400

Eagle Wine & Liquor
3345 M St. NW
Washington, DC
(202) 333-5500

Georgetown Tobacco
3144 M St. NW
Washington, DC
(202) 338-5100

Georgetown Wine Cellar
1635 Wisconsin
Ave. NW
Washington, DC
(202) 333-3308

Grand Havana Room
1220 19th St. NW
Washington, DC
(202) 293-6848

JR Tobacco
1667 K St. NW
Washington, DC
(202) 833-3766

JW Marriot/Garden Terrace Lounge
1331 Pennsylvania
Ave. NW
Washington, DC
(202) 626-1342

Les Halles
1201 Pennsylvania
Ave. NW
Washington, DC
(202) 347-6848

W. Curtis Draper
640 14th NW
Washington, DC
(202) 638-2555

Wide World of Wines & Cigars
2201 Wisconsin
Ave. NW
Washington, DC
(202) 333-7500

Florida

BOCA RATON & VICINITY

Bennington Tobacconist
Royal Palm Plaza,
501 SE Mizner
Blvd., Boca Raton
(561) 391-1372

Carmody Fine Wine & Liquor
6060 SW 18th St.
Boca Raton
(561) 394-3766

Crown Liquors & Wine Merchants
22191 Powerline Rd.
Boca Raton
(407) 391-6009

Crown Liquors & Wine Merchants
757 S. Federal Hwy.
Boca Raton
(407) 394-3828

MDK News & Tobacco
23014 Sandalfoot
Plaza Dr.
Boca Raton
(561) 883-0086

PS Cigars
19575 8A S. State
Rd. 7, Boca Raton
(561) 482-9070

Sabatino's Gourmet Market
8177 W. Glades Rd.
Boca Raton
(561) 852-9289

Smoker's Gallery
302 Town Center
Boca Raton
(561) 416-1330

Tinder Box International
5250 Town Center Circle
Boca Raton
(561) 338-8606

Crown Liquors & Wine Merchants
306 S. Federal Hwy.
Deerfield Beach
(954) 427-5274

Fort Lauderdale Swap Shop
1515 SE 10th St.
Deerfield Beach
(954) 698-0022

City News II
14530 S. Military Trail, Delray
(561) 496-3166

Beers Unlimited
4428 Cortez Rd. W.
Bradenton
(941) 761-0502

Smoke & Snuff
205 Desoto Sq. Mall
Bradenton
(941) 747-9700

DAYTONA BEACH & VICINITY

Tinder Box
2455 W. International Speedway
Daytona Beach
(904) 253-0708

Tobacco Exotica
749 W. International Speedway
Daytona Beach
(904) 255-3782

Tobacco Exotica
3404 S. Atlantic
Daytona Beach Shores
(904) 761-2400

La Havana Cabana Inc.
324-B Flagler Ave.
New Smyrna Beach
(904) 426-5400

DESTIN

Day Dream Trading Company
300 E. Hwy. 98
Destin
(850) 654-8020

Harbor Cigars
1021 Hwy. 98 E.
Destin
(850) 650-3111

Seaside Cigar
285 Hwy. 98 E.
Destin
(850) 650-1600

FORT LAUDERDALE & VICINITY

The Cigar Place
1478 Coral Ridge Dr., Coral Springs
(954) 255-5280

Sips and Cigars Inc.
9838 W. Sample Rd.
Coral Springs
(954) 340-8860

67 Liquors
5479 N. Federal Hwy.
Fort Lauderdale
(954) 771-9000

67 Liquors
1311 SE 17th St.
Fort Lauderdale
(954) 767-9099

Beverages, & More!
1740 N. Federal Hwy.
Fort Lauderdale
(954) 563-5846

Cigar Outlet
401 E. Commercial Blvd.
Fort Lauderdale
(954) 772-8711

Cigar Wrapper
2345 NE 26th St., Rte. 1, Walgreens Plaza
Fort Lauderdale
(954) 561-4722

City News Stand
4400 Bougainvilla Dr.
Fort Lauderdale
(954) 776-0940

Crown Liquors & Wine Merchants
2850 N. Federal Hwy.
Fort Lauderdale
(954) 566-5322

Crown Liquors & Wine Merchants
3518 N. Ocean Blvd.
Fort Lauderdale
(954) 566-2337

Havana Republic
1360 Weston
Fort Lauderdale
(954) 384-6333

Macabi Smoke & Beanery
1225 E. Las Olas Blvd.
Fort Lauderdale
(954) 764-8566

Riverside Hotel— The Gift Shop
620 E. Las Olas Blvd.
Fort Lauderdale
(954) 467-0671

Smoker's Gallery
2356 E. Sunrise Blvd.
Fort Lauderdale
(954) 561-0002

Smokin Moes Cigar Emporium
1850 SE 17th St.
Fort Lauderdale
(888) 640-MOES

Papa's Cigars
4405 Sheridan St.
Hollywood
(954) 986-1414

Crown Liquors & Wine Merchants
5000 N. University Dr., Lauderhill
(305) 741-7070

67 Liquors
1585 E. Oakland Park Blvd.
Oakland Park
(954) 565-0407

Announcing a grand merger
of two renowned cigar retailers…

…Offering You One of the Nation's Largest Selections of Super Premium Cigars, Humidors, Lighters and Pens

20 Locations to Serve You

Smoker's Gallery

FLORIDA:

The Falls	The Galleria	Sawgrass Mills
Miami, FL	Ft. Lauderdale, FL	Sunrise, FL
(305) 378-2300	(954) 561-0002	(800) 226-2632
Town Center	Boyton Beach Mall	The Gardens
Boca Raton, FL	Boyton Beach,FL	Palm Beach Gardens, FL
(561) 416-1330	(561) 736-5533	(561) 694-9440

Simply Cigars

CONNECTICUT:	Montgomery Mall	Northshore Mall	Woodland
Crystal Mall	Bethesda, MD	Peabody, MA	Grand Rapids, MI
Waterford, CT	301-365-0042	978-532-5052	49508
860-701-0436	**MASSACHUSETTS:**	**MICHIGAN:**	616-975-3019
ILLINOIS:	Cambridgeside Galleria	Briarwood Mall	**OHIO:**
Stratford Square	Cambridge, MA	Ann Arbor, MI	Tuttle Crossing
Bloomingdale, IL	617-374-9442	734-213-6058	Dublin, Oh
630-235-3111	Emerald Square Mall	Lakeside	614-761-8930
Woodfield Mall	N. Attleborough, MA	Sterling Heights, MI	
Schaumburg, IL	810-247-3109	810-247-3109	
847-995-8209	Natick Mall	Twelve Oaks Mall	
MARYLAND:	Natick, MA	Novi, MI	
Anapolis Mall	508-651-9050	248-380-2614	
Anapolis, MD			
410-571-1775			

Smoker's Gallery and Simply Cigars are wholly owned companies of Windsor Capital Corp.
(NASDAQ: Bulletin Board "WDSC")

Aficionado's Premium Cigars
112 S. Flamingo Rd.
Pembroke Pines
(954) 431-9800

Beverages, & More!
11854 Pines Blvd.
Pembroke Pines
(954) 433-4636

Florida Tobacco Book & Novelty
7948 Pines Blvd.
Pembroke Pines
(954) 963-4358

Crown Liquors & Wine Merchants
7620 Peters Rd.
Plantation
(305) 475-9750

Sal's Smoke Shops
8130 W. Broward Blvd.
Plantation Isles
(954) 452-7655

Cigars By Juan
2900 W. Sample Rd.
Pompano Beach
(954) 984-8939

Famous Players
2100 E. Atlantic Blvd.
Pompano Beach
(954) 785-0100

White Ash
3201 E. Atlantic Blvd.
Pompano Beach
(954) 786-0290

Smoker's Gallery
12801 W. Sunrise Blvd., Sunrise
(954) 846-2631

FORT MYERS & VICINITY

Cape Smoke Shop
3512 Del Prado Blvd., Cape Coral
(941) 549-8809

Gourmet Captiva
14820 Captiva Dr.
Captiva Island
(941) 472-4200

Cigarettes And Things
16450 S. Tamiami Trail, Fort Myers
(941) 267-9777

The Downtown Tobacco Shoppe
2235 1st St.
Fort Myers
(941) 337-4662

Sir Richards
Christmans Village, 2320 McGregor Blvd., Fort Myers
(941) 332-7722

Smoke & Snuff
139 Edison Mall
Fort Myers
(941) 939-2626

Beach Tobacco Candy & Nut
19041 San Carlos Blvd.
Fort Myers Beach
(941) 463-5177

Discount Cigarettes Etc.
17105 San Carlos Blvd.
Fort Myers Beach
(941) 482-1947

Disc Cafe
2330 Palm Ridge Rd.
Sanibel
(941) 395-0446

FORT PIERCE & VICINITY

The Brass Pipe
2573 S. US 1
Fort Pierce
(407) 461-7451

Roy's Wine & Liquor
720 US Hwy. 1
Fort Pierce
(407) 461-3097

Coffman's Tobacco Shop
4320 SE Federal Hwy., Stuart
(561) 287-5060

The Rufuge
2196 SE Ocean Rd.
Stuart
(561) 221-1981

Beach Beverages
1025 Easter Lily Lane, Vero Beach
(561) 234-5555

The Gourmet Center
Horizon Outlet Center, 1710 94th Dr., Vero Beach
(561) 567-9760

The Pipe Den
1426 20th St.
Vero Beach
(561) 569-1154

Modern Age Tobacco & Gift
214 NW 13th St.
Gainesville
(352) 371-4733

Smoke & Snuff
C-4 The Oaks Mall, 6451 W. Newberry Rd., Gainesville
(352) 331-3696

JACKSONVILLE & VICINITY

The Ritz-Carlton - Gift Shop
4750 Amelia Island Pkwy.
Amelia Island
(904) 277-1100

The Wharf
973 Atlantic Blvd.
Atlantic Beach
(904) 246-8616

Island Tobacco & Trade
214 Centre St.
Fernandina Beach
(904) 261-7222

Broudy's Liquors
353 Marshlanding Pkwy.
Jacksonville
(904) 273-6119

Chefs Market II
4520-2 San Juan Ave., Jacksonville
(904) 387-1700

Cigar Box
9501 Arlington
   Expy.
Jacksonville
(904) 721-0458

Edward's Pipe &
Tobacco
5566-23 Ft. Caroline
   Rd., Jacksonville
(904) 745-6368

Edward's of San
Marco
2016 San Marco
   Blvd.
Jacksonville
(904) 396-7990

Le Baron Gifts &
Cigars Inc.
1567 University
   Blvd. W.
Jacksonville
(904) 448-1899

Nicotine
1021-B Park St.
Jacksonville
(904) 354-0009

Smoke & Snuff
2540 The Avenues
   Mall
Jacksonville
(904) 363-2161

Tobacco Cove
3849 Bay Meadows
   Rd., Jacksonville
(904) 731-2890

The Tobacco Shop
17 N. Ocean St.
Jacksonville
(904) 355-9319

Tobacco Village
4940 Blanding Blvd.
Jacksonville
(904) 771-3200

The Wine Club/
Edgewood Village
1188 S. Edgewood
   Ave.
Jacksonville
(904) 389-9997

Eight 'til Late
241 3rd St.
Neptune Beach
(904) 241-1127

Eight 'til Late
832-16 A1A N.
Ponte Vedra
(904) 285-5356

KEY WEST &
VICINITY

Key West Havana
Cigar
1117 Duval St.
Key West
(800) 217-4884

Kings Treasure
Tobacco of Key
West
106 Duval St.
Key West
(305) 294-4477

La Tobacoria
326 Duval St.
Key West
(305) 294-3200

Scents & Cigars
3122 N. Federal
   Hwy.
Lighthouse Point
(954) 784-1177

Edward's Pipe &
Tobacco Shop
2118 S. Florida Ave.
Lakeland
(941) 687-4168

Ybor Cigar &
Spirits
5263 S. Florida Ave.
Lakeland
(941) 619-6799

MELBOURNE &
VICINITY

Grumpy's Cigar
Pub
9 Stone St.
Cocoa Village
(407) 631-5430

Vlass's Curiosity
Shop
974 Pine Tree Dr.
Indian Harbor Beach
(407) 777-9460

Tobacerie
1700 W. New Haven
   Ave.
Melbourne
(407) 768-0170

MIAMI &
VICINITY

Havana Cigar
Emporium &
Lounge
18833 Biscayne
   Blvd., Aventura
(305) 466-0220

Mike's Cigars
1030 Kane
   Concourse
Bay Harbor
(305) 866-2277

Ed's Smokers
Emporium
4181 NW 66th
   Place
Coconut Creek
(954) 421-5672

Havana Ray's
3399 Virginia St.
Coconut Grove
(305) 446-4003

Bill's Pipe &
Tobacco Shop
2309 Ponce De Leon
   Blvd.
Coral Gables
(305) 444-1764

Cigar Depot
1536 S. Dixie Hwy.
Coral Gables
(305) 665-0102

Crown Liquors &
Wine Merchants
6731-51 Red Rd.
Coral Gables
(305) 669-0225

Gables Cigar
Company
2222 Ponce De Leon
   Blvd.
Coral Gables
(888) CIGAR 42

A & B Cigars
6551 SW 40th St.
Miami
(305) 665-2727

Canterbury Export
Trading
5409 NW 72nd Ave.
Miami
(305) 863-1881

Casa Habana
2509-A NW 72 St.
Miami
(305) 593-5051

Cigar Box
19501 Biscayne
Blvd., Miami
(305) 936-8808

**The Cigar
Factory—Home of
Don Réne**
2761 NW 79th Ave.
Miami
(305) 463-7448

Cigar World Inc.
7286 SW 40th
Miami
(305) 261-8002

Cigars & Things
4008 SW 57th Ave.
Miami
(305) 666-1350

Doral Cigar Shop
9769 NW 41st St.
Miami
(305) 436-5701

El Credito Cigars
1106 SW 8th St.
Miami
(305) 858-4162

**Fisher Island
Market**
1 Fisher Island Dr.
Miami
(305) 535-6599

**Harriel's Tobacco
Shoppe**
11401 S. Dixie Hwy.
Miami
(305) 252-9010

Safeway
10871 NW 33rd St.
Miami
(305) 513-9939

**King's Treasure
Tobacco**
401 Biscayne Blvd.
Miami
(305) 374-5593

Lola's Cigars
8343 NW 12th St.
Miami
(305) 436-5652

Macabi Cigars
5861 Sunset Dr.
Miami
(305) 662-4417

Macabi Cigars
3473 SW 8th St.
Miami
(305) 446-2606

Macabi Cigars
13989 S. Dixie Hwy.
Miami
(305) 259-7009

**Miami Havana
Cigars**
1071 SW 8th St.
Miami
(305) 285-6990

**Nick's Cigar
Company**
7167 W. Flagler St.
Miami
(305) 266-9907

**Oceanika Tobacco
Shop**
World Traders
Corporation, 1426
NW 82nd Ave.
Miami
(305) 639-9510

Rich's Wine Cellar
6702 Main St.
Miami
(305) 819-7454

Rio Cigars
7902 NW 36th St.
Miami
(305) 994-3599

Smoke Shop
1601 Biscayne Blvd.
Miami
(305) 358-1886

Smoker's Gallery
8888 SW 136th St.
Miami
(305) 378-2300

Stogies Inc.
10101 SW 72nd St.
Miami
(305) 279-4990

Stogies of Kendall
11612 N. Kendall
Dr., Miami
(305) 598-9820

Tabacos Inc.
9450 Sunset Dr.
Miami
(305) 595-1922

Timber Box
7801 NW 37th St.
Miami
(415) 244-9560

Tobacco News
22 E. 3rd Ave.
Miami
(305) 358-6865

Tobacco World
221 N. N. West
Miami
(305) 607-4295

Cigar Connection
534 Lincoln Road
Mall
Miami Beach
(305) 594-2288

Cy's At Sobe
1504 Alton Rd.
Miami Beach
(305) 532-5301

Holy Smoke
1052 Ocean Dr.
Miami Beach
(305) 674-9390

Smokers Notch
425 Washington
Ave.
Miami Beach
(888) 53-SMOKE

**South Beach News
& Tobacco**
710 Washington
Ave.
Miami Beach
(305) 673-3002

**Crown Liquors &
Wine Merchants**
12555 Biscayne
Blvd.
North Miami
(305) 892-9463

Cigar Locator
17813 Biscayne
Blvd.
North Miami Beach
(305) 931-1900

Smokers World
20097 Biscayne
Blvd.
North Miami Beach
(305) 931-1117

Los Passion De La Vie
613 Lincoln Rd.
South Miami Beach
(305) 672-1174

NAPLES & VICINITY

Bonita Smoke Shop
3300 Bonita Beach Rd.
Bonita Springs
(941) 495-9296

Tobacco Road
26831 S. Tamiami Trail
Bonita Springs
(941) 947-8121

Bill Henry's Tobacco Road
200 Goodlette Rd. S., Naples
(941) 262-2098

Cigarettes and Things
975 Imperial Gulf Course, Naples
(941) 594-0777

Heaven
2950 Tamiami Trail N., Naples
(941) 649-6373

Rick's Discount Cigarettes & Cigars
8793 Tamiami Trail E., Naples
(941) 774-2888

Smoke & Snuff
G3-A Coastland Center, 1988 Tamiami Trail
Naples
(941) 649-5599

Smoke Shop
4625 Tamiami Trail N., Naples
(941) 435-1862

Zoom Zone Caliente
8525 Radio Rd.
Naples
(941) 455-3755

OCALA

Smoke & Snuff
Paddock Mall
Ocala
(352) 237-2883

Smoke & Snuff
608 West Oaks Mall, 9401 W. Colonial Dr., Ocala
(407) 521-9511

Thoroughbred Tobacco Company
44 SE 1st Ave.
Ocala
(352) 380-0629

ORLANDO & VICINITY

Spirits
1146 W. State Rd.
Altamonte Springs
(407) 682-3033

The Sosa Family Cigar Company
1502 East Lake Buenal Vista Drive
Downtown Disney, West Side
Lake Buena Vista
(800) 773-7412

Cigar Bazaar
3865 Lake Emma Rd., Lake Mary
(407) 444-0403

The Tobacco Merchant
1877 W. State Rd.
Longwood
(407) 767-0050

The Cigar Bar
108 E. 3rd Ave.
Mount Dora
(352) 735-CGAR

Art's Premium Cigars
1235 N. Orange Ave., Orlando
(407) 895-9772

Church Street Cigar Company
Church Street Market
Orlando
(407) 365-1751

Eastwood Liquor
1963 S. Trail
Orlando
(407) 249-8220

Lee's Liquor
4100 Town Center
Orlando
(407) 850-2435

Metro Cigars
2457 S. Hiawasse
Orlando
(407) 294-8888

Ol' Times
124 W. Pine St.
Orlando
(407) 425-7879

**Pipe & Pouch
Smoke Shop**
53 N. Orange Ave.
Orlando
(407) 841-7980

Smoke & Snuff
The Florida Mall
Orlando
(407) 826-5053

Eastside Cigars
Oakwood Village,
 1759 W. Broadway
Oviedo
(407) 365-6665

**Lee's Liquor Three
Inc.**
761 N. Orange Ave.
Winter Park
(407) 645-3395

PALM BEACH &
VICINITY

**Crown Liquors &
Wine Merchants**
564 SE 15th Ave.
Boynton Beach
(407) 734-9463

Dan's News
640 E. Ocean Ave.
Boynton Beach
(407) 737-0345

Smoker's Gallery
801 N. Congress
 Ave.
Boynton Beach
(407) 736-5533

**The Ritz-Carlton -
Gift Shop**
100 S. Ocean Blvd.
Manalapan
(407) 533-6000

**LJ Fine Cigars &
Tobacco**
11585 N. US Hwy. 1
North Palm Beach
(800) 486-1919

**The Breakers News
& Gourmet**
1 S. County Rd.
Palm Beach
(561) 655-6611

**Palm Beach
Tobacco**
1649 Forum Place
Palm Beach
(561) 616-2611

**Carmines Gourmet
Market**
2401 PGA Blvd.
Palm Beach Gardens
(407) 775-0105

Smoker's Gallery
3101 PGA Blvd.
Palm Beach Gardens
(407) 694-9440

Smoke Inn
Village Square
 Shopping Center,
 241 US Hwy. 1
Tequesta
(561) 745-0600

**Super Duper Liquor
Store**
614 Belvedere Rd.
West Palm Beach
(561) 802-4443

PANAMA CITY
& VICINITY

**Jim's Pipe &
Tobacco Shop**
2400 Lisenby Ave.
Panama City
(904) 785-1022

**Classic Cigar &
Wine Company**
72 Central Square
Seaside
(770) 886-1670

PENSACOLA &
VICINITY

Cigar Emporium
300 Mary Esther
 Blvd.
Mary Esther
(850) 243 9040

**Grand Reserve
Cigar & Smoke
Shop**
210 S. Palafox Place
Pensacola
(850) 429-0078

Tinder Box
Cordova Mall, 5100
 N 9th Ave.
Pensacola
(850) 477-4131

Smoke & Snuff
865 Port Charlotte
 Train Center, 1441
 Tamiami Trail
Port Charlotte
(941) 627-5640

SARASOTA &
VICINITY

**Bennington
Tobacco**
5 Filmore Dr.
Sarasota
(941) 388-1562

Holy Smoke
3100 N. Washington
 Blvd.
Sarasota
(941) 351-4606

Le Cigar
1345 Main St.
Sarasota
(941) 36-CIGAR

Smoke & Snuff
Sarasota Sq. Mall,
 820 Tamiami Trail
Sarasota
(941) 921-6147

The Smoke Shop
106 Paradise Plaza
Sarasota
(941) 955-6433

Smokin' Joe's
1467 Main St.
Sarasota
(941) 365-3556

The Cigar Room
121 Tamiami Trail
 N., Venice
(941) 485-0837

**Chesser's Gap
Spirits**
726 Fleming St.
Sebastian
(561) 589-1889

Orlando's *Smokin'* Club & Café

Join Us for a Cigar, a Sandwich or a Membership

Art's features Central Florida's Largest Selection of
Premium Cigars and Smoking Accessories including;
Dunhill • Elie Bleu humidors
Colibri S.T. Dupont pens and lighters • Montblanc
Scheaffer • Montegrappa writing instruments
Tumi luggage • Polo leather goods

Humidor and Café is open to the public

1235 N. Orange Ave., Orlando FL 32804 • 1-888-770-ARTS • Fax (407) 895-7177

Private Club Room • Full Service Bar • Casual Café • Memberships Available

St. Jorge Tobacco Shoppe
62 Spanish St.
St. Augustine
(904) 825-2681

Eleni's Coffee & Tea Company
1400 Village Square Blvd.
Tallahassee
(904) 668-3385

Smoke & Snuff
2055 Governors Sq. Mall
Tallahassee
(850) 877-8489

TAMPA/ ST. PETERSBURG & VICINITY

Smoke & Snuff
666 Brandon Town Center
Brandon
(813) 654-2566

Curbside Cafe & Cigar
4499 126th Ave. N.
Clearwater
(813) 896-1180

Famous Cigars
25032 US Hwy. 19 N., Clearwater
(813) 796-2442

Havana Cigar Company
28471 US Hwy. 19 N., Clearwater
(813) 725-8815

Mr. D's Pipe & Tobacco
Countryside Mall, 27001 US Hwy. 19 N., Clearwater
(813) 796-1220

Smoke & Snuff
104 Clearwater Mall
Clearwater
(813) 796-1668

Smokers Paradise
1251 S. Missouri Ave., Clearwater
(813) 446-2231

Smokers Paradise
1251 S. Missouri Ave., Clearwater
(813) 446-2231

Tobacco Depot
23038 State Rd. 54
Lutz
(813) 948-3844

Only The Best
5546 Main St.
New Port Richey
(813) 844-5100

The Tobacco Hut
Elfers Square, 4036
S. Madison St.
New Port Richey
(813) 842-2139

Harr's Surf-n-turf
3235 Tampa Rd.
Palm Harbor
(813) 787-6758

Smoke & Snuff
611 Gulfview Sq.
Mall, 9409 US 19
Port Richey
(813) 849-4746

**Wholly Smokes/
Unique Gifts**
11840 US Hwy. 19
N., Port Richey
(813) 863-0374

Beers Unlimited
1490 S. Pasadena
Ave.
South Pasadena
(813) 345-9905

Central Cigars
273 Central Ave.
St. Petersburg
(813) 898-2442

**House of Pipes &
Cigars**
2525 9th St. N.
St. Petersburg
(813) 823-3762

Smoke & Snuff
886 Tyrone Sq. Mall
St. Petersburg
(813) 381-9527

**Berns Fine Wines/
Spirits**
1992 S. Howard
Ave., Tampa
(813) 250 9463

**Cammarata Cigar
Company**
4830 W. Kennedy
Tampa
(813) 287-2654

**Charlie's Wine
Cellar**
533 S. Howard Ave.
Tampa
(813) 254-1395

Cigar Elegante
1910 W. Platt St.
Tampa
(800) 962-2495

**Edward's Pipe &
Tobacco**
3235 Henderson
Blvd., Tampa
(813) 872-0723

**Edwards Pipe &
Tobacco**
3235 Henderson
Blvd., Tampa
(813) 872-0723

**Gonzalez Havano
Cigar Company**
3304 W. Columbus
Dr., Tampa
(813) 348-0343

**Hometown News &
Cigars**
1441 E. Fletcher
Ave., Tampa
(813) 977-6740

**The Hyde Park
Cafe**
1806 W. Platte St.
Tampa
(813) 254-CAFE

Metropolitan Inc.
2014 E. 7th Ave.
Tampa
(813) 248-3304

Paul's Liquor Inc.
19018 Bruce B.
Downs Blvd.
Tampa
(813) 632-0053

Simons Market
3225 S. Macdill Ave.
Tampa
(813) 839-2521

Smoke & Snuff
2015 Tampa Bay
Center
Tampa
(813) 879-7071

Smoke & Snuff
339 W. Shore Plaza
Tampa
(813) 282-8776

Tampa Rico Cigars
1901 N. 13th St
Tampa
(813) 874-8997

Thompson & Co.
5401 Hanger Court
Tampa
(813) 884-6344

Tinder Box
12358 University
Square Mall
Tampa
(813) 971-0623

**Vincent & Tampa
Cigar Company**
2503 21st St.
Tampa
(813) 248-1511

Georgia

**Joe's Smoke House
& Gift Shop**
2827A Meredyth Dr.
Albany
(912) 888-3646

McLane Southeast
Athena Industrial
Park, Hwy. 29 N.
Athens
(706) 549-4520

**Modern Age
Tobacco & Gift**
1087 Baxter St.
Athens
(706) 549-6360

ATLANTA &
VICINITY

Vintage Bottle Shop
1720 Mars Hill Rd.
Acworth
(770) 428-9686

Cigar Merchant
9850 Nesbit Ferry
Alpharetta
(770) 552-1942

Clubhouse Cigars
6000 Medlock
Bridge Pkwy.
Alpharetta
(800) 646-9330

Smokin' Post
28 Milton Ave.
Alpharetta
(770) 619-0019

Tinder Box
North Point Mall,
1204 N. Point
Circle
Alpharetta
(770) 569-0059

Buckhead Fine Wine
3906 Roswell Rd.
Atlanta
(404) 231-8566

Cigar Box
3393 Peachtree Rd.
NE Cart T109
Atlanta
(404) 266-9901

Edward's Pipe & Tobacco
3137 Piedmont Rd.
Atlanta
(404) 292-1721

Happy Hermans
204 Johnson Ferry
Rd., Atlanta
(404) 256-3354

Harris Teeter
Sage Hill Shopping
Center, 1799
Briarcliff Rd. NE
Atlanta
(404) 607-1189

The Humidor Inc.
4400 Ashford
Dunwoody Rd.,
Perimeter Mall
Atlanta
(770) 448-5424

Jax Beer & Wine
5901 Roswell Rd.
Atlanta
(404) 252-1443

Orvis
Buckhead Square,
3255 Peachtree
Rd. NE
Atlanta
(404) 841-0093

The Ritz-Carlton - Gift Shop
181 Peachtree St.
NE, Atlanta
(404) 659-0400

Sherrin's Tinder Box At Lenox
3393 Peachtree Rd.
Atlanta
(404) 231-9853

The Tobacco Loft
2900 Peachtree Rd.
Atlanta
(404) 467-0000

Tobacos Gran Columbia
4200 Paces Ferry Rd.
Atlanta
(770) 805-0838

Edward's Pipe & Tobacco
444 N. Indian Creek
Dr., Clarkston
(404) 292-1721

Edwards Pipe & Tobacco
444 N. Indian Creek
Dr., Clarkston
(404) 292-1721

Scottish Tobacco
425 Sigmund Rd.
Conyers
(770) 922-5066

Mistic Dreams
6229 Sairburn
Douglasville
(770) 489-9490

Tinder Box
Gwimett Place, 2100
Pleasant Hill Rd.
Duluth
(770) 813-1248

The Cigar Merchant
2472 Jett Ferry Rd.
Dunwoody
(770) 671-1777

Starship Enterprises
1188 Central Ave.
East Point
(404) 766-6993

Atlanta Tobacco
1980 Hwy. 54 W.
Fayettville
(770) 486-1354

Southeast Tobacco Outlet
1513 W. McIntosh
Rd., Griffin
(770) 229-1666

Modern Age Tobacco & Gift
7000 Tara Blvd.
Jonesboro
(770) 472-1587

Bullocks Wine & Spirits
3612 Sandy Plains
Rd., Marietta
(770) 565-0017

Cigar Emporium
4719 Lower Roswell
Rd., Marietta
(770) 579-8280

Cubana Cigar Company
3000 Canton Hills
Dr., Marietta
(770) 973-3090

Minks Beer & Wine
2555 Delk Rd.
Marietta
(770) 952-2337

Sherlocks
2156 Roswell Rd.
Marietta
(770) 971-6333

Sherlocks
135 Barrett Pkwy.
Marietta
(770) 426-6744

This That & The Other
2040 Cobb Pkwy. S.
Marietta
(770) 984-8801

The Ultimate Cigar
1381 Morrow
Industrial Blvd.
Morrow
(770) 968-9622

**Georgia Cigar,
Tobacco & Coffee
Company**
773 Hwy. 138
Riverdale
(770) 996-8182

North End Cigars
900 Mansell Rd.
Roswell
(770) 642-2108

Tobacco City
2500 Old Alabama
Rd., Roswell
(770) 650-0520

Cigar Emporium
1525 E. Park Place
Stone Mountain
(770) 879-7090

Platinum Package
3121 Peachtree
Pkwy.
Suwanee
(770) 886-2254

**Up In Smoke Fine
Cigars**
3983 Lavista Rd.
Tucker
(770) 414-0033

Tinder Box
Coastal Retail
Systems, 8632
Main St.
Woodstock
(770) 517-0105

Tobacco Outlet
6845 Hwy. 92
Woodstock
(770) 592-8744

AUGUSTA &
VICINITY

**Marcella's Fine
Cigars & Tobacco**
2921 Washington
Rd., Augusta
(706) 737-0477

Tobacco & Gifts
Anderson Plaza, 592
Bobby Jones Expy.
Augusta
(706) 860-8386

Tobacco Land
Augusta Mall, 3450
Wrightsboro Rd.
Augusta
(706) 738-8381

**Discount Cigarette
Outlet**
4573-B Cox Rd.
Evans
(706) 860-9361

**Harvard Wine &
Beverage**
110 Old Evans Rd.
Martinez
(706) 855-0060

**Sweet Briar Smoke
Shop**
5592 H Whitesville
Rd., Columbus
(706) 322-6467

**Classic Cigar &
Wine Company**
1605 Woodridge
Court
Cumming
(904) 650-3355

Jax Beer & Wine
928 Market Place
Blvd., Cumming
(770) 888-8036

Smitty's Tobacco
975 Dawsonville
Hwy., Gainesville
(770) 539-9006

Tinder Box
400 Barrett Pkwy.,
Town/Ctr. Cobbs
Kennesaw
(770) 428-9075

MACON &
VICINITY

Old South Tobacco
3706 Mercer
University Dr.
Macon
(912) 477-5426

Cork Shoppe
1887 N. Columbia
St., Milledgeville
(912) 452-2335

**Southern Smokers
Outlet**
6073 Peachtree
Pkwy., Norcross
(770) 242-6605

SAVANNAH

**Habersham
Beverage**
4618 Habersham St.
Savannah
(912) 354-6477

Savannah Cigars
308 W. Congress St.
Savannah
(912) 233-2643

Tinder Box
244 Bull St.
Savannah
(912) 232-6184

**Ye Olde Tobacco
Shop**
131 W. River St.
Savannah
(912) 236-9384

**Ye Olde Tobacco
Shop**
280 Eisenhower Dr.
Savannah
(800) 596-1425

**Victor Sinclair
Cigars**
201 Redfern Village
St. Simons Island
(912) 634-1192

Hawaii

HAWAII &
VICINITY

Kipuka Smoke Shop
308 Kam Ave.
Hilo
(808) 961-5082

MAUI &
VICINITY

**Connoisseur Food
& Wine**
444 Hana Hwy.
Kahului
(808) 871-9463

Stantons of Maui
Maui Mall
Kahului
(808) 877-3711

Hava Cigar
1993 S. Kihei Rd.
Kihei
(808) 879-8823

Sir Wilfred's of Lahaina
Hahaina Cannery
    Mall, 1221
    Honoapiilani Hwy.
Lahaina
(808) 667-1941

OAHU &
VICINITY

Cigar Emporium Inc.
98-199 Ram Hwy.,
    Union A-9
Aiea
(808) 484-5757

Alfred Dunhill Limited
Waikiki Trade
    Center, 2365
    Kalakaua Ave.
Honolulu
(808) 971-2026

Davidoff of Geneva
1200 Ala Moana
    Blvd., Wade
    Center
Honolulu
(808) 593-2224

Don Pablo Smoke Shop
1 Aloha Tower Dr.
Honolulu
(808) 537-6900

Don Pablo Smoke Shop
1430 Kona St.
Honolulu
(808) 944-1600

Havana Cabana
1131 Nuuanu Ave.
Honolulu
(808) 524 4277

Premium Cigar Company
1137 12th Ave.
Honolulu
(808) 737-6662

R. Field Wine Co.
1200 Ala Moana
    Blvd.
Honolulu
(808) 596-9463

Tobacco's of Hawaii
512-101 Atkinson
    Dr., Honolulu
(808) 942-7833

Vintage Cigar Parlor
602 Kailua Rd.
Kailua
(808) 261-7833

Don Pablo Smoke Shop
Waiau Center, 98-
    450 Kam Hwy.
Pearl City
(808) 484-1488

Idaho

BOISE

Havana House Ltd.
220 W. Jefferson St.
Boise
(208) 343-2907

Sturman's Smoke Shop
218 N. 10 St.
Boise
(208) 338-3225

Tobacco Connection
725 Vista Ave.
Boise
(208) 342-6330

COEUR D'
ALENE &
VICINITY

Hunters
2108 N. 4th
Coeur d' Alene
(208) 765-8095

Cast & Blast
9521 N.
    Government Hwy.
Hayden
(208) 772-3748

Signature Cigars
11010 Avondale
    Loop Rd.
Hayden Lake
(208) 772-4666

H & J Tobacco
301 Main St.
Lewiston
(208) 798-0871

Pend-Oreille Wine Sellers
206 N. 1st
Sandpoint
(208) 265-8116

Illinois

BLOOMINGTON

Cigarette Express
Market Square, 1510
    W. Market St.
Bloomington
(309) 828-7025

Famous Liquors
1404 E. Empire
Bloomington
(309) 663-8303

Smoker's Choice Inc.
1212 Towanda Ave.
Bloomington
(309) 828-1581

Cigar Czar
719 N. Convent
Bourbonnais
(888) I-SMOKE 1

Yester Year Tobacconist
200 W. Monroe
Carbondale
(618) 457-8495

Bacca Cigar Company
Round Barn Center,
    1912-B Round
    Barn Rd.
Champaign
(217) 356-3239

Jon's Pipe Shop
509 E. Green St.
Champaign
(217) 344-3459

Calliope Court
706 Jackson Ave.
Charleston
(217) 348-1905

CHICAGO &
VICINITY

Payless Tobacco
709B W. Lake St.
Addison
(708) 628-8177

Arlington Pipe &
Cigar Shop
3 W. Davis St.
Arlington Heights
(847) 255-2263

John's Smoke Shop
18 S. River
Aurora
(708) 897-3920

Tinder Box
1462 Fox Valley
Center
Aurora
(630) 898-9450

Payless Tobacco
227 N. NW Hwy.
Barrington
(847) 842-1080

Up In Smoke Cigar
Shop
557 Hough St.
Barrington
(847) 842-0875

P J Discount
202 W. Irving Park
Rd., Bensonville
(630) 350-2000

Premium Tobacco
Corp
3118 S Oak Park
Ave., Berwyn
(708) 749-1475

Tinder Box
6500 W. Cermak Rd.
Berwyn
(708) 484-4840

C & R Tobacco
132 Ridge Ave.
Bloomingdale
(630) 582-8638

Simply Cigars
Stratford Mall, NE
(Corner. Army
Trail & Gary Dr.)
Bloomingdale
(630) 235-3111

Tobacco Country
7235 W. 87th St.
Bridgeview
(708) 430-1918

Neopolitan Cigar
Company
9014 W. 31st St.
Brookfield
(708) 387-0472

Binny's Beverage
Depot
124 McHenry Rd.
Buffalo Grove
(847) 459-2200

Cigar Exchange
470 Half Day Rd.
Buffalo Grove
(847) 808-4444

Payless Tobacco
1169 Old McHenry
Rd., Buffalo Grove
(847) 821-8552

Payless Tobacco
1485 Fair Oak Rd.
Carol Stream
(630) 830-2005

Egor's Tobacco &
Gift Shop
2 Wisconsin Ave.
Carpentersville
(847) 428-7707

Alfred Dunhill
Limited
Water Tower Place,
835 N. Michigan
Ave., Chicago
(312) 467-4455

Around the World
1044 W. Belmont
Chicago
(773) 327-7975

Blue Havana
2709 N. Clark St.
Chicago
(773) 542-8262

Blue Havana
854 W. Belmont
Ave., Chicago
(773) 348-5000

Casey's Liquors
1444 W. Chicago
Ave., Chicago
(312) 243-2850

Chalet
405 W. Armitage
Chicago
(312) 266-7155

Chalet
1531 E. 53rd St.
Chicago
(773) 324-5000

Something special delivered right to your door

from sam's

the world's best selection of:

fine wine

spirits

champagne

beer

cigars

cigar accessories

gift baskets

glassware

and, of course, more!

Call for a complimentary catalog, or let our knowledgable staff help you place your order over the phone. Now you can also order on the internet at **www.sams–wine.com**

Sam's Wines & Spirits
is located in Chicago
tel 312.664.4394
toll free 800.777.9137
www.sams–wine.com

SAM'S DELIVERS WORLDWIDE!

Chalet
3000 N. Clark
Chicago
(773) 935-9400

Chalet
40 E. Delaware
Chicago
(312) 787-8555

The Cigar Spot at Bigsby & Kruthers
605 N. Michigan
Ave., Chicago
(312) 397-0430

Double Corona
2058 W. Chicago
Ave., Chicago
(312) 342-7820

Eastgate Wine & Spirits
446 W. Diversy
Pkwy., Chicago
(312) 327-1210

English Pipe Shop
15 S. La Salle St.
Chicago
(312) 263-3922

Four Friends Cigar Shop
3516 S. Halsted Ave.
Chicago
(773) 927-5963

Four Seasons/Gift Shop
120 E. Delaware
Place
Chicago
(312) 280-8800

Gold Coast Tobacco
1 E. Erie
Chicago
(312) 255-8750

Gold Standard
3000 N. Clark
Chicago
(312) 935-9400

Good Fellas Cigar Shop
5539 W. Montrose
Ave., Chicago
(312) 286-9747

Iwan Ries & Company
19 S. Wabash Ave.
Chicago
(312) 372-1306

Jack Schwartz Importer
175 W. Jackson
Chicago
(312) 782-7898

Little Havana Cigar Co.
50 W. Adams St.
Chicago
(312) 857-1170

Old Chicago Smoke Shop
10 S. La Salle St.
Chicago
(312) 236-9771

Orvis
142 E. Ontario St.
Chicago
(312) 440-0662

Ralph's Cigars & Tobacco on Taylor St.
1032 W. Taylor St.
Chicago
(312) 829-0672

Rubovits Cigars
320 S. La Salle St.
Chicago
(312) 939-3780

Sam's Wine & Spirits
1720 N. Marcey St.
Chicago
(312) 664-4394

Up Down Tobacco
1550 N. Wells St.
Chicago
(312) 337-8505

Utopia Cigars
6355 W. Montrose
Chicago
(773) 725-1810

Valuemost Liquors
3263 N. Pulaski Rd.
Chicago
(312) 725-4151

Worldwide Tabacco
1587 N. Milwaukee
Chicago
(773) 862-2226

Southtown RX
1533 Chicago Rd.
Chicago Heights
(708) 755-3500

Chiko Club Liquors
5202 W. 25th St.
Cicero
(708) 656-5111

Popela's Cigars
5620 W. Cermak Rd.
Cicero
(708) 652-8009

Prestige Wine & Liquors
1423 W. 55th St.
Countryside
(708) 354-6969

Cardinal Wine & Spirits
305 Virginia St.
Crystal Lake
(815) 459-4050

Smoker's News
2671 Mannheim Rd.
Des Plaines
(847) 699-6622

Tribeca Cigar Company
5229 Main St.
Downers Grove
(630) 241-1200

Pied Piper Tobacco Shop
557 N. McLean
Blvd., Elgin
(847) 695-8670

Prairie Rock Brewery
127 S. Grove
Elgin
(847) 622-8888

The Smokin' Fox
269 S. State St.
Elgin
(847) 608-9903

Total Beverage
7330 W. North Ave.
Elmwood Park
(708) 456-2112

Evanston Pipe & Tobacco
923 Davis St.
Evanston
(847) 328-0208

Evanston First Liquors
1019 Davis St.
Evanston

Silver Outlaw
9500 S. Western St.
Evergreen Park
(708) 425-7022

Smokey Bear
8701 S. Kedzie Ave.
Evergreen Park
(708) 499-0222

Chalet
71 N. Greenbay Rd.
Glencoe
(847) 835-3900

D'Artagnan's Cellar
Carillon Sq., 1486
Waukegan Rd.
Glenview
(847) 998-0303

Stogies
1226 E. Lake St.
Hanover Park
(630) 837-6828

Hickory Tobacco
4514 S. Robert Rd.
Hickory Hills
(708) 233-6060

Tobacco City
8613 W. 95th St.
Hickory Hills
(708) 599-4943

Binny's Beverage Depot
153 Skokie Valley Hwy.
Highland Park
(847) 831-5400

Markus International Inc.
484 Hillside Dr.
Highland Park
(847) 43-FLAME

Old Chicago Smoke Shop
221 Skokie Valley Rd.
Highland Park
(847) 831-3310

Great Ash
5 N. 105 Rte. 53
Itasca
(630) 773-2520

Wine & Cigar Shop
884 S. Rand Rd.
Lake Zurich
(847) 438-1922

Suburban News and Concession
3300 W. Devon Ave.
Lincolnwood
(847) 679-5577

Famous Liquors
105 E. Roosevelt Rd.
Lombard
(630) 629-3330

Tinder Box
205 Yorktown
  Center
Lombard
(630) 495-2555

Tobacco Plus Inc.
4718 W. Lincoln
  Hwy., Matteson
(708) 748-5227

Gold Standard
4610 W. Elm St.
McHenry
(815) 385-3200

Tobacco and Gift City
3281 W. 115th St.
Merrionette Park
(708) 489-5700

Gold Eagle Liquors
1721 Golf Rd.
Mount Prospect
(847) 437-3500

Binny's Beverage Depot
790 Royal St.
  George
Naperville
(630) 717-0100

Gentleman's Delight
24 W. 500 Maple
  Ave.
Naperville
(630) 961-2496

Premier Tobacco
1292 Rickert Dr.
Naperville
(630) 428-0026

Total Beverage
1163 E. Ogden Ave.
Naperville
(630) 428-1122

Goldfinger Super Sales
7227 N. Harlem
  Ave., Niles
(847) 647-7460

Tobacco Express
5050 N.
  Cumberland Ave.
Norridge
(708) 452-8159

Cigar Heaven Inc.
2750 Dundee Rd.
Northbrook
(847) 564-9600

Hopwerx
9607 SW Hwy.
Oak Lawn
(708) 636-1699

Oak Park Cigar
823 S. Oak Park
  Ave., Oak Park
(708) 848-6909

Smoker's Haven
15806 S. Harlem
  Ave.
Orland Park
(708) 633-8331

Burning Ambitions
19 N. Bothwell
Palatine
(847) 358-0200

Puff 'n' Stuff
20434 N. Rand Rd.
Palatine
(847) 550-0055

Paylos Tobacco
10160 S. Roberts Rd.
Palos Hills
(708) 598-7996

Around the World Cigar & Gifts
31 ½ S. Prospect
  Ave.
Park Ridge
(847) 292-1219

Gold Standard
3121 Thatcher
River Grove
(708) 456-7400

Carlucci Restaurant
6111 N. River Rd.
Rosemont
(847) 518-0990

Binny's Beverage Depot
323 W. Golf Rd.
Schaumburg
(847) 882-6000

Country Sports Cards and Fine Cigars
2261 W.
  Schaumburg Rd.
Schaumburg
(847) 534-9576

Habana Cigar House
1404 E. Golf Rd.
Schaumburg
(847) 517-4444

Simply Cigars
Woodfield Mall
Schaumburg
(847) 995-8209

Binny's Beverage Depot
5100 W. Dempster
  St., Skokie
(847) 674-4200

Cigar King Downtown Skokie
8016 Lincoln
Skokie
(800) CIGAR-51

Gift & Tobacco Emporium
Village Crossing
  Shopping Center,
  7140 N. Carpenter
Skokie
(847) 674-4283

Tinder Box
125-E Old Orchard
  Center, Skokie
(847) 677-6717

34th Street Cigars
83 E. 34th St.
Steger
(708) 756-7494

South Side Cigars
30 E. 34th St.
Steger
(708) 754-6312

Best Tobacco
310 E. State St.
Sycamore
(815) 899-9164

Tobacco City
7943 W. 171st St.
Tinley Park
(708) 532-1850

Tinder Box
211 Hawthorne
 Center
Vernon Hills
(847) 362-6655

Al's Smoke Shop
Inc.
1 E. Park Blvd.
Villa Park
(708) 279-2215

Eight To Eight
Tobacco Shop
330 E. St. Charles
 Rd.
Villa Park
(630) 993-1234

Tinder Box
1116 Spring Hill
 Mall
West Dundee
(847) 428-6444

White Ash Cigar
Company
838 E. Ogden Ave.
Westmont
(630) 205-1750

G & G Pharmacy
925 E. Roosevelt Rd.
Wheaton
(630) 668-6477

Jorgio Cigars
600 S. Country Farm
 Rd., Wheaton
(630) 690-7490

Stogies
6300 Kingery Hwy.
Willowbrook
(630) 455-4100

Willowbrook
Liquors
6920 S. Rte. 83
Willowbrook
(630) 654-0988

Cigary International
139 Skokie Blvd.
Wilmette
(888) 244-2795

Tobacco World Inc.
11302 S. Harlem
 Ave., Worth
(708) 448-0002

Moore's Tobacco
Shop
8 Fountain Place
Danville
(217) 431-3271

Kerry Tobacco
1752 Sycamore Rd.
De Kalb
(815) 758-5200

Famous Liquors
1321 N. Oakland
Decatur
(217) 428-0632

Blanquart Jewelers
2322 Troy Rd.
Edwardsville
(618) 656-6030

Tinder Box
255 St. Clair Square
Fairview Heights
(618) 632-6160

Cigarette Depot/
Freeport
302 N. Galena Ave.
Freeport
(815) 235-3183

Warco
400 W. State
Jacksonville
(217) 245-9528

The Tobacco Shop
301 S. Jefferson
Jerseyville
(618) 498-7473

Tinder Box
Joliet Mall, 1034
 Louis, Joliet
(815) 439-1190

Tobacco For Less
616 N. State St.
Litchfield
(217) 324-4641

MOLINE &
VICINITY

Baker Street
South Park Mall,
 4500 16th St.
Moline
(309) 762-9267

Cut 'n' Puff Pipe/
Tobacco Shop
1417 5th Ave.
Moline
(309) 762-1819

Rudy's Cigars
Edgebrook Center,
 1641 N. Alpine
 Rd., Rockford
(815) 223-2351

Tinder Box
Cherry Vale Mall
Rockford
(815) 332-4656

SPRINGFIELD

Cigars For
Aficionado's
717 N. Grand Ave.
 E., Springfield
(217) 523-4357

Epicures Choice
Smoke Shop
Myers Building 1 W.
 Old State Capital
 Plaza
Springfield
(217) 523-9350

Famous Liquors
724-E S. Grand Ave.
Springfield
(217) 528-4377

WAUKEGAN &
VICINITY

The Humidor
552 Main St.
Antioch
(414) 862-6396

Aromas Cigars Ltd.
6170 W. Grand
Gurnee
(847) 856- 8408

International House
of Wine
11302 W. Rte. 12
Richmond
(815) 678-4573

Tool Shed
417 Railroad Ave.
Round Lake
(847) 546-6222

Tool Shed, Jr.
519 W. Rollins Rd.
Round Lake Beach
(847) 740-8665

Gold Standard
1501 N. Lewis
Waukegan
(847) 244-5200

Schrank's Smoke 'n Gun
2010 Washington
St., Waukegan
(847) 662-4034

Harbor Bacco 'n' Beans
1707 7th St
Winthrop Harbor
(847) 731-7001

Indiana

Angola Tobacco Shop
2998 N. Wayne St.
Angola
(219) 665-9142

BLOOMINGTON & VICINITY

The Briar & The Burley
College Mall, 2968
E. 3rd St.
Bloomington
(812) 332-3300

Karton King
435 S. Walnut St.
Bloomington
(812) 339-8422

Men's Toy Shop Inc.
Old Colonial
Building, 131 N.
Van Buren
Nashville
(812) 988-6590

Discount Tobacco Shack
2516 Central Ave.
Columbus
(812) 378-4711

7th Street Cigar Company
1632 7th St.
Columbus
(812) 375-6798

Flying Dragon Cigar Shop
500 N. Nappanee St.
Elkhart
(219) 293-6239

Briar 'n' Bean
Eastland Mall, 800
N. Greenriver Rd.
Evansville
(812) 479-8736

FORT WAYNE

Riegel's Pipe & Tobacco
624 S. Calhoun St.
Fort Wayne
(219) 424-1429

Riegel's Pipe & Tobacco
Georgetown Sq.,
6556 E. State
Blvd.
Fort Wayne
(219) 493-2806

Tinder Box
10510 Tidewater
Trail
Fort Wayne
(219) 471-3091

GARY & VICINITY

Black Tie Smokes
203 Broadway
Chesterton
(219) 921-5330

Theodore James Tobacconist
1076 Joliet St.
Dyer
(219) 864-8800

Tinder Box
2217 Southlake Mall
Merrillville
(219) 769-4770

Cigarette Discount Outlet
4211 Franklin St.
Michigan City
(219) 931-1507

The Golden Leaf
232 W. 4th St.
Michigan City
(219) 872-9692

Munster Smoke Shop
822 Ridge Rd.
Munster
(219) 836-1993

Cigarette Discount Outlet
2814 Talumet Ave.
Valparaiso
(219) 477-2726

Triangle Liquors
3210 N. Talumet
Valparaiso
(219) 477-4849

INDIANAPOLIS & VICINITY

Kahns Fine Wine Market Place
313 E. Carmel Dr.
Carmel
(317) 251-9463

The Cigar Box
7437 N. Shadeland
Ave.
Indianapolis
(317) 841-9992

Cigars & Such
8335 Allison Point
Trail
Indianapolis
(317) 596-3280

Discount Tobacco & Cigars
3801 Lafayette Rd.
Indianapolis
(317) 387-9700

Hardwickes Pipe & Tobacco
24 N. Meridian St.,
Monument Circle
Indianapolis
(317) 635-7884

Hardwickes Pipe & Tobacco
743 Broad Ripple
Ave.
Indianapolis
(317) 257-5915

Kahn Fine Wine & Spirits
5369 N. Keystone
Ave.
Indianapolis
(317) 251-9463

Phoenix Discount
Tobacco & Tan
3940 S. Keystone
Ave.
Indianapolis
(317) 783-7366

Pipe Puffer Smoke
Shop
2306E S. County
Line Rd.
Indianapolis
(317) 881-2957

Tinder Box
Washington Sq.
Mall, 10202 E.
Washington St.
Indianapolis
(317) 899-2811

Tinder Box
6020 E. 82nd
Indianapolis
(317) 845-0806

Tobacco Barn
5302 W. 10th &
Lindhurst
Indianapolis
(317) 481-9700

Tobacco Express
5310 N. Keystone
Ave.
Indianapolis
(317) 475-1444

Tobacco Outlet
8613 N. Michigan
Rd., Indianapolis
(317) 334-9700

The Tobacco Shop
Lafayette Shoppes,
4660 W. 38th St.
Indianapolis
(317) 299-6010

Valley Mills Shell
4887 Kentucky Ave.
Indianapolis
(317) 856-4870

Village Smoke Shop
8910 S. Meridian St.
Indianapolis
(317) 888-8122

Wine Gallery
4026 E. 82nd St.
Indianapolis
(317) 576-0108

Ybor's/Gibsons
Indiana
49 W. Maryland St.
Indianapolis
(317) 951-1621

The Liquor Store
758 Westfield Rd.
Noblesville
(317) 770-9199

Bogie's Stogies
604 Columbia St.
Lafayette
(765) 742-6771

MUNCIE

Edgar Warren Cigar
Co.
Muncie Mall, 3501
N. Granville Ave.
Muncie
(765) 288-7463

Sal's Tobacco Pipe
& Coffee
3319 N. Everbrook
Lane
Muncie
(765) 286-7257

Smokin' Joes
3808 Riggin Rd.
Muncie
(765) 284-5250

NEW ALBANY &
VICINITY

Youngstown Cigar
Shoppe
1411 Youngstown
Shop Center
Jeffersonville
(812) 284-6044

Kaiser's Tobacco
Store
415 E. Oak St.
New Albany
(812) 945-2651

Smoke House
60 S. Broadway
Peru
(317) 473-9917

Edgar Warren Cigar
Co.
312 E. High St.
Portland
(219) 726-3035

Low Bob's East
4521 National Rd. E.
Richmond
(317) 935-1305

SOUTH BEND &
VICINITY

Granger Tobacco
12634 State Rd. 23
Granger
(219) 271-7070

Tinder Box
110 University Park
Mall
Mishawaka
(219) 277-3440

Club Lasalle
115 W. Colfax Ave.
South Bend
(219) 288-1155

Havanna Joe's
2036 S. Bend Ave.
South Bend
(219) 273-9153

Wabash Cigar Store
Inc.
815 Wabash Ave.
Terre Haute
(812) 232-1249

Iowa

Regal Liquors
2880 Devils Glen
Rd., Bettendorf
(319) 332-0957

Jefferson Street
Cigar Shop
208 Jefferson St.
Burlington
(319) 754-6698

Tobacco Outlet Plus
124 Collins Rd.
Cedar Rapids
(319) 377-0622

DAVENPORT

Baker Street
Northpark Mall, 320
W. Kimberly Rd.
Davenport
(319) 391-4055

Tobacco Outlet Plus
902 W. Kimberly Rd.
Davenport
(319) 445-0459

Tobacco Outlet Plus
401 E. Locust St.
Davenport
(319) 323-8681

DES MOINES & VICINITY

C & C Smoker's Outlet
121 N. Ankeny
Blvd.
Ankeny
(515) 964-9755

Cigar Source
3305 Ingersoll Ave.
Des Moines
(515) 279-1439

David's Briar Shoppe
944 Merle Hay Mall
Des Moines
(515) 278-8701

Tobacco Outlet
3814 Douglas Ave.
Des Moines
(515) 279-7813

Tobacco Outlet Plus
400 Euclid
Des Moines
(515) 280-6895

Tobacco Outlet Plus
1242 E. 14th St., E.
Town Plaza
Des Moines
(515) 262-0020

Tobacco Outlet Plus
4503 SW 9th St.
Des Moines
(515) 285-1399

Tobacco Outlet Plus
6535 Douglas Ave.
Urbandale
(515) 334-9524

Hy-Vee Food Store
1725 74th St.
West Des Moines
(515) 226-8753

JT's Fine Wine & Spirits
5010 E.P. True Pkwy.
West Des Moines
(515) 244-2997

Regal Liquors
1925 Grand Ave.
West Des Moines
(515) 327-0703

Tinder Box
Valley West Mall,
1551 Valley West
Dr.
West Des Moines
(515) 225-6011

Tobacco Outlet Plus
1540 W. 22nd St.,
Westowne Center
West Des Moines
(515) 226-3280

Pipe Inn
Kennedy Mall
Dubuque
(319) 556-5175

Tobacco Outlet Plus
806 Wacker Dr.
Dubuque
(319) 582-4607

Stogies Smoke Shop
100 N. Court
Fairfield
(515) 472-9878

Tobacco Outlet Plus
2307-B 5th Ave.
Fort Dodge
(515) 955-3159

IOWA CITY & VICINITY

Coralville Liquor Store
411 2nd St.
Coralville
(319) 354-2313

John's Grocery
401 E. Market St.
Iowa City
(319) 337-2183

Tobacco Outlet Plus
90 Sturgis Corner
Dr., Iowa City
(319) 356-6122

Hy-Vee Food Store
3600 Business Hwy.
Marion
(319) 377-4803

Tobacco Outlet Plus
2500 S. Center St.
Marshalltown
(515) 753-8625

Tobacco Outlet Plus
1522 S. Federal Ave.
Mason City
(515) 421-1750

Tobacco Outlet Plus
1111 N. Quincy
Ottumwa
(515) 683-9033

Regal Liquors
2818 N. Court
Ottumwa
(515) 683-4142

National Cigar
617 Sycamore St.
Waterloo
(319) 234-5958

Tobacco Outlet Plus
1505 E. San Marnan
Dr., Waterloo
(319) 234-6821

Kansas

KANSAS CITY & VICINITY

Tobacco Road Smoke Shop
8155 State Ave.
Kansas City
(913) 334-4567

Cigar & Tabac Limited
6898 W. 105th St.
Overland Park
(913) 642-9500

The Cigar Box
5275 W. 95th St.
Overland Park
(913) 642-3443

Klein's Premium Cigars
7524 W. 119th St.
Overland Park
(913) 451-2122

Mel's Party Shop
7709 W. 63rd St.
Overland Park
(913) 262-4184

Street Corner News
11505 W. 95th
Overland Park
(913) 888-9198

The Pittsburgh Smoker's Outlet Store
201 S. Broadway
Pittsburg
(313) 232-5770

Overland Cigar & Tobacco
730 S. Kansas Ave.
Topeka
(913) 233-0808

Cheers & Beers Connection
3300 N. Rock Rd.
Wichita
(316) 636-2433

Old Town Cigars Inc.
1217 E. Douglas
Ave., Wichita
(316) 267-8744

Kentucky

Ashland Beverage Center
744 Winchester
Ave., Ashland
(606) 329-2866

Bowling Green Pipe & Tobacco Shoppe
434 E. Main St.
Bowling Green
(502) 843-9439

Tobacco Row
2608 Burlington
Pike
Burlington
(606) 586 5403

CINCINNATI, OH & VICINITY

Tinder Box
1020 Florence Mall
Florence
(606) 525-6067

The Party Source
524 W. 6th St.
Newport
(606) 291-2250

Discount Tobacco
869 Jamestown St.
Columbia
(502) 384-1237

Tobacco Mart
2872 US Hwy. 41 N.
Henderson
(502) 827-9406

Ervin's Discount Tobacco Center Inc.
604 Crystal Place
La Grange
(502) 222 7040

LEXINGTON

Fayette Cigar Store
137 E. Main St.
Lexington
(606) 252-6267

Lansdowne Wine & Liquor
3329 Tates Creek
Rd., Lexington
(606) 266-8475

Liquor Barn
921 Beaumont
Centre Pkwy.
Lexington
(606) 223-1400

Liquor Barn
3040 Richmond Rd.
Lexington
(606) 252-8800

Schwab's Pipes 'n Stuff
Lexington Mall,
Richmond Rd.
Lexington
(606) 266-1011

Straus Tobacconist
Hyatt Gift Shop,
410 W. Vine
Lexington
(606) 252-5142

LOUISVILLE & VICINITY

Cox's Smokers Outlet
6825 Central Ave.
Crestwood
(502) 243-1450

The Busted Case
Brownsboro Rd.
Louisville
(502) 423-0019

Cigar Friendly
St. Matthews
Station, 3900
Shelbyville Rd.
Louisville
(502) 893-7445

Cox's Smokers Outlet
294 N. Hubbards
Lane
Louisville
(502) 897-5289

Ervin's Discount Tobacco Center Inc.
4222 Bishop Lane
Louisville
(502) 479 7233

Kremer's Smoke Shoppe
333 S. Preston St.
Louisville
(502) 584-3332

Kremer's Smoke Shoppe East
2420 Lime Kilin
Lane, Louisville
(502) 426-7665

Old Town Wine & Spirit
1529 Bardstown Rd.
Louisville
(502) 451-8591

Oxmoor Smoke Shoppe
7900 Shellyville Rd.
Louisville
(502) 426-4706

Paul's J. House of Cigars
1227 Bardstown Rd.
Louisville
(502) 458-2009

Rodgers Cigar Supply
Mall St. Matthews,
5000 Shelbyville
Rd., Louisville
(502) 895-8488

Up In Smoke Ltd. Cigar Shop
1431 Bardstown Rd.
Louisville
(502) 451-1118

Grand Ashe Tobacco USA
6914 Carslaw Court
Prospect
(502) 228-7804

Cigar Emporium
Westland Park Plaza,
2702 Fredricka St.
Owensboro
(502) 691-0802

The Cigar Connection
1860 Georgetown
Rd., Owenton
(502) 484-4569

Louisiana

BATON ROUGE

The Burning Leaf
11848 Coursey Blvd.
Baton Rouge
(504) 292-9004

Churchill's
7949 Jefferson Hwy.
Baton Rouge
(504) 927-4211

Friends & Company
100 France St.
Baton Rouge
(504) 381-0000

Havana House of Cigar
676 Jefferson Hwy.
Baton Rouge
(504) 930-0309

Kenilworth Superfoods
7355 Highland Rd.
Baton Rouge
(504) 767-0074

Phillip's Bayou Humidor
1152 S. Acadian
Thruway
Baton Rouge
(504) 343-1152

COVINGTON & VICINITY

Jewel Caterers & Gourmet
201 N. New
Hampshire St.
Covington
(504) 892-5746

Main Street Tobacco Shop
410 Main St.
Madisonville
(504) 845-7608

Tobacco Plus
115 E. 1st
Crowley
(318) 783-8696

The Cigar Merchant
1001 Coolidge Blvd.
Lafayette
(318) 233-9611

Piper's Haven
2480 W. Congress
Lafayette
(318) 235-4757

The Cigar Specialist
4315 Common St.
Lake Charles
(318) 480-0201

Shop-A-Lot
2707 Hazel St.
Lake Charles
(318) 433-2846

NEW ORLEANS & VICINITY

Smokin' Joes
8340 W. Judge Perez
Chalmette
(504) 277-0060

Discount Depot
712 Terry Pkwy.
Gretna
(504) 392-2696

Imperial Trading Company
701 Edwards Ave.
Harahan
(800) 743-9243

Cafe Havana
3216 W. Esplanade
Metairie
(800) 489-6738

Don Juan Cigar Co., Inc.
3200 Severn Ave.
Metairie
(504) 889-2600

Martin's Wine Cellar
714 Elmire Ave.
Metairie
(504) 896-7300

Tinder Box
Lakeside Shopping
Center, 3301
Veterans Blvd.
Metairie
(504) 834-5801

Cigar Emporium of New Orleans
5243 Canal Blvd.
New Orleans
(504) 483-6009

Dos Jefes Uptown Cigar Shop
5700 Magazine St.
New Orleans
(504) 899-3030

The Epitome
729 St. Louis
New Orleans
(504) 523-2844

The Humidor Room
137 Robert E. Lee
Blvd.
New Orleans
(504) 28-CGARS

Martin's Wine Cellar
38-27 Barronne St.
New Orleans
(504) 899-7411

Mayan Import Company
3009 Magazine St.
New Orleans
(504) 269-9000

New Orleans Cigar Co.
201 St. Charles Ave.
New Orleans
(504) 524-9631

Up In Smoke
Riverwalk
   Marketplace
New Orleans
(504) 524 2770

SHREVEPORT &
VICINITY
Tobacco Rack
120 Bossier
   Crossroad
Bossier City
(318) 752-2981

M.A.'s Smoke House
1736 E. 70th St.
Shreveport
(318) 797-3138

Tobacco Discount House
4422 Youree Dr.
Shreveport
(318) 861-2243

Tobacco Rack
750 Southfield Rd.
Shreveport
(318) 861-7765

Habano's of Slidell
1561-A Gause Blvd.
Slidell
(504) 645-9463

The Humidor
451 Red Oak St.
Slidell
(504) 645-9060

The Tobacco Pouch
700-A St. Mary St.
Thibodaux
(504) 447-3170

Maine

BANGOR & VICINITY

The Calabash
663 Stillwater Ave.
Bangor

Welch's Beverage & Tobacco
546 Hammond St.
Bangor
(207) 945-0112

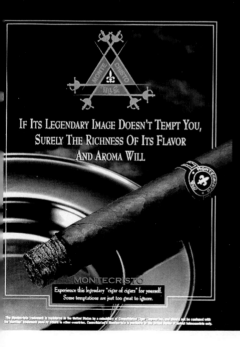

Burby & Bates
7 Oak St.
Orono
(207) 866-2533

The Digital Humidor
469 Elm St., Rte. 1
Biddeford
(207) 283-8506

La Conque At Manor Inn
Battle Ave.
Castine
(207) 326-4335

Fortune Cigars
8 Western Ave.
Kennebunkport
(207) 967-8129

Smoke Outlet @ Welcome Center
Main Outlet Mall,
345 US Rte. 1
Kittery
(207) 439-6666

PORTLAND & VICINITY

Justino's
21 Main St. (Rear)
Freeport
(207) 846-0882

The Calabash Habana Cafe
398 Fore St.
Portland
(207) 874-4055

Joe's Smoke Shop
665 Congress St.
Portland
(207) 773-3656

Smoke and Mirrors
207 Chute Rd.
Windham
(207) 892-7128

Maryland

ANNAPOLIS & VICINITY

A. Fader & Son
Annapolis Plaza
Annapolis
(410) 841-5155

Annapolis Cigar Company
121 Main St.
Annapolis
(410) 295-7400

Leader Drugs
609 Taylor Ave.
Annapolis
(410) 841-6773

Simply Cigars
Annapolis Mall,
2002 Annapolis
Annapolis
(410) 571-1775

Port Tack Limited
1264 Bay Dale Dr.
Arnold
(301) 974-0800

BALTIMORE & VICINITY

A. Fader & Son
Eastpoint Mall
Baltimore
(410) 282-6622

A. Fader & Son
107 E. Baltimore
Baltimore
(410) 685-5511

Cigar Landing
201 E. Pratt St. at
Inner Harbor
Baltimore
(410) 659-9442

Cross St. Tobacco Co.
1065 S. Charles St.
Baltimore
(410) 727-0074

Max's Trading Company
733 S. Broadway
Baltimore
(410) 675-6297

Ropewalk Tavern
1209 S. Charles St
Baltimore
(410) 727-1298

Rotunda Wine & Spirits
711 W. 40th St.
Baltimore
(410) 467-7777

Wells Liquors
6310 York Rd.
Baltimore
(410) 435-2700

Windsor Club
7 N. Calvert St.
Baltimore
(410) 332-0700

A. Fader & Son
40 W. Shopping
Center, 728 N.
Rolling Rd.
Catonsville
(410) 744-9090

Cranbrook Liquors Inc.
588 Cranbrook Rd.
Cockeysville
(410) 666-8248

Jason Liquors
National Pike, 9339
Baltimore Rd.
Ellicott City
(410) 465-2424

Ronnie's Beverage Warehouse
1514 Rock Spring
Rd., Forest Hill
(410) 838-4566

Valley Tobacco Company
Hunt Valley Mall,
118 Shawn Rd.
Hunt Valley
(410) 771-3493

Rolling Road Tobacco Warehouse
1421 York Rd.
Lutherville
(410) 339-7072

A. Fader & Son
Valley Village
Shopping Center
Owings Mills
(410) 363-7799

Grand Ritchie Cigars
8149-D Ritchie
Hwy., Pasadena
(410) 544-0988

A. Fader & Son
25 W. Alleghany
Towson
(410) 828-4555

BEL AIR

Black Jack Cigar Company
504 Hanna Way
Bel Air
(410) 638-1574

Decker Wine & Spirits
401 Baltimore Pike
Bel Air
(410) 879-4400

South Station Gourmet
16 Bel Air S. Pkwy.
Bel Air
(410) 569-2337

JB Sims Fine Tobaccos
4914 St. Elmo Ave.
Bethesda
(301) 656-7123

Simply Cigars
Montgomery Mall,
Democracy Blvd.
& I-270
Bethesda
(301) 365-0042

King Contrivance Smoke Shop
8630 Guilford Rd.
Columbia
(410) 290-7860

EASTON & VICINITY

Town & Country Liquors
28248 St. Micheal's Rd.
Easton
(410) 822-1433

Chesapeake Trading Company
102 Talbot St.
Saint Michaels
(410) 745-9797

Oasis Liquors
2013 Pulaski Hwy.
Edgewood
(410) 679 2600

Davidus Cigars, Ltd.
1015 W. Patrick St.
Frederick
(301) 662-6606

GAITHERSBURG & VICINITY

Tinder Box
347 Kentlends Blvd.
Gaithersburg
(301) 881-8322

Tobacco Shack
12615-D Wisteria Dr., Germantown
(301) 972-2905

Avery Peirson's Upperbay
Shoppers of Lonsdale, 32 S. Main St.
North East
(410) 287-3733

Greene Turtle
11601 Coastal Hwy.
Ocean City
(410) 723-2128

94th Street Beer, Wine & Deli
9301 Coastal Hwy.
Ocean City
(410) 524-7037

The Humidor
Padonia Village Shopping Center, 33 E. Padonia Rd.
Timonium
(410) 666-3212

WASHINGTON, DC VICINITY

Capital Plaza Smoke Shop
6200 Anapolis Rd.
Landover Hills
(301) 341-2614

Davidus Cigars, Ltd.
3116 Olney-Sandy Spring Rd.
Olney
(301) 260-0788

Davidus Cigars, Ltd.
7737 Tuckerman Lane, Potomac
(301) 983-6646

Shelly's Woodroast
1699 Rockville Pike
Rockville
(301) 984-3300

Signature Cigars
1598 Rockville Pike
Rockville
(301) 984-2008

Massachusetts

Colonial Spirits
69 Great Rd.
Acton
(508) 263-7775

ANDOVER VICINITY

The Cigar Emporium
800 Turnpike St.
North Andover
(508) 470-0300

Den Rock Liquor Mart
North Andover Mall, Winthrop Ave.
North Andover
(508) 683-2216

Messina's Liquors
117 Main St.
North Andover
(508) 686-9649

The Vineyard
554 Turnpike St.
North Andover
(508) 688-5005

BOSTON & VICINITY

The Cigar Emporium at Auburndale Liquors
2102 Commonwealth Ave., Rte. 30
Auburndale
(617) 244-2772

Bauer Liquors
337 Newbury St.
Boston
(718) 262-0083

Brookline Liquor Mart
1354 Commonwealth Ave., Boston
(617) 731-6644

Charles St. Liquor
143 Charles St.
Boston
(617) 523-5051

Cigar Landing II
Faneuil Hall Mkt.
  Place, Quincy
  Mkt. Bldg.
Boston
(617) 723-0147

Cigar Masters
176 Newbury St.
Boston
(617) 266-4400

David P Ehrlich
27 Court Sq.
Boston
(617) 227-1720

**Gloucester Street
Cigar Company**
34 Gloucester St.
Boston
(617) 424-1000

The Humidor
800 Boylston St.
Boston
(617) 262-5510

**L J Peretti
Company**
2 1/2 Park Sq.
Boston
(800) 797-9LJP

**Martini's Smoke
Shop**
325 Hanover St.
Boston
(617) 726-6666

Richard's Liquors
175 Wolcott Sq.
Boston
(617) 364-3745

**State Street Smoke
Shop Inc.**
107-A State St.
Boston
(617) 227-7576

**Waterfront Beer
& Wine**
379 Commercial St.
Boston
(617) 523-4055

Milton's
250 Granite St.
Braintree
(781) 848-1880

Martignetti's
1650 Soldiers Field
Rd., Brighton
(617) 782-3700

Brookline News & Gift
313 Harvard St.
Brookline
(617) 566-9634

The Cigar Emporium at Busa Liquors
182 Cambridge St.
Burlington
(617) 272-1050

Harvard Provisions Company
94 Mount Auburn
St., Cambridge
(617) 547-6684

Simply Cigars
Cambridgeside
Galleria, 100
Cambridgeside Pl.
Cambridge
(617) 374-9442

K B Tobacco
168 Everett Ave.
Chelsea
(617) 889-0012

The Cigar Emporium at Curtis Liquors
790 Rte. 3-A
Cohasset
(617) 383-9800

Global News & Tobacco Company
268 Bennington St.
East Boston
(617) 568-9740

Two Guys Smoke Shop
423 Broadway
Everett
(617) 387-6691

Tobacco Shed
400 Cochituate Rd.
Framingham
(508) 875-9851

The Wine Vault
2 Fairbanks St.
Framingham
(508) 875-6980

The Cigar Emporium at Busa Liquors
55 Bedford St.
Lexington
(617) 862-1400

Cal's News Store
53 Central Ave.
Lynn
(617) 595-9277

Highland Smoke Shop
132 Highland Ave.
Malden
(781) 397 7401

Pleasant Smoke Shop
428 Main St.
Malden
(617) 321-3593

Palumbo Liquors
547 Main St.
Medfield
(508) 359-4453

Atlas Liquors
156 Mystic Ave.
Medford
(617) 395-4400

Tufts Square Tobacco
468 Main St.
Medford
(617) 391-1820

Powers Package Store
4 South Ave.
Natick
(508) 653-6832

Simply Cigars
Natick Mall, Rte. 9
& Speen St.
Natick
(508) 651-9050

The Cigar Emporium at Upper Falls Liquors
Higland Ave.
Newton
(617) 969-9200

Pipe Rack
1247-49 Center St.
Newton Center
(617) 969-3734

Marty's Wine, Gourmet Food & Tobacco
675 Washington St.
Newtonville
(617) 332-1230

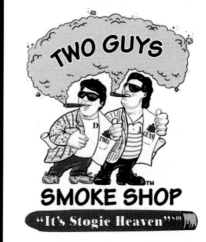

273

Kappy's
175 Andover St.
Peabody
(508) 532-2330

Simply Cigars
Northshore Mall,
  Rtes. 128 & 114
Peabody
(508) 532-5052

Richard's Liquor
301 Quincy Ave.
Quincy
(617) 376-0709

The Smoke Shop
618 Hancock St.
Quincy
(617) 472-9997

ABC The Cigar Store
170 Revere St.
Revere
(617) 289-4959

Stoneham News & Smokeshop
416 Main St.
Stoneham
(617) 438-9777

Mark's Smoke Shop
360 Main St.
Wakefield
(617) 245-1211

Watch City Cigar Company
853 Main St.
Waltham
(617) 891-6281

Vahey's Liquors
392 Main St.
Watertown
(617) 894-9578

The Cigar Emporium at Post Road Liquors
44 Boston Post Rd.
Wayland
(508) 358-4300

Tinder Box International
45 Central St.
Wellesley
(617) 431-0777

The Cigar Emporium at Curtis Liquors
Bedford St.
Weymouth
(617) 383-9800

Cigar Landing II
10 Tower Office Park
  Suite 419
Woburn
(617) 723-0147

Tobacco Shed
Woburn Mall, 300
  Mishawum Rd.
Woburn
(617) 933-0231

- -

CB Perkins
Village Mall, 95
  Washington St.
Canton
(617) 575-1411

CAPE COD

Brewster Package Store
2655 Main St.
Brewster
(508) 896-3412

Cape Cod Package Store
1495 Falmouth Rd.
Centerville
(508) 775-2065

The Epicure
538 Main St.
Chatham
(508) 945-0047

Cape and Island Tobacco Co., Inc.
303 Main St.
Falmouth
(508) 540-7724

Norman's Liquors/ Kappy's
21 Spring Bars Rd.
Falmouth
(508) 548-2600

Cape Cod Mall Liquors
226 Falmouth Rd.,
  Rte. 28
Hyannis
(508) 790-4770

Doc James Tobacco
420 Rte. 134
South Dennis
(508) 760-1223

Little Thumb Pipe Rack
307 Main St.
West Dennis
(508) 394-8955

- -

Franklin News
36 Main St.
Franklin
(508) 528-8263

Liquor World
365 W. Central St.
Franklin
(508) 528-0138

Dad's Cigars
34 Chapman St.
Greenfield
(888) 244-2760

Groton Market
235 Main St.
Groton
(508) 448-6387

B & F Tobacco
1775 Washington
St., Hanover
(617) 826-1344

Cigars Etc.
1090 Washington
St., Hanover
(617) 826-1344

**Hopkinton Wine &
Spirit**
77 W. Main St.
Hopkinton
(508) 435-1292

Ipswich News Co.
14 Market St.
Ipswich
(978) 356-3313

**Smoke Showing
Premium Cigars**
657 Central St.
Leominster
(978) 840-9500

Wyman's Liquors
30 Pleasant St.
Leominster
(508) 537-5537

LENOX &
VICINITY

Domaney's Liquors
66 Main St.
Great Barrington
(413) 528-6093

**Great Barrington
News & Tobacco**
284 Main St.
Great Barrington
(413) 528-9794

Trotta's Liquors
490 Main St.
Great Barrington
(413) 528-3490

**Najaime Wine &
Liquor**
444 Pittsfield, Lenox
Rd., Lenox
(413) 637-1220

**Nejaime's Wine
Cellar**
27 Church St.
Lenox
(413) 637-2221

Dub's Liquor
30 Chauncy St., Rte.
106, Mansfield
(508) 339-3454

Town News
165 N. Main St.
Mansfield
(508) 539-6744

Bolton St. Liquors
147 Bolton St.
Marlborough
(508) 485-3985

MARTHA'S
VINEYARD

Trader Fred's
249D State Rd.
Edgartown
(508) 627-8004

Jim's Package Store
Circuit Ave. Ext.
Oak Bluffs
(508) 693-0236

Pop and Cork
1-A Cape Rd.
Mendon
(508) 634-3133

Liquor World
Star Market Plaza, 9
Midway Rd., Rte.
109, Milford
(508) 478-1700

Up In Smoke
136 Main St.
Milford
(508) 478-8678

**Nantucket Wine
& Spirit**
Sparks Ave.
Nantucket
(508) 228-1136

Circle B Liquors Inc.
527-A Church St.
New Bedford
(508) 995-8708

Simply Cigars
Emerald Square
Mall, Rtes. 1 &
1275
North Attleboro
(508) 643- 9597

Big Y Wines
122 N. King St.

Northhampton
(413) 584-7775

**Pembroke Center
Liquors**
44 Mattakeesett
Pembroke
(781) 293-9665

PLYMOUTH &
VICINITY

Solitude's
Independence Mall
Kingston
(617) 585-4300

**Summer Hill Smoke
Shop**
161 Summer St.
Kingston
(617) 585-5588

**Brennan's Smoke
Shop**
28 Main St.
Plymouth
(508) 746-5711

Hunter's Restaurant
380 Winthrop St.
Rehoboth
(508) 252-3233

Yankee Spirits
167 Market St.
Rockland
(617) 878-0226

**Tobacco
International Ltd.**
162 Newbury Port
Tpke., Rte. 1
Rowley
(508) 948-2626

Red Lion Smoke Shop
94 Washington St.
Salem
(508) 745-2050

Little Cuban Smoke Shop
1 Prospect St.
Seekonk
(508) 336-2583

Yankee Spirits
628 Washington St.
South Attleboro
(508) 399-5860

South Egermont Spirit Shop
71 Main St.
South Egermont
(413) 528-1490

SPRINGFIELD & VICINITY

Scrappys Liquor Locker
577 East St.
Chicopee
(413) 594-9553

Aurora Borealis
25 King St.
Northampton
(413) 585-9533

The Blue Collar Cigar Com.
354 Coolie St.
Springfield
(413) 796-3908

Civic Center Convenience
1365 Main St.
Springfield
(413) 746-0889

Dave's Smoke Shop
900 Main St.
Springfield
(413) 739-4089

Phoenix Tobacconist
1676 Main St.
Springfield
(413) 731-8322

Have A Cigar
1270 Memorial Ave.
West Springfield
(413) 827-7699

Stogies
1771 Riverdale Rd.
West Springfield
(413) 781-0333

Town & Country
1119 Riverdale St.
West Springfield
(413) 736-4694

Harringtown News & Gifts
2 Galleria Mall Dr.
Taunton
(508) 880-9301

WORCESTER & VICINITY

Holden Wine & Spirits
160 Reservoir St.
Holden
(508) 829-6632

Armeno Coffee Roasters
75 Otis St.
Northborough
(508) 393- 2821

Havana House
45 W. Main St.
Northborough
(508) 393-7075

Friendly Discount Liquor
135 Providence Rd.
Northbridge
(508) 234-7951

Yankee Spirits
376 Main St., Rte. 20, Sturbridge
(508) 347-2231

Julio's Liquor
140 Boston Turnpike Rd., Rte. 9
Westborough
(508) 366-0569

Highland Emporium
146 Highland St.
Worcester
(508) 756-1989

The Owl Shop
416 Main St.
Worcester
(508) 753-0423

Palley Cash-n-Carry
1049 Main St.
Worcester
(508) 752-2811

Michigan

Chaloner & Company
108 W. Maumee St.
Adrian
(517) 263-9803

Tobacco Avenue
102 E. Erie
Albion
(517) 626-3431

ANN ARBOR & VICINITY

Blue Heron Fine Foods & Wines
882 W. Eisenhower Pkwy.
Ann Arbor
(313) 662-2270

Simply Cigars
Briarwood Mall, 100 Briarwood Circle
Ann Arbor
(313) 213-6058

Smoker's Depot
1760 Plymouth Rd.
Ann Arbor
(313) 669-9277

Village Corner
601 S. Forest Ave.
Ann Arbor
(313) 995-1818

Smokers Depot
10006 E. Grand River, Brighton
(810) 220-2701

Smokers Express
1799 Washtenaw Ave., Ypsilanti
(313) 480-0705

The Party Store SW
1950 W. Columbia Ave., Battle Creek
(616) 965-6703

Mid-town
9714 Red Arrow Hwy., Bridgman
(616) 465-6622

Marina Village
Party Store
47240 Jefferson Ave.
Chesterfield Towns
(810) 598-0999

DETROIT &
VICINITY

Smokers Only
9095 Allen Rd.
Allen Park
(313) 381-0480

Smoky's Cigarette
& Cigars
3029 E. Walton
Blvd.
Auburn Hills
(810) 373-7174

Tinder Box
2761 University Dr.
Auburn Hills
(810) 377-6840

Smoky's Cigarettes
& Cigars
2727 S. Woodward
Berkley
(810) 546-8431

Big Rock Chop &
Brew House
245 S. Eton
Birmingham
(248) 647-7774

Churchills of
Birmingham
142 S. Woodward
Birmingham
(810) 647-4555

Bloomfield
Gourmet
1081 W. Lons Lake
Rd.
Bloomfield Hills
(810) 647-5570

Miner's of
Bloomfield
41 W Longlake Rd.
Bloomfield Hills
(810) 644-0514

H & I Smokers
42090 Ford Rd.
Canton
(313) 844-3003

Smoker's Express
45156 Ford Rd.
Canton
(313) 459-7270

Smoker's Ultra
6760 E. 10 Mile Rd.
Center Line
(810) 758-0185

Tobacco Road
6684 Dixie Hwy.
Clarkston
(810) 620-7177

Parkway Beverage
37031 Groesbeck
Hwy.
Clinton Township
(810) 468-1631

Smoke-n-Paradise
36562 Moravian
Clinton Township
(801) 792- 0231

Smoker's Express
3050 Union Lake Rd.,
Commerce Twp.
(248) 360-6992

Dearborn Tobacco
Company
22085 Michigan
Ave., Dearborn
(313) 562-1221

Hill & Hill
Tobacconists
Fairlane Town
Center Mall,
18900 Michigan
Ave.
Dearborn
(313) 441-3959

The Ritz-Carlton
Gift Shop
Fairlane Plaza, 300
Town Center Dr.
Dearborn
(313) 441-2000

VIP Smokers Inc.
7118 Greenfield Rd.
Dearborn
(313) 581-9966

Puff-n-Stuff
25446 Ford Rd.
Dearborn Heights
(313) 278 7731

New Center
Tobacco & Snack
3011 W. Grand
Blvd., Detroit
(313) 873-7833

Smoker's Bargain
150 Michigan Ave.
Detroit
(313) 964-5283

Walters-Watkins
Tobacco
122 W. Lafayette
Blvd., Detroit
(313) 965-5326

Smoker's City Stop
Inc.
18814 9 Mile Rd.
East Pointe
(810) 772-7405

Smoker's Paradise
20853 Kelly Rd.
Eastport
(810) 445-1818

Cigar Emporium
33185 Grand River
Farmington
(810) 426-7271

Farmington Hills
Wine & Liquor
24233 Orchard Lake
Rd.
Farmington Hills
(248) 476-0682

Smokers & More
38499 W. 10 Mile
Rd.
Farmington Hills
(248) 442-2499

Smokes 'n More
29429 W. 12 Mile
Rd.
Farmington Hills
(248) 476-5190

Hill & Hill
Tobacconists
19529 Mack Ave.
Grosse Pointe
(313) 259-3388

H S I Cigar
19818 Mack Ave.
Grosse Pointe Wood
(313) 417-1940

Smoker's World
135 W. Highland
Rd., Highland
(810) 889-3900

Ed's Broadway Gift
2 S. Broadway
Lake Orion
(248) 693-4220

Smokers Cigarette King
28927 S. Fold Rd.
Lathrup Village
(248) 557-8908

Down River Smoker's Center
3416 Fort St.
Lincoln Park
(313) 388-2297

Smoky's Cigarette & Cigar
16705 Middlebelt
Rd., Livonia
(313) 513-2622

Wine Barrel Plus
30303 Plymouth Rd.
Livonia
(313) 522-9463

Smokers Outlet of Madison Hts.
160 W. 12 Mile
Madison Heights
(810) 414-7007

Trader Toms Tobacco Shop
43249 W. Seven
Mile Rd.
Northville
(810) 348-8333

Simply Cigars
Twelve Oaks Mall,
27500 Novi Rd.
Novi
(248) 380-2614

Smoker's Express
45029 Pontiac Trail
Novi
(248) 926-9744

Smoker's Merchant
Pheasant Run Plaza,
39877 Grand
River, Novi
(248) 473-4485

Vic's Market Wine Shop
42875 Grand River
Novi
(248) 305-7333

Vintage Wine Shop
4137 Orchard Lake
Rd., Orchard Lake
(313) 626-3235

Cap 'n' Cork
40644 W. Five Mile
Rd., Plymouth
(313) 420-0055

Smokers Only
585 S. Main St.
Plymouth
(313) 453-5644

Wellington Ltd .
14 Forest Place
Plymouth
(313) 453-8966

Smokers Shop
19158 Fort St.
Riverview
(313) 479-0404

Tobacco Town
18080 Fort St.
Riverview
(313) 246-3460

Red Wagon Wine Shop
2940 S. Rochester
Rd., Rochester
(248) 852-9307

Vintage Reserve One
417-B Main St.
Rochester
(248) 651-1649

Churchills
1416 Walton Blvd.
Rochester Hills
(248) 652-1335

Little Havana Tobacconist
3068 Walton Blvd.
Rochester Hills
(248) 375-5435

Embassy Wine & Cigar
29010 Beaconsfield
Rd., Roseville
(810) 771-7880

Smokers Outlet Inc.
18655 E. 10 Mile
Rd., Roseville
(810) 772-3999

Casablanca Tobacconist
720 E. 14 Mile Rd.
Royal Oak
(810) 585-9599

Churchill's
21425 Great Mack
Ave.
St. Clair Shores
(810) 775-3181

Smokers Express
47079 Van Dyke
Shelby Township
(810) 254-7272

Hayes Market
22580 Telegraph
Southfield
(810) 352-2216

Humidor One/ Panache
20000 W. Ten Mile
Rd., Southfield
(810) 356-4600

JR Tobacco
28815 Northwestern
Hwy., Southfield
(248) 357-2340

Majestic Market Inc.
25877 Lahser
Southfield
(810) 352-8556

Old Wooden Indian Tobacco
13260 Northline St.
Southgate
(313) 282-1379

Casablanca Tobacconist
33126 Dequindre
Rd.
Sterling Heights
(810) 268-5577

Simply Cigars
Lakeside, 14000
Lakeside Circle
Sterling Heights
(810) 247-3109

Smokers Outlet
43089 Van Dyke
Sterling Heights
(810) 997-4030

Smoker's Choice
3275 West Rd.
Trenton
(313) 671 6000

**Hill & Hill
Tobacconists**
Oakland Mall, 662
W. 14 Mile Rd.
Troy
(810) 585-0621

Smoker's Outlet
5086 Rochester Rd.
Troy
(810) 528-8018

Tobacco Emporium
2981 E. Big Beaver
Rd., Troy
(810) 689-1840

Tobacco Road
1148 E.W. Maple
Rd., Walled Lake
(810) 926-9266

**Smoker's Plus of
Warren**
3665 E. 12 Mile Rd.
Warren
(810) 558-8730

Smokers Only IX
4646 Walton Blvd.
Waterford
(248) 674-1199

Smokers Outlet
5154 Highland Rd.
Waterford
(248) 674-4880

Tobacco Village
6628 Cooley Lake
Rd., Waterford
(248) 366-8377

Lil' Havana
6690-A Orchard
Lake Rd.
West Bloomfield
(810) 539-0190

Ricks Liquor Mart
67660 M 152
Dowagiac
(616) 424-6200

FLINT &
VICINITY

Smoker's Kastle
1235 S. Center Rd.
Burton
(810) 743-6050

Smokers Outlet
1447 N. Leroy Rd.
Fenton
(810) 750-5523

Paul's Pipe Shop
647 S. Saginaw St.
Flint
(810) 235-0581

Port of Call
G-4225 Miller Rd.
Flint
(810) 732-2793

Oliver T's
1553 E. Hill Rd.
Grand Blanc
(810) 695-6550

Smoker Stop
2213 Hill Rd.
Grand Blanc
(810) 603-2471

**Smokers Palace-
Lapeer**
1045 Summit St.
Lapeer
(810) 667-3337

**Gary's Cigars and
News**
334 W. Main St.
Galland
(517) 731 1299

GRAND RAPIDS
& VICINITY

**Bib Buck Brewery
& Steakhouse**
2500 28th St. SE
Grand Rapids
(616) 954-9635

**Buffalo Tobacco
Traders**
952 E. Fulton St.
Grand Rapids
(616) 451-8090

**Elliotts News &
Tobacco**
21 Ottawa Ave. NW
Grand Rapids
(616) 235-6400

**Martha's Vineyard
Limited**
200 Union North E.
Grand Rapids
(616) 459-0911

Simply Cigars
Woodland, 28th St.
& E. Beltline Rd.
Grand Rapids
(616) 975-3019

**Smitty's Speciality
Beverage**
1489 Lake Dr. SE
Grand Rapids
(616) 451-0640

Smoker's Express
3927 28th St. SE
Grand Rapids
(616) 977-0199

Tuttle's
3835 28th St. SE
Grand Rapids
(616) 942-6990

Smoker's Express
224-C 28th St. SW
Wyoming
(616) 261-9456

JACKSON &
VICINITY

The Cigar Box
124 N. Main St.
Brooklyn
(517) 592-9064

Frank's
418 1st St.
Jackson
(517) 784-4387

KALAMAZOO &
VICINITY

**AA Tiffany Spirit
Shoppe**
1714 W. Main St.
Kalamazoo
(616) 381-1414

Corner Bar
1030 E. Vine St.
Kalamazoo
(616) 385-2028

Kalamazoo Brewing Company
427 ½ E. Michigan Ave.
Kalamazoo
(616) 382-2338

Tinder Box
Crossroads Mall,
6650 S. Westnedge
Kalamazoo
(616) 327-3447

Portage City Wine Cellar
7628 S. Westnedge
Portage
(616) 323-8466

Serafino's
8004 N. 32nd St.
Richland
(616) 629-4721

LANSING & VICINITY

Campbells Smoke Shop Inc.
207 Mac Ave.
East Lansing
(517) 332-4269

J. Scott Smokers Club
855 S. Latson Rd.
Howell
(517) 552-0835

Smokers Depot-Howell
1235 E. Grand River
Howell
(517) 546-2646

Smokers Hub
Kensington Valley Factory S., 1475 N. Burkhart Rd.
Howell
(517) 545-5577

The Humidor
117 S. Washington Sq., Lansing
(517) 484-3434

Mac's
207 S. Washington Sq., Lansing
(517) 487-0670

Dusty's Cellar
1839 Grand River Ave., Okemos
(517) 349-5150

Tinder Box
5100 Marsh Rd.
Okemos

Surroundings
423 River St.
Manistee
(616) 723-0637

French Town Liquor Shoppe
3616 N. Dixie Hwy.
Monroe
(313) 289-9952

Cigar Club Mt. Pleasant
110 N. Fancher
Mount Pleasant

MUSKEGON & VICINITY

JD's Super Stop
115 N. 3rd St.
Ferrysburg
(616) 842-7121

Hostetter's News Agency
135 Washington St.
Grand Haven
(616) 842-3920

Good For What Ales You
475 Whitehall Rd.
North Muskegon
(616) 719-2537

Barrel Craft
305 E. Mitchell St.
Petoskey
(616) 347-3322

Smokey's of Richmond
67365 Main St.
Richmond
(810) 727-5834

SAGINAW & VICINITY

Smokers Palace II
705 North Euclid Ave., Bay City
(810) 667-4410

Tobacco Outlet
Eastlawn Plaza, 971 S. Saginaw Rd.
Midland
(800) 618-7679

Daves Smokin' Post
3986 Bay Rd.
Saginaw
(517) 790-0066

Austin's Pipe & Tobacco
539 Ashmun St.
Sault Ste. Marie
(906) 632-1775

Double Corona
406 State St.
St. Joe
(616) 683-2044

TRAVERSE CITY

Folgarelli Import Market
424 W. Front St.
Traverse City
(616) 941-7651

Nolan's Tobacco
336 E. Front St.
Traverse City
(616) 946-2640

Smokers Den
1073 S. Airport Rd.
Traverse City
(616) 946-2742

Smoker's Paradise
161 N. Wayne Rd.
Westland
(313) 326-8304

Minnesota

Smoke Shoppe & Booknook
109 Washington St.
Brainerd
(218) 829-5830

Hilltop Smoke Shop
1069 Madison Ave.
Mankato
(507) 386-1706

Park Lane Smoke Shop
412 Park Lane
Mankato
(507) 389-9829

MINNEAPOLIS/
ST. PAUL &
VICINITY

Legacy Cigar Company
Mall of America,
   6124 W. Market
Bloomington
(612) 851-0021

Street Corner News
Mall of America,
   119 E. Broadway
Bloomington
(615) 858-9826

Tobacco Outlet Plus
7814 Portland Ave.
   S., Town &
   Country Shopping
   Center
Bloomington
(612) 884-1058

Tobacco Warehouse
Valley West
   Shopping Center,
   10602-B France
   Ave.
Bloomington
(612) 703-0366

Smoker's Haven
2030 W. County Rd.
Burnsville
(612) 892-0401

Tobacco Warehouse
2125 Hwy. 13 S.
Burnsville
(612) 890-8606

Cigars Unlimited, Inc.
2996 111th Ave.
   NW
Coon Rapids
(612) 323-0752

Wholey Smokes
3067 Coon Rapids
   Blvd. NW
Coon Rapids
(612) 323-3319

Smoker's Haven
7280 Point Douglas
   Rd., Cottage
   Grove
(612) 458-6909

Tobacco Warehouse
2149-C Cliff Rd.
Eagan
(612) 454-8971

E P Tobacco
16366 Wagner Way
Eden Prairie

Smoker's Haven
582 Prairie Center
   Dr.
Eden Prairie
(612) 826-1969

Cigar Importers Limited
7029 Amundson
   Ave., Edina
(612) 942-8785

Smoker's Haven
1148 W. Broadway
Forest Lake
(612) 982-1808

The Smoke Shop
809 Sibley Memorial
   Hwy., Lilydale
(612) 457-4953

The Good Life
90 Mahtomedi
Mahtomedi
(612) 429-7841

Depot Liquor
1010 Washington
   Ave. S.
Minneapolis
(612) 339-4040

Golden Leaf Limited
Calhoun Sq., 3001
   Hennepin Ave. S.
Minneapolis
(612) 824-1867

Lewis Pipe & Tobacco
512 Niccollet Mall
Minneapolis
(612) 332-9129

Smoke Depot
4941 France Ave. S.
Minneapolis
(612) 920-2235

South Lyndale Liquor
5300 Lyndale Ave.
   S., Minneapolis
(612) 827-5811

Surdyk' S Liquors
303 E. Hennepin
Minneapolis
(612) 379-3232

Tobacco Road
Foshay Tower, 831
   Marquette Ave.
Minneapolis
(612) 333-1315

Tobacco Shop
2900 Hennepin Ave.
   S., Minneapolis
(612) 825-3380

Tobacco Warehouse
Parkway Plaza
   Shopping Center,
   4727 Hiawatha
   Ave., Minneapolis
(612) 724-8142

Broviak Company
West Ridge Market,
   11300 Wayzata
   Blvd.
Minnetonka
(612) 938-0445

Haskell's Inc
12900 Wayzata Blvd.
Minnetonka
(612) 544-4456

Smoker's Haven
7912 Bass Lake Rd.
New Hope
(612) 504-4500

Tobacco Outlet Plus
3550 Winnetka Ave.
   N., Winnetka
   Commons
New Hope
(612) 544-6994

Smoker's Haven
1640 Hastings Ave.
Newport
(612) 768-8310

Smoker's Haven
2231 11th Ave. E.
North St. Paul
(612) 773-5935

Smoker's Haven
7029 10th St.
Oakdale
(612) 578-1029

Tobacco Outlet Plus
3475 W. Terrace
Mall, 3475 W.
Broadway
Robbinsdale
(612) 521-4223

Up In Smoke
333 N. Concord
Exchange
South St. Paul
(612) 552-9559

**Central Park
Warehouse**
8101 Hwy. 65
Springlake Park
(612) 780-8246

U.S. Tobacco
8320 Hwy. 7
St. Louis Park
(612) 933-0133

**Grand Tobacco
Company**
670 Grand Ave.
St. Paul
(612) 224-6972

**Griggs Cooper &
Co**
489 N. Pryor Ave.
St. Paul
(612) 646-7821

**MGM Liquor
Warehouse**
1124 Larpenteur
Ave. W.
St. Paul
(612) 487-1006

Smoker's Haven
1677 Grand Ave.
St. Paul
(612) 690-7660

Stogies On Grand
961 Grand Ave.
St. Paul
(612) 944-8690

Tobacco Outlet Plus
898 Arcade St.,
Seegor Sq.
St. Paul
(612) 778-8391

Tobacco Outlet Plus
Hillcrest Shopping
Center, 1662
White Bear Ave.
St. Paul
(612) 772-8520

Tobak & News Inc.
2140 Ford Pkwy.
St. Paul
(612) 698-3835

Up In Smoke
Minnesota World
Trade Center, 444
Cedar St. Skyway
St. Paul
(612) 298-9652

**Boozemart Wine &
Spirits**
131 E. Wentworth
West St. Paul
(612) 457-6111

Smoker's Haven
1981 Whitaker Ave.
White Bear Lake
(612) 426-6400

Smoker's Haven
1981 Whitaker Ave.
White Bear Lake
(612) 426-6400

Tobacco Outlet Plus
1580 Woodlane Dr.
Woodbury
(612) 578-7780

Churchill's
Birchwood Mall,
4350 24th Ave.
Port Huron
(810) 385-1920

Cigar Rack
416 Huron Ave.
Port Huron
(810) 989-7225

West End Liquors
1430 W. Main
Red Wing
(612) 388-9425

ST. CLOUD &
VICINITY

**G & W Coffee &
Tobacco**
21 Wilson Ave. NE
St. Cloud
(320) 654-6111

**Westside Discount
Liquor**
45 N. Waite Ave.
Waite Park
(320) 253-9511

**Westgate Liquor &
Cigars**
1429 W. Service Dr.
Winona
(507) 454-1111

Mississippi

BILOXI &
VICINITY

The Epitome
Edgewater Mall,
2600 W. Beach
Blvd., Biloxi
(601) 388-2022

Cigar Vault
Hancock Bank Bldg.,
2510 14th St.
Gulfport
(228) 868-8770

**Smokey's Discount
Tobacco**
2961 Bienville Blvd.
Ocean Spring
(601) 872-5322

**Dyre-Kent Drug
Company**
109 1st St.
Grenada
(601) 226-5232

JACKSON &
VICINITY

Rez Smoke Shop
115 Village Square
Brandon
(601) 992-2882

The Country Squire
1855 Lakeland Dr.
Jackson
(800) 222-8976

Creative Cards
2440 N. Hills St.
Meridian
(601) 483-0544

John's Premium Cigars
301 Woodrun Dr.
Richland
(601) 853-0243

Missouri

The Discount Smokes
2430 Grand
Carthage
(417) 358-3455

Jon's Pipe Shop
42 N. Central Ave.
Clayton
(314) 721-1480

JR Cigars
4 N. Central Ave.
Clayton
(314) 727-5667

Hemingway's
Nifong Square
    Shopping Center,
    10 W. Nifong
Columbia
(573) 443-2726

Nostalgia Shop
819 E. Walnut
Columbia
(573) 874-1950

Cigarettes For Less
506 N. Truman
Blvd.
Crystal City
(314) 464-4920

Tinder Box
147 Jamestown Mall
Florissant
(314) 741-0899

Welcome Smokers
2111 Mission Blvd.
Jefferson City
(573) 635-7045

T J Boggs Tobacconist
205 W. 20th St.
Joplin
(417) 623-1804

KANSAS CITY & VICINITY

Berbiglia
1101 E. Bannister
Kansas City
(816) 942-0070

Boardwalk Cigar & Coffee
6232 NW Barry Rd.
Kansas City
(816) 587-0560

Diebel's Sportsmens Gallery
Country Club Plaza,
    426 Ward Pkwy.
Kansas City
(816) 931-2988

Havana Moon, Inc.
1614 W. 39th St.
Kansas City
(816) 756-3367

The Outlaw Cigar Company
6234 N. Chatham
Ave.
Kansas City
(816) 505-2442

Royal Chieftan Cigars
Kansas City Station
    Casino, 8201 NE
    Birmingham
Kansas City
(816) 414-7418

Gomers Northland Fine Wines
8995 NW 45 Hwy.
Parkville
(816) 746-0400

JJ's Specialty Store
794 Hwy. HH
Lake Ozark
(573) 365-6989

Welcome Smokers
130 Terra Lane
O'Fallon
(314) 978-3714

OSAGE BEACH

Kenilworth House
5926 Hwy. 54
Osage Beach
(573) 348-4791

Martini's
1522 Nichols Rd.
Osage Beach
(573) 348-2100

Welcome Smokers
4 Kings Plaza
Osage Beach
(314) 569-2294

PADUCAH & VICINITY

Tobacco Lane
265 West Park Mall
Cape Girardeau
(573) 651-3414

Jug Store Liquors
Rte. 2, Box 2418
Pineville
(417) 226-4430

Red X General Store
2401 W. Platte Rd.
Riverside
(816) 741-8074

SPRINGFIELD & VICINITY

TJ's Books and Bytes
1004 Spur Dr.
Marshfield
(888) 352-9837

Brown Derby
2023 S. Glenstone
Springfield
(417) 881-1215

Don Johnson's Tobacco World
1420 S. Glenstone
Springfield
(417) 890-1978

The Humidor Ltd.
Brentwood Center,
    2728 S. Glenstone
Springfield
(417) 887-9619

Just For Him
1334 E. Battlefield
Springfield
(417) 886-8380

John Dengler, Tobacconist
700 S. Main St.
St. Charles
(314) 946-6899

Tinder Box
6227 Mudrivers Mall
Dr., St. Charles
(314) 798-2224

**ST. LOUIS &
VICINITY**

Welcome Smokers
19 Grasso Plaza
Affton
(314) 631-1211

Smoke Shop
1389 Jeffco Blvd.
Arnold
(314) 296-5523

Welcome Smokers
523 Jeffco Blvd.
Arnold
(314) 282-9910

**Brown Derby Wine
Cellar**
14125 Clayton Rd.
Chesterfield
(314) 207-9563

**Discount Smoke
Shop**
11754 Manchester
Rd., De Peres
(314) 822-6557

Welcome Smokers
15642 Manchester
Rd., Ellisville
(314) 227-4995

Welcome Smokers
3524 Lemay Ferry
Rd., Lemay
(314) 845-3680

Welcome Smokers
176 Weldon Pkwy.
Maryland Heights
(314) 569-2294

Welcome Smokers
176 Weldon Pkwy.
Maryland Heights
(314) 569-2265

Tinder Box
412 Northwest Plaza
St. Ann
(314) 298-7134

**The Adam's Mark
Hotel - Gift Shop**
4th & Chestnut
St. Louis
(314) 241-7400

**Briars & Blends
Ltd.**
6008 Hampton Ave.
St. Louis
(314) 351-1131

JR Cigars
710 Olive St.
St. Louis
(314) 231-4434

**Joel's Shell Food
Mart**
1815 Arsonal St.
St. Louis
(314) 772-1977

The Ritz-Carlton
100 Carondelet
Plaza, St. Louis
(314) 863-6300

Smoke Shop
3134 Telegraph Rd.
St. Louis
(314) 487-9992

Street Corner News
900 Crestwood Plaza
St. Louis
(314) 918-7795

**Town & Country
Tobacco**
13933 Manchester
Rd., St. Louis
(314) 227-0707

Welcome Smokers
10544 Page Blvd.
St. Louis
(314) 423-2264

H S B Tobacconist
6362 Delmar at
Westgate
University City
(314) 721-1483

Montana

**Bee's Tobacco
Outlet**
409 W. Main St.
Belgrade
(406) 388-0987

BILLINGS

The Cigarette Store
1302-24th St., W.
Billings
(406) 655-9678

The Cigarette Store
249 Main St.
Billings
(406) 254-6166

Fun For All
Rimrock Mall, 300
S. 24th St. W.
Billings
(406) 652-6747

Stogies
2717 1st Ave. N.
Billings
(406) 248-6879

Smoker Friendly
1520 3rd St. NW
Great Falls
(406) 771-0806

HELENA

Cigarette Store
1530 Cedar St.
Helena
(406) 443-3158

Smoker Friendly
1530 Cedar St.
Helena
(406) 443-3158

Maine News
9 N. Last Chance
Gulch, Helena
(406) 442-6424

Tobacco Emporium
1425 11th Ave.
Helena
(406) 443 5944

Tobacco Junction
1701 Hwy. 93 S.
Kalispell
(406) 752-1339

**Bill's Pipe &
Tobacco Shop**
136 E. Broadway St.
Missoula
(406) 728-2781

Nebraska

Cigar Humidor
17 E. 21st St.
Kearney
(308) 236-9945

The Still
5560 South 48
Lincoln
(402) 423-1875

Teds Tobacco
Ward's 61st & O St.,
#2 Gateway
Lincoln
(402) 467-3350

CGR Enterprises
5136 Erskine St.
Omaha
(402) 598-4930

Cigarros
13110 Birch Dr.
Omaha
(402) 496-9595

David's Briar Shop
10000 California St.
Omaha
(402) 397-4760

David's Briar Shop
Oak View Mall
Omaha
(402) 697-0771

Dundee Cigars & Tobacco
614 N. 50th St.
Omaha
(402) 553-2117

Nickleby's Smoke Ring
2464 S. 120
Omaha
(402) 330-4556

S. G. Roi
503 S. 11th St.
Omaha
(402) 341-9264

Tobacco Hut
13766 Millard Ave.
Omaha
(402) 895-1016

Regal Liquors
Cornhusker Plaza
South Sioux City
(402) 494-2246

Sherm's Smoke Shop
100 W. 6th St.
South Sioux City
(402) 494-7952

Nevada

Carsons Cigar Company
318 N. Carson
Carson City
(702) 884-4402

Tahoe Cigar Co.
Incline Village, 805
Tahoe Blvd.
Lake Tahoe
(702) 832-8471

Beverages, & More!
1437 W. Sunset Rd.
Henderson
(702) 456-1158

Mr Bill's Pipe & Tobacco
1014 W. Sunset Rd.
Henderson
(702) 434-4423

Alfred Dunhill Limited
Form Shops @
Caesars Palace,
3500 Las Vegas
Blvd. S.
Las Vegas
(702) 650-2992

Beverages, & More!
2610 S. Decatur
Blvd., Las Vegas
(702) 367-6778

Churchill's Tobacco Emporium
3144 N. Rainbow
Blvd., Las Vegas
(702) 645-1047

Cigar Express Inc.
2250 E. Tropicana
Las Vegas
(702) 369-1100

Cigar Maestro of Las Vegas
3700 S. Las Vegas
Blvd., Las Vegas
(702) 736 8484

Cigar Mania
7400 S. Las Vegas
Blvd., Las Vegas
(702) 361-9837

Don Pablo Cigar Company
3025 Las Vegas Blvd.
S., Las Vegas
(702) 369-1818

Don Yeyo
510 E. Fremont
Las Vegas
(702) 384-9262

Ed's Pipes, Tobacco & Gifts
Maryland Sq., 3661
S. Maryland Pkwy.
Las Vegas
(702) 734-1931

Hamilton
3790 Las Vegas Blvd.
S., Las Vegas
(702) 740-6400

Hiland's Gift & Tobacco
Meadows Mall, 4300
Meadows Mall
Las Vegas
(702) 878-7720

Las Vegas Cigar Company
3755 S. Las Vegas
Blvd., Las Vegas
(800) 432-4277

Le Cigar & Pipe
5116 W. Charleston
Blvd., Las Vegas
(702) 880-9880

Malecon Tobacco Co.
3900 Paradise Rd.
Las Vegas
(702) 735-8633

Mr. Bill's Pipe & Tobacco
3220 N. Jones Blvd.
Las Vegas
(702) 395-7264

Mr. Bill's Pipe & Tobacco
2550 S. Rainbow
Blvd., Las Vegas
(702) 362-4427

Mr. Bill's Pipe & Tobacco
4632 S. Maryland
Las Vegas
(702) 739-8840

Mr. Bill's Pipe & Tobacco
4441 W. Flamingo
Rd., Las Vegas
(702) 221-9771

Mr. Bill's Pipe & Tobacco
4510 E. Charleston
Blvd., Las Vegas
(702) 459-3400

Pheasant Tobacconist
2800 W. Sahara
Las Vegas
(702) 368-1700

Putt-n-Puff
The Riviera Hotel &
Casino
2901 Las Vegas Blvd.
S., Las Vegas
(702) 794-4047

Rio Suite Hotel & Casino
3700 W. Flamingo
Rd., Las Vegas
(702) 247-7969

Royal Cigar Society
3900 S. Paradise Rd.
Suite J
Las Vegas
(702) 732-4411

Scarpe
3200 Las Vegas Blvd.
S.
Las Vegas
(702) 369-3500

Smoker's Paradise East
6235 S. Pecos
Las Vegas
(702) 434-6444

Spirits Plus Liquor Store
4880 W. Flamingo
Rd.
Las Vegas
(702) 873-6000

Stogies Shop
4169 S. Maryland
Pkwy.
Las Vegas
(702) 737-8649

Tinder Box
3536 Maryland
Pkwy.
Las Vegas
(702) 737-1807

Tobacco Road I
3650 E. Flamingo
Rd., Las Vegas
(702) 435-8511

RENO

French Quarter
270 Lake St.
Reno
(702) 772-8383

Tinder Box
3950 Mayberry Dr.
Reno
(702) 787-2215

Tinder Box
Park Lane Mall, 186
E. Plumb Lane
Reno
(702) 826-2680

New Hampshire

Tobacco Town
76 Rte. 101A
Amherst
(603) 672-8653

The Hudson News/ News Shop
Steeple Gate Mall
Concord
(603) 226-2833

The News Shop
Steeple Gate Mall
Concord
(603) 226-2833

LACONIA & VICINITY

Black Cat Coffee & Cigars
17 Veterans Sq.
Laconia
(603) 528-3233

Paugus Variety
1325 Union Ave.
Laconia
(603) 527-1900

Fermentation Station
72 Main St.
Meredith
(603) 279-4028

MANCHESTER

Candia Road Convenience & Smoke
836 Candia Rd.
Manchester
(603) 669-6565

The Hudson News/ News Shop
Mall of New
Hampshire, 1500
S. Willow St.
Manchester
(603) 622-1782

NASHUA & VICINITY

Twin Smoke Shop
128 Rockingham
Rd.
Londonderry
(603) 421-0242

Castro's Back Room
182 Main St.
Nashua
(603) 881-7703

The Hudson News/ News Shop
310 Daniel Webster
Hwy., Nashua
(603) 897-1096

The News Shop
310 Daniel Webster
Hwy., Nashua
(603) 891-1867

Hudson News/ News Shop
Fox Run Mall
Newington
(603) 897-1999

Steele's Stationers
40 Main St.
Peterborough
(603) 924-7203

Cigars Etc.
9 Plaistow Rd.
Plaistow
(603) 382-3636

Federal Cigar
1 Market Sq.
Portsmouth
(603) 436-5363

**The Hudson News/
News Shop**
99 Rockingham Park
   Blvd., Salem
(603) 890-3699

**Two Guys Smoke
Shop**
309 S. Broadway
Salem
(888) 2CIGARS
   (224-4272)

**The Gold Leaf
Tobacconist**
920 Lafayette Rd.
Seabrook
(603) 474-7744

**The Village
Tobacconist**
Miracle Mile Plaza
West Lebanon
(603) 448-2000

New Jersey

ATLANTIC/
CAPE MAY COS.

**AC Souvenir &
Gift**
2700 Boardwalk
Atlantic City
(609) 345-6655

Have A Cigar
Ocean One Mall, 1
   Atlantic Ocean
Atlantic City
(609) 449-1899

**Trump Plaza Hotel
and Casino**
Front Page Gift
   Shop, Mississippi
   Ave. & Boardwalk
Atlantic City
(609) 441-6751

**Northfield News &
Tobacco**
Rte. 9 & Tilton Rd.
Northfield
(609) 641-9112

Your Cigar Box
703 Tilton Rd.
Northfield
(609) 645-3345

Circle Liquor Store
1 MacArthur Circle
Somers Point
(609) 927-2921

BERGEN/
PASSAIC COS.

Garden State News
461 Palisade Ave.
Cliffside Park
(201) 941-1146

**Mr. & Mrs. Cigar
Corp.**
1162 Main Ave.
Clifton
(973) 574-9330

**Richfield Video,
Cigars & Magazines**
1350 Clifton Ave.
Clifton
(973) 778-4122

**Rowe-Manse
Emporium**
1065 Bloomfield
   Ave., Clifton
(973) 472-8170

Azucar Restaurant
10 Dempsey Ave.
Edgewater
(201) 886-0747

Smokers World Ltd.
126 Engle St.
Englewood
(201) 567-1305

Bern Stationers
24-24 Fairlawn Ave.
Fairlawn
(201) 797-1311

The Cigar Room
200 Main St.
Fort Lee
(201) 947-5835

Smokin'
2450 Lemoine Ave.
Fort Lee
(201) 944-0234

The Smoke Stack
326 Main St.
Hackensack
(201) 498-0332

Cigar Den
202 Boulevard
Hasbrouck Heights
(201) 288-4277

Garden State News
106 Broadway
Hillsdale
(201) 664-2225

**Main Tobacco &
Confectionery**
83 Main St.
Little Falls
(973) 812-1382

Cigar Emporium
607 Ridge Rd.
Lyndhurst
(201) 438-8760

Beverage Barn
224 Livingston St.
Northvale
(201) 768-8848

**Fairway Smoke
Shop**
168 Paris Ave.
Northvale
(201) 784-8163

Garden State News
216 Old Tappan Rd.
Old Tappan
(201) 664-7987

**Good Spirits of
Paramus**
67A Ridgewood
   Ave., Paramus
(201) 261-3000

John David Limited
Garden State Plaza
Paramus
(201) 368-1975

JR Tobacco
184 17 N.
Paramus
(201) 288-7676

The Cigar Box
476 Rte. 17 N.
Ramsey
(201) 236-0111

Cigar World
Interstate Shopping
   Center, Ramsey
(201) 934-1142

**Exquisite Wine
Liquor**
230 Main St.
Ridgefield
(201) 641-1218

Smokers Paradise
577 Bergen Blvd.
Ridgefield
(201) 840-8999

Tobacco Shop Inc.
10 Chestnut St.
Ridgewood
(201) 447-2204

**Park Avenue Cigar
Shop**
46 Park Ave.
Rutherford
(201) 842-8398

City Cigar
181 South St.
Saddle Brook
(201) 587-0728

The Cigar Car
174 Selvage Ave.
Teaneck
(201) 837-1981

**Havana Cigar
Hecho A Mano**
26 Washington St.
Tenafly
(201) 816-8990

Havana Cigar
Hecho A Mano, 26
Washington St.
Tenafly
(201) 816-8990

**Totowa Tobacco
Inc.**
330 Union Blvd.
Totowa
(973) 389-8004

**Town Centre
Smoke Shop**
1512 Union Valley
Rd., West Milford
(973) 728-5901

Stogie's Ltd.
50 Madison Ave.
Westwood
(201) 666-1234

**Enrico's Cigar
Hideaway**
290 Godwin Ave.
Wyckoff
(201) 891-8901

BURLINGTON/
MERCER COS.

**Columbus Discount
Smoke Shop**
Columbus Farmers
Market, 2919 Rte.
206 S.
Columbus
(609) 267-4495

Shoprite Liquors
3161 Quaker Bridge
Rd., Hamilton
(609) 587-2849

**Pipe & Tobacco
Shop**
797 Rte. 33
Hamilton Square
(609) 587-6375

**Hopewell House &
Wine Shop**
48 W. Broad St.
Hopewell
(609) 466-1937

**Tinder Box
International**
501 Rte. 73 S.
Marlton
(610) 668-4220

Finlay's Cigars
560 Stokes Rd.
Medford
(609) 268-2489

**Holy Smoke Cigar
Shop**
1 N. Main St.
Medford
(609) 654-1233

**John's Greeting
Center**
356 Rte. 33
Mercerville
(609) 586-7050

Liquor Fair
Rte. 38
Mount Holly
(609) 267-4012

See-Gars
115A Creek Rd.
Mount Laurel
(609) 608-0280

**Main Street Cigars,
Inc.**
16 N. Main St.
Pennington
(609) 737-8557

**A Little Taste of
Cuba**
70 Witherspoon St.
Princeton
(609) 683-8988

PJ Smokes
3535 Rte. 1
Princeton
(609) 243-9394

**Windsor Cigar
Company**
33 Heights Town
Rd., Princeton
(609) 936-0600

Lee's Pharmacy
940 Parkway Ave.
Trenton
(609) 406-1901

**Princeton Avenue
Cigar**
1258 Princeton Ave.
Trenton
(609) 396-9610

**Smoke's Cigar &
Tobacco**
1679 Hamilton Ave.
Trenton
(609) 890-6090

**Churchill Cigar
Parlor**
4327 S. Broad St.
Yardville
(609) 585-6565

CAMDEN/
GLOUCESTER
COS.

Village Tobacco
41 Clementon Rd.
Berlin
(609) 768-5181

**Delmonte's News
Agency**
2999 Mount
Ephraim Ave.
Camden
(609) 962-6929

**Track Town Smoke
Shop**
2111 Rte. 70 W.
Cherry Hill
(609) 662-0214

Largest Walk In Humidor Room In South Jersey

Over 100 Brands of Cigars - Private Cigar Vaults

We Ship Worldwide (800) 486-8948

Davidoff - Montecristo - Cohiba
Appointed Merchant

Frank Vincent
Karen & Lou Silver
Creators of Public Enemy Cigars

Home of the Public Enemy

Track Town Smoke Shop
2111 Rt. 70, Cherry Hill, NJ 08002
Ph.609-662-0214   Fx.609.662.5909

CB Perkins
Deptford Mall
Deptford
(609) 848-3363

Monster Beverage
1299 N. Delsea Dr.
Glassboro
(609) 881-2580

Groucho's Cigars
3 Kings Hwy. E.
Haddonfield
(609) 795-1982

Scott's Smoke Shop
345 Pennsauken
Mart, Rte. 130 &
Rte. 73
Pennsauken
(609) 662-6447

**Greentree Tobacco
Company**
Greentree Rd. &
Rte. 42, 110-G
Greentree Rd.
Turnersville
(609) 374-4010

**CUMBERLAND/
SALEM COS.**

**Rebel Valley
Custom Humidor &
Cigar**
744 N. Delsea Dr.
Vineland
(609) 205-0046

**Rebel Valley Cigar
Superstores**
744 N. Delsea Dr.
Vineland
(609) 205-0046

**Williams
Continental
Tobacco Shop**
137 S. Delsea Dr.
Vineland
(609) 692-8034

**ESSEX/
HUDSON COS.**

Brookdale Buy-Rite
1057 Broad St.
Bloomfield
(973) 338-7090

Sanj's Smoke Shop
419 Broad St.
Bloomfield
(973) 743-0693

The Smoke Shop
235 Hudson St.
Hoboken
(201) 217-1701

White Ash
77 River St.
Hoboken
(201) 653-4088

**Livingston Bottle
King**
19 S. Livingston
Ave., Livingston
(973) 994-4100

**Madison Shoppers
Liquor**
277 Eisenhower
Pkwy.
Livingston
(973) 922-4441

**Wine Cellar of
Millburn**
279 Millburn Ave.
Millburn
(973) 379-0123

International Cigars
Newark Intl.
Airport, Terminal
B, Newark
(973) 622-8812

**Franklin Cigar Club
Bar & Restaurant**
522 Franklin Ave.
Nutley
(973) 661-2400

Secaucus Liquors
115 Plaza Center
Secaucus
(201) 867-7428

**Brick Church
Collection**
The Mall at Short
Hills
Short Hills
(973) 379-6920

**Liquortown USA
Inc.**
25 Valley St.
South Orange
(973) 762-9682

Cuban Aliados
Cigars Inc.
329 48th St.
Union City
(201) 348-0189

Havana Post Cigars
905 Summit Ave.
Union City
(201) 348-8999

Angelbecks
621 Valley Rd.
Upper Montclair
(201) 744-1375

The Tobacco Store
405 Bloomfield Ave.
Verona
(973) 857-2266

Universal Cigar Co.
707 Bloomfield Ave.
Verona
(973) 857-9002

Waterway Cafe
at Pershing Circle
Weehawken
(201) 902-8738

Le Johns Liquors
7 Northfield Rd.
West Orange
(973) 736-0120

HUNTERDON/
WARREN/
SUSSEX COS.

Clinton Wine &
Spirits
57 Laneco Plaza
Clinton
(973) 735-9655

Smokey Joe's Inc.
125 Main St.
Flemington
(908) 788-0560

The Jigger Shop
190 Main St.
Hackettstown
(908) 852-3080

Cigars Unlimited
Jefferson Village
Square, 725 Rte.
15 S.
Lake Hopatcong
(973) 663-5411

Bottle King
121 Water St.
Newton
(973) 383-4484

Phillips Fine Wines
Inc.
17 Bridge St.
Stockton
(609) 397-0587

MONMOUTH/
OCEAN COS.

Colonial Tobacco
Shop
1403 Wickapecko
Dr.
Asbury Park
(732) 774-6830

Barnegat Gourmet
& Gift
690 E. Bay Ave.
Barnegat
(888) 698-1944

Clancy's News &
Tobacco
256 Atlantic City
Blvd.
Beachwood
(732) 349-1416

Stogies & Bogies
96 Leonardville Rd.
Belford
(732) 495-2260

Village Tobacco
114 Main St.
Bradley Beach
(732) 774-7055

Bottazzi's Red Lion
Inn
2545 Hooper Ave.
Brick
(732) 477-1230

Cigars Plus
2140-1 Rte. 88
Brick
(732) 295-9795

Brielle Pharmacy
602 Higgins Ave.
Brielle
(732) 528-5400

Eatontown Smoke
Shop
21 Main St.
Eatontown
(732) 542-1855

County Seat
Tobacco
11 South St.
Freehold
(732) 845-4944

Mr. Pipe
Freehold Raceway
Mall, 3710 Hwy. 9
Freehold
(732) 303-9500

Spirit Unlimited
Rte. 9 & Adelphia
Rd., Freehold
(732) 462-3738

Spirit Unlimited
138 Village Center
Dr., Freehold
(732) 409-3060

Lighthouse Cigars
Airport Plaza, 1350
Hwy. 36
Hazlet
(732) 888-8118

Sasha's Boutique
1 Bay Ave.
Highlands
(732) 872-8788

Lincroft Village
Cigars
665 Newman
Springs Rd.
Lincroft
(732) 842-9777

Court Liquors
Foodtown Shopping
Center, 1 W. End
Court, Long Branch
(732) 870-9859

Have A Cigar
14 Susan Lane
Manahawkin
(609) 449-1899

Spirit of '76 Wine & Liquors
119 Taylor Ave.
Manasquan
(732) 223-3180

Spirit Unlimited
116 Third Ave.
Neptune
(908) 776-5292

Cigar City
1903 Hwy. 35
Oakhurst
(888) 300-7477

Smoke 'n' More
2005 Rte. 35 N.
Oakhurst
(732) 660-0600

Crates Wine & Liquor
14 N. Bridge Ave.
Red Bank
(732) 747-1485

Recollection
Gallery Mall 2-40
Bridge Ave.
Red Bank
(732) 747-3858

The Red Pipe
39½ Broad St.
Red Bank
(732) 842-6633

Tinder Box International
68 White St.
Red Bank
(732) 530-0006

Cigar Box
Treasure Island Plaza
Shrewsbury
(732) 460-1480

The Spring Lake Bottle Shop
1400 3rd Ave.
Spring Lake
(732) 449-5525

Amaryllis Cigars & Gifts
1608 Rte. 37
Toms River
(732) 506-0719

The Cigar Box
Ocean County Mall,
1201 Hooper Ave.
Toms River
(732) 286-7769

Cigar Depot
10 Washington St.
Toms River
(732) 914-2292

EZ Liquors
35 Rte. 37 E.
Toms River
(732) 341-3444

Monaghan's Liquors
1617 Rte. 37 E.
Toms River
(732) 270-6060

Senor Cigar
1231 Rte. 166
Toms River
(732) 286-5299

MORRIS/
SOMERSET COS.

Petrocks Liquor
419 Amwell Rd.
Belle Mead
(201) 359-2333

CB Perkins
Bridgewater
Commons Mall,
400 Commons
Way
Bridgewater
(908) 707-8787

The Chatham Wine Shop
465 Main St.
Chatham
(973) 635-0088

United Card & Smoke Shop
13 Broadway
Denville
(973) 627-6718

Ronecto Market Inc
1070 Rte. 6
Ledgewood
(201) 927-8300

Shop Rite Liquors
60 Beaver Brook Rd.
Lincoln Park
(973) 694-4420

Garden State News Village
43 Main St.
Madison
(973) 660-9600

Shoppers Liquor/ Madison
121 Main St.
Madison
(973) 822-0200

Spirits of The Valley
1990 Washington
Valley Rd.
Martinsville
(732) 302-0011

Flintlock Room
6 Hilltop Rd.
Mendham
(973) 543-1861

Morris Plains Bottle King
246 Littleton Rd .
Morris Plains
(201) 285-1226

Cutter's Restaurant
67 Morris St.
Morristown
(973) 644-4749

Tobacco Hut
31 Rte. 206
Raritan
(908) 725-4440

Cedar Grove Wine & Liquor
120 Cedar Grove
Lane
Somerset
(732) 560-0009

McAleary's
10 E. Main St.
Somerville
(908) 526-3991

JR Tobacco
301 Rte. 10 E.
Whippany
(973) 887-0800

MIDDLESEX/
UNION COS.

Puff and Stuff
21 E. North Ave.
Cranford
(908) 272-6989

Brunswick Hilton Towers
3 Tower Center
Blvd.
East Brunswick
(732) 828-2000

Market Place Wines & Spirits
647-G Hwy 18 S.
East Brunswick
(732) 432-9393

Mr. Pipe
Brunswick Square
Mall
East Brunswick
(732) 257-0200

John David Ltd
453 Menlo Park
Edison
(732) 494-8333

Bayway Liquors
639 Bayway Ave.
Elizabeth
(908) 353-6300

Easy Video
3391 Hwy 27
Franklin Park
(732) 422-4300

Kingston Wine & Liquors
3391 State Hwy.
Franklin Park
(908) 422-2324

Stoagie's
37 Gillane
Iselin
(732) 283-5535

Tobacco Barn
Middlesex Mall,
6739 Hadley Rd.
South Plainfield
(908) 753-7855

Florez Tobacconist
34 Maple St.
Summit
(908) 589-1600

Shoppers Discount Liquors
8 Millburn Ave.
Springfield
(973) 376-0005

Shopper's Discount Liquor
2321 Rte. 22
Union
(908) 964-5050

Smokers Delight
1053 Stuyvesant
Ave., Union
(908) 810-7352

Sir Puff's Cafe
43 Elm St.
Westfield
(908) 317-5900

Mr. Pipe's Smoke Shop
320 Woodbridge
Center
Woodbridge
(732) 636-7626

New Mexico

ALBUQUERQUE & VICINITY

Kelly Liquors
2621 Tennessee NE
Albuquerque
(505) 293-3270

Laru Ni Hati
3413 Central Ave.
NE, Albuquerque
(505) 255-1575

Pueblo Pipe Shop & Men's Gifts
2685 Louisana Blvd.
NE, Albuquerque
(505) 881-7999

Smoker's Depot
7600 Jefferson St.
NE, Albuquerque
(888) 296-8736

**Smoker'
s Depot**
8212 Montgomery
NE, Albuquerque
(505) 292-6641

Stag Tobacconist of Albuquerque
11200 Montgomery
NE, #27
Albuquerque
(505) 237-9366

Tinder Box
6600 Menaul Blvd.
NE, Albuquerque
(505) 883-6636

Tobacco Road LLC
1300-A Juan Tabo
Blvd. NE
Albuquerque
(505) 237-2002

Mountain Cigar & Coffee Company
12147 Hwy. 14 N.
Cedar Crest
(505) 286-2016

Tobacco Unlimited
2001 E. Lohman
Ave. #12
Las Cruces
(505) 541-9795

Siano's
2318 Sudderth Dr.
Ruidoso
(505) 257-9898

Santa Fe Cigar Co.
518 Old Santa Fe
Trail, Santa Fe
(505) 982-1044

Stag Tobacconist of New Mexico
189 Paseo de Peralta
Santa Fe
(505) 982-3242

Freud's Cigar Company
1384 Paeo Del
Pueblo Sur
Taos
(505) 751-1223

New York

ALBANY & VICINITY

Edleez Tobacco
Stuyvesant Plaza
Albany
(518) 489-6872

Habana Premium Cigar Club
Colonie Center
Albany
(518) 482-1351

Black Dog Cigar & Gift
44 Broad St.
Kinderhook
(518) 758-9150

Love of the Leaf
595 Loudon Rd.
Latham
(518) 786-9241

Biscor Ltd.
Rotterdam Square
  Mall, 93 W.
  Cambell Rd.
Schenectady
(518) 346-2796

Orion Boutique
169 Jay St.
Schenectady
(518) 346-4902

BINGHAMTON & VICINITY

Parlor City Smoke Shop
46 Court St.
Binghamton
(607) 722-4643

Wolcott's Beverage & Tobacco
1007 Union Center
  Hwy., Endicott
(607) 754-4261

BUFFALO & VICINITY

Bernstone's Cigar Store
275 Main St.
Buffalo
(716) 852-2135

Sans Souci
1783 Hertel Ave.
Buffalo
(716) 836-3248

Virgil Avenue Tobacconist
6 Virgil Ave.
Buffalo
(716) 873-6461

McBurney's
716 Main St.
East Aurora
(716) 652-4011

Havana Harry's
5472 Broadway
Lancaster
(716) 685-9901

Mario's
2304 Pine Ave.
Niagara Falls
(716) 282-4391

Bellezia Tobacco Shop
4549 Main St.
Snyder
(716) 839-5381

Smokers Haven
1167 Union
West Seneca
(716) 675-6195

Tinder Box
8212 Transit Rd.
Williamsville
(716) 689-2914

The Party Store
540 N. Main St.
Canandaigua
(716) 394-2894

Valvano's Central News
185 S. Main St.
Canandaigua
(716) 394-1176

Edleez Tobacco West
4 W. Main St.
Fredonia
(716) 672-4470

Tobacco Road
28 Main St.
Geneseo
(716) 243-5580

Baroody's Cigar Store
372 Exchange St.
Geneva
(315) 789-3133

Urban Town News
25 N. Main St.
Jamestown
(716) 483-5371

With Pipe & Book
91 Main St.
Lake Placid
(518) 523-9096

LONG ISLAND: NASSAU CO.

Don Gabriel Cigar
52-A Glencover Rd
East Hills
(516) 625-0517

The Wine Cellar
169 W. Merrick Rd.
Freeport
(516) 377-8888

Tobacco Plaza
70 Forest Ave.
Glen Cove
(516) 671-9037

Cigar Shop Limited
215 Middleneck Rd.
Great Neck
(516) 487-4830

Tobacco Plaza Limited
80 Northern Blvd.
Great Neck
(516) 829-7134

Hicksville Humidors
126 Broadway
Hicksville
(516) 933-0898

Smoke Stax
240 N. Broadway
Hicksville
(516) 938-8347

Pop's Wine & Spirits
265 Long Beach Rd.
Island Park
(516) 431-0025

Zubair Tobacco
315 Rockaway Tpke.
Lawrence
(516) 371-6213

Manhasset Humidors
69 Plandome Rd.
Manhasset
(516) 627-7066

Fortune Smoke Shop
1701 Merrick Rd.
Merrick
(516) 868-2342

Tobacco Junction
428 Jericho Tpke.
Mineola
(516) 741-3385

Smoke Stax
914 Jericho Tpke.
New Hyde Park
(516) 354-1166

Oceanside Cigar Company
3559 Long Beach
Rd., Oceanside
(516) 763-9611

Tobacco Connection
3224 Long Beach
Rd., Oceanside
(516) 763-4300

Cigar Den
377-12 S. Oyster Bay
Rd., Plainview
(516) 938-5050

Lee's Smoke Shop
553 Port
Washington Blvd.
Port Washington
(516) 883-3039

Michael Anthony's Fine Cigars
61 Main St.
Port Washington
(516) 944-0864

P & P Smoke Shop
600 Merrick Rd.
Rockville Center
(516) 536-1513

Trinity East Smoke Shop
215 Sunrise Hwy.
Rockville Center
(516) 678-1822

One Stop Smoke Shop
4007 Merrick Rd.
Seaford
(516) 783-5375

Maxim Smoke
406 Jericho Tpke.
Syosset
(516) 921-4513

Merrick Enterprise
120 E. Merrick Rd.
Valley Stream
(516) 872-9796

Mom's Cigars
126 E. Sunrise Hwy.
Valley Stream
(516) 825-0901

Sunrise Tobacco
3300 Sunrise Hwy.
Wantagh
(516) 783-8646

Fortune Smoke Stax
485 Hempstead
Tpke.
West Hempstead
(516) 481-0280

Fortune Smoke Shop
527 Old Country
Rd., Westbury
(516) 997-8109

JMP Mini Mart Corp
22 Hillside Ave.
Williston Park
(516) 248-4563

LONG ISLAND: SUFFOLK CO.

North Folk Tobacco
Main Rd.
Aquebogue
(516) 722-2660

One Stop Smoke Shop
2425 Middle
Country Rd.
Centereach
(516) 467-8653

One Stop Smoke Shop
6214 Jericho Tpke.
Commack
(516) 462-9192

Coram Smoke Shop
337 Middle County
Rd., Coram
(516) 736-1959

Kristy's Smoke Shop
1836 Deer Park Ave.
Deer Park
(516) 242-7421

The Cigar Box
10 Main St. Parish
Mews
East Hampton
(516) 324-8844

London Jewelers
2 Main St.
East Hampton
(516) 329-3939

A & D Tobacco
2031 Jericho Tpke.
East Northport
(516) 499-2330

The Westside Deli
653 Montawk Hwy.
East Quogue
(516) 653-6343

Aladdin's Tobacco Shop
260 Main St.
East Setauket
(516) 689-9418

Stogies and Tales Inc.
220 Main St.
Farmingdale
(516) 753-2596

Colonial Drugs
100 Front St.
Greenport
(516) 477-1111

Huntington Humidor
8 New St.
Huntington
(516) 423-8599

Marx Brothers Tobacconists
264 Main St.
Huntington
(516) 427-2624

NY Finest Smoke and Convenience Inc.
1803 New York Ave.
Huntington Station
(516) 673-5058

Townhouse Smoke
517-A E. Jericho Tpke.
Huntington Station
(516) 351-7131

Trade Winds Cigar
454 Main St.
Islip
(516) 277-6088

KV's Premium Imported Cigars, Pipes & Cigarettes
470 Hawkins Ave.
Lake Ronkonkoma
(516) 467-8473

Lindy's Smoke Shop
260 E. Sunrise Hwy.
Lindenhurst
(516) 957-0287

S & T Smoke Shoppe
394 Old Walt Whitman Rd.
Melville
(516) 549-3928

Supersale of Melville
825 Rte. 110
Melville
(516) 385-0190

Jim Smoke Shop II
331 Rte. 25A
Mount Sinai
(516) 331-4370

Roompam Cards And Smoke Inc.
50 Deer Shore Sq.
North Babylon
(516) 667-7977

Doc James Tobacco
1019 Fort Salonga Rd., Northport
(516) 757-9291

Jim's Smoke Shop
582 Sunrise Hwy. W.
Patchogue
(516) 331-4370

Quogue Country Market
146 Jessup Ave.
Quogue
(516) 653-4191

EJ Tobacco
1699 Rte. 25
Ridge
(516) 345-0398

Sunshine General Store
37 E. Main St.
Riverhead
(516) 727-3599

The Cigar Bar
1 Bay St.
Sag Harbor
(516) 725-2575

Fortune Tobacco
281 Middle Country Rd., Selden
(516) 732-1701

Mr. Tobacco Store
126 E. Main St.
Smithtown
(516) 724-7463

Nichalex Cigar Corp.
95 New York Ave.
Smithtown
(516) 724-5748

Udall Stationary
795 Udall Rd.
West Islip
(516) 731-3979

Card House
809 Rte. 208
Monroe
(914) 782-3333

NEW YORK CITY: BRONX

La Casa Grande Tobacco
2344 Arthur Ave.
Bronx
(718) 364-4657

SF Cigars
2084 White Plains Rd., Bronx
(718) 829-0461

NEW YORK CITY: BROOKLYN

86 Smoke Shop
1953 86th St.
Brooklyn
(718) 714-9289

Barney's Smoke Shop
76 Court St.
Brooklyn
(718) 875-8355

Cigar Box
1701 Ave. Z
Brooklyn
(718) 934-5766

Good Newsstand
1836 Rockaway Pkwy.
Brooklyn
(718) 763-1926

Harvey's Cards & Gifts
3042 Ave. U
Brooklyn
(718) 648-0105

JGP Cigars
9212 3rd Ave.
Brooklyn
(718) 238-2224

See Gar
404-B 7th Ave.
Brooklyn
(718) 499-8303

NEW YORK CITY:
MANHATTAN

**Alfred Dunhill
Limited**
450 Park Ave.
New York
(212) 753-9292

**Angelo & Maxi's
Steakhouse**
233 Park Ave. S.
New York
(212) 220-9200

**Arnold's Tobacco
Shop**
323 Madison Ave.
New York
(212) 697-1477

Barclay - Rex Inc.
70 E. 42nd St.
New York
(212) 962-3355

Barclay - Rex Inc.
7 Maiden Lane
New York
(212) 962-3355

Barclay - Rex Inc.
570 Lexington Ave.
New York
(212) 888-1015

**The Big Cigar
Company**
193-A Grand St.
New York
(212) 966-9122

**Bleeker Cigar
Company**
322 Bleeker St.
New York
(212) 352-1278

**Broadway Office
Products**
1412 Broadway
New York
(212) 354-7530

Cigar Emporium
541 Warren St.
New York
(518) 828-5014

The Cigar Inn
1314 1st Ave.
New York
(212) 717-7403

Cigar Landing
89 South St., Pier 17
New York
(212) 406-3886

**Coopers Classic
Cars and Cigars**
41 W. 58th St.
New York
(212) 588-8888

**Davidoff of Geneva
(NY)**
535 Madison Ave.
New York
(212) 751-9060

**De La Concha
Tobacconist**
1390 Ave. of The
    Americas
New York
(212) 757-3167

Eastside Cigars
969 3rd Ave.
New York
(212) 755-3255

**Famous Smoke
Shop**
55 W. 39th St.
New York
(212) 221-1408

Florio's
192 Grand St.
New York
(212) 226-7610

Gigi Tobacco
Manhattan Mall,
    Lower Level, 100
    W. 33rd
New York
(212) 643-9478

**Grand Havana
Room**
666 5th Ave., 39th
    Fl., New York
(212) 245-1600

H R Scott
64 Exchange Place
New York
(212) 422-3046

J & F Tobacco
500 Lexington Ave.
New York
(212) 935-9800

Jay Kos
986 Lexington Ave.
New York
(212) 327-2382

JR Tobacco
11 E. 45th St.
New York
(212) 983-4160

JR Tobacco
219 Broadway
New York
(212) 233-6620

La Rosa Cigars
862 6th Ave.
New York
(212) 532 7450

**Maxwell's Daily
Grind**
40 Water St. Plaza
New York
(212) 269-6444

**Mom's Cigars
House of Oxford**
172 5th Ave.
New York
(212) 243-1996

Mustang Grill
1633 2nd Ave.
New York
(212) 744-9194

Nat Sherman
500 5th Ave.
New York
(212) 246-5500

OK Cigars
383 W. Broadway
New York
(212) 965-9065

**Packman Tobacco
Co.**
304 W. 39th St.
New York
(212) 714-2300

**Park Avenue
Liquors**
292 Madison Ave.
New York
(212) 685-2442

QC Cigar Co. Inc.
1 World Trade Ctr.,
    Concourse Level
New York
(718) 406-3434

QC Cigar Co. Inc.
198 Broadway
New York
(718) 852-8487

Rhyme & Reason
419 Park Ave. S.
New York
(212) 328-2540

St. Regis Hotel
2 E. 55th St.
New York
(212) 339-6711

Smoker's Choice
1 Beekman St.
New York
(212) 285-0937

The Smoking Shop
45 Christopher St.
New York
(212) 929-1151

**The Stock
Exchange Luncheon
Club**
11 Wall St. 7th Fl.
New York
(212) 344-6855

Trumpets Cigar Bar
Grand Hyatt New
    York, Park Ave. at
    Grand Central
New York
(212) 883-1234

**The Wall Street
Humidor**
18 Warren St.
New York
(212) 96-CIGAR

NEW YORK CITY:
QUEENS

Discount Magazines
23-22 30th Rd.
Astoria
(718) 726-3087

The Gift Source
90-15 Queens Blvd.
Elmhurst
(718) 592-0400

Puff-n-Stuff
161-10 Northern
    Blvd., Flushing
(718) 321-3908

**B & A Newsstand
& Grocery Inc.**
55-47 69th St.
Maspeth
(718) 898-0044

**Maspeth Express
Minimart**
69-28 Grand Ave.
Maspeth
(718) 397-5633

**45th Street Smoke
Shop**
4520 Queens Blvd.
Sunnyside
(718) 937-4426

NEW YORK CITY:
STATEN ISLAND

Carmine's Cigars
1671 Richmond Rd.
Staten Island
(718) 351-6637

Cigar Aficionado
965 Richmond Rd.
Staten Island
(718) 761-1234

Empire Smoke Shop
1398 Forest Ave.
Staten Island
(718) 815-4444

Gigi's Tobacco Ltd
Staten Island Mall,
   2655 Richmond
   Ave., Staten Island
(718) 982-0013

Smokin Bean
1722 Hylan Blvd.
Staten Island
(718) 980-7113

**Tobacco & Gift
Emporium**
3277 Richmond
   Ave.
Staten Island
(718) 948-2899

Factory 370
117 Main St.
Oneida
(315) 363-4807

POUGHKEEPSIE
& VICINITY

Harley Designs
Farmingdale Rd.,
   Rte. 94
Blooming Grove
(914) 496-7230

**Fishkill Beer &
Soda**
169 Main St.
Fishkill
(914) 897-5412

Smokes For Less
Rte. 82
Hopewell Junction
(914) 226-2622

**Uptown Cigar
Company**
42 N. Front St.
Kingston
(914) 340-1142

**Hudson Valley
Cigars**
475 Temple Hill Rd.
New Windsor
(914) 562-1762

**Tommy's Smoke
Shop**
768 Broadway
Newburgh
(914) 569-9255

The Brown Leaf
Kalyto Plaza, 63 E.
   Main St.
Pawling
(914) 855-0141

**O'Leary's Smoke
Shop**
Poughkeepsie Plaza
   Mall, South Rd.
Poughkeepsie
(914) 471-5736

Smokes For Less
2 Raymond Ave.
Poughkeepsie
(914) 471-6602

United Smoke Shop
2 E. Market St.
Rhinebeck
(914) 876-7185

**Thruway Shopping
Center**
78 Oak St.
Walden
(914) 778-3535

**Slick Leathers &
Cigars**
54 Tinker St.
Woodstock
(914) 679-7039

ROCHESTER &
VICINITY

Bahama Bob's
135 Packetts
   Landing
Fairport
(716) 223-7490

The Havana Room
1220 Fairport Rd.
Fairport
(716) 385-4420

Hickey's
19 S. Main St.
Pittsford
(716) 385-1780

**Pittsford Village
Market**
57 N. Main St.
Pittsford
(716) 264-1060

**Dewey Avenue
Smoke Shop**
1405 Dewey Ave.
Rochester
(716) 458-8824

Havana House, Inc.
365 N. Washington
   St., Rochester
(716) 586-0620

J & J Newsstand
428 Greece Ridge
   Center
Rochester
(716) 227-0270

J & J Newsstand
231 Irondequoit
   Mall Dr.
Rochester
(716) 266-1870

**Nestor's Cigar
Corner**
3485 W. Henrietta
   Rd., Rochester
(716) 427-7240

Old City Hall
Wandtke
Restaurant &
Humidor Club
30 W. Broad St.
Rochester
(716) 454-1641

Paco's Cigars
768 Monroe Ave.
Rochester
(716) 256-1090

Park Oxford Cigar
Company
365 Park Ave.
Rochester
(716) 271-3850

Twelve Corners
Apothecary
1832 Monroe Ave.
Rochester
(716) 244-8600

Panateri & Son
Cigar
5 Caroline St.
Saratoga Springs
(518) 885-0296

Saratoga Cigar &
Pipe
130 S. Broadway
Saratoga Springs
(518) 584-4716

Mountain Service
Dist.
40 Lake St.
South Fallsburg
(914) 434-5674

**SYRACUSE &
VICINITY**

Nick's Fine Cigars
523 S. Main St.
North Syracuse
(315) 458-5624

Little Havana
Trading Co.
Rear 5 E. Genesee
St., Skaneateles
(315) 685-4845

Kieffers Cigar Store
851 N. Salinas St.
Syracuse
(315) 475-3988

Mallard Tobacconist
208 Walton St.
Syracuse
(315) 475-5839

Olympic News
Gallery
441 S. Salina St.
Syracuse
(315) 424-1336

Rocky's Newsstand
447 N. Salina St.
Syracuse
(315) 422-1997

Ball's Card Shop
2 Lafayette St.
Utica
(315) 733-7005

Pipes Unlimited
19 Auburn Ave.
Utica
(315) 735-2588

The Cigar Shop
Carbone Plaza, 605
Coffeen St.
Watertown
(315) 779-8460

Demar Cigar
Company
Salmon Run Mall
Watertown
(315) 788-3605

**WESTCHESTER/
ROCKLAND CO.**

Bavarian Beverage
Center
643 Sawmill River
Rd., Ardsley
(914) 693-3339

Doc James Tobacco
110 Kraft Ave.
Bronxville
(914) 961-4868

Hudson River
Cigars Inc.
Essel Bourne Rd.
Cold Spring
(914) 265-4675

One Stop
159 Fisher Ave.
Eastchester
(914) 779-9600

Maxis Smoke Shop
253-22 Union Tpke.
Floral Park
(718) 343-5000

Hartsdale Wines &
Liquor
218 E. Hartsdale
Ave., Hartsdale
(914) 723-3535

Tinder Box
International
161 S. Central Ave.
Hartsdale
(914) 328-0222

Winetasters of
Larchmont
100 Chatsworth
Ave.
Larchmont
(914) 834-0800

Old Time Cigar &
Sweets
571 Rte. 6
Mahopac
(914) 621-3541

Boston Road Cigars
164 E. Boston Post
Rd., Mamaroneck
(914) 831-4006

CB Perkins
Galleria At Crystal
Run, One Galleria
Dr., Middletown
(914) 692-4518

Smokers Harbor
49 S. Moger Ave.
Mount Kisco
(914) 666-2648

Nyack Tobacco
Company
140 Main St.
Nyack
(914) 358-9300

Westchester
Tobacco
189 Main St.
Ossining
(914) 941-1185

Village Smoke Shope
12 E. Central Ave.
Pearl River
(914) 735-2638

Varmax Liquor Pantry Inc.
16 Putnam Ave.
Port Chester
(914) 937-4930

Cigar Box of Scarsdale
44 E. Parkway
Scarsdale
(914) 428-0900

Mom's Cigars
1119 Central Park
Ave., Scarsdale
(914) 723-3088

Zachy's Wine & Liquor
16 E. Pkwy.
Scarsdale
(914) 723-0241

Doc James Tobacco
Rte. 132
Shrub Oak
(800) 41SMOKE

The Market Place Smoke Shop
31 Springvalley
Market Place
Spring Valley
(914) 356-3717

Mainstreet Cigars
84 Main St.
Tarrytown
(914) 366-4381

Cigars & Sweets
Rosehill Shopping
Center, 632
Columbus Ave.
Thornwood
(914) 747-0029

John David Limited
Galleria Mall, 100
Main St.
White Plains
(914) 761-0180

Main Street Smoke Shop
175 Main St.
White Plains
(914) 682-2947

Up In Smoke
100 Main St.
White Plains
(914) 681-1913

White Plains Tobacconist
148 Mamaroneck
Ave., White Plains
(914) 686-5538

Ajit K Corporation
944 Central Park
Ave., Yonkers
(914) 963-9826

Cigar World
777-B Central Park
Ave., Yonkers
(914) 423-0771

North Carolina

Tobacco Road Outlet
1818 N. Sand Hills
Blvd.
Aberdeen
(910) 695-4344

Asheboro Wholesale Grocery
228 W. Ward St.
Asheboro
(910) 625-5570

ASHEVILLE & VICINITY

Bonnie's Little Corner
1 Park Sq. SW
Asheville
(704) 252-1679

Cigar Box
Biltmore Sq. Mall,
800 Brevard Rd.
Asheville
(704) 670-1177

Hunter Banks Company
29 Montford Ave.
Asheville
(704) 252-3005

Pipes Limited
3 S. Tunnel
Asheville
(704) 298-2392

Sir Toms Tobacco Emporium
129 W. 4th Ave.
Hendersonville
(704) 697-7753

Expressions In Boone
195 New Market
Center, Boone
(704) 262-1816

Highland Newsstand
Shops at Shadow
Line, 240
Shadowline Dr.
Boone
(704) 264-5850

Pipes By George
15 The Courtyard,
431 W. Franklin
St., Chapel Hill
(919) 967-5707

CHARLOTTE & VICINITY

Cigars Etcetera
3712 E.
Independence
Blvd.
Charlotte
(704) 532-9853

Cutters Cigar Bar
Charlotte Marriot
City, 100 W. Trade
St.
Charlotte
(704) 333-9000

The Humidor
BB&T Center,
Overstreet Mall,
200 S. College St.
Charlotte
(704) 334-3449

McCranies Pipe Shop
4143 Park Rd.
Charlotte
(704) 523-8554

Tinder Box
South Park Mall,
4400 Sharon Rd.
Charlotte
(704) 366-5164

Tinder Box
Eastland Mall, 5521
    Central Ave.
Charlotte
(704) 568-8798

Carolina Wine &
Beverage
20832 Catawba Ave.
Cornelius
(704) 892-0406

Tinder Box
11025 Carolina
    Place Pkwy.
Pineville
(704) 542-6115

DURHAM &
VICINITY

Carving Tree
Gallery
8513 Roxboro Rd.
Bahama
(919) 620-9077

Tinder Box
242 S. Square Mall,
    4001 Chapel Hill
    Blvd., Durham
(919) 489-7765

Anstead's Tobacco
337 Cross Creek
    Mall, Fayetteville
(910) 864-5705

Adam Samuels
Tobacco
245 W. Garrison
    Blvd., Gastonia
(704) 864 8334

GREENSBORO &
VICINITY

International House
Limited
108 Holly Hill Mall
Burlington
(910) 584-3895

GSO Wine
Warehouse
2212 Battleground
    Ave.
Greensboro
(910) 288-2002

Just One More
3722-G
    Battleground Ave.
Greensboro
(910) 282-2900

Pleasures &
Treasure
229 Four Seasons
    Town Centre
Greensboro
(910) 855-1301

Tobacco USA
1305 Coliseum Blvd.
Greensboro
(910) 292-5130

Iloco Mart
1010 N. Main St.
High Point
(910) 883-7623

Pleasures And
Treasures
Oak Hollow Mall,
    921 Eastchester
    Dr., High Point
(910) 282-3023

GREENVILLE

Jefferson's
505 Red Banks Rd.
Greenville
(919) 756-6196

Onix Tobacco Shop
505 S. Evans St.
Greenville
(919) 413-0900

Village Vineyard
729 Red Banks Rd.
Greenville
(919) 355-6714

The Tobacco Shop
1315 E. Main St.
Havelock
(919) 447-8282

The Tobacco Shop
803-B E. Main St.
Havelock
(919) 447-8282

Pipes Limited
174 Valley Hills
    Mall, Hickory
(704) 328-8002

NC Cigarette &
Cigar Outlet
976 Clover Leaf
    Plaza, Kannapolis
(704) 786-2120

Havana Day
Dreaming
2701 N. Croatan
    Hwy.
Kill Devil Hills
(919) 480-3934

Syd's Tobacco
Company
108 E. Murphy St.
Madison
(336) 548-1973

Island Tobacco
5000 S. Croatan
    Hwy., Nags Head
(919) 441-1392

Armstrong Grocery
Co.
1201 Broad St.
New Bern
(919) 638-1822

Wine Plus
3310 Trent Rd.
New Bern
(919) 635-5200

RALEIGH &
VICINITY

Cary Tobacco
Outlet
8045-B Chapel Hill
    Rd., Cary
(919) 461-0704

J. Gilbert's
1913 Arboretum
    Trace, Cary
(919) 859-1793

Cigar & Tobacco
Emporium
5167-l Hwy. 42
Garner
(919) 773-2215

Angus Barn
9401 Glenwood
    Ave., Raleigh
(919) 787-3505

Grapes, Beans & Hops
Crabtree Valley Mall, 4325 Glenwood Ave.
Raleigh
(919) 786-0467

Harris Teeter
501 Oberlin Rd.
Raleigh
(919) 828-9216

Pipes By George
1209 Hillsborough St., Raleigh
(919) 829-1167

Tinder Box
Crabtree Valley Mall, 4325 Glenwood Ave.
Raleigh
(919) 787-1310

The Tobacco Shack
2930 Capital Blvd.
Raleigh
(919) 871-0202

JR Tobacco
67 Jr Rd.
Selma
(919) 965-5055

JR Tobacco
I-95 & Rte.70
Selma
(919) 965-0000

Tobacco Road Smoke Shop
915-1 Old Boiling Springs Rd.
Shelby
(704) 487-0621

Matchbox
157 E. New Hampshire Ave.
Southern Pines
(910) 692-5545

JR Tobacco
1515 E. Broad St.
Statesville
(704) 838-0092

WILMINGTON & VICINITY

Davis & Sons Smokers Emporium
Longleaf Mall, Shipyard Blvd.
Wilmington
(910) 791-6688

JL's Smoke Shop
220 N. Front St.
Wilmington
(910) 254-4556

Koolies
11 N. Lumina Ave.
Wrightsville
(910) 256-2525

WINSTON-SALEM & VICINITY

R & A Smoke Shop
916-B Randolph St.
Thomasville
(910) 476-9346

Carolina Tobacco Emporium
801 Silas Creek Pkwy.
Winston-Salem
(336) 750-0160

Garner's Tobacco Shop
114-E Reynolda Village
Winston-Salem
(910) 725-7611

Harris Teeter
420-22 S. Stratford Rd., Winston-Salem
(910) 723-2305

Harris Teeter
1955 N. Peace Haven Rd.
Winston-Salem
(910) 760-0116

Pipes Etc.
Thruway Shopping Center, 385 Lower Mall Dr.
Winston-Salem
(910) 723-1269

Tinder Box
Hanes Mall, 3320 Silas Creek Pkwy.
Winston-Salem
(910) 945-9068

North Dakota

BISMARCK

Captain Jack's
808 2nd St.
Bismarck
(701) 223-6546

MVP Sports
114 N. 5th St.
Bismarck
(701) 258-8806

Tobacco Row
404 E. Bowen Ave.
Bismarck
(701) 255-9339

FARGO

Crown Liquors
3051 25th St. S.
Fargo
(701) 298-3260

Empire Liquor
4861 13th Ave. S.
Fargo
(701) 282-2882

Happy Harrys Bottle Shop
1125 19th Ave. N.
Fargo
(701) 235-4661

Smoke Shop
1525 S. University Dr., Fargo
(701) 298-7824

Up In Smoke
107½ Broadway
Fargo
(701) 476-0195

Happy Harry's
2051 32nd Ave. S.
Grand Forks
(701) 780-0902

Market Place Liquor
1930 S. Broadway
Minot
(701) 839-7580

Ohio

AKRON & VICINITY

The Pipe Rack
2200 Manchester Rd., Akron
(330) 745-9022

Smoke Inn
3900 Medina Rd.
Akron
(888) SMOKE-3

The Smokers Den
1163 E. Tallmadge
Ave., Akron
(330) 633-3141

The United Cigar
Company
The Everett
Building, 3 N.
Main St.
Akron
(330) 535-7474

Village Tobacconist
Summit Mall, 3265
W. Market
Akron
(330) 864-3929

Campus Wine
Cellar
1655 E. Main St.
Kent
(330) 673-1589

Downtown Tobacco
44 Public Sq.
Medina
(330) 722-9096

Stogies
135 E. Main
Ravenna
(330) 296-6256

Tinker Box
236 W. Main St.
Ravenna
(330) 296-6165

Oakway Cigar &
Tobacco
7291 Roberts Rd.
Athens
(614) 593-7169

Tobacco For Less
751 E. State St.
Athens
(614) 593-8091

Wine Reserve
16785 Chillicothe
Rd., Bainbridge
(216) 543-3339

A R M Cigar Store
7125 Southern Blvd.
Boreman
(330) 758-2886

Discount Cigarette
Mart
55 Pearl Rd
Brunswick
(330) 273-1290

CANTON &
VICINITY

Briarpatch
2880 Whipple Ave.
NW, Canton
(330) 477-2511

Duncan Hill/Careys
Smoke
7835 Freedom Ave.
NW, Dock Door C
North Canton

Boston Stoker
Washington Sq., 14
W. Whipp Rd.
Centerville
(513) 439-2400

The Smokehouse
264 N. Main St.
Centerville
(937) 438-1927

CINCINNATI &
VICINITY

Burning Desires
7833 Cooper Rd.
Cincinnati
(513) 984-2876

Carousel Tobacco
Shoppe
8001 Reading Rd.
Cincinnati
(513) 821-5350

Cincinnati
Tobacconist
617-D Vine St.
Cincinnati
(513) 621-9932

The Cincinnati
Smoke Shop
2717 Erie Ave.
Cincinnati
(513) 533-4999

The Smoke Store
2824 Jefferson
Cincinnati
(513) 871-4367

Straus Tobacconist
410 Walnut St.
Cincinnati
(513) 621-3388

Tinder Box
Tri-County Mall,
11700 Princeton
Pike
Cincinnati
(513) 671-8966

Tinder Box
7875 Montgomery
Rd., Cincinnati
(513) 891-3380

Tinder Box
Eastgate Mall, 4601/
B-316 Eastgate
Blvd.
Cincinnati
(513) 752-7359

Tom's Cigar Store
135 Main St.
Hamilton
(513) 896-1724

Doc's Smoke Shop
12 W. Mulberry St.
Lebanon
(513) 932-9939-

CLEVELAND &
VICINITY

Sirnas Market &
Deli/Mainline
7307 Aurora Rd.
Aurora
(216) 562-5221

Tobacco Pouch
26 N. Main St.
Chagrin Falls
(216) 247-5365

Cousin Cigar Co.
1828 Euclid Ave.
Cleveland
(216) 781-9390

Dad's Smoke Shop
17112 Lorain Ave.
Cleveland
(216) 671-3663

Havana Cigar
2720 E. 79th St.
Cleveland
(216) 751-4867

Havana Cigar
13204 Shaker Sq.
Cleveland
(216) 751-4867

Huntington Building Cigar Store
Huntington Bank
  Building, 925
  Euclid Ave.
Cleveland
(216) 621-5420

Mayfield Smoke Shop
12307 Mayfield Rd.
Cleveland
(216) 229-1588

McBill Beverages Inc.
1015 E. 18th St.
Cleveland
(216) 531-1299

Old Erie Tobacco Co.
The Arcade, #150,
  401 Euclid Ave.
Cleveland
(216) 861-0487

Sam Klein Cigar Co.
1834 E. 6th St.
Cleveland
(216) 621-2673

Smoking Room
2238 Lee Rd.
Cleveland
(216) 321-8888

Moniti Inc.
20550 Lorraine Rd.
Fairview Park
(216) 333-0057

Beverage Square House of Fine Wines, Beer & Tobacco
13340 Madison Ave.
Lakewood
(216) 226-8796

Jo Vann's Tobacco Shop
6260 May Field Rd.
Mayfield Heights
(216) 442-4775

Box Office Movies
7557 Pearl Rd.
Middleburg Heights
(216) 243-6233

Tinder Box
434 Great Northern
  Mall
North Olmsted
(216) 572-3668

Wine World
27600 Lorain Rd.
North Olmsted
(216) 779-7571

Parma Heights Smoke Shop
6647 Pearl Rd.
Parma Heights
(216) 886-3449

Cigar Cigars
21802 Center Ridge
  Rd., Rocky River
(216) 333-5454

Cheese and Wine Etc.
20140 Van Aken
  Blvd.
Shaker Heights
(216) 283-7260

Paragon Cigar Company
155 Southpark
  Center
Strongsville
(216) 572-1339

Churchill's Smoke Shop
4050 Erie St.
Willoughby
(216) 975-8364

Cousins Cigar
28400 Chagrin
Woodmere
(216) 464-9396

COLUMBUS & VICINITY

Barclay Pipe & Tobacco
1677 W. Lane Ave.
Columbus
(614) 486-4243

Burning Leaf
1044 S. High St.
Columbus
(614) 443-5323

Humidor Plus
6157 Cleveland Ave.
Columbus
(614) 891-9463

La Luna Tobacconist
1767 Hill Rd. N.
Columbus
(614) 864-6254

The Original Smokers' Haven
1097 Bethel Rd.
Columbus
(614) 538-9534

Pipes & Pleasures
4244 E. Main St.
Columbus
(614) 235-6422

Premium Cigar Company
400 N. High St.
Columbus
(614) 221-4555

Tinder Box
4236 Westland Mall
Columbus
(614) 276-2904

Simply Cigars
5043 Tuttle Crossing
  Blvd., Dublin
(614) 761-8930

Stogies & Stix
6788 Preimeter Loop
  Rd., Dublin
(614) 336-9590

Hey Have A Cigar, Co.
1151 N. Hamilton
  Rd., Gahanna
(614) 478-1000

Emporium Downtown
154 W. Main St.
Lancaster
(614) 653-5717

Burning Needs Cigar Emporium
232 E. Olentangy St.
Powell
(614) 593-7169

Smoke-n-Save
111 Westerville
Plaza, Westerville
(614) 818-9884

**DAYTON &
VICINITY**

Tinder Box
2727 Fairfield
Commons
Beaver Creek
(513) 429-1172

Tobacco Wharf
3464-A New
Germany Trebein
Rd., Beaver Creek
(513) 426-0633

Boston Stoker
8341 N. Main St.
Dayton
(513) 836-2200

Fred's Fine Tobacco
458 Patterson Rd.
Dayton
(937) 294-9866

**Oakwood Kettering
Smoke Shop**
2970 Far Hills Ave.
Dayton
(937) 294-2100

**Smoker's Paradise/
Coffee**
3200 N. Main St.
Dayton
(937) 277-8556

Tinder Box
2700 Miamisburg
Centerville Rd.
Dayton
(937) 433-2841

Tobacco Man
4958 Springboro Rd.
Dayton
(937) 298-6751

Boston Stoker
University Snoppes,
2624 Colonel
Glenn Hwy.
Fairborn
(513) 426-1005

Jungle Jims Markets
5440 Dixie Hwy.
Fairfield
(513) 829-1918

The Smokehouse
6067 Brandt Pike
Huber Heights
(937) 233-8153

The Smokehouse
4626 Wilmington
Pike, Kettering
(937) 643-1996

**King's Rook 4 Pipe
Shop**
110 E. Main St.
Tipp City
(513) 667-6821

Boston Stoker
10855 Engle Rd.
Vandalia
(513) 890-6401

Steve & Edey's
686 W. National Rd.
Vandalia
(937) 898-2776

C J Original
1500 N. Clinton St.
Defiance
(419) 782-8998

Executive Cigar Inc.
15655-M State Rte.
170, East Liverpool
(330) 382-0200

City News
738 Broadway
Lorain
(216) 246-9097

Tobacco Road
12 S. Main St.
Mansfield
(419) 522-6218

**The Holiday Inn
French Quarter**
PO Box 268
Perrysburg
(419) 874-3111

Arisen Merchandise
145 W. Main St.
Springfield
(513) 323-1791

Prime Fuel
330 W. North St
Springfield
(937) 324-8187

TOLEDO & VICINITY

Cigar Affair
101 E. Wayne St.
Maumee
(419) 891-0109

Smoker's Hub
5813 Monroe St.
Sylvania
(419) 885-6002

Port Royale
3301 W. Central
Toledo
(419) 537-1491

Smoker's Express
5801 Telegraph Rd.
Toledo
(419) 254-7272

Zips Tobacco Outlet
3251 Alexis Rd.
Toledo
(419) 474-6333

....

The Cigar Box
13528 US Hwy. 52
West Portsmouth
(614) 355-1040

Low Joes Discount Tobacco
1334 Rombach Ave.
Wilmington
(937) 382-7383

YOUNGSTOWN & VICINITY

Plaza Book & Smoke Shop
Boardman Plaza,
 Boardman
 Canfield Rd.
Boardman

(330) 726-9493

Girard Book & News
101 N. State St.
Girard
(330) 799-1050

Ohio Cigar
410 Robbins Ave.
Niles
(330) 544-7900

Plaza Book & Smoke Shop
6000 Mahoning
 Ave., Youngstown
(330) 799-1050

Oklahoma

Havana Leaf Tobacco
3322 S. Broadway
Edmond
(405) 330-9478

Dave's Pipe & Tobacco Shop
216 W. Maple St.
Enid
(405) 237-1666

Plantations
3335 W. Main
Norman
(405) 364-5152

Royal Pipe & Tobacco
105 E. Boyd St.
Norman
(405) 364-5151

OKLAHOMA CITY & VICINITY

The Cigar Brokers
12404 SE 15th
Choctaw
(405) 810-8566

A-OK Discount Cigarettes
4517 S.
 Pennsylvania Ave.
Oklahoma City
(405) 681-2288

ABC Tobacco
4508 S. May
Oklahoma City
(405) 685-1716

Jose's Party Stand
10902 N. Penn Ave.
Oklahoma City
(405) 752-7380

Plantations
7000 Crossroads
 Blvd.
Oklahoma City
(405) 631-2511

R & K Cigars
Quail Plaza
 Shopping Center,
 10904-J N. May
 Ave.
Oklahoma City
(405) 752-2772

Tobacco Exchange
French Market Mall,
 2828 NW 63rd
Oklahoma City
(405) 843-1688

The Tobacco Room
7400 N. May Ave.
Oklahoma City
(405) 843-1010

TULSA

Fogue & Bates Inc.
6929 E. 71st St.
Tulsa
(918) 488-0818

Mecca Coffee Company
1143 E. 33rd Place
Tulsa
(918) 749-3509

Park Hill & Villines Cigars
5111-A S. Lewis
Tulsa
(918) 749-2229

Ric's Fine Cigars
1224 N. Lewis
Tulsa
(918) 584-1090

Tobacco Pouch
5800 S. Lewis
Tulsa
(918) 742-1660

Vintage Cigar Company
8929 S. Memorial
Tulsa
(918) 250-8999

Oregon

Island Imports of Ashland
111 E. Main St.
Ashland
(541) 488-3382

Timber Valley Tobaccos
3355 SW Cedar
Hills Blvd.
Beaverton
(503) 644-3837

BEND &
VICINITY

Specialty Cigar
906 NW Harriman
St., Bend
(541) 389-1001

Redmond Smoke & Gift
245 SW 6th
Redmond
(541) 923-6307

Ray's Food Place
500 W. Hwy. 20
Sisters
(541) 549-2222

The Briar Shoppe
278 Valley River
Center
Eugene
(541) 343-4738

Tobacco Outlet
11723 Northeast
Div., Gresham
(503) 661-2290

Pappy's Tobacco Road
910-A N. Coast
Hwy., Newport
(541) 265-8384

PORTLAND & VICINITY

Domestic Gourmet
12044 SE Sunnyside
Rd.
Clackamas
(503) 698-3176

82nd Avenue Tobacco & Pipe
400 SE 82nd Ave.
Portland
(503) 255-9987

Burlingame Grocery
8502 SW Terwillger
Blvd.
Portland
(503) 246-0711

Cascade Cigar & Wine
528 SW Madison
Portland
(503) 790-9045

KC's Tobacco Town
8200 SW Barber
Blvd.
Portland
(503) 774-0858

Liner & Elsen Ltd. Wine
202 NW 21st Ave.
Portland
(503) 241-9463

Paul's Trading Co.
1409 Jantzen Beach
Center, Portland
(503) 283-4924

Pauls Trading Co.
9986 SE Washington
St., Portland
(503) 255-4471

Rich's Cigar Store
801 SW Alder St.
Portland
(503) 228-1700

T Whittaker Tobacco's
1123 Lloyd Center
Portland
(503) 654-4812

The Tobacco Shack
6835 N. Fessenden
Portland
(503) 286-4527

Tinder Box of Oregon
9614 SW
Washington
Square Rd.
Tigard
(503) 639-8776

Sun River Country Store
Sun River Village
Mall, Sun River
(541) 593-8113

Pennsylvania

ALLENTOWN &
VICINITY

G & E Smoke Shop
960 E. Hamilton St.
Allentown
(610) 821-9677

Pat's News
327 S. New St.
Bethlehem
(610) 865-6233

Tinder Box
3926 Linden St.
Bethlehem
(610) 882-9195

Grandfather's Den
1325 Chestnut St.
Emmaus
(610) 967-6254

Nemacolin Woodlands Resorts
Rte. 40 E.
Farmington
(412) 329-6013

Collins Tobacco
205 Lehigh Valley
Mall
Whitehall
(610) 264-7911

Tobacco Village
1225 Schadt Ave.
Whitehall
(610) 434-1555

BUCKS CO. &
VICINITY

Classic Cigar Parlor
12 N. Main St.
Doylestown
(215) 348-2880

Country Food Market
203 W. State St.
Doylestown
(215) 348-8845

A Little Taste of Cuba
102-A S. Main St.
New Hope
(215) 862-1122

Robusto's of New Hope
115 S. Main St.
New Hope
(215) 862-9266

Classic Cigar Parlor
14 S. State St.
Newtown
(215) 860-9442

Neds Cigar Store
4 S. State St.
Newtown
(215) 968-6337

Tobacco Outlet II
201 Station Rd.
Quakertown
(215) 538-3665

El Cabana Cigar
101 Clearview
Circle
Butler
(412) 285 0037

High End Cigars
Rte. 1 at Rte. 100
Chadds Ford
(610) 388-2110

JM Boswell's Pipe & Tobacco
586 Lincoln Way
Chambersburg
(717) 264-1711

GW Pipe Dreams
10 N. 5th Ave.
Clarion
(814) 227-2340

Cigarette Express
20734 Rte. 19
Cranberry Township
(412) 772-7810

Maloney Distributing Inc.
575 Walnut
Danville
(717) 275-2120

The Cigar Shoppe
4525 Henry St.
Easton
(610) 258-3206

The Cigar Shoppe
125-129 N. 3rd St.
Easton
(610) 252-6229

Guiseppe's Fine Tobacco and Coffee House
1210 W. 26th St.
Erie
(814) 459-2554

Top 5 Selections Inc.
3751 W. 26th St.
Erie
(800) 867-3483

Smoke Shop
114 S. Easton Rd.
Glenside
(215) 886-7415

Michael Ashton Tobacco
11 Center Square
Hanover
(717) 632-9004

HARRISBURG & VICINITY

Johnsons Pipe Shop
151 S. Hanover St.
Carlisle
(717) 243-8260

Capital Cigars
3406 Walnut St.
Harrisburg
(717) 657-8020

Little Habana Cigar Shop
881 Eisenhower
Blvd.
Harrisburg
(717) 939-3811

Pipe Den
Harrisburg E Mall
Harrisburg
(717) 564-8425

TGI Fridays
3882 Union Deposit
Rd., Harrisburg
(717) 652-4227

Tinder Box
219 N. 2nd St.
Harrisburg
(717) 232-7166

Tobacco Mart
900 Market St.
Lemoyne
(717) 975-0994

Grand Smoke Shop
231 W. Mine St.
Hazleton
(717) 454-2202

Quik Picks & Paks
218 Laurel Mall
Hazleton
(717) 459-3099

Hershey's Cigar Den
20 Briarcrest Square
Hershey
(717) 520-5944

Ken's Cigar & Tobacco
517 Allegheny St.
Hollidaysburg
(814) 695-6650

Port of Entry
978 Philadelphia St.
Indiana
(412) 465-6778

LANCASTER & VICINITY

Tobacco Palace Inc.
311 Park City
Center
Lancaster
(717) 397-7569

Tobacco Road
154 N. Prince St.
Lancaster
(717) 293-8688

Tobacco World
Crossroads Plaza, Rd.
Mount Pleasant
(412) 547-7166

Wingenroth Pipe Shop
638 Cumberland St.
Lebanon
(717) 273-7727

C + C Cigar Shoppe
115 Market St.
Lewisburg
(717) 523-8017

The Country Boys
624 W. Harford
Milford
(717) 296-5000

Pennsylvania News and Tobacco
Mill Pond Shopping Center, 1-D S. Pennsylvania Ave.
Morrisville
(215) 295-4004

United Cut Rate
19 E. Bridge St.
Morrisville
(215) 295-3835

PHILADELPHIA & VICINITY

Tinder Box
3 Bala Plaza E.
Bala-Cynwyd
(800) 846-3372

Keystone News
2854 Street Rd.
Bensalem
(215) 638-3605

Tobacco Country
107 Neshaminy Mall
Bensalem
(215) 357-6615

The Smoking Stogie
610 Lancaster Ave.
Berwyn
(610) 725-1777

J M Cigars
27 Marchwood Rd.
Exton
(610) 363-3063

Burdicks Hatboro News
206 S. York Rd.
Hatboro
(215) 675-9960

Claude's Cigars
59 S. York Rd.
Hatboro
(215) 672-6642

Hatboro Beverages
201 Jacksonville Rd.
Hatboro
(215) 675-1078

Kathie's Smoke Shop
106 Maple Ave.
Hatboro
(215) 675-0259

Rebel Valley Cigar Superstars
542 Lancaster Ave.
Haverford
(610) 581-7665

Tinder Box
391 W. Lancaster Ave., Haverford
(610) 896-4511

Widmers Tobacco Shop
Macdade Mall
Holmes
(610) 586-3857

Rebel Valley Cigar Superstores
537 Easton Racks
Horsham
(215) 328-0500

Tinder Box
Marketplace Huntington Valley, 2082 County Line Rd.
Huntington Valley
(215) 396-1982

School House Cigar
2118 W. Main St.
Jeffersonville
(610) 630-6300

Ye Olde Tobacco Barrell
King of Prussia Plaza
King of Prussia
(610) 265-4544

CB Perkins
Oxford Valley Mall, 2300 E. Lincoln Hwy.
Langhorne
(215) 750-1775

Mainly Cigars
4335 Main St.
Manayunk
(215) 508-1111

Glen Center Pharmacy
Genuardis Shopping Center, 1969 Norristown Rd.
Maple Glen
(215) 643-2880

CB Perkins
Granite Run Mall, 1067 W. Baltimore Pike, Media
(610) 627-1472

Rose's Newsstand
117 S. Olive
Media
(610) 565-9015

Prime Cigars
822 Montgomery Ave.
Narberth
(888) PRIME-79

Black Horse Cigars
1515 Ridge Pike
Norristown
(610) 279-7676

Hill Crest Tobacco
120 W. Germantown Pike
Norristown
(610) 279-8610

Black Cat Cigar Company
1518 Sansom St.
Philadelphia
(215) 563-9850

Chestnut Smoke Shop
27 S. 8th St.
Philadelphia
(215) 923-1699

City Cigars
2417 S. 11th St.
Philadelphia
(215) 551-3662

Harry's Smoke Shop
15 N. 3rd St.
Philadelphia
(215) 925-4770

Holts
12270 Townsend Rd.
Philadelphia
(215) 676-8778

Max's Tobacconists The Pipe Rack
8433-C Germantown Ave.
Philadelphia
(215) 242-3625

McKeown's
Beverage Company
Inc.
6828-58 Rising Sun
Ave., Philadelphia
(215) 342-6677

Philadelphia Cigar
& Tobacco
2506 Welsh Rd.
Philadelphia
(215) 464-1810

Silver Star Casino
Hwy. 16 W.
Philadelphia
(800) 922-9988

Smokin-Java
524 S. 3rd St.
Philadelphia
(215) 440-0776

Tinder Box
International
12027 Elmore Rd.
Philadelphia
(215) 632-2729

Tobacco Village
North East Plaza,
7300 Bustleton
Ave.
Philadelphia
(215) 745-7040

Gentleman's
Quarters Tobacco
and Gifts
1149 Lancaster Ave.
Rosemont
(610) 525-5127

Cigars Unlimited
1004 Bethlehem
Pike
Spring House
(215) 295-3835

Gateway Smoke
Shop
269 E. Swedesford
Rd., Wayne
(610) 971-2500

PITTSBURGH &
VICINITY

Tobacco World
638-B Rostraver Rd.
Belle Vernon
(412) 930-0112

Tobacco World
Gabriel Brothers
Plaza, 160 Finley
Rd., Belle Vernon
(412) 930-0112

Jernigan's Tobacco
Village
Westmoreland Mall
Greensburg
(412) 838-1090

Big Dog Cigars
140 Main St.
Imperial
(412) 695-2994

Holy Smoke
2603 Leechburg Rd.
Lower Burrell
(724) 334-6665

Leaf And Bean
3525 Washington
Rd., McMurray
(412) 942-6670

Migliore's Hardware
627 Midland Ave.
Midland
(412) 643-8122

Frank Jernigan
Tobacco Village
147 Monroeville
Mall, Monroeville
(412) 372-4114

Tobacco Barn
1771 Golden Mile
Hwy., Monroeville
(412) 733-5405

Bower Hill Cigar
Shop
1121 Bowere Hill
Rd., Mount
Lebanon
(412) 278-4457

Plaza News Plus
1901 Lincoln Hwy.
North Versailles
(412) 824-6999

Allegheny
Smokeworks
318 Freeport Rd.
Pittsburgh
(412) 828-6653

Bloom Cigar
Company
54 S. 12th St.
Pittsburgh
(412) 431-4277

Darla's Coffee
House
8501 Perry Hwy.
Pittsburgh
(412) 367-8151

Jernigan's Tobacco
Village
1500 Washington
Rd., 2501 The
Galleria
Pittsburgh
(800) 554-8952

Market Street Cigar
Shoppe
107 Market St.
Pittsburgh
(412) 338-CGAR

Old Allegheny
Shoppe
613 Caste Village
Shopping Center
Pittsburgh
(412) 881-6969

Pittsburgh Cigar
Company
8623 Old Perry Hwy.
Pittsburgh
(412) 635-7784

Poor Richards
Freight House
Shops, Station Sq.
Pittsburgh
(412) 281-1133

R & R Cigar
345 Butler St.
Pittsburgh
(412) 781-1077

Uncle Mike's Cigar
Heaven
1102 Northway Mall
Pittsburgh
(412) 367-SMOKE

The Smoke Shop
Franklin Mall
Washington
(412) 228-3266

Tinder Box
Century III Mall,
3075 Clairton Rd.
West Mifflin
(412) 653-1177

La Habana Cabana
1985 Lincoln Way
White Oak
(412) 664-6002

POTTSTOWN &
VICINITY

Cigar Haven
Trappe Shop Center,
130 W. Main St.
Collegville
(610) 970-1437

Cole Tobaccoland
213 High St.
Pottstown
(610) 323-6060

READING &
VICINITY

**Kensington
Tobacconist**
600 Penn Ave.
West Reading
(610) 373-5001

Tobacco Land
Berkshire Mall
Wyomissing
(610) 372-6571

SCRANTON &
VICINITY

Dunmore Cigar
622 E. Drinker St.
Dunmore
(717) 344-9721

**Up In Smoke
Tobacco & More**
766 E. Drinker St.
Dunmore
(717) 341-5448

**Discount Tobacco
Shop**
1129 Main St.
Peckville
(717) 383-6944

Markowitz Brothers
256 Wyoming Ave.
Scranton
(717) 342-0315

Montage Tobacco
632 Davis St.
Scranton
(717) 342-3388

Sunshine News
546 Spruce St.
Scranton
(717) 347-4337

Pete's News Plus
Rear 59 E. Tioga St.
Tunkhannock
(717) 836-7001

**Smokin Joes
Tobacco Inc.**
270 W. Roosevelt
Hwy., Waymart
(717) 282-9085

Hot Tropix
103 Shenango St.
Sharpsville
(412) 962-4811

The Cigar Shop
231 E. Beaver Ave.
State College
(814) 231-0828

Tobacco World
72 Lebanon Ave.
Uniontown
(412) 438-3534

WILKES-BARRE
& VICINITY

**Back Mountain
Tobacco**
324 Memorial Hwy.
Dallas
(717) 675-2663

Plaza Smoke Shop
190 S. Wyoming
Ave., Kingston
(717) 287-4478

Smoke Signals
120 S. River St.
Plains
(717) 822-5058

El Humidor
525 Scott St.
Wilkes-Barre
(717) 822-3544

Leo Matus
46 Public Sq.
Wilkes-Barre
(717) 822-3613

Tobacco Center
21 W. Church St.
Williamsport
(717) 322-7766

YORK

Cigar World
3400 Eastern Blvd.
York
(717) 840-1716

Custom Blends
2559 S. Queen St.
York
(717) 741-4972

Franklin Steven's Jeweler
180 Memory Lane
York
(717) 757-6075

Hains Pipe Shop
225 S. George St.
York
(717) 843-2237

Rhode Island

Bag Piper Smoke Shoppe
8A Pier Market
 Plaza
Narragansett
(401) 783-0555

NEWPORT & VICINITY

Humidor
182 Thames St.
Newport
(401) 842-0270

Seagar
400 Thames St.
Newport
(401) 846-6365

Wellington Square Liquor
580 Thames St.
Newport
(800) 898-WINE

Allen Wine & Spirits
3001 E. Main Rd.
Portsmouth
(401) 683-4030

PROVIDENCE & VICINITY

Jolly Roger's Smoke Shop
230-D Waseca Ave.
Barrington
(401) 245-9393

Humidor
1500 Oaklawn Ave.
Cranston
(401) 463-5949

Barbato & Sons Candy Company
65 Newport Ave.
East Providence
(401) 434-3004

Dapper Dave's Smoke Shop
1465 Atwood Ave.
Johnston
(401) 751-8499

Mr. Cigar
1622 Mineral Spring
 Ave.
North Providence
(401) 353-5200

Headlines
270 Wickenden St.
Providence
(401) 274-6397

Red Carpet Smoke Shop
108½ Waterman St.
Providence
(401) 421-4499

Sir Winston's Tobacco Emporium
341 S. Main St.
Providence
(401) 861-5700

Town Wine & Spirits
179 Newport Ave.
Rumford
(401) 434-4563

WARWICK & VICINITY

Cigar Box Ltd.
164 Main St.
East Greenwich
(401) 886-5555

Regency Cigar Emporium
752 Main St.
East Greenwich
(401) 884-7665

Thorpes Discount Liquors Wines & Spirits
609 Main St.
East Greenwich
(401) 885-4485

Joyal's Liquors
90 W. Warwick Ave.
West Warwick
(401) 822-0536

Up In Smoke
116 Granite Center
Westerly
(401) 348-0534

South Carolina

Pipe Dreams
Aiken Mall, 2441
 Whiskey Rd. S.
Aiken
(803) 642-0080

Piedmont Tobacco Company
3300 N. Main St.
Anderson
(864) 224-4004

CHARLESTON & VICINITY

The Smoking Lamp
197 E. Bay St.
Charleston
(803) 577-7339

Tinder Box International
177 Meeting St.
Charleston
(803) 853-3720

Tobaccos, Teas & Spirits
364 King St.
Charleston
(803) 853-3513

Harris Teeter
920 Houston N.
 Cutt Blvd.
Mount Pleasant
(803) 881-1983

Smoky's Tobacco Shop
5720 Northwoods
 Mall
North Charleston
(803) 553-4447

COLUMBIA

4 Morganelli's Inc.
3155 Forest Dr.
Columbia
(803) 787-5651

The Cigar Box
100 Columbiana
Circle
Columbia
(803) 749-4341

Gourmet Shop
724 Saluda Ave.
Columbia
(803) 799-9463

Groff Jewelers
107 Harbison Blvd.
Columbia
(803) 781-6905

Intermezzo
2015 Devine St.
Columbia
(803) 799- 2276

**The Tobacco
Merchant**
278-K Harbison
Blvd., Columbia
(803) 749-5499

Boda Pipes
McAllister Square
Mall, 225 S.
Pleasantburg
Greenville
(864) 242-1545

Harris Teeter
Roper Mountain Rd.
Greenville
(864) 987-9103

**Martine Specialty
Beer**
580 Bypass 72 NW
Greenwood
(864) 227-1170

MYRTLE BEACH & VICINITY

Tinder Box
2501 N. Kings Hwy.
Myrtle Beach
(803) 272-2336

Tinder Box
10177 N. Kings
Hwy.
Myrtle Beach
(803) 272-2336

Tinder Box
Broadway at The
Beach
Myrtle Beach
(803) 444-5690

Cigar Company
4914 Hwy. 17 S.
North Myrtle Beach
(803) 361-9666

Nick's Cigar World
2705 Hwy. 17 S.
North Myrtle Beach
(803) 361-8266

**Buchanan Tobacco
Shop**
The Litchfield
Exchange, Hwy. 17
S., Pawleys Island
(803) 237-5416

General Store
1985 E. Main
Spartanburg
(864) 585-6328

**The Tobacco
Merchant**
1600 Reidville Rd.
Spartanburg
(864) 587-1566

South Dakota

Doc James Tobacco
668 Main St.
Deadwood
(605) 578-1969

Tobacco Warehouse
1937 Dakota Ave. S.
Huron
(605) 353-1296

Tobacco Warehouse
4901 N. Main
Mitchell
(605) 996-0031

Miller Liquors
101 Military Rd.
North Sioux City
(605) 232-4616

Tobacco Warehouse
680-B N. Lacross
Rapid City
(605) 343-7742

**Eastwold
Smokeshop**
112 E. 10th St.
Sioux Falls
(605) 334-3418

**Tobacco Road
Smoke Shop**
901 Broadway
Yankton
(605) 665-7057

Tennessee

Tobacco Harbor
3051 Kirby Whitten
Bartlett
(901) 382-8266

CHATTANOOGA

**Beer and Wine
Maker Shops**
2336 Frazier Ave.
Chattanooga
(423) 267-2337

**Chattanooga
Billards Club**
110 Jordan Dr.
Chattanooga
(423) 499-3883

Tinder Box
Hamilton Place
Mall, 2100
Hamilton Place
Blvd.
Chattanooga
(423) 894-7843

Tobacco Mart
4011 C-3 Brainerd
Rd., Chattanooga
(423) 493-9056

Briar & Bean
Governors Square,
2801 Wilma
Rudolph Blvd.
Clarksville
(615) 552-6465

**Colonial Country
Club**
2736 Countrywood
Pkwy., Cordova
(901) 388-6150

The Memphis Cigar Company
680-46 Germantown Pkwy.
Cordova
(901) 624-5400

Fred Stokers & Sons Inc.
3846 Sharon Hwy. 89, Dresden
(901) 364-5419

L & J Discount Tobacco Outlet
2608 W. Market St.
Johnson City
(423) 975-6911

Shamrock Beverage & Tobacco
300 W. Walnut St.
Johnson City
(423) 926-8511

KNOXVILLE & VICINITY

The Gatlin-Burlier Tobacconist
603 Skyline Dr.
Gatlinburg
(615) 436-9177

Jim's Pipes & Gifts
6925-B Maynardville Hwy.
Knoxville
(423) 922-3914

Smokin Joes
6110 Papermill Rd.
Knoxville
(423) 584-9010

Smoking Joes
5236 Broadway
Knoxville
(423) 281-2002

Smokys Pipe & Tobacco & Cigars
143 Montvue Center
Knoxville
(423) 693-8371

W.A. Stogies
508 Lovell Rd.
Knoxville
(423) 671-4630

Panther Pipe Shop
1937 S. Economy Rd., Morristown
(423) 581-7473

S & W Cigars
3145 Parkway
Pigeon Forge
(423) 453-4741

The Cigar Club
21-48 N. Gallatin Rd., Madison
(615) 859-2425

The Smoke Shop
1011 S. Gallatin Pike, Madison
(615) 860-8253

MEMPHIS & VICINITY

Cigar Depot
3133 Forest Hill, Irene Rd.
Germantown
(901) 755-7279

Lansky Brothers
92 S. Front St.
Memphis
(901) 525-5401

The Memphis Cigar Company
7859 Farmington Blvd., Memphis
(901) 758-2535

Select Smoke Shop
5043 Park Ave.
Memphis
(901) 685-7788

The Smoke Shop
4770 Poplar Ave.
Memphis
(901) 335-6664

Tinder Box
2760 N. Germantown Pkwy., Memphis
(888) 6-STOGIE

Tinder Box
4477 Mall of Memphis
Memphis
(901) 795-0360

The Tobacco Bowl
152 Madison Ave.
Memphis
(901) 525-2310

Tobacco Corner Limited
669 S. Mendenhall
Memphis
(901) 682-3326

Wizards
2025 Madison Ave.
Memphis
(901) 726-6843

Three Ten Pipe Shop
109 E. Main St.
Murfreesboro

(615) 893-3100

NASHVILLE & VICINITY

Uptown's Smoke Shop
1745 Galleria Blvd.
Franklin
(615) 771-7027

Bluegrass Beverages
555 E. Main St.
Hendersonville
(615) 824-3437

Arcade Smoke Shop
11 Arcade
Nashville
(615) 726-8031

Discount Tobacco
2501 Lebanon Rd.
Nashville
(615) 889-1321

Midtown Beverages & More
1608 Church St.
Nashville
(615) 327- 3874

Mosko's Inc.
2204 Elliston Place
Nashville
(615) 321-3377

Smoke Depot
563 Stewart Ferry Pike, Nashville
(615) 391-4171

Uptown's Smoke Shop
3900 Hillsboro Rd.
Nashville
(615) 292-6866

H & W Tobacco
119 Main St.
Parsons
(901) 847-3454

Texas

**Cowan Pipe &
Tobacco**
Wolftin Sq. N., 2497
I-40 W.
Amarillo
(806) 355-2821

The Smoke Shop
2201 S. Western A
Amarillo
(806) 353-6331

AUSTIN &
VICINITY

BR News
3208 Guadalupe
Austin
(512) 454-9110

Cedar Valley Liquor
12009 Hwy. 290 W.
Austin
(512) 288-4937

Cigar Palace
121 W. 8th St.
Austin
(512) 472-2277

Heroes & Legacies
3663 Bee Caves Rd.
Austin
(512) 306-8200

Heroes & Legacies
10000 Research
Blvd., Austin
(512) 343-6600

**Hill Country Wine
& Spirits**
701 Capitol of Texas
Austin
(512) 347-1299

Pipe World
2160 Highland Mall
Austin
(512) 451-3713

Pipe World
2525 W. Anderson
Lane, Austin
(512) 451-5347

Planet K Cigars
9411 N. IH-35
Austin
(512) 837-5337

**Reuben's Wine &
Spirits**
11637 Research
Blvd., Austin
(512) 345-2866

Texas Tobacconist
115-T E. 6th
Austin
(512) 479-8741

Wiggy's
1130 W. 6th
Austin
(512) 474-9463

Smoker's Discount
605 S. Bell Blvd.
Cedar Park
(512) 331-9474

Butch Hoffer
136 Parkdale
Beaumont
(409) 892-9311

The Cigar Stop
2370-1 North Expy.
Brownsville
(956) 544-6044

J.J.'s Package Stores
1219 N. Texas Ave.
Bryan
(409) 822-1042

**Little Havana Cigar
Company**
3100 Briarcrest
Bryan
(409) 776-7600

Mr. Smoke's
114 Truly Plaza
Cleveland
(281) 592-8586

J.J.'s Package Stores
1600 Texas Ave. S.
College Station
(409) 260-2068

Tobacco World
1220 Airline Rd.
Corpus Christi
(512) 992-4427

D's Pipes Etc.
200n 15th St.
Corsicana
(903) 874-8661

DALLAS &
VICINITY

Centennial Liquor
15055 Inward Rd.
Addison

Chilly Mart
14885 Inwood
Addison
(972) 991-6304

Cigar Shop & More
4285 Beltline Rd.
Addison
(972) 661-9136

Red Coleman's
14733 Inwood Rd.
Addison
(214) 233-8967

Sigel's
15003 Inwood Rd.
Addison
(972) 387-9873

Cigarettes For Less
801 S. Greenville
Ave., Allen
(972) 727-6824

Centennial Liquors
1827 W.
Mockingbird Lane
Dallas
(214) 630-5004

Centennial Liquors
400 Medallion
Center, Dallas
(214) 692-7609

Centennial Liquors
5709 W. Lovers Lane
Dallas
(214) 352-4161

Centennial Liquors
8123 Preston Rd.
Dallas
(214) 361-6697

Centennial Liquors
101 Turtle Creek
Village
Dallas
(214) 520-0645

Centennial Liquors
1600 W. Northwest
Hwy., Dallas
(972) 556-0637

Centennial Liquors
2271 W. Northwest
Hwy., Dallas
(214) 350-0061

Centennial Liquors
6312 La Vista Dr.
Dallas
(214) 821-6294

Edward's Pipe &
Cigar
15757 Coit Rd.
Dallas
(214) 774-1655

Golden Leaf
Tobacco
2932 Main St.
Dallas
(214) 741-5700

Lone Star Cigars,
Inc.
1302 Elm St.
Dallas
(214) 74-SMOKE

Lone Star Cigars,
Inc.
13305 Montfort Dr.
Dallas
(214) 392-4427

Magdalena Cigar
Company Inc.
2820 Greenville
Ave., Dallas
(214) 826-8101

Marty's
3316 Oak Lawn
Dallas
(214) 526-0900

Midway Drive In
318 Cadiz, Dallas
(214) 428-2077

Midway Liquor
316 Cadiz, Dallas
(214) 565-9287

Nicole's Tobacco
Shop
3611-A Greenville
Ave., Dallas
(214) 821-3740

Orvis
Preston Oaks
Shopping Court,
10720 Preston Rd.
Dallas
(214) 265-1600

Pipe Dream Cigar
& Tobacco
7728 S. Loop 12
Dallas
(214) 398-8056

Pipe Dream Cigar
& Tobacco
4706 Maple Ave.
Dallas
(214) 520-8000

Pipe Dream Cigar
& Tobacco
2416 W. Ledbetter
Dallas
(214) 339-7977

Pipe Dream Cigar
& Tobacco
1921 Greenville
Ave., Dallas
(214) 827-0519

Pogo's Wine &
Spirits
Inwood Village
Shopping Center,
5360 W. Lovers
Lane, Dallas
(214) 350-8989

Red Coleman's
2030 Empire Central
Dallas
(214) 350-4300

Red Coleman's
7560 Greenville
Ave., Dallas
(214) 363-0201

Red Coleman's
2131 W. NW Hwy.
Dallas
(214) 556-1611

Servi Cigar Inc.
3840 W. Northwest
Hwy.
Dallas
(214) 350-1496

Sigel's
2960 Anode Lane
Dallas
(214) 350-1271

Sigel's
5757 Greenville
Ave., Dallas
(214) 739-4012

Sigel's
506 S. Industrial
Dallas
(214) 748-1866

Sigel's
5636 Lemmon (at
Inwood)
Dallas
(214) 352-2291

Sigel's
6750 Abrams Rd.
Dallas
(214) 343-4399

Sigel's
1441 W.
Mockingbird
Dallas
(214) 637-3616

Sir Elliot's Tobacco
18101 Preston Rd.
Dallas
(214) 250-4650

Tobacco Club Inc.
4043 Trinity Mills
Rd., Dallas
(972) 306-2880

Tobacco Gallery
8453 Kate St.
Dallas
(214) 692-9214

Tobacco Lane
Preston Wood Mall,
5301 Belt Line Rd.
Dallas
(972) 239-1521

Up In Smoke
534 N. Park Mall
Dallas
(214) 368-0433

Up In Smoke
2032 Valley View
Center
Dallas
(214) 934-3618

Tobacco Lane
Northeast Mall
Hurst
(817) 284-7251

**A Carousel of
Flowers, Gifts &
Tobacco**
2450 N. Beltline
Irving
(972) 255-2850

Granada Market
387 E. Las Colinas
Blvd., Irving
(972) 830-8445

**Up in Smoke/
Tobacco Lane**
3621 Irving Mall
Irving
(972) 255-8812

Tobacco Club
1705 W. University
McKinney
(972) 562-2500

Sir Elliot's Tobacco
2176 Town East
Mall
Mesquite
(972) 681-4959

Beverage City
1100 Preston Rd.
Plano
(972) 964-8660

Black Tack
3115 Parker Rd.
Plano
(972) 596-2505

Bon Viviant Market
1801 Preston Rd.
Plano
(972) 818-1177

Chilly Mart
540 Centennial
Richardson
(972) 699-3999

Oasis Liquors
538 Centennial
Richardson
(972) 705-9800

Sigel's
909 Abrams
Richardson
(972) 480-8484

Tobacco Town
800 E. Arapaho Rd.
Richardson
(972) 231-4454

Chilly Mart
2335 Interstate 30
Rockwall
(972) 771-4127

Sigel's
2325 E. Interstate 30
Rockwall
(972) 771-0385

EL PASO

**Airline
International
Luggage & Gifts**
Southern Park Mall
El Paso
(915) 833-9960

Cigar Gallery
6310 N. Mesa A-3
El Paso
(915) 587-7657

Pipes & Gifts
6254 Edgemere
El Paso
(915) 778-5950

Tobacco Tin
Sunland Park Mall,
750 Sunland Park
Dr., El Paso
(915) 584-0945

FORT WORTH &
VICINITY

**Pipe Dream Cigar
& Tobacco**
1308 S. Cooper St.
Arlington
(817) 469-8986

Tobacco Lane
2911 E. Division St.
Arlington
(817) 640-3210

Tobacco Lane
Parks Mall, 3811 S.
Cooper
Arlington
(817) 784-0022

**Baxters Gourmet
Marketplace**
5604 Colleyville
Blvd.
Colleyville
(817) 498-2675

Majestic Liquors
4520 Camp Bowie
Fort Worth
(817) 731-0634

Majestic Liquors
6801 Randol Mill
Rd., Fort Worth
(817) 451-8011

Majestic Liquors
5600 E. I-20
Fort Worth
(817) 478-2661

Majestic Market
1111 Jacksboro Hwy.
Fort Worth
(817) 335-5252

Puff-n-Stuff
4800 S. Hullen
Fort Worth
(817) 294-0600

Ronnie's
2701 S. Hulen
Fort Worth
(817) 927-0101

Strand Market
215 Tremont
Galveston
(409) 763-5177

HOUSTON &
VICINITY

**Texana Cigar
Company**
730 Main
Chappell Hill
(888) 845-0853

Mr. Smoke's
1029 N. Loop
Conroe
(409) 760-2727

**Richard's Fine
Cigars and More**
2506 Center St.
Deer Park
(281) 476-4590

#10 Downing Street
2549 Kirby
Houston
(713) 523-2290

**Alfred Dunhill
Limited**
Galleria II, 5085
    Westheimer Rd.
Houston
(713) 961-4661

**Antique Pipe
Shoppe**
6366 Richmond
    Ave., Houston
(800) 925-2442

**Bobalu's Cigar
Company**
2146 Portsmouth
Houston
(713) 520-8373

The Briar Shoppe
2412 Times Blvd.
Houston
(713) 529-6347

**Churchill &
Company**
2727 Kirby Dr.
Houston
(713) 523-4574

**Cigars Pipes &
More**
14520 Memorial Dr.
Houston
(713) 493-9196

Copperfield Liquor
12850 Memorial Dr.
Houston
(713) 461-6242

**Greenway Pipe &
Tobacco**
5 Greenway Plaza E.,
Houston
(713) 626-1613

**Hearthstone
Tobacco Mart**
6176 N. Hwy. 6
Houston
(713) 345-9199

**Jeffery Stone
Limited**
5000 Westheimer
    Rd., Houston
(713) 621-2812

**Jeffrey Stone
Limited**
9694 Westheimer
    Rd., Houston
(713) 783-3555

Lone Star Tobacco
3741 FM 1960 W.
Houston
(713) 444-2464

**Mandalas
Warehouse Liquors**
4310 Richmond
Houston
(713) 621-5314

**McCoy's Fine
Cigars & Tobacco**
1201 Louisiana
Houston
(713) 739-8110

Orvis
5858 Westheimer
    Rd., Houston
(713) 783-2111

Paradise Gift Store
1200 McKinney
Houston
(713) 650-8708

Paradise Gift II
600 Travis
Houston
(713) 228-7818

**Richards Liquor &
Fine Wines**
1701 Brun
Houston
(713) 529-6266

**Richmond Avenue
Cigar**
3301 Fondren Rd.
Houston
(713) 975-9057

**Self Indulgence
Cigar Company**
710 N. Post Oak Rd.
Houston
(713) 957-2100

Smoke Inn
9435 Jones Rd.
Houston
(281) 807-7500

The Smoke Ring
17050 Hwy. 3
Houston
(713) 332-9871

Spec's Warehouse
2410 Smith St.
Houston
(713) 526-8787

Tobacco Depot
22446 State Hwy.
  249, Houston
(281) 379-2776

Tobacco Habana
6513-B Westheimer
Houston
(713) 266-5508

Atascocita Liquors
5311 FM 1960 E.
Humble
(713) 852-4845

Magnolia Foods
619 Magnolia Blvd.
Magnolia
(409) 356-2700

Stogies
606 Long View
Sugar Land
(281) 242-4525

**The Beverage
Shoppe**
4775 W. Panther
  Creek
The Woodlands
(713) 363-9463

The Cigar Firm
503 El Dorado
Webster
(281) 488-4778

Cigar Box
2501 S. W.S. Young
  Dr., Killeen
(817) 526-6811

Tobacco Tin
Brazos Mall
Lake Jackson
(409) 297-5771

Up In Smoke
2086 Vista Ridge
  Mall
Lewisville
(214) 315-1300

R & R Tobacco
612 W. Marshall
Longview
(903) 236-9905

LUBBOCK

Elwood Cigars
1113A University
  Ave., Lubbock
(806) 762-2442

Smokers Haven
1915 19th St.
Lubbock
(806) 744-0017

Smokers Haven
S. Plains Mall, 6002
  Slide Rd.
Lubbock
(806) 799-2489

MCALLEN

Casa Petrides
222 S. Broadway
McAllen
(956) 631-5219

Galliden
2403 N. 10th
McAllen
(956) 618-3374

Smokers Island
1226 North St.
Nacogdoches
(409) 560-0611

**Seazar's Fine Wine
& Spirits**
651 S. Walnut
New Braunfels
(210) 829-7151

Tobacco Haus
180 W. San Antonio
  St., New Braunfels
(210) 620-7473

Mr. Smoke's
Lot 4 FM 1485 W.
New Caney
(281) 689-7094

Colonel's Pipe Shop
3544 Knickerbocker
  Rd., San Angelo
(915) 944-3322

**Discount Tobacco
Shop**
3304 Knickerbocker
  Rd., San Angelo
(915) 947-8350

**SAN ANTONIO
& VICINITY**

The Cigar Club
17115 Fawn Brook
  Dr., San Antonio
(210) 805-8580

**Cigars Solamente
Club**
205 N. Presa
San Antonio
(210) 227-3377

Club Humidor
11745 IH-10 W.
San Antonio
(210) 558-7700

Gabriel's
4445 Walzem Rd.
San Antonio
(210) 655-3966

The Humidor
6900 San Pedro
San Antonio
(210) 824-1209

The Humidor
112 N. Star Mall
San Antonio
(210) 308-8545

The Humidor
204-J Alamo Plaza
San Antonio
(210) 472-2875

**Joe Saglibeni Fine
Wine**
638 W. Rhapsody
San Antonio
(210) 349-5149

Latin Gold
Rivercenter Mall,
  849 E. Commerce
San Antonio
(800) 496-3814

**Megusta Cigar
Company**
4714 Broadway
San Antonio
(210) 732-4427

**Mike's Beverage
Warehouse**
14906 Jones-
  Maltsberger
San Antonio
(210) 829-7151

Seazar's Fine Wine & Spirits
6422 N. New
Braunfels
San Antonio
(210) 822-6094

Seazar's Fine Wine & Spirits
16625 Huebner Rd.
San Antonio
(479) 0315-

Swig Martini Bar
111 W. Crockett
San Antonio
(210) 476-0005

Aroma's
4936 Windsor Hill
Windcrest
(210) 590-1802

Hill Country Humidor
122 N. LBJ
San Marcos
(512) 396-7473

Tobacco Gallery
4800 N. Parkway
Sherman
(903) 892-8854

Market Wine & Spirit
110 N. IH 35
Sound Rock
(512) 310-0486

Tobacco Junction
1330 SW HK
Dodgen Loop
Tempo
(254) 742-1160

Dale's House of Cigars
1214 Main St.
Texarkana
(903) 793-3274

Don's Humidor
1412 N. Valley Mills
Dr., Waco
(817) 772-3919

Cigars & Tobacco Etc.
4208 Kemp Blvd.
Wichita Falls
(817) 691-2347

Zach's Classic Cigars
310 Wimberly Sq.
Wimberly
(512) 847-1296

Utah

Tobacco Products International
4227 S. Highland
Dr., Holladay
(801) 278-8508

Tinder Box
Fashion Place Mall,
6191 S. State
Murray
(801) 268-1321

Crawford-Bennett Trading
419 Main St.
Park City
(801) 649-0101

Jeanie's Smoke Shop
156 S. State St.
Salt Lake City
(801) 322-2817

Knuckleheads Tobacco & Gifts
443 E. 4th S.
Salt Lake City
(801) 533-0199

Tinder Box
2A26 Crossroads
Plaza, 50 S. Main
St., Salt Lake City
(801) 355-7336

Vermont

Smoker's Den & Discount Beverage Center
214 Hunt St.
Bennington
(802) 442-2861

BURLINGTON & VICINITY

Garcia Tobacco Shop
Burlington Square
Mall
Burlington
(802) 658-5737

Lilydale Inc
1350 Shelburne Rd.
South Burlington
(802) 658-5896

Orvis
Historic Rte. 7A
Manchester
(802) 362-3750

Middlebury Tobacco & News Emporium
3 Court St.
Middlebury
(802) 388-2442

Fired Up
3 Sterling Hill Rd.
South Barre
(802) 476-4700

Discount Beverage
157 Marlboro Rd.
West Brattleboro
(802) 254-4950

The Hermitage
457-B Cold Brook
Rd., Wilmington
(802) 464-3511

Virginia

ALEXANDRIA

Bostetter's Wine & Gourmet
3690-J King St.
Alexandria
(703) 820-8600

Cigar Club International
2869 Duke St.
Alexandria
(703) 823-2234

Cigar Palace
4711-A Eisenhower
Ave.
Alexandria
(703) 751-6444

John Crouch Tobacconist
215 King St.
Alexandria
(703) 548-2900

Total Beverage
Landmark Plaza,
  6240 Little River
  Tpke.
Alexandria
(703) 941-1133

ARLINGTON &
VICINITY

**Automobilliards
Corp**
4000 Fairfax
Arlington
(703) 807-0091

The Cigar Vault
1500 Wilson Blvd.
Arlington
(703) 276-7225

Tobacco Barns
Fashion Centre
  Pentagon City,
  1200 S. Hayes St.
Arlington
(703) 415-5554

Brewtopia
Centreville Square
  Shopping Center
Centreville
(703) 830-0300

The Cigar Vault
Centreville Sq.
  Shopping Center,
  14011-B St.
  Germain Dr.
Centreville
(703) 968-9102

Total Beverage
Greenbriar Twin
  Center, 13055-C
  Lee Jackson Hwy.
Chantilly
(703) 817-1177

**Havana Cigar Chest
Co.**
3920 Fairview Dr.
Fairfax
(800) 709-2289

**John B. Hayes
Tobacconist**
11755-l Fair Oaks
  Mall, Fairfax
(703) 385-3033

Tobacco Barns
6208-K Leesburg
  Pike, Falls Church
(703) 536-5588

The Wine Seller
9912-C Georgetown
  Pike, Great Falls
(703) 759-0430

Wine Seller
304 Elden St.
Herndon
(703) 471-9649

The Cigar Club
1774-U
 International Dr.
McLean
(703) 734-4303

**Georgetown
Tobacco**
Tysons Corner
 Center
McLean
(703) 893-3366

**The Ritz-Carlton -
Gift Shop**
1700 Tysons Blvd.
McLean
(703) 506-4300

The Cigar Vault
Concord Shopping
 Center, 6127-D
 Backlick Rd.
Springfield
(703) 644-9442

Tobacco Barns
6568 Springfield
 Mall
Springfield
(703) 971-1933

Orvis
8334-A Leesburg
 Park, Vienna
(703) 556-8634

**Side Track Tobacco
Shop**
300 Randall St.
 Expy., Bristol
(540) 466-8450

**Artesanias
Mexicanas
Carmelita's**
316 E. Main St.

Charlottesville
(804) 979-0936

Tobacconist & Gift
214 Zan Rd.
Charlottesville
(804) 973-9065

Tobacco Barns
2745 Metro Plaza
Dale City
(703) 492-2260

Tobacco Barns
2626 Riverside Dr.
Danville
(804) 797-9055

**Fredericksburg
News & Tobacco**
719-A Caroline St.
Fredericksburg
(540) 371-3715

The Tobacco Bar
Westwood Center,
 1915 Plank Rd.
Fredericksburg
(540) 373-4533

**Grundy Tobacco
Company**
Rte. 460, E. Main St.
Grundy
(540) 935-5576

**Radisson Hotel
Hampton**
700 Settlers Landing
 Rd., Hampton
(757) 727-9700

The Smoke House
47 E. Queensway
Hampton
(757) 722-4185

Peace Pipe Inc.
Dukes Plaza, 2193 S.
 Main St.
Harrisonburg
(540) 433-7473

**Leesburg Emporium
& Smoke Shop**
205 Harrison St. SE
Leesburg
(703) 777-5557

**Washington Street
Purveyors**
9 E. Washington St.
Lexington
(540) 464-9463

MANASSAS &
VICINITY

Tobacco Barns
Manassas Mall, 8300
 Sudley Rd.
Manassas
(703) 330-9753

The Grapevine
389 W. Shirley Ave.
Warrenton
(540) 349-4443

**Olde Towne
Tobacco**
Stone Cellar, 29
 Main St.
Warrenton
(540) 341-7600

The Smokehouse
14 Bridge St.
Martinsville
(540) 638-3619

**Smokehouse of
Middleburg**
4 N. Madison St.
Middleburg
(540) 687-8787

NORFOLK &
VICINITY

**Emerson's of
Norfolk**
124-A Crossways
 Shopping Center
1412 Greenbriar
 Pkwy.
Chesapeake
(757) 424-1665

Harris Teeter
Greenbriar Market,
 1216 Greenbriar
 Pkwy.
Chesapeake
(757) 382-7300

**Emerson's of
Norfolk**
116 Grandby St.
Norfolk
(757) 624-1520

**Emerson's Fine
Tobacco**
880 N. Military
 Hwy.
Norfolk
(757) 461-6848

**CJ's Discount
Tobacco Outlet**
2504 S. Front St.
Richlands
(540) 963-1416

RICHMOND &
VICINITY

**Silk Leaf
Connection**
106 S. Center St.
Ashland
(804) 798-4667

The Mug & Chalice
6523 Centralia Rd.
Chesterfield
(804) 796-5552

Stogies
4040-F Cox Rd.
Glen Allen
(804) 527-1919

**Bucksnort Tobacco
And Tea**
7 E. Franklin St.
Richmond
(804) 788-4748

The Cigarette Store
6841 Forrest Hill
   Ave., Richmond
(804) 323-6413

Cork & Kegs
7110-A Patterson
   Ave., Richmond
(804) 288-0816

**Island Tobacco &
Gifts**
1601 Willow Lawn
   Dr., Richmond
(804) 285-5604

**The Mailbox &
Tobacco Store**
11266 Patterson
   Ave., Richmond
(804) 754-2280

Tinder Box
Three James Center,
   1051 E. Cary St.
Richmond
(804) 343-1827

**Tobacco House
Limited**
3138 W. Cary St.
Richmond
(804) 353-4675

**Tobacconist of
Richmond**
11521-H Midlothian
   Tpke., Richmond
(804) 378-7756

**Wine & Beer
Village**
7021 Three Chopt
   Rd., Richmond
(804) 673-0006

ROANOKE &
VICINITY

Tobacco Alley
120 Wilson St.
Blacksburg
(540) 951-3154

Milan Brothers
106 S. Jefferson St.
Roanoke
(540) 344-5191

Select Leaf Tobacco
325 Garysonville Rd.
Stafford
(540) 720-2928

VIRGINIA
BEACH

**Blue Pete's
Restaurant**
1400 N. Muddy
   Creek Rd.
Virginia Beach
(757) 426-2005

Churchill Cigars
1294 Great Neck Rd.
Virginia Beach
(757) 481-0346

J & M Imports
2973 Shore Dr.
Virginia Beach
(804) 496-5500

P J Baggan Wine
960 Laskin Rd.
Virginia Beach
(804) 491-8900

**Old Dominion
Tobacconist**
1505-B Richmond
   Rd., Williamsburg
(757) 220-9200

**Williamsburg Fine
Cigars**
106 Edward-Dyatt
   Dr., Williamsburg
(757) 258-3715

Cigar Haven
7 N. Loudon St.
Winchester
(540) 662-9269

Smoker's Friend
835 Main St.
Wytheville
(540) 228-7833

**York Tobacco
Company**
2231 Rte. 17
Yorktown
(757) 596-2120

Washington

Seaport Cigar & Tobacco
1003 8th St.
Anacortes
(360) 299-8341

Trading Post @ March Point
823 S. March Point
Rd., Anacortes
(360) 293-5632

Irby's Fine Cigars
713 W. Main St.
Battleground
(360) 666-4877

BELLINGHAM & VICINITY

Fairhaven Smoke Shop
1213 Harris Ave.
Bellingham
(360) 647-2379

Puffenstuff's Tobacconists & Gift
302 W Champion
St., Bellingham
(360) 647-3477

International Market Place
1733 H St.
Blaine
(360) 332-5909

M & R Tobacco
202 S. Tower St.
Centralia
(360) 736-4933

G & W Retail
950 Post Lane
Clarkston
(509) 758-6247

EVERETT & VICINITY

The Great Northwest Trading Company
2908 Wetmore Ave.
Everett
(206) 339-2614

Smokin' Sams
12811 8th Ave. W.
Everett
(206) 347-1971

Smokin' Deal
1227-A State Ave.
Marysville
(360) 653-0182

Celestial Treasures
135 Spring St.
Friday Harbor
(360) 378-6960

OLYMPIA & VICINITY

Le Bon Vie
5826 Pacific Ave. S.
Lacey
(360) 493-1454

The Spar Cafe Bar & Tobacco Merchant
114 E. 4th Ave.
Olympia
(360) 357-6444

SEATTLE & VICINITY

Tinder Box
10150 Main St.
Bellevue
(206) 451-8544

Fine Wines Limited
710 NW Gilman
Blvd., Issaquah
(206) 392-6242

Tinder Box
1810 12th Ave. NW
Issaquah
(206) 771-8418

The Grape Choice
220 Kirkland Ave.
Kirkland
(425) 827-7551

Smoke 'n' Cigar
12443 116th Ave.
NE, Kirkland
(425) 814-8149

Smoker's Choice
13520 100th Ave.,
NE, Kirkland
(206) 823-9232

Tobacco Patch
125 Central Way
Kirkland
(425) 739-4782

H G Tobacco & Snuff
5800 198th St.
Lynnwood
(425) 774-4002

Tinder Box
222 Alderwood
Mall, 3000-184th
St. SW
Lynnwood
(425) 771-8418

Cigar Cigar
15918 27 Dr. SE
Mill Creek
(206) 337-3683

Fine Wines
16535 NE 76th St.
Redmond
(425) 869-0869

Redmond Cigar & Tobacco
15788 Redmond
Way
Redmond
(425) 409-4348

Smoker's Choice
15161 NE 24th St.
Redmond
(206) 641-8421

Arcade Smoke Shop
1522 5th Ave.
Seattle
(206) 587-0159

Bad Habits Tatoo and Tobacco Parlor
4310 SW Alaska St.
Seattle
(206) 933-0368

Cigar Mania
West Lake Center,
400 Pine St.
Seattle
(206) 748-0328

Downtown Cigar
Store
310 Columbia St.
Seattle
(206) 624-2794

G & G Cigar Store
Inc.
Smith Tower, 504
2nd Ave.
Seattle
(206) 623-6721

International Cigars
& News
1522 3rd Ave.
Seattle
(206) 382-9284

Kirsten Limited
1900 W. Knickerson
Seattle
(206) 286-0851

Larry's Market
100 Mercer St.
Seattle
(206) 213-0778

Market Tobacco
Patch & Games
1906 #6 Pike Place
Seattle
(206) 728-7291

Nickel Cigar
89 Yesler Way
Seattle
(206) 622-3204

Pete's Supermarket
58 E. Lynn
Seattle
(206) 322-2660

Stogies
555 Northgate Mall
Seattle
(206) 440-7899

Tom's University
Smoke Shop
4140 University
Way NE
Seattle
(206) 632-9260

Tinder Box
751 S. Center
Tukwila
(206) 243-3443

Tobacco II
University Pipe
Square, 703
University City
Mall
Spokane
(509) 928-9531

Tobacco World
W-621 Mallon Ave.
Spokane
(509) 326-4665

TACOMA &
VICINITY

Young's Pipe &
Tobacco
29500 Pacific Hwy.
S., Federal Way
(206) 839-1653

Smoker's Choice
24817 Pacific Hwy.
S., Kent
(206) 641-8421

Tinder Box
3500 S. Meredian
Puyallup
(253) 435-0178

Mike's Smoke Shop
101 Pioneer Way E.
Tacoma
(253) 627-8959

Puro Mundo
763 Broadway
Tacoma
(253) 272-0565

Tinder Box
Tacoma Mall, 4502
S. Steele St.
Tacoma
(253) 472-9993

City Grill East
916 SE 164th Ave.
Vancouver
(360) 253-5399

Kev's Cigars &
Tobacco
516 SE Chkalov Dr.
Vancouver
(360) 883-4966

Vashon Thriftway
9740 SW Bark Rd.
Vashon Island
(206) 463-2100

Little Brown Smoke
Shack
3201 Goodman Rd.
Yakima
(509) 457-6404

West Virginia

Appalachian Books
& Cigar Company
331 Neville St.
Beckley
(304) 255-7688

Budget Tapes &
Records
3708 McCorkle
Charleston
(304) 925-8273

The Squire Tobacco
Unlimited
30 Capitol St.
Charleston
(304) 345-0366

La Fontaine's
Tobacco
Frederick Building
Lobby, 940 4th
Ave.
Huntington
(304) 523-7879

Stephen Street
Emporium
306 W. Stephen St.
Martinsburg
(800) 249-9130

Crumbakers
232 Grand Central
Mall
Parkersburg
(304) 422-3393

Churchill's
1102 Market St.
Wheeling
(800) 735-8477

Gumby's Cigarettes
95 Edginton Lane
Wheeling
(304) 242-0002

Wisconsin

APPLETON & VICINITY

Appleton Souvenir Cigar
415 W. College Ave.
Appleton
(414) 830-8349

The Cigar Vault
10 College Ave.
Appleton
(414) 954-8984

Tobacco Outlet Plus
241 N. Casaloma Dr.
Grand Chute
(920) 991-0916

Tobacco Shack
2221 Advance Dr.
Beloit
(608) 363-0577

EAU CLAIRE & VICINITY

Tobacco Outlet Plus
304 River St. W.
Chippewa Falls
(715) 720-7176

The Coffee Grounds
3460 Mall Dr.
Eau Claire
(715) 834-1733

GREEN BAY & VICINITY

Tobacco Outlet Plus
2349 Oneida St.
Ashwaubenon
(920) 405-8741

Bosse's News & Tobacco
220 Cherry St.
Green Bay
(920) 432-8647

Bosse's News & Tobacco
933 Anderson Dr.
Green Bay
(920) 405-9120

Blowin' Smoke
107 W. Milwaukee
Janesville
(608) 757-9510

KENOSHA & VICINITY

Andrea's Tobacconist
2401 60th St.
Kenosha
(414) 657-7732

Tenuta's
3203 52nd St.
Kenosha
(414)657-1012

Tobacco Outlet Plus
2111 22nd Ave.,
Villa Capri S.
Kenosha
(414) 652-5781

Bruno's Liquors
524 Broad St.
Lake Geneva
(414) 248-6059

LA CROSSE

Briar Patch
519 Main St.
La Crosse
(608) 784-8839

Tobacco Outlet Plus
2216 State Hwy. 16
La Crosse
(609) 779-4433

MADISON & VICINITY

Aficionado
702 N. Midvale Blvd.
Madison
(608) 236-0555

Capital Cigars
20 S. Carroll St.
Madison
(608) 259-9959

Ciabo Associates
640 W. Washington Ave., Madison
(608) 251-7288

The Cigar Shop at Gerhardt
4620 Cottage Grove Rd., Madison
(608) 221-3688

Ken Tobacco, Books, Etc.
434 State St.
Madison
(608) 294-9210

Knucklehead's
254 -A W. Gilman St., Madison
(608) 284-0151

The Tasting Room
6325 Monona Dr.
Madison
(608) 223-1641

The Tobacco Bar
6613 Seybold Rd.
Madison
(608) 276-7668

Tobacco Outlet Plus
3868 E. Washington Ave., Madison
(608) 249-9637

Tobacco Outlet Plus
2401-B W. Broadway St., Monona
(608) 221-3005

MILWAUKEE & VICINITY

Jack's Tobacco And Mcs
Brookfield Plaza Shopping Center,
13640-A W. Capitol Dr.
Brookfield
(414) 783-7473

Premier Cigars Inc.
18900 W. Bluemound Rd.
Brookfield
(414) 938-2313

V Richards
17165 W. Bluemound Rd.
Brookfield
(414) 784-8303

Otto's Wine Cask Inc.
4600 W. Brown Deer Rd.
Brown Deer
(414) 354-5831

Elm Grove Liquor
15380 Watertown
 Plank
Elm Grove
(414) 784-3545

**Cream City Cigar
Company**
5900 N. Port
 Washington Rd.
Glendale
(414) 967-0735

Tobacco Outlet Plus
5497-A S. 76th St.
Greendale
(414) 423-7056

Tobacco World
4818 S. 76th St.
Greenfield
(414) 281-1935

Bert's In Bay View
2523 E. Oklahoma
 Ave.
Milwaukee
(414) 744-8478

**East Town
Pharmacy**
788 N. Jefferson St.
Milwaukee
(414) 271-4441

**Edward's Pipe &
Tobacco**
400 W. Silver Spring
 Dr., Milwaukee
(414) 964-8212

Green Tree Liquors
6945 N. Point
 Washington Rd.
Milwaukee
(414) 352-8282

Metropolitan Liquor
5350 N. Sherman
 Blvd.
Milwaukee
(414) 463-9710

Uhle's Pipe Shop
114 W. Wisconsin
 Ave.
Milwaukee
(414) 273-6665

Tobacco Outlet Plus
3628 S. Moorland
 Rd., New Berlin
(414) 784-8102

The Smokers Club
927 Milwaukee Ave.
South Milwaukee
(414) 570-9911

The Ambassador
327 W. Main St.
Waukesha
(414) 547-9009

Tobacco Outlet Plus
11702-A W. North
 Ave., Wauwatosa
(414) 476-3509

**Little Havana Cigar
Shop**
9505 W. Greenfield
 Ave., West Allis
(414) 258-8219

Tobacco Outlet Plus
2830 Church St.
Stevens Point
(715) 341-6942

**The Great White
Tobacco Co.**
210 S. Water St.
Watertown
(920) 206-1072

Tobacco Outlet Plus
1041 S. 3rd Ave.
Wausau
(715) 849-1028

Tobacco Outlet Plus
1802 Stewart Ave.
Wausau
(715) 845-0937

**The Cigarette
Outlet**
2021 W. Washington
 St., West Bend
(414) 338-8556

Wyoming

**Lane's Tobacco &
Gifts**
Eastridge Mall, 601
 SE Wyoming Blvd.
Casper
(307) 577-5209

JACKSON

The Liquor Store
520 W. Broadway
Jackson
(307) 733-4466

Orvis
485 W. Broadway
Jackson
(307) 733-5407

Tobacco Row
120 N. Cache
Jackson
(307) 733-4385

**Uncle Mike's Fine
Cigars & Tobacco**
1940 Main St.
Torrington
(307) 532-7779

INTERNATIONAL

Andorra

La Casa del Habano
Plaça Co-Princeps,
Escaldes-Ergordany
Andorra La Vella
376 869 225

Argentina

La Casa del Habano
Viamontes No. 524,
1st Floor, Apt. 1
Buenos Aires
54 1 315 4085

Australia

**Benjamins &
Daniels Fine Shop**
10 Strand Central,
250 Elizabeth St.
Melbourne
61 3 9663 2879

**J & D of
Alexander's**
7A-459 Toorak Rd.
Melbourne
61 3 271 477

**Victorian Cigar
Room**
St. Kilda Rd.
Melbourne
61 3 98 50 94 47

**Alexander's Cigar
Divan**
Crown Ltd. (lower
ground level), 8
Whiteman St.
Southbank
61 3 9292 7842

**Alexander's Cigar
Divan**
Intercontinental
Hotel, 119
Macquarie St.
Sydney
61 2 9252 0280

**Wal Baranow's
Cuban Cigars**
Cook St. Preston,
3072, Victoria
61 3 9478 6549

Austria

Christian Kozlik
Potzleinsdorfer Str
59, Vienna
43 1 479 34 46

**Unternehmensbereich
Wein**
Ikera Waren-
handelsgesell,
Schaft Mbh
Maculangasse6
Vienna
43 1 250 55 630

Bahrain

La Casa del Habano
Shop. No. 8 Le
Royal Meridiem
Manama
973 580 400

Bermuda

Chatham House
63 Front St.
Hamilton
(441) 292-8422

**The Dockyard
Humidor**
Hamilton
(441) 295-3961

Tienda De Tabaco
The Emporium
Building, 69 Front
St., Hamilton
(441) 292-4411

Brazil

Faria Lima
Av. Brigadeirog 2232
Sao Paolo
55 11 815 5835

Siqueira
Teodoro Sampaio,
201-B Sao Paolo
Sp Pinhe, Ros Sp
Sao Paolo
55 11 814 9720

La Casa del Habano
Alameda Lorena
1821, Sao Paolo
55 11 883 7344

Ranieri Pipes
Alameda Lorena
1221, Sao Paolo
55 11 577 5420

Canada

ALBERTA

**Hub Cigar &
Newsstand**
10345 82nd Ave.
Edmonton
(403) 439-0144

Shefield & Sons
West Edmonton
Mall, Edmonton
(403) 444-1104

BRITISH
COLUMBIA

Cola
2015 Paramount
Crest
Abbottsford
(604) 504-0977

**Old Village Cigar &
Tobacco**
7961 Rosewood
Burnaby
(604) 524-1358

**Shefield & Sons
Tobacconist**
17-935 Marine Dr.
North Vancouver
(604) 986-5775

**Shefield & Sons
Tobacconist**
320-A 4741 Lakelse
Ave., Terrace
(604) 635-9661

I HRS Cigar Bar
5887 Main St.
Vancouver

**Alpha Tobacco,
House of Cigars**
927 Denman St.
Vancouver
(604) 688-1555

D & J's Daily Stop
925 Davie St.
Vancouver
(604) 687-5954

Green Trees Emporium
172 W. 2nd Ave.
Vancouver
(250) 752-0347

Havana Restaurant
1212 Commercial
Dr., Vancouver
(604) 253-9119

La Casa del Habano
980 Robson St.
Vancouver
(604) 609-0511

Lilac
605 Robson St.
Vancouver
(604) 669-8111

Marble Arch Hotel
518 Richards St.
Vancouver
(604) 681-5435

R.J. Clarke Tobacconist
3 Alexander St.
Vancouver
(604) 687-4136

Cabin Fever
1001 Douglas St.
Victoria
(800) 711-1156

Casa de Malahato
1441 Store St.
Victory
(250) 383-0812

Canadian Cigar Company
1557-A Marine Dr.
West Vancouver
(604) 878-0995

Shefield & Sons Tabacconist
712 Park Royal N.
West Vancouver
(604) 926-7011

Listel Hotel
4121 Village Green
Whistler
(604) 932-3433

Memories
4249 Village Stroll
Whistler
(604) 932-6439

Whistler Cigar Company
103-4338 Main St.
Whistler
(604) 905-2423

MANITOBA

Thomas Hinds Tobacconist
96-185 Carlton St.
Winnipeg
(204) 942-0203

NOVA SCOTIA

MacDonald Tobacco & Gifts
Barrington Mall,
1903 Barrington
St., Halifax
(902) 429-6872

ONTARIO

Havana Tobacconist
Stone Rd. Mall, 435
Stone Rd.
Guelph
(519) 837-9193

Lil' Habanas
79 Dunlop St. W.
Barrie
(888) 728-1111

Smalley's Cigar Store
132 Hurontario St.
Collingwood
(705) 445-1666

Roxanne's
3 King St. W.
Harrow
(519) 738-4925

The King City Outpost
Hwy. 400 N.
King City
(905) 832-2305

Thomas Hinds Tobacconist
8 King St. E.
Kitchener
(519) 744-3556

Cuban Pete Cigar Company
609 Richmond St.
London
(519) 641-8919

Smoker's Factory Outlet
38 Adelaide St. N.
London
(519) 679-8445

Smokin Joes
785 Wonderland Rd.
S., London
(519) 471-0279

Wiff N Puff
Westmount
Shopping Center,
785 Wonderland
Rd., London
(519) 472-1244

International House of Cigars
1900 Dundas St. W.
Mississauga
(905) 855-3836

Bells Corner Minimart
72 Robertson Rd
Nepean
(613) 828-4812

The Cuban Connection Inc.
42 Antares Dr.
Nepean
(613) 727-1775

Copa-Habana Cuban & World Cigars
5930 Victoria Ave.
Niagara Falls
(905) 354-4530

Copa-Habana Cuban & World Cigars/Cigar Bar
6580 Lundys Lane
Niagara Falls
(905) 374-1103

Copa-Habana Cuban & World Cigar
5711 Victoria Ave.
Niagara Falls
(905) 354-8576

Chandra's Specialty
Cigar Shop (est.
1982)
240 Sparks St., Level
A, West Tower
Ottawa
(613) 234-4490

Port Sandfield
Marina
LT R#2
Port Sandfield
(705) 765-3147

Real Fakes
14402 Niagara Pkwy.
Queenstown
(905) 262-5904

Chubby's Smoke
House
504-625 Roselawn
Ave., Toronto
(416) 785-8669

Cuban Pete (Forest
Hill)
394 Spadina Rd.
Toronto
(519) 641-8919

Groucho &
Company
150 Bloor St. W.
Toronto
(416) 922-4817

Havana House
87 Avenue Rd.
Toronto
(416) 927-9070

La Casa del Habano
170 Bloor St. W.
Toronto
(416) 926-9066

Thomas Hinds
Tobacconist
392 Eglinton Ave.
W., Toronto
(416) 481-6909

Thomas Hinds
Tobacconist
8 Cumberland St.
Toronto
(416) 927-7703

Tobacco Haven
595 Bay St.
Toronto
(416) 593-6655

Touch of Class
630 Mount Pleasant
Toronto
(416) 487-5535

The Wine
Establishment
250 The Esplanade
Toronto
(416) 861-1462

Winston & Holmes
138 Cumberland St.
Toronto
(800) 465-2035

Havana Tobacconist
Bayview Village
Shopping Center,
2901 Bayview
Ave., Willowdale
(416) 733-9736

Havana Heaven
Fine Cigars &
Accesories
21 Chatham St. E.
Windsor
(519) 252-4447

La Casa del Habano
473 Ouellette Ave.
Windsor
(519) 254-0017

Ray & Kim's Super
Convenience
352 Ouellette Ave.
Windsor
(519) 977-1256

Star Light
Convenience &
Smoke Shop
780 Dundas St.
Woodstock
(519) 421-1953

Starlight Smoke
780 Dundas
Woodstock
(519) 421-1953

PRINCE
EDWARD
ISLAND

Cuban Cigar
Importers
93 Water St.
Charlottetown
(902) 628-1910

QUEBEC

Cigar Emporium
3525 St. Laurent St.
Montreal
(514) 281-6658

La Casa del Habano
1434 Sherbrooke
Ouest
Montreal
(514) 849-0037

Vinum Design
1480 City Councilor
Montreal
(514) 985-3200

SASKATCHEWAN

**Cigar Venue on
Louise Avenue**
1038 Louise Ave.
Saskatoon
(306) 249-4321

Smoke & Ashes
Midtown Plaza
Saskatoon
(306) 652-1117

Caribbean

ANTIGUA, W.I.

La Casa del Habano
Heritage Quay, No.
45, St. Johns
(809) 462-2677

ARUBA

La Bonbonniere
Holland Aruba Mall,
Havenstraat No. 6
Oranjestaad
297 8 20297

La Casa del Habano
Royal Plaza
Oranjestaad
297 8 25355

**RC Gift Shop &
Drug Store**
Windham Aruba
Resort, Lower
Lobby Shopping
Arcade
Oranjestaad
297 825 699

BAHAMAS

Burns House Ltd.
JFK Dr.
Nassau
(242) 323-6444

Graycliff
West Hill St.
Nassau
(242) 322-2797

La Casa del Habano
Hotel Graycliff
Nassau
(809) 322-2796

**Pink Flaimingo
Trading Company**
Bay & Charlotte St.
Nassau
(242) 322-7891

**Tropique
International
Smoke Shop**
Marriot Crystal
Palace Arcade, W.
Bay St.
Nassau
(809) 327-7292

CUBA

La Casa del Habano
Fábrica Partagás,
Industria No. 250
Habana Vieja
537 33 8060

La Casa del Habano
Museo del Tabaco,
Mercaderes No.
120, Habana Vieja

La Casa del Habano
Ave. 1ra. esq. 64
Varadero, Matanzas
537 5 66 7843

CURAÇAO, N.A.

Lord's Inc.
Schottegatweg Oost
#82, Promenade
Shopping Center
599 462-7476

DOMINICAN
REPUBLIC

C & P Cigar Club
Ave. 27 De Febrero
Santo Domingo
809 563 6774

GUADELOUPE,
F.W.I.

La Casa del Habano
Center St. John
Perse No. 54
Pointe-à-Pitre
590 894 216

PUERTO RICO

Genfy Zatata
Iomas Verdes Ave.
Bayamon
(787) 786-2352

Pleasures
M 73 Santa Juanita
Ave., Bayamon
(787) 798-9700

La Casa del Habano
18 N. 23 Condado
Moderno
Caguas
(787) 783-2060

Cigar Box
Isla Verde #5900 L-6
Carolina
(787) 728-6970

Cigar Cellar
Calle 4, #102, Villar
Mar, Carolina
(787) 726-4001

The Ritz-Carlton
La Isla Verde, 6961
State Rd.
Carolina
(787) 253-1700

Tobacco Shop
Isla Verde Mall, 2nd
Level, Carolina
(787) 253-0865

Fun Times
152 Barbosa Ave.
Catano
(787) 788-1345

**International House
of Cigars**
B-2 Tabonuco St.
Guaynabo
(787) 782-6871

Smoker's Suite
Road#1 Km 21.1,
La Muda Rd.
Guaynabo
(787) 720 1200

And Cigars
311 F.D. Roosevelt
Ave., Hato Rey
(787) 756-6344

Tobacco Shop
Plaza Las Americas,
1st Level
Hato Rey
(787) 759-8062

Luigi's Cigar Box
128 Palma Nova
Plaza
Humacao
(787) 850-3500

**Wine & Liquor
Gallery**
Marginal Urb., San
Salvador, Manati
(787) 884-0109

**Good Times Smoke
Shop**
McKinley #74 -
Oeste, Mayaguez
(809) 265-2380

**Elvis Spirit &
Smoke Shop**
La Calle Shopping
Mall, Fortaleza St.
Old San Juan
(787) 725-1306

**Smt. Pr. Duty Free,
Inc.**
Pier #1, Paseo
Gilberto,
Concepcion De
Gracia No1
Old San Juan
(305) 477-0515

Tobacco Shop
Plaza Del Caribe
Mall
Ponce
(787) 842-6881

Cigar Shop
Plaza Los
Muchachos, 201
Fortaleza
San Juan
(787) 725-4977

**EMV International
House of Cigars**
1203 Americo
Miranda Ave.,
Rpto. Metro
San Juan
(787) 782-6871

El Barco
Borinquen Towers
San Juan
(787) 781-5525

**International Cigar
Trader**
804 Condado Ave.
San Juan
(787) 289-0052

La Boutique du Vin
10 Chardon Ave.
San Juan
(787) 250-0008

The Smoker's Suite
El San Juan Hotel,
6073 Isla Verde
Ave.
San Juan
(809) 791-6002

V I Cigar Society
120 Calle Gardenia
A, Estancia De La
Fuente
Toa Alta
(787) 782-4908

ST. BARTHÉLEMY

P & G Associates
Gustavia
590 27 50 62

**Le Comptoir du
Cigare**
6 General de Gaulle
Gustavia
590 275 062

La Casa del Habano
Villa Creole
St. Jean
590 276 689

ST. CROIX,
U.S.V.I.

Baci Duty Free
55 Company St.
Christiansted
(888) SEE-BACI

**Steeles Smokes &
Sweets**
1102 Strand St.
Christiansted
(809) 773-3366

ST. JOHN,
U.S.V.I.

Shady Days
13-B Wharfside
Village
(809) 693-7625

ST. MAARTEN/
ST. MARTIN

La Casa del Habano
Port La Royal, Rue
de La Liberte 71
Marigot
590 877 910

La Casa del Cigarro
Marina Port La
Royal, BP 445
Marigot
590 879 048

Le Cigare
Rue de la Liberté,
BP 1020
Marigot
590 877 910

**The New
Amsterdam Store**
66 Front St.
Philipsburg
599 5-22787

ST. THOMAS,
U.S.V.I.

Ah Riise
37 Main St.
(809) 776-2303

Captain's Corner
#8A Dronnigens
Gade
(809) 774-8435

**Dazzlers Duty Free
Shop**
Hazen Sight Mall
(809) 777-4335

Gregory's
PO Box 9071
(809) 777-5480

Shell Seeker Inc.
Captain Corner
(809) 774-8435

Cyprus

La Casa del Habano
Higa Fereou, Str.
No. 4, Limassol
357 5 747 341

Czech Republic

La Casa del Habano
Hotel
  Intercontinental,
  Nan. Curicovych
  43/5, Prague
42 2 488 1544

Denmark

W O Larsen A/S
9 Amagertorv, Dk
  1160, Copenhagen
45 3 312 2050

**Alfred & Christian
Petersen**
Norgesvej 10
Horsens
45 7 561 2000

Egypt

La Casa del Habano
Hotel Semiramis
  Intercontinental
Cairo
20 2 354 9608

France

**La Casa Del
Habano**
169 Blvd. St.
  Germain Paris
75006
45 49 24 30

A La Civette
157 Rue Saint
  Honore
Paris
33 1 42 960 499

Boutique 22
22 Ave. Victor Hugo
Paris
33 1 45 01 8141

La Casa del Habano
69 Blvd. St.
  Germain
Paris
33 1 45 49 24 30

La Cave A Cigares
14 Blvd. Haussmann
Paris
33 1 47 70 73 6

**La Civette
Desquatretemp**
Centre Commercial
  Des 4, Casier 102,
  Cedex 25, Paris
33 1 47 74 75 28

La Tabagie
CC Montparnasse
Paris
33 1 45 38 65 1

Germany

Zigarien Herzog
Ludwig Kirchplatz 1
Berlin
49 886 823 40

**The Cigar Cabinet
@ Hotel Land**
Poststrasse 70,
  Meerbusch
Düsseldorf
49 2132 911294

Cigar Cabinet
Hotel Landsknecht
  Holding,
  Poststrasse 70
Düsseldorf
49 2132 911294

**Zigarren-und
Pfeifenhaus**
Konig Und
  Schubert,
  Lavesstrabe 71
Hanover
49 511 321 984

Shiraz Wein & Co.
Theatinerstr. 38
Munchen
49 89 22 35 87

Dachauer Str. 7
Filiale Bauerstr 1 U,
  Turkenstr 43
Munich
49 89 550 4448

Alte Tabakstube
Schillerplatz 4
Stuttgart
49 711 292 729

Pfeifen Archive
Cal Wer Passage
Stuttgart
49 711 299 1555

Greece

La Casa del Habano
258 Kifissias Ave.
Athens, Psichico
30 1 677 3438

Balli-Davidoff
1-3 Spiromilou St.
Athens
30 1 323 5325

La Casa del Habano
1-3 Spyromiliov St.
Athens
30 1 323 5325

**Ranios S.A. Havana
Cigars**
6 Tsakalof St.
Athens
30 1 364 3500

Mefisto
6 Xanthoy St.
Kolonaki
30 1 721 8084

**Ranios S.A. Havana
Cigars**
125 Karaiskou St.
Piraeus
30 1 422 5536

Honduras

**Tabaco Fino Cigar
Shop**
Hotel Honduras
Maya
504 20 08 13

Hong Kong

Aficionado Cigarros
14-15 Wo On Lane,
  1st Fl., Hong Kong
852 252 535 00

**Cohiba Cigar Divan
(La Casa del
Habano)**
The Mandarin
  Oriental Hotel
Hong Kong
852 2522 0111, ext.
  4074

**Wine Establishment
Co. Lt. Shop**
103 The Royal
  Garden, 69 Mody
  R., Tsimshatsui E.
Kowloon
852 2 722 0039

Hungary

Finn Trading Ltd.
Hegedus Gyula U 75
1133 Budapest
140 1996

**Magyar
Szivarforgalmazas**
Tuzer Ut Ca 43
Budapest
36 3055 2551

Indonesia

La Casa del Habano
The Mandarin
Oriental, Jakarta
Jakarta
62 21 314 1307

Ireland

The Decent Cigar
46 Grafton St.
Dublin 2
353 1 549 363

**Gibney's-Cheers
Takehome**
New St., Malahide
Dublin
353 1 845 0606

JJ Fox
119 Grafton St.
Dublin 2
353 1 677 0533

Terroiris Limited
103 Morehampton
Rd., Donnybrook
Dublin 4
353 1 667 1311

Israel

Har Zahav
Canion Molcha,
The Jerusalem
Mall, Jerusalem
972 2 679-3515

**Gold Mount,
A.K.A. Har Zahav**
Jerusalem Mall,
Kanion Molcho
Jeusalem
972 2 679-3515

Cigarim
194 Dizengoff
Tel Aviv
972 3 527-0707

Italy

Achille Savinelli Srl
Via Dogana 3
Milano
39 2 875 900

Ivory Coast (Côte d'Ivoire)

Afrique-Tabacs
04 Bp 748 Abidjan
04
Abidjan
225 21 63 00

Lebanon

La Casa del Habano
Achrafieh Cassine
Square - Notre
Dame Center
Beirut
961 1 328 568

La Casa del Habano
Zalka Hwy., Arz
Center - Abu
Jawde Bldg.
Beirut
961 3 741 503

Luxembourg

La Civette
22B Av Porte-Neuve
352 221 321

Malaysia

Lim & Hooi
Umno Building, 3rd
Floor, Jalan Segget
8000 Johore
Bahru
60 7 222 1788

Havana Club
Marriott Kuala
Lumpur, 183 Jalan
Bukit Bintang
Kuala Lumpur

Havana Club
Shopping Centre,
No. 50 Jalan
Sultan Ismail
Kuala Lumpur
60 3 245 5996

Mexico

Havana House
Avenue Cabo San
Lucas 72, Entre
Esquire A Surdan
Baja California Su
52 114 32 308

Incorp SA de CV
La Calle 8, Av De
Las Naciones, Piso
1733, Col. Napoles
52 5 488 0400

**Casa del Tabaco SA
de CV**
Presidente Mazarik
393
Colonia Polanco D.F.
52 5 576 7263

**Havana Cabana-
Cuban Cigar**
Blvd Costero #609
Cona Centro
115 261 740 569

Monte Pala Palatino
233 Colonia Fuente
Del Valle
Garca Garcia Nl
52 832 9307

**Barcena Cigar
House**
Monte Pala Palatino,
233 Colina Fuente
Del Valle
Garca Garcia, N.l.
52 8 335 4104

Amaris Tobacco
La Gran Plaza de
Guadalajara,
Segundo Nivel
Avenida
Guadalajara
52 3 636 6518

La Casa del Habano
Plaza Loreto
Altamirano No.
46, Col. Tizapan
San Angel
Mexico, D.F.
52 5 616 1430

La Casa del Habano
Plaza Mazaryk,
   Presidente
   Mazaryk 393, Col.
   Polanco
Mexico, D.F.
52 5 282 1046

La Casa del Habano
Plaza Flaming, Zona
   Hotelera Cancun
Quintana Roo,
   Cancun
52 9 88 52929

**Amigos Smoke
Shop**
Calle M Doblado Y
   Morelos
San Jose del Cabo
52 114 21 138

La Casa del Habano
Pasco de los Heroes
   No. 95, Zona Rio
Tijuana, B.C.

La Villa Del Tabaco
02015 Ent
   Revolucion y
   Madero Zona
   Centro
Tijuana, B.C.
52 668 58 558

New Zealand

**Ohauiti Wines &
Spirits**
150 Ohauiti Rd.
   Tauranga
64 754 43 3215

**Havana House
Cigars Limited**
11-19 Customs St.
   W., Auckland
64 9 357 0037

The Cigar Bar Ltd.
Shop 5 Beach St.
Steameewharf
64 3 441 8064

Norway

Sol Cigar Company
Drammensun #8
Oslo
47 22 441 347

Philippines

Forth & Tay
New World Hotel
   Shopping Arcade,
   Pasay Rd. &
   Makati Ave.
Makati City, Manila
63 2 811 6870

**Tabac Inc., Hotel
Sofitel**
Lobby, Grand Blvd.,
   1990 Roxas Blvd.
Manila
63 2 526 8588

**Tabac On Wilson
Street**
152 Wilson St,
   Greenhills
San Juan City,
   Manila
63 2 822 6656

Portugal

**Empor Importacao e
Export**
Rua Joao Dos
   Santos, Lote
Lisboa
(351) 1-364 6820

Puerto Rico

Cigar Box
Isla Verde, #5900
Carolina
(787) 728-6970

Cigar Box
Isla Verde #5900 L-6
Carolina
(787) 728-6970

Tobacco Shop
Isla Verde Mall
Carolina
(787) 253-0865

Tobacco Shop
Plaza Las Americas
Hato Rey
(787) 759-8062

Tobacco Shop
Plaza Del Caribe
   Mall
Ponce
(787) 842-6881

Republic of Panama

The Cigar Shoppe
Miramar Inter-
   Continental
   Hotel, Miramar
   Plaza
Panama
(507) 214-1000 X6

Saudi Arabia

La Casa del Habano
Palestine Rd.
Al Hamra, Jeddah
966 2 665 8227

La Casa del Habano
Saladin St.
Al Malaz, Riyadh
966 1 476 3114

La Casa del Habano
Prince Sultan St.
Olaya, Riyadh
966 1 465 037

Singapore

**The Oak Cellars
Pte. Ltd.**
10 Jalan Besar 08-07,
   Sim Lim Tower
65 296 2111

The Oaks Cellars
Tanglin Mall, 163
   Tanglin Rd.
65 835 3411

Havana Club
Glorient Trading 41
   Yatvas St.
789 6580

Havana Club
Main Lobby,
   Singapore Marriott
   Hotel, 320
   Orchard Rd.
Singapore

South Africa

**Wesley's—The
Cock 'n Bull**
20 Tyger Valley
   Centre
Bellville Cape
27 21 94 82 400

Wesley's
Sanlam Plaza
Bloemfontein
27 51 48 46 58

**Horrell's
Tobacconist**
Piazza Level, Golden
    Acre, Adderly St.
Cape Town
27 21 45 1890

Wesley's
Golden Acre Plaza
Cape Town
27 21 21 50 90

**Wesley's—The
Cock 'n Bull**
Covendish Square
Cape Town
27 21 61 14 32

**Wesley's—The
Cock 'n Bull**
143 V & A
    Waterfront
Cape Town
27 21 21 18 60

**Wesley's—Zoggy's
Durban**
87 Gardiner St.
Durban
27 31 30 40 866

Wesley's
Vincent Park Centre
East London
27 431 57 873

Wesley's
The Mall
Johannesburg
27 11 880 1150

Wesley's
Garden Pavillion,
    Carlton Centre
Johannesburg
27 11 33 11 050

Wesley's
The Rosebank Mall
Johannesburg
27 11 88 01 150

Wesley's
Bank City, Pritchard
    St., Johannesburg
27 11 63 32 510

**Wesley's Pipe &
Tobacco-Swaziland
Jewelers**
The Mall
Mbabane
27 9268 42 460

Wesley's
Buster Brown Centre
Nelspruit
27 1311 53 308

**Wesley's—The
Cock 'n Bull**
The Square
Plettenberg Bay
27 4457 30 335

Wesley's
24 Shoprito
    Chockers Mall,
    Greenacres
Port Elizabeth
27 41 34 20 36

Spain

Gimeno Tabacs
Rambla de Les Flors
Barcelona
34 3 302 9083, 318
    4947

**Casa Central Del
Tabaco**
Alcala 44
Madrid
34 91 521 0420

Sweden

**Broberg s
Tobakshandel AB**
Arkaden Box 111 10
Goteborg
46 31 153 614

**Broberg's
Tobakshandel AB**
Sturegallerian 39
Stockholm
46 31 611 69 00

Cigarrummet
Gotgatan 9
Stockholm
46 08 641 8588

Switzerland

Eden Tabac Cigares
Rue du Grand Lancy
    6, Acacias
41 22 342 27 57

Davidoff
Centralbahnplatz 9
Basel
41 61 23 11 52

Davidoff
Steinenvorstadt 2
Basel
41 61 22 87 37

Kagi
2 Place du Theatre
Berne
41 22 31 37 03

**Jacky Bonvin S.A.
Cigares**
Crans
41 27 481 26 34

Alfred Dunhill
Rue de Rhône 59
Geneva
41 22 312 42 60

**Comptoirs du
Rhône**
2 Rue du Rhône 59
Geneva
41 22 312 14 22

**Eden Confederation
Emile SA**
Rue de la
    Confederation 8
Geneva
41 22 311 96 41

**Gesto Cigars
International**
2 Rue Vallin
Geneva
41 22 741 1089

Raffi's
2-3 Place
    Longemalle
Geneva
41 22 31 97 40

Tabac Rhein
1 Rue du Mont-
    Blanc, Geneva
41 22 32 97 64

Davidoff
2 Rue de Rive
Genva
41 22 310 90 41

Davidoff
Hotel Savoy,
   Poststrasse 12
Zürich
41 1 211 48 00

Durr
Bahnhofplatz 6
Zürich
41 1 211 63 23

La Casa del Habano
Bleicherweg 18
Zürich
41 1 202 1211

Tabak
Schwarzenbach
Hauptbahnof
Zürich
41 1 211 63 25

Taiwan

David Mann Cigar
Club
Lane 140,
   Minsheng, E. Rd.
   Sec. 3
Taipei
88 6271 92688

Thailand

Au Bon Plaisir S.A.
20/12-15 Rvamrodec
   Village, Lumpini
   Pathumwan, Soi
   Ruamndee
   Ploencht Rd.
Bangkok
66 2 255 1084 6

Bangkok Gem &
Jewelry
Tr. 322 Surawong
   Rd., Bangkok
66 2284 2216

The Davidoff Shop
Hilton International
   Hotel
Bangkok
66 2 253 0123

Havana Club
(Thailand) Co. Ltd.
Main Floor, J.W.
   Marriott Hotel,
   Sukhumvit Soi 2,
   Plong Toey
Bangkok

La Casa del Habano
The Oriental
   Bangkok, 48 Ave.
Bangkok
66 2 267 1596

Zeltex Pacific Co.
Ltd.
137/7 Soi
   Naksuwan, Noni,
   Chongnonsi
   Yannawa
Bangkok
66 2 294 9163

Turkey

Pogep Inc.
Sulunlu Sok No 3, 1
   Levent
Istanbul
9012122641929

UK

Tobacco World
78 Northgate St.
Cheshire
44 1244 348 821

Berry Brothers &
Rudd
Heathrow Airport,
   Terminal 3
Hounslow
44 181 564 8363

Alfred Dunhill
Limited
30 Duke St., St.
   James
London
44 171 4999566

Alfred Dunhill
Pipes Ltd.
32 St. Andrews Rd.
London
44 181 498 4000

Benson & Hedges
13 Old Bond St.
London
44 171 493 1825

Berry Brothers &
Rudd
3 St. James St.
London
44 171 396 9600

Davidoff of London
35 St. James St.
London
44 171 930 3079

Desmond Sautter
106 Mount St.
London
44 171 4994866

Dunhill
32 St. Andrews Rd.
London
44 181 498-4000

Harvey Nichols
Knightsbridge
London
44 171 235 5000

JJ Fox London
19 St. James St.
London
44 171 493 9009

Monte's
164 Sloane St.
London
44 171 245 0892

Monte's
10th Floor,
   Boatwater House
   W., 114
   Knightsbridge
London
44 171 245 0890

Sautter of Mayfair
106 Mount St.
London
44 171 499 4866

Uruguay

Classic Duo/Conrad
Hilton Hotel
Rbla. William Pda.4,
   Centro
   Commercial. Loc.6
Punta Del Este
598 42 91348

CHAPTER 15

Cigar-Friendly Restaurants

The cigar-friendly restaurants that follow are divided into two sections: United States and International. Restaurants in the United States are listed alphabetically by state, then by metropolitan area, then by city. International restaurants are listed alphabetically by country, and then by city (or, in the case of Canada, by province and then by city; or, in the case of the Caribbean, by island and then by city).

Each listing details where cigar-smoking is allowed inside the restaurant and what type of cuisine is served, if any. A listing that contains "Humidor" indicates that cigars are available at the restaurant. If the primary role of the establishment is not that of a public, full-service restaurant—for example, if it's a coffee bar, nightclub or private club—that fact is noted in bold at the end of the listing.

The restaurant information was provided by the restaurants themselves in a questionnaire prepared by Cigar Aficionado. Each listing was checked as close to the publication date as possible, but changes occur all the time, so it's best to call ahead.

UNITED STATES

Alabama

Blue Monkey Lounge
1318 Cobb Lane
Birmingham
(205) 933-9222
• *Throughout the lounge. Humidor. Cuisine: lite fare—cheeses, salads, sandwiches.* **Cocktail lounge.**

Montgomery Brewing Co. & Cafe
12 W. Jefferson St.
Montgomery
(334) 834-2739
• *Smoking section. Humidor. Cuisine: features steak, seafood, & pasta.*

North River Yacht Club
New Watermelon Rd., Tuscaloosa
(205) 345-0202
• *All areas. Humidor. Cuisine: international.* **Private club.**

Alaska

Bernie's Cafe & Lounge
626 O St.
Anchorage
(907) 276-8088
• *All areas. Humidor.* **Lounge.**

Chilkoot Charlie's
2435 Spenard Rd.
Anchorage
(907) 272-1010
• *All areas. Humidor. Cuisine: open menu.* **Nightclub.**

Chena Hot Springs Resort
206 Driveway
Fairbanks
(907) 369-4111
• *Bar. Cuisine: Intercontinental featuring game meats.*

Arizona

PHOENIX & VICINITY

The Discovery Lounge at Boulders
34631 N. Tom Darlington Dr.
Carefree
(602) 488-9009
• *Bar/lounge. Humidor. Cuisine: hors d'oeuvres only.* **Bar/lounge.**

Copper Canyon Brewing & Alehouse
5945 W. Ray Rd.
Chandler
(602) 705-9700
• *Bar and patio. Humidor. Cuisine: pub fare, seafood, steaks, & burgers.*

Wigwam Resort
300 Wigwam Blvd.
Litchfield Park
(602) 935-3811
• *In the Arizona Bar and Kachina Lounge. Humidor. Cuisine: three restaurants serving southwestern, American, & Continental.*

Doubletree Paradise Valley Resort
5401 N. Scottsdale Rd.
Paradise Valley
(602) 947-5400
•*Loggia lobby bar and patio. Humidor. Cuisine: southwestern.* **Bar.**

Another Pointe in Tyme at The South Mountain Hilton
7777 S. Pointe Pkwy.
Phoenix
(602) 431-6472
•*Bar, private rooms, and patio. Humidor. Cuisine: American.*

Christopher's/ Christopher's Bistro
2398 E. Camelback Rd., Phoenix
(602) 957-3214
•*Smoking section, private room, and patio. Humidor. Cuisine: French at Christopher's; Continental at the Bistro.*

Different Pointe of View at the Pointe Hilton Tapatio Cliff
11111 N. 7th St.
Phoenix
(602) 863-0912
•*Patio. Humidor. Cuisine: regional American.*

Morton's of Chicago
Shops at the Esplanade/2501 E. Camelback Rd., Ste. 1. Phoenix
(602) 955-9577
•*Bar/lounge, smoking section, and patio. Humidor. Cuisine: steakhouse.*

Pointe in Tyme at the Pointe Hilton Tapatio Cliff
11111 N. 7th St.
Phoenix
(602) 866-6348
•*Bar, lounge, and patio. Humidor. Cuisine: American bistro.*

The Ritz-Carlton
2401 E. Camelback Rd., Phoenix
(602) 468-0700
•*Bar after 5pm. Humidor. Cuisine: lite fare.* **Bar.**

Tarbell's
3213 E. Camelback Rd., Phoenix
(602) 955-8100
•*Private dining room. Humidor. Cuisine: American bistro.*

Wrong Number Lounge
4041 N. 40th St.
Phoenix
(602) 955-9886
•*All areas.* **Bar.**

SCOTTSDALE

Cafe Patou
7000 E. Shea Blvd.

Scottsdale
(602) 951-6868
•*Bar/lounge and private rooms. Humidor. Cuisine: French.*

Marco Polo's Supper Club
8606 E. Shea Blvd.
Scottsdale
(602) 483-1900
•*Bar and patio after 10pm. Humidor. Cuisine: Northern Italian with Oriental flair.*

Marquessa at the Scottsdale Princess Hotel
757 E. Princess Dr.
Scottsdale
(602) 585-4848
•*Dining room and lounge at the grille. Humidor. Cuisine: contemporary steak & seafood.* **Bar/cigar bar.**

Remington's at The Scottsdale Plaza Resort
7200 N. Scottsdale Rd., Scottsdale
(602) 951-5101
•*Lounge and lounge patio. Humidor. Cuisine: American regional.*

Thirsty Camel Bar at the Phoenician Resort
6000 E. Camelback Rd., Scottsdale
(602) 941-8200
•*Patio. Humidor. Cuisine: Mediterranean/southwest.*

TUCSON

Anthony's in the Catalinas
6440 N. Campbell Tucson
(520) 299-1771
•*Bar/lounge and patio. Humidor. Cuisine: Continental.*

Box Seats Grill & Pub
8848 E. Tanque Verde, Tucson
(520) 760-6699
•*Patio and smoking section. Cuisine: American.*

Charles Restaurant
6400 E. El Dorado Circle, Tucson
(520) 296-7173
•*Lounge. Humidor. Cuisine: Continental.*

El Charro Cafe
311 N. Court Ave.
Tucson
(520) 622-1922
•*Cigar lounge. Humidor. Cuisine: Mexican/Tucson.*

El Charro Cafe at El Mercado
6310 E. Broadway
Tucson
(520) 745-1922
•*Cigar lounge. Humidor. Cuisine: Mexican/Tucson.*

Sheraton El Conquistador Resort & Country Club
10000 N. Oracle Rd.
Tucson
(520) 544-5000
•Lobby lounge. Humidor. Cuisine: nine restaurants at the resort featuring such cuisine as Southwestern, steak, cafe/light fare, and California. **Resort.**

Suite 102
5350 E. Broadway
Tucson
(520) 745-9555
•Cigar lounge, smoking section in bar, and patio. Humidor. Cuisine: upscale American eclectic.

Arkansas

The Mast
201 E. Cedar
El Dorado
(870) 881-8100
•All areas. Humidor. Cuisine: Italian & steaks.

Coach's Sports Grill
2588 N. Gregg Ave.
Fayetteville
(501) 582-5625
•All areas including a private cigar lounge. Humidor. Cuisine: traditional, yet upscale sports bar menu featuring ribs, steaks, chicken, pasta, and fish specialties.

James at the Mill at the Inn at the Mill
3906 Greathouse Springs Rd.
Johnson
(501) 443-1400
•Smoking section, patio, and private room. Humidor. Cuisine: Ozark Plateau.

LITTLE ROCK

Andre's Hillcrest
605 N. Beechwood
Little Rock
(501) 666-9191
•Smoking section in dining room and patio. Humidor. Cuisine: Continental.

Cafe Saint Moritz
225 E. Markham
Little Rock
(501) 372-0411
•Smoking dining room, bar, and private rooms for private parties. Humidor. Cuisine: Continental.

Capital Bar & Grill at The Capital Hotel
111 W. Markham
Little Rock
(501) 374-7474
•Bar. Humidor. Cuisine: American.

California

NOTE: As of January 1, 1998, California State Law prohibits smoking in all public places. However, the restaurants below responded to our questionnaire. We suggest you confirm a restaurant's policy before lighting up.

ANAHEIM & VICINITY

Mama Cozza's
2170 W. Ball Rd.
Anaheim
(714) 635-0063
•Bar. Cuisine: Italian.

Mr. Stox
1105 E. Katella Ave.
Anaheim
(714) 634-2994
•Bar/lounge and patio. Humidor. Cuisine: Continental.

The Cellar
305 N. Harbor Blvd.
Fullerton
(714) 525-5682
•Bar area and private rooms. Humidor. Cuisine: classic French.

Aroma Italiano Coffee House & Fine Cigars
1948 N. Tustin
Orange
(714) 282-2382

•Heated patio. Humidor. Cuisine: pastries & desserts only. **Coffee bar/cigar bar.**

The Hobbit
2932 E. Chapman Ave., Orange
(714) 997-1972
•Separate cigar lounge. Humidor. Cuisine: Continental.

The Cigar Cafe
21550-A Yorba Linda Blvd.
Yorba Linda
(714) 693-2427
•Cigar bar. Humidor. Cuisine: Japanese featuring a sushi bar & microbrewery.

The Ballard Store Restaurant & Bar
2449 Baseline Ave.
Ballard
(805) 688-5319
•Wine cellar. Humidor. Cuisine: American & French.

COSTA MESA & VICINITY

Amici Trattoria
655 Anton Blvd., Suite C
Costa Mesa
(714) 850-9399
•Patio. Humidor. Cuisine: Mediterranean.

The Golden Truffle
1767 Newport Blvd.
Costa Mesa
(714) 645-9858
•Patio. Cuisine: French/Caribbean.

Habana Restaurant & Bar
2930 Bristol St.
Costa Mesa
(714) 556-0176
•Bar and patio.
Humidor. Cuisine:
Cuban.

The Cigar Room Inc.
16400 Pacific Coast
Hwy. (Peters
Landing on the
water)
Huntington Beach
(562) 592-5290
•All areas. Humidor.
Cuisine: monthly cigar
dinners—menu varies.
Private cigar club
with public facilities.

Bistango
19100 Von Karman
Ave., Irvine
(714) 752-5222
•Patio and bar/lounge
after 10pm. Humidor.
Cuisine: contemporary California.

Chanteclair
18912 MacArthur
Blvd., Irvine
(714) 752-8001
•Bar and grill room.
Humidor. Cuisine:
French.

The Ritz
880 Newport Center
Dr.
Newport Beach
(714) 720-1800
•Bar/lounge. Humidor. Cuisine: Continental/French.

Twin Palms Newport Beach
630 Newport Center
Dr., Newport Beach
(714) 721-8288
•Patio and bar area.
Humidor. Cuisine:
California Coastal.

Windows on the Bay
2241 W. Coast Hwy.
Newport Beach
(714) 722-1400
•Patio. Humidor.
Cuisine: gourmet.

Morton's of Chicago
1661 W. Sunflower
Ave., Suite C-5
Santa Ana
(714) 444-4834
•Bar. Humidor. Cuisine: steakhouse.

Pizzaioli Ristorante Italiano
3920 Grand Ave.,
Unit. A, Chino
(909) 590-5454
•Patio. Humidor.
Cuisine: Italian.

Hennessey's Tavern
34111 La Plaza
Dana Point
(714) 488-0121
•Bar and patio.
Humidor. Cuisine:
American.

The Ritz-Carlton, Laguna Niguel
One Ritz Carlton Dr.
Dana Point
(714) 240-2000

•Cigar bar "The
Library." Humidor.
Cuisine: dinner is
available in any of the
hotel's three restaurants. Cigar bar.

Brix Dining Cafe and Bar
6763 N. Palm Ave.
Fresno
(209) 435-5441
•Patio. Humidor.
Cuisine: bistro.

Il Vesuvio
7089 N. Marks
Fresno
(209) 446-1443
•Patio. Humidor.
Cuisine: Italian.

Wente Vineyards Restaurant
5050 Arroyo Rd.
Livermore
(510) 456-2450
•Veranda. Humidor.
Cuisine: American.

LOS ANGELES & VICINITY

Beverly Hilton Hotel
9876 Wilshire Blvd.
Beverly Hills
(310) 274-7777
•Bar (separate from
restaurant) and lobby
lounge. Humidor.
Cuisine: Polynesian.

Grand Havana Room
301 N. Canon Dr.
Beverly Hills
(310) 446-4925
•Bar/lounge. Humidor. Cuisine: American. Private club.

Hamiltons at The Wine Merchant
9713 Santa Monica
Blvd.
Beverly Hills
(310) 278-0347
•All areas. Humidor.
Cuisine: appetizers,
desserts, salads, sandwiches. Bar/cigar
bar/entertainment/
retail wine store.

Lawry's The Prime Rib
100 N. La Cienega
Blvd.
Beverly Hills
(310) 652-2827
•Lounge. Cuisine:
American.

McCormick & Schmick's Seafood Restaurant
206 N. Rodeo Dr.
Beverly Hills
(310) 859-0434
•Patio. Humidor.
Cuisine: seafood.

The Peninsula Beverly Hills
9882 Santa Monica
Blvd. S.
Beverly Hills
(310) 551-2888
•Bar. Humidor. Cuisine: Continental.

The Regent Beverly Wilshire
9500 Wilshire Blvd.
Beverly Hills
(310) 275-5200
•Cigar lounge.
Humidor. Cuisine:
Continental.

The Stinking Rose- A Garlic Restaurant
55 N. La Cienega
Beverly Hills
(310) N-LA-ROSE
•*Cigar lounge "Tobacco Road," and outside patio. Humidor. Cuisine: California/Italian.*

Havana Studios
245 E. Olive Ave.,
   Suite 100
Burbank
(818) 557-7600
•*All areas. Humidor.* **Private club.**

Pepper's Restaurant
13101 Crossroads
   Pkwy. S.
City of Industry
(562) 692-4445
•*Bar/lounge and patio. Humidor. Cuisine: Mexican.*

Ceegar Gallery & Lounge
109 E. Broadway
Glendale
(818) 507-0500
•*Lounge. Humidor. Cuisine: pub fare.* **Coffee bar.**

Hennessey's Tavern
8 Pier Ave.
Hermosa Beach
(310) 372-5759
•*Bar/lounge and patio. Humidor. Cuisine: American.*

Lighthouse Cafe
30 Pier Ave.
Hermosa Beach
(310) 376-9833
•*Bar/lounge. Humidor. Cuisine: American.*

Blue Cafe
210 The Promenade
Long Beach
(562) 983-7111
•*All areas. Humidor. Cuisine: deli sandwiches/burgers.* **Bar/ live music.**

Moose McGillycuddy's Pub & Cafe
190 Marina Dr.
Long Beach
(562) 596-8108
•*Patio. Cuisine: American.*

Mum's Restaurant & Club Cohiba
144 Pine Ave.
Long Beach
(562) 437-7700
•*Cigar bar, patio, and rooftop. Humidor. Cuisine: International.*

Nino's Ristorante Italiano
3853 Atlantic Ave.
Long Beach
(562) 427-1003
•*Smoking dining room, patio, and private parties. Cuisine: Italian.*

Phil Trani's
3490 Long Beach
   Blvd., Long Beach
(562) 426-3668
•*Bar. Humidor. Cuisine: creative Cuisine.*

Bel-Air Hotel Dining Room
701 Stone Canyon
   Rd., Los Angeles
(310) 472-1211
•*Lounge and terrace. Humidor. Cuisine: French & California.*

Bernard's Restaurant at The Regal Biltmore
506 S. Grand Ave.
Los Angeles
(213) 612-1580
•*Bar/lounge and patio (Fountain Court) Humidor. Cuisine: Continental.*

Cafe Pinot
700 W. 5th St.
Los Angeles
(213) 239-6500
•*Outdoor garden only. Humidor. Cuisine: French bistro.*

Campanile
624 S. La Brea Ave.
Los Angeles
(213) 938-1447
•*Bar/lounge. Humidor. Cuisine: Mediterranean.*

Checkers
535 S. Grand Ave.
Los Angeles
(213) 624-0000
•*Lobby. Cuisine: California.*

Fénix at the Argyle
8358 Sunset Blvd.
Los Angeles
(213) 848-6677
•*Patio. Humidor. Cuisine: French/Californian.*

Four Seasons Hotel
9500 Wilshire Blvd.
Los Angeles
(310) 275-5200
•*Bar. Humidor. Cuisine: French-Californian.*

Friars Club of California
9900 Santa Monica
   Blvd., Los Angeles
(310) 553-0850
•*Lounge. Humidor. Cuisine: Continental.* **Private club.**

Gardens Restaurant, Window's Bar & Lounge at the Four Seasons
300 S. Doheny Dr.
Los Angeles
(310) 273-2222
•*Outside sections. Humidor. Cuisine: California.*

L'Orangerie
903 N. La Cienega
   Blvd., Los Angeles
(310) 652-9770
•*Bar/lounge. Humidor. Cuisine: contemporary French.*

Lola's
945 N. Fairfax Ave.
Los Angeles
(213) 736-5652
•*Bar and patio. Cuisine: American.*

McCormick & Schmick's Seafood Restaurant
633 W. 5th St.
Los Angeles
(213) 629-1929
•*Bar/lounge (after 9pm) and patio anytime. Humidor. Cuisine: seafood.*

Monty's Steak House
1100 Glendon Ave.
Los Angeles
(310) 208-8787
•*Bar/lounge. Humidor. Cuisine: California.*

Morton's of Chicago
435 S. LaCienega Blvd., Los Angeles
(310) 246-1501
•*Bar. Humidor. Cuisine: steakhouse.*

Pinot Hollywood
1448 N. Gower St.
Los Angeles
(213) 461-8800
•*Bar, martini lounge, cigar bar, private room, and patio. Humidor. Cuisine: California/French bistro.*

Taix French Restaurant
1911 Sunset Blvd.
Los Angeles
(213) 484-1265
•*Bar/lounge. Humidor. Cuisine: country French.*

The Tower
1150 S. Olive St.
atop the Trans-America Center
Los Angeles
(213) 746-1554
•*Bar/lounge and private room. Cuisine: Continental/French.*

Bambú
3835 Cross Creek Rd., Malibu
(310) 456-5464
•*Patio Monday-Sunday; all areas on Tuesday for private cigar club. Humidor. Cuisine: eclectic California & sushi bar.*

The Ritz-Carlton
4375 Admiralty Way
Marina del Rey
(310) 823-1700
•*Bar. Humidor. Cuisine: Provencale.* **Bar.**

Brio Bistro
24050 Camino del Avion
Monarch Beach
(714) 443-1476
•*Patio. Humidor. Cuisine: Italian.*

Il Sogno
863 Swarthmore Ave.
Pacific Palisades
(310) 454-6522
•*Patio. Cuisine: French/Italian.*

Bistro 45
45 S. Mentor Ave.
Pasadena
(818) 795-2478
•*Terrace. Humidor. Cuisine: California-French.*

The Humidor
70 N. Raymond Ave.
Pasadena
(626) 584-6383
•*Bar & patio. Humidor. Cuisine: seafood.* **Private cigar lounge.**

The Maryland Bar at the Doubletree Hotel-Pasadena
191 N. Los Robles Ave., Pasadena
(818) 792-2727
•*Bar/lounge, private room, and patio. Humidor. Cuisine: American & northern Italian.*

McCormick & Schmick's Seafood Restaurant
111 N. Los Robles Ave., Pasadena
(818) 405-0064
•*Patio. Humidor. Cuisine: seafood.*

Twin Palms
Pasadena
101 W. Green St.
Pasadena
(818) 577-2567
•*Bar and patio after 10pm. Humidor. Cuisine: California Coastal.*

Zona Rosa Caffe
15 S. El Molino Ave.
Pasadena
(626) 793-2334
•*Outside patio. Humidor.* **Coffee bar.**

Magic Lamp Inn
8189 Foothill Blvd.
Rancho Cucamonga
(909) 981-8659
•*Bar, lounge, and private rooms. Humidor. Cuisine: American/Continental.*

H.T. Grill
1710 S. Catalina Ave.
Redondo Beach
(310) 316-6658
•*Patio. Humidor. Cuisine: California.*

Ports O'Call Restaurant
Berth 76, Worldport LA, San Pedro
(310) 833-3553
•*Patio. Humidor. Cuisine: California-casual cuisine featuring fresh seafood.*

Drago Ristorante
2628 Wilshire Blvd.
Santa Monica
(310) 828-1585
•*Wine cellar. Cuisine: Italian.*

Michael's
1147 3rd St.
Santa Monica
(310) 451-0843
•*Bar/lounge and patio. Humidor. Cuisine: California/ French.*

Remi
1451 3rd St. Promenade
Santa Monica
(310) 393-6545
•*Private rooms and patio. Humidor. Cuisine: Italian.*

Röckenwagner
2435 Main St.
Santa Monica
(310) 399-6504
•*Patio. Humidor. Cuisine: contemporary French/California.*

Schatzi on Main
3110 Main St.
Santa Monica
(310) 399-4800
•*Patio. Humidor. Cuisine: California.*

World Cafe
2820 Main St.
Santa Monica
(310) 392-1661
•*Patio. Cuisine: California with a Continental flair.*

Romeo et Juliette
1198 Pacific Coast
Hwy., Suite E
Seal Beach
(562) 430-2331
•*Outdoor patio. Humidor. Cuisine: cafe-style.* **Coffee bar.**

The Bistro Garden at Coldwater
12950 Ventura Blvd.
Studio City
(818) 501-0202
•*Bar and private fireside room for private functions. Humidor. Cuisine: Continental/ French.*

Pinot Bistro
12969 Ventura Blvd.
Studio City
(818) 990-0500
•*Patio. Humidor. Cuisine: French bistro.*

Aioli Restaurant
1261 Cabrillo Ave.
Torrance
(310) 320-9200
•*Bar, patio, and banquet room. Humidor. Cuisine: Mediterranean/California.*

The Viper Room
8852 Sunset Blvd.
West Hollywood
(310) 358-1880
•*All areas.* **Nightclub.**

MONTEREY & VICINITY
Covey Quail Lodge Resort
8205 Valley Greens
Dr., Carmel
(408) 624-1581
•*Patio. Humidor. Cuisine: Euro-California.*

Pacific's Edge Restaurant at the Highlands Inn
Hwy. 1 (3.8 miles
south), Carmel
(408) 624-3801
•*Bar/lounge. Humidor. Cuisine: California with a French influence.*

Rio Grill
101 Crossroads
Carmel
(408) 625-5436
•*Patio. Humidor. Cuisine: American grill with a southwest twist.*

The Whaling Station Inn
763 Wave St.
Monterey
(408) 373-3778
•*Outside only. Humidor. Cuisine: prime steak & seafood.*

The Bay Club/Inn at Spanish Bay at The Pebble Beach Resort
2700 17 Mile Dr.
Pebble Beach
(408) 647-7433

•*Patio. Humidor. Cuisine: Northern Italian.*

NAPA & VICINITY
Bistro Don Giovanni
4110 St. Helena
Hwy., Napa
(707) 224-3300
•*On lawn adjacent to the restaurant. Humidor. Cuisine: French/ Italian.*

Mustards Grill
7399 St. Helena
Hwy., Napa
(707) 944-2424
•*Patio (dubbed the "Cigar & Wildlife Preserve"). Humidor. Cuisine: American.*

Auberge du Soleil
180 Rutherford Hill
Rd., Rutherford
(707) 963-1211
•*Bar. Humidor. Cuisine: wine country.*

The Restaurant at Meadowood at the Meadowood Resort
900 Meadowood
Lane, St. Helena
(707) 963-3646
•*Patio. Humidor. Cuisine: wine country.*

Showley's at Miramonte
1327 Railroad Ave.
St. Helena
(707) 963-1200

•*Outdoor patio.
Humidor. Cuisine:
California.*

PALM SPRINGS & VICINITY

Morton's of Chicago
74-880 Country
Club Dr.
Palm Desert
(760) 340-6865
•*Bar. Humidor. Cuisine: steakhouse.*

The Ritz-Carlton
68900 Frank Sinatra
Dr.
Rancho Mirage
(760) 321-8282
•*Bar. Humidor. Cuisine: Mediterranean.*
Cigar bar.

SACRAMENTO

Ciao Yama and Dawson's at The Hyatt Regency Sacramento
1209 L St.
Sacramento
(916) 443-1234
•*Patio and other designated areas. Humidor. Cuisine: Japanese (Ciao Yama); upscale chophouse (Dawson's).* **Nightclub.**

Harlows Restaurant & Nightclub
2708 J St.
Sacramento
(916) 441-4693

•*"Momo Lounge" over the bar. Humidor. Cuisine: modern American.*

Mace's
501 Pavillion Lane
Sacramento
(916) 922-0222
•*Bar/lounge and patio. Humidor. Cuisine: American.*

Morton's of Chicago
521 L St.
Sacramento
(916) 442-5091
•*Bar. Humidor. Cuisine: steakhouse.*

The Pig's Ear Pub
1987 S. Diners
Court
San Bernardino
(909) 889-1442
•*Bar and patio. Humidor. Cuisine: British—fish & chips, roast beef, & other pub food.*

SAN DIEGO & VICINITY

Hennessey's Tavern
2777 Roosevelt St.
Carlsbad
(760) 729-6951
•*Bar and outside patio. Humidor. Cuisine: American.*

Il Forno Bistro & Bar
909 Prospect St.,
#190, La Jolla
(619) 459-5010

•*Bar, lounge, and patio. Humidor. Cuisine: Italian.*

Top O' The Cove
1216 Prospect St.
La Jolla
(619) 454-7779
•*Front patio. Humidor. Cuisine: Continental.*

Baci's
1955 W. Morena
Blvd., San Diego
(619) 275-2094
•*Outside. Humidor. Cuisine: Italian.*

El Bizcocho
17550 Bernardo
Oaks Dr.
San Diego
(619) 487-1611
•*Patio. Humidor. Cuisine: French/California.*

Grant Grill Lounge at the U.S. Grant Hotel
326 Broadway
San Diego
(619) 239-6806
•*Lounge area. Humidor. Cuisine: Continental.*

Osteria Panevino
722 5th Ave.
San Diego
(619) 595-7959
•*Patio. Humidor. Cuisine: Tuscan.*

Prego Ristorante
1370 Frazee Rd.
San Diego
(619) 294-4700

•*Heated courtyard surrounded by olive trees, fountains, & herb garden in a Tuscan setting. Humidor. Cuisine: regional Italian.*

Trattoria Portobello
715 4th Ave.
San Diego
(619) 232-4440
•*Bar. Humidor. Cuisine: contemporary Italian.*

SAN FRANCISCO & VICINITY

Papa Georges Restaurant and Tavern
2320 S. Cabrillo
Hwy.
Half Moon Bay
(650) 726-9417
•*Outside patios and tavern. Humidor. Cuisine: Continental.*

Dal Baffo Restaurant
878 Santa Cruz Ave.
Menlo Park
(650) 325-1588
•*Bar/lounge and cigar bar. Humidor. Cuisine: Continental.*

Garden Grill and Red Terrier Pub
1626 Elma St.
Menlo Park
(415) 325-8981
•*Pub and patio. Humidor. Cuisine: British & California.*

Terrace Cafe
1100 El Camino
  Real, Millbrae
(415) 742-5588
•*Patio. Cuisine:
American.*

**Orsi's (Ristorante
Orsi)**
340 Ignacio Blvd.
Novato
(415) 883-0960
•*Bar. Cuisine: Italian.*

Alioto's Restaurant
8 Fisherman's Wharf
San Francisco
(415) 673-0183
•*Bar, lounge, and
private rooms. Humidor. Cuisine: Sicilian
specialties.*

**The Big Four
Restaurant at The
Huntington Hotel**
1075 California St.
San Francisco
(415) 771-1140
•*Bar. Humidor. Cuisine: contemporary
American.*

Cypress Club
500 Jackson St.
San Francisco
(415) 296-8555
•*Bar and private
rooms. Humidor.
Cuisine: American.*

Essex Supper Club
847 Montgomery St.
San Francisco
(415) 397-5969

•*"Bacchus Wine Cellar" (floor devoted to
cigar smoking).
Humidor. Cuisine:
California.*

Fournou's Ovens
905 California St.
San Francisco
(415) 989-3500
•*Lounge. Humidor.
Cuisine: Mediterranean.*

Fumé Restaurant
101 Cyril Magnin
San Francisco
(415) 788-3863
•*Cigar bar. Humidor.
Cuisine: Japanese.*
Cigar bar.

**George's Global
Kitchen**
340 Division St.
San Francisco
(415) 864-4224
•*Dining room during
smoker nights only and
patio. Humidor. Cuisine: American—on
smoker nights California & French are
served.*

The Gold Club
650 Howard
San Francisco
(415) 536-0300
•*All areas. Humidor.
Cuisine: features
salmon, pasta, &
steak.* **Upscale gentleman's club.**

**Harrington's Bar &
Grill**
245 Front St.
San Francisco
(415) 392-7595
•*Bar. Cuisine: American.*

**Harry Denton's
Starlight Room**
450 Powell St.
San Francisco
(415) 395-8595
•*Bar/lounge area.
Humidor. Cuisine:
light fare featuring
caviar, Caesar salads,
shrimp, & crabcakes.*
Nightclub.

**Morton's of
Chicago**
400 Post St.
San Francisco
(415) 986-5830
•*Bar/lounge. Humidor. Cuisine: steakhouse.*

Murray's
740 Sutter St.
San Francisco
(415) 474-6478
•*Cigar room. Humidor. Cuisine: farm
fresh California &
American provincial.*

**The Park Grill at
the Park Hyatt
Hotel**
333 Battery St.
San Francisco
(415) 296-2933
•*Bars only. Humidor. Cuisine: California/Pacific Rim &
Continental.*

The Ritz-Carlton
600 Stockton St.
San Francisco
(415) 296-7465
•*Ritz-Carlton Bar
from 6pm until closing. Humidor. Cuisine: contemporary
French.* **Cigar bar.**

Stars
150 Redwood Alley
San Francisco
(415) 861-7827
•*Special facility, the
"Stellar Cigar Society
Smoke Room." Humidor. Cuisine: Californian/New American.*

Timo's Norte
900 N. Point St.
San Francisco
(415) 440-1200
•*Bar, smoking room,
and outside on a
heated patio. Humidor. Cuisine: Spanish
tapas.*

Vendetta
12 Tillman Place
San Francisco
(415) 397-7755
•*Cigar smoking room-
members only. Humidor.* **Smoking club &
retail men's apparel
and cigars.**

Barley & Hopps
201 S. B St.
San Mateo
(650) 348-7808
• *Billiards parlor.
Humidor. Cuisine:
American regional
with BBQ specialties.*

**Wave's
Smokehouse &
Saloon**
65 Post St.
San Jose
(408) 885-9283
• *Upstairs, outdoors,
and patio. Humidor.
Cuisine: BBQ.*

Cafe Roma
1819 Osos St.
San Luis Obispo
(805) 541-6800
• *Patio. Humidor.
Cuisine: Italian.*

Wine Cask
813 Anacapa St.
Santa Barbara
(805) 966-9463
• *Heated outdoor patio
only. Humidor. Cui-
sine: California.*

**Wine Cask
Intermezzo**
813 Anacapa St.
Santa Barbara
(805) 966-9463
• *Front patio. Humi-
dor. Cuisine: light
bistro, featuring break-
fast, lunch, & a light
dinner menu.*

**Santa Cruz
Brewing Co. &
Front St. Pub**
516 Front St.
Santa Cruz
(408) 429-8838
• *Beer Garden
(heated). Humidor.
Cuisine: pub fare.*

Garlic Brothers
6629 Embarcadero
Stockton
(209) 474-6585
• *Outside deck.
Humidor. Cuisine:
California.*

**Vintage Press
Restaurant**
216 N. Willis St.
Visalia
(209) 733-3033
• *Bar, lounge, private
rooms, and patio.
Humidor. Cuisine:
American.*

Colorado

The Greenbriar
Lefthand Cyn & 36
Boulder
(303) 440-7979
• *Bar. Humidor. Cui-
sine: American.*

Laudisio
2785 Iris Ave.
Boulder
(303) 442-1300
• *Cigar lounge. Humi-
dor. Cuisine: Italian.*

COLORADO
SPRINGS

Primitivo Wine Bar
28 S. Tejon St.

Colorado Springs
(719) 473-4900
• *Cigar bar, patio, and
private rooms. Humi-
dor. Cuisine: Mediter-
ranean.*

**Stars Club & Cigar
Bar at The
Broadmoor**
PO Box 1429
Colorado Springs
• *All smoking areas.
Humidor.*
Nightclub.

DENVER &
VICINITY

Avenue Grill
630 E. 17th Ave.
Denver
(303) 861-2820
• *Lounge and smoking
section. Humidor.
Cuisine: traditional
grilled cuisine in the
manner of a San Fran-
cisco-style bar & grill.*

**Churchill Cigar Bar
at The Brown
Palace Hotel**
321 17th St., Denver
(303) 297-3111 ext.
  3339
• *All areas. Humidor.
Cuisine: American.*
Cigar bar.

**Del Frisco's Double
Eagle Steak House**
8100 E. Orchard Rd.
Denver
(303) 796-0100

• *Cigar lounge and
smoking section in
main dining room.
Humidor. Cuisine:
USDA prime aged
beef & seafood.*

Morton's of Chicago
1710 Wynkoop St.
Denver
(303) 825-3353
• *Smoking area and
bar. Humidor. Cui-
sine: steakhouse.*

Shakespeare's
2375 15th St.
Denver
(303) 433-6000
• *All areas. Humidor.
Cuisine: American
bistro.*

Tante Louise
4900 E. Colfax Ave.
Denver
(303) 355-4488
• *Select areas of the
dining room and
lounge. Humidor.
Cuisine: contempo-
rary French.*

Trinity Grille
1801 Broadway
Denver
(303) 293-2288
• *Bar area. Humidor.
Cuisine: American.*

Trois Enoteca
1730 Wynkoop St.
Denver
(303) 293-2887
• *Cigar room. Humi-
dor. Cuisine: fabulous
appetizers, soups, &
salads.* **Wine & cigar
bar.**

The Divide Grill atop Cooper Creek Square
Main St. - Hwy. 40
Winter Park
(970) 726-4900
•*Bar area. Humidor. Cuisine: Black Angus steaks, fresh seafood, & pasta.*

Smokin' Moe's Ribhouse & Saloon
Courtyard at Cooper
 Creek Square
Downtown Winter
 Park - Hwy. 40
Winter Park
(970) 726-4600
•*Bar area and specified section of the restaurant. Humidor. Cuisine: Oklahoma/Texas BBQ featuring hickory smoked ribs, chicken, brisket, & chops.*

FORT
COLLINS &
VICINITY
Marie's Inn
400 Mountain Ave.
Berthoud
(970) 532-2648
•*Smoking room. Cuisine: Czech-German & American.*

Nico's Catacombs
115 S. College Ave.
Fort Collins
(970) 484-6029
•*Bar, lounge, and private rooms after 9:30pm. Cuisine: American/Continental.*

New Sheridan Hotel Restaurant & Bar
231 W. Colorado
Telluride
(970) 728-3911
•*Bar and pool hall. Humidor. Cuisine: steak, game, seafood, pasta.*

Club Chelsea
304 Bridge, Vail
(970) 476-5600
•*Smoking room and smoking section. Humidor. Cuisine: snacks are available.* **Nightclub/bar.**

Connecticut

Hat City Ale House & Cigar Bar
253 Main St.
Danbury
(203) 790-4287
•*All areas. Humidor.* **Beer bar/cigar bar.**

Peppercorn's Grill
357 Main St.
Hartford
(860) 547-1714
•*Lounge and bar after 10pm. Humidor. Cuisine: Italian.*

Tollgate Hill Inn
Rte. 202 & Tollgate
 Rd., Litchfield
(860) 567-4545
•*Bar and patio. Humidor. Cuisine: American.*

Eli Cannon's Tap Room
695 Main St.
Middletown
(860) 347-3547
•*Tap room and outdoor courtyard. Cuisine: American.*

NEW HAVEN
& VICINITY
Callahan's Restaurant
1027 S. Main St.
Cheshire
(203) 271-1993
•*All areas. Humidor. Cuisine: American.*

Scribner's
31 Village Rd.
Milford
(203) 878-7019
•*Bar/lounge. Cuisine: seafood.*

Barkies Grill and Rotisserie
220 College St.
New Haven
(203) 752-1000
•*Lounge area. Humidor. Cuisine: American.*

The Brewery
458 Grand Ave.
New Haven
(203) 773-5297
•*Bar and smoking section. Humidor. Cuisine: American grill.*

Scoozzi Trattoria & Wine Bar
1104 Chapel St.
New Haven
(203) 776-8268

•*Bar, lounge, and patio. Humidor. Cuisine: innovative Italian.*

Le Bon Coin
223 Litchfield Tpke.
New Preston
(203) 868-7763
•*Bar. Cuisine: French.*

The Fumè: Cigar Bar, Restaurant, & Nite Club
7 Wall St., Norwalk
(203) 899-0222
•*Bar, lounge, and cigar bar. Humidor. Cuisine: American grill featuring steak & seafood.*

Old Lyme Inn
85 Lyme St.
Old Lyme
(860) 434-2600
•*Bar and library sitting area. Cuisine: classic American.*

La Bretagne Restaurant
2010 W. Main St.
Stamford
(203) 324-9539
•*Bar/lounge. Cuisine: French.*

WATERBURY
Bacco's Restaurant
1230 Thomaston
 Ave., Waterbury
(203) 755-0635
•*Bar. Humidor. Cuisine: Italian.*

Cafe 4 Fifty 7
457 W. Main St.
Waterbury
(203) 574-4507
•*Bar area. Cuisine: Italian specializing in fish & pasta.*

Carmen Anthony's Steakhouse
496 Chase Ave.
Waterbury
(203) 757-3040
•*Bar. Humidor. Cuisine: steakhouse.*

Restaurant Promis/ Club Boca Chica
1563 Post Rd. E.
Westport
(203) 256-3309
•*Bar and Club Boca Chica (smoking dining room). Humidor. Cuisine: Continental.*

Madeleines Restaurant
1530 Palisado Ave.
Windsor
(860) 688-0150
•*Bar. Humidor. Cuisine: French.*

Delaware

DOVER & VICINITY
Blue Coat Inn
800 N. State St.
Dover
(302) 674-1776
•*Designated smoking sections. Cuisine: American.*

Paradiso Restaurant
1151 E. Lebanon
Rd./Rte. 10 Plaza
Dover
(302) 697-3055
•*Smoking section and cappacino bar. Humidor. Cuisine: Northern Italian.*

Rose & Crown Restaurant & Pub
108 2nd St., Lewes
(302) 645-2373
•*Cigar lounge and in main area of restaurant after conclusion of dinner service. Humidor. Cuisine: seafood, steaks, & pastas.*

Columbus Inn
2216 Pennsylvania
Ave., Wilmington
(302) 571-1492
•*Bar, adjoining club room, and 3 private dining rooms. Humidor. Cuisine: new American.*

Harry's Savoy Grill
2020 Naaman's Rd.
Wilmington
(302) 475-3000
•*Bar, grill room, and patio. Humidor. Cuisine: American featuring beef & seafood.*

District of Columbia

Butlers-The Cigar Bar
10th & H. Sts., NW
Washington, D.C.
(202) 637-4765
•*All areas. Humidor. Cuisine: American.*
Cigar bar.

Café Atlantico
405 8th St. NW
Washington, D.C.
(202) 393-0812
•*Bar and cigar smoking dinner tables. Humidor. Cuisine: Nuevo Latino.*

The Capital Grille
601 Pennsylvania
Ave.
Washington, D.C.
(202) 737-6200
•*Bar/lounge, smoking sections, and wine room for private use. Humidor. Cuisine: steakhouse, specializing in dry-aged steak.*

Capitol View Club at the Hyatt Regency
400 New Jersey Ave.
NW
Washington, D.C.
(202) 783-2582
•*Lounge. Humidor. Cuisine: American— steaks, seafood, pasta.*
Private club.

Grand Havana Room
1220 19th St. NW
Washington, D.C.
(202) 955-4575
•*Bar/lounge. Humidor. Cuisine: American.* **Private club.**

i Ricchi
1220 19th St. NW
Washington, D.C.
(202) 835-0459
•*Smoking areas. Cuisine: authentic regional Italian/Tuscan.*

J. Paul's
3218 M St. NW
Washington, D.C.
(202) 333-3450
•*Bar area and large smoking section. Humidor. Cuisine: American saloon.*

John Hay Room at the Hay Adams Hotel
800 16th St. NW
Washington, D.C.
(202) 638-6600
•*Lounge. Humidor. Cuisine: American.*

La Brasserie
239 Massachusetts
Ave. NE
Washington, D.C.
(202) 546-9154
•*Bar. Cuisine: French.*

La Colline
400 N. Capitol St.
NW
Washington, D.C.
(202) 737-0400
•*Smoking section.
Humidor. Cuisine:
French.*

**Les Halles
Restaurant**
1201 Pennsylvania
Ave. NW
Washington, D.C.
(202) 347-6848
•*3rd level dining room
and bar/lounge.
Humidor. Cuisine:
French/American
steakhouse.*

**Les Pinasse at the
Sheraton Carlton**
923 16th St. NW &
K St.
Washington, D.C.
(202) 638-2626
•*Library lounge.
Humidor. Cuisine:
Continental.*

**Melrose at the Park
Hyatt Washington**
24 & M Sts.
Washington, D.C.
(202) 955-3899
•*"Melrose Bar" and
the lounge. Humidor.
Cuisine: contemporary
American.*

**The Monocle on
Capitol Hill**
107 D St. NE
Washington, D.C.
(202) 546-4488

•*Bar and smoking
section of dining room.
Humidor. Cuisine:
American.*

**Morton's of
Chicago**
3251 Prospect St.
NW
Washington, D.C.
(202) 342-6258
•*Bar, lounge, and
parts of the dining
room. Humidor. Cui-
sine: steakhouse.*

Nathan's
3150 M St. NW
Washington, D.C.
(202) 338-2000
•*Bar (with late night
dancing in back).
Humidor. Cuisine:
Northern Italian/new
American.*

**Ozio Martini &
Cigar Lounge**
1835 K St. NW
Washington, D.C.
(202) 822-6000
•*All areas. Humidor.
Cuisine: Continental
& international tapas.*

Renaissance Hotel
999 9th St. NW
Washington, D.C.
(202) 898-9000
•*Bar. Humidor. Cui-
sine: Mediterranean.*

Sam & Harry's
1200 19th St. NW
Washington, D.C.
(202) 296-4333

•*Smoking section.
Humidor. Cuisine:
American.*

**Seasons Restaurant
at the Four Seasons
Hotel**
2800 Pennsylvania
Ave. NW
Washington, D.C.
(202) 342-0810
•*Bar/lounge, smoking
section, private room
and patio. Humidor.
Cuisine: contemporary
American.*

Sesto Senso
1214 18th St. NW
Washington, D.C.
(202) 785-9525
•*Bar/lounge, smoking
section, and cigar bar.
Humidor. Cuisine:
Italian.*

Shelly's Back Room
1331 F St. NW
Washington, D.C.
(202) 737-3003
•*All areas. Humidor.
Cuisine: casual Amer-
ican fare (burgers,
soups, salads, sand-
wiches, NY strip,
salmon).* **Tavern.**

**Tunnicliff's
Restaurant**
222 7th St. SE
Washington, D.C.
(202) 546-3663
•*Bar, living room,
patio, and front tables
in the restaurant.
Humidor. Cuisine:
Cajun & American.*

Florida

**Boca Raton Hotel
& Club**
501 E. Camino Real
Boca Raton
(561) 395-3000
•*El Lago Lounge.
Humidor. Cuisine:
Continental, Italian,
& seafood available at
the hotel's restaurants.*

**Maxwell's
Chophouse**
501 E. Palmetto Park
Rd., Boca Raton
(561) 347-7077
•*Grill and club room.
Humidor. Cuisine:
steak & seafood (lob-
ster in club & ham-
burgers in grill room).*

**Bobby's Bistro &
Wine Bar**
447 Mandalay Ave.
Clearwater Beach
(813) 446-WINE
•*Smoking section,
bar, and patio. Humi-
dor. Cuisine: diverse
menu, featuring such
items as elk, buffalo,
& snook.*

**Bernkastel
Festhaus at the
Adams Mark
Resort**
100 N. Atlantic
Ave., Suite 27
Daytona Beach
(904) 255-8300

Was Your Favorite
"Cigar-friendly" Restaurant Listed?

If your favorite "cigar-friendly" restaurant was not included in this book, let the editors of *Cigar Aficionado* know by simply filling out the form and dropping it in the mail.

Restaurant Name _____

Address _____

City/State/Zip _____

Tel _____ Fax _____

Thank you for your help.

CF06

Business Reply Mail
FIRST-CLASS MAIL PERMIT NO. 5366, NEW YORK, N.Y

POSTAGE WILL BE PAID BY ADDRESSEE

Cigar Aficionado
387 Park Avenue South
New York, NY 10157-0198

•*All areas. Humidor.
Cuisine: German
sausages & gourmet
sandwiches; offers 47
draft beers.*

**Huddleston's
Blind Pig Pub**
148 W. New York
   Ave.
DeLand Junction
(904) 736-3450
•*All areas. Humidor.
Cuisine: pub fare.*

Destin Chops
320 Hwy. 98 E.
Destin
(904) 654-4944
•*Bar and designated
smoking area. Humidor. Cuisine: steak.*

FORT
LAUDERDALE
& VICINITY
**Churchill's
Restaurant & Pub**
Pine Lake Plaza/
   10076 Griffin Rd.
Cooper City
(954) 680-0226
•*Pub and private dining room. Humidor.
Cuisine: Euro-American.*

**The Melting Pot—
A Fondue
Restaurant**
10374 W. Sample
   Rd.
Coral Springs
(954) 755-6368
•*Bar area. Humidor.
Cuisine: fondue.*

Burt & Jack's
Berth 23, Port Everglades
Fort Lauderdale
(954) 522-5225
•*Cocktail lounge and
patio. Humidor. Cuisine: sophisticated
American.*

Canyon
1818 E. Sunrise
   Blvd.
Fort Lauderdale
(954) 765-1950
•*All areas after 9pm.
Cuisine: gourmet
American/Southwestern.*

**Harbor Beach at
the Marriott Hotel**
3030 Holiday Dr.
Fort Lauderdale
(954) 525-4000
•*Bar. Humidor. Cuisine: eclectic seafood.*

Mark's Las Olas
1032 E. Las Olas
   Blvd.
Fort Lauderdale
(954) 463-1000
•*Bar, lounge, and
outdoors. Humidor.
Cuisine: contemporary American featuring Florida seafood.*

Petaluma
2861 E. Commercial
   Blvd.
Fort Lauderdale
(954) 771-8336
•*All areas. Humidor.
Cuisine: Italian/Continental.*

**Playoffs Sports
Grill**
3001 E. Commercial
   Blvd.
Fort Lauderdale
(954) 772-7890
•*Skybox area. Humidor. Cuisine: steaks,
chops.*

**Smoke Chophouse
& Cigar Emporium**
2863 E. Commercial
   Blvd.
Fort Lauderdale
(954) 489-1122
•*All areas. Humidor.
Cuisine: steak, chops,
& seafood.*

**Smugglers of Las
Olas, Martini &
Cigar Club**
609 E. Las Olas
   Blvd.
Fort Lauderdale
(954) 767-0029
•*Cigar bar. Humidor.
Cuisine: American.*

Studio One Cafe
2447 E. Sunrise
   Blvd.
Fort Lauderdale
(954) 565-2052
•*Dining room after
9pm and patio. Cuisine: American,
French, & Mediterranean.*

Veranda
2122 2nd St.
Fort Myers
(941) 332-2065
•*Piano lounge.
Humidor. Cuisine:
elegant Southern.*

Max & Meg's
122 N. 2nd. St.
Fort Pierce
(561) 467-0065
•*Smoking section of
dining room and in the
bar area. Humidor.
Cuisine: burgers to
Black Angus steaks to
seafood.*

JACKSONVILLE
& VICINITY
The Ritz-Carlton
4750 Amelia Island
   Pkwy.
Amelia Island
(904) 277-1100
•*Bar/lounge, private
room, and patio.
Humidor. Cuisine:
Grill is fine dining;
Cafe serves Continental.*

**The Blue Anchor
Pub**
10550 Old St.
   Augustine Rd.
Jacksonville
(904) 262-1592
•*All areas. Humidor.
Cuisine: pub fare.*

**TPC (Tournament
Players Club) at
Sawgrass**
110 TPC Blvd.
Ponte Vedra
(904) 273-3242
•*Throughout the clubhouse. Humidor. Cuisine: American,
Caribbean, & Continental, specializing in
seafood. **Private
club.***

KEY LARGO & VICINITY

Uncle's Restaurant
M.M. 80, Islamorada
(305) 664-4402
•Smoking area and patio. Humidor. Cuisine: fresh pasta, steak, chicken, Italian, seafood, & wild game.

Snook's Bayside Restaurant and Patrick's Waterfront Bar
M.M. 99.9 (behind Largo Honda)
Key Largo
(305) 453-3799
•At bars only. Humidor. Cuisine: features seafood, certified beef, veal, & chicken.

KEY WEST

Ernest's Cafe
832 Whitehead St.
Key West
(305) 296-9624
•Bar/lounge and Cafe. Humidor. Cuisine: lite fare.

Flagler's Restaurant at The Marriot's Casa Marina Hotel
1500 Reynold's St.
Key West
(305) 296-3535
•Smoking section of dining room and lounge. Humidor. Cuisine: steakhouse.

Louie's Backyard
700 Weddell Ave.
Key West
(305) 294-1061

•Deck only. Humidor. Cuisine: eclectic.

The Ocean View
1435 Simonton St.
Key West
(305) 296-5000
•Outdoor restaurant. Humidor. Cuisine: Continental, featuring fresh seafood.

Blue Water Bay
State Rd. 26
Melrose
(352) 475-1928
•Bar and smoking section. Humidor. Cuisine: features seafood & certified black angus.

MIAMI & VICINITY

Cafe Tu Tu Tango
Cocowalk/3015 Grand Ave., Suite 2510
Coconut Grove
(305) 529-2222
•Patio. Humidor. Cuisine: eclectic & multinational appetizers.

Caffe Abbracci
318 Aragon Ave.
Coral Gables
(305) 441-0700
•Bar. Humidor. Cuisine: Italian.

The Heights
2530 Ponce de Leon
Coral Gables
(305) 461-1774

•Cigar terrace only. Humidor. Cuisine: contemporary American with southwest & Asian influences.

Rusty Pelican Restaurant
3201 Rickenbacker Causeway
Key Biscayne
(305) 361-3818
•Bar, outside patio, and at private functions. Humidor. Cuisine: Continental, seafood.

Casa Juancho Restaurant
2436 SW 8th St.
Miami
(305) 642-2452
•Dining room, bar, lounge, and private rooms. Humidor. Cuisine: Spanish, specializing in seafood.

Hotel Casa de Campo
2600 SW 3rd Ave., #300, Miami
(809) 523-3333
•All areas. Humidor. Cuisine: American, Mexican, & Dominican, specializing in seafood & steak.

Le Pavillon Restaurant at the Hotel Intercontinental
100 Chopin Plaza
Miami
(305) 577-1000

•Lobby lounge and Oak Room bar. Humidor. Cuisine: Continental & French.

Morton's of Chicago
1200 Brickell, Miami
(305) 400-9990
•All areas. Humidor. Cuisine: steakhouse.

Speakeasy Les Deux Foutaines at the Ocean Front Hotel
1238 Ocean Dr.
Miami
(305) 672-7878
•Outside terrace overlooking Ocean Dr., inside dining area, and Speakeasy lounge bar. Humidor. Cuisine: seafood. **Bar/cigar bar.**

Cafe Royal at The Hotel Sofitel Miami
5800 Blue Lagoon Dr., Miami Beach
(305) 264-4888
•"Le Fumoir" cigar lounge and bar; private parties in the Limoges room. Humidor. Cuisine: French classical.

The Forge
432 Arthur Godfrey Rd., Miami Beach
(305) 538-8533
•Smoking section. Humidor. Cuisine: American/Continental.

i Paparazzi
940 Ocean Dr.
Miami Beach
(305) 531-3500
•*Patio. Humidor.
Cuisine: Italian.*

Jimmy at Cuba Club
432 Arthur Godfrey
Rd., Miami Beach
(305) 604-9798
•*All areas. Humidor.
Cuisine: Continental.*

Joe's Stone Crab
227 Biscayne St.
Miami Beach
(305) 673-0365
•*Bar and lounge.
Humidor. Cuisine:
seafood.*

The Strand
671 Washington St.
Miami Beach
(305) 532-2340
•*The Living Room:
all areas. Humidor.
Cuisine: American
with a twist of French.*

Yuca
501 Lincoln
Miami Beach
(305) 532-9822
•*Smoking section,
bar, and lounge.
Humidor. Cuisine:
innovative Cuban.*

Chef Allen's
19088 NE 29th Ave.
North Miami Beach
(305) 935-2900
•*Bar and smoking
section. Humidor.
Cuisine: new world.*

Heaven
The Hibiscus Cen-
ter/2950 N. Tamia-
mi Trail
Naples
(941) 649-6373
•*All areas. Humidor.
Cuisine: nouveau.*
Cigar bar.

Terra
1300 3rd St. S.
Naples
(941) 262-5500
•*Smoking area. Cui-
sine: Mediterranean.*

Maison & Jardin
430 S. Wymore Rd.
Altamonte Springs
(407) 862-4410
•*Lounge, patio, and
private dining rooms.
Humidor. Cuisine:
Continental.*

**The Green Parrot
Pub & Eatery**
280 E. Semoran
Blvd.
Casselberry
(407) 332-1599
•*All areas. Cuisine:
upscale casual.*

**Pleasure Island Jazz
Company**
PO Box 10,150
Lake Buena Vista
(407) 828-5665
•*In the cigar area.
Humidor. Cuisine:
Continental.* **Night-
club.**

Cuban-to-Go
1605 Lee Rd.
Orlando
(407) 578-8888
•*Patio. Humidor.
Cuisine: Cuban.*

Morton's of Chicago
7600 Dr. Philips
Blvd., Orlando
(407) 248-3485
•*Smoking area and
bar. Humidor. Cui-
sine: steakhouse.*

**O'Keefe's Irish Pub
Restaurant**
115 S. Rockingham
Ave., Tavares
(352) 343-2157
•*Smoking area and
bar area. Humidor.
Cuisine: Irish & Con-
tinental world cuisine.*

**Four Seasons
Restaurant**
2800 S. Ocean Blvd.
Palm Beach
(561) 582-2800
•*Bar/lounge. Humi-
dor. Cuisine: south-
eastern regional.*

**The Leopard Room
Restaurant &
Supper Club at the
Chesterfield Hotel**
363 Cocoanut Row
Palm Beach
(561) 659-5800
•*All areas after dinner;
bar and lounge before
dinner. Humidor. Cui-
sine: Continental.*

Sheldon's
9501 Harding Ave.
Bay Harbour
(305) 866-6251
•*Bar. Humidor. Cui-
sine: American.*

**Panama City
Brewery & Café**
11040 Hutchison
Blvd. (Middle
Beach Rd.)
Panama City Beach
(904) 230-BREW
•*Special section for
cigar smokers. Humi-
dor. Cuisine: features
fresh seafood prepared
in Southwestern- &
Floridian-style; also,
steaks, chicken, pizza,
salad, fresh desserts,
& homebrewed beers.*

**The Colony
Restaurant at the
Colony Beach
Hotel & Resort**
1620 Gulf of Mexico
Dr., Longboat Key
(941) 383-5558
•*Lounge. Humidor.
Cuisine: regional
American.*

**Zeno's Italian
Restaurant**
267 US Hwy. 27 N.
Sebring
(941) 471-9844
•*Outside. Humidor.
Cuisine: Italian.*

TAMPA & VICINITY

Armani's at The Hyatt Regency Westshore
6200 Courtney Campbell Causeway, Tampa
(813) 281-9165
•*Lounge and terrace. Humidor. Cuisine: Northern Italian.*

Bern's Steakhouse
1208 S. Howard Ave., Tampa
(813) 251-2421
•*Bar/lounge and the dessert Room. Humidor. Cuisine: American, specializing in steak.*

Columbia Restaurant & Cafe Cigar Bar
2117 E. 7th Ave. Tampa
(813) 248-4961
•*Cafe cigar bar. Humidor. Cuisine: Spanish.*

Le Bordeaux
1502 S. Howard Ave., Tampa
(813) 254-4387
•*Lounge and courtyards. Humidor. Cuisine: French.*

Bernini
1702 E. 7th Ave. Ybor City
(813) 248-0099
•*All areas. Humidor. Cuisine: innovative Italian.*

WEST PALM BEACH & VICINITY

The Ritz-Carlton
100 Ocean Blvd. Manalapan
(561) 533-6000
•*Bar/lounge and lobby lounge. Humidor. Cuisine: Mediterranean & Continental.*

John Bull English Pub
801 Village Blvd. West Palm Beach
(561) 697-2855
•*Cigar room at all times and smoking section of dining room after 10pm. Humidor. Cuisine: English pub/ American grill.*

Morton's of Chicago
777 S. Flagler West Palm Beach
(561) 835-9664
•*Smoking section, lounge, and private rooms. Humidor. Cuisine: steakhouse.*

Georgia

ATLANTA & VICINITY

103 West
103 W. Paces Ferry Rd. Atlanta
(404) 233-5993
•*Lounge. Humidor. Cuisine: new American with a French influence.*

The Abbey
163 Ponce de Leon Ave. Atlanta
(404) 876-8532
•*Bar, lounge, and private rooms. Humidor. Cuisine: Continental.*

Bone's Restaurant
3130 Piedmont Rd. Atlanta
(404) 237-2663
•*Bar and smoking section. Humidor. Cuisine: steak & seafood.*

Bugatti Restaurant at the Omni Hotel
100 CNN Center Atlanta
(404) 818-4450
•*Smoking area of dining room and bar. Humidor. Cuisine: Northern Italian.*

Cafe Intermezzo
1845 Peachtree Rd. Atlanta
(404) 355-0411
•*In Loggia (special smoking room-dining available), bar, and patio. Humidor. Cuisine: international bistro & European coffeehouse items.* **European coffeehouse.**

Cheyene Grill & The Clubhouse
2391 Peachtree Rd. Atlanta
(404) 842-1010

•*Martini room. Humidor. Cuisine: American grill.*

Chops
70 W. Paces Ferry Rd. Atlanta
(404) 262-2675
•*Bar area and smoking section. Humidor. Cuisine: steak, seafood, lobster.*

Filibuster's
1049 Juniper St. Atlanta
(404) 875-6634
•*Smoking section and bar area. Humidor. Cuisine: traditional American.*

Four Seasons Hotel
75 14th St. Atlanta
(404) 881-9898
•*Bar/lounge. Humidor. Cuisine: new American.*

The Mansion
179 Ponce de Leon Ave. Atlanta
(404) 876-0727
•*Smoking section, smoking parlour, and garden courtyard. Humidor. Cuisine: American/Continental.*

The Martini Club
1140 Crescent Ave. Atlanta
(404) 873-0794
•*All areas. Humidor.* **Nightclub/piano bar/nightly jazz.**

Morton's of Chicago
303 Peachtree St.
    NE Atlanta
(404) 577-4366
•*Smoking section,
bar, lounge, and foyer.
Humidor. Cuisine:
steakhouse.*

Morton's of Chicago, Buckhead
Peachtree Lenox
    Building/3379
    Peachtree Rd. NE
    Atlanta
(404) 816-6535
•*Bar, dining room,
and private dining
rooms. Humidor.
Cuisine: steakhouse,
lobster, seafood.*

The Ritz-Carlton, Atlanta
181 Peachtree St.
    NE Atlanta
(404) 659-0400
•*Bar. Humidor. Cui-
sine: haute-fusion
French.*

The Ritz-Carlton, Buckhead
3434 Peachtree Rd.
    Atlanta
(404) 237-2700
•*Bar. Humidor. Cui-
sine: Continental.*

Tongue & Groove
3055 Peachtree Rd.
    Atlanta
(404) 261-2325
•*All areas. Humidor.
Cuisine: Pan-Pacific/
Sushi.* **Nightclub/
sushi bar.**

Veni Vidi Vici
41 14th St. Atlanta
(404) 875-8424
•*Bar/lounge. Humi-
dor. Cuisine: Italian.*

Winfield's at the Galleria Mall
1 Galleria Pkwy.
    Atlanta
(770) 955-5300
•*Bar/lounge. Cuisine:
American/Continental.*

Havana Club
247 Buckhead Ave.
Buckhead
(404) 869-8484
•*All areas. Humidor.
Cuisine: Cuban.*

Moniker's Restaurant at Embassy Suites
4700 Southport Rd.
College Park
(404) 767-1988
•*Smoking section
and bar. Cuisine:
Continental.*

Marra's Seafood Grill
1782 Cheshire
    Bridge Rd.
Northeast Atlanta
(404) 874-7347
•*Lounge, patio, and
private room. Humi-
dor. Cuisine: seafood
grill.*

Hackett's at the Holiday Inn Skytop Convention
20 US 411 E., Rome
(706) 295-1100

•*Smoking area. Cui-
sine: American/Conti-
nental/Southern.*

----

45 South at the Pirate's House
20 E. Broad St.
Savannah
(912) 233-1881
•*Lobby lounge and
late night after dinner.
Cuisine: contempo-
rary American.*

Bogart's Classic Cigar Parlour
405 W. Congress St.
Savannah
(912) 238-1311
•*All areas. Humidor.
Cuisine: lite fare.*
Cigar bar/bar.

Hawaii

MAUI

Fish and Games Grill
4405 Honoapiilani
    Hwy., Lahaina
(808) 669-3474
•*Bar. Humidor. Cui-
sine: Continental,
Classical French.*

Swan Court at the Hyatt Regency Maui
200 Nohea Kai Dr.
Lahaina
(808) 661-1234
•*Lounge. Humidor.
Cuisine: Continental
with an Island/Pacific
Rim flare.*

Reilley's Steaks & Seafood
2290 Kaanapali
    Pkwy., Lahania
(808) 667-7477
•*Bar/lounge. Humi-
dor. Cuisine: steak &
seafood.*

OAHU

Caffe Pronto
131 Kaiulani Ave.
Honolulu
(808) 923-0111
•*Patio. Humidor.
Cuisine: pastries.* **Coffee bar.**

Kapalua Bay Club
1 Kapalua Bay Dr.
Honolulu
(808) 669-8008
•*Poolside. Humidor.
Cuisine: American &
Mediterranean.*

L'Italiano
1330 Ala Moana
    Blvd., Honolulu
(808) 591-0105
•*All areas. Humidor.
Cuisine: French &
Italian.*

Murphy's Bar & Grill
2 Merchant St.
Honolulu
(808) 531-0422
•*Bar only during the
day; throughout
restaurant in the
evening. Humidor.
Cuisine: American.*

O'Tooles Irish Pub
902 Nuuanu St.
Honolulu
(808) 536-6360
•*Bar. Humidor. Cuisine: American.* **Bar.**

Idaho

Mugger's Brewpub
516 2nd St. S.
Twin Falls
(208) 733-2322
•*All areas (except Bistro). Humidor. Cuisine: pub fare.*

Illinois

University Inn - Sneakers Lounge
302 E. John St.
Champaign
(217) 384-2100
•*Smoking section. Cuisine: fine cuisine.*

CHICAGO & VICINITY

Bice Ristorante
158 E. Ontario St.
Chicago
(312) 664-1474
•*Bar, private rooms, and patio. Humidor. Cuisine: Northern Italian/Milanese.*

B.L.U.E.S. Etc...
1124 W. Belmont
Chicago
(312) 549-9416
•*All areas. Humidor.* **Blues club.**

Buddy Guy's Legends
754 S. Wabash

Chicago
(312) 427-1190
•*All areas. Humidor. Cuisine: Cajun, Creole, & soul food*

Cafe Ba Ba Reeba!
2024 N. Halsted St.
Chicago
(773) 935-5000
•*Cigar Lounge, bar, and private rooms only. Humidor. Cuisine: Spanish.*

Chicago Chop House
60 W. Ontario St.
Chicago
(800) 229-2356,
 (312) 787-7100
•*Main bar. Humidor. Cuisine: steakhouse.*

Coco Pazzo
300 W. Hubbard
Chicago
(312) 836-0900
•*Cigar section. Humidor. Cuisine: Italian.*

Como Inn
546 N. Milwaukee
Chicago
(312) 421-5222
•*Bar. Humidor. Cuisine: Northern Italian.*

Diaggi's Italian Bistro
1723 N. Halstead St.
Chicago
(312) 266-8900
•*All areas after 9pm. Humidor. Cuisine: Italian.*

Entre Nous at the Fairmont Hotel
200 N. Columbus Dr., Chicago
(312) 565-7997
•*Bar and private rooms on Monday nights. Humidor. Cuisine: regional American with a French twist.*

Erie Cafe
536 W. Erie St.
Chicago
(312) 266-2300
•*Bar and reserved private dining area. Humidor. Cuisine: steak, seafood, Italian.*

Fly Me to the Moon
3400 N. Clark
Chicago
(773) 528-4033
•*Cigar bar (and all areas after 11pm). Humidor. Cuisine: Italian with a Greek influence.*

Four Seasons Hotel
120 E. Delaware
Chicago
(312) 280-8800
•*Bar/lounge and private rooms. Humidor. Cuisine: American.*

Gene & Georgetti
500 N. Franklin St.
Chicago
(312) 527-3718
•*Bar area. Cuisine: American steakhouse.*

Gibsons
1028 N. Rush St.

Chicago
(312) 266-8999
•*Bar/lounge. Humidor. Cuisine: steakhouse specializing in fresh seafood.*

Green Dolphin St.
2200 N. Ashland
Chicago
(773) 395-0066
•*Bar, jazz club, and patio. Humidor. Cuisine: fine dining.*

Harry's Velvet Room
534 N. Clark St.
Chicago
(773) 772-3663
•*All areas. Humidor. Cuisine: American.*

Havana
230 W. Kinzie
Chicago
(312) 595-0101
•*Bar, cigar bar, and private room. Humidor. Cuisine: Cuban.*

Iron Mike's Grille at the Tremont Hotel
100 E. Chestnut
Chicago
(312) 587-8989
•*Smoking parlour and bar. Humidor. Cuisine: regional.*

Jesse Livermore's
401 S. LaSalle St.
Chicago
(312) 786-5272
•*All areas.* **Bar.**

**Jilly's Bistro/
Jilly's Retro Club**
1007 N. Rush
Chicago
(312) 664-1001
•*All areas. Humidor.*
**Bar/cigar bar/night-
club.**

**Kirzie Street
Chophouse**
400 N. Wells St.
Chicago
(312) 822-0191
•*Bar. Humidor. Cui-
sine: classic American
steakhouse.*

**Magnum's Steak &
Lobster**
225 W. Ontario St.
Chicago
(312) 337-8080
•*Piano bar and lounge
at all times/smoking
section after 10pm.
Humidor. Cuisine:
steaks, chops, seafood.*

Millennium
832 W. Randolph
Chicago
(312) 455-1400
•*Cigar bar. Humidor.
Cuisine: steakhouse.*

**Morton's of
Chicago**
1050 N. State St.
Chicago
(312) 266-4820
•*Smoking section,
bar, lounge, and pri-
vate rooms. Humidor.
Cuisine: steakhouse.*

Nick's Fishmarket
1 First National
Plaza, Chicago
(312) 621-0200
•*Bar/lounge. Humi-
dor. Cuisine: seafood/
steaks/pasta.*

**O'Brien's
Restaurant & Bar**
1528 N. Wells St.
Chicago
(312) 787-3131
•*Piano bar. Humidor.
Cuisine: steak &
seafood.*

**The Outpost
Restaurant & Bar**
3438 N. Clark
Chicago
(773) 244-1166
•*Dining room after
service, bar, and out-
door cafe (weather
permitting). Cuisine:
American-style bistro.*

**P.J. Clarke's-
Chicago**
1204 N. State Pkwy.
Chicago
(312) 664-1650
•*Bar/lounge and pri-
vate room. Humidor.
Cuisine: American.*

**Printer's Row
Restaurant**
550 S. Dearborn St.
Chicago
(312) 461-0780
•*Lounge and private
dining room. Humi-
dor. Cuisine: Ameri-
can fine dining.*

**The Pump Room at
The Ambassador
East Hotel**
1301 N. State Pkwy.
Chicago
(312) 266-0360
•*Bar/lounge. Humi-
dor. Cuisine: Ameri-
can/Continental.*

Rico's of Chicago
626 S. Racine
Chicago
(312) 421-7262
•*Bar. Humidor.
Cuisine: Italian (fine
dining).*

The Ritz-Carlton
160 E. Pearson St.
Chicago
(312) 266-1000
•*Cigar bar (Trianon)
and Terrace Green-
house. Humidor. Cui-
sine: contemporary
French.*

Saloon Steakhouse
200 E. Chestnut
Chicago
(312) 280-5454
•*Bar. Humidor. Cui-
sine: classic American
steakhouse.*

Scoozi!
410 W. Huron St.
Chicago
(312) 943-5900
•*Bar. Cuisine: Italian.*

Seasons Bar
120 E. Delaware
Chicago
(312) 280-8800

•*Bar. Humidor. Cui-
sine: Asian-style hors
d'oeuvres.* **Bar.**

Shaw's Crab House
21 E. Hubbard St.
Chicago
(312) 527-2722
•*Bar. Cuisine:
seafood.*

Shelly's Back Room
192 E. Walton St.
Chicago
(312) 255-9900
•*All areas. Humidor.
Cuisine: American.*

Sorriso
321 N. Clark
Chicago
(312) 644-0283
•*Dining room and
bar. Humidor. Cui-
sine: American &
Italian.*

Spago Chicago
520 N. Dearborn St.
Chicago
(312) 527-3700
•*Cigar bar and pri-
vate room. Humidor.
Cuisine: American.*

**Stouffer Riviere
Hotel**
1 W. Wacker
Chicago
(312) 372-7200
•*Lobby Court
Lounge. Cuisine: lite
fare.* **Bar.**

Tailgators Sports Bar
2263 N. Lincoln
Chicago
(773) 348-7200
•*All areas. Humidor. Cuisine: American pub fare.*

Tania's Restaurant
2659 N. Milwaukee
Ave., Chicago
(773) 235-7120
•*Dining room, bar, lounge, and private rooms. Humidor. Cuisine: Cuban, Spanish, Puerto Rican & Mexican.*

Pete Miller's Steakhouse
1557 Sherman Ave.
Evanston
(847) 328-0399
•*Smoking area, bar, jazz lounge, and billiard room. Humidor. Cuisine: steakhouse.*

The Living Room
801 E. Butterfield
Rd., Lombard
(630) 368-0069
•*2/3 of dining area. Humidor. Cuisine: tapas & eclectic appetizers.*

Cypress Inn
1352 Shermer Rd.
Northbrook
(847) 272-8787
•*Smoking section and bar. Cuisine: pub fare.* **Pub.**

Ken's Guest House
9848 SW Hwy.
Oaklawn
(708) 422-4014
•*Bar, lounge, and private rooms. Cuisine: American, specializing in seafood & steak.*

PJ's Courthouse Grille
202 W. State St.
Sycamore
(815) 895-9253
•*Bar and smoking section in dining room. Humidor. Cuisine: casual grille/American.*

Scalawag's
313 W. State St.
Sycamore
(815) 895-4333
•*Bar/lounge. Cuisine: American.*

Morton's of Chicago
1 Westbrook Corporate Center, 22nd & Wolf Rds.
Westchester
(708) 562-7000
•*Bar/lounge, smoking section, and private dining rooms. Humidor. Cuisine: steakhouse.*

Courtright's
8989 Archer Ave.
Willow Springs
(708) 839-8000
•*Lounge. Humidor. Cuisine: American.*

Porter's Steakhouse and Cigar Bar
1000 Eastport Plaza Dr. , Collinsville
(618) 345-2400;
cigar bar: (618) 345-2929
•*Smoking section in dining room, cigar bar, and private rooms. Humidor. Cuisine: steak.*

Prairie Rock Brewing Co.
127 S. Grove Ave.
Elgin
(847) 622-8888
•*Smoking area in dining room, cigar bar, and main bar. Humidor. Cuisine: American eclectic.*

Benjamin's
103 N. Main St.
Galena
(815) 777-0467
•*Bar, booths, and tables in the bar. Humidor. Cuisine: American.*

Maurie's Table
2360 Glenwood Ave.
Joliet
(815) 744-2619
•*Dining room and bar. Humidor. Cuisine: American, Italian, & pizza.*

Pauley's Pub & Eatery
500 S. Washington
Kankakee
(815) 932-2211

•*All areas. Humidor. Cuisine: American.*

Uptown Grill
601 1st St.
LaSalle
(815) 224-4545
•*Bar and smoking sections. Humidor. Cuisine: American bistro.*

Carlucci Rosemont
6111 N. River Rd.
Rosemont
(847) 518-0990
•*Bar. Humidor. Cuisine: regional Italian.*

Morton's of Chicago
9525 W. Bryn Mawr
Rosemont
(847) 678-5155
•*Smoking section and bar. Humidor. Cuisine: steakhouse.*

ROCKFORD

Cafe Patou
3929 Broadway
Rockford
(815) 227-4100
•*Bar/lounge and private rooms. Humidor. Cuisine: French.*

The City Club of Rockford/Blue Smoke Cigar Lounge
555 N. Court St.
Rockford
(815) 966-6966
•*Lounge and cigar lounge. Humidor. Cuisine: Continental.*

Giovanni's Restaurant & Banquet Facility
610 N. Bell School
Rd., Rockford
(815) 398-6411
•*Bar/lounge, private room, and banquet rooms. Humidor. Cuisine: Continental.*
....

Baur's Restaurant
620 S. 1st St.
Springfield
(217) 789-4311
•*Dining room and lounge. Humidor. Cuisine: Continental, featuring German specialities.*

Indiana

The Jungle Restaurant and Fat Cats Bar & Cigar Lounge
415 Main St.
Evansville
(812) 425-5282
•*All areas of "Fat Cats" on the lower level; smoking section of restaurant. Humidor. Cuisine: American bistro—featuring steaks, chops, & seafood.*

INDIANAPOLIS & VICINITY

Carvers Steaks & Chops
780 US 31 N
Greenwood
(317) 887-6380

•*Lounge and smoking section. Humidor. Cuisine: steaks, chops, seafood.*

Bench Warmers at the Holiday Inn Select North
3850 De Pauw Blvd.
Indianapolis
(317) 872-9790
•*Bar and private rooms. Humidor. Cuisine: appetizers, sandwiches, salads.*
Sports bar.

The Restaurant at the Canterbury
123 S. Illinois St.
Indianapolis
(317) 634-3000
•*Bar area. Humidor. Cuisine: Continental.*

Henry Grattan Pub
745 Broad Ripple
Ave.
Indianapolis
(317) 257-6030
•*All areas. Cuisine: American/Irish.*

Keystone Grill
8650 Keystone
Crossing
Indianapolis
(317) 848-5202
•*Bar and smoking section. Humidor. Cuisine: American steak & seafood.*

The Marker Restaurant at the Adam's Mark Hotel
2544 Executive Dr.
Indianapolis
(317) 248-2481

•*Smoking section. Cuisine: fine dining.*

Philabuster's
50 S. Capital
Indianapolis
(317) 231-3970
•*All areas. Humidor. Cuisine: American.*

Ruth's Chris Steak House
9445 Three L Rd.
Indianapolis
(317) 844-1155
•*Bar area. Humidor. Cuisine: steakhouse.*

St. Elmo Steak House
127 S. Illinois St.
Indianapolis
(317) 635-0636
•*Bar and private rooms. Humidor. Cuisine: steakhouse.*

Sullivan's Steakhouse
3316 E. 86th St.
Indianapolis
(317) 580-1280
•*Bar and lounge. Humidor. Cuisine: steakhouse.*

J. Gingers Steakhouse at the Radisson Hotel at Star Plaza
800 E. 81st Ave.
Merrillville
(219) 769-6311
•*Smoking section. Humidor. Cuisine: features Black Angus steaks.*

Rich O's Public House
3312 Plaza Dr.
New Albany
(812) 949-2804
•*All areas. Humidor. Cuisine: four styles of pizza, lasagnas, barbeque sandwiches.*

SOUTH BEND & VICINITY

Mishawaka Brewing Co.
3703 N. Main St.
Mishawaka
(219) 256-9993
•*Bar. Humidor. Cuisine: English pub-style.*

La Salle Grill
115 W. Colfax
South Bend
(800) 382-9323,
(219) 288-1155
•*Smoking section, private room, and cigar bar. Humidor. Cuisine: modern American.*
....

Orion's Restaurant
1700 Rozella Rd.
Warsaw
(219) 269-9100
•*Bar/lounge. Humidor. Cuisine: regional.*

Up For Grabs Restaurant & Bar
1923 Calumet Ave.
Whiting
(219) 659-4508
•*All areas. Humidor. Cuisine: sandwiches to seafood.*

Iowa

Eight Hundred One Steak & Chop House
801 Grand Ave.
Des Moines
(515) 288-6000
•*Bar. Humidor. Cuisine: prime steaks, lobster, fresh fish.*

Embassy Club
801 Grand Ave.
Des Moines
(515) 244-2582
•*Bar/lounge. Humidor. Cuisine: American & French.* **Private club.**

The Tobacco Bowl
111 S. Dubuque
Iowa City
(319) 338-5885
•*All areas. Humidor. Cuisine: pastries.* **Coffee bar.**

Kansas

Grain Bin Supper Club
1301 E. Fulton
Garden City
(316) 275-5954
•*All areas. Humidor. Cuisine: American.*

The Woodlands
9700 Leavenworth Rd.
Kansas City
(913) 299-9797
•*Smoking areas. Cuisine: American.*

Auntie Mae's Parlor
616 N. 12th St.
Manhattan
(913) 539-8508
•*All areas. Humidor. Cuisine: lite fare.* **Bar.**

Lucky Bar & Grille
710 N. Manhattan Ave., Manhattan
(913) 776-9090
•*Bar/lounge and smoking area. Humidor. Cuisine: pizzas, pastas, & sandwiches.*

La Mediterranee
9058-B Metcalf Ave.
Overland Park
(913) 341-9595
•*Bar. Humidor. Cuisine: classical French.*

Mort's Cigar & Martini Lounge
923 E. 1st St.
Wichita
(316) 262-1785
•*All areas. Humidor. Cuisine: sandwiches.* **Cigar bar.**

Kentucky

Coach House Restaurant
855 S. Broadway
Lexington
(606) 252-7777
•*Bar. Humidor. Cuisine: Continental & French.*

LOUISVILLE
Azalea
3612 Brownsboro Rd., Louisville
(502) 895-5493
•*Private room. Humidor. Cuisine: new American fusion.*

Bobby J's
1314 Bardstown Rd.
Louisville
(502) 452-2665
•*"Mermaid" lounge, the upstairs cigar bar, and the cigar dining room. Humidor. Cuisine: American & Italian.*

Brasserie Deitrich
2862 Frankfort Ave.
Louisville
(502) 897-6076
•*Lounge. Humidor. Cuisine: French.*

The Oakroom at the Seelbach Hotel
500 4th Ave.
Louisville
(502) 585-3200
•*At private dinners in "Oakroom Anteroom." Humidor. Cuisine: Kentucky fine dining.*

Porcini
2730 Frankfort Ave.
Louisville
(502) 894-8686
•*Bar. Cuisine: Italian featuring fresh pastas, hand-tossed gourmet pizzas, & veal specialties.*

Jeremiah's Restaurant & Brew Pub
225-27 Broadway
Paducah
(502) 443-3991
•*Lounge and brewpub. Humidor. Cuisine: steakhouse, seafood.*

Louisiana

Drakes The Restaurant
5837 Essen Lane
Baton Rouge
(504) 767-9600
•*All areas of dining room with bar (nonsmoking dining room available). Humidor. Cuisine: contemporary Creole.*

Juban's Restaurant
3739 Perkins Rd.
Baton Rouge
(504) 346-8422
•*Bar. Humidor. Cuisine: Creole.*

NEW ORLEANS & VICINITY
Charley G's Seafood Grill
111 Veterans Blvd.
Metairie
(504) 837-6408
•*Bar area, private dining rooms, and at some smoking tables. Humidor. Cuisine: contemporary South Louisiana, specializing in grilled seafood.*

Antoine's
713 St. Louis St.
New Orleans
(504) 581-4422
•*Main dining room
and private banquet
rooms. Cuisine:
French/Creole.*

**Arnaud's
Restaurant**
813 Bienville St.
New Orleans
(504) 523-5433
•*Cigar bar and pri-
vate dining rooms.
Humidor. Cuisine:
Creole.*

Brennan's
417 Royal St.
New Orleans
(504) 525-9711
•*Smoking areas.
Humidor. Cuisine:
French/Creole.*

**Broussard's
Restaurant**
819 Conti St.
New Orleans
(504) 581-3866
•*Banquet rooms,
courtyard patio, and
main dining room late
in the evening. Humi-
dor. Cuisine: nouvelle
Creole.*

Cafe Havana
842 Royal St.
New Orleans
(504) 569-9006
•*All areas. Humidor.*
**Coffee bar/cigar
shop.**

**Cafe Rue Bourbon
Restaurant**
241 Rue Bourbon at
   Bienville
New Orleans
(504) 524-0114
•*Smoking section, pri-
vate room, and wine
room. Cuisine: Cajun.*

**The Court of
Two Sisters**
613 Royal St.
New Orleans
(504) 522-7261
•*Smoking section of
dining room and bar/
cocktail area. Humi-
dor. Cuisine: Cajun,
Creole, & French.*

**Dos Jefes Uptown
Cigar Bar**
5535 Tchoupitoulas
   St., New Orleans
(504) 899-3030
•*All areas. Humidor.
Cuisine: lite fare—
appetizers & desserts.*
Cigar bar/jazz club.

Emeril's Restaurant
800 Tchoupitoulas
   St., New Orleans
(504) 528-9393
•*Bar and dining
room. Humidor. Cui-
sine: American &
Creole.*

Galatoire's
209 Bourbon St.
New Orleans
(504) 525-2021
•*Dining room. Cui-
sine: French.*

The Grill Room
300 Gravier St.
New Orleans
(504) 522-1992
•*Polo Lounge. Humi-
dor. Cuisine: Conti-
nental.*

**Kabby's at the
Riverside Hilton**
2 Poydras
New Orleans
(504) 584-3880
•*Smoking section.
Humidor. Cuisine:
Continental.*

**Louis XVI
Restaurant at the
Saint Louis Hotel**
730 Rue Bienville
New Orleans
(504) 581-7000
•*Bar/lounge, private
room, and patio. Cui-
sine: classic French.*

**Maximo's Italian
Grill**
1117 Decatur St.
New Orleans
(504) 586-8883
•*Bar/lounge and
smoking section.
Humidor. Cuisine:
modern, innovative
Italian.*

**Mint Julep Lounge
at the Hyatt
Regency**
500 Poydras Plaza
New Orleans
(504) 561-1234
•*All areas. Humidor.
Cuisine: appetizers
only.* **Sports bar.**

**The Rib Room at
the Omni Royal
Orleans Hotel**
621 St. Louis St.
New Orleans
(504) 529-5333
•*Smoking room
"Escoffier" adjacent to
restaurant. Humidor.
Cuisine: American,
Continental, New
Orleans Creole.*

**Sazerac Bar at The
Fairmont Hotel**
123 Barrone St.
New Orleans
(504) 529-7111
•*Bar. Humidor. Cui-
sine: elegant French &
Continental.*

**Top of the Dome
Steakhouse at the
Hyatt Regency
32nd Floor**
500 Poydras Plaza
New Orleans
(504) 561-1234
   x2755
•*10pm to 12am only.
Humidor. Cuisine:
steakhouse.*

**Windsor Court
Hotel**
300 Gravier St.
New Orleans
(504) 523-6000
•*Polo Lounge.
Humidor. Cuisine:
Continental.*

Maine

The Greenhouse Restaurant
193 Broad St.
Bangor
(207) 945-4040
•Smoking dining room and lounge. Cuisine: American.

Cork Inc.: Wine Bar, Espresso Cafe, Gallery & Restaurant
37 Bayview St., 2nd Fl., Camden
(207) 230-0533
•Bar and smoking section on Tuesday evenings only 7pm-10pm. Humidor. Cuisine: steak, poultry, seafood, & pasta.

La Conque at The Manor Inn
Battle Ave., Box 276
Castine
(207) 326-4335
•Smoking section, cigar/espresso bar, and cocktail lounge. Humidor. Cuisine: American, French, & Mediterranean.

Maryland

BALTIMORE & VICINITY

Baltimore Brewing Company
104 Albemarle St.
Baltimore
(410) 837-5000

•Bar area/smoking section. Humidor. Cuisine: American.

The Brass Elephant
924 N. Charles St.
Baltimore
(410) 547-8480
•Lounge and private dining rooms Cuisine: Northern Italian.

Corks
1026 S. Charles St.
Baltimore
(410) 752-3810
•Cellar room. Humidor. Cuisine: American eclectic.

Da Mimmo Finest Italian Cuisine
217 S. High St.
Baltimore
(410) 727-6876
•Lounge. Humidor. Cuisine: Italian.

Edgar's Billiard Club
1 E. Pratt St., Plaza Level, Baltimore
(410) 752-8080
•All areas except non-smoking. Humidor. Cuisine: lite fare/Continental cuisine.

Explorer's Lounge at the Harbour Court Hotel
550 Light St.
Baltimore
(410) 234-0550
•Bar and lounge area. Humidor. Cuisine: nouvelle American.

The Fishery Restaurant
1717 Eastern Ave.
Baltimore
(410) 327-9340
•Bar/lounge, smoking section, and private room. Humidor. Cuisine: Spanish & Italian, featuring Maryland seafood.

La Scala Italian Restaurant
411 S. High St.
Baltimore
(410) 783-9209
•Godfather Lounge Humidor. Cuisine: Italian.

Little Havana
1325 Key Hwy.
Baltimore
(410) 837-9903
•Bar. Humidor. Cuisine: new Cuban.

Max's on Broadway
737 S. Broadway
Baltimore
(410) 276-2850
•All areas. Humidor. Cuisine: bar food. **Bar.**

Pickles Pub
520 Washington Blvd., Baltimore
(410) 752-1784
•All areas. Humidor. Cuisine: pub fare.

The Prime Rib
1101 N. Calvert St.
Baltimore
(410) 539-1804

•Bar. Humidor. Cuisine: features prime aged beef & fresh seafood.

Ropewalk Tavern
1209 S. Charles St.
Baltimore
(410) 727-1298
•All areas. Humidor. **Cigar bar.**

Ruth's Chris Steak House
600 Water St.
Baltimore
(410) 783-0033
•Smoking rooms and lounge. Humidor. Cuisine: steak, seafood.

Sisson's Restaurant & Brewery
36 E. Cross St.
Baltimore
(410) 539-2093
•Bar area. Cuisine: Cajun & Creole.

Water Street Exchange
110 Water St.
Baltimore
(410) 332-4060
•Bar and patio. Humidor. Cuisine: Continental.

Windows
202 E. Pratt St.
Baltimore
(410) 547-1200
•Lounge. Humidor. Cuisine: contemporary American.

Windsor Club
7 N. Calvert St.
Baltimore
(410) 332-0700
•*All areas. Humidor.
Cuisine: light fare.*
Private cigar club.

**Patrick's Pub &
Restaurant**
550 Cranbrook Rd.
Cockeysville
(410) 683-0604
•*Bar/lounge. Humidor. Cuisine: Continental.*

**Hersh's
Orchard Inn**
1528 E. Joppa Rd.
Towson
(410) 823-0384
•*Bar/lounge. Cuisine: Continental.*

Westminster Inn
5 S. Center St.
Westminster
(410) 857-4445
•*Cigar lounge and
Courtyard Restaurant. Humidor. Cuisine: New American/
Continental.* **Bed &
breakfast.**

**The Red Horse
Restaurant**
996 W. Patrick St.
Frederick
(301) 663-3030
•*Cigar lounge. Humidor. Cuisine: steak &
seafood.*

Nick's Airport Inn
Rte. 11 N.
Hagerstown
(301) 733-8560
•*Lounge. Humidor.
Cuisine: Continental.*

**The Inn at
Perry Cabin**
308 Watkins Lane
St. Michaels
(800) 722-2949,
(410) 745-2200
•*All areas. Humidor.
Cuisine: Continental.*

**St. Michael's Crab
House**
305 Mulberry St.
St. Michaels
(410) 745-3737
•*Tavern. Humidor.
Cuisine: seafood/beef/
chicken.*

Fred's Grapevine
410 Thompson
Creek Mall, Rte.
50 E.
Stevensville
(410) 643-4640
•*Bar and smoking
section. Humidor.
Cuisine: Italian &
American.*

**Antrim 1844
Country Inn**
30 Treventon Rd.
Taneytown
(800) 858-1844
•*Bar. Humidor. Cuisine: regional.*

**Parioli Ristorante
& Cigar Lounge**
4800 Elm St.
Bethesda
(301) 951-8600
•*Cigar bar, lounge,
smoking section of dining room, patio, and
private rooms. Humidor. Cuisine: Italian.*

Old Angler's Inn
10801 McArthur
Blvd., Potomac
(301) 365-2425
•*Bar, lounge, private
rooms, and patio.
Humidor. Cuisine:
contemporary American.*

**Shelly's Back Room
at Shelly's
Woodroast**
1699 Rockville Pike
Rockville
(301) 984-3300
•*Bar/lounge area and
private cigar room.
Humidor. Cuisine:
American.*

Massachusetts

Anthony's Pier 4
140 Northern Ave.
Boston
(617) 682-6262
•*Bar and lounge.
Humidor. Cuisine:
American, specializing
in seafood.*

Biba Restaurant
272 Boylston St.
Boston
(617) 426-7878
•*Bar/lounge. Humidor. Cuisine: eclectic
American.*

The Capital Grille
359 Newbury St.
Boston
(617) 262-8900
•*Dining rooms, bar,
and private rooms.
Humidor. Cuisine:
steak.*

Four Seasons Hotel
200 Boylston St.
Boston
(617) 351-2071
•*Bristol Lounge
smoking areas. Humidor. Cuisine: Continental.*

Grill 23 & Bar
161 Berkeley St.
Boston
(617) 542-2255
•*All smoking areas.
Humidor. Cuisine:
American, specializing
in prime aged beef,
seafood, & rotisserie
cooking.*

**Julien Restaurant
at the Hotel
Meridien Boston**
250 Franklin St.
Boston
(617) 451-1900
•*Bar/lounge area.
Humidor. Cuisine:
French.*

Legal C-Bar
27 Columbus Ave.
Boston
(617) 426-5566
•*Bar and lounge.
Humidor. Cuisine:
Caribbean/world
cuisine.*

Locke-Ober
3 Winter Place
Boston
(617) 542-1340
•*Dining room,
lounge, and Yvonne's
(private club).
Humidor. Cuisine:
Continental.*

**Morton's of
Chicago**
1 Exeter Plaza
Boston
(617) 266-5858
•*Smoking section.
Humidor. Cuisine:
steakhouse.*

Oskar's
107 South St.
Boston
(617) 542-6756
•*Bar/lounge, smok-
ing section, and pri-
vate room. Humidor.
Cuisine: creative
American.*

**Punch Bar at the
Sheraton Boston
Hotel and Towers**
39 Dalton St.
Boston
(617) 236-2000

•*All areas. Humidor.
Cuisine: dining avail-
able in the hotel's
restaurant.* **Cigar
bar.**

The Ritz-Carlton
15 Arlington St.
Boston
(617) 536-5700
•*Bar/lounge and pri-
vate rooms. Humi-
dor. Cuisine: French
Continental.* **Bar.**

**Seasons at The
Bostonian Hotel**
Faneuil Hall Market
  Place, Boston
(617) 523-3600
•*Atrium lounge and
smoking area after
9:30pm. Humidor.
Cuisine: new Ameri-
can.*

Chez Henri
1 Shepard St.
Cambridge
(617) 354-8980
•*Bar. Humidor. Cui-
sine: French/Cuban.*

**Upstairs at the
Pudding**
10 Holyoke St.
Cambridge
(617) 864-1933
•*Bar, herb garden ter-
race, and waiting area
only. Cuisine: hand-
crafted with Italian
influences.*

**Dockside
Restaurant**
229 Centre St.
Malden
(781) 321-3000

•*Bar and smoking
section in dining room.
Cuisine: American.*

**Robert's Grub, Pub
& Pool**
342-344 Moody St.
Waltham
(617) 894-6666
•*All areas. Humidor.
Cuisine: features
BBQ, steak, stir fry,
fresh pasta, sirloin
burgers, & more.*

CAPE COD
VICINITY

**The Trowbridge
Tavern & Ale
House**
100 Trowbridge Rd.
Bourne
(508) 759-1776
•*Bar. Humidor. Cui-
sine: American.*

**The Joe's Beach
Road Bar & Grille
at the Barley Neck
Inn & Lodge**
5 Beach Rd.
East Orleans
(508) 255-0212
•*Bar/lounge. Humi-
dor. Cuisine: French
& traditional New
England.*

**Bobby Byrne's
Restaurant & Pub**
Rte. 28
Hyannis
(508) 775-1425
•*Throughout pub and
bar. Humidor. Cui-
sine: Continental/
American.*

Puff The Magic
649 Main St.
Hyannis
(508) 771-9090,
   (888) 87-4CIGAR
•*All areas. Humidor.*
**Bar/cigar bar/coffee
bar/nightclub.**

Sun Tavern
500 Congress St.
Duxbury
(617) 837-4100
•*Tavern section.
Humidor. Cuisine:
country Continental.*

St. James Irish Pub
91 Purchase St.
Fall River
(508) 672-6951
•*All areas. Humidor.
Cuisine: pub fare.*
Pub.

Castle Restaurant
1230 Main St.
Leicester
(508) 892-9090
•*Bar/lounge. Humi-
dor. Cuisine: Ameri-
can/Continental.*

Blantyre Hotel
16 Blantyre Rd.
Lenox
(413) 637-3556
•*Music room and
patio. Humidor. Cui-
sine: American/
French.*

Cobblestones
91 Dutton St.
Lowell
(508) 970-2282

•*Bar and smoking room. Humidor. Cuisine: eclectic American.*

The Chanticleer
9 New St., Siaconset
Nantucket
(508) 257-6231
•*Bar. Humidor. Cuisine: traditional French.*

Silks at the Stonehedge Inn
160 Pawtucket Blvd.
Tyngsboro
(978) 649-4400
•*Bar and library. Humidor. Cuisine: French Continental/ nouvelle American.*

Moby Dick Wharf Restaurant & Marina
1 Bridge Rd.
Westport Point
(508) 636-6500
•*West deck. Humidor. Cuisine: French-style seafood.*

Michigan

The Real Seafood Company
341 S. Main St.
Ann Arbor
(313) 769-5960
•*Bar and lounge area. Humidor. Cuisine: premium seafood.*

DETROIT & VICINITY

Big Rock Chop & Brew House
245 S. Eton
Birmingham
(248) 647-7774
•*Bar, lounge, smoking section in dining room, cigar bar, patio, and private rooms. Humidor. Cuisine: steaks & chops.*

Dick O'Dow's Irish Pub & Restaurant
160 W. Maple St.
Birmingham
(248) 642-1135
•*Pub area. Humidor. Cuisine: Irish American.*

Carl's Chop House
3020 Grand River
Detroit
(313) 833-0700
•*Smoking section. Humidor. Cuisine: American steakhouse.*

Caucus Club
150 W. Congress
Detroit
(313) 965-4970
•*Bar/lounge and smoking section. Humidor. Cuisine: American/ Continental.*

Joe Meur's
2000 Gratiot Ave.
Detroit
(313) 567-1088
•*Bar room only. Humidor. Cuisine: seafood.*

Opus One
565 E. Larned
Detroit
(313) 961-7766
•*Bar/lounge. Humidor. Cuisine: American with a French flair.*

The Rattlesnake Club
300 River Place
Detroit
(313) 567-4400
•*Bar/lounge and private dining rooms. Humidor. Cuisine: contemporary American.*

Vivio's
2460 Market St.
Detroit
(313) 393-1711
•*Bar room only. Humidor. Cuisine: American.*

The Whitney
4421 Woodland
Ave., Detroit
(313) 832-5700
•*Third floor. Humidor. Cuisine: American.*

Ginopolis' on the Grill
27815 Middlebelt
Rd.
Farmington Hills
(248) 851-8222
•*Bar/lounge. Humidor. Cuisine: American & Greek featuring seafood and the famous "Montgomery Inn ribs."*

MacKinnon's Restaurant
126 E. Main St.
Northville
(248) 348-1991
•*Bar/lounge and cigar bar. Humidor. Cuisine: French.*

Cheers on the Channel
6211 Point Tremble
Pearl Beach
(810) 794-9017
•*Lounge area where food is available (seats 20). Humidor. Cuisine: French/American.*

Pike Street Restaurant
18 W. Pike, Pontiac
(248) 334-7878
•*Bar, lounge, and private rooms. Humidor. Cuisine: American & French.*

Rochester Chop House
306 Main St.
Rochester
(248) 651-2266
•*Special highly ventilated room. Humidor. Cuisine: steak, veal, & seafood.*

**Goodnite Gracie
next to D'Amato's
Neighborhood
Restaurant**
224 Sherman Dr.
Royal Oak
(248) 544-7490
•*All areas. Humidor.
Cuisine: dinner available at D'Amato's.*
**Cocktail & cigar
lounge.**

**Chianti Villa
Italiana**
28565 Northwestern
Hwy., Southfield
(248) 350-0055
•*Bar/lounge. Cuisine:
Italian.*

**Excalibur
Restaurant**
28875 Franklin Rd.
Southfield
(248) 358-3355
•*All areas. Humidor.
Cuisine: American/
Continental.*

Golden Mushroom
18100 W. 10 Mile
Rd., Southfield
(248) 559-4230
•*Bar/lounge. Humidor. Cuisine: Continental.*

**Morton's of
Chicago**
One Towne Square
Southfield
(248) 354-6006
•*Smoking section.
Humidor. Cuisine:
steakhouse.*

**Ruth's Chris
Steak House**
755 W. Big Beaver
Rd., Troy
(248) 269-8424
•*Lounge. Humidor.
Cuisine: American.*

**Shula's Steak
House at the Troy
Marriott**
200 W. Big Beaver
Rd., Troy
(248) 680-9616
•*Lounge. Humidor.
Cuisine: steakhouse.*

Spectadium
2511 Livernois
Troy
(248) 362-4030
•*All areas. Humidor.
Cuisine: American
classic pub fare.* **Bar/
nightclub.**

**Laredo Steak
House**
2324 S. Ballenger
Flint
(810) 234-1271
•*Smoking section of
the dining room and
bar. Cuisine: steak,
featuring baby back
ribs, and large cuts of
USDA choice beef.*

**Big Buck Brewery
& Steakhouse**
2500 28th St. SE
Grand Rapids
(616) 954-9635
•*Smoking section of
dining room and in the
bar. Humidor. Cuisine: American:
steaks, game, pasta,
fresh seafood.*

Lakos Downtown
188 Monroe NW
Grand Rapids
(616) 459-4135
•*Bar/lounge. Humidor. Cuisine: classic
American & French.*

**Whirligig at the
Hilton**
2000 Holiday Inn
Dr., Jackson
(517) 783-2681
•*Smoking section.
Cuisine: American.*

KALAMAZOO
& VICINITY
**Arcadia Brewing
Company**
103 W. Michigan
Ave., Battle Creek
(616) 963-9520
•*Bar. Humidor. Cuisine: wood-fired oven
cuisine.*

Corner Bar
1030 E. Vine
Kalamazoo
(616) 385-2028
•*All areas except non-
smoking. Humidor.
Cuisine: grill & pub
fare.*

Knight Cap
320 E. Michigan
Ave., Lansing
(517) 484-7676
•*All areas. Cuisine:
steak & seafood.*

**Herman's Garland
Resort**
Rte. 1, Box 364 M
Lewiston
(517) 786-2211

•*Lounge and grille.
Humidor. Cuisine:
American.*

Fonte d'Amore
32030 Plymouth Rd.
Livonia
(313) 422-0770
•*All areas. Humidor.
Cuisine: Abruzzo-
style Italian.*

**Laredo Steak
House**
350 E. 14 Mile Rd.
Madison Heights
(248) 583-1077
•*Smoking section of
the dining room and in
the bar. Cuisine:
steak, featuring baby
back ribs, and large
cuts of USDA choice
beef.*

**Muskegon Country
Club**
2801 Lakeshore Dr.
Muskegon
(616) 755-3737
•*Bar/lounge. Humidor. Cuisine: Continental.* **Private club.**

**O'Farrell
McGuire's Irish
Pub**
120 E. Michigan
Paw Paw
(616) 657-3654
•*Bar. Humidor. Cuisine: Irish.* **Pub.**

PETOSKEY & VICINITY

Rowe Inn
6303 C-48
Ellsworth, E. Jordan Rd.
Ellsworth
(616) 588-7351
•*Wine cellar and outside patio. Humidor. Cuisine: regional.*

Arboretum
7075 S. Lakeshore Dr.
Harbor Springs
(616) 526-6291
•*Bar, lounge, and private rooms. Humidor. Cuisine: American.*

Bar Harbor
100 State St.
Harbor Springs
(616) 526-2671
•*All areas. Humidor.*
Tavern.

Park Garden Cafe
432 E. Lake St.
Petoskey
(616) 347-0101
•*Bar/lounge. Cuisine: American.*
....

Treasure Island
924 N. Niagara St.
Saginaw
(517) 755-6577
•*Bar. Humidor. Cuisine: fine dining & saloon.*

Andiamo Lakefront Bistro
24026 Jefferson Ave.
St. Clair Shores
(810) 773-7770

•*Bar and patio. Humidor. Cuisine: Italian/American.*

Minnesota

MINNEAPOLIS/ ST. PAUL & VICINITY

Captain's Quarters at The Radisson South
7800 Normandale Blvd., Bloominton
(612) 835-7800
•*All areas. Humidor. Cuisine: Continental.*

Shorewood
6161 Hwy. 65 NE
Fridley
(612) 571-3444
•*Lounge. Humidor. Cuisine: Grecian & American.*

Brit's Pub & Eating Establishment
1110 Nicollet Mall
Minneapolis
(612) 332-3908
•*Upstairs dining area, bar, lounge, and near fireplaces. Humidor. Cuisine: British.*

Crowne Plaza North South
618 2nd Ave. S.
Minneapolis
(612) 338-2288
•*Smoking section and lounge. Cuisine: gourmet Continental & American classic.*

D'Amico Cucina
100 N. 6th St.

Minneapolis
(612) 338-2401
•*Lounge. Humidor. Cuisine: modern Italian.*

Huberts
601 Chicago Ave.
Minneapolis
(612) 332-6062
•*Bar/lounge, private room, and patio. Cuisine: American.*

Jimmy's Steak & Spirits
3675 Minnehaha Ave. S.
Minneapolis
(612) 729-9635
•*All areas. Humidor. Cuisine: steaks, pub fare.*

Manny's Steak House at the Hyatt Regency
1300 Nicolett Mall
Minneapolis
(612) 339-9900
•*Bar. Humidor. Cuisine: American steakhouse.*

Minneapolis Cafe
2730 W. Lake St.
Minneapolis
(612) 672-9100
•*Bar area and on the patio in the summer Humidor. Cuisine: Mediterranean.*

Morton's of Chicago
555 Nicollet Mall
Minneapolis
(612) 673-9700

•*Lounge and dining room. Humidor. Cuisine: steakhouse.*

Murray's
26 S. 6th St.
Minneapolis
(612) 339-0909
•*Lounge. Humidor. Cuisine: American.*

Nye's Polonaise Room
112 E. Hennepin
Minneapolis
(612) 379-2021
•*Bar/lounge. Humidor. Cuisine: Polish/American.*

Schiek's Palace Royale
115 S. 4th St.
Minneapolis
(612) 341-0054
•*All areas. Humidor. Cuisine: American.*
Nightclub.

Table of Contents
1310 Hennepin Ave.
Minneapolis
(612) 339-1133
•*Bar and lounge area. Humidor. Cuisine: contemporary American.*

Chang O'Hara's Bistro
498 Selby, St. Paul
(612) 290-2338
•*All smoking areas. Humidor. Cuisine: American bistro fare—influenced with spices from around the world.*

Forepaugh's
276 S. Exchange St.
St. Paul
(612) 224-5606
•*Bar/lounge. Cuisine: French.*

The St. Paul Grill at The St. Paul Hotel
350 Market St.
St. Paul
(612) 22 GRILL
•*Bar area. Humidor. Cuisine: American.*

Sweeney's Saloon
96 N. Dale St.
St. Paul
(612) 221-9157
•*All areas. Cuisine: American.* **Bar.**

Town & Country Club
300 Mississippi River
    Blvd. N., St. Paul
(612) 646-7121
•*Bar/lounge, smoking section, patio, and private rooms. Humidor. Cuisine: American.* **Private club.**

Missouri

KANSAS CITY
American Restaurant
25th & Grand
Kansas City
(816) 426-1133
•*Private dining rooms and cocktail lounge area. Humidor. Cuisine: American.*

Cafe Allegro
1815 W. 39th St.

Kansas City
(816) 561-3663
•*Bar. Humidor. Cuisine: contemporary seasonal.*

Fedora Cafe & Bar
210 W. 47th St.
Kansas City
(816) 561-6565
•*Bar/lounge. Cuisine: Continental.*

Harry's Bar & Tables
501 Westport Rd.
Kansas City
(816) 561-3950
•*All areas. Humidor. Cuisine: upscale casual—prix fixe lunch, tapas dinners.*

J.J.'s Restaurant
910 W. 48th St.
Kansas City
(816) 561-7136
•*Bar. Humidor. Cuisine: American/ Continental.*

Majestic Steakhouse
931 Broadway
Kansas City
(816) 471-8484
•*Main dining room, jazz club, and private dining room. Humidor. Cuisine: American, featuring steaks.*

Plaza III Jazz Club
4749 Pennsylvania
    Ave., Kansas City
(816) 753-0000
•*Bar and jazz club. Cuisine: steakhouse.*

River Market Brewing Company
500 Walnut
Kansas City
(816) 471-6300
•*Bar and billards parlor. Humidor. Cuisine: eclectic brewpub cuisine.*

Savoy Grill at the Savoy Hotel
219 W. 9th St.
Kansas City
(816) 842-3890
•*All areas and bar. Humidor. Cuisine: lobster & steak.*

Zola
4113 Pennsylvania
Kansas City
(816) 561-9191
•*All areas. Cuisine: comtemporary American.*

Nearly Famous Deli & Pasta House
1828 S. Kentwood
Springfield
(417) 883-3403
•*Smoking section and patio. Cuisine: American, French, & Italian.*

ST. LOUIS & VICINITY
Annie Gunn's
16806 Chesterfield
    Airport Rd.
Chesterfield
(314) 532-7684
•*All areas. Humidor. Cuisine: American.*

Bernard's Bar & Bistro
26 N. Meramec
Clayton
(314) 727-7004
•*Bar. Humidor. Cuisine: American/ Continental.*

John P. Fields
26 N. Central
Clayton
(314) 862-1886
•*Smoking section, patio, and cigar bar. Humidor. Cuisine: American Continental.*

Morton's of Chicago
7822 Bonhomme
    Ave., Clayton
(314) 725-4008
•*Dining room and bar. Humidor. Cuisine: steakhouse.*

Seven Gables Inn
26 Meramec
Clayton
(314) 863-8400
•*Bar and patio. Humidor. Cuisine: American.*

Gerard's
1153 Colonnade
    Center, Des Peres
(314) 821-0458
•*Smoking section. Humidor. Cuisine: Continental.*

Wilbut & Gil's
Clayton Center/
    1308 Clarkson
Ellisville
(314) 391-3200

•*All areas. Humidor. Cuisine: upscale American.*

Growler's Pub at the Heritage Inn
1600 Heritage
    Landing
St. Charles
(314) 939-9900
•*Smoking section, bar, and snug. Humidor. Cuisine: casual Cuisine.*

Cardwell's
8100 Maryland
St. Louis
(314) 726-5055
•*Bar and patio. Cuisine: American.*

Cheshire Inn
7036 Clayton Ave.
St. Louis
(314) 647-7300 ext.
    601
•*Private room, bar, and cigar bar. Humidor. Cuisine: American.*

Dierdorf & Harts Steakhouse
323 Westport Plaza
St. Louis
(314) 878-1801
•*Bar and lounge. Humidor. Cuisine: steakhouse with a contemporary flair.*

Jake's Steaks
707 Clamorgan
    Alley, St. Louis
(314) 621-8184

•*Smoking area of dining room and bar. Humidor. Cuisine: southwestern.*

LoRusso's Cucina
3121 Watson
St. Louis
(314) 647-6222
•*Piano lounge. Humidor. Cuisine: Italian.*

Noonday Club
1 Metropolitan
    Square, St. Louis
(314) 231-8452
•*All areas. Humidor. Cuisine: Continental.*
Private club.

The Ritz-Carlton
100 Carondelet
    Plaza, St. Louis
(314) 863-6300
•*Cigar club (members only) and lobby lounge. Humidor. Cuisine: American.*

Station Grill at the Hyatt Regency
1 St. Louis Union
    Station, St. Louis
(314) 231-1234
•*Grandhall lounge and Station Grill bar. Humidor. Cuisine: steaks, seafood.*

Tony's
410 Market St.
St. Louis
(314) 231-7007
•*Cocktail lounge. Humidor. Cuisine: Gourmet Italian.*

Wilbur & Gil's
639 Westport Plaza
    Dr., St. Louis
(314) 514-0466
•*All areas. Humidor. Cuisine: upscale American.*

Montana

The Grand Hotel
139 McLeod St.
Big Timber
(406) 932-4459
•*Bar. Cuisine: American/Continental.*

BILLINGS

Jake's
2701 1st Ave. N.
Billings
(406) 259-9375
•*Bar, smoking section, and casino. Humidor. Cuisine: steaks, ribs, chops.*

Lamplighter
75 27th St. W.
Billings
(406) 652-6773
•*Bar/lounge. Humidor. Cuisine: pub fare.*

Montana Brewing Co.
113 N. Broadway
Billings
(406) 252-9200
•*Bar. Humidor. Cuisine: American featuring wood-fired pizzas, burgers, & pastas.*

Nebraska

Misty's Restaurant & Lounge
6235 Havelock Ave.
Lincoln
(402) 466-8424
•*Lounge. Humidor. Cuisine: steakhouse.*

Top Hat
736 W. Cornhusker
Lincoln
(402) 479-9935
•*All areas. Humidor. Cuisine: American.*

OMAHA

Le Cafe de Paris
1228 S. 6th St.
Omaha
(402) 344-0227
•*Smoking area. Cuisine: French.*

Omaha Prime
415 S. 11th St.
Omaha
(402) 341-7040
•*Upstairs cigar room and downstairs cigar bar. Humidor. Cuisine: USDA prime steaks & chops.*

Passport
1101 Jackson St.
Omaha
(402) 344-3200
•*Lounge and cigar room. Humidor. Cuisine: steakhouse.*

Vivace
1108 Howard St.
Omaha
(402) 342-2050
•Bar. Cuisine: contemporary Italian with a Mediterranean influence.

Nevada

LAS VEGAS

Caesars Palace Hotel
3570 Las Vegas Blvd.
Las Vegas
(702) 731-7110
•All areas. Humidor. Cuisine: 19 restaurants offer a wide range of cuisines.

Carver's
2061 Sunset
Las Vegas
(702) 433-5801
•Smoking section and lounge area. Humidor. Cuisine: steakhouse.

Fiore at the Rio Hotel
3700 W. Flamingo
Las Vegas
(702) 252-7777
•Cigar terrace only. Humidor. Cuisine: European cuisine prepared in a new American-style.

Morton's of Chicago
3200 Las Vegas Blvd. S., Las Vegas
(702) 893-0703

•Dining room (smoking section) and bar. Humidor. Cuisine: steakhouse.

Ruth's Chris Steak House
3900 Paradise Rd.
Las Vegas
(702) 791-7011
•Bar/lounge. Humidor. Cuisine: steakhouse.

Ruth's Chris Steak House
4561 W. Flamingo Rd., Las Vegas
(702) 248-7011
•Dining room and lounge. Humidor. Cuisine: steakhouse.

Sfuzzi
3200 S. Las Vegas Blvd., B-11
Las Vegas
(702) 699-5777
•Bar and private room. Humidor. Cuisine: Italian.

Spago Las Vegas at The Forum Shops at Caesars
3500 Las Vegas Blvd. S., Las Vegas
(702) 369-6300
•Private dining rooms. Humidor. Cuisine: California.

The Tillerman
2245 E. Flamingo Rd., Las Vegas
(702) 731-4036

•Bar, lounge, and patio. Cuisine: seafood.

Tommy Rocker's Cantina & Grill
4275 S. Industrial
Las Vegas
(702) 261-6688
•All areas. Humidor. Cuisine: American, Mexican & BBQ.

RENO

The Christmas Tree
20007 Mount Rose Hwy., Reno
(702) 849-0127
•Bar, lounge, and patio. Humidor. Cuisine: unique American.

Harrah's Steak House
210 N. Center St.
Reno
(702) 788-2929
•Lounge and cigar bar. Humidor. Cuisine: tableside cooking—steak & seafood.

The Men's Club of Reno
270 Lake St., Reno
(702) 786-7800
•All areas. Humidor. Cuisine: Continental, featuring steaks, seafood, & other specialties including live Maine lobster. **Gentlemen's club.**

Rapscallion
1555 S. Wells, Reno
(702) 323-1211

•Bar area. Humidor. Cuisine: seafood.

New Hampshire

Tony Clamato's Ristorante
15 Court St., Keene
(603) 357-4345
•Bar and lounge. Humidor. Cuisine: Italian.

Black Cat Coffee & Cigars
17 Veterans Sq.
Laconia
(603) 528-3233
•All areas. Humidor. Cuisine: lite fare featuring homemade specialties including soups, sandwiches, salads, pastries & desserts.

Stark Mill Brewery & Restaurant
500 Commercial St.
Manchester
(603) 622-0000
•Large lounge area and bar. Humidor. Cuisine: steaks, seafood, pizza, salads, sandwiches.

Wild Rover
21 Kosciuszko St.
Manchester
(603) 669-7722
•Bar area. Cuisine: variety of dishes.

Scottish Lion Inn & Restaurant
Rte. 16
North Conway
(888) 356-4945,
    (603) 356-6381
•*Blackwatch Pub only (special room for cigars & pipes). Humidor. Cuisine: International.*

Woodstock Inn & Brewery
Main St. Rte. 3
North Woodstock
(603) 745-3951
•*All areas of the brewpub. Humidor. Cuisine: wide variety of pub fare.*

Barnstormers Restaurant
27 International Dr.,
    Pease Intl.
    Trade Port
Portsmouth
(603) 433-6700
•*Sports and piano bars. Cuisine: steak & seafood.*

Legends 1291
Town Square
Waterville Valley
(603) 236-4678
•*All areas. Humidor. Cuisine: American.*

The Seven Barrel Brewey Pub
Rte. 12-A at I-89,
    exit 20
West Lebanon
(603) 298-5566
•*Smoking section. Cuisine: British pub fare.* **Pub.**

New Jersey

ATLANTIC/ CAPE MAY COS.

The Ram's Head Inn
9 W. White Horse
    Pike, Absecon
(609) 652-1700
•*Bar, art gallery, and courtyard. Humidor. Cuisine: Continental.*

Trump Plaza Hotel & Casino
Boardwalk at Missis-
    sippi
Atlantic City
(609) 441-6000
•*All smoking areas. Humidor. Cuisine: variety available.*

BERGEN/ PASSAIC COS.

Azúcar
10 Dempsey Ave.
Edgewater
(201) 886-0747
•*All areas. Humidor. Cuisine: Cuban.*

Smoke Chophouse & Cigar Emporium
36 Engle St.
Englewood
(201) 541-8530
•*All areas. Humidor. Cuisine: steak, chops, lobster, chicken; lunch menu features the "Macanudo" and "Cohiba" burgers.*

The Park Steakhouse
151 Kinderkamack
    Rd., Park Ridge
(201) 930-1300

•*Private dining room for smokers only and bar. Humidor. Cuisine: steakhouse.*

Saints Cafe
827 Teaneck Rd.
Teaneck
(201) 833-1160
•*All areas. Humidor. Cuisine: American eclectic.*

ESSEX/ HUDSON COS.

Seven Hills Restaurant
88 Washington St.
Bloomfield
(973) 743-5331
•*Bar/lounge and private rooms. Humidor. Cuisine: Italian-American.*

Pronto Cena Ristorante
87 Sussex St.
Jersey City
(201) 435-0004
•*Smoking section and bar. Humidor. Cuisine: authentic Tuscan-Italian.*

Paparazzi
The Mall at Short
    Hills, Short Hills
(973) 467-5544
•*Bar and smoking section in dining room. Humidor. Cuisine: Northern Italian.*

MERCER CO.

Barley's at the Forrestal Hotel
100 College Rd. E.
Princeton
(609) 452-7800
•*Bar and cigar bar. Humidor. Cuisine: American bar menu.*

Diamond's
132 Kent St.
Trenton
(609) 393-1000
•*All areas. Humidor. Cuisine: Italian, prime aged steak, Maine lobsters & fresh seafood.*

MONMOUTH/ OCEAN COUNTIES

Giamano's Restaurant & Cigar Room
301 Main St.
Bradley Beach
(732) 775-4275
•*Bar, lounge, smoking section in dining room, and cigar bar. Humidor. Cuisine: fine Italian.*

Havana
409 Easy Ave.
Highlands
(732) 708-0290
Lounge and Cigar bar. Humidor. Cuisine: Cuban

Basil T's Brewpub & Italian Grill
183 Riverside Ave.
Redbank
(732) 842-5990
•*Bar and smoking section in dining room. Humidor. Cuisine: Italian & pizza.*

Basil T's Brewpub & Italian Grill
1171 Hooper Ave.
Toms River
(732) 244-7566
•*Bar, smoking section in dining room and cigar lounge. Humidor. Cuisine: Italian & pizza.*

MORRIS/
HUNTERDON/
SOMERSET COS.

Conservatory at the Madison Hotel
1 Convent Rd.
Morristown
(973) 285-1800
•*Bar/lounge. Humidor. Cuisine: American.*

Verve American Bar & Restaurant
18 E. Main St.
Somerville
(908) 707-8655
•*Bar. Humidor. Cuisine: Provencial American.*

Luigi's Restaurant
Roxbury Mall/275-230 Rte. 10
Succasunna
(973) 584-2881

•*Bar and front room. Humidor. Cuisine: Italian.*

Season's Restaurant
644 Pascack Rd.
Washington Township
(201) 664-6141
•*Lounge area. Humidor. Cuisine: Continental.*

The Ryland Inn
Rte. 22 W.
Whitehouse
(908) 534-4011
•*Cigar lounge only. Humidor. Cuisine: modern regional French.*

UNION/
MIDDLESEX
COS.

Al Dente Ristorante
1665 Stelton Rd.
Piscataway
(732) 985-8220
•*Cigar bar, bar, lounge, and private rooms. Humidor. Cuisine: authentic & creative Italian.*

Ginamarie's Ristorante
514 Park Ave.
Scotch Plains
(908) 322-3133
•*Cigar bar, bar, and lounge. Humidor. Cuisine: Authentic & Creative Italian.*

Stage House Inn
366 Park Ave.

Scotch Plains
(908) 322-4224
•*Cocktail lounge and bar. Humidor. Cuisine: French/ American.*

New Mexico

Ranchers Club at the Albuquerque Hilton
1901 University Blvd. NE
Albuquerque
(505) 884-2500
•*Dining room smoking section after dinner and in the lounge. Humidor. Cuisine: American, specializing in seafood & steak.*

Billy Crews
1200 Country Club Rd., Santa Teresa
(505) 589-2071
•*All areas. Humidor. Cuisine: American.*

New York

Mansion Hill Inn
115 Philip St.
Albany
(518) 465-2038/
(888) 299-0455
•*Dining room, courtyard, and guestrooms. Humidor. Cuisine: American regional.*

BINGHAMTON
& VICINITY

Sportmen's Club
190 Main St.
Binghamton
(607) 722-9751

•*All areas. Humidor. Cuisine: pub fare.*
Sports bar/cigar bar.

Yesterday's
907 Vestal Pkwy. E.
Vestal
(607) 785-3313
•*Bar/lounge. Cuisine: American.*

BUFFALO &
VICINITY

The Dakota Grill & Cigar Bar and Ciao
4224 Maple Rd./
Maple Ridge Plaza
Amherst
(716) 834-6600
•*Cigar bar. Humidor. Cuisine: steaks, fresh fish & chicken at The Grill; Italian Trattoria at Ciao.*

Adam's Steak & Seafood
204 Como Park Blvd., Buffalo
(716) 683-3784
•*Bar/lounge. Cuisine: American, specializing in seafood & steak.*

The Riverside Inn-"On the water"
115 S. Water St.
Lewiston
(716) 754-8206
•*Smoking area in dining room and in pub. Humidor. Cuisine: classic American steakhouse.*

Pierce's 1894 Restaurant
228 Oakwood Ave.
Elmira Heights
(607) 734-2022
•Bar and lounge. Humidor. Cuisine: American/Continental.

The White Inn
52 E. Main St.
Fredonia
(716) 672-2103
•Bar/lounge. Cuisine: American. **Country inn.**

John Thomas Steakhouse
1152 Danby Rd.
Ithaca
(607) 273-3464
•Lounge and deck (weather permitting) where food and drink are available. Humidor. Cuisine: steakhouse.

Wiltwyck Golf Club
404 Stewart Lane
Kingston
(914) 331-0700
•Bar/lounge. Humidor. **Private golf club.**

The Horned Dorset Inn
Rte. 8
Leonardsville
(315) 855-7898
•Cigar bar. Humidor. Cuisine: French.

LONG ISLAND
—NASSAU CO.

E.T. Quigg's
2807 Merrick Rd.

Bellmore
(516) 785-9559
•All areas. Humidor. Cuisine: pub fare. **Pub.**

Jonathan's Creative American
3000 Jericho Tpke.
Garden City Park
(516) 742-7300
•Cigar lounge seating 50 people. Humidor. Cuisine: American & International.

Nassau Country Club
St. Andrews Lane
Glen Cove
(516) 676-0554
•Main bar, adjoining lounge areas, and card room. Humidor. Cuisine: Continental. **Private club.**

Brick Cafe
157 Lakeview Ave.
Lynbrook
(516) 599-9669
•Dining room and bar. Humidor. Cuisine: American.

Eleanor Rigby's
133 Mineola Blvd.
Mineola
(516) 739-6622
•Bar and designated tables in smoking section. Humidor. Cuisine: Continental.

Bryant & Cooper Steakhouse
2 Middleneck Rd.
Roslyn
(516) 627-7270

•Large bar area. Humidor. Cuisine: steakhouse.

Hemingway's American Bar & Grill
1885 Wantagh Ave.
Wantagh
(516) 781-2700
•Bar/smoking area. Humidor. Cuisine: American/Continental.

LONG ISLAND
—SUFFOLK CO.

Cavanaugh's
255 Blue Point Ave.
Blue Point
(516) 363-2666
•All areas. Humidor. Cuisine: pub fare.

The Palm
94 Main St.
East Hampton
(516) 324-0411
•Bar/lounge. Humidor. Cuisine: steakhouse.

Chesterfield's
330 New York Ave.
Huntington
(516) 425-1457
•All areas. Humidor. **Jazz/blues lounge.**

The Dock
1 Town Rd.
Montauk
(516) 668-9778
•Bar. Humidor. Cuisine: seafood, pasta & burgers.

Jerry's Restaurant & Tap Room
1575 Montauk Hwy.
Oakdale
(516) 567-0055
•Bar. Humidor. Cuisine: American.

American Hotel
Main St.
Sag Harbor
(516) 725-3535
•Bar and lobby. Humidor. Cuisine: French.

The Cigar Bar
2 Main St.
Sag Harbor
(516) 725-2575
•Throughout the living room setting and at the bar. Humidor. Cuisine: cocktail foods including caviar, foie gras & gravlax. **Cigar bar.**

NEW YORK CITY
— BROOKLYN

Lundy Bros. Restaurant
1901 Emmons Ave.
Brooklyn
(718) 743-0022
•Bar/lounge, smoking section, patio and cigar bar. Humidor. Cuisine: features seafood & steakhouse.

Mike & Tony's Bar & Grill
239 5th Ave.
Brooklyn
(718) 857-2800
•Bar. Humidor. Cuisine: steak & seafood.

The River Cafe
1 Water St.
Brooklyn
(718) 522-5200
•*Bar/lounge and private room. Humidor. Cuisine: American/ Continental.*

Cigargoyles
7 Old Fulton St.
Brooklyn Heights
(718) 254-0656
•*All areas. Humidor. Cuisine: Black Angus steaks, seafood & pasta.*

NEW YORK CITY
— MANHATTAN
1st Ave.
361 1st Ave. (corner of 21st & 1st)
(212) 475-9068
•*All areas. Humidor. Cuisine: American.*

21 Club
21 W. 52nd St.
(212) 582-7200
•*Lounge. Humidor. Cuisine: American.*

53rd St. Cigar Bar
53rd St. & 7th Ave.
(212) 581-1000, ext. 5276
•*Cigar bar. Humidor. Cuisine: Continental.*

The Alamo
304 E. 48th St.
(212) 759-0590
•*Bar. Humidor. Cuisine: Mexican/Texan.*

Alva
36 E. 22nd St.
(212) 228-4399

•*Bar/lounge. Humidor. Cuisine: contemporary American bistro.*

An American Place
2 Park Ave.
(212) 684-2122
•*Bar. Cuisine: regional American.*

Angelo & Maxie's Steakhouse
233 Park Ave. S.
(212) 220-9200
•*Cigar bar. Humidor. Cuisine: steakhouse.*

Armstrong's
875 10th Ave.
(212) 581-0606
•*Bar area. Humidor. Cuisine: eclectic.*

Beekman Bar and Books
889 1st Ave.
(212) 980-9314
•*All areas. Humidor. Cuisine: hors d'oeuvres only.* **Bar/cigar lounge.**

Ben Benson's Steakhouse
123 W. 52nd St.
(212) 581-8888
•*Bar/lounge. Humidor. Cuisine: steakhouse.*

Bice
7 E. 54th St.
(212) 688-1999, 593-0665 (office)
•*Bar and lounge area. Humidor. Cuisine: Italian.*

BlackFinn Bar and Restaurant
994 2nd Ave.
(212) 355-6993
•*All areas. Humidor. Cuisine: Cajun.*

The Box Tree Restaurant
250 E. 49th St.
(212) 758-8320
•*Bar, smoking section, and private rooms. Humidor. Cuisine: steakhouse, French.*

Boxers
190 W. 4th St.
(212) 633-BARK
•*Bar. Cuisine: American bar & grill.*

Brew's
156 E. 34th St.
(212) 889-3369
•*Bar. Humidor. Cuisine: American, specializing in steak.*

The Bubble Lounge
228 W. Broadway
(212) 431-3433
•*Bar area and half room. Humidor. Cuisine: caviar & other hors d'oeuvres only.* **Champagne bar.**

Bull & Bear Restaurant at The Waldorf Astoria
301 Park Ave.
(212) 872-4606
•*Bar. Humidor. Cuisine: American, specializing in steak.*

Butlers Restaurant
1407 Broadway
(212) 575-1407
•*Upstairs. Humidor. Cuisine: American.*

Cafe Aubette
119 E. 27th St.
(212) 686-5500
•*All areas, but encouraged in the back room. Humidor. Cuisine: innovative American appetizers and dessert at night; European espresso bar in the afternoon.* **Cafe.**

Café des Artistes
1 W. 67th St.
(212) 877-3500
•*The Parlor. Humidor. Cuisine: country French.*

Cafe Pierre at The Pierre Hotel
2 E. 61st St.
(212) 940-8195
•*Bar/rotunda. Cuisine: Continental & French.*

Cal's
22 W. 21st St.
(212) 929-0740
•*Bar. Cuisine: Continental.*

Campagna
24 E. 21st St.
(212) 460-0900
•*Bar area. Humidor. Cuisine: Italian.*

Carnegie Bar and Books
156 W. 56th St.
(212) 957-9676
•*All areas. Humidor. Cuisine: hors d'oeuvres only.* **Bar/cigar lounge.**

Chiam
160 E. 48th St.
(212) 371-2323
•*Bar and wine cellar. Humidor. Cuisine: Chinese.*

The Cigar Room at Trumpets at The Grand Hyatt Hotel
Grand Central Station
(212) 850-5999
•*Cigar room, restaurant, and lounge. Humidor. Cuisine: Continental.*

Cinquanta
50 E. 50th St.
(212) 759-5050
•*One floor for smokers. Humidor. Cuisine: Italian.*

Cité
120 W. 51st St.
(212) 956-7100
•*Bar. Cuisine: steakhouse.*

City Crab & Seafood Co.
235 Park Ave. S.
(212) 529-3800
•*Main floor and cigar lounge. Humidor. Cuisine: seafood.*

City Wine & Cigar Co.
62 Laight St.
   (Tribeca)
(212) 334-2274
•*Cigar restaurant—so most areas. Humidor. Cuisine: food from cigar producing regions.*

Club Macanudo
26 E. 63rd St.
(212) 752-8200
•*All areas. Humidor. Cuisine: American with a Latin influence.* **Cigar bar.**

Coco Pazzo
23 E. 74th St.
(212) 794-0205
•*Bar area. Humidor. Cuisine: Italian.*

The Conservatory at the Mayflower Hotel
15 Central Park W.
(212) 641-1173
•*Bar/lounge. Cuisine: Continental.*

Corsica
310 W. 4th St.
(212) 691-8541
•*Bar. Cuisine: Corsican/Mediterranean.*

Da Antonio Ristorante
157 E. 57th St.
New York
(212) 588-1545
•*Private rooms. Humidor. Cuisine: Italian*

Dakota Bar & Grill
1576 3rd Ave.
(212) 427-8889
•*Bar area. Cuisine: American.*

Decade: A State of Mind & Spirit
1117 1st Ave. at
   61st St.
(212) 835-5979
•*All areas. Humidor. Cuisine: contemporary American.*

Delano Drive Restaurant
E. 25th St. & the
   East River (FDR
   Drive; on the
   river)
(212) 683-3001
•*Bar area. Humidor. Cuisine: steaks, fresh fish, pasta.*

Divine Bar
244 E. 51st. St.
(212) 319-9463
•*All areas. Humidor. Cuisine: Mediterranean tapas.* **Lounge/wine bar.**

Drake Cafe & Bar at the Drake Swiss Hotel
440 Park Ave.
(212) 756-3925
•*Bar. Humidor. Cuisine: Innovative American.*

Elaine's Restaurant
1703 2nd Ave.
(212) 534-8114

•*Dining room and bar. Humidor. Cuisine: Italian.*

Filli Ponte Ristorante
39 Debrosses St.
(212) 226-4621
•*Cigar lounge and Beca Bar. Humidor. Cuisine: regional Italian.*

Florio's of Little Italy
192 Grand St.
New York
(212) 226-7610
•*Bar/lounge, cigar bar, and smoking area. Humidor. Cuisine: Italian.*

Flowers
21 W. 17th St.
(212) 691-8888
•*Tapas lounge and rooftop dining room. Humidor. Cuisine: exotic Continental.*

Frank's Restaurant
85 10th Ave.
(212) 243-1349
•*Bar, smoking section, and private party room. Humidor. Cuisine: steakhouse.*

Frankie & Johnnie's
269 W. 45th St.
(212) 997-9494
•*Cigar bar. Humidor. Cuisine: steakhouse.*

Fresco by Scotto
34 E. 52nd St.
(212) 935-3434
•*Bar area and party room. Humidor. Cuisine: modern Tuscan.*

Gallagher's Steak House
228 W. 52nd St.
(212) 245-5336
•*Bar and smoking section. Humidor. Cuisine: steakhouse.*

Giovanni
47 W. 55th St.
New York
(212) 262-2828
•*Cigar room and at bar after 10pm. Humidor. Cuisine: Northern Italian (Venetian).*

Grand Havana Room
666 5th Ave.
(212) 245-1600
•*Bar/lounge. Humidor. Cuisine: American. Private club.*

Granville
40 E. 20th St.
(212) 253-9088
•*Bar and lounge area. Humidor. Cuisine: modern Creole.*

Greatest Bar on Earth & The Skybox
One World Trade Center, 107 Fl.
(212) 524-7107

•*Skybox cigar lounge after 7pm and at 3 bars. Humidor. Cuisine: world-view theme/international.*

Grill 53 at the Hilton Hotel and Towers
1335 Ave. of the Americas
(212) 261-5770
•*Lounge. Humidor. Cuisine: steak & seafood.*

The Grotto Lounge at Limoncello Restaurant
777 7th Ave.
(212) 582-7932
•*All areas. Humidor. Cuisine: Italian. Cigar bar.*

Halcyon
151 W. 54th St.
(212) 468-8736
•*Bar/lounge. Cuisine: American.*

Harbour Lights
South Street Seaport, Pier 17, 3rd Fl.
(212) 227-2800
•*Separate room for smokers only. Humidor. Cuisine: American & seafood.*

Harry's at Hanover Square
1 Hanover Square
(212) 425-3412
•*Bar. Cuisine: Continental.*

Havana Tea Room & Cigar House
265 E. 78th St.
(212) 327-2012
•*All areas. Humidor. Cuisine: English tea/ Cuban sandwiches/ extensive dessert menu. English tea service & cigar house.*

Heartland Brewery
35 Union Square N.
(212) 645-3400
•*Smoking section and bar. Humidor. Cuisine: American Continental.*

Home
20 Cornelia St.
(212) 243-9579
•*Garden only. Cuisine: American neighborhood.*

Hudson Bar and Books
636 Hudson St.
(212) 229-2642
•*All areas. Humidor. Cuisine: elegant light fare. Bar/cigar lounge.*

Hudson River Club
4 World Financial Center
(212) 786-1500
•*Bar, lounge, and private rooms. Humidor. Cuisine: regional.*

Il Monello
1460 2nd Ave.
(212) 535-9310

•*Bar/lounge and private room. Humidor. Cuisine: Italian.*

Il Toscanaccio
7 E. 59th St.
(212) 935-3535
•*Bar/lounge. Humidor. Cuisine: Tuscan.*

Il Valentino Restaurant
330 E. 56th St.
(212) 355-0001
•*Bar/lounge and outdoor dining room. Cuisine: Tuscan.*

Jake's Steakhouse
1155 3rd Ave.
(212) 879-9888
•*Bar. Humidor. Cuisine: steak.*

John Street Bar & Grill
17 John St.
(212) 349-3278
•*All smoking areas and private rooms. Humidor. Cuisine: American pub fare.*

Jubilee
347 E. 54th St.
(212) 888-3569
•*Smoking area near the bar. Cuisine: French.*

Keens Steakhouse
72 W. 36th St.
(212) 947-3636
•*Bar and private party rooms. Humidor. Cuisine: steakhouse.*

La Granita
1470 2nd Ave.
(212) 717-5500
•*Special separate
room. Cuisine: Italian/Tuscan.*

Le Bar Bat
311 W. 57th St.
(212) 307-7228
•*All three levels.
Humidor. Cuisine:
American grill.*

Le Cirque 2000
455 Madison Ave.
(212) 303-7788
•*Bar, lounge, and private dining room.
Humidor. Cuisine:
French/Continental.*

Le Colonial
149 E. 57th St.
(212) 752-0808
•*Bar/lounge area.
Cuisine: Vietnamese.*

Le Madri
168 W. 18th St.
(212) 727-8022
•*Bar and patio.
Humidor. Cuisine:
Italian.*

Le Marais
150 W. 46th St.
(212) 869-0900
•*Bar and upstairs
area. Humidor. Cuisine: French steakhouse.*

Le Veau d' Or
129 E. 60th St.
(212) 838-8133
•*All areas. Humidor.
Cuisine: French.*

**Les Célébrités at
the Hotel Nikko**
155 W. 58th St.
(212) 484-5113
•*Private dining room.
Humidor. Cuisine:
French.*

**Lexington Bar and
Books**
1020 Lexington Ave.
(212) 717-3902
•*All areas. Humidor.
Cuisine: cocktail cuisine.* **Bar/cigar
lounge.**

**Maggie's Place
Restaurant & Bar**
21 E. 47th St.
(212) 753-5757
•*Bar area. Humidor.
Cuisine: nouvelle
American.*

Manhattan Grille
1161 1st Ave.
(212) 888-6556
•*Separate private
cigar smoking dining
room (seats 60-70).
Humidor. Cuisine:
American.*

**Mark's Restaurant
and Bar**
25 E. 77th St.
(212) 879-1864
•*Bar and private
rooms. Humidor.
Cuisine: French Continental.*

Marti Kebab
1269 1st Ave.
(212) 737-6104
•*Private room. Cuisine: Turkish.*

Merchant NY
1125 1st Ave.
(212) 832-1551
•*Entire floor devoted to
cigar lounge. Humidor.
Cuisine: nouvelle
American Continental.*

Michael's
24 W. 55th St.
(212) 767-0555
•*Bar/lounge. Humidor. Cuisine: American.*

Minetta Tavern
113 MacDougal St.
(212) 475-3850
•*Bar. Humidor. Cuisine: Northern Italian.*

**Monkey Bar at the
Hotel Elysee**
60 E. 54th St.
(212) 838-2600
•*Bar. Humidor. Cuisine: American cuisine
Vidal.*

Moran's Restaurant
146 10th Ave.
(212) 627-3030
•*Bar and private
rooms. Humidor.
Cuisine: American,
specializing in seafood
& steak.*

**Morton's of
Chicago**
551 5th Ave.
(212) 972-3315
•*Bar. Humidor. Cuisine: steakhouse.*

North Star Pub
93 South St.
(212) 509-6757

•*All areas. Humidor.
Cuisine: British.*

**O'Flaherty's
Ale House**
334-336 W. 46th St.
(212) 246-8928
•*Bar and in dining
room when the kitchen
closes. Cuisine: international Irish pub
fare.*

O'Nieal's Grand St.
174 Grand St.
(212) 941-9119
•*Bar/lounge and after
dinner in the dining
area. Humidor. Cuisine: upscale American with French influences.*

**Oak Bar at the
Plaza Hotel**
768 5th Ave.
(212) 546-5330
•*Bar. Humidor. Cuisine: certified Black
Angus meats.* **Bar.**

Oceana
55 E. 54th St.
(212) 759-5941
•*Bar/lounge. Humidor. Cuisine: seafood.*

The Odeon
145 W. Broadway
(212) 233-0507
•*Bar. Cuisine:
European/American.*

Old Homestead
56 9th Ave.
(212) 242-9040
•*Bar and cocktail
area. Humidor. Cuisine: steak & seafood.*

Oyster Bar
Grand Central Terminal
(212) 490-6650
•*Saloon bar. Humidor. Cuisine: seafood.*

Palio
151 W. 51st St.
(212) 245-4850
•*Bar only (separate from restaurant). Humidor. Cuisine: Italian.*

Palm
837 2nd Ave.
(212) 687-2953
•*Bar only (and at some tables). Humidor. Cuisine: American featuring steak & lobster.*

Park Avenue Cafe
100 E. 63rd St.
(212) 644-1900
•*Bar. Humidor. Cuisine: American.*

Patroon
160 E. 46th St.
(212) 883-7373
•*Cigar lounge. Humidor. Cuisine: American/Continental.*

The Post House
28 E. 63rd St.
New York
(212) 935-2888
•*Bar. Humidor. Cuisine: American, specializing in steak.*

Pravda
281 Lafayette St.
(212) 226-4696

•*All areas. Humidor. Cuisine: Russian-inspired.*

Rainbow Room
30 Rockefeller Plaza
(212) 632-5000
•*Rainbow Promenade bar. Humidor. Cuisine: American-inspired Continental.*

Raoul's
180 Prince St.
(212) 966-3518
•*Garden room and bar. Humidor. Cuisine: French.*

Remi
145 W. 53rd St.
(212) 581-4242
•*Bar, private party rooms, and outdoor atrium garden. Humidor. Cuisine: Venetian/northern Italian.*

Ristorante Bruno
240 E. 58th St.
(212) 688-4190
•*Smoking section of dining room. Humidor. Cuisine: Italian.*

Runyon's
932 2nd Ave.
(212) 223-9592
•*Bar and some tables. Humidor. Cuisine: American steakhouse.*

Russian Samovar
256 W. 52nd St.
(212) 757-0168

•*Bar area and upstairs cigar bar. Humidor. Cuisine: Russian.*

Ruth's Chris Steak House
148 W. 51st St.
(212) 245-9600
•*Lounge and private rooms. Humidor. Cuisine: steakhouse.*

San Domenico
240 Central Park South
(212) 265-5959
•*Bar and lounge. Humidor. Cuisine: Italian.*

Señor Swanky's
287 Columbus Ave.
(212) 501-7000
•*Bar, lounge, cigar bar, and patio. Humidor. Cuisine: Mexican.*

SettaMoMA at the Museum of Modern Art
12 W. 54th St.
(212) 708-9710
•*Bar/lounge and smoking section. Cuisine: Italian.*

Sheila Clancy's
922 3rd Ave.
(212) 688-4646
•*Bar. Cuisine: Continental.*

Slaughtered Lamb Pub
182 W. 4th St.
(212) 727-3350

•*Smoking section. Cuisine: Old English Tavern/American.*

Smith & Wollensky
797 3rd Ave.
(212) 753-1530
•*At one of the three bars and also a small section in the bar area. Humidor. Cuisine: steakhouse.*

Spy
101 Greene St.
(212) 343-9000
•*All areas. Humidor. Cuisine: upscale hors d'oeuvres. **Nightclub/ bar.***

St. Regis Hotel— King Cole Bar & Astor Court
2 E. 55th St.
(212) 339-6857
•*Bar and Cognac Room. Humidor. Cuisine: upscale bistro. **Bar.***

Tapastry
575 Hudson St.
(212) 242-0003
•*Bar and lounges. Humidor. Cuisine: American tapas with California & southwestern influences in a Spanish style.*

Tatou
151 E. 50th St.
(212) 753-1144
•*Cigar bar and near the bar in main dining room. Humidor. Cuisine: French/American.*

Ten's World Class Cabaret
35 E. 21st St.
(212) 254-2444
• *All areas. Humidor.
Cuisine: American/
Continental.* **Gentleman's club.**

Third Floor Cafe
315 5th Ave.
(212) 481-3669
• *Smoking section.
Cuisine: lunch menu
& evening hors d'oeuvres.* **Cafe.**

Torre di Pisa
19 W. 44th St.
(212) 398-4400
• *Cigar room only
(seats 28). Humidor.
Cuisine: Italian.*

Torremolinos Restaurant
230 E. 51st St.
(212) 755-1862
• *Bar. Cuisine: Spanish & Continental.*

Tse Yang
34 E. 51st St.
(212) 688-5588
• *Bar and private
rooms. Humidor.
Cuisine: gourmet
Peking- & Shanghai-
style Chinese.*

Twins Restaurant
1712 2nd. Ave. (at
89th St.)
(212) 289-1777
• *Bar area. Humidor.
Cuisine: American
with a Mediterranean
influence.*

Typhoon Brewery
22 E. 54th St.
(212) 754-9006
• *Bar. Humidor. Cuisine: upscale Thai.*

Victor's Cafe 52
236 W. 52nd St.
(212) 586-7714
• *Bar. Humidor. Cuisine: Cuban.*

Wall Street Kitchen & Bar
70 Broad St.
(212) 797-7070
• *Bar/lounge. Humidor. Cuisine: eclectic
American.*

The Water Club
East River & FDR
(just north of E.
23rd St.)
(212) 683-3333
• *Bar and upper deck.
Humidor. Cuisine:
American, specializing
in seafood.*

Webster Hall
125 E. 11th St.
(212) 606-4202
• *Havana Lounge.*
Nightclub.

West 63rd Street Steakhouse
44 W. 63rd St.
(212) 246-6363
• *Bar, lounge, and private rooms. Humidor.
Cuisine: steakhouse.*

NEW YORK CITY — QUEENS

Piccola Venezia Ristorante
42-01 28 Ave.
Astoria
(718) 721-8470
• *Private room and bar
area. Humidor. Cuisine: Italian.*

Caffe on the Green
201-10 Cross Island
Pkwy., Bayside
(718) 423-7272
• *Bar and smoking
section. Humidor.
Cuisine: Italian.*

Uncle Jack's Steakhouse & Cigar Bar
39-40 Bell Blvd.
Bayside
(718) 229-1100
• *All areas. Humidor.
Cuisine: eclectic steakhouse featuring Black
Angus & Kobe beef.*

Calla Larga
247-63 Jamaica Ave.
Bellerose
(718) 343-2185
• *Smoking section in
dining room. Humidor. Cuisine: Northern Italian.*

Rosso Bianco New York
104-08 Metropolitan
Ave., Forest Hills
(718) 793-0748
• *All areas. Humidor.
Cuisine: light menu.*
Bar/cigar lounge.

Maxfield's Restaurant
5 Market St.
Potsdam
(315) 265-3796
• *Bar. Humidor. Cuisine: pasta, steaks, &
seafood.*

La Pavillon
230 Salt Point Tpke.
Poughkeepsie
(914) 473-2525
• *Bar/lounge and private rooms. Cuisine:
French.*

Oasis Mediterranean Bistro
365 Park Ave.
Rochester
(716) 271-0090
• *Cigar bar, patio,
and private rooms.
Humidor. Cuisine:
Mediterranean.*

Thendara Inn & Restaurant
4356 E. Lake Rd.
Rochester
(716) 394-4868
• *Bar/lounge and
patio. Humidor. Cuisine: American, Continental, French.*

Wandtke's Old City Hall Restaurant & Humidor Club
30 W. Broad St.
Rochester
(716) 454-1641
• *Cigar & martini bar.
Humidor. Cuisine:
American*

43 Phila Bistro
43 Phila St.
Saratoga Springs
(518) 584-2720
•*Smoking section and bar. Humidor. Cuisine: upscale American bistro.*

The Inn at Speculator
Rte. 8, Box 163
Speculator
(518) 548-3811
•*Pub room. Humidor. Cuisine: American, Continental, French, Mediterranean, & Mexican; specializing in seafood & steak.*

Clark's Ale House
122 W. Jefferson St.
Syracuse
(315) 479-9859
•*All areas. Cuisine: pub fare.* **Bar.**

Danzer's Restaurant
153 Ainsley Dr.
Syracuse
(315) 422-0089
•*Smoking section and bar. Cuisine: German.*

Pascale Restaurant
204 W. Fayette St.
Syracuse
(315) 471-3040
•*Bar and private room. Humidor. Cuisine: Mediterranean.*

Riley's For the Fun of It
312 Park St.
Syracuse
(315) 471-7111
•*Bar. Humidor. Cuisine: American.*

Alexander Hamilton Inn & Alexander's Cigar Bar
21 W. Park Row
Clinton
(315) 853-5555
•*Smoking section, bar, and cigar bar. Humidor. Cuisine: international/Continental.*

Beardslee Castle
Rte. 5, Little Falls
(315) 823-3000
•*Bar, grill, and smoking section. Humidor. Cuisine: creative American.*

Jack Appleseed's Tavern
147 N. Genesee
Utica
(315) 797-7979
•*Smoking section and bar. Cuisine: American.*

Lock, Stock & Barrel
35 Bardonia Rd.
Bardonia
(914) 623-6323

•*Bar and lounge area. Humidor. Cuisine: American.*

Hoppfields Restaurant
954 Old Post Rd., Rte. 121, Bedford
(914) 234-3374
•*Bar and private dining room. Humidor. Cuisine: American.*

Tomaso's at the Bedford Village Inn
Rte. 22
Bedford Village
(914) 234-6739
•*Bar area. Humidor. Cuisine: Italian.*

Arch Restaurant
Rte. 22
  Brewster
(914) 279-5011
•*Bar/lounge. Humidor. Cuisine: Continental, modern French, eclectic.*

Crabtree's Kittle House
11 Kittle Rd.
Chappaqua
(914) 666-8044
•*Bar. Humidor. Cuisine: progressive American.*

Louisiana Cajun Cafe
25 Cedar St.
Dobbs Ferry
(914) 693-9762
•*Bar. Humidor. Cuisine: Cajun/Creole.*

Old Drovers Inn
Old Rte. 22
Dover Plains
(914) 832-9311
•*Library parlor. Humidor. Cuisine: traditional & contemporary American.*

Depuy Canal House
Rte. 213, High Falls
(914) 687-7700
•*Bar and cabaret. Humidor. Cuisine: nouvelle American.*

Broadway Bar & Grill
8 S. Broadway
Irvington
(914) 591-9861
•*All areas. Humidor. Cuisine: American, steak, seafood.*

Marco
Rte. 6
Lake Mahopac
(914) 621-1648
•*Lounge. Humidor. Cuisine: nouvelle.*

The Black Bass Grille
2 Central Ave., Rye
(914) 967-6700
•*Bar area. Humidor. Cuisine: American.*

Gregory's Steak Pub
324 Central Ave.
White Plains
(914) 684-8855
•*Bar. Humidor. Cuisine: Italian.*

**The Lazy Boy
Saloon & Ale
House**
154 Mamaroneck
    Ave., White Plains
(914) 761-0272
•*Cigar bar. Humidor.
Cuisine: American.*

North Carolina

**Crippen's County
Inn & Restaurant**
239 Sunset Dr.
Blowing Rock
(704) 295-3487
•*Patio. Humidor. Cuisine: new American.*

**Southend Brewery
& Smokehouse**
161 E. Bay St.
Charleston
(803) 853-4677
•*Bar on the 1st floor
and also in the 3rd
floor "Harborview Bar
& Billiard" room.
Humidor. Cuisine:
American smokehouse
featuring wood-oven
pizzas, hardwood grill
& fresh seafood.*

CHARLOTTE
& VICINITY
**Alston's Steaks &
Seafood**
1812 South Blvd.
Charlotte
(704) 342-1088
•*Main dining room
(smoking section),
bar, and private dining
rooms. Humidor.
Cuisine: prime steak
and fresh seafood.*

**H. Dundee's
Steakhouse**
8128 Providence Rd.
4508 Independence
    Blvd. (2 locations)
Charlotte
(704) 543-6299,
    536-5003
•*Bar and smoking
section. Humidor.
Cuisine: steakhouse.*

**The Lamplighter
Restaurant**
1065 E. Moorehead
    St., Charlotte
(704) 372-5343
•*Bar/lounge and private rooms. Humidor.
Cuisine: American,
French, & Continental.*

**The Men's Club of
Charlotte**
444 Tyvola Rd.
Charlotte
(704) 525-8525
•*All areas. Humidor.
Cuisine: Continental,
featuring steaks,
seafood, & other specialties including live
Maine lobster. **Gentlemen's club.***

**Morton's of
Chicago**
227 W. Trade St.
Charlotte
(704) 333-2602
•*All areas. Humidor.
Cuisine: steakhouse.*

Palm Restaurant
6705 Phillips Place
    Court
Charlotte
(704) 552-7256

•*Bar, lounge, smoking section in dining
room, and private
rooms. Humidor.
Cuisine: steak & lobster.*

**Pewter Rose
Restaurant &
Cigar Bar**
1820 South Blvd
Charlotte
(704) 332-8149
•*In cigar bar at all
times and on the
restaurant patio.
Humidor. Cuisine:
eclectic American featuring seafood, pasta,
& steak.*

Props
911 E. Morehead St.
Charlotte
(704) 333-2226
•*All areas. Humidor. Cuisine: new
American.*

**Southend Brewery
& Smokehouse**
2100 South Blvd.
Charlotte
(704) 358-4677,
    (800) 828-4677
•*Smoking section, bar,
and patio. Humidor.
Cuisine: American
smokehouse featuring
wood-oven pizzas.*

Swing 1000
1000 Central Ave.
Charlotte
(704) 334-4443
•*Cigar bar and private
rooms. Humidor. Cuisine: gourmet dining.*

**The Townhouse
Restaurant**
1011 Providence Rd.
Charlotte
(704) 335-1546
•*Bar, lounge, and
smoking section in dining room. Humidor.
Cuisine: modern
American.*

**The City Club of
Gastonia**
532 S. New Hope
    Rd., Gastonia
(704) 865-1980
•*All areas. Humidor.
Cuisine: American.
Private club.*

Nana's Restaurant
2514 University Dr.
Durham
(919) 493-8469
•*Bar/lounge. Humidor. Cuisine: American.*

**Vinnie's Tap &
Grille Room**
4015 University Dr.
Durham
(919) 493-0004
•*All areas. Humidor.
Cuisine: steakhouse.*

Lucky 32
1421 Westover Terrace
Greensboro
(910) 370-0707
•*Grill Room & Bar
and outside patio.
Cuisine: American-
style menu featuring a
small section that
changes monthly.*

... On the Verandah
1536 Franklin Rd.
(overlooking Lake
Sequoyah on US
64), Highlands
(704) 526-2338
•*Wine bar and
deck. Humidor.
Cuisine: contempo-
rary American.*

House of Wang
710 W. Vernon Ave.
Kinston
(919) 527-7897
•*Lounge. Humidor.
Cuisine: Chinese/
International.*

**King's Restaurant,
Inc.**
Hwy. 70 E., Kinston
(800) 332-6465
•*All areas. Cuisine:
family-style country
BBQ.*

RALEIGH &
VICINITY

**Prestonwood
Country Club**
300 Prestonwood
Pkwy., Cary
(919) 467-2566
•*Pub and lounge.
Humidor. Cuisine:
American. **Private
country club.***

Angus Barn
US 70 W. at Avia-
tion Pkwy.
Raleigh
(919) 787-3505
•*"Wild Turkey" bar
& lounge. Humidor.
Cuisine: steak &
seafood; French cui-
sine in wine cellar.*

**Black Marlin
Seafood Grille &
Bar**
428 Daniels St.
Raleigh
(919) 832-7950
•*Cigar bar, bar,
lounge, and smoking
section in dining room.
Humidor. Cuisine:
new American/
seafood.*

**The Capital City
Club**
411 Fayetteville
Street Mall
Raleigh
(919) 832-5526
•*Lounge and private
rooms. Humidor.
Cuisine: American/
Continental. **Private
club.***

It's Prime Only
5509 Edwards Mill
Rd., Raleigh
(919) 420-0224
•*Smoking section.
Humidor. Cuisine:
steakhouse.*

Lucky 32
832 Spring Forest
Rd., Raleigh
(919) 876-9932
•*Grill Room & Bar.
Cuisine: American-
style menu featuring a
small section that
changes monthly.*

**Vinnie's Steak
House & Tavern**
7440 Six Forks Rd.
Raleigh
(919) 847 7319

•*All areas. Humidor.
Cuisine: steakhouse.*

WILMINGTON
& VICINITY

The Faded Rose
8 N. Front St.
Wilmington
(910) 762-2969
•*Cigar lounge and
bar. Humidor. Cui-
sine: New Orleans-
style.*

**Vinnie's Steak
House & Tavern**
1900 Suite Z, Cumi-
na Station/East-
wood Rd.
Wrightsville Beach
(910) 256-0995
•*Smoking area.
Humidor. Cuisine:
steakhouse.*

Lucky 32
109 S. Stratford Rd.
Winston-Salem
(910) 777-0032
•*Grill Room & Bar
and outside patio.
Cuisine: American-
style menu featuring a
small section that
changes monthly.*

**New Town Bistro
& Cigar Bar**
420 Jonestown Rd.
Winston-Salem
(910) 659-8062
•*Bar, patio, and
smoking section.
Humidor. Cuisine:
bistro.*

North Dakota

Mama Lola's
124 N. 3rd St.
Grand Forks
(701) 775-5454
•*Bar. Humidor. Cui-
sine: Northern Italian.*

Ohio

AKRON &
VICINITY

**Winking Lizard
Tavern**
511 E. Aurora Rd.
Macedonia
(330) 467-6200
•*Bar. Humidor. Cui-
sine: casual American
tavern.*

**The Olde Loyal
Oak Tavern &
Restaurant**
3044 Wadsworth Rd.
Norton
(330) 825-8280
•*Specified area of the
main dining room,
bar, lounge, and pri-
vate rooms. Humidor.
Cuisine: American/
Continental.*

CINCINNATI
& VICINITY

**Celestial
Restaurant**
1071 Celestial St.
Cincinnati
(513) 241-4455
•*Bar/lounge. Humi-
dor. Cuisine: Conti-
nental & French.*

Cricket Lounge
601 Vine St.
Cincinnati
(513) 381-3000
•*Bar. Humidor. Cuisine: lite fare and restaurant menu available in bar.*

Havana Martini Club
580 Walnut Ave.
Cincinnati
(513) 651-2800
•*All areas. Humidor. Cuisine: lunch only—American cuisine.* **Cigar bar/bar/nightclub.**

The Heritage Restaurant and The Stein & Vine Pub
7664 Wooster Pike
Cincinnati
(513) 561-9300
•*Bar, patio, and private rooms. Humidor. Cuisine: regional American with southwest, Cajun, & seafood specialties; sandwiches, salads, & snacks in the pub.*

The International Bar & Grill at the Best Western
11911 Sheraton Lane, Cincinnati
(513) 671-6600
•*Smoking section, bar, and lounge. Cuisine: American, Chinese, Continental, French, Mexican, & Spanish.*

The Montgomery Inn at The Boathouse
925 Eastern Ave.
Cincinnati
(513) 721-7427
•*All areas. Humidor. Cuisine: American.*

Morton's of Chicago
Tower Place, 28 W. 4th St., 105
Cincinnati
(513) 241-4104
•*Lounge and smoking section in dining room. Humidor. Cuisine: steakhouse.*

Orchids
35 W. 5th St.
Cincinnati
(513) 564-6465
•*Bar, lounge, and private rooms. Humidor. Cuisine: American with an International Flair.*

The White House Inn
4940 Muhlhausern Rd., Hamilton
(513) 860-1110
•*Tavern. Cuisine: American.*

CLEVELAND & VICINITY
Ristoranti Giovanni's
25550 Chagrin Blvd.
Beachwood
(216) 831-8625
•*Lounge. Humidor. Cuisine: Northern Italian.*

Baricelli Inn
2203 Cornell Rd.
Cleveland
(216) 791-6500
•*Inn sitting area, lobby, and at private parties. Humidor. Cuisine: Continental.* **Inn.**

John Q's Steakhouse
55 Public Square
Cleveland
(216) 861-0900
•*Lounge. Humidor. Cuisine: steakhouse.*

The Lincoln Inn
75 Public Square
Cleveland
(216) 621-9085
•*Lounge. Humidor. Cuisine: fresh seafood, Black Angus steaks, Italian dishes, & chicken specialties.*

Morton's of Chicago
230 Huron Rd. NW
Cleveland
(216) 621-6200
•*Bar and smoking section. Humidor. Cuisine: steakhouse.*

The Ritz-Carlton
1515 W. 3rd St.
Cleveland
(216) 623-1300
•*Lounge after 5pm. Humidor. Cuisine: American.*

Rider's Inn
792 Mentor Ave.
Painesville
(216) 354-8200
•*Pub. Cuisine: American.*

Chez Francois
555 Main St.
Vermilion
(216) 967-0630
•*Bar/lounge and dining room after 9:30pm. Humidor. Cuisine: French.*

Eddie's Place
28601 Chagrin Blvd.
Woodmere
(216) 591-1545
•*Bar. Humidor. Cuisine: southern Italian.*

COLUMBUS & VICINITY
Bravo! Cucina
3000 Hayden Rd.
Columbus
(614) 791-1245
•*Bar. Humidor. Cuisine: Italian.*

Fifty Five at Crosswoods
55 Hutchinson Ave.
Columbus
(614) 846-5555
•*Lounge area. Humidor. Cuisine: upscale American, featuring fresh seafood.*

Morton's of Chicago
2 Nationwide Plaza
Columbus
(614) 464-4442
• *Bar/lounge and smoking section. Humidor. Cuisine: steakhouse.*

The Refectory
1092 Bethel Rd.
Columbus
(614) 451-9774
• *Lounge, private rooms, and patio. Humidor. Cuisine: French.*

Otie's Old Hilliard Inn & Pub
5344 Center St.
Hilliard
(614) 876-6044
• *Pub. Humidor. Cuisine: home-cooked American.*

The Bogey Inn Restaurant & Sports Site
6013 Glick Rd.
Powell
(614) 889-0150
• *Bar area, patio, and some sit down areas. Humidor. Cuisine: mixed.*

Miss Kitty's Steakhouse and Grand Saloon
4336 Medina Rd.
Copley
(330) 666-7429

• *All areas except non-smoking. Humidor. Cuisine: steakhouse, seafood.*

Mad Anthony's at the Greenville Inn
851 E. Martin St.
Greenville
(937) 548-3613
• *Smoking section and lounge. Humidor. Cuisine: American.*

Courthouse Cafe
110 S. Broadway
New Philadelphia
(330) 343-7896
• *Smoking section. Cuisine: American.*

Citi Lounge
114 Louisiana Ave.
Perrysburg
(419) 872-6437
• *All areas after 10:30pm, and in the loft "Exhale Room" Humidor. Cuisine: Italian.*

Springfield Grille
7413 Tiffany S.
Boardman
(330) 726-0895
• *Bar area. Humidor. Cuisine: American, featuring fire-grilled steaks & seafood.*

Alberini's
1201 Youngstown
Rd., Niles
(330) 652-5895

• *Private cigar smoking room, bar, and lounge. Humidor. Cuisine: Italian.*

The Outer Limits Nightclub & Cigar Bar
10125 Market St.
North Lima
(330) 549-3320
• *All areas. Humidor. Cuisine: light "pub" fare.* **Nightclub/cigar bar.**

Boat Yard Ltd.
3163 Belmont Ave.
Youngstown
(216) 759-7892
• *Bar and patio. Humidor. Cuisine: Italian, specializing in seafood.*

Oklahoma

Old Germany Restaurant
15920 SE 29th
Choctaw
(405) 390-8647
• *Wine cellar room. Humidor. Cuisine: German.*

Nikz At The Top
United Founders
Tower /5900
Mosteller Dr.
Oklahoma City
(405) 843-7875

• *Both lounges (including a separate cigar lounge) as well as 25% of the restaurant seating. Humidor. Cuisine: American Continental with a French influence.*

The Polo Grill
2038 Utica Square
Tulsa
(918) 744-4280
• *Wine cellar. Humidor. Cuisine: American.*

Oregon

Crossings at the Riverhouse
3075 N. Hwy. 97
Bend
(541) 389-8810
• *Bar and lounge. Humidor. Cuisine: premier steakhouse.*

The Brazen Bean
2075 NW Glisan
Portland
(503) 294-0636
• *All areas. Humidor. Cuisine: European (first course).* **Cigar bar.**

The Heathman Hotel
1001 SW Broadway
at Salmon
Portland
(503) 241-4100

•*Cigar room on mezzanine level. Humidor. Cuisine: Pacific Northwest & French.*

Jake's Famous Crawfish
401 SW 12th Ave.
Portland
(503) 226-1419
•*Bar. Humidor. Cuisine: seafood.*

Jake's Grill at the Governor Hotel
611 SW 10th St.
Portland
(503) 220-1850
•*Bar. Humidor. Cuisine: steak, pasta, salads, & seafood.*

McCormick & Schmick's Seafood Restaurant
235 SW 1st Ave.
Portland
(503) 224-7522
•*Bar/lounge. Humidor. Cuisine: seafood.*

The Sports Den at the Shilo Inn
9900 SW Canyon Rd., Portland
(503) 297-6125
•*Cigar bar. Humidor. Cuisine: Pacific Northwest.*

Touché Restaurant & Bar
1425 NW Glisan
Portland
(503) 221-1150

•*Billiard room only. Humidor. Cuisine: Italian & Mediterranean.*

Pennsylvania

Hartefeld National
1 Hartefeld Dr.
Avondale
(800) 240-7373,
   (610) 268-8800
•*Irish Pub and Walker Cup dining room. Humidor. Cuisine: traditional American.*

JC Dunphy's
433 N. 21st
Camp Hill
(717) 761-3663
•*Smoking section and bar. Humidor. Cuisine: steak, seafood, pasta, sandwiches.*

Kokomos Sports Bar & Grill
3721 Market St.
Camp Hill
(717) 731-9602
•*All areas. Humidor. Cuisine: pub fare.*

Prudhomme's Lost Cajun Kitchen
519 Cherry St. (Rte. 462), Columbia
(717) 684-1706
•*Bar and cigar bar. Humidor. Cuisine: Cajun.*

The Black Horse Restaurant & Tavern
Rte 272 & PA Tpke.
   Exit 21
Denver
(717) 336-6555
•*Bar and lounge. Humidor. Cuisine: certified Angus beef, fresh seafood.*

HARRISBURG & VICINITY

Appalachian Brewing Company
50 N. Cameron St.
Harrisburg
(717) 221-1080
•*Smoking areas. Humidor. Cuisine: gourmet brick oven pizza, sandwiches, soups, salads, appetizers, desserts.*

Cantone's Southern Italian Restaurant
4701 Fritchey St.
Harrisburg
(717) 652-9976
•*Bar and smoking section. Humidor. Cuisine: Italian.*

Maverick Restaurant
1851 Arsenal Blvd.
Harrisburg
(717) 233-7688
•*Bar, lounge, and smoking section. Humidor. Cuisine: Continental.*

Nick's 1014 Cafe
1014 N. 3rd St.
Harrisburg
(717) 238-8844

•*All areas. Humidor. Cuisine: seafood, steak, pasta, Italian specialties.*

Scotts' Bar & Grille
212 Locust St.
Harrisburg
(717) 234-7599
•*Smoking section and bar. Humidor. Cuisine: American/Continental.*

Forebay Lounge at the Hershey Lodge & Convention Center
Rte. 322 & University Dr.
Hershey
(717) 533-3311
•*Bar and lounge. Humidor. Cuisine: raw bar, sandwiches, salads.* **Bar.**

The Hotel Hershey—Iberian Lounge
Box 400 Hotel Rd.
Hershey
(717) 533-2171
•*Bar, lounge, and cigar bar. Humidor. Cuisine: new American.*

Al Mediterraneo
288 E. Main St.
Hummelstown
(717) 566-5086
•*Bar, patio, and private rooms. Humidor. Cuisine: Mediterranean.*

Caddy Shack
800 Orrs Bridge Rd.
Mechanicsburg
(717) 975-0940
•*Bar and smoking section. Humidor. Cuisine: casual American.*

Alfred's Victorian
38 N. Union St.
Middletown
(717) 944-4929
•*Bar/lounge and patio. Humidor. Cuisine: Continental & Northern Italian.*

Angelina's Ristorante
449 S. Front St.
Wormleysburg
(717) 761-6000
•*Bar, lounge, smoking section and deck. Humidor. Cuisine: Italian.*

Catalanos
461 S. Front St.
Wormleysburg
(717) 763-7905
•*Bar. Cuisine: gourmet.*

LANCASTER & VICINITY

Gallo Rosso
337 N. Queen St.
Lancaster
(717) 392-5616
•*Bar. Humidor. Cuisine: upscale Northern Italian.*

Market Fare Restaurant
50 W. Grant St.
Lancaster
(717) 299-7090

•*Bar. Humidor. Cuisine: new American.*

Roadhouse Cafe
700 E. Chestnut St.
Lancaster
(717) 393-5555
•*All areas but nonsmoking. Humidor. Cuisine: American with southwestern flair.*

Strawberry Hill
128 W. Strawberry St., Lancaster
(717) 393-5544
•*Bar room and private rooms. Humidor. Cuisine: American, Continental, French, & Mediterranean.*

The Watering Trough
905 W. Main St.
Mount Joy
(717) 653-6181
•*Lounge. Humidor. Cuisine: Continental, salads, & sandwiches.*

The Washington House at the Historic Strasburg Inn
1 Historic Dr.
Strasburg
(717) 687-7691
•*Tavern. Humidor. Cuisine: French colonial.*

Springfield Grille
1553 Perry Hwy.
Mercer
(412) 748-3589

•*Bar area. Humidor. Cuisine: American, featuring fire-grilled steaks & seafood.*

PHILADELPHIA & VICINITY

King George II Inn
102 Radcliff St.
Bristol
(215) 788-5536
•*Tavern. Humidor. Cuisine: Continental.*

Country Squire Diner/Restaurant
2560 W. Chester Pike, Broomall
(610) 356-3030
•*Smoking section after 9pm. Humidor. Cuisine: American.*

America Bar & Grill
499 E. Uwchlan Ave., Rte. 113
Chester Springs
(610) 280-0800
•*Bar and surrounding area. Humidor. Cuisine: American.*

The Park Ridge at Valley Forge
480 N. Gulph Rd.
King of Prussia
(610) 337-1800
•*Bar/lounge. Humidor. Cuisine: American.*

The General Layfayette Inn & Brewery
646 Germantown Pike
Lafayette Hill
(610) 941-0600

•*Bar area and upstairs cigar lounge. Humidor. Cuisine: fine dining.*

D'Ignazio's Town House Restaurant
117 Veterans' Square
Media
(610) 566-6141
•*Bar. Humidor. Cuisine: steaks, seafood, pasta.*

Italian Village Restaurant
902 MacDade Blvd.
Milmont Park
(610) 237-0200
•*Cigar lounge. Humidor. Cuisine: Italian.*

D'Ignazio's Nottingham Inn
Old U.S. 1 & Rte. 272, Nottingham
(610) 932-4050
•*Back of dining room and bar area. Humidor. Cuisine: American, Italian, local.*

Chris's Cafe
1421 Sansom St.
Philadelphia
(215) 568-3131
•*All areas. Humidor. Cuisine: seafood. **Jazz club.***

Ciboulette at The Bellevue Building
200 S. Broad St.
Philadelphia
(215) 790-1210
•*Bar/lounge, cigar bar, and private room. Humidor. Cuisine: contemporary French.*

Dickens Inn
421 S. 2nd St.
Philadelphia
(215) 928-9307
•*All bar areas. Humidor. Cuisine: English & Continental.*

Dilullo Centro
1407 Locust St.
Philadelphia
(215) 546-2000
•*Bar/lounge. Cuisine: Northern Italian.*

The Happy Rooster
119 S. 16th St.
Philadelphia
(215) 563-1481
•*All areas. Humidor. Cuisine: American/ Continental.*

Jack's Firehouse
2130 Fairmount
Ave., Philadelphia
(215) 232-9000
•*Bar area. Cuisine: American regional.*

Le Bar Lyonnais at Le Bec Fin
1523 Walnut St.
Philadelphia
(215) 496-9606
•*Bar Lyonnais after 9:30pm Humidor. Cuisine: classic French with nouvelle influences.*

London Grill
2301 Fairmount
Ave., Philadelphia
(215) 978-4545
•*Bar/lounge. Humidor. Cuisine: new American.*

McGillin's Olde Ale House
1310 Drury Lane
Philadelphia
(215) 735-5562
•*Dining room, bar, and lounge. Cuisine: American.*

Mia's Restaurant & Wine Bar at The Warwick Hotel
1701 Locust St.
Philadelphia
(215)545-4655
•*Lounge. Humidor. Cuisine: Mediterranean.*

Morton's of Chicago
1 Logan Square
Philadelphia
(215) 557-0724
•*Throughout restaurant. Humidor. Cuisine: steakhouse.*

Old Original Bookbinder's Restaurant
125 Walnut St.
Philadelphia
(215) 925-7027
•*Bar. Cuisine: seafood.*

Palm Restaurant at the Hyatt Hotel at the Bellevue
200 S. Broad St.
Philadelphia
(215) 546-7256
•*Bar. Humidor. Cuisine: American, specializing in steak.*

Park Hyatt at the Bellvue
Broad & Walnut Sts.
Philadelphia
(215) 893-1776
•*Library lounge. Humidor. Cuisine: at Founder's: eclectic French with Traditional Asian influences.* **Bar.**

Philip's Italian Restaurant
1145 S. Broad St.
Philadelphia
(215) 334-0882
•*All areas. Humidor. Cuisine: Italian & American.*

The Ritz-Carlton
17th & Chestnut
Sts. at Liberty
Plaza, Philadelphia
(215) 563-1600
•*"The Grill Bar" only. Humidor. Cuisine: contemporary American.* **Bar.**

Seven Stars Inn
Rte. 23 & Hoffecker
Rd., Phoenixville
(610) 495-5205
•*Lounge, bar, and special cigar society dining room that seats 22 people. Humidor. Cuisine: steaks, seafood.*

Log Cabin Inn
430 Perry Hwy.
Harmony
(412) 452-4155
•*Bar. Humidor. Cuisine: American, specializing in seafood & steak.*

The Carlton
One Mellon Bank
Center, Pittsburgh
(412) 391-4099
•*Smoking section, bar, and lounge. Humidor. Cuisine: steaks, fresh seafood, veal, & pasta.*

The Colony Restaurant & Lounge
corner of Cochran &
Greentree Rds.
Pittsburgh
(412) 561-2060
•*Bar, lounge, and private rooms. Humidor. Cuisine: steak & seafood.*

Heaven
107 6th St.
Pittsburgh
(412) 338-2720
•*All areas except restaurant dining area. Humidor. Cuisine: steak & seafood.*

Le Mont
1114 Grandview
Ave., Pittsburgh
(412) 431-3100
*Front dining room,
lounge, and private
rooms. Humidor.
Cuisine: contemporary American.*

Louis Tambellini
Restaurant
860 Sawmill Run
Blvd., Pittsburgh
(412) 481-1118
*Large bar area.
Humidor. Cuisine:
seafood.*

Morton's of
Chicago
625 Liberty Ave.
Pittsburgh
(412) 261-7141
*Bar and private
rooms. Humidor.
Cuisine: steakhouse.*

Roland's Seafood
Grill
1904 Pennsylvania
Ave., Pittsburgh
(412) 261-3401
*All areas. Humidor.
Cuisine: seafood.*

Siena
430 Market Square
Pittsburgh
(412) 338-0955
*Bar/lounge. Humidor. Cuisine: modern
American.*

- - - - - - - - - - - - - - - - - -

Tink's Cafe
519 Linden St.
Scranton
(717) 346-8465

*All areas. Humidor.
Cuisine: American.*
Nightclub.

Rhode Island

The Clarke Cooke
House
Bannister's Wharf
Newport
(401) 849-2900
*In the three bars and
in one dining room.
Humidor. Cuisine:
Continental.*

PROVIDENCE
Atomic Grill
99 Chestnut St.
Providence
(401) 621-8888
*Smoking areas.
Humidor. Cuisine:
nouvelle.*

The Capital Grille
1 Cookson Place
Providence
(401) 521-5600
*Dining room, bar,
and lounge. Humidor.
Cuisine: American,
specializing in steak.*

Capriccio
2 Pine St.
Providence
(401) 421-1320
*Lounge and smoking
section. Humidor.
Cuisine: European.*

Sikar Cafe and
Smoking Lounge
190 Atwells Ave.
Providence
(401) 273-SIKAR
(7452)

*All areas. Humidor.
Cuisine: pastries.* **Coffee bar.**

South Carolina

Restaurant Million
2 Unity Alley
Charleston
(803) 577-3141
*Lounge and atrium.
Humidor. Cuisine:
French low country.*

Alberto's Trattoria
2016 Augusta Rd.
Greenville
(864) 233-8868
*Bar and private
rooms. Humidor.
Cuisine: Continental
Italian.*

Commons Bar at
the Hyatt Regency
Greenville
220 N. Main St.
Greenville
(864) 235-1234
*All areas. Humidor.
Cuisine: appetizers
only.* **Bar.**

Inn on the Square
104 Court St.
Greenwood
(864) 223-4488
*Pub and private
rooms. Humidor.
Cuisine: southern
American nouveau.*

The Gentleman's
Club
1 Dunnigan's Alley
Hilton Head
(803) 842-3340

*All areas. Humidor.
Cuisine: appetizers
only.* **Adult entertainment.**

New York Prime
405 28th Ave. N.
Myrtle Beach
(803) 448-8081
*Smoking section in
dining room and bar
area. Humidor. Cuisine: New York-style
prime steaks.*

H. Dundee's
Steakhouse
2455 Cherry Rd.
Rock Hill
(803) 325-7661
*Dining room, bar,
and lounge. Humidor.
Cuisine: steak.*

South Dakota

SIOUX FALLS
& VICINITY
Alcester
Steakhouse
Junction of Hwys. 11
& 13, Alcester
(605) 934-2974
Bar/lounge. Humidor. Cuisine: steakhouse.

Sioux Falls
Brewing Co.
431 N. Phillips Ave.
Sioux Falls
(605) 332-4847
*Pub. Humidor.
Cuisine: hand-crafted
cuisine.*

Theo's Great Food
601 W. 33rd St.
Sioux Falls
(605) 338-6801
•Lounge. Humidor.
Cuisine: American,
Continental, French,
& Mediterranean.

Tennessee

**Chattanooga
Billiard Club**
110 Jordan Dr.
Chattanooga
(423) 499-3883
•All areas of club.
Humidor. Cuisine:
traditional American.

**Chattanooga
Billiard Club**
725 1/2 Cherry St.
Chattanooga
(423) 267-7740
•All areas of club.
Humidor. Cuisine:
traditional American.

**Baker-Peters
Jazz Club**
9000 Kingston Pike
Knoxville
(423) 690-8110
•All areas except non-
smoking dining room.
Humidor. Cuisine:
certified Angus beef,
seafood, chicken.

Regas
318 N. Gay St.
Knoxville
(423) 637-9805
•Bar/lounge area.
Humidor. Cuisine:
steak & seafood.

**Arthur's at The
Union Station
Hotel**
1001 Broadway
Nashville
(615) 255-1494
•Smoking section.
Humidor. Cuisine:
Continental.

**Belle Meade
Brasserie**
101 Page Rd.
Nashville
(615) 356-5450
•Bar area and late
evening in the smoking
dining room. Humi-
dor. Cuisine: new
American.

**Blackstone
Restaurant &
Brewery**
1918 West End Ave.
Nashville
(615) 327-9969
•Bar. Humidor. Cui-
sine: American.

The Bound'ry
711 20th Ave. S.
Nashville
(615) 321-3043
•Bar/lounge and
patio. Humidor.
Cuisine: upscale
international.

**Cafe Coco Coffee
House**
210 Louise Ave.
Nashville
(615) 329-2871

•Humidor room,
front and back patios.
Humidor. Cuisine:
pizza, pasta, sand-
wiches.

**F. Scott's
Restaurant &
Jazz Bar**
2210 Crestmoore
Rd., Nashville
(615) 269-5861
•Lounge. Humidor.
Cuisine: American
with southwestern &
Pacific influences.

Ivory's Lounge
2200 Elm Hill Pike
Nashville
(615) 883-9770
• All areas. Humidor.
Cuisine: bar food.
**Nightclub/live
entertainment.**

Mario's
2005 Broadway
Nashville
(615) 327-3232
•Cocktail lounge.
Humidor. Cuisine:
Northern Italian.

**The Merchants
Restaurant**
401 Broadway
Nashville
(615) 254-1892
•Lounge. Humidor.
Cuisine: American.

Mere Bulles
152 2nd Ave. N.
Nashville
(615) 256-1946

•Bar/lounge. Humi-
dor. Cuisine: Conti-
nental & seafood with
a French twist.

**Morton's of
Chicago**
641 Church St.
Nashville
(615) 259-4558
•Smoking section, bar
area, and private
rooms. Humidor.
Cuisine: steakhouse.

**Ruth's Chris
Steak House**
2100 W. End Ave.
Nashville
(615) 320-0163
•Bar/lounge. Humidor.
Cuisine: steakhouse.

**Snaffles at Lowes
Vanderbilt Plaza
Hotel**
2100 W. End Ave.
Nashville
(615) 320-1700
•Bar, lounge, cigar
bar, patio, and private
rooms. Humidor.
Cuisine: American.
Cigar bar.

Sunset Grill
2001-A Belcourt
Ave., Nashville
(615) 386-3663
•Lounge and patio.
Humidor. Cuisine:
American.

Valentino's
1907 W. End Ave.
Nashville
(615) 327-0148
•*Smoking section and bar. Humidor. Cuisine: Northern Italian.*

Wild Boar
2014 Broadway
Nashville
(615) 329-1313
•*Cocktail lounge. Humidor. Cuisine: contemporary French.*

Texas

AUSTIN & VICINITY

Chambers Bar at the Omni Austen Hotel Downtown
700 San Jacinto
Austin
(512) 476-3700
•*Bar and cigar bar. Humidor. Cuisine: Texas Cuisine.* **Cigar bar.**

Louie's 106 Grill & Tapas Bar
106 E. 6th St.
Austin
(512) 476-1997
•*Private room. Humidor. Cuisine: Spanish & Mediterranean.*

Sfuzzi
311 W. 6th St.
Austin
(512) 476-8100
•*Bar. Humidor. Cuisine: Northern Italian.*

The Yellow Rose
6528 N. Lamar
Austin
(512) 458-2106
•*All areas. Humidor. Cuisine: American.*

Hoffbrau Steaks
2310 N. 11th St.
Beaumont
(409) 892-6911
•*Bar/lounge, smoking section, private room, and outdoor beer garden. Humidor. Cuisine: steakhouse, seafood.*

Steak & Ale
315 I H-10
Beaumont
(409) 832-3441
•*Smoking section. Humidor. Cuisine: American.*

BROWNSVILLE & VICINITY

The Artichoke Delicatessen & Beer
108 E. Elizabeth
Brownsville
(956) 544-7636
•*All areas. Humidor. Cuisine: pasta, pizza, and a variety of flatbread wrap sandwiches.*

Marcello's Italian Restaurant
110 N. Tarmada
Port Isabel
(956) 943-7611
•*Cigar bar. Humidor. Cuisine: Italian.*

Padre Island Brewing Co.
3400 Padre Blvd.
South Padre Island
(956) 761-9585
•*Smoking areas. Humidor. Cuisine: American.*

DALLAS & VICINITY

Flying Saucer
14999 Montfort
Addison
(972) 934-2537
•*Indoor beer garden. Humidor. Cuisine: pub fare.*

Morton's of Chicago
14831 Midway Rd.
Addison
(972) 233-5858
•*Bar/lounge and smoking section. Humidor. Cuisine: prime steakhouse.*

Old Chicago
4060 Beltline Rd.
Addison
(972) 490-3900
•*Bar, patio, and banquet rooms. Humidor. Cuisine: pizza/pasta.*

Monet's Restaurant & Catering
5005 Colleyville
Blvd., Suite 240
Colleyville
(817) 498-5525
•*Bar. Humidor. Cuisine: French Continental.*

Addison Point
4578 Belt Line Rd.
Dallas
(972) 661-2230
•*All areas. Cuisine: American burger joint.* **Sports bar.**

Bob's Steak & Chop House
4300 Lemmon Ave.
Dallas
(214) 528-9446
•*Bar and designated smoking dining rooms. Humidor. Cuisine: American, specializing in steak.*

Bugatti
3802 W. Northwest Hwy., Dallas
(214) 350-2470
•*Cigar room. Humidor. Cuisine: Italian.*

Cabaret Royale
10723 Composite Dr., Dallas
(214) 350-0303
•*All areas. Humidor. Cuisine: American & southwestern.*

Del Frisco's Double Eagle Steak House
5251 Spring Valley Rd. at Dallas North Tollway
Dallas
(972) 490-9000
•*Smoking section in dining room, bar, lounge, and cigar bar. Humidor. Cuisine: USDA prime aged beef & seafood.*

Dick's Last Resort
West End Market
  Place
Dallas
(214) 747-0001
•All areas. Humidor.
Cuisine: ribs, steak,
& shrimp.

**Four Seasons
Resort & Club**
4150 N. MacArthur
  Blvd., Dallas
(214) 717-0700
•Smoking section in
bar and lounge.
Humidor. Cuisine:
new American.

The Harder Bar
1909 Greenville
  Ave., Dallas
(214) 824-8200
•All areas. Humidor.
Bar.

**Javier's Gourmet
Mexicano
Restaurant**
4912 Cole Ave.
Dallas
(214) 521-4211
•Cigar bar and smok-
ing section. Humidor.
Cuisine: Continental/
Mexico City-style.

Les Saisons
165 Turtle Creek
  Village, Dallas
(214) 528 1102
•Bar area. Humidor.
Cuisine: French.

The Lodge
10530 Spangler Rd.
Dallas
(972) 506-9229

•All areas. Humidor.
Cuisine: American
featuring seafood,
steaks, and exotic
meats. **Gentleman's
club.**

**Mansion on Turtle
Creek**
2821 Turtle Creek
  Blvd., Dallas
(214) 559-2100
•Bar and lounge area.
Humidor. Cuisine:
southwestern.

Matt's No Place
6326 La Vista Dr.
  (Lakewood)
Dallas
(214) 823-9077
•Smoking section and
bar area. Humidor.
Cuisine: steaks, wild
game, seafood.

**The Men's Club of
Dallas**
2340 W. Northwest
  Hwy., Dallas
(214) 956-8800
•All areas. Humidor.
Cuisine: Continental,
featuring steaks,
seafood, & other spe-
cialties including live
Maine lobster. **Gen-
tlemen's club.**

**Morton's of
Chicago**
50l Elm St., Dallas
(214) 741-2277
•Smoking section,
bar, and private
rooms. Humidor.
Cuisine: steakhouse.

**Mr. G's at the
Hyatt Regency**
DFW International
  Pkwy., DFW Air-
  port, Dallas
(972) 453-1234
•Dining room and
public areas. Humi-
dor. Cuisine: premium
cuts of steak & fresh
seafood.

Nana Grill
2201 Stemmons Fwy.
Dallas
(214) 761-7479
•Bar and private din-
ing rooms. Humidor.
Cuisine: American.

**Newport's Seafood
Restaurant**
703 McKinney Ave.
Dallas
(214) 954-0220
•Bar and private
room. Humidor. Cui-
sine: seafood.

The Palm
701 Ross Ave.
Dallas
(214) 698-0470
•Bar and private din-
ing room. Cuisine:
steak & lobster.

**Pyramid Room at
the Fairmont Hotel**
1717 N. Akard St.
Dallas
(214) 720-5249
•Bar. Humidor. Cui-
sine: classical & new
American.

**Routh Street
Brewery & Grill**
3011 Routh St.
Dallas
(214) 922-8835
•Main bar and Bier
Garten. Humidor.
Cuisine: Texas-hill-
country cuisine.

**Trail Dust
Steak House**
10841 Composite
  Dr., Dallas
(214) 357-3862
•Only private cigar
dinners or reservations
for cigar dinners. Cui-
sine: steak.

West End Pub
211 N. Record, Suite
  109, Dallas
(214) 748-5711
•All areas. Humidor.
Cuisine: pub fare.
Bar.

**Wizards Sports
Cafe**
747 S. Central Expy.
Dallas
(972) 235-0371
•All areas. Humidor.
Cuisine: steaks, salad,
brisket, burgers,
wings, etc...

**Sneaky Pete's—
Lewisville**
2 Eagle Point Dr.
Lewisville
(972) 434-2500
•Bar, patio & private
rooms. Humidor.
Cuisine: steak &
seafood.

Carmen's at The Radisson Hotel
2211 I-35E N.
Denton
(817) 381-0263
•Smoking section.
Cuisine: Italian. **Bar.**

Cafe Central
109 N. Oregon
El Paso
(915) 545-CAFE
•Bar. Humidor. Cuisine: eclectic contemporary, including fresh seafood, prime steaks, lamb, & pasta.

FORT WORTH

The Ancho Chile
3413 W. 7th St.
Fort Worth
(817) 877-3413
•Dining room after hours, bar/lounge, and private room. Humidor. Cuisine: contemporary ranch.

Del Frisco's Double Eagle Steak House
812 Main St.
Fort Worth
(817) 877-3999
•Smoking section in dining room, bar, lounge, and cigar bar. Humidor. Cuisine: USDA prime aged beef & seafood.

Flying Saucer
111 E. 4th St.
Fort Worth
(817) 336-7470

•Indoor beer garden, "Half-Acre" gaming parlor. Humidor. Cuisine: pub fare.

Gaido's Restaurant
3800 Seawall
Galveston
(409) 762-9625
•Smoking section and bar. Cuisine: seafood.

HOUSTON

Big John's Neighborhood Bar
6150 Wilcrest at Harwin, Houston
(281) 498-3499
•All areas. Humidor. Cuisine: pub fare featuring imported beer and steaks.

Brennan's
3300 Smith St.
Houston
(713) 522-9711
•Bar. Humidor. Cuisine: southwestern/American.

The Brownstone
2736 Virginia
Houston
(713) 520-5666
•Terrace & club. Humidor. Cuisine: Continental.

Cent'anni Gran Ristorante
2128 Portsmouth
Houston
(713) 529-4199
•Smoking section and bar. Humidor. Cuisine: Italian.

Clive's The Grille
517 Louisiana St.
Houston
(713) 224-4438
•Lounge. Humidor. Cuisine: fine seafood & steaks.

Colorado Bar & Grill
6710 SW Fwy.
Houston
(713) 781-1122
•All areas. Cuisine: features steaks, pizza, & sandwiches. **Upscale gentlemen's club.**

DeVille, Terrace Cafe, Lobby Lounge at the Four Seasons Hotel
1300 Lamar St.
Houston
(713) 650-1300
•Bar. Humidor. Cuisine: DeVille serves American with an Italian flair; Terrace Cafe serves reasonably priced light-American.

Downing Street Ltd., No. 10
Kirby Oaks Center/ 2549 Kirby Dr.
Houston
(713) 523-2291
•All areas. Humidor. Cuisine: appetizers featuring specialty sandwiches, caviar, and imported cheeses. **Cigar bar/tobacco emporium/bar/coffee bar/nighclub.**

The Ginger Man
5607 Morningside Blvd., Houston
(713) 526-2770
•All areas. Humidor. **Tavern.**

La Colombe d'Or
3410 Montrose Blvd.
Houston
(713) 524-7999
•Bar and library. Humidor. Cuisine: French/Continental.

La Reserve at the Omni Houston
4 Riverway
Houston
(713) 871-8177
•Bar, lounge, and private rooms. Humidor. Cuisine: creative Continental.

Matthias' Restaurant & Pub
3755 FM 1960 W.
Houston
(281) 537-5837
•All areas. Humidor. Cuisine: American.

Maxey & Jake's
907 Westheimer
Houston
(713) 524-3839
•All areas. Humidor. Cuisine: American with a southwestern flair.

Montesano Ristorante Italiano
6009 Beverly Hill Lane, Houston
(713) 977-4565

Smoking section, bar/lounge, and fireplace room. Humidor. Cuisine: Italian.

Morton's of Chicago
Centre at Post Oak/
5000 Westheimer
Houston
(713) 629-1946
Bar and smoking section in dining room. Humidor. Cuisine: steakhouse.

Pappas Bros. Steakhouse
5839 Westheimer
Houston
(713) 780-7352
Bar/lounge and smoking section. Humidor. Cuisine: steakhouse.

Rainbow Lodge
1 Birdsall
Houston
(713) 861-8666
Bar, lounge, and private rooms. Humidor. Cuisine: American.

The Ritz-Carlton
1919 Briar Oaks
Lane, Houston
(713) 840-7600
Dining room, bar, lounge, and private rooms. Humidor. Cuisine: American with a southwest influence.

The Roxy
5351 W. Alabama
Houston
(713) 850-7103

All areas. Humidor. **Nightclub.**

Ruth's Chris Steak House
6213 Richmond
Ave., Houston
(713) 789-2333
Lounge area. Humidor. Cuisine: steakhouse.

Shooters Billiards & Sports Cafe
6306 Richmond
Ave., Houston
(713) 952-9628
Pool hall. Humidor. Cuisine: appetizers only.

Truluck's Steak & Stone Crab
5919 Westheimer
Houston
(713) 783-7270
Bar/lounge. Humidor. Cuisine: steak & stonecrabs.

The Velvet Elvis
3303 Richmond
Ave., Houston
(713) 520-0434
All areas. Humidor. Cuisine: American.

Blank & Company
203 1/2 E. Main
Nacogdoches
(409) 560-0776
Anywhere, anytime. Cuisine: steakhouse.

SAN ANTONIO & VICINITY

Grey Moss Inn
19010 Scenic Loop
Rd., Grey Forest
(210) 695-8301
Patio. Cuisine: steakhouse.

Barcelona Cafe
4901 Broadway
San Antonio
(210) 822-6129
Cigar bar and patio areas. Humidor. Cuisine: Mediterranean.

Morton's of Chicago
300 Crockett St.
San Antonio
(210) 228-0700
Smoking section, bar, and private rooms. Humidor. Cuisine: steakhouse.

Polo's at the Fairmont Hotel
401 S. Alamo
San Antonio
(210) 224-8800
Bar. Humidor. Cuisine: southwestern.

The Vault
314 E. Commerce,
Suite 100
San Antonio
(210) 475-0031
All areas. Humidor. Cuisine: Continental.

Cricket's Grill & Draft House
211 Mary St., Waco
(254) 754-4677

Smoking section and pool table/game area. Humidor. Cuisine: American.

Harbour Texas Marina
Airport Park, Lake
Waco, Waco
(254) 754-1642
Smoking section. Cuisine: features steak and catfish.

Rock Bottom Brewery
4050 Beltline Rd.
West Addison
(972) 404-7456
Cigar bar, private room, and patio. Humidor. Cuisine: pub fare.

Vermont

Main Street Grill & Bar
118 Main St.
Montpelier
(802) 229-9202
Smoking room off of pub. Cuisine: American.

La Poule a Dents
Main St., Norwich
(802) 649-2922
Patio (summer only). Humidor. Cuisine: French.

Ye Olde England Inne
433 Mountain Rd.
Stowe
(802) 253-7064
• *Private dining rooms. Cuisine: European/game.*

Hermitage Inn
Coldbrook Rd.
Wilmington
(802) 464-3511
• *Cabaret area (bar and main dining room are included). Humidor. Cuisine: Continental.*

Virginia

Michael's Bistro & Taphouse
1427 University Ave.
Charlottesville
(804) 977-3697
• *Bar during dinner and all areas after 10pm. Humidor. Cuisine: regional American.*

The Riverview— A Steak & Seafood Restaurant
1101 Sophia St.
Fredericksburg
(540) 373-6500
• *Captain Irvin's lounge. Cuisine: steak (featuring Black Angus), seafood, chicken, & pastas.*

Defazio's of Innsbrook
4032-B Coz Rd.
Glen Allen
(804) 747-5500

• *Bar and lounge. Cuisine: Italian, pasta, chicken.*

The Cigar Lounge at Oasis Winery
14141 Hume Rd.
Hume
(540) 635-3103
• *Back patio. Humidor. Cuisine: variety of cheese & meat/ soup/sandwiches.* **Winery.**

Cafe France
3225 Old Forest Rd.
Lynchburg
(804) 385-8989
• *Dining room after 9:45pm. Humidor. Cuisine: nouvelle American.*

The Dumbwaiter American Bistro
117 W. Tazewell St.
Norfolk
(757) 623-3663
• *Lounge. Humidor. Cuisine: American regional with a neo-southern accent.*

RICHMOND & VICINITY

Ruth's Chris Steak House
11500 Huguenot Rd.
Midlothian
(804) 378-0600
• *Smoking lounge. Humidor. Cuisine: steakhouse.*

Havana '59
16 N. 17th St.
Richmond
(804) 649-2822

• *Bar/lounge, smoking section, and outdoor rooftop dining. Humidor. Cuisine: Cuban.*

Rare Old Times
10602 Patterson Ave., Richmond
(804) 750-1346
• *All areas. Humidor. Cuisine: Irish pub fare.*

The Tobacco Co. Restaurant
1201 E. Cary St.
Richmond
(804) 782-9431
• *Dining room, bar, and lounge. Humidor. Cuisine: American.*

Corned Beef & Co. Bar and Grill
107 S. Jefferson St.
Roanoke
(540) 342-3354
• *Cigar bar, smoking section in dining room, private rooms, and patio. Humidor. Cuisine: American/pizza/ pasta.*

Coyote Cafe & Cantina
972 Laskin Rd.
Virginia Beach
(757) 425-8705
• *Bar area and back room. Humidor. Cuisine: southwestern featuring nightly chalkboard specials.*

Croc's
620 19th St.
Virginia Beach
(757) 428-5444

• *Bar and patio at all times; all areas after 11pm. Humidor. Cuisine: Caribbean inspired featuring steak, pasta, seafood, & gator bites!*

WASHINGTON, DC VICINITY

Bullfeathers
112 King St.
Alexandria
(703) 836-8088
• *Bar area. Humidor. Cuisine: American steakhouse & seafood.*

Morrison House
116 S. Alfred St.
Alexandria
(703) 838-8000
• *Library only. Humidor. Cuisine: contemporary American.*

Blue 'n Gold Brewing Company
3100 Clarendon Blvd., Arlington
(703) 908-4995
• *Bar. Humidor. Cuisine: French Creole-based.*

Coco's Casa Mia Ristorante
3111 Columbia Pike
Arlington
(703) 920-5450
• *Bar, lounge, and smoking section. Humidor. Cuisine: American & Italian.*

The Ritz-Carlton
1250 S. Hayes St.
Arlington
(703) 412-2760

•Bar/lounge. Humidor. Cuisine: Continental.

Evans Farm Inn and The Sitting Duck Pub
1696 Chain Bridge
Rd., McLean
(703) 356-8000
•Number of smoking sections. Humidor. Cuisine: American with Continental specialties.

The Ritz-Carlton
1700 Tysons Blvd.
McLean
(703) 506-4300
•Bar and lobby lounge after 5:30pm. Humidor. Cuisine: American/Continental.

Morton's of Chicago
8075 Leesburg Pike
Vienna
(703) 883-0800
•Bar/lounge and smoking section. Humidor. Cuisine: steakhouse.

Phillips Seafood Grill
8330 Boone Blvd.
Vienna
(703) 442-0400
•Bar/lounge and patio. Humidor. Cuisine: seafood.

- - - - - - - - - - - - - - - - - - - -

Piper's
136 Creekside Lane
Winchester
(540) 662-2900

•Pub (and private room when available). Humidor. Cuisine: American.

Washington

Palmer's Restaurant & Pub
201 E. Washington
St.
La Conner
(360) 466-4261
•Bar, lounge, and patio/sidewalk only. Cuisine: Continental.

The Spar Cafe & Bar
114 4th Ave. E.
Olympia
(360) 357-6444
•Bar/lounge, smoking section, and cigar bar. Humidor. Cuisine: American.

SEATTLE

Bandoleone
2241 Eastlake Ave.
E., Seattle
(206) 329-7559
•Bar area and in dining area after 10pm and all areas every Monday on "Havana Night." Humidor. Cuisine: fine Latin.

Bookstore Bar at The Alexis Hotel
1007 1st Ave.
Seattle
(206) 382-1506
•All areas. Humidor. Cuisine: new American.

El Goucho
2505 1st Ave.
Seattle
(206) 728-1337
•Cigar bar and private rooms for club. Humidor. Cuisine: steakhouse.

F.X. McRory's Steak, Chop & Oyster House
419 Occidental Ave.
S., 501, Seattle
(206) 623-4800
•Bar. Humidor. Cuisine: steaks.

Georgian Room at the Four Seasons Hotel
411 University St.
Seattle
(206) 621-7889
•Terrace lounge. Humidor. Cuisine: regional.

McCormick's Fish House & Bar
722 4th Ave.
Seattle
(206) 682-3900
•Patio and bar. Humidor. Cuisine: fresh seafood.

Metropolitan Grill
820 2nd Ave.
Seattle
(206) 624-3287
•Bar and private dining rooms. Humidor. Cuisine: American steakhouse.

Pike Pub & Brewery
1415 1st Ave.
Seattle
(206) 622-6044
•Two ventilated cigar rooms. Humidor. Cuisine: traditional European fare & northwest seafood; recipes made with beer or a beer byproduct.

Ray's Boathouse
6049 Seaview Ave.
NW, Seattle
(206) 789-3770
•Smoking section of cafe lounge. Cuisine: Pacific Northwest & seafood.

Tini Bigs Lounge
100 Denny, Seattle
(206) 284-0931
•All areas. Humidor. Cuisine: mixed cultural.

- - - - - - - - - - - - - - - - - - - -

City Grill Restaurant
605 NE 78th St.
Vancouver
(360) 574-2270
•Bar, patio, private rooms, and banquet rooms. Humidor. Cuisine: steaks, seafood, pasta.

City Grill Restaurant
916 NE 164th Ave.
Vancouver
(360) 253-5399
•*Bar, patio, private rooms, and banquet rooms. Humidor. Cuisine: steaks, seafood, pasta.*

John Horan House
2 Horan Rd.
Wenatchee
(509) 663-0018
•*Outside dining area. Humidor. Cuisine: American, specializing in seafood & steak.*

West Virginia

The Anvil Restaurant
1270 Washington St., Harpers Ferry
(304) 535-2582
•*Bar/lounge. Cuisine: seafood.*

The Red Fox Inn Restaurant
Snowshoe Rd.
Snowshoe
(304) 572-1111
•*Bar/lounge. Humidor. Cuisine: wild game, prime rib, seafood.*

Greenbrier Hotel
300 Main St.
White Sulphur Springs
(304) 536-1110
•*Lounges. Humidor. Cuisine: American, Continental, Classical.*

The Old White Club at The Greenbriar Resort
White Sulphur Springs
(304) 536-1110
•*Cocktail lounge. Humidor. Cuisine: hors d'oeuvres in cocktail lounge only.*

Wisconsin

Jimmie's White House Inn
5776 Main St.
Butte des Morts
(414) 582-7211
•*Old Antique bar and private rooms. Humidor. Cuisine: American, specializing in steak.*

Studio Grille
1318 Racine St.
Delavan
(414) 728-0456
•*Bar/lounge and smoking section. Humidor. Cuisine: American.*

Alfred's Supper Club
506 Hill St.
Green Lake
(800) 664-3631,
  (414) 294-3631
•*Dining room, bar, and private rooms. Humidor. Cuisine: American & Mediterranean.*

The Fox & Hounds
1298 Friess Lake Rd.
Hubertus
(414) 251-4100

•*Bar area and at private parties. Humidor. Cuisine: Continental.*

Horse & Plow at The American Club
Highland Dr.
Kohler
(920) 457-8000
•*Bar. Humidor. Cuisine: American & Mexican/Tex-Mex.*

Kirsch's Restaurant at the French Country Inn
Hwy. 50 W.
Lake Geneva
(414) 245-5756
•*Bar, lounge, and patio. Humidor. Cuisine: American, Continental, French.*

The Bistro at The Madison Concourse Hotel
1 W. Dayton St.
Madison
(608) 257-6000
•*Bar and Solitaire Room. Humidor. Cuisine: Continental.* **Bar.**

The Cardinal Bar & Dance Club
418 E. Wilson St.
Madison
(608) 251-0080
•*All areas. Humidor.* **Bar/dance club.**

Inn on Maritime Bay
101 Maritime Dr.
Manitowoc
(920) 682-7000

•*Smoking section. Humidor. Cuisine: American, specializing in Continental, seafood, & steak.*

Johnny's Bar & Grill
3161 Hwy. 51
Mercer
(715) 476-2516
•*All areas. Humidor. Cuisine: pub fare.*

MILWAUKEE & VICINITY

Grenadier's
747 N. Broadway
Milwaukee
(414) 276-0747
•*Bar. Humidor. Cuisine: Continental.*

Romans' Pub
3475 S. Kinnickinnic Ave.
Milwaukee
(414) 481-9264
•*All areas. Humidor. Cuisine: snacks only.* **Bar.**

Shaker's Cigar Bar
422 S. 2nd St.
Milwaukee
(414) 272-2427
•*All areas. Humidor. Cuisine: Caribbean, Cuban or Japanese served at events.* **Cigar bar.**

Steakhouse 100
37238 Valley Rd.
Oconomowoc
(414) 567-1111

•*Bar/lounge. Humidor. Cuisine: steakhouse.*

Ambassador Club
2339 Silver Nail Village, Suite A
Pewaukee
(414) 513-8888
•*All areas. Humidor.*
Jazz & cigar bar.

Ambassador Club
327 W. Main St.
Waukesha
(414) 547-9009
•*All areas. Humidor.*
Jazz & cigar bar.

Steakhouse 100
10725 W. Greenfield Ave., West Allis
(414) 771-2223
•*Bar/lounge. Humidor. Cuisine: steakhouse.*
- - - - - - - - - - - - - - - - - - -

Fifty Two Stafford, An Irish Guest House
52 Stafford St.
Plymouth
(920) 893-0552
•*Smoking section and bar. Humidor. Cuisine: American/ Continental.*

HOBNOB
277 S. Sheridan Rd.
Racine
(414) 552-8008
•*Smoking section and bar. Humidor. Cuisine: American featuring fresh fish & meats.*

Cavalier Room Restaurant & Lounge
70 N. Stevens St.
Rhinelander
(715) 362-7100
•*Lounge and private rooms. Cuisine: American.*

The Wagon Wheel Supper Club
3901 N. 6th St.
Wausau
(715) 675-2263
•*Bar area from 5pm to 10pm. Humidor. Cuisine: features beef, game, chops, & seafood.*

Wausau Club
309 McClellan St.
Wausau
(715) 845-2131
•*Private dining club. Humidor. Cuisine: Continental.* **Private dining club.**

Cafe Calamari
10 E. Geneva St.
Williams Bay
(414) 245-9665
•*Bar and smoking section of dining room. Humidor. Cuisine: Gourmet Italian.*

Kirsch's on the Bay
57 N. Walworth Ave.
Williams Bay
(414) 245-2333
•*Bar. Humidor. Cuisine: steak & seafood.*

INTERNATIONAL

Austria

Academie
Untere Viaduktgasse
45, Vienna
43 1 71 38 256
•*All areas. Humidor.
Cuisine: French
kitchen.*

**Korso at the Bristol
Hotel**
Karntner Ring 1
Vienna
43 1 51 51 60
•*All areas. Humidor.
Cuisine: traditional
Austrian & interna-
tional.*

**La Scala at The
Vienna Plaza**
Schottenring 11
Vienna
43 1 31 39 00
•*Smoking sections.
Humidor. Cuisine:
Austrian.*

**Restaurant
Steirereck**
Rasumofskygasse 2
Vienna
43 1 71 33 168
•*Bar/lounge and
smoking section.
Humidor. Cuisine:
new Austrian.*

Belgium

'T Fornuis
Reyndersstraat 24
Antwerp
32 3 23 36 270

•*Bar and after dinner.
Humidor. Cuisine:
French.*

Bruneau
ave. Broustin 75
Brussels
32 2 42 76 978
•*All areas. Humidor.
Cuisine: French.*

Comme Chez Soi
23 place Rouppe
Brussels
32 2 51 22 921
•*Smoking areas and
private salons. Humi-
dor. Cuisine: French.*

**La Maison du
Cygne**
Grand Place 9
Brussels
32 2 51 18 244
•*All areas (there's a
small nonsmoking sec-
tion). Humidor. Cui-
sine: French.*

La Truffe Noire
12 blvd. de La Cam-
bre, Brussels
32 2 64 04 422
•*All areas. Humidor.
Cuisine: French &
Italian.*

**Les 4 Saisons at the
Royal Windsor**
rue Duquesnoy 5
Brussels
32 2 50 55 100
•*Smoking section.
Humidor. Cuisine:
classic French.*

Maison du Boeuf
blvd. du Waterloo 38
Brussels
32 2 50 41 111
•*All areas. Humidor.
Cuisine: Continental
& international.*

**Sea Grill
J. Le Divellec**
rue Fossé-aux-Loups
47, Brussels
32 2 22 73 120
•*Smoking section, bar
and atrium lounge.
Humidor. Cuisine:
French/seafood.*

Villa Lorraine
ave. du Vivier d'Oie
75, Brussels
32 2 37 43 163
•*Bar and part of din-
ing area. Humidor.
Cuisine: French.*

**Rudy's
Fonduehuisje**
St. Maartenstraat
12-C, Leuven
32 16 20 44 20
•*All areas. Humidor.
Cuisine: Swiss.*

Brazil

**Havana Club at the
Renaissance São
Paulo Hotel**
Alameda Santos
São Paulo
55 11 3069 2233

•*Bar, lounge, and
cigar bar. Humidor.
Cuisine: Nuevo
Latino.* **Cigar bar.**

Canada

ALBERTA
Osteria de Medici
201 Lost Plaza NW
Calgary
(403) 283-5553
•*Private room.
Humidor. Cuisine:
Italian.*

**Tasmanian
Ballroom &
Havana's Cigar
Lounge**
1215 1st St. SW
Calgary
(403) 266-1824
•*All areas. Humidor.*
**Nightclub/private
club (guests are
welcome).**

**Booker Martuni's
at The Palace
Casino**
Entrance 9, West
Edmonton Mall
Edmonton
(403) 481-2265
•*Bar, lounge, and
smoking section of din-
ing room. Humidor.
Cuisine: beef,
seafood, chicken,
pasta.*

BRITISH COLUMBIA

Bacchus Ristorante & Lounge
845 Hornby St.
Vancouver
(604) 689-7777
•*Cigar room, smoking section, and private rooms. Humidor. Cuisine: Northern Italian.*

La Gavroche
1616 Alberni St.
Vancouver
(604) 685-3924
•*Private rooms. Cuisine: contemporary French.*

Bearfoot Bistro
4121 Village Green
Whistler
(604) 932-3433
•*Air tight cigar room. Humidor. Cuisine: fusion.*

NOVA SCOTIA

Jon Alan's Steak & Chop House
5523 Spring Garden Rd., Halifax
(902) 422-5267
•*Cigar bar. Humidor. Cuisine: steak & chops.*

Joe's Warehouse & Food Emporium
424 Charlotte St.
Sydney
(902) 539-6686
•*Smoking section, bar, and private dining room. Cuisine: steak & seafood.*

ONTARIO

Calhoon's Steakhouse
135 Bayfield St.
Barrie
(705) 727-1520
•*Bar and smoking area. Humidor. Cuisine: steakhouse.*

Lil' Habanas
79 Dunlop St. W.
Barrie
(705) 728-1872
•*All areas. Humidor. Cuisine: sandwiches available.* **Cigar bar.**

Rockwater Brewing Company
Galleria Mall
London
(519) 672-2739
•*Bar and smoking section. Humidor. Cuisine: roadhouse/ fine dining steakhouse.*

Victoria House Cigar Club
5448 Victoria Ave.
Niagara Falls
(905) 371-2238
•*Two cigar lounges. Humidor. Cuisine: Italian, Cajun.*

Lake Obabika Lodge
P.O. Box 10
River Valley
(705) 858-1056
•*Bar, lounge, and balcony. Humidor. Cuisine: international gourmet.*

Barberian's Steak House Tavern
7 Elm St., Toronto
(416) 597-0335
•*Bar and smoking section. Humidor. Cuisine: steakhouse.*

Bindi Ristorante
3241 Yonge St.
Toronto
(416) 487-2881
•*Cigar lounge. Humidor. Cuisine: Italian.*

Brass Rail Tavern
701 Yonge St.
Toronto
(416) 924-1241
•*Designated smoking areas. Humidor. Cuisine: Italian.* **Exotic gentlemen's club.**

George Bigliardi's
463 Church St.
Toronto
(416) 922-9594
•*Dining room, bar, and private rooms. Humidor. Cuisine: Italian, specializing in seafood & steak.*

Opus Restaurant
37 Prince Arthur Ave., Toronto
(416) 921-3105
•*Bar area. Humidor. Cuisine: European & Mediterranean.*

Prego della Piazza
150 Bloor St. W.
Toronto
(416) 920-9900

•*Enoteca bar only. Humidor. Cuisine: Italian.*

The Senator
249 Victoria St.
Toronto
(416) 364-7517
•*Dining room, club, and cigar lounge. Humidor. Cuisine: steakhouse.*

Shark City Bar & Grill
117 Eglinton Ave. E.
Toronto
(416) 488-7899
•*All smoking sections. Humidor. Cuisine: Eurasian.*

The School of Fine Dining
4121 14th Ave.
Unionville
(905) 477-1161
•*Lounge. Humidor. Cuisine: steak & seafood.*

QUEBEC

Beaver Club at The Queen Elizabeth Hotel
900-B, Montreal
(514) 861-3511
•*Smoking section. Humidor. Cuisine: French.*

La Mas des Oliviers
1216 rue Bishop
Montreal
(514) 861-6733
•*Special room only. Humidor. Cuisine: French.*

Le Lutetia
1430 rue de La Montagne
Montreal
(514) 288-5656
•Special smoking area in lobby. Humidor. Cuisine: French.

Les Caprices de Nicolas
2072 Drummond
Montreal
(514) 288-1112
•Smoking section and patio. Humidor. Cuisine: modern French.

Modavie Restaurant-Bar
1, St. Paul St. W.
Montreal
(514) 287-9582
•All areas. Humidor. Cuisine: world cuisine (fusion).

Monte Cristo Cigar Bar Lounge
1466 A Crescent
Montreal
(514) 288-9696
•All areas. Humidor. Cigar bar/lounge/private club.

Opus II at the Westin
1050 Scherook St.
Montreal
(514) 849-6787
•Bar after 9pm. Cuisine: breakfast buffet, lunch; hors d'oeuvres only after lunch.

Quelli Della Notte
6834 St.-Laurent (Upper Little Italy), Montreal
(514) 271-3929
•Lounge and cigar bar. Humidor. Cuisine: fine Italian regional cuisine & Japanese Sushi.

Whisky Cafe
5800 St.-Laurent
Montreal
(514) 278-2646
•Bar and lounge. Humidor. Cuisine: caviar, foie gras, smoked salmon, cheeses. Bar/cigar lounge.

L'Inox
37 St. Andrè
Quebec City
(418) 692-2877
•All areas. Cuisine: pub fare.

Pub St.-Alexandre
1087 St.-Jean
Quebec City
(418) 694-0015
•Bar and second floor. Cuisine: pub fare.

Bistro à Champlain
75 Chemin Masson
Sainte-Marguerite du Lac Masson
(514) 228-4988
•Smoking lounge. Humidor. Cuisine: French.

Hampton's Cigar Lounge at the Sheraton Cavalier Hotel
612 Spadina Cres East, Saskatoon
(304) 584-1855
•Cigar bar. Humidor. Cuisine: European. Bar/cigar bar.

Caribbean

BAHAMAS

Graycliff
W. Hill St.
Nassau
(242) 322-2797
•All areas including the lounge, patio, and private rooms. Humidor. Cuisine: mostly French.

BARBADOS, B.W.I.

Mango's
West End #2 Queen St., Speightstown, St. Peter
(246) 422-0704
•Dining room (covered by a veranda & overlooking the ocean), bar, and cigar bar. Humidor. Cuisine: specializes in fresh seafood & fish.

ST. CROIX, U.S.V.I.

The Galleon
5000 Estate Southgate
Christiansted
(809) 773-9949

•All areas. Humidor. Cuisine: Continental, northern Italian & French cuisines.

The Great House at Villa Madeleine
Box 3109
Christiansted
(809) 778-7377
•All areas. Humidor. Cuisine: Caribbean, Mediterranean & Continental.

ST. LUCIA, W.I.

Charthouse Restaurant
PO Box 144
Castries
(758) 452-8115
•Bar at all times (dining room baring no complaints). Humidor. Cuisine: steak, seafood, spare ribs.

ST. MAARTEN/ST. MARTIN

Shivsagar
20 Frontstreet
Phillipsburg
599 5 22299
•All areas. Cuisine: Indian.

Pelican Reef Steak & Seafood House
Pelican Resort Club
Simpson Bay
599 5 43021
•All areas. Humidor. Cuisine: steak & seafood.

ST. THOMAS, U.S.V.I.

Randy's Bistro
Raphune Hill - Al
  Cohen Plaza
(809) 777-3199
• *All areas including
the bar and patio.
Humidor. Cuisine:
Italian/Mediterranean/
American.*

TURKS & CAICOS ISLANDS, B.W.I.

**Banana Boat
Caribbean Grill**
Turtle Cove Marina
Providenciales
(809) 941-5706
• *All areas of this
open-air marina side
setting/dining room.
Humidor. Cuisine:
Caribbean, with
Yucatan & Jamaican
influences.*

**Tiki Hut Cabana
Bar and Grill at the
Turtle Grove Inn**
Turtle Cove Marina
Providenciales
(809) 941-5341
• *All areas. Humidor.
Cuisine: Caribbean.*

Denmark

Restaurant Kanalen
Wilders Plads
Copenhagen
45 3 295 1330
• *All areas. Humidor.
Cuisine: Danish &
French.*

Kommandanten
NY Adelgade 7
Copenhagen
45 3 312 0990
• *All areas. Cuisine:
Danish & French.*

Nouvelle
Gammel Strand 34
Copenhagen
45 3 313 5018
• *All areas. Humidor.
Cuisine: French.*

Finland

Lord a la Carte
Lönnrotinkatu 29
Helsinki
358 9 68 01 680
• *All areas. Humidor.
Cuisine: classic
Finnish.*

France

**Restaurant La Belle
Otéro & Carlton
Casino Club at the
Hôtel Carlton
International**
58 blvd. Croisette
Cannes
33 4 92 99 51 00
• *Dining room and
near the piano bar.
Humidor. Cuisine:
French Mediter-
ranean, specializing in
seafood.*

**La Côte at the
Hôtel Carlton
International**
58 blvd. Croisette
Cannes
33 4 93 06 40 06

• *Smoking section in
dining room. Humi-
dor. Cuisine: French
Gastronomique.*

**La Palme d'Or at
Hotel Martinez**
73 blvd. Croisette
Cannes
33 4 92 98 74 14
• *All smoking areas.
Humidor. Cuisine:
French.*

Paul Bocuse
Collonges-au-Mont-
  d'Or, Lyons
33 4 7 24 29 090
• *All areas. Humidor.
Cuisine: traditional
French.*

Alain Ducasse
59 ave. Raymond
  Poincare, Paris
33 1 47 27 12 27
• *Lounge. Humidor.
Cuisine: French.*

Apicius
122 ave. Villiers
Paris
33 1 43 80 19 66
• *All areas. Humidor.
Cuisine: French.*

Au Trou Gascon
40 rue Taine, Paris
33 1 43 44 34 26
• *Bar. Humidor. Cui-
sine: southwest
French.*

**Bristol at The
Hôtel Bristol**
112 rue Faubourg St-
  Honoré, Paris
33 1 53 43 43 00

• *Bar/private room/
restaurant Humidor.
Cuisine: Gas-
tronomique French.*

Carre des Feuillants
14 rue de Castiglione
Paris
33 1 42 86 82 82
• *Smoking section.
Humidor. Cuisine:
French.*

Chez Pauline
5 rue Villédo, Paris
33 1 42 96 20 70
• *All areas. Humidor.
Cuisine: contempo-
rary/classic French.*

Chiberta
3 rue Arsène-Hous-
  saye, Paris
33 1 45 63 77 90
• *All areas. Humidor.
Cuisine: Gas-
tronomique French.*

Drouant
18 place Gaillon
Paris
33 1 42 65 15 16
• *All smoking areas.
Humidor. Cuisine:
traditional French.*

**Espadon at the
Hotel Ritz**
15 place Vendôme
Paris
33 1 43 16 30 80
• *Smoking areas.
Humidor. Cuisine:
traditional French.*

Faucher
123 ave. de Wagram
Paris
33 1 42 27 61 50
•*All areas. Humidor.
Cuisine: grand
French.*

Fifteen Montaigne
Maison Blanche
15 ave. Montaigne
Paris
33 1 47 23 55 99
•*All areas. Humidor.
Cuisine: Gas-
tronomique French.*

Gérard Besson
5 rue Coq Héron
Paris
33 1 42 33 14 74
•*All areas. Humidor.
Cuisine: French.*

Goumard-Prunier
9 rue Duphot, Paris
33 1 42 60 36 07
•*All smoking sections.
Humidor. Cuisine:
seafood.*

Grand V'efour
17 rue Beaujolais
Paris
33 1 42 96 56 27
•*Smoking section.
Humidor. Cuisine:
traditional & modern
French.*

Guy Savoy
18 rue Troyon, Paris
33 1 43 80 40 61
•*All areas. Humidor.
Cuisine: Gas-
tronomique (classic)
French.*

Hôtel Plaza
Athénée
25 ave. Montaigne
Paris
33 1 53 67 65 00
•*Areas of Le Relais,
Le Regence, Bar
Anglais, and banquet
facilities. Humidor.
Cuisine: Gas-
tronomique at
Regence.*

Jacques Cagna
14 rue Grands
    Augustins, Paris
33 1 43 26 49 39
•*All areas. Humidor.
Cuisine: French.*

Joséphine
117 rue Cherche-
    Midi, Paris
33 1 45 48 52 40
•*Lounge. Humidor.
Cuisine: traditional
French.*

L'Ambroisie
9 place des Vosges
Paris
33 1 42 78 51 45
•*All smoking areas.
Humidor. Cuisine:
traditional French.*

La Cagouille
10 place Constantin
    Brancusi, Paris
33 1 43 22 09 01
•*All areas. Humidor.
Cuisine: seafood.*

La Couronne at the
Hôtel Warwick
5 rue Berri, Paris
33 1 45 63 78 49

•*Bar and restaurant.
Humidor. Cuisine:
gourmet.*

La Mare
1 rue Daru, Paris
33 1 43 80 20 00
•*All areas. Humidor.
Cuisine: French, spe-
cializing in seafood.*

La Table d'Anvers
2 place d'Anvers
Paris
33 1 48 78 35 21
•*All areas. Humidor.
Cuisine: nouvelle
French.*

Lasserre
17 ave. Franklin D.
    Roosevelt, Paris
33 1 43 59 53 43
•*Smoking section.
Humidor. Cuisine:
traditional French.*

Laurent
41 ave. Gabriel
Paris
33 1 42 25 00 39
•*Bar and smoking
section. Humidor.
Cuisine: Bourgeoise
Allégée.*

Le Doyen
Dutuit 8, Paris
33 1 44 70 24 23
•*Bar and smoking
section. Humidor.
Cuisine: French.*

Le Grand V'efour
17 rue de Beaujolais
Paris
33 1 42 96 56 27

•*Smoking section.
Humidor. Cuisine:
contemporary French.*

Le Meurice at the
Hôtel Meurice
228 rue Rivoli, Paris
33 1 44 58 10 50
•*All areas. Humidor.
Cuisine: traditional
French.*

Le Petit Colombier
42 rue Acacias, Paris
33 1 43 80 28 54
•*Fireplace salon.
Humidor. Cuisine:
traditional French.*

Le Sormani
4 rue Gén-Lanrezac
Paris
33 1 43 80 13 91
•*Dining room. Humi-
dor. Cuisine: Italian.*

Ledoyen
Carré Champs-
    Elysées, Paris
33 1 53 05 10 00
•*All areas. Humidor.
Cuisine: French.*

Les Ambassadeurs
at the Hôtel Crillon
10 place Concorde
Paris
33 1 44 71 16 16
•*All areas. Humidor.
Cuisine: French.*

Les Elysées at the
Hôtel Vernet
25 rue Vernet, Paris
33 1 44 31 98 98
•*Under the dome-
glass Eiffel. Humidor.
Cuisine: Provençal.*

Manoir de Paris
6 rue Pierre Demours
Paris
33 1 45 72 25 25
•*Bar. Humidor. Cuisine: French.*

Mercure Galant
15 rue Petits-
   Champs, Paris
33 1 42 96 98 89
•*All areas. Humidor.
Cuisine: French.*

**Restaurant Morot-
Gaudry**
8 rue de la Cavalerie
Paris
33 1 45 67 06 85
•*All areas. Humidor.
Cuisine: classic
French.*

**Restaurant Opéra-
Café de la Paix at
the Grand Hôtel
Inter-Continental**
5 place Opéra, Paris
33 1 40 07 30 10
•*Smoking section.
Humidor. Cuisine:
Gastronomique (classic) French.*

Pharamond
24 rue Grande-
   Truanderie, Paris
33 1 42 33 06 72
•*All areas. Humidor.
Cuisine: French.*

Pile ou Face
52 bis rue Notre-
   Dames-des-Vic-
   toires, Paris
33 1 42 33 64 33
•*All areas. Humidor.
Cuisine: French.*

Pré Catelan
Route de Suresnes
Paris
33 1 45 24 55 58
•*In one dining room.
Humidor. Cuisine:
international & classical French.*

Récamier
4 rue Récamier, Paris
33 1 45 48 86 58
•*All areas. Humidor.
Cuisine: French.*

Taillevent
15 rue Lamennais
Paris
33 1 45 61 12 90
•*All areas. Humidor.
Cuisine: French.*

Tour d'Argent
15 quai Tournelle
Paris
33 1 43 54 23 31
•*Special cigar smoking
section. Humidor.
Cuisine: French.*

Côte d'Or
2 rue Argentine
Saulieu
33 3 80 90 53 53
•*Lobby. Humidor.
Cuisine: traditional
French.*

Au Crocodile
10 rue Outre
Strasbourg
33 3 88 32 13 02
•*Smoking section.
Humidor. Cuisine:
Gastronomique.*

French Polynesia

Bali Hai Huahine
Sare
Huahine, Tahiti
689 68 84 77
•*All areas. Cuisine:
French, American &
local cuisines.*

Bali Hai Moorea
BP26 Maharepa
Moorea, Tahiti
689 56 13 59
•*All areas. Cuisine:
French, American &
local cuisines.*

Germany

**Brenner's Park
Restaurant &
Oleander Bar at
The Schwarzwald**
Schillerstrasse 6,
   Lichtenthaler
   Allee
Baden Baden
49 7 221 9000
•*All smoking areas.
Humidor. Cuisine:
Continental.*

**Schloss Thiergarten
Hotel &
Restaurant**
Oberthiergärtner
   Strasse 36
Bayreuth
49 9 209 9840
•*All areas. Humidor.
Cuisine: German.*

**Hotel &
Restaurant
Landsknecht**
Post Str. 70, 40667
   Meerbusch
Düsseldorf
49 21 32 93350
•*All areas. Humidor.
Cuisine: international.*

**Restaurant
Schiffchen**
Kaiserswerther
   Markt 9
Düsseldorf
49 21 140 1050
•*All areas. Humidor.
Cuisine: French.*

Victorian
Köenigstrasse 3-A
Düsseldorf
49 21 186 550 20
•*All areas. Humidor.
Cuisine: French, new
German.*

**Schassberger Spa &
Resort Hotel
Ebnisee**
Winnender 10
Ebnisee
49 7 184 2920
•*Bar. Humidor. Cuisine: French & traditional German.*

La Grappa
Rellinghauserstrasse
   4, Essen
49 20 123 1766
•*All areas. Humidor.
Cuisine: French, Italian, seafood.*

Restaurant Français
Bethmannstrasse 33
Frankfurt
49 69 215 118
•*All areas. Humidor.
Cuisine: French.*

**Weinhaus
Brückenkeller**
Schützenstrasse 6
Frankfurt
49 69 29 80 070
•*Bar/lounge. Humidor. Cuisine: German & Continental.*

**Wald-und
Schlosshotel
Friedrichsruhe**
Friedrichsruhe
49 79 41 608 70
•*Bar/lounge, private room, and lobby. Humidor. Cuisine: French.*

**Hotel/Restaurant
Zur Traube**
Bahnstrasse 47
Grevenbroich
49 21 816 8767
•*All areas. Humidor. Cuisine: French.*

Le Canard
Elbchaussee 139
Hamburg
49 40 88 05 057
•*All areas. Humidor. Cuisine: nouvelle Cuisine.*

Grill Restaurant at the Munich Park Hilton
Am Tucherpark 7
Munich
49 89 3845 261

•*Cigar lounge, restaurant, and bar. Humidor. Cuisine: Continental with a touch of local flavor.*

**Königshof at the
Hotel Königshof**
Karlsplatz 25
Munich
49 89 551 36 142
•*Restaurant and bar. Humidor. Cuisine: Continental.*

Tantris
Johann-Fichtestrasse 7, Munich
49 89 362 061
•*All areas. Humidor. Cuisine: international.*

**Landgasthof-
Metzgerei Paulus**
Prälat-Faber-Straße 2-4
Nonnweiler-Sitzerath
49 6873 91011
•*All areas. Humidor. Cuisine: regional cuisine accompanied by a huge wine-by-the-glass program.*

Hotel Wilder Mann
Hauptstrasse 37
Rückersdorf
49 911 9501 0
•*All areas. Cuisine: German.*

**Rüdesheimer
Schloss**
Drosselgasse
Rüdesheim am Rhein
49 6 722 90500
•*All areas. Humidor. Cuisine: regional.*

**Restaurant
Backmulde**
Karmeliterstrasse 11-13, Speyer
49 62 32 715 77
•*All areas. Humidor. Cuisine: French & Mediterranean w/ regional flavor.*

Die Ente vom Lehel at the Hotel Nassauer Hof
Kaiser-Friedrichplatz 3/4, Wiesbaden
49 61 113 3666
•*Bar all evening and dining room after dinner. Humidor. Cuisine: French & German.*

Hotel Waldhaus
Kiefernweg 12
Winterberg
49 2 981 2042
•*Restaurant and hotel rooms. Humidor. Cuisine: new German.*

Greece

Gevfis
Kifissias 317, Kifissia
Athens
30 1 800 1402

•*Bar. Humidor. Cuisine: Greek haute-cuisine.*

**Restaurant Kona
Kai in the Athens
Ledra Marriott
Hotel**
115 Syngrou Ave.
Athens
30 1 934 7711
•*All areas. Humidor. Cuisine: Polynesian & Teppanyaiki Japanese.*

Guatemala

Jake's
17 Calle 10-40 Zona 10
Guatemala City
502 2 368 0351
•*All areas. Humidor. Cuisine: Continental.*

Hong Kong

Brown's Restaurant & Wine Bar
Exchange Square Tower II
Central Hong Kong
852 2523 7003
•*All areas. Humidor. Cuisine: American/ Continental.*

Petrus
Island Shangri-La Hotel
Pacific Place, Supreme Court Rd.
852 2877 3838
•*Smoking section. Humidor. Cuisine: French.*

Panorama Western Fine Dining Room at the New World Hotel
4/F New World Hotel
22 Salisbury Rd.
Tsimshatsui,
    Kowloon
852 2369 4111
• *Bar/lounge and smoking section. Humidor. Cuisine: Continental.*

The Peninsula Hotel
Salisbury Rd.
Tsimshatsui,
    Kowloon
852 2366 6251
• *Smoking section. Humidor. Cuisine: French, Chinese, Mediterranean, & Euro-Asian.*

Ireland

Le Coq Hardi
35 Pembroke Rd.,
    Pallsbridge, Dublin
353 1 668 4130
• *Dining room, bar, lounge, and private rooms. Humidor. Cuisine: French, specializing in seafood.*

Israel

Coffee Bar Emporium
13 Yad-Harutsim
Tel-Aviv
972 3 688 9696
• *Smoking section. Humidor. Cuisine: French & Italian.*

Italy

Osteria Solferino
Via Solferino, 18
    Bardolino
    (Verona)
39 457 211 020
• *All areas. Humidor. Cuisine: local Veneto dishes.*

Hotel Dominik Relais & Chateaux
Rapp Gardens
Bressanone
39 472 830 144
• *Large terrace, bar, and lobby. Humidor. Cuisine: traditional South Tyrolean with a Mediterranean influence.*

La Taverna
Piazza Castello 2
Colloredo di Monte
    Albano
39 43 28 89 045
• *Dining room and bar. Humidor. Cuisine: Mediterranean.*

Enoteca Pinchiorri
Via Ghibellina 87
Florence
39 55 24 27 77/2
• *After dinner only. Humidor. Cuisine: traditional—yet creative—Italian.*

Lorenzo
Via Carducci 61
Forte dei Marmi
39 5 848 4030
• *All areas. Humidor. Cuisine: Tuscan.*

A Riccione
Via Taramelli 70
Milan
39 2 66 86 807
• *All areas. Cuisine: seafood.*

Ristorante Sadler
Troilo 14, Milan
39 2 58 10 44 51
• *All areas. Cuisine: original Italian.*

Scaletta
Piazza Porta Genova
    3, Milan
39 2 58 10 02 90
• *All areas. Cuisine: Italian.*

Checchino dal 1887
Via Monte Testaccio
    30, Rome
39 6 57 46 318
• *All areas. Cuisine: Roman.*

Papa Giovanni
Via dei Sediari 4
Rome
39 6 68 80 48 07, 68
    65 308
• *After dessert is served only. Humidor. Cuisine: typical Roman.*

Relais le Jardin at the Hotel Lord Byron
Via G. De Notaris 5
Rome
39 6 32 20 404
• *Bar/lounge. Cuisine: Mediterranean & traditional Italian.*

Restaurant Sans Souci
Via Sicilia 20/24
Rome
39 6 48 21 814
• *Bar/lounge and smoking section. Humidor. Cuisine: French & Italian.*

Japan

Shooters Sports Cafe
1-2-14 Izumi,
    Higashi-Ku
Nagoya
81 52 953 7774
• *All areas. Humidor. Cuisine: pasta, Tex-Mex, burgers & more.*

Chez Wada
2-10-14 Nishi Shin-
    saibashi Chou-Ku,
    Osaka
81 6 212 1780
• *All areas. Humidor. Cuisine: French.*

Luxembourg

Patin d'Or
40 route de Bettem-
    bourg
Luxembourg
352 226 499
• *All areas. Humidor. Cuisine: French.*

St-Michel
rue Eau 32
Luxembourg
352 223 215
• *All areas. Humidor. Cuisine: French.*

Mexico

La Noria Restaurant
Playa El Medano at
    Hotel Hacienda
Cabo San Lucas
52 11 43 06 63
•*All areas. Humidor.*
Cuisine: upscale Mexican.

Pazzo's Cabo
Morelos y Niños
    Heroes S/N
Cabo San Lucas
52 11 43 43 13
•*All areas. Humidor.*
Cuisine: Italian,
pizza, & seafood.

El Sombrero
Centro Comercial
    Los Patios, Ixtapa
52 755 30439
•*All areas. Humidor.*
Cuisine: upper Mexican & International.

Champs Elysees
Reforma 316
Mexico City
52 5 533 3698
•*All areas. Humidor.*
Cuisine: French.

Circulo del Sureste
Lucerna 12 Col.
    Juárez
Mexico City
52 5 535 2704/535
    2741
•*All areas (a non-*
smoking section is
available). Humidor.
Cuisine: traditional
Mexican & international.

The Men's Club of Mexico City
#54 Varsovia
Mexico City
52 5 533 2224
•*All areas. Humidor.*
Cuisine: Continental,
featuring steaks,
seafood, & other specialties including live
Maine lobster. **Gentlemen's club.**

Mirabeau Restaurant
Ave Vasconalos Sol. 6
    Monterrey
Mexico
52 8 338 8880
•*All areas. Humidor.*
Cuisine: French

Monaco

La Coupole at the Hôtel Mirabeau
1 ave. Princess
    Grace
Monte Carlo
377 92 16 6565
•*Smoking area.*
Humidor. Cuisine:
nouvelle French.

l'Hôtel de Paris
Place du Casino
Monte Carlo
377 92 16 2966
•*American Bar, Cote*
Jardin, Salle Empire,
Louis XV, and main
lobby. Humidor. Cuisine: Mediterranean
& Provençal.

Netherlands

Christophe
Leliegracht 46
Amsterdam
31 20 625 0807
•*All areas. Humidor.*
Cuisine: French.

Le Restaurant Tout Court
Runstraat 13
Amsterdam
31 20 625 8637
•*All areas. Humidor.*
Cuisine: French.

Vermeer at Golden Tulip Barbizon Palace Hotel
Prins Hendrikkade
    59-72, Amsterdam
31 20 556 4885
•*All areas. Humidor.*
Cuisine: French.

Kaatje bij de Sluis
Browerstraat 20
Blokzijl
31 527 291 833
•*All areas. Humidor.*
Cuisine: French.

Restaurant/Hotel Savelberg
Oosteinde 14
Eh Voorburg
31 70 387 2081
•*All areas. Humidor.*
Cuisine: French.

De Oude Rosmolen
Duinsteeg 1, Hoorn
31 229 214 752
•*All areas. Humidor.*
Cuisine: French.

Norway

Bagatelle
Bygdy Alle 3, Oslo
47 2 244 0990
•*Bar/lounge and*
smoking section.
Humidor. Cuisine:
Norwegian fish,
seafood, & game.

Bar & Cigar
CJ Hambros Plass
Oslo
47 22 20 43 18
•*All smoking areas.*
Humidor. **Cigar bar.**

Portugal

Casa da Comida
Travessa das Amoreiras 1
Lisbon
351 1 388 5376
•*All areas. Humidor.*
Cuisine: Portugese.

Coventual
Praça das Flores 45
Lisbon
351 1 609 196
•*All areas. Cuisine:*
Portugese.

Tagide
Largo da Academia
    Nacional de Belas
    Artes 1820, Lisbon
351 1 342 0720
•*Dining room, bar,*
lounge, and private
rooms. Humidor.
Cuisine: Continental
& French.

Puerto Rico

Perichi's at the Hotel Parador
Carr 102, KN 14.3,
 HC01 Box 16310
Cabo Rojo
(787) 851-0620
•*Bar/lounge. Humidor. Cuisine: American, Caribbean, Continental, & Spanish.*

The Cigar Bar at The El San Juan Hotel & Casino
6073 Isla Verde Ave.
San Juan
(809) 791-1000
•*All areas. Humidor. Cuisine: American, Chinese, Italian, Japanese, & Mexican.*

Johnny's Restaurant
208 Domenech Ave.
San Juan
(787) 763-2793
•*Bar/lounge and smoking section. Humidor. Cuisine: international, Cuban & Puerto Rican.*

Spain

Botafumeiro
Grand de Gràcia 81
Barcelona
34 3 218 4230
•*All areas. Humidor. Cuisine: Spanish & international.*

Ca L'Isidre
Les Flors 12
Barcelona
34 3 441 1139
•*All areas. Humidor. Cuisine: seasonal.*

Jaume de Provença
Provença, 88
Barcelona
34 3 430 00 29
•*All areas. Humidor. Cuisine: Mediterranean.*

La Dama
Ave. Diagonal 423
Barcelona
34 3 202 0686
•*All areas. Humidor. Cuisine: international.*

Neichel
Ave. de Pedralbes 16
bis., Barcelona
34 3 203 8408
•*All areas. Humidor. Cuisine: Mediterranean.*

Via Veneto
Ganduxer 10-12
Barcelona
34 3 200 7244
•*All areas. Humidor. Cuisine: Catalan.*

Cabo Mayor
37 Ramón Jiménez
Madrid
34 3 350 8776
•*Different private rooms. Humidor. Cuisine: Spanish, specializing in seafood from Cantabria.*

El Cenador del Prado
Prado 4, Madrid
34 1 4 29 15 61
•*All areas. Humidor. Cuisine: cocina Española.*

El Olivo
General Gallegos 1
Madrid
34 1 359 1535
•*All areas. Humidor. Cuisine: Mediterranean.*

Jockey
Amador de Los Ríos
 6, Madrid
34 1 319 2435
•*All areas. Humidor. Cuisine: Continental.*

La Mission
Comandante Zorita
 6, Madrid
34 1 533 2757
•*All areas. Humidor. Cuisine: Spanish.*

La Trainera
Lagasca 60, Madrid
34 1 576 0575
•*All areas. Humidor. Cuisine: seafood.*

Las Cuatro Estaciones
General Ibañez
 Ibero SA
Madrid
34 1 553 6305
•*All areas. Humidor. Cuisine: Spanish.*

Switzerland

The Griffins Club
36 blvd. Helvetique
Geneva
41 22 735 12 18
•*All areas. Humidor. Cuisine: French.*

La Cigogne at the Hôtel de la Cigogne
17 place Longemalle
Geneva
41 22 818 40 40
•*All areas. Humidor. Cuisine: French.*

Le Chat Botte
Hôtel Beau Rívage
13 Mont-Blanc
Geneva
41 22 716 69 20
•*All areas. Humidor. Cuisine: Gastronomique (classic) French.*

Le Cygne
19 Quai Mont-Blanc
Geneva
41 22 908 90 81
•*All areas. Humidor. Cuisine: Gastronomique French.*

Restaurant Wiesental
Zürichstrasse 25
Winkel
41 1 860 15 00
•*All areas. Humidor. Cuisine: Italian.*

Taverna Catalana
Glockengasse 8
Zürich
41 1 221 12 62
•*All areas. Humidor.
Cuisine: Mediter-
ranean & Spanish.*

Taiwan, R.O.C.

**Cigar Tribune
Restaurant**
3 Lane 186, Chung-
Shan N. Rd., Sec.
6, Taipei
886 2 2832 8335
•*All areas. Humidor.
Cuisine: Continental.*

Thailand

**Bourbon Street
Restaurant & Bar**
29/4-6 Sukhumvit
Soi 22 Washing-
ton Sq.
Bangkok
66 2 259 0328 9
•*Smoking section,
bar, and cigar bar.
Humidor. Cuisine:
Cajun Creole &
South Louisiana/New
Orleans-style Ameri-
can.*

United Kingdom

**Terrace at the
Waldos**
Cliveden Taplow
Berkshire
44 1628 668 561
•*Bar/lounge, private
room, and patio.
Humidor. Cuisine:
English & French.*

**The New Mill
Restaurant and
Grill**
New Mill Rd.,
Eversley
Hampshire
44 173 473 2105
•*Bar. Humidor. Cui-
sine: British.*

Annabel's
44 Berkeley Square
London
44 171 629 1096
•*All areas. Humidor.
Cuisine: French, Ital-
ian, & English. **Pri-
vate nightclub.***

**Bentleys Seafood
Restaurant**
11-15 Swallow St.
London
44 171 734 4756
•*All areas. Humidor.
Cuisine: seafood.*

**The Berkley
Restaurant**
Wilton Place
London
44 171 235 6000
•*Dining room, bar,
lounge, and private
rooms. Humidor.
Cuisine: French/mod-
ern British.*

**Bibendum at The
Michelin House**
81 Fulham Rd.
London
44 171 581 5817
•*All areas. Humidor.
Cuisine: modern
British.*

**Blue Print Cafe at
The Deskin
Museum**
Butlers Wharf
London
44 171 716 0716
•*All areas. Humidor.
Cuisine: modern
British. **Cafe.***

Bombay Brasserie
Courtfield Rd.
London
44 171 370 4040
•*Smoking section.
Humidor. Cuisine:
Indian.*

**The Butlers Wharf
Chop-House**
The Butlers Wharf
Building, 36-E
Shad Thames
London
44 171 403 3403
•*All areas. Humidor.
Cuisine: British.*

**Cafe Nico at The
Grosvenor House**
Grosvenor Park
Lane, London
44 171 499 6363
•*Smoking section.
Humidor. Cuisine:
English bistro.*

Cantina del Ponte
The Butlers Wharf
Building, 36-C
Shad Thames
London
44 171 403 5403
•*Back area of dining
room. Humidor. Cui-
sine: Mediterranean.*

Caviar House
161 Piccadilly
London
44 171 409 0445
•*All areas. Humidor.
Cuisine: caviar,
smoked salmon, &
other seafood.*

Cecconi Restaurant
5-A Burlington Gar-
dens, London
44 171 434 1509
•*All areas. Humidor.
Cuisine: Italian.*

**Christopher's/The
American Grill**
28 Wellington St.
London
44 171 240 4222
•*All areas. Humidor.
Cuisine: American.*

City Circle
10 Basinghall St.
London
44 171 600 8479
•*All areas. Humidor.
Cuisine: Continental.*

Corney & Barrow
44 Cannon St.
London
44 171 248 1700
•*All areas. Humidor.
Cuisine: modern
British. **Wine bar.***

**The English
Garden Restaurant**
10 Lincoln St.,
Chelsea, London
44 171 584 7272
•*Smoking areas.
Humidor. Cuisine:
English.*

The English House Restaurant
3 Milner St.,
 Chelsea, London
44 171 584 3002
•*Smoking areas. Humidor. Cuisine: English.*

Finos Wine Cellar
123 Mount St.
London
44 171 491 1640
•*All areas. Humidor. Cuisine: English/Continental.*

Four Seasons Hotel
Hamilton Place,
 Park Lane, London
44 171 499 0888
•*All areas. Humidor. Cuisine: French with an international influence.*

Gattis Restaurant
1 Finsbury Ave.
London
44 171 247 1051
•*Small area only. Humidor. Cuisine: Italian.*

Green's Restaurant & Oyster Bar
36 Duke St., St.
 James's, London
44 171 930 4566
•*All areas. Humidor. Cuisine: traditional English.*

Greenhouse Restaurant
27-A Hays Mews
London
44 171 409 1017

•*All areas. Humidor. Cuisine: English.*

The Grill Room at the Dorchester
53 Park Lane
London
44 171 629 8888
•*All areas. Humidor. Cuisine: English.*

Grill St. Quinten
3 Yeomans Row
London
44 171 581 8377
•*Most areas. Cuisine: French.*

Halcyon Hotel & Restaurant
81 Holland Park
London
44 171 221 5411
•*The Room: bar, restaurant, and private room. Humidor. Cuisine: British & French.*

Harry's Bar
26 S. Audley St.
London
44 171 408 0844
•*All areas. Humidor. Cuisine: Italian. **Private luncheon & dining club.***

Howard Hotel
Temple Place
London
44 171 836 3555
•*All areas. Humidor. Cuisine: French & English.*

Interlude
5 Charlotte St.

London
44 171 637 0222
•*All smoking areas and private room (nonsmoking is available). Humidor. Cuisine: modern European.*

La Tante Claire Restaurant
68 Royal Hospital
 Rd., London
44 171 352 6045
•*Bar area. Humidor. Cuisine: French.*

The Lanesborough
1 Lanesborough
 Place, London
44 171 259 5599
•*All areas. Humidor. Cuisine: international. **Bar.***

Le Pont de la Tour
The Butlers Wharf
 Building, 36-D
 Shad Thames
London
44 171 403 8403
•*All areas. Humidor. Cuisine: British, modern European, & French.*

Les Saveurs
37-A Curzon St.,
 Mayfair, London
44 171 491 8919
•*Bar. Humidor. Cuisine: French.*

Mark's Club
46 Charles St.
London
44 171 499 2936

•*All areas. Humidor. Cuisine: English & French. **Private luncheon & dining club.***

Mezzo
100 Wardour St.
London
44 171 314 4000
•*All areas. Cuisine: British, French, & Asian.*

Monte's
164 Sloane St.
London
44 171 245 0892
•*All areas. Humidor. Cuisine: Mediterranean. **Private club (temporary membership available).***

Mosimann's
Belgrave Square, 11-
 B W. Halkin St.
London
44 171 235 9625
•*All areas. Humidor. Cuisine: Continental & French. **Private club.***

Motcombs Club
5 Halkin Arcade, W.
 Halkin St.
London
44 171 235 5532
•*All areas. Humidor. Cuisine: modern Oriental.*

The No. 1 Cigar Club of London
1 Percy St., London
44 171 636 8141
•*All areas. Humidor. Cuisine: modern British.* **Private club.**

Pine Bar at the Britannia Intercontinental
Grosvenor Square
London
44 171 629 9400
•*Bar area. Humidor. Cuisine: light snacks.* **Bar.**

Poissonnerie de l'Avenue
82 Sloane Ave.
London
44 171 589 2457
•*All areas. Humidor. Cuisine: French seafood.*

Quaglino's
16 Bury St., London
44 171 930 6767
•*Throughout restaurant, bar, and private dining room. Humidor. Cuisine: British.*

Rules Restaurant
35 Maiden Lane
London
44 171 836 5314
•*All areas. Humidor. Cuisine: British, specializing in game animals.*

Sale e Pepe Restaurant
9 Pavilion Rd.
London
44 171 235 0098
•*All areas. Humidor. Cuisine: Italian.*

Savoy Grill at the Savoy
1 Savoy Hill
London
44 171 836 4343
•*All areas. Humidor. Cuisine: English/Continental.*

Scalini Restaurant
1-2-3 Walton St.
London
44 171 225 2301
•*All areas. Humidor. Cuisine: Italian.*

Scott's Restaurant
20 Mount St.
London
44 171 629 5248
•*Bar. Humidor. Cuisine: modern British.*

Sheekey's Restaurant
28/32 St. Martins
Court, London
44 171 240 2565
•*Smoking section. Humidor. Cuisine: seafood.*

Signor Sassi
14 Knightsbridge
Gardens, London
44 171 584 2277
•*All areas. Cuisine: Italian.*

Simpsons-in-the-Strand
100 Strand, London
44 171 836 9112
•*All areas. Humidor. Cuisine: traditional British.*

The Square
6-10 Breuton St.,
Mayfair, London
44 171 495 7100
•*Bar and lounge (late after dinner in the dining room). Cuisine: modern French.*

Toto Restaurant at the Walton House
Walton St., London
44 171 589 2062
•*All areas. Humidor. Cuisine: Italian.*

Trader Vic Restaurant at The London Hilton
Park Lane, London
44 171 208 4113
•*All areas. Humidor. Cuisine: island-style.*

Tramp
40 Jermyn St.
London
44 171 734 0565
•*All areas. Humidor. Cuisine: modern English.* **Exclusive club.**

Wig & Pen Club
229 Strand, London
44 171 583 7255
•*All areas. Humidor. Cuisine: traditional English.* **Gentleman's dining club.**

Wiltons Restaurant
55 Jermyn St.
London
44 171 629 9955
•*All areas (with consideration to other diners). Humidor. Cuisine: features deluxe fish & game.*

Hambleton Hall
Hambleton,
Oakham, Rutland
44 1572 756 991
•*Bar and drawing room. Humidor. Cuisine: English.* **Country house.**

The Whitehorse at Chilgrove
Chichester
West Sussex
44 1243 535 219
•*Bar all day and restaurant during coffee. Humidor. Cuisine: English/French.*

Personal Tasting Log

(paste your cigar bands here)	Name _____
	Size _____
	Price _____
	Notes _____
	_____
	_____
	_____
	Name _____
	Size _____
	Price _____
	Notes _____
	_____
	_____
	_____
	Name _____
	Size _____
	Price _____
	Notes _____
	_____
	_____
	_____
	Name _____
	Size _____
	Price _____
	Notes _____
	_____
	_____
	_____

PERSONAL TASTING LOG

Name _____
Size _____
Price _____
Notes _____
_____
_____

Name _____
Size _____
Price _____
Notes _____
_____
_____

Name _____
Size _____
Price _____
Notes _____
_____
_____

Name _____
Size _____
Price _____
Notes _____
_____
_____

Name _____
Size _____
Price _____
Notes _____
_____
_____

PERSONAL TASTING LOG

Name _____

Size _____

Price _____

Notes _____

_____

_____

Name _____

Size _____

Price _____

Notes _____

_____

_____

Name _____

Size _____

Price _____

Notes _____

_____

_____

Name _____

Size _____

Price _____

Notes _____

_____

_____

Name _____

Size _____

Price _____

Notes _____

_____

_____

GILBERT

Name _____
Size _____
Price _____
Notes _____
_____
_____

Name _____
Size _____
Price _____
Notes _____
_____
_____

Name _____
Size _____
Price _____
Notes _____
_____
_____

Name _____
Size _____
Price _____
Notes _____
_____
_____

Name _____
Size _____
Price _____
Notes _____
_____
_____